THE INTERNATIONAL LAW OF RESPONSIBILITY FOR ECONOMIC CRIMES

To my grandchildren, Elinge and Anne-Marlyse

The International Law of Responsibility for Economic Crimes

Holding State Officials Individually Liable for Acts of Fraudulent Enrichment

NDIVA KOFELE-KALE
SMU Dedman School of Law, USA

ASHGATE

Published by
Ashgate Publishing Limited
Gower House
Croft Road
Aldershot
Hampshire GU11 3HR
England

Ashgate Publishing Company
Suite 420
101 Cherry Street
Burlington, VT 05401-4405
USA

Ashgate website: http://www.ashgate.com

British Library Cataloguing in Publication Data
Kofele-Kale, Ndiva
The international law of responsibility for economic crimes : holding state officials individually liable for acts of fraudulent enrichment
1. Unjust enrichment (International law) 2.Misconduct in office
I.Title
345'.02323

Library of Congress Cataloging-in-Publication Data
Kofele-Kale, Ndiva.
The international law of responsibility for economic crimes : holding state officials individually liable for acts of fraudulent enrichment / Ndiva Kofele-Kale.-- [2nd ed.].
p. cm.
Includes index.
ISBN 0-7546-4757-9
1. Political corruption. 2. Heads of state. 3. Unjust enrichment (International law) I. Title.

KS5261.K64 2006
345'-235--dc22

200600433

ISBN-10: 0 7546 4757 9
ISBN-13: 978 0 7546 4757 7

Printed and bound in Great Britain by MPG Books Ltd. Bodmin, Cornwall.

Contents

Preface

The problem of 'Grand' Corruption (I prefer the term 'indigenous spoliation' or '*patrimonicide*' because both capture the exceptional gravity and magnitude of the plunder of national resources that takes place), the misuse of public power by *high-ranking* state officials for private gain, has finally been '*outed*.' The veil that once shrouded this subject from public view, particularly the probing view of multilateral institutions and national legislatures, is now lifted. It has taken over ten years to get here. When the first edition of this work was published in 1995 there was only a solitary multilateral convention against corruption by public officials or private individuals. Now we can count at least seven, with several still in the draft stage. This is clearly progress but the journey is far from over. Indigenous spoliation has yet to be contained and much ground remains to be covered.

The mobilization of a global effort in the fight against high-level official corruption was motivated by two factors. First, the grudging acceptance that the corruption of public officials is a practice not confined to the Third World alone but occurs everywhere, even in some of the most economically developed and prosperous regions of the world. More especially, the increasing realization that corruption flourishes in countries where a transparent and accountable culture is lacking; central institutions are weak; legal rules are simply not enforced or non-existent; and weak market participants do not operate under an internationally accepted set of principles or standards. Second, the widespread recognition that corruption is a threat to the stability of societies and retards the progress (social, economic or political) of countries, particularly developing countries and those with economies in transition. In the words of United Nations Secretary General Kofi Annan at the signing ceremony for the United Nations Convention against Corruption: 'Corruption hurts the poor disproportionately – by diverting funds intended for development, undermining a government's ability to provide basic services, feeding inequality and injustice, and discouraging foreign investment and aid.'

Some four years ago, it was suggested to me that I might undertake the task of preparing a second edition. The project appealed to me, the more so as the global fight against corruption had entered into high gear, so to speak. I felt that it would be illuminating and useful to assess how far this international effort has gone and to draw attention to a few uncharted areas that continue to pose some difficulties in the global war against Grand Corruption.

This then is the genesis of this new edition. As will be seen, there have been major revisions of six of the ten chapters from the first edition. I have revised Chapter 2, 'Indigenous Spoliation as an International Crime,' extensively to take into account the more significant evolving state practice with respect to legal regimes of responsibility. The revised chapter now incorporates (1) revisions to the Draft of Code of Crimes which the International Law Commission (ILC) submitted for adoption to the United Nations General Assembly in 1996 and (2) changes to the ILC Draft Articles on State Responsibility following the work of Rapporteur James Crawford. In the first edition Article 19's dual regime of state responsibility was arguably state practice in this area. This is no longer the case. This article reflected Special Rapporteur Robert Ago's multinational view of international law and his belief that some state acts were so serious as to be criminal in nature. Although this view was the more progressive one, it did not garner sufficient support to gain the approval of the ILC. Over time sovereign opposition to the dual regime of responsibility entrenched in Article 19 gathered steam to the point where it was necessary to revisit the subject. The demise of Article 19 and its replacement with Article 40 will be traced and discussed in great depth in this chapter.

I have revised Chapter 5 which presents recent additions to the international legal regime to combat corruption. The 1995 European Union Convention on the Protection of the European Communities' Financial Interests and its two additional Protocols represent the first of numerous multilateral expressions of a commitment to combat the problem of official corruption. These were followed by the 1996 Inter-American Convention Against Corruption, the 1997 Organization for Economic Cooperation and Development Convention on Combating Bribery of Foreign Public Officials in International Business Transactions, the 1999 Council of Europe Criminal Law Convention on Corruption together with its Additional Protocol and, finally, the 2003 Council of Europe Civil Law Convention on Corruption. In addition to these *Euro-American* instruments, the dawn of the new millennium also saw the birth of two anti-corruption treaties in *Africa*, the 2001 South African Development Community Protocol Against Corruption and the African Convention on Preventing and Combating Corruption of September 2002, as well as the first *global* anti-corruption instrument, the 2004 United Nations Convention against Corruption. Both the African and UN conventions will likely cause a major sea change in the global war against corruption upon entry into force. The former speaks to the needs of a continent whose modern history of statehood is littered with unimaginable acts of indigenous spoliation: a continent that has watched helplessly over the last four decades or so as an estimated $400 billion or more of its scarce development resources have been looted by its *own* leaders, elected as well as appointed, and stashed away in foreign banks. The latter, with its clearly articulated and hopefully enforceable provisions for the recovery and repatriation of looted assets, holds out the promise of a comprehensive *international* legal instrument to combat corruption. These developments are examined in some detail in this chapter.

I have also made changes in Chapter 6 by updating state practice since 1995. Particular attention is placed on the legal problems dogging the former President of Zambia and former government ministers that are related to their alleged involvement in looting their respective national economies; Nigeria's investigations of a former head of state and the government's attempts to recover sovereign funds looted by the late military ruler, General Sani Abacha and members of his family; the lifting of President Estrada of the Philippines' immunity, his impeachment in the Senate and subsequent trial for acts of indigenous spoliation.

In revising Chapter 8 on 'Judicial Barriers to Holding Heads of State Individually Liable for Acts of Indigenous Spoliation,' I have included changes in bank secrecy laws, particularly the Swiss Government's willingness to waive its blocking statutes to permit victim States to recover stolen funds, and recent developments on the Foreign Sovereign Immunities Act and the Act of State defense and their implications for piercing the veil of sovereign immunity in indigenous spoliation cases. The discussion on the doctrine of individual responsibility in Chapter 9 has been substantially revised to include changes contained in the final version of the Draft Code of Crimes against the Peace and Security of Mankind that the ILC submitted to the United Nations General Assembly in 1996 for adoption.

The discussion in Chapter 10 on the legal basis of jurisdiction over crimes of indigenous spoliation has been updated also to include the more significant scholarly contributions on the subject that have been published during the past ten years. The revised Chapter 10 also explores opportunities for public interest legal action and strategies to pursue legal remedies for corruption arising from indigenous spoliation. Finally, the recommendations in the concluding chapter have been revised to include what could very well be emerging 'soft law' in the form of standards, codes and guiding principles adopted by the International Monetary Fund and the World Bank in the fight against corruption. The inclusion of all this new material has regrettably resulted in practically doubling the size of the original book.

The central argument articulated in the first edition remains unchanged. There I argued that the most effective way to combat corruption involving high-ranking state officials is by elevating it to the status of a crime of universal interest, that is, a crime under international law that: (a) entails individual responsibility and punishment; and (b) is subject to universal jurisdiction. The appeal of high-level corruption as a crime that shocks the conscience of humankind lies in the essential attributes of a universal crime. Drawing from the jurisprudence of the Nuremberg Tribunal, a crime of universal interest exhibits three crucial basics. First, jurisdiction over this crime is universal and any state may participate in its repression even though it was not committed in its territory, was not committed by one of its nationals, or was not otherwise within its jurisdiction to prescribe and enforce. The ubiquity of jurisdiction guarantees that those who divert national assets into their private bank accounts can run but will find no place to hide.

Acknowledgments

My thanks are due to my colleagues Joseph Norton (James L. Walsh Distinguished Faculty Fellow in Financial Institutions and Professor of Law at SMU Dedman School of Law), Professor Chris Okeke of Golden Gate University College of Law and Dr. Roberto MacLean (onetime Ambassador Extraordinary and Plenipotentiary of Peru to the United States and former Judge of the Supreme Court of Peru) who were among the first group of publicists to grasp the significance of this emerging field of international economic law and who not only encouraged me in this venture but likewise drew my attention to certain lacunae in the text of the first edition. My debt to them is immense! Thanks are also due to my research assistants, past and present, at SMU Dedman School of Law: Ms. Victoria Roa (LL.M. 2004) and Ms. Seema Sharma (LL.M. 2004, J.D. 2006), and to Carolyn Yates and Sharon Magill for preparing a camera-ready copy of the manuscript. I acknowledge the immense contribution of Ms. Yolanda Eisenstein (J.D. 2004) who prepared most of the revisions to chapter 2 and, in the process, became an expert on the International Law Commission's Articles on State Responsibility. Last, but by no means least, I must express my warmest gratitude to John B. Attanasio (Dean and William Hawley Atwell Professor of Constitutional Law, SMU Dedman School of Law) for having provided me with two generous research grants in the summers of 2003 and 2004 that allowed me to complete the revision of this new edition. I am also deeply grateful to him for the financial support of my research assistants.

The first edition of this book was originally published by Kluwer Law International under its International Economic Development Law series. Kluwer discontinued the series following a merger with Aspen Publishers of New York while I was in the throes of revising the book for a second edition. Luckily for me, Ashgate Publishing Limited came to the rescue and agreed to publish the second edition. I am immensely grateful to Ms. Alison Kirk, Senior Commissioning Editor, for her favorable recommendation to the Board of Editors of Ashgate Publishing Limited.

I need hardly say that the views expressed in this book are my own personal views and do not engage anyone else.

Ndiva Kofele-Kale
SMU Dedman School of Law
Dallas, TEXAS
August 2005

Chapter 1

Introduction

THE NATURE OF THE PROBLEM

Colony is a petroleum-rich country blessed with vast deposits of gold, diamonds and other precious minerals. It gained its independence from Empire in 1965. Independence was followed by five years of civil strife. In 1970, *le maréchal* Pangloss with the help of 'the firm' overthrew a fragile civilian government and installed himself President-for-Life. From the beginning he used Colony's vast mineral wealth as his personal preserve and within two decades had accumulated an estimated $5 billion, an amount almost twice Colony's entire foreign debt! In early 1990, bowing to pressure from major Western aid donors, Pangloss allowed political parties to organize and shortly thereafter held Colony's first multiparty parliamentary elections. These were immediately followed by Presidential elections, also the first since *maréchal* seized power in 1970. Pangloss lost the elections to his ex-wife, Candide, a former World Bank official and Colony's first ambassador to Empire. An attempted putsch by the Presidential Guard to return Pangloss to power fizzled; Pangloss was implicated in this *coup manqué* and placed under house arrest pending trial before a military tribunal. After complicated negotiations, Pangloss was allowed to choose between a life in exile to one under his former wife. Preferring the former, the Marshall sought and was immediately granted political asylum in the United States where his eldest son was serving as Colony's ambassador. Pangloss left Colony on a chartered French Concorde – since he no longer had access to the Presidential jet – accompanied by two of his four wives (a third having had a change of heart decided to throw in her lot with Candide), children, in-laws, assorted relatives and his closest associates. He also took along several crates filled with currency, jewels, precious stones, negotiable instruments and, thrown in for good measure, numerous trunks containing 150 of his bespoke hats and turbans.

With Pangloss gone the new government began to assess the wreckage. Left behind, a shocked President Candide soon discovered, was an economy that had been brusquely ransacked and almost completely destroyed with the balance of payments registering a current account deficit of 11% of GDP compared to a surplus of 7% five years previously; GDP falling by an alarming 9% on average the previous 3 years and likely to fall a further 6-7% that year; investments and imports at about 30% and 20%, respectively, below their levels three years previously; a fall in export earnings, together with internationally uncompetitive domestic interest rates which encouraged capital flight in the last three years of Marshall Pangloss's administration, resulting in a dramatic decline in Colony's net foreign reserves from $5 billion in June 1985 to minus $3.2 billion on the eve of the presidential elections; a severe drop in government revenues and a sizeable deficit equivalent to 15% of GDP in government operations; and to top it all, a foreign debt of $3 billion. The situation was bleak.

The details of the problem are hypothetical, yet its substance is very real. Colony could just as easily pass for the Philippines under Ferdinand Marcos or the Romania of Nicolae Ceausescu or Jean-Claude (Baby Doc) Duvalier's Haiti or the Shah's Iran or the Paraguay of Stroessner; and the fictional Marshall Pangloss lives through the likes of Teodoro Obiang Nguema of Equatorial Guinea, or the Sani Abachas of Nigeria.

The issues raised by this conduct – the sacking of national treasuries by the very people in whom the public trust is placed, the subsequent flight of these individuals to safe havens in Europe and America to live out their remaining years in luxury and the attempts by the victim states to recover spoliated sovereign assets – represent a complex and under-analyzed area of international law. But it is one likely to take on increasing significance in this decade as the democratization process proceeds in States that were formerly under authoritarian rule and as the new governments are pressured by populations increasingly conscious of their fundamental economic rights to go after former rulers. In countries that have been injured by this kind of massive looting of their wealth and resources, this practice has become the single most important obstacle to economic development.[1] In each of the countries discussed in this study, the confusion of public finance with private financial interests of constitutionally-responsible officials has had fatal consequences for the vast majority of the population. This tradition of plundering the national treasury has brought about human suffering on a tragic scale, rolled back the little gains in economic advancement and given ground to those who advocate a return to the age of imperial rule.[2]

Fraudulent enrichment by heads of states and other top State officials have become a permanent factor in the political life of many countries. Their lethal effects on the world economy have been acknowledged and international policy makers have begun to take tentative steps to bring these activities under international discipline. Although the response to the problem of indigenous spoliation has been slow when contrasted to the international preoccupation with efforts aimed at protecting and preserving for future generations endangered

1 See also Joseph Nye, 'Corruption and Political Development: a cost-benefit analysis,' in *Political Corruption: A Handbook*, 966 (Arnold J. Heidenheimer, Michael Johnson & Victor T. Le Vine eds, 1989); Robert Williams, *Political Corruption in Africa* (1987).

2 See Paul Johnson, 'Colonialism's Back – and Not a Moment Too Soon,' *The New York Times Magazine*, 18 April 1993/Section 6, 22, 43–44.

species such as the Nile crocodile, the Asian and African elephant and leopard,[3] the whale,[4] the rain forest, stolen art, and so on,[5] at least the problem has been

---

[3] See for example s. 7(a)(2) of the Endangered Species Act, 16 USCS s. 1536(a)(2) which requires each federal agency to consult with the United States Secretary of the Interior to ensure that any action authorized, funded, or carried out by such agency is not likely to jeopardize the continued existence of any endangered or threatened species. See also Michael J. Glennon, 'Has International Law Failed the Elephant?' *American Journal of International Law*, 84, 1 (1990).

[4] See Anthony D'Amato & Sudhir K. Chopra, 'Whales: Their Emerging Right to Life,' *American Journal of International Law*, 85, 21 (1991).

[5] One is not downplaying the importance of animal preservation except to suggest that such efforts must be put in some perspective and context. The author is a Cameroonian national whose ethnic group, the Bakweri, live on the slopes of Mt. Cameroon, the highest mountain in West Africa. The Bakweri are traditionally hunters and farmers and Fako, as they call their mountain, is where they have their farms and have done all their hunting since time immemorial. Fako is also home to a variety of wildlife ranging from the lowly porcupine to the majestic African elephant. The Bakweri have hunted and continue to hunt and trap these animals much as their ancestors did. In times past the game hunted was for subsistence, but with the advent of colonization and the introduction of the modern economy, Bakweri traded their catch for money to pay their taxes among other things. Recent efforts by the Cameroon government armed with grants from foreign groups to turn the mountain into a wildlife reserve have been met with bewilderment and resistance from the Bakweri. They cannot understand how the source of their livelihood, their very existence could be taken away from them in the name of wildlife preservation. The author has been approached by many of the affected people for legal help to stop what they consider to be foolishness on the government's part. The point of this narrative is to underscore the fact that definitions of human rights are culture-bound and conflicts in values arise when one tries to impose one culture's definition of human rights on another's. The inevitable clash between the Bakweri and the central government results from the attempt to juxtapose the so-called universal human right to a quality environment with the right of peoples to pursue their traditional practices without outside interference; it results from the attempt to pit the concern of the universally-minded environmentalist for the state of the earth a century hence against the concern of subsistence farmers and hunters for their survival a month hence. Preserving all the elephants in Mt. Cameroon will not change the quality of life of the vast majority of the Cameroonian population if at the same time its rulers are emptying the national treasury and carting the money to banks in Europe and America. I can speak with authority for the Bakweri of Cameroon who are resisting government efforts to turn their hunting ground into a wildlife preservation. They see such attempts as an infringement of some of their basic human rights. Whose values and judgment should prevail: the universalist who states the case for all mankind or the communalist who retorts that the universalist cannot speak for his people? For an examination of how these issues have been dramatically played out in a court of law, see, for example, Mabo v. Queensland (No. 2) 175 CLR 1 (1992) (Where the High Court of Australia held that Australia was not *terra nullius* when first occupied and that significant pre-settlement indigenous land rights continued to exist under the common law of Australia); see also Gerard P.J. McGinley, 'Natural Resource Companies and Aboriginal Title to Land: The Australian Experience

recognized. To be sure, international condemnation of the trafficking of stolen cultural property[6] and the steps taken by the community of nations to stem this illicit trade represents the kind of response one would have expected for a problem such as indigenous spoliation.[7] And the attempts made thus far to criminalize the illicit taking and movement of cultural property[8] and to define it as an international crime in the Draft International Criminal Code[9] provide a model to which advocates of bringing indigenous spoliation under some kind of international discipline would aspire. Clearly, if the plunder of cultural assets can engage international concern, then the organized and systematic theft of a nation's wealth and resources by its leaders deserves no less. If this demonstrated concern for the illicit trafficking in art objects is justified on grounds that such activities destroy a nation's cultural patrimony, the theft of its wealth and natural resources has similar consequences; in its wake, an economy plundered and pillaged with the consequential deferment into a distant future of the expectations of entire populations of ever enjoying the good life. But the discussion of this problem has somehow been ceded to newspaper columnists, editorial writers and lawyers representing successor governments trying to sue in foreign courts to get back some of the spoliated funds.[10]

Mabo and its Aftermath,' *International Law*, 28, 695 (1994). For a sensitive treatment of the subject, see Jonathan S. Adams & Thomas O. McShane, *The Myth of Wild Africa: Conservation Without Illusion* (1992) (decrying the adoption of European-inspired preservationist policies that restrict local access to land and game while noting that the imposition of western ideas of wildlife conservation has prevented the emergence of an indigenous policy based on African values).

6 See, for example, The Pennsylvania Declaration Decision of Curators of the University Museum, University of Pennsylvania (1 April 1970); The Harvard Report (29 November 1971).

7 See L. Potter & B. Zagaris, 'Toward a Common US-Mexican Cultural Heritage in the Recovery and Return of Stolen Cultural Property,' *Transnational Lawyer*, 5, 627 (1992); L. Prott & P. O'Keefe, *National Legal Council of Illicit Traffic in Cultural Property* (UNESCO) (1983); and Halina Niec, 'Legislative Models of Protection of Cultural Property,' *Hastings Law Journal*, 27, 1089 (1976).

8 See James A.R. Nafziger, 'International Penal Aspects of Crimes Against Cultural Property and the Protection of Cultural Property,' in *International Criminal Law*, 525 (M. Cherif Bassiouni ed., 1986).

9 See M. Cherif Bassiouni, *International Criminal Law: A Draft Criminal Code*, 98–99 (1980).

10 See Weiner, 'Recovering Wealth from Dictators Is Not Easy,' *The Washington Times*, 24 September 1990, at A7, col. 1; Drogin, 'Corruption; Manila Under Fire for Its Deals on Marcos Assets,' *The Los Angeles Times*, 24 November 1990, at A3, col. 1; Tempest, 'Ex-Despots Can't Bank on the Swiss,' *The Los Angeles Times*, 31 January 1990, at 1, col. 1; Hetzer, 'The Pols & Pariahs; The Wealth That Leaves No Tracks,' *Fortune*, 12 October 1987, at 189; Kraar, 'Where Do You Hide $10 Billion? Aquino Wants to Know,' *Fortune*, 14 September 1987, at 97 (Marcos's 'declared net income over 22 years [in office] was just $224,750.'); Frontline, *In Search of the Marcos Millions*, at 2 (PBS television

The apparent neglect of this important subject matter in part is a reflection of the nature of the scholarship in this area. Discussions of the consequences of high level political corruption in the last two decades have been shaped by what Laurence Whitehead terms a *realpolitik* stance.[11] This paradigm, which has dominated the writings of American political scientists, avoids any outright condemnation of political corruption, preferring instead a 'balance sheet' approach which strains to break down the social costs and benefits of political corruption. Adherents to the *realpolitik* school do not see corruption as a problem to be overly concerned about, given, as they claim, its functional or utilitarian role in any political system and, more particularly, in developing Third World countries.[12]

---

broadcast, May 26, 1987; transcript no. 511); *Marcos Bid to Stash Gold in Australia, Newspaper Report*, Associated Press, 5 March 1986.

At its 81st Annual Meeting in 1987, the American Society of International Law broke new ground when it devoted an entire panel to address the problem of indigenous spoliation; see Abram Chayes, 'Pursuing the Assets of Former Dictators,' *Proceedings of the 81st Annual Meeting of the American Society of International Law*, 394 (1987) (Michael P. Malloy ed., 1990) [hereinafter ASIL Proceedings]. A couple of years later, the remarkable humanist, Michael Reisman, in a piece that appeared in the American Journal of International Law, attempted to draw attention once again to this scourge. In that brief commentary, Reisman decried the preoccupation of traditional scholarship with the exploitation of the natural wealth of developing countries by giant multinational corporations while ignoring internal forms of wealth exploitation. As he argued, the 'ritual of condemnation of foreign corporations' spoliations of the resources of developing countries and their elevation to the level of international concern have obscured the problem of spoliations by national officials of the wealth of the states of which they are temporary custodians. The effects of this neglect have been much confusion and paralysis about the status of funds spoliated by high government officials and cached abroad. It was time, Reisman reasoned, to harness 'international law to restrain and recapture' spoliated wealth. See W. Michael Reisman, 'Harnessing International Law to Restrain and Recapture Indigenous Spoliations,' *American Journal of International Law*, 83, 56–57 (1989).

[11] See Laurence Whitehead, 'On Presidential Graft: the Latin American Evidence,' in *Corruption: Causes, Consequences and Control*, 146, 154 (Michael Clarke ed. 1983). Whitehead's realpolitik school is also referred to as the functionalist paradigm by other political scientists. See Edward van Roy, 'On the Theory of Corruption,' *Economic Development and Cultural Change*, 19, 87 (1970); Arnold J. Heidenheimer, 'Introduction,' in *Political Corruption: Readings in Comparative Analysis*, 479 (Arnold J. Heidenheimer ed.. 1970); Samuel P. Huntington, *Political Order in Changing Societies*, 69 (1968).

[12] See Nye, *supra* note 1. (Advances the argument that corruption is a necessary element in the development of nations because in the early stages of development, societies lack the infrastructures necessary to make things work. Entrepeneurs who bend the rules can bring together the resources they need to create development. The system becomes dysfunctional only when a middle class and/or a student population emerges, because those groups, more than anyone else, believe in morality and law!) But see Sinnathamby Rajaratnam, 'Bureaucracy versus Kleptocracy,' in *Political Corruption: A Handbook*, 546 (Arnold J. Heidenheimer, Michael Johnston & Victor T. Levine eds, 1989) (arguing that kleptocracy has led to economic anarchy, political instability, and the eventual replacement

They tend therefore to view corruption as a lesser of two evils,[13] touting as one of its beneficial consequences its contribution to the non-violent resolution of social conflicts.[14]

Functionalists, in fact, posit an inverse relationship between corruption and political instability by arguing that the average costs of political corruption are likely to diminish over the life of a regime as it becomes more secure. Thus, it is better for a country to retain a corrupt person as president for an extended period rather than changing presidents fairly frequently in order to minimize the cost of presidential fortunes.[15] In a system where presidential graft is a way of life, as is the case in much of the Third World, each change in leadership sets in motion a wave of corruption as the new president will try to amass his own wealth in the shortest possible time. Though this can be ruinous to a country's economy, to adherents of the *realpolitik* school, overall political corruption is the lesser of evils.[16] It is reasoned that once presidential graft has become established, it can be relied upon as a substitute for violent conflict.

But others have argued instead that in embracing this socially beneficial formulation of corruption academics have unwittingly conferred the stamp of respectability on political corruption in general and presidential graft in

---

of democracy by civilian or military autocracies). At the time this article was written, the author was the minister of foreign affairs and labor of Singapore and well-placed to know the destructive effects of high-level corruption.

13 See Whitehead, *supra* note 11, at 156.

14 *Id.*, at 156.

15 An unidentified supporter of a South American dictator is quoted in 1956 as saying that: 'It is cheaper for the country that he should be president for life, because he has made his fortune and is satisfied. When we changed presidents every few years, the cost of presidential fortunes used to ruin us.' See 'Towards a Grammar of Graft,' *Economist*, 15 June 1957, at 959, col. 2.

16 Available evidence would tend to refute this thesis. For example, throughout the 20 or so years that Ferdinand Marcos was President of the Philippines, his country was plagued by an increasingly challenging communist insurgency. Some analysts saw a direct connection between the flow of funds out of the Philippines – estimated as high as $30 billion since the 1950s – and the rising tide of guerilla war. A Western diplomat in the Philippines was convinced that 'the mind-boggling manipulation of the economy by less than 1 percent of the population has created fertile ground for the communists' appeal among the 99 percent who are have-nots.' A Western economic analyst was even more blunt: 'The exploitation of the vast underclass by the handful of rich with political and military connections - the very people who are investing huge fortunes overseas – must be viewed as a fundamental contributing factor to the insurgency.' These views were echoed by a senior Filipino corporate executive who put it this way: 'The poor have lost all hope. They are ripe for anything that offers change. The insurgency is a direct reflection of the maldistribution of wealth, and the salting of dollars overseas is but one example of how horribly twisted things are.' Quoted in *Congressional Record-Senate*, 7 November 1985, 31165, cols. 2 & 3.

particular,[17] an imprimatur which may very well explain why international policy-makers have been slow to condemn the practice. Yet, to the victims of presidential graft there is nothing academic about this pestilence. Soon after becoming Prime Minister of Ghana in 1969, Dr. Kofi Busia, an Oxford-educated sociologist no less – who would himself go down in ignominy a few years later under the weight of corruption charges leveled against him[18] – acknowledged that high-level official corruption was the biggest threat to the national economy.[19] For Ghana as well as numerous other countries, longevity in office has never been known to dampen a president's acquisitive tendencies. Whitehead cites the case of Trujillo whose 'acquisitiveness was never dimmed by satiation'[20] even after 31 years as President of the Dominican Republic. He may also have included in Trujillo's company, Mobutu of Zaire, Marcos of the Philippines, Stroessner of Paraguay, the Duvaliers, *père et fils*, of Haiti, who ruled their countries, respectively, for 30 years, 21 years, 31 years, and 30 years – during which period none of these dictators showed any signs of slowing down the pace of personal aggrandizement.

To suggest to the citizens of these countries – the teeming Haitians adrift in the high seas in leaky makeshift vessels making one last desperate attempt to escape from the wrenching poverty that is Haiti, or to Filipinos who must travel thousands of miles away from home in search of menial jobs in the more prosperous Gulf States, or the millions of poverty stricken Zaireans, Equato-guineans and Cameroonians who have no hope of ever escaping their fate – that high-level official corruption has some broad redeeming social value is to invite their boos and jeers and to risk being dismissed as unhinged, for these human flotsam and jetsam are the immediate casualties of indigenous spoliation.[21] What would one

---

17 See Whitehead, *supra* note 11, at 159.

18 Busia was the target of the Taylor Assets Committee set up by the National Redemption Council. For a fuller discussion on commissions of inquiry, see Chapter 6 infra.

19 See Herbert H. Werlin, 'The Roots of Corruption - the Ghanaian Enquiry,' *Journal of Modern African Studies*, 10, 247, 251 (1972) (hereinafter cited as 'Roots of Corruption').

20 See Whitehead, *supra* note 11, at 157.

21 Sometime in December 1993 government employees in Cameroon went on strike to protest against deep salary cuts (between 50–70%), unpaid arrears and other related grievances. *See* Memorandum submitted by Public Service Employees of the South West Province through the Prime Minister, Head of Government to His Excellency the Head of State, President of the Republic, in Reaction to the Recent Salary Cuts, 29 December 1993 (on file at SMU School of Law). Much of the public school system was closed down because striking teachers refused to teach; the judiciary in some provinces stopped administering justice while government hospitals continued their long tradition of abandoning the sick. The government complained of not having money to pay state employees or to service its internal debts and the international community has refused to come to its rescue citing among other things gross mismanagement, excessive corruption in high places, and persistent human rights abuses. See 'Democracy in West Africa: Moins ca change,' *Economist*, 22 January 1994, at 45–46. Cameroonians have been asking for quite

think of a doctor who devotes the better part of his examination of a patient with high fever doing a cost-benefit analysis of the disease? Surely you would expect the physician to attempt to lower the patient's body temperature and to do everything medically possible to discover the underlying infection responsible for producing the fever with a view toward eliminating it?[22] The conventional wisdom of treating this problem as an exercise in 'balance sheet balancing' is ripe for reassessment.

---

some time now where all their national wealth went. Striking public service employees thought they had the answer. In their memorandum to the government, they called attention to the 'known and proven cases of embezzlement of public funds where protected culprits have remained unpunished and the funds unrecovered . . . [and] the mass stashing of public funds in foreign banks and businesses by, again, the very known privileged persons.' *Id.*, at 2. Newspaper accounts of a long history of illegal trafficking of capital out of Cameroon riveted the public for one brief week in August 1990. See 'Probe the Alleged Embezzlers,' *Cameroon Post*, No. 39 Wed. 8 August–15 August 1990, 1; 'Qu'est ce qui ne va pas dans le système Biya,' *International News Hebdo,* No. 91 du 01/8/1990, 4–6. It was revealed that in the thirty years since independence, an estimated 1,610 billion CFA francs (CFAF), roughly $5,313 million, have been embezzled by public officials and safely stashed away in European banks. *Id.* Of this amount, 650 billion CFAF or $2,145 million, left the country during a four-year period, 1986–1990. See P-J. Tedga, 'Enterprises Publiques, Etat et Crise au Cameroun: Faillite d'un Systeme, 246–56 (1990). These figures need to be put in some perspective. Cameroon's export receipts for the period 1985–1990 have averaged about 587 billion CFAF ($1,937 million), that is, about 63 billion CFAF less than the amount of public funds allegedly stolen during this same period. Cameroon's total external debt in 1990 was an estimated 1,470 billion CFAF (not including external payment arrears). In fiscal year 1 July 1989 to 30 June 1990 alone a total of 55 billion CFAF were earmarked for debt amortization: 43 billion CFAF for interest payments and 12 billion CFAF toward principal repayments. If as much as 75% of the estimated 650 billion CFAF that left Cameroon illegally between 1986–90 were repatriated, that amount would be enough to cover her service obligations *ceteris paribus* for the next several years. And if only 50% of these assets were freed and applied to the external debt, it would reduce it by about 22 percent. Put differently, private Cameroonian wealth abroad is enough to wipe out the country's external debt! Even if there is some quibbling over the exact amount, it is really beyond dispute that substantial sums of money have snaked their way out of the national territory for parts unknown. No less a personage than the country's Minister of Finance conceded this point during his highly publicized appearance before the National Assembly in December 1990. See Peut-on repatrier nos capitaux? *Cameroon Tribune*, no. 4782, Lundi 10 decembre 1990, 1; see also 'Qu'est-ce qui fait fuir nos capitaux?' *Id.*, at 6. The public outrage stirred by these revelations of systematic looting of the national patrimony by so few and for so long has been understandably harsh. Much of this huge fortune was diverted into the pockets of the ruling elite with the Biya family allegedly heading the pack of plunderers. See for example, Gerard Mpessa Moulongo, 'Chronique d'un pillage annonce,' *Jeune Afrique Economie*, no. 151, janvier 1992, 175–83 (presents a who's who of prominent Cameroonians, public servants as well as private businessmen, who have mulcted the national treasury).

22 Werlin in discussing corruption in Ghana employs the metaphor but in a slightly different form. See 'Roots of Corruption,' *supra* note 19, at 250.

In the face of the outrageous practices just described, what should the international legal system do? What should other States that have not personally and directly been harmed by these activities do? What obligations do they owe to the injured State and its peoples? International attention needs to be drawn to this persistent problem of economic plunder in general and high level official graft in particular: the problem of indigenous spoliation. In line with this belief, the book will advance and attempt to confirm the thesis that acts of indigenous spoliation by high-ranking government officials violate the law of nations and should be treated as international economic crimes. These acts violate (1) convention-based obligations imposing on States parties a duty to promote individual economic rights within their domestic spheres, and (2) convention-based obligations imposing on States parties a duty to promote and protect fundamental human rights and freedoms. Finally, acts of indigenous spoliation violate international customary law. The widespread establishment, by States that have been victims of indigenous spoliation, of commissions of inquiry to investigate corrupt officials and the adoption of domestic legislation making indigenous spoliation an economic crime reflect State practice expressing existing international legal expectation relative to the obligations of constitutionally-responsible officials in the promotion of individual economic rights.

A DEFINITION OF INDIGENOUS SPOLIATION

For purposes of this study, indigenous spoliation is defined as an illegal act of *depredation* which is committed for private ends by *constitutionally responsible rulers, public officials* or *private individuals.*[23] Such terms as 'embezzlement' or

---

[23] The definition of corruption is much narrower; the focus is on the illegitimate use of power for private ends by a particular group of people who hold public trust: heads of states and governments, other high-ranking constitutionally elected and appointed leaders. The circle of persons liable for acts of indigenous spoliation tracks the list of possible offenders in Article IV of the Convention on the Prevention and Punishment of the Crime of Genocide, 9 December 1948, *United Nations Treaty Series*, 78 277. There was much discussion during the drafting of the Genocide Convention on the circle of persons liable for persecution under the convention. Should monarchs be included? Can the plea of acts of states be raised by an accused to abort any persecution? What about hiding behind a command of the law or superior orders? These were some of the questions the drafters grappled with. In the end, the final version of the Convention put to rest many of these concerns. Article IV stipulates that persons committing acts punishable under the Convention shall be punishable regardless of whether they are 'public officials or private individuals.' Some concern was raised whether this definition was not only limiting but imprecise as well in that there are persons who act on behalf of the State, such as Members of Parliament, who do not qualify as officials *strictu sensu.* The comment to article IV of the draft Convention prepared by the UN Secretary-General ('Those committing genocide shall be punished, be they rulers, public officials or private individuals') sought to clarify this

'misappropriation' or 'corruption' or 'graft' or 'fraudulent enrichment' have been, and continue to be, used to describe the widespread practice of office holders confusing the public fisc with their private accounts,[24] but these concepts do not adequately convey the full force of the relatively new phenomenon of indigenous spoliation.[25] If anything, they signify only the raw act of depredation but not its

---

point: '[t]he perpetration of genocide can indeed be the act of statesmen, officials or individuals. The heaviest responsibility is that of statesmen or rulers in the broad sense of the word, that is to say, heads of state, ministers and members of legislative assemblies, whose duty it is to abstain from organizing genocide personally and from provoking it and to prevent its commission by others.' See 'Draft Convention on the Crime of Genocide,' *United Nations Economic and Social Council Report*, 4, at 35, UN Doc. E/447 (1947). In the final version of Article IV that was adopted by the General Assembly the words 'constitutionally responsible' are added to qualify 'rulers.' It has been observed that the inclusion of 'constitutionally responsible rulers' among the circle of persons liable for persecution under the Convention explicitly excludes the plea of acts of state. See Robinson Nehemiah, *The Genocide Convention; Its Origins and Interpretation*, 22 (1949). As to the defense of superior orders, the comment on draft Article V suggests that the Article puts paid to that option and that it will no longer be possible for offenders 'to take shelter behind a command of the law or superior orders.' *See* Draft Convention, at 36. This provision, however, never made it into the final document that was adopted by State parties.

24 Kleptocracy has been offered as a substitute. See for example, Stanislav L. Andreski, *The African Predicament: A Study in the Pathology of Modernisation*, 93 ff (1968) (pointing out that the essence of kleptocracy is that the functioning of the organs of authority is determined by the mechanisms of supply and demand rather than the laws of regulation). The ordinary meaning associated with the term 'kleptocracy' is a ruling body or order of thieves. According to the Oxford English Dictionary, a kleptocracy also refers to a nation ruled by a government of thieves. Again, like the other terms, 'kleptocracy' only succeeds in describing the act of thieving but fails to convey its effects on the society. See *The Oxford English Dictionary*, 8, 477 (J.A. Simpson & E.S.C. Weiner eds, 2d ed. 1989). Others have taken to referring to these countries as 'vampire states'. See generally Jonathan Frimpong-Ansah, *The Vampire State in Africa: The Political Economy of Decline in Ghana* (1992) (arguing that Ghana's decline is due to the exploitation of the farmers, in particular the cocoa growers, first by colonial rule and then by the Ghanaian state).

25 Consider, for example, some of the startling disclosures that were made in three Commissions of Inquiry set up by the military government that overthrew a civilian one in Sierra Leone in 1991: the Beccles-Davis Commission of Inquiry headed by Justice Samuel Beccles-Davis investigated the assets and other related matters of the former President, Vice Presidents, Ministers, Ministers of State and Deputy Ministers who served in the Momoh administration between June 1986 and 22 September 1991; the Lynton Nylander Commission probed the financial activities of the various machinery which supported the government during this period, that is, government ministries, local authorities, parastatals including public corporations and the Bank of Sierra Leone; and the Marcus-Jones Commission headed by Justice Laura Marcus-Jones examined the assets and other related matters of all public officers, members of boards and employees of parastatals including public corporations, members of the armed and police forces.

One of the first witnesses to appear before the Beccles-Davis Commission was the former Inspector-General of Police, Mr. James Bambay Kamara, who disclosed that he had substantial money in several local and overseas bank accounts and occasionally kept between Le10,000 and Le20,000 in his office, which he used to help people. Kamara admitted that he owned over 30 pieces of property in the country including one which was bought for Le7.5 million less than two weeks before the coup that ejected him from office. The acquisitions were all made between 1974 and 1991 but at the time of the coup Mr. Kamara's monthly salary including allowances was Le18,042! It was also revealed that Kamara awarded Le96 million contract to an uncle of ex-president Momoh for the purchase of uniforms for the Security Services Division (SSD). A 50 percent deposit of the contract sum was deposited in a local bank, but up to the ousting of Momoh there was no sign of the SSD uniforms. Another example of phantom contracts that was brought to the attention of the Lynton Nylander Commission of Inquiry was the award of a $20 million contract to SIEMENS for the rehabilitation of the Sierra Leone Broadcasting Service. The contract was never performed though the contractors were paid Le66 million on the instructions of the former minister of information and broadcasting.

Fake contracts, kickbacks, assets out of step with salaries, and outright conversion of public funds were the order of the day in Sierra Leone. Take the case of Mr. Michael Abdulai, the former Minister of Transport and Communication, who also appeared before the Beccles-Davis Commission. His cabinet portfolio gave him jurisdiction over the country's sea and inland waters ports. In 1987 Abdulai executed a Memorandum of Understanding and Consultancy Agreement with Hamburg Ports Consultancy (HPC), the managers of the Sierra Leone Ports Authority (SLPA). The agreement provided that Abdulai would be paid in secret, a lump sum of $100,000 each year and that irrespective of change in status, profession or occupation or in the event of death or incapacitation, the money would be directed to his next of kin. In addition to all of this Abdulai also received a 10% commission on all purchases made overseas by the SLPA.

A former diplomat and government minister, Aiah M'bayo, told the Beccles-Davis Commission that the Algerian government had donated $4 million, 500 tons of fuel and a ship load of provisions, as Algeria's own contribution to the hosting of the OAU summit in Sierra Leone. But contrary to the intentions of the Algerian government, the money was distributed among some of Sierra Leone's ambassadors. M'bayo who negotiated for this OAU aid package and had the donation passed through him received for his efforts $25,000 and admitted before the commission that the package never benefitted Sierra Leone as a country! Other ministers and top public servants who testified before these commissions revealed huge assets that were out of step with their salaries. One senior official was found to own five homes and Le6 million in two bank accounts but could not account for the source of his wealth. Another with a salary of Le41,722 a month plus Le8500 allowance could boast two expensive foreign cars (a Mercedes Benz and a Volvo), a satellite dish costing Le2 million, a house under construction on which he had already spent Le17 million and shares in several local companies. He too could not tell the commission how he acquired his wealth. A former Foreign Minister, Alhaji Abdul Karim Koroma, owned a huge mansion in an exclusive Freetown suburb, a BMW car bought in 1988 for 25,000 pounds sterling and a satellite dish bought in 1991 for $8,000. He at least gave a glimpse into how he came by some of his wealth: selling food aid meant for starving Sierra Leonians and converting the money into his personal account. This is precisely what he did with the proceeds from the sale of Italian food aid! He was not alone in this practice. Other former ministers and some

effect, which is the destruction of the social, economic and moral foundation of the victim nation. What has been taking place in the last two decades or so is a coordinated plan whose effect, if not objective, is the destruction of the essential foundations of the economic life of a society. It is the systematic looting and stashing in foreign banks of the financial resources of a State; the arbitrary and systematic deprivation of the economic rights of the citizens of a nation by its leaders, elected and appointed, in military regimes as well as civilian governments in Africa, Asia, Latin America and Eastern Europe, on a scale so vast and never before seen in history. This activity deserves a new name, for, as Raphael Lemkin[26] argued some five decades ago when he introduced the word 'genocide' into the lexicon of political discourse, a new crime deserves a new name.[27] Thus, like

---

public servants close to ex-president Momoh acquired huge amounts from United States PL480 Fund for agricultural projects and community development and converted such monies to their own use.

This kind of graft contributed in no small measure to the classification of Sierra Leone as the poorest of the poor. This is not ordinary, run of the mill corruption but graft of a different order; the kind that can literally bankrupt a country's economy, arrest its development and condemn its people to a life of poverty and misery.

[26] Lemkin was one of three experts – the other two were Professor Donnedieu de Vabres of the University of Paris and Professor Pella, President of the International Association of Penal Law – who assisted Professor Humphrey, Director of the Division of Human Rights at the UN in preparing a draft convention on genocide. See *Draft Convention on Genocide*, at 15. Raphael Lemkin was a Polish-Jew who escaped from Nazi-occupied Poland and traveled to the United States where he pursued his twin passions of philology and international law. Lemkin spent much of the war trying to get the US authorities to understand the enormity of what was happening to European Jewry. He believed that once genocide was recognized in international and national law, it would inevitably be the more forcefully opposed by the community of nations. He had little success at first, but with the Holocaust and revelations of what the Nazis had done during World War II to specific groups, such as Jews and gypsies, the world became more receptive to outlawing such unconscionable behavior. Lemkin was an important figure behind the Convention on the Prevention and Punishment of the Crime of Genocide. Adopted by the United Nations on 9 December 1948 and entered into force on 12 January 1951. For a sympathetic treatment of Lemkin, see Samantha Power, *A Problem From Hell: America and the Age of Genocide* (2002).

[27] See Raphael Lemkin, 'Genocide – A Modern Crime,' *Free World*, 9, 39 (April 1945); see also Raphael Lemkin, 'Genocide,' *American Scholar*, 15, 227 (1946); and Raphael Lemkin, 'Genocide as a Crime under International Law,' *American Journal of International Law*, 41, 145 (1947). It may be argued that the depredations complained of here pale in comparison to the horrors of ethnic cleansing in Bosnia-Herzegovina or the killing fields of Cambodia and Kurdish Iraq, the kinds of physical destruction that shock the conscience of mankind and for which Lemkin's term 'genocide' is reserved. Be that as it may, recognition that spoliation by indigenous rulers is offensive is a step forward in the evolution of international law as it pertains to respect for the rights and obligations of individuals. Here is an activity whose effects are immediate as capital flight, particularly the

Lemkin before me, the author has immodestly taken the liberty of inventing the word '*patrimonicide*' as the name for this new international economic crime. The word comes from combining the Latin words '*patrimonium*' meaning '[t]he estate or property belonging by ancient right to an institution, corporation, or class; especially the ancient estate or endowment of a church or religious body'[28] and, of course, '*cide*' meaning killing. For is not indigenous spoliation the destruction (or killing, if you please) of the sum total of a nation's endowment; the laying waste of the wealth and resources belonging by right to her citizens; the denial of their heritage?

As Lemkin pointed out in his 1945 article, the crime of the Nazis 'in wantonly and deliberately wiping out whole peoples [was] not utterly new in the world. It [was] only new in the civilized world as we have come to think of it. It [was] so new in the traditions of civilized man that he [had] no name for it.'[29] So it is with indigenous spoliation, an ancient practice that has taken on some distinctively new features. Although political leaders have historically misappropriated the wealth of their peoples, three things separate the old from this new generation of 'economic crimes of former dictators.'[30] First, unlike past depredations where the wealth remained in the territory for recycling, the modern context is characterized by 'great mobility of wealth and the capacity to hide and disguise it.'[31] A Filipino senior executive of a multinational oil company operating in the Philippines said it all: 'If only these people kept their money here and reinvested it in productive enterprises, our problems would be a lot more manageable.'[32] So much then for the argument that this practice has a socially beneficial side to it.

---

massive amounts involved here, have immediate macro- and micro-economic consequences. The victims are easily identifiable: unemployed and underemployed college and university graduates whom the economy simply cannot absorb; ordinary citizens who cannot count on services from any of the social agencies, etc., undernourishment, high infant mortality rates, and so on.

28 See *The Oxford English Dictionary*, 11, 349 (J.A. Simpson & E.S.C. Weiner eds, 1989); see also *Oxford Latin Dictionary*, 1310 (P.G.W. Glare ed., 1983) (the property of a paterfamilias, private or personal possessions, estate, fortune).

29 *Id.*

30 See 'ASIL Proceedings' *supra* note 10, at 395. Presidential corruption is an old problem. Hugh Thomas' CUBA: THE PURSUIT OF FREEDOM (documents presidential corruption in Cuba dating back to the turn of the century during the administration of President Gomez ending with Fulgencio Batista's second time around as President of Cuba. Edwin Lieuwen also documents gross presidential graft in Venezuela covering a span of five decades), see also Edwin Lieuwen, VENEZUELA (1961).

31 See 'ASIL Proceedings' *supra* note 10, at 395; see also Hetzer, 'The Pols & Pariahs; The Wealth That Leaves No Tracks,' *Fortune*, 12 October 1987, at 189; Kraar, 'Where Do You Hide $10 Billion? Aquino Wants to Know,' *Fortune*, 14 September 1987, at 97.

32 Pete Carey et al., 'Marcos Topi Associates Stash Personal Fortunes Overseas,' *San Jose Mercury News*, in Congressional Record, 31, 170 (1985).

A second feature of the modern version of indigenous spoliation is the amount of wealth involved, usually billions of dollars. So stupendous are the amounts of wealth involved that one commentator was moved to describe these depredations as going beyond shame and almost beyond imagination.[33] Indeed, this private buildup of assets abroad is usually so large in relation to the total external debts of the countries from which these funds were spoliated that in some cases it even exceeds their total foreign debt.[34] A study by Morgan Guaranty Trust Company comparing the external assets and debt of six major debtor countries found that in 1985 Venezuelans had accumulated $54 billion of assets abroad; enough to wipe out their country's foreign debt of $38 billion; in that same year while Argentina's external debt was $49 billion, the private wealth held abroad by Argentinians was $33 billion; Mexicans had accumulated abroad $60 billion against the country's $97 billion foreign debt; for the Philippines, the foreign debt was $26 billion while private foreign wealth stood at $11 billion; Brazil and Nigeria owed, respectively, $106 billion and $20 billion to their foreign creditors as against $30 billion and $12 billion, respectively, in foreign assets held by their citizens.[35]

Finally, what is also new about contemporary indigenous spoliation is the social and economic devastation that follows when capital of the magnitude described above is allowed to leave any country, but particularly a capital-poor developing one. It is fairly certain that the ultimate losers and victims are the ordinary citizens.[36] The economies lose out because the accumulation of these substantial assets abroad has the effect of draining resources, both domestic and

---

[33] See D. Delamaide, *Debt Shock: The Full Story of the World Credit Crisis*, 60 (1984); see also C. Braeckman, *Le Dinosaure* (1990).

[34] See Rimmer de Vries, 'LDC Debt: Debt Relief or Market Solutions?' *World Financial Markets*, 1, 6 (Sept. 1986).

[35] *Id.*

[36] Commenting on the real estate buying spree of the Marcoses in the United States, Congressman Stephen Solarz noted that such actions cheat the Philippines in two ways: 'In the first place, President Marcos' salary is roughly $5,700 a year. That is, so far as we know, his only known public and legitimate source of income. It suggests either that he has a very good investment adviser, or that the resources he has acquired for the purpose of purchasing these properties have been corruptly obtained. The corrupt practices he has engaged in and encouraged have made him one of the world's richest men while impoverishing millions of people in his own country and greatly accentuating the prospects for progress on the part of the Communist-dominated New People's Army. Second, the hundreds of millions if not billions of dollars he has acquired represent resources that would otherwise be available to meet the basic needs of the Filipino people and to generate the kind of economic growth that can serve as an antidote to communism.' *Investigation of the Philippine Investments in the United States, Hearings before the Subcommittee on Asian and Pacific Affairs of the Committee on Foreign Affairs, House of Representatives*, 99th Cong. 1st & 2nd Sess., 263 (1985 & 1986) (Statement of Stephen Solarz, Chairman of the Subcommittee) [hereinafter Philippine Hearings].

external, that might otherwise have been used for domestic investment.[37] As resources are funneled into private accounts abroad, governments, state enterprises, central banks, and private-sector companies are forced to borrow from foreign lenders.[38] These external borrowings create new liabilities which must be paid off by governments whose economies are already overburdened with debt.[39] The whole of Africa spends four times more on the interest on its debts than on health.[40] Burundi, which has been described as a 'wretchedly poor country,'[41] uses up 30 per cent of its budget each year to service its external debts.[42] The price of these outflows of foreign exchange to the West is 'billions of dollars-worth of unsurfaced roads, unpurified water and untreated illnesses.'[43] And yet, these governments cannot count on the earnings on the accumulation of private assets to assist them in meeting their debt-servicing obligations since these earnings are not repatriated and therefore unavailable for this purpose.[44]

Focus on Heads of States and Other High-Ranking Officials

The focus of this study is not on the garden variety corruption but on the illegitimate use of power for private ends by a particular group of people who hold public trust: heads of state and government as well as other high-ranking constitutionally elected and appointed leaders. The focus on this group is justified on pragmatic as well as jurisprudential grounds.

Jurisprudential Basis for Heads of State Liability

The rule holding heads of state individually responsible for crimes that shock the

---

37 *Id.*

38 *Id.* According to the London-based *Economist,* Africa's debt in 1993 has more than tripled since 1980 as a result of new borrowings, and more importantly, because of the build-up of unpaid interest over the past decade. The result is that Africa has been able to meet only half of its debt-servicing obligations. See 'African debt: Borrowed time,' *Economist*, 22 May 1993 at 46.

39 *Id.* In order to keep up payments on their debts, many third world governments use up scarce foreign exchange. Uganda spends two-thirds of all foreign currency it earns from exports on servicing its debts. It has been estimated that the average share for sub-Saharan Africa is about a fifth.

40 *Id.*

41 *Id.*

42 *Id.*

43 *Id.*

44 *Id.* It is estimated that if the assets held by private-sector residents were yielding an average of 6 per cent annual return, the earnings, if repatriated, would generate foreign exchange sufficient to pay roughly one-third of the interest owed on the total external obligations of Argentina, Brazil, Mexico, Venezuela, Philippines, and Nigeria.

conscience of mankind is found in both treaty law and customary international. The rule of international law, which under certain circumstances heads of state are immunized from liability, cannot, the Nuremberg Tribunal held, 'be applied to acts which are condemned as criminal by international law. The authors of these acts cannot shelter themselves behind their official position in order to be freed from punishment in appropriate proceedings.'[45] This principle was subsequently codified in the Principles of Law Recognized in the Charter of the Nuremberg Tribunal and the Judgment of the Tribunal[46] as well as numerous other international instruments.[47]

Arthur Watts, in his Hague lectures, has acknowledged that 'the idea that individuals who commit international crimes are internationally accountable for them has become an accepted part of international law … It can no longer be doubted that as a matter of general customary international law a Head of State will personally be liable to be called to account if there is sufficient evidence that he authorized or perpetrated such serious international crimes.'[48] Through its work in the progressive development and codification[49] of international law, the International Law Commission has also recognized that the principle of head of state liability for crimes that shock the conscience of mankind has risen to the level of customary international law.[50]

---

[45] 'International Military Tribunal (Nuremberg) Judgment and Sentence,' *American Journal of International Law*, 41, 220–21 (1947).

[46] See 'Principles of Law Recognized in the Charter of the Nuremberg Tribunal and Judgment of the Tribunal.' Adopted by the UN International Law Commission, 2 August 1950. UN Doc. A/1316, *British Yearbook of International and Comparative Law*, 2, 374 (1950) (Principle III); see also 'Charter of the International Military Tribunal for the Far East' (Article 6).

[47] See for example Convention on the Prevention and Punishment of the Crime of Genocide. Concluded at New York, 9 December 1948. Entered into force, 12 January 1951. 78 UNTS 277 (Article IV); Statute of the International Tribunal (for the Prosecution of Persons Responsible for Various Violations of Humanitarian Law Committed in the Territory of the Former Yugoslavia). Annex to the Secretary-General's Report on Aspects of Establishing an International Tribunal for the Prosecution of Persons Responsible for Serious Violations of International Humanitarian Law Committed in the Territory of the Former Yugoslavia, UN Doc. S/25704 (3 May 1993), reprinted in 32 ILM 1159 (1993) (Article 7(2)); United Nations Security Council Resolution 955 on Establishing an International Tribunal for Rwanda (with Annexed Statute). Adopted 8 November 1994. SC Res. 955, UN SCOR, 49th Sess., 3453rd mtg., at 15, UN Doc. S/RES/955 (1994) (Article 6(2)); Rome Statute for the International Criminal Court. Adopted by the UN Diplomatic Conference of Plenipotentiaries on the Establishment of an International Criminal Court. A/CONF.183/9, 17 July 1998 (Article 27).

[48] See Sir Arthur Watts, *Recueil des Cours*, 82–4 (1994).

[49] Article 15 of the Statute of the International Law Commission defines codification as 'the more precise formulation and systematization of rules of international law in fields where there already has been extensive state practice, precedent and doctrine.'

[50] See Draft Articles on the Code of Offences against the Peace and Security of

The rule excluding head of state immunity for particularly heinous international crimes also finds support from the writings of the most highly qualified publicists. Over two centuries ago, Emmerich de Vattel in his Law of Nations acknowledged the 'great guilt of a sovereign who undertakes an unjust war' because he would be:

> … chargeable with all the evils, all the horrors, of the war; all the effusions of blood, the desolation of families, the rapine, the violence, the revenge, the burnings, are his works and his crimes. He is guilty towards the enemy, of attacking, oppressing, massacring them without cause, guilty towards his people, of drawing them into acts of injustice, exposing their lives without necessity, without reason, towards that part of his subjects whom the war ruins, or who are great sufferers by it, of losing their lives, their fortune, or their health. Lastly, he is guilty towards all mankind, of disturbing their quiet, and setting a pernicious example.[51]

These views were echoed at the close of the First World War by a group of leading publicists in a report they presented to the 1919 Preliminary Peace Commission.[52] On the issue of charging high-ranking members of former enemy forces for crimes against humanity, this blue chip panel stated that:

> [I]n the hierarchy of persons of authority, there is no reason why rank, however exalted, should in any circumstances protect the holder of it from responsibility when that responsibility has been established before a properly constituted tribunal. This extends even to the case of heads of states. An argument has been raised to the contrary based upon the alleged immunity, and in particular the alleged inviolability of a sovereign of a state. But this privilege, where it is recognized, is one of practical expedience in municipal law, and is not fundamental. However, even if, in some countries, a sovereign is exempt from being prosecuted in a national court of his own country the position from an international point of view is quite different … If the immunity of a sovereign is claimed to extend beyond the limits above stated, it would involve laying down the principle that the greatest outrages against the laws and customs of war and the laws of humanity, if proved against him, could in no circumstances be punished. Such a conclusion would shock the conscience of civilized mankind.[53]

Mankind. Adopted by the International Law Commission, 4 December 1954, *Yearbook of International Law Commission*, 150 (1954) (Article 3); and Draft Code of Crimes against the Peace and Security of Mankind. Adopted by the International Law Commission, 5 July 1996. Report of the International Law Commission on its Forty-Eighth Session. UN GAOR, 51st Sess., Supp. No. 10, at 9. UN Doc. A/51/10 (1996) (Article 7).

51 See Emmerich de Vattel, *The Law of Nations*, Book III, Chap. XI, §184 (1758) (Joseph Chitty, ed., 1883); see also Quincy Wright, 'The Legal Liability of the Kaiser,' *American Political Science Review*, 13, p120, 126 (1919).

52 See Commission on the Responsibility of the Authors of the War and on Enforcement of Penalties, 29 March 1919, Carnegie Endowment for International Peace, Division of International Law, Pamphlet No. 32, reprinted in *American Journal of International Law*, 14, 95 (1920) (Supp.)

53 *Id.*, at 116.

The rule that individuals notwithstanding their official position, even as head of state, is also recognized by contemporary publicists as the cornerstone of individual responsibility for crimes which shock the conscience of mankind.[54] There is therefore an emerging international consensus in favor of a rule that heads of state and other high-ranking officials are not immune for crimes against humanity and other serious international law crimes.

Pragmatic Grounds for Singling Out Heads of State

There are pragmatic reasons for paying so much emphasis on the criminal responsibility of heads of state. As Whitehead observed in the case of Latin America that:

> … the office of the presidency generally concentrates so much power and responsibility in the person of a single leader that an accurate analysis of political corruption must personalise and must devote special attention to the Chief Executive. Indeed, in a significant number of extreme cases, the head of state has harnessed the whole apparatus of state power to the task of advancing his own personal enrichment until it seems as though the first aim of political activity in certain countries ... is to facilitate the systematic 'extraction of surplus' on his behalf.[55]

The chief executive presides over the plunder of the state's resources; while limited corruption can always escape presidential scrutiny, 'but on a large-scale systematic basis it normally must require at least his tacit acquiescence and, more likely, his personal supervision.'[56] This view is consistent with what others have observed in the presidential regimes in Africa. In Ghana, for instance, the Apaloo Commission of Inquiry and several other commissions appointed to investigate high-level corruption during Kwame Nkrumah's administration revealed that he 'sat at the apex of the pyramid of government and party officials who had succeeded in institutionalizing political corruption at the highest levels.'[57] This assessment is shared by Stephen Riley whose study of corruption in Sierra Leone unveiled a substantial, systematic and systemic 'web of corruption … centred around the president [Siaka Stevens], his two vice-presidents, a range of senior ministers and parastatal heads, coupled with a group of potential economic beneficiaries.'[58] Graft

---

[54] Seefor example, Virginia Morris and Michael P. Scharf, *The International Criminal Tribunal for Rwanda*, 1, 246, 249 (1997); André Huet and Renée Koering-Joulin, *Droit Pénal International*, 54–5 (1994); Claude Lombois, *Droit Pénal International*, 142, 162, 506 (1971); Georg Schwarzenberger, *International Law as Applied by International Courts and Tribunals*, 2, 508 (1968).

[55] See Whitehead, *supra* note 11, at 147–8.

[56] *Id.*, at 148.

[57] See Victor T. Le Vine, *Political Corruption: The Ghana Case*, 29 (1975); see also Samuel Ikoku, *Le Ghana de Kwame Nkrumah*, 111 (1971).

[58] See Stephen Riley, ''The land of waving palms': political economy, corruption

at the presidential level is merely mirrored, on a smaller scale, by officials at all levels of government making chief executives the appropriate target for corruption inquiries.

However, given their intimate involvement in the organized plunder of national resources, it is not surprising therefore that such inquiries as well as laws prohibiting corruption almost always target low-level officials, rarely looking into what an American political scientist has described as 'the politically dangerous areas of the Presidency, the party, and the activities of the country's ministerial oligarchs'[59] – a view shared by another political scientist with respect to corruption investigations in Sierra Leone. Riley found this exercise useful only 'as evidence in areas of low-level, incidental and systematic corruption; they are not, however, and cannot for political reasons be used as evidence in cases of high-level systemic corruption. It is unlikely that a corrupt regime will investigate itself; it is only possible when there is a change of regime, and then the exercise is politically suspect (as an apologia for the current regime).'[60]

Finally, in light of the prevailing Western academic view that corruption is socially beneficial, a reminder of how the vast amounts of state funds routinely stolen by heads of state continue to exact a heavy financial toll on national economies might result in a reassessment of this thesis. Of five Latin American presidents ousted between 1952 and 1961, their reported fortunes, obtained mostly

---

inquiries and politics in Sierra Leone,' in *Corruption: Causes, Consequences and Control*, 190, 202 (Michael Clarke ed. 1983). Subsequent commissions of inquiry corroborate Stephen Riley's assessment. See Sierra Leone Government, White Paper on the Report of the Justice Beccles Davies Commission of Inquiry, Vol. 1, August, 1993.

59 Le Vine, *supra* note 57, at 23.

60 See Riley, *supra* note 58, at 195. Le Vine offers an identical explanation for Ghana: 'Statutes appear to have relatively little effect thus far on corruption. One reason may be that in Ghana those charged with eliminating corruption were tainted with it; indeed, under such circumstances, both investigations and remedial legislation tend to be ineffective and pointless, or to become elaborate exercises in hypocrisy.' See Le Vine, *supra* note 57, at 80. The Ghanaian novelist, Ayi Kwei Armah, is even more forthright in his dismissal of post-coup corruption inquiries in his country as no better than a net 'made to catch only the small, dispensable fellows, trying in their anguished blindness to leap and to attain the gleam and the comfort the only way these things can be done. And the big ones floated free, like all the slogans.' See Ayi Kwei Armah, THE BEAUTYFUL ONES ARE NOT YET BORN 180 (1969); see also Roots of Corruption, *supra* note 19, at 248. When corruption became so widespread and common in the Philippines, President Marcos in 1984 appointed a commission headed by then Trade and Industry Minister Roberto V. Ongpin to investigate persistent allegations that high-ranking officials close to the First Family were exporting huge amounts of illegally obtained state funds to safe havens abroad. The commission found that an estimated $1 billion was drained out of the Philippines in 1983 and about $2 billion in 1984. Few Filipinos had any confidence in the commission: '[it] was appointed by the president, and it will concentrate only on small operators. To expect otherwise would be silly self-deception,' said a consultant to a leading Philippine bank. See Congressional Record-Senate, 7 November 1985, 31165, col. 3.

through graft, has been placed at between $1.8 and $2.6 billion[61] against a total foreign debt of about $2 billion for the five countries.[62] More recently, Alfredo Stroessner who ruled Paraguay for 34 years until he was deposed in 1989 is believed to have salted away a fortune in foreign banks. The amount of state funds spoliated during this period by his associates have been quite spectacular. Take the case of a former roving ambassador Gustavo Gramont Berres, who fled to Europe when Stroessner was overthrown, and is alleged to have embezzled $60 million in public funds and was wanted in Paraguay to stand trial.[63] Or, the case of 36 former officials whose assets, the combined worth of which was estimated at $550 million, equivalent to one quarter of Paraguay's foreign debt![64] Latin American heads of states are not unique in this as a similar picture of corrupt enrichment by constitutionally responsible leaders also emerges in Africa. In the early 1960s, for example, Maurice Yameogo, first president of Upper Volta (now Burkina Faso) was tried for embezzling £1,212,000 during his spell in office.[65]

Sani Abacha, Ferdinand Marcos, Mobutu Sese Seko and Trujillo are long gone but indigenous spoliation has survived them. It has been kept alive by such new kleptocrats as Teodoro Obiang Nguema Mbasogo of Equatorial Guinea.

Beginning in 1996, President Obiang saw his tiny impoverished central African country become the third largest exporter of oil in Sub-Saharan Africa, after Nigeria and Angola, producing 500,000 barrels of petroleum a day and raking in about $5.5 billion dollars in oil revenues annually.[66] With a population of 523,051 these earnings would translate to a per capita income of $5,300,[67] a figure that is

---

61 Miguel Aleman of Mexico, $500–$800 million; Juan Peron of Argentina, $500–$700 million; Marcos Perez Jimenez of Venezuela, over $250 million; Cuba's Fulgencio Batista, $100–$300 million; and Rafael Trujillo of the Dominican Republic, $500 million. *See* Whitehead, *supra* note 11, at 146, 150.

62 *Id.*

63 See 'US Judge orders former Paraguayan ambassador held without bond,' *Reuters*, Tuesday, 4 June 1991, AM cycle.

64 See Municipal elections again postponed; Delay in compiling electoral rolls as voters unresponsive, Latin American Regional Reports: Southern Cone, 18 October 1990, 7. Of the total, $12 million were recouped in cash, properties and cattle from three high-ranking military officers: Gen. Hugo Dejesus Araujo, former social welfare director; Gen. Roberto Knopfelmacher, former president of the state oil company, Petropar; and Gen. Alcebiades Britez, former director of the national police. *Id.*

65 See Ruth First, *Power in Africa*, 103 (1970). Maurice Yameogo was President of Upper Volta from 5 August 1960 until 1966 when he was deposed by a military coup led by Lt. Col. Sangole Lamizana, his successor.

66 See Peter Maass, *A Touch of Crude*, MotherJones.com News (Jan./Feb. 2005) [hereinafter 'Maass']. Available on www.motherjones.com (last visited 26 February 2005).

67 See CIA, World Factbook–Equatorial Guinea. Available on www.cia.gov/cia/publications/factbook (last visited 27 February 2005); see also IMF, Republic of Equatorial Guinea: 2003 Article IV Consultation– Staff Report; Staff Statement; Public Information Notice on the Executive Board Decision; and Statement by the Executive

misleading, at best, since the average Equatoguinean scrapes by on roughly $2 a day; 30 percent of the population is unemployed; four of every ten children under age five suffer from malnutrition; for every 1,000 babies born to Equatoguinean mothers 101 die at birth; few ever get to visit a doctor since the country can only boast 125 physicians; and only 44 percent of the population has access to safe water. Yet, the Obiang government spends less than 2 percent, or a miserly $106 per capita, of the national budget for health service, one of the lowest in Sub-Saharan Africa.[68] Government commitment to the education of Equatoguineans is equally shameful – devoting 1.6 percent of total public expenditure for the period 1999–2001 on education.[69] Yet when in 1997 Equatorial Guinea received its first oil payments of $190 million, Obiang diverted $96 million into his private account.[70] This was just the tip of the iceberg, as a 2003 United States Senate investigation would subsequently uncover.[71]

President Obiang has chosen to use with impunity the patrimony of the Equatoguinean people to enrich himself and his family while denying them the basic fruits of development in the process. The US Senate Permanent Sub-Committee on Investigations discovered that Riggs Bank managed more than 60 accounts and Certificates of Deposits (CDs) for the Equatorial Guinea Government, its officials and their family members with balances and outstanding loans that together approached $700 million in 2003.[72] At least half of these accounts functioned as private banking accounts for senior Equatoguinean officials and members of their family.[73] Signatories to a number of standard business checking accounts in the name of the '*Republica de Guinea Ecuatorial– Tresoreria Genera*' were President Obiang; his son, Gabriel M. Obiang Lima, Secretary of State Mines and Energy; and his nephew, Melchor Esono Edjo, Secretary of State for Treasury and Budget. Two signatures, one of which had to be the President, were required to withdraw funds from these accounts.[74] President Obiang was also the beneficial owner of one account at this American bank and two CDs, with values in excess of $15 million, opened in the name of a Bahamian offshore shell corporation.[75] Not to be outdone, the President's first wife, Constancia Mangue Nsue, owned three CDs and maintained several accounts (one jointly with her

---

Director for the Republic of Equatorial Guinea (December 2003), IMF Country Report No. 03/385.

68 *Id.*

69 See UNDP, Human Development Reports. Available on http://hdr.undp.org/statistics/data/cty/cty_(last visited 27 February 2005).

70 See United States Senate Permanent Sub-Committee Investigations, Money Laundering and Foreign Corruption: Enforcement and Effectiveness of the Patriot Act. Case Study Involving Riggs Bank, 1, 39 (15 July 2004) [hereinafter 'Riggs Case Study'].

71 *Id.*

72 *Id.*, at 37.

73 *Id.*, at 46.

74 *Id.*, at 40.

75 *Id.*, at 42.

brother, Teodoro Biyogo Nsue, Equatorial Guinea's ambassador to the United States). Regular payments were made into these accounts by oil companies doing business in Equatorial Guinea.[76]

In addition to siphoning oil revenues and directing them to their private accounts, President Obiang, his sons and family members also control a number of companies in strategic sectors of the Equatoguinean economy: the only construction company and importer of construction-related materials (Abayak); a forestry company with exclusive rights of exploiting and exporting timber (Grupo Sofana); a company that provides security services (SONAVI); the national telecommunications company, Nusiteles G.E.; majority ownership interest in the state-owned Guinea Equatorial Oil & Gas Marketing Ltd. (GEOGAM); and 25 percent ownership in a liquid gas plant.[77]

This account of spoliation in Equatorial Guinea would not be complete without a discussion of how a head of state and his family members flaunt this stolen wealth: expensive homes in exclusive suburbs in the United States – a $7.5 million (only $300,000 less than Equatorial Guinea's external debt in 2001) penthouse apartment in Southern California for a playboy son, Teodoro Nguema Obinag, a $2.6 million mansion for President Obiang himself, a $1.5 million second residence for one of his several wives and for good measure a bank charge card with a *daily* limit of $10,000 – a $30 million presidential jet[78] while the son had to make do with a fleet of Ferraris, Lamborghinis and Bentleys.[79] Decent people reading these snippets should be sufficiently revolted by these excesses to want to do something to put an end to the crime of indigenous spoliation.

DOMESTIC CONSEQUENCES OF INDIGENOUS SPOLIATION

Haiti is considered today as not only underdeveloped but by almost any standard the most impoverished country in the Western hemisphere.[80] In a 1979 book *Peasants and Poverty. A Study of Haiti*, Lundahl described the relentless despoliation of the Haitian environment and people by a small class on a scale never before seen in the Western hemisphere since the Spanish Conquest.[81] One estimate puts this class at between 1 and 2 percent of the population, roughly

---

[76] *Id.*

[77] *Id.*, at 48–50.

[78] *Id.*, at 42.

[79] Maass, *supra* note 66.

[80] See A. Dupuy, *Haiti in the World Economy: Class, Race, and Underdevelopment since 1700*, 184 (1988).

[81] M. Lundahl, *The Haitian Economy: Man, Land and Markets*, 399 (1983). See also J. DeWind & D.H. Kinley III, *Aiding Migration: The Impact of International Development Assistance on Haiti*, 16 (1988).

24,000 people in a population of 5.9 million.[82] This class has appropriated 44 percent of the national income and owns 40 percent of the country's wealth.[83] Lundahl and others[84] contend that successive Haitian dictators but most notably under the Duvaliers (père et fils), established a predatory relation with the Haitian economy. They devised numerous strategies and deployed the entire machinery of the state, including all its repressive apparatus, to extract wealth from the economy: 'The treasury has continued to be legitimate prey for the cliques in power, and power is viewed as a means to reach the prey.'[85] As a result of this predatory relationship, it is estimated that between 1960 and 1967 as much as 87 percent of the government's expenditures were paid out directly or indirectly to Francois Duvalier's supporters.[86]

While in power from 1957 to 1971, Papa Doc Duvalier officially received a modest presidential salary of only $20,000 per annum. Yet, during the first few years in office, he was able to purchase two mansions for $575,000, amassed some $400,000 and stashed another $1.5 million in a Swiss bank account.[87] In 1963, according to estimates by the International Commission of Jurists, Duvalier and his close collaborators mulcted the Haitian treasury of about $10 million per year. The august body concluded that the only reason for this pillage was 'to place the country under tribute in order to ensure the future affluence of those in power.'[88] The plunder of the Haitian economy continued unabated under the regime of Duvalier (*fils*). Nothing was spared, no funds were sacred; not even foreign aid. International development assistance earmarked for economic development was systematically diverted away from the genuinely needy.[89] From 1973 through 1983, $477 million of international aid went to Haiti, of which amount the United States contributed $213.6 million.[90] During the first four years of Jean-Claude Duvalier's rule, official aid increased more than tenfold, reaching $59.3 million in

---

82 Dupuy, *supra* note 80, at 184.

83 *Id.*

84 *Id.* See also DeWind & Kinley, *supra* note 81.

85 Lundahl, *supra* note 81, at 399.

86 See DeWind & Kinley, *supra* note 81, at 20.

87 See Lundahl, *supra* note 81, at 345.

88 Quoted in B. Diederich & A. Burt, *Papa Doc: Haiti and its Dictator*, 257 (1969), cited in Lundahl, *supra* note 81, at 345.

89 See DeWind & Kinley, *supra* note 81, at 40. In an extensive review of United States AID programs undertaken in Haiti during the period 1973–1981, the US General Accounting Office somberly concluded that: 'The AID program to date has had a limited impact on Haiti's dire poverty.' See 'US General Accounting Office, Assistance to Haiti: Barriers, Recent Program Changes, and Future Options, Report ID-82-13,' 22 February 1982, at 6–7, cited in DeWind & Kinley, *supra* note 81, at 46.

90 See 'World Bank, Country Program Paper, Haiti 21–22' (1983), cited in DeWind & Kinley, *supra* note 81, at 41–42.

1975. By the early 1980s, this amount had almost doubled again, in excess of $100 million per year.[91]

But true to its predatory character, Haiti's ruling class pocketed close to one-third of all foreign aid and as much as 80 percent of the US-provided assistance in the years preceding Jean-Claude's rise to power. During 1977–1978 alone, $69 million, an amount equal to 63 percent of all recorded central government revenues in 1978, were misappropriated by the Haitian government.[92] Students of Haiti see a direct connection between the predatory state and Haiti's poverty.[93] They point out that wealth extracted from the national economy has never been used to finance public services or economic development programs likely to benefit the masses of Haitians. Accumulated wealth has been used instead to maintain the opulent lifestyle of the ruling class and to 'feed the ravenous appetite of the repressive state security apparatus.'[94] During the three decades the Duvaliers were in power, the standard of living of the majority of Haitians declined significantly. The per capita GDP declined from about $80 in 1950–1951 to $74 in 1967–1968 while the per capita income went down from $67 in 1962 to $62 in 1967. Haiti in 1967 had the highest infant mortality rate in the Americas (147 per 1000) with 50 percent of children dying before the age of 5; the lowest life expectancy (47.5 years); a generalized malnutrition and the lowest per capita consumption of calories and protein (1700/40); a total of 332 medical doctors or 0.68 doctors per 10,000 inhabitants (in contrast to 1 per 6700 persons in Guatemala, the next lowest); 0.67 hospital beds for every 1,000 people (compared with 1.9 per 1,000 in the Dominican Republic). Only 2.6 percent of all houses (12.1 percent in Guatemala) and 21 percent of all urban residences (43 percent in Guatemala) had pipe-borne water, and only 0.1 percent had indoor sanitation. There were 17.4 kilowatt hours of electricity per capita (compared with 164 for the Dominican Republic); 1 telephone per 1,000 inhabitants (compared with 63 in Barbados), almost all of them in the capital of Port-au-Prince; and 200 miles of paved roads[95] and 2,000 miles of unpaved roads in a country the size of Maryland.

Some two decades after these grim statistics were recorded, the situation had become much worse. When compared to her Caribbean neighbors in 1985, Haiti's infant mortality rate of 123 per 1,000 remained the highest and was lowest in life expectancy (53 years), literacy rate (23 percent), in ratio of access of population to pipe-borne water (21 and 3 percent, respectively) and in per capita income

---

[91] See P.E. English, *Canadian Development Assistance to Haiti*, 24–26 (1984).

[92] *Id.*, at 7, cited in DeWind & Kinley, *supra* note 81, at 50.

[93] See DeWind & Kinley, *supra* note 81, at 20; Dupuy, *supra* note 80, at 185ff.

[94] See DeWind & Kinley, *supra* note 81, at 18. For a more flattering view of Papa Doc Duvalier, see D. Nicholls, *From Dessalines to Duvalier. Race, Colour and National Independence in Haiti*, 237, 246 (1979).

[95] See R.I. Rotberg & C.K. Clague, HAITI: THE POLITICS OF SQUALOR, 6–11 (1971), cited in Dupuy, *supra* note 80 at 165.

($310).[96] By this time, Haitians as a whole were consuming 20 percent fewer calories and 30 percent less protein (40 percent and 50 percent, respectively, in the rural areas) than the daily recommended amounts.[97] One-third of all children under five years old were chronically malnourished and 90 percent of child deaths were attributed to malnutrition and gastroenteritis.[98]

Although in the 1980s 90 percent of the Haitian population earned less than $150, and fewer than 20 percent of the workers employed full time received the official minimum wage of $3 per day,[99] their President Jean-Claude Duvalier, his wife Michele, and their close associates were estimated to have filched over $505 million from the public treasury. Like his father before, Jean-Claude employed a variety of means to generate government revenue which was then siphoned into the private bank accounts of his family and close collaborators. Lundahl has identified the three methods of choice employed by the predatory state to extract money from the national economy. Duties on foreign trade and excise taxes on consumption were the primary source for government revenue. Invariably, the burden for these tributes fell on the shoulders of the rural peasants who constitute the overwhelming majority of Haiti's consumers. It was common to apply duties disproportionately to imported basic necessities such as kerosine, cotton textiles, soap, flour, fish, and rice, or to tack on excise taxes on basic consumer goods produced in Haiti such as flour, cigarettes or oil knowing fully that these taxes and duties would be borne by the poorest segment of the Haitian population. In contrast, imported luxury goods, usually beyond the purchasing reach of the poor, such as fine liquors, were allowed in with almost no duty, while excise taxes on luxury foods yielded only a fraction (1/50th to be exact) of that on basic foods.[100]

Lundahl concludes that

> The wealth extracted from peasants by taxation accounts for much of the impoverishment of rural Haiti. Although most of the government's revenues came from peasants, less than eight percent of government expenditures could be said to have been returned to the agricultural sector during Duvalier's first 10 years in power.[101]

It is worth keeping in mind that 77 percent of the Haitian population lives in rural areas[102] and agriculture remains the largest sector of the national economy

---

96 See Tom Barry, Beth Wood, & Deb Preusch, *The Other Side of Paradise: Foreign Control in the Caribbean*, x–xi (1984); *The World Bank 1987*, 202, 258, 260, cited in Dupuy, *supra* note 80, at 184.

97 Dupuy, *supra* note 80, at 184.

98 *Id.*

99 See R. Prince, *Haiti: Family Business*, 51 (1985); and M. Hooper 36 (1987), cited in Dupuy, *supra* note 80, at 184.

100 *Id.*, at 395.

101 *Id.*, at 310.

102 See Lundahl, *supra* note 81, at 23 (placing the figure at 80 percent); see also Dupuy, *supra* note 80, at 180.

engaging 75–80 percent of the total population.[103]

Another method favored by the predatory state for generating government revenue was through a system of extortion euphemistically called 'voluntary contributions.' Businessmen, government deputies, army officers, and government employees were required to make 'voluntary' contributions to the exchequer. The money was later diverted for other purposes.[104] A final source of government revenue was through the imposition of a series of compulsory payments for so-called 'economic liberation' bonds, vehicle inspection, pension funds, lotteries, literacy funds, and so forth. One writer described one of the more ingenious schemes employed by the state to raise funds: it involved billing telephone holders several hundred dollars for the previous decade even though the phones had not operated on the promise that the funds generated would be used to restore services.[105]

On the other side of the Atlantic corrupt enrichment by domestic elites and its consequences on the mass of the population has followed the same script as in Haiti. Ghana, which became the first colony in black Africa to gain its independence from Great Britain on 6 March 1957, according to Professor Le Vine, 'inherited a large foreign exchange balance, a sizable budgetary surplus, a relatively efficient economy, and a windfall in tax revenues, which had come to about 30 percent above estimates because of changes in the structure of the tax system.'[106] But by 1963 this once prosperous economy had begun to falter badly.[107]

Le Vine and several other scholars who have studied this period in Ghanaian history attribute this decline to extensive corruption by top State officials.[108] The

---

103 See Lundahl, 1983, *supra* note 81, at 23.

104 DeWind & Kinley, *supra* note 81, at 19.

105 *Id.*, at 20.

106 See Le Vine, *supra* note 57, at 19.

107 *Id.*, at 25.

108 *Id.* See also T. Peter Omari, *Kwame Nkrumah: The Anatomy of an African Dictatorship* (1970); Henry Bretton, *The Rise and Fall of Kwame Nkrumah: A Study of Personal Rule in Africa* (1966). This is not to suggest that political corruption was new to Ghana. As early as 1948 the Watson Commission which was appointed to enquire into disturbances in the colony made the following observation: '[i]t would be idle to ignore the existence of bribery and corruption in many walks of life in the Gold Coast admitted to us by every responsible African to whom we addressed the question. That it may be widespread as further responsibility devolves upon the African is a possibility which cannot be denied.' See Aiken Watson, *Chairman, Report of the Commission to Inquire into Disturbances in the Gold Coast*, 8 (1948) (hereinafter cited as 'Watson Report'), quoted in Le Vine, *supra* note 57, at 12. Against this backdrop, Professor Le Vine's conclusion that by the end of the 1960s Ghana had developed a 'culture of political corruption' is intended to underscore the fact that both in scope and extent corruption in the 1960s was unprecedented in Ghanaian history. *Id.* This view finds support in the following observation carried in *The Legon Observer,* a publication of a group of faculty at the University of Ghana, Legon: 'Massive material corruption seems to have taken hold of the new class of (West) African

growth of political corruption was painstakingly monitored and reported in a series of audit reports prepared by the principal auditors of governmental accounts first of the Gold Coast Colony and later for independent Ghana.[109] These audit reports revealed an 'unmistakable pattern of increasing corruption over the years' coincidentally corresponding to the increased indigenization of the civil service and government;[110] something the Watson Commission had predicted back in 1948.[111]

On the eve of Ghana's independence, amidst the euphoria of imminent African rule, the auditor-general commented on the financial irresponsibility of the nation's rulers in these sober words:

> The habit of liberality with Government funds, acquired during the period of buoyant revenue, is difficult to reverse whilst the formidable list of losses and frauds gives a disquieting commentary on standards of integrity. Difficulty has been experienced in relating claims for expenses incurred overseas by Ministers and other representatives of Government to the scales approved by Finance Committee.[112] Confirmation of this view could be found in the reports of several commissions of inquiry which were set up to look into improprieties in high governmental circles.[113] A decade or so later, the view that corruption had worked its way through every facet of the Ghanaian government

---

politicians and their followers since they began to come into power. It is so widespread as to be universal, at least in this area.' *See* 'Corruption in African Public Life,' *Legon Observer 1*, no. 5, 2 September 1966, at 7 quoted in Le Vine, *supra* note 57, at 12.

[109] See Gold Coast Colony, *Report of the Auditor for the Year 1938–39* (1940); Gold Coast Colony, *Report of the Director of Audit for the Financial Year Ended 31st March, 1948* (1949); Gold Coast, *Report of the Director of Audit on the Accounts of the Gold Coast for the Financial Year Ending 31st March, 1951* (1952); Gold Coast, *Report of the Auditor-General on the Accounts of the Gold Coast for the Financial Period Ended 30th June, 1956* (1957); Ghana, *Report of the Auditor-General on the Accounts of Ghana for the Financial Year Ended 30th June, 1958* (1960); Ghana, *Report and Financial Statements by the Accountant General and Report Thereon by the Auditor-General for the Year Ended 30th September, 1962* (1965); Ghana, *Report by the Auditor-General on the Accounts of Ghana for the Period 1st January, 1965 to 30th June, 1966* (1968); Ghana, *Report by the Auditor-General on the Accounts of Ghana: First Report for 1971, Local Authorities and Educational Institutions, 1967–68, 1968–69* (1971). *Second Report for 1971, Treasury Accounts, 1967–68, 1968–69* (1971). *Third Report for 1971, Public Boards and Corporations, 1967–68, 1968–69* (1971).

[110] Le Vine, *supra* note 57, at 16.

[111] Watson Commission, *supra* note 84, at 8.

[112] See Ghana, *Report of the Auditor-General on the Accounts of Ghana for the Financial Year Ended 30th June, 1956*, 8 (1955–56), quoted in Le Vine, *supra* note 57, at 20–21.

[113] See Sir Arku Korsah, Commissioner, *Report of the Commission of Inquiry into Mr. Braimah's Resignation and Allegations Arising Therefrom* (1954); O. Jibowu, Chairman, *Report of the Commission of Enquiry into the Affairs of the Cocoa Purchasing Company, Ltd.* (1956).

received additional confirmation from the reports of another set of investigatory commissions.[114] The Akainyah Commission which was appointed to enquire into allegations of improprieties in the issuance of import licenses concluded its report with this observation: 'It is unfortunate and pathetic that the love of money has become an obsession with some of us, and drives us to any length to get rich quick without stopping to think of the consequences. So long as we can get the money, we do not care whether or not our country is plunged into bankruptcy.'[115] In the National Assembly, representatives of the Ghanaian people had also taken note of this sad state of affairs and let it be known that they disapproved of this enveloping culture of kleptocracy. The following statement by Mr. B.E. Kusi is fairly representative of this view:

> We here are the caretakers of national funds and it is our duty to see that those people who have charge of this money should account for any loss. Are we to sit down and look on when those people in charge of the money are unable to account for no less than £G150,000? The President, in the Government's policy statement, told us recently that they were going all out to provide free secondary education for our children; and they will inevitably put money into the hands of some of us to carry out the policy. If no exemplary action is taken now in respect to those who have misused the sum of £G150,000, it is likely that anybody who will be trusted with money in the future to carry out the government's educational policy will put that money in his pocket. If no action is taken to bring those concerned to book, I will not take the Government serious [sic] and I will not take the statement of the President seriously. Many children go about in the streets because they cannot get accommodation in secondary schools, while those who have charge of the money send their children to international schools and to universities. Most of them ride in Mercedes Benz 220[s] and yet call themselves socialists. This is very bad. If we want to build a socialist country, then we must let the President know that we are serious about the use of public funds and that we do not pay

---

[114] See A.A. Akainyah, Commissioner, *Report of the Commission of enquiry into Alleged Irregularities and Malpractices in Connection with the Issue of Import Licenses* (1964) (hereinafter cited as 'Akainyah Commission Report'); Willie E. Abraham, Chairman, *Report of the Commission of Enquiry into Trade Malpractices in Ghana* (1965); Justice Ollenu, *Report of the Commission of Enquiry into Irregularities and Malpractices in the Grant of Import Licenses* (1967); Justice Ollenu, Commissioner, *Summary of the Report of the Commission of Enquiry into Irregularities and Malpractices in the Grant of Import Licenses* (1967) (hereinafter cited as 'Ollenu Commission Report').

[115] See 'Akainyah Commission Report,' *Id.*, at 38. It is one of the ironies of life that Justice Akainyah would himself become the target of a second commission of inquiry charged to investigate the same activities that led to the establishment of the Akainyah Commission! See Ollenu Commission Summary Report, *supra* note 114, at 12, 22. As a result of adverse findings made against Justice Akainyah and an accomplice by the Ollenu Commission of Inquiry, the Attorney-General of Ghana, in exercise of his powers under the Corrupt Practices (Prevention) Act, 1964 (Act 230), brought charges against them in the High Court. Both were convicted and sentenced to various terms of imprisonment and their subsequent appeal to the Court of Appeals was dismissed. See Akainyah and Another v. The Republic, [1968] GLR 548, CA.

> mere lip-service to socialism [Mr. B.E. Kusi, commenting on some £G150,000 for which the Ghana Educational Trust could not account].[116]

It is possible that when he made this statement in parliament Mr. Kusi was unaware of the President's own role in the misuse of public funds. In fact the auditor-general had already identified President (then Prime Minister) Nkrumah as one high-ranking official who was in the 'habit of liberality with Government funds' who in the 1956 financial year had exceeded his official budget by 200 percent.[117] Nkrumah's involvement in the fleecing of the Ghanaian treasury would be revealed after he was overthrown.

When on 24 February 1966, Ghana's Army and Police overthrew the civilian government of President Nkrumah, political corruption had become commonplace involving all levels of government, from ministers of state down to the lowly clerks.[118] One of the first acts by the National Liberation Council (NLC) was to appoint a commission of inquiry headed by Mr. Justice Fred Apaloo of the Supreme Court to investigate former President Nkrumah's assets.[119] All in all, the NLC appointed over 40 commissions, committees, special audit teams, and other investigative bodies charged with probing the public and private activities of the Nkrumah regime.[120] Almost all reached the same conclusion that corruption was not only confined to the hoi polloi of society but had worked its way through the upper levels of government as well. So endemic it had become that Professor Le Vine could confidently assert that Ghana was in the grip of an 'incipient Ghanaian culture of political corruption.'[121] He was able to point to an abundance of evidence in support of his observation. For instance, the Jiagge Assets Commission which investigated the assets of specified persons uncovered some spectacular abuses of office by high-ranking Government and Party officials. It eventually rendered judgments against twenty-one of them[122] requiring the culpable public servants to forfeit ill-gotten properties and to pay to the State substantial sums of money.[123]

---

116 Quoted in Le Vine, *supra* note 57, at 22–23.

117 *Id.*, at 20.

118 *Id.*, at 27.

119 See Fred Apaloo, Chairman, *Report of the Commission to Enquire into the Kwame Nkrumah Properties* (1967).

120 See Le Vine, *supra* note 57, at 27; see also 'Roots of Corruption,' *supra* note 19, at 251. Others, however, have placed the number of commissions at 76, see *Ghana, Parliamentary Debates*, Wednesday, 24 June 1970, col. 1164 (Statement of B.K. Adama, Minister of State for Parliamentary Affairs).

121 *Id.*, at 37.

122 See *White Paper on the Report of Jiagge Commission of Inquiry into the Assets of Specified Persons*, no. 3/69 (1969).

123 *Id.* The exchange rate for the new cedi at that time was $1.00 = NC 1.02. See Le Vine, *supra* note 57, at 62. At the high end of the scale was Krobo Edusei, a former government minister, who was required to pay back NC635,739.27. Lucy Anin, a former

Describing the scope of corruption in the Philippines, one expert wrote: '… the magnitude of the amounts involved, and the damage done to both the government and the economy make the corruption of the Marcos regime a singular and one would hope, unique experience in Philippine history.'[124] By the time the regime collapsed in early 1986 the Philippines had suffered through several years of the worst political and economic crises in its history.

Corruption and favoritism had spread throughout the government and society like cancer; the economy had been ravaged by greed and mismanagement; the welfare of most Filipinos had declined significantly; the communist threat cited by Marcos as a reason for imposing martial law had grown ominously and society was polarized as never before.[125]

While it might be difficult to talk of the effects of corrupt enrichment in causation terms, there can be no question that such practices have contributed to the numerous problems victim states are experiencing. There is arguably a link between indigenous spoliation and political instability. Virtually every State that has fallen prey to this pestilence has experienced some form of social upheaval at some point in its political history. As the preceding discussion demonstrates the benefits of fraudulent enrichment usually accrue to a small highly visible oligarchy who live in a state of triumphant opulence. Conversely, the costs of high level graft are almost always borne by the rest of society. But continued plunder gradually erodes the legitimacy of any government which must then resort to force and coercion to govern. Political oppression quickly becomes the means to extract support, financial and otherwise, from the populace.[126] However, once the

---

member of parliament, was required to pay NC1,108.75, an amount which fell at the lowest end of the scale. In between were: A.E. Inkumsah, a former minister of trade and Deputy Speaker of the National Assembly – NC124,666.23; Komlah Gbedemah, former minister of finance – NC35,929.80; B.E.Kwaw-Swanzy, former minister – NC17,030.35; A.H. Suleimana, former member of parliament and a CPP official – NC12,326.26; J.E. Hagan, former member of parliament and regional commissioner – NC53,480.80; E.Tachie-Menson, former minister – NC45,171.27; F.K.D. Goka, former minister – NC56,121.07; Salifu Yakubu, former member of parliament and CPP official – NC15,714.91; Sulemana K. Tandoh, former ambassador and member of parliament – NC12,589.50; A.K. Puplampu, former minister of agriculture – NCI 12,261.90; M. Appiah-Danquah, former minister, ambassador and secretary-general of the United Ghana Farmers' Cooperatives Council – NC82,374.57; G.Y. Odoi, former general manager of the Cocoa Purchasing Company, and manager of GNCC – NC27,925.10; E.C.D. Asiama, former director of the Research Bureau of the Ministry of External Affairs – NC51,793.27.

124 See D.G. Timberman, *A Changeless Land: Continuity and Change in Philippine Politics*, 76 (1991).

125 *Id.*

126 In 1974 Ceausescu of Romania decided to build a palace for his wife in Olanesti, a resort town famous for its mineral water reservoirs in the mountains of Romania. When the palace was completed and Ceausescu paid his wife a visit in 1988 he complained about the proximity to the village. His solution was to move the entire village to another site. See *Free*

opportunity presents itself as was the case in the Philippines in 1986 and Romania in 1989 the dispossessed are very likely to turn against their corrupt rulers. The frequency of military coups and other extra-constitutional methods of regime change lends further support for the view that persistent and unrestrained corruption by high-ranking officials invariably lead to serious social instability. In coup after coup the justifications usually given by the military leaders is the need to put an end to high-level corruption. The 1992 military coup that overthrew the civilian government of President Momoh of Sierra Leone justified its actions as corrective measures intended 'to eradicate corruption, mismanagement and in-discipline' in government and 'to restore morality, accountability, transparency and good government in the body politic… .'[127]

Finally, corruption on a vast scale can sap the strength of any economy leading to a collapse from within. This thesis has been advanced by Arkady Vaksberg, a leading writer for the *Literary Gazette*, a Moscow newspaper that has long enjoyed a privileged readership in Russia, to explain the downfall of the Soviet Union.[128] His thesis is that, during Leonid Brezhnev's tenure as supreme leader of the Communist party and *de facto* head of the Communist patrimonium, corruption among public office holders reached staggering proportions, penetrating the highest ranks of the State. Corruption was so extensive, Vaksberg argued, that it seriously affected the government's ability to manage the economy and may well have contributed towards its collapse a few short years later.

In the face of these outrageous acts by constitutionally responsible rulers, what should the international legal system do? What should other States that have not personally and directly been harmed by this practice of fraudulent enrichment do? What obligations do they owe to the victim State and its peoples? These are some of the questions this study intends to address.

The analysis is presented in two parts. Part I situates the problem of fraudulent enrichment by heads of States and other high-ranking public officials in the context of decades-long efforts at elaborating and developing a regime of law to deal with international crimes by individuals. An attempt is made here to trace the emergence and progressive evolution of an international legal norm which imposes a fiduciary duty on constitutionally-responsible rulers with respect to the exercise and disposal of national wealth and natural resources for the exclusive benefit of the peoples whom they govern. The conventions and state practice which provide the basic building blocks of this embryonic norm are examined. The second part of

---

Romania, 11 January 1989 issue.

127 See Beccles Davies Commission, *supra* note 25, at 1. Professor Tignor points out 'the frequent regime changes which have occurred in Africa in the last several decades have been accompanied by charges of gross administrative malfeasance and promises to introduce honest government'. Robert L. Tignor, 'Political Corruption in Nigeria Before Independence,' *Journal of Modern African Studies*, 31, 175 (1993).

128 *See* Arkady Vaksberg, THE SOVIET MAFIA (John Roberts & Elizabeth Roberts, trans. 1991).

the volume explores some of the limitations that municipal law as well as international law has placed on the imposition of individual criminal responsibility for the crime of indigenous spoliation. It discusses a framework for holding high-ranking State officials personally liable for the violation of some fundamental international community interests, explores the various constituencies that have genuine legal interests in protecting these fundamental rights and who therefore have a right and a duty to vindicate them. Finally, Part II examines some of the procedural elements required by international and municipal law before these rights can be judicially redressed.

PART I

INDIGENOUS SPOLIATION AS AN INTERNATIONAL ECONOMIC CRIME

Chapter 2

Indigenous Spoliation as an International Crime

THE CHARACTER OF CRIMES

Crime is a wrong not merely against the individual but also against society.[1] But what makes a particular kind of conduct 'criminal'? If conduct is viewed as shameful or unethical does that make it a crime in the legal sense of the term? Does it satisfy the basic elements of a crime? In international law, wrongful conduct that rises to the level of international crimes is usually the product of conventional and customary international law.[2] The crimes established through this process are usually enforced through national criminal laws.[3] As a consequence, the contents and penal characteristics of an international criminal law convention have been shaped and determined by this system of indirect enforcement.[4] It has now come to be accepted that the recognition in an international criminal law convention that certain conduct rises to the level of an international crime imposes a duty upon state parties to the convention to criminalize the prohibited conduct.[5]

Since international criminal law is enforced by national tribunals as national law,[6] it is helpful to look at how 'crime' is conceptualized in domestic law to get a

---

1 See Sarkar, 'The Proper Law of Crime in International Law,' in *International Criminal Law*, 50 (G.O.W. Mueller & Edward Wise eds, 1965).

2 See Cherif Bassiouni, 'Characteristics of International Criminal Law Conventions,' in *International Criminal Law*, 1, 2 (M. Cherif Bassiouni ed., 1986) (hereinafter cited as 'Criminal Law Conventions').

3 *Id.* at 3.

4 *Id.*

5 *Id.*

6 See G.O.W. Mueller & Douglas J. Besharon, *Evolution and Enforcement of International Criminal Law*, in *International Criminal Law*, 59, 70 (M. Cherif Bassiouni ed., 1986). 'A variety of countries have included *verbatim*, international crimes (and international standards of criminal justice) in their penal codes and others are penalizing, as municipal crimes, violations of international criminal law.' Examples abound: *piracy* in addition to being declared unlawful under international law is also a crime under municipal law. For a compilation of national legislations on piracy, see generally *American Journal of International Law*, 16, pt. V (Supp. 1932); Working Draft No. 744–1, 17 November 1969, prepared for the 17th session of the Legal Committee of the International Civil Aviation Organization. Treaties proscribing crimes of terror violence (hijacking, hostage taking,

sense of what must go into the elaboration of the concept of international crime. Generally, crime as a normative concept can be defined in formal or legal terms, or in naturalistic, material terms. The definition of crime in formal or legal terms involves some act that a sovereign has termed criminal and to which will subject an individual to criminal proceedings. J.W.C. Turner and Robert Perkins provide a fairly succinct and complete definition:

> [T]he nature of crime will elude true definition, nevertheless, it is a broadly accurate description to say that nearly every instance of crime presents all of the three following

---

terrorism) or those punishing so-called crimes against social interests (for example, theft of cultural property) all rely on municipal laws for their criminalization, see generally Convention For the Suppression of Unlawful Seizure of Aircraft, signed at The Hague, 16 December 1970, 860 UNTS 105, 22 UST. 1641, TIAS No. 7192 (entered into force 14 October 1971; entered into force with respect to the United States 14 October 1971), Arts. IV, VII; Convention for the Suppression of Unlawful Acts Against the Safety of Civil Aviation, signed at Montreal, 23 September 1971, 24 UST 565, TIAS No. 7570 (entered into force 26 January 1973; entered into force with respect to the United States 26 January 1973), Arts. 3, 5; International Convention Against the Taking of Hostages, done at New York, 17 December 1979, UNGA Res. 34/146.34, UNGOAR Supp. (No. 46) at 245 (1980), Arts. 2, 4(a), 5; Convention on the Prevention and Punishment of Crimes Against Internationally Protected Persons, Including Diplomatic Agents, done at New York, 14 December 1973, UNGA Rex. 3166 (XXVIII), 28 UNGAOR Supp. (No. 30), at 146, UN Doc. A/9030, 28 UST 1975, TIAS No. 8532 (entered into force 20 February 1977; entered into force with respect to the United States 20 February 1977), Art. 3. For a discussion of municipal controls over the theft of cultural property, see generally L. Prott & P. O'Keefe, *National Legal Control of Illicit Traffic in Cultural Property*, UNESCO Doc. CLT-83/WS/16 (1983). For a sample of specific national laws, *see* [United States] National Stolen Property Act, 18 USC §§2311–2318 (1976). Sections 2314 and 2315 have been held to be applicable to stolen art objects. Section 2314 provides:

> Whoever transports in interstate or foreign commerce any goods, ware merchandise, securities or money, of value of $5,000 or more, knowing the same to have been stolen, connected or taken by fraud ... shall be fined not more than $10,000 or imprisoned not more than 10 years or both.

18 USC §2314; Act on the Regulation of Importation of Pre-Columbian Monumental or Architectural Sculpture or Murals, 19 USC §§2091–2095 (1975); [Mexico] Ley Federal Sobre Monumentos y Zonas Arqueologicas, Artisticas e Historicas, *Diaro Oficial* [DO], 312, 16 (1972); [United Kingdom] Import, Export and Customs Powers (Defence) Act, 1939, 2 & 3 Geo. 6, ch. 69, and administrative regulations thereunder; Ancient Monuments Consolidation and Amendment Act, 1913, 3 & 4 Geo. 5, ch. 32 §12; Ancient Monuments Act, 1931, 21 & 22 Geo. 5, ch. 16 §§6–8; [France] Act of 31 December 1913 (1914), *Journal Officiel de la Republique Francaise* [JO] 129, [1951] *Recueil Periodique et Critique* [DP] IV 153 (Fr.) reprinted in *UNESCO, Index of National Legislations on the Protection of Cultural Heritage*, 29 (1969) (Fr.); Decree of Nov. 30, 1944, JO 1585, [1945] Recueil Sirey [S.Jur.] 1713 (Fr.).

> characteristics: (1) (sic) that it is a harm, brought about by human conduct, which the sovereign power in the State desires to prevent; (2) that among the measures of prevention selected is the threat of punishment; (3) that legal proceedings of a special kind are employed to decide whether the person accused did in fact cause the harm, and is, according to law, to be held legally punishable for doing so.[7]

Perkins similarly suggests that a 'crime' is 1) 'any social harm' 2) 'defined and made punishable by law' 3) through 'a process that is primarily used for the prosecution and disposition of persons whose conduct resulting in social harm is classed as criminal.'[8] Some commentators believe the definition of crime depends on whether the offense can be pursued by the sovereign as opposed to the injured party.[9] Others place the key determination of the definition of crime on whether or not it is an act capable of being followed by criminal proceedings with one of the types of outcomes known to follow these proceedings (that is, punishment).[10]

The attempt to define 'crime' based on a 'natural' or 'material' definition has largely depended on discovering some intrinsic quality that could be used to set criminal conduct apart from non-criminal conduct. Actions involving moral culpability or some special or serious harm to the whole community, considered as a community, in its social aggregate capacity have been cited as examples of a 'natural' definition of crime.[11] While some acts are clearly of a nature to be found to be a crime under the 'natural' definition, society for the most part has been unable to make a discernable list of just what qualities and actions will result in a crime. Not surprisingly, therefore, society has criminally sanctioned some acts, such as gross indecency and homosexuality, even when they do not necessarily harm society. Other acts that affect society, like breach of contract and negligence, are left to civil law remedies.[12]

A key element of these various definitions of 'crime' is the focus on the performance of some 'act' by a person or entity in order to be found culpable of committing a crime. The bulk of national penal laws are geared towards punishing conduct found to be in breach of a common or statutory law. The word 'conduct' is proactive. It implies some act or action. Can a person be found culpable when his conduct does not involve any action, rather an omission to act? Can a person's conduct be a crime when it does not violate any law? These are jurisprudential questions society has long struggled to answer. Certain omissions to act are found to be a crime and in some penal codes the failure to render aid is a crime; for instance, the failure to provide care and nourishment to a child or elderly person in one's care.

However, conduct that does not violate any law cannot be found to be a crime

---

7 *See* Edward Wise, *International Crimes and Domestic Criminal Law*, *DePaul Law Review*, 38, 923, 924, n. 4 (1989)[hereinafter 'Wise'].

8 *Id.*, at 924 citing R. Perkins & R. Boyce, *Criminal Law*, 12 (3rd ed. 1982).

9 *Id.*, at 924, n. 5 citing John Austin, *Lectures on Jurisprudence*, 417 (3rd ed. 1869).

10 *Id.*, at 924, n. 4 citing B. Williams, *The Definition of a Crime*, 128–130 (1955).

11 *Id.*, at 925.

12 *Id.*, at 925, n. 8 citing P.J. Fitzgerald, *Criminal Law and Punishment*, 4 (1962).

by the formal definition of crime. Conduct only translates into crime when it has been defined and made punishable by law and that person can be subjected to some form of legal proceeding to determine guilt and punishment. Therefore, it follows that if no criminal proceedings follow the conduct, no crime has been committed. Developing a definition of 'international crime' can best be done only by analogy to the definition of 'crime' applied in domestic law. 'An international crime is an act that international law prohibits and provides should be followed by consequences more or less closely analogous to the proceedings and punishments that characterize the operation of domestic criminal law.'[13] The problem with the definition of international crime just provided is that it conflicts with the domestic law definition of crime.

To call conduct a 'crime' implies that it is liable to be followed by criminal proceedings and punishment. But there are no international criminal proceedings, or international agencies empowered to inflict punishment on states. Further, the institutions of internal law allow for the distinction between civil and criminal proceedings and between civil and criminal liability. No such distinction exists in international law.[14] It is also difficult to conceive of a whole nation being guilty of a 'crime.' It would seem an impossible task trying to hold a whole nation responsible for actions taken by its government, for example. But, and as will shortly be discussed at some length, the International Law Commission's (Commission or ILC)[15] use of the term 'international crime,' taken in context with the whole Draft Articles on State Responsibility is meant to convey the idea that some wrongs are of such concern to the entire international community that they are more closely analogous to criminal responsibility. The International Court of Justice in the Barcelona Traction Case[16] judgment lent its support to the idea that certain wrongs are of concern to the whole international community and then cited the types of wrongful acts that affect and warrant the attention of the entire international community: acts of aggression, acts of genocide, protection from slavery and racial discrimination. But overall there is no precise test for determining what kind of conduct may be regarded as falling within the 'international crime' category.

---

13 See Wise, *supra* note 7, at 926.

14 *Id.*, at 927.

15 In 1947, the General Assembly established the Committee on the Progressive Development of International Law and its Codification, which recommended the creation of the International Law Commission (ILC or Commission). The work of the ILC, as determined by its statute, is primarily focused on public international law, although it is not precluded from working in the field of private international law. The purpose of the Commission is twofold: to promote the 'progressive development' and 'codification' of international law. The statute distinguishes the ILC's two objectives. Progressive development is 'the preparation of draft conventions on subjects which have not yet been sufficiently developed in the practice of States,' while codification is 'the more precise formulation and systematization of rules of international law in fields where there already has been extensive State practice precedent and doctrine' Art. 15.

16 1970 ICJ Rep., at 32.

Some publicists contend that the definition of international crime extends only to conduct defined in multilateral conventions such as 1) aggression, 2) war crimes, 3) unlawful use or emplacement of weapons, 4) crimes against humanity, 5) genocide, 6) racial discrimination and apartheid, 7) slavery and related crimes, 8) torture, 9) unlawful human experimentation, 10) piracy, 11) aircraft hijacking, 12) threat and use of force against internationally protected persons, 13) taking of civilian hostages, 14) drug offenses, 15) international traffic in obscene publications, 16) destruction or theft of national treasures, 17) environmental protection, 18) unlawful use of the mails, 19) interference with submarine cables, 20) falsification and counterfeiting, 21) bribery of foreign public officials, and 22) theft of nuclear materials.[17] Anything outside this list is not considered an international crime.

Identifying a criminal wrong in international law with a desire to suppress that wrong does not impart the same types of remedies available within the scope of domestic law. The doctrine of *ubi jus ibi remedium* (where there is a right there has to be a remedy) does not seem to apply as easily as it would apply to domestic law in civil and criminal cases. Yet the Commission recognized that the international community has a legal interest, along with the individually-harmed state, to address the breach:

> ... that the responsibility engaged by the breach of these obligations is engaged not only in regard to the State which was the direct victim of the breach: it is also engaged in regard to all the other members of the international community, so that, in the event of a breach of these obligations, every State must be considered justified in invoking - probably through judicial channels – the responsibility of the State committing the internationally wrongful act.[18]

The problem remains, though, that international law has no central authority empowered to initiate criminal proceedings or impose punishment. Nor does international law allow individual States to act as self-appointed representatives of the international community in fixing responsibility or inflicting punishment. The final paradox relates to the responsibility of states but as one commentator lamented: 'It is common wisdom that states, although they are the major subjects of international law, cannot be held to criminal liability.'[19]

The issue of an appropriate mechanism for the settlement of disputes and the implementation (*mettre en oeuvre*) of international criminal responsibility, whether of States or private individuals, has been around for quite some time. A valiant attempt to finally put this matter to rest was the International Law Association's proposal, some sixty years ago, for the creation of an international criminal court. More recently, the International Law Commission, within the framework of its

---

17 M. Cherif Bassiouni, *A Draft International Criminal Code and Draft Statute for an International Criminal Court*, 21–65 (1987).

18 See 'Report of the International Law Commission on the Work of its 28th Session,' *International Law Commission Yearbook*, 1976, vol. 2, pt. 2, at 99.

19 See Cherif Bassiouni, *International Criminal Law – Enforcement*, 14 (1987).

work on the draft Code of Crimes against the Peace and Security of Mankind, has again taken up the issue of an international criminal jurisdiction to address draft code crimes.

At its forty-sixth session in 1991, the General Assembly requested the Commission to explore this subject and to give some thought to the possibility of establishing an international criminal court or other international trial mechanism.[20] The Commission took this mandate seriously and at its forty-fourth session in 1992 the Special Rapporteur devoted the whole of his tenth report to the question of the possible establishment of an international criminal jurisdiction.[21] A Working Group was appointed by the Commission which subsequently recommended that an international criminal court be established by a statute in the form of a multilateral treaty with States as parties. If established this court would be able to exercise, at least in its initial phase, jurisdiction over private persons. In addition to the draft code crimes, the court's jurisdiction would extend to crimes defined in international conventions and agreements.[22] However, some Commission members were of the view that custom and general principles of law as well as the court's own case law could in certain cases also constitute a source of applicable law.[23] The Working Group also recommended that a State could become a party to the statute establishing the international tribunal without necessarily becoming a party to the draft Code of Crimes.

When the Commission met at its forty-fifth session a year later, the Special Rapporteur presented his eleventh report which, like its predecessor, was entirely devoted to the question of a draft statute of an international criminal court.[24] The Special Rapporteur acknowledged in his report that the question of an international criminal jurisdiction continued to present a problem of great complexity. He hoped, however, that his report 'would raise for consideration, and determination in a pragmatic manner, the difficult questions, many of which were of considerable legal and political sensitivity, which the Commission would need to satisfactorily resolve if the statute was to succeed in its purpose.'[25] Among the difficult and politically sensitive issues to which the Special Rapporteur adverted was the perennial question of jurisdiction *ratione materiae*. So contentious has this issue been in the past that no agreement could be reached at this session on the list of crimes that would form the subject of such jurisdiction.[26] It was, however, settled that until a code of crimes is adopted, the next best solution would be to have the subject-matter jurisdiction of the proposed court to be established by special agreements between State parties, or by individual acceptance.

---

[20] See Official Records of the General Assembly, Forty-sixth session, UN GAOR,46th Sess., Supp. No. 10, at Chap. II, Sect. C, UN Doc. A/46/10 (1991).

[21] See Report of the International Law Commission on the work of its forty-fifth session, UN GAOR, 48th Sess., Supp. No. 10, at 23, UN Doc. A/48/10 (1993).

[22] *Id.*, at 24.

[23] *Id.*, at 28.

[24] *Id.*, at 26.

[25] *Id.*

[26] *Id.*, at 28.

Parallel to the debate over the establishment of an international criminal tribunal has been the debate over the elaboration of an international criminal code with the goal of developing a system of codes and criminal proceedings similar in effect to those existing in domestic law.[27] But perhaps the greatest obstacle to securing approval of an international criminal code by the majority of countries is the great divergence within and among their various legal systems. A criminal code or penal statute, whether domestic or international, is only the first, albeit critical, step. However, it is the ability to enforce the provisions of the code that ultimately determines its effectiveness. Enforcement remains an important deterrence to criminal acts in and to itself. This idea is best illustrated by the common law maxim: a law badly enforced is worse than no law at all. But in international law, what and whom do you enforce against? Does one hold the State and its government responsible or its people? Simply using compensation and reparations as a remedy against a State hardly seems appropriate in every situation. Penalties and sanctions, if applied by whatever means, often are politically-motivated as opposed to penal-driven.[28] Besides, what rights does an international tribunal have against an individual violator when the domestic court has not had a chance to adjudicate the alleged breach?

The doctrine of exhaustion of remedies holds that individuals must have exhausted their avenues of redress in domestic legal systems before turning to international adjudication. This presupposes the existence of State-provided remedies.[29] As a general rule, remedies must be both effective and adequate. The determination of when a remedy is effective, taking into account that effectiveness will vary depending on specific conditions, is in large part based on the jurisprudence on exhaustion of remedies. Remedies are ineffective when domestic laws do not afford adequate relief or when the injured party is prevented from having recourse to them. The remedy is also ineffective if the courts are not independent or the proceeding takes too long[30] to dispose of the dispute. These are the many issues that intrude in any discussion of international crimes and their ubiquity suggests that even though the term 'crime' has been borrowed from domestic law, no attempt has been made to confuse its domestic law meaning from its international law meaning. An international crime is not the same thing as a domestic law crime.

---

27 *Id.*

28 See for example, Bernhard Graefrath, 'International Crimes – A Specific Regime of International Responsibility of States and its Legal Consequences,' in *International Crimes of State: An Analysis of Article 19 of the ILC's Draft Articles on State Responsibility*, 161, 163 (Joseph H.H. Weiler, Antonio Cassese & Marina Spinedi eds, 1989) (voicing his apprehension that the attribution of criminal responsibility to sovereign States would open the door for political abuse) [hereinafter 'Weiler, Cassese & Spinedi'].

29 Naomi Roht-Arriaza, 'State Responsibility to Investigate and Prosecute Grave Human Rights Violations in International Law,' *California Law Review*, 78, 449, 463 (1990).

30 *Id.*

THE ILC'S ATTEMPTS AT DEFINING AN INTERNATIONAL CRIME

Regimes of Responsibility in International Law

Largely through the work of the International Law Commission an attempt has been made to offer a framework for conceptualizing internationally wrongful conduct that could rise to state or individual responsibility. In two separate draft instruments the Commission has come up with two distinct types of wrongful conduct which give rise to some kind of responsibility and one to which it attaches the term 'international' crime. In earlier drafts the first set of paradigms of wrongful conduct international crime was broken down into 'crimes of state' or 'international crimes' proper and 'international delicts;' these were codified in the Draft Articles on State Responsibility (Draft Articles). The second paradigm is what the ILC terms 'crimes under international law,' that is, crimes *by* individuals, defined and elaborated in the Draft Code of Crimes Against the Peace and Security of Mankind (Draft Code of Crimes). An examination of the Draft Articles and the Draft Code of Crimes is necessary in order to discover what under current State practice constitutes wrongful conduct that engages international action. But, more important for our purposes, it is an opportunity to isolate the brightline tests against which reasoned judgments can be made as to whether indigenous spoliation qualifies as an international economic crime. In the process of isolating the crucial definitional basics of an international crime, an attempt will be made to discover whether the ILC paradigms of an international crime compete with or complement each other.

Codification of State Responsibility

State responsibility was one of the original topics for codification by the ILC.[31] Work began in 1956 under the Cuban jurist, F.V. García Amador, who called state responsibility a 'vast and complex' area of international law with 'glaring inconsistencies of traditional doctrine and practice.'[32] His comments proved to be prophetic not only for his term, but for the project itself as codification got off to a slow start.[33] The original focus of the draft articles was to be state responsibility for injuries to aliens and their property. It would cover the substantive rules of the international law of diplomatic protection.[34] This narrow approach to state responsibility generated criticisms that it was inadequate, particularly from the Soviet Union and the Socialist countries.[35] As a result of the dissatisfaction with

---

31 See [1956] *International Law Commission Yearbook*, at 174.

32 *Id.*, at 52.

33 See James Crawford, *The International Law Commission's Articles on State Responsibility: Introduction, Text and Commentaries*, 1–60 (2002) (history of the work of the International Law Commission on State Responsibility) [hereinafter 'Crawford'].

34 See Crawford, *supra* note 33, at 1–60.

35 See *International Crimes of State: A Critical Analysis of the ILC's Draft Article 19 on State Responsibility*, 12–15 (Joseph H. Weiler, Antonio Cassese & Marina Spinedi ed.

the scope of the draft articles and distractions from other ILC projects, little progress was made during García Amador's tenure.[36]

García Amador left the ILC in 1961 and was succeeded by Ago of Italy who had chaired an inter-sessional subcommittee that reconsidered the scope of the codification of state responsibility.[37] Various proposals were presented, but it was eventually agreed that all of the general rules of state responsibility should be codified.[38] In addition, the draft articles should promulgate secondary, rather than primary, rules.[39] Secondary rules are the general rules that define the conditions of an internationally wrongful act and its consequences. Primary rules define the rule and the actual content of the obligation it imposes, which the Commission felt went beyond the scope of the draft articles. In 1963, the ILC approved Ago's approach and appointed him Special Rapporteur.[40]

Work continued under Ago until 1979, at which time the ILC provisionally adopted 35 draft articles making up 'Part One, Origin of International Responsibility.'[41] This section laid out the general principles of state responsibility: the basic premises of responsibility; the elements of an internationally wrongful act; the parameters of attribution and culpability; the definition of an international breach; and various circumstances affecting a breach.[42]

The Old Regime of State Responsibility

Article 19 of the Draft Articles on State Responsibility contains ILC's earlier paradigms of internationally wrongful conduct – crimes and delicts. Crimes constituted the most serious breaches of international law and everything that remained was a delict. Article 19 was a product of Ago's multinational view of international law and his belief that some state acts were so serious as to be criminal in nature. His view was a more progressive one, but had enough support to gain the approval of the Commission. Interestingly, Special Rapporteur García Amador had expressed the same opinion in his first report to the General Assembly in 1956.[43] He stressed that international criminal responsibility had become 'well defined and widely acknowledged' since World War II and 'must be admitted as one of the consequences' of the breach of certain international obligations.[44] At the time, the Commission did not accept his proposition.

1989).

36 See *Id.*

37 See Crawford, *supra* note 33, at 1–60.

38 See *Id.*

39 See *Id.*

40 See *Id.*

41 See [1979] *International Law Commission Yearbook*, pt. 2, at 91, UN Doc. A/CN.4/SER.A/1979/Add.1 [hereinafter 1979 Yearbook].

42 *Id.*

43 *See* 1956 Yearbook, *supra* note 31, at 105.

44 *Id.*

Although article 19 was unanimously adopted by the Commission in 1976 that consensus is nowhere reflected in the discordant debate that has dogged it since its adoption. Nevertheless, draft Article 19 represents one of the most valiant attempts to stake out the contours of conduct considered wrongful in the international sense, to which responsibility attaches to the State *qua* state. The text of the draft Article 19, titled 'International Crimes and International Delicts,' as approved in 1976[45] reads as follows:

> 1. An act of a State which constitutes a breach of an international obligation is an internationally wrongful act, regardless of the subject-matter of the obligation breached.
>
> 2. An internationally wrongful act which results from the breach by a State of an international obligation so essential for the protection of fundamental interest of the international community that its breach is recognized as a crime by that community as a whole constitutes an international crime.
>
> 3. Subject to paragraph 2, and on the basis of the rules of international law in force, an international crime may result, inter alia, from:
>
> (a) serious breach of an international obligation of essential importance for the maintenance of international peace and security, such as prohibiting aggression;
>
> (b) serious breach of an international obligation of essential importance for safeguarding the right of self-determination of peoples, such as that prohibiting the establishment or maintenance by force of colonial domination;
>
> (c) a serious breach on a widespread scale of an international obligation of essential importance for safeguarding the human being, such as those prohibiting slavery, genocide and apartheid;
>
> (d) serious breach of an international obligation of essential importance for the safeguarding and preservation of the human environment, such as those prohibiting massive pollution of the atmosphere or of the seas.

Any internationally wrongful act which is not an international crime in accordance with paragraph 2 constitutes an international delict.[46] Paragraph 1 simply affirmed the fact that the subject matter of a breach is irrelevant to whether or not the breach is internationally wrongful. This premise is supported in state practice and the jurisprudence of the international community. Paragraph 2 defined an international

---

[45] See [1976] *International Law Commission Yearbook*, pt.2, 95–122 UN Doc. A/CN.4/SERA.A/1976/Add.1 [hereinafter 1976 Yearbook] (commentary to article 19). *See* [1996] *International Law Commission Yearbook*, 58–65 UN Doc. A/CN.4/SERA/A/1996 (hereinafter 1996 Yearbook) (draft articles approved on the first reading in 1996), available at http://www.cam.ac.uk/RCIL/ILCSR/stateresp.htm. See also UN Doc. A/CN.4/L.600 (11 August 2000), available at www.cam.ac.uk/RCIL/ILCSR/statresp.htm. (draft articles approved on the second reading in 2001).

[46] 1976 Yearbook, *supra* note 45 at 95.

crime as the breach of an international obligation that is so essential for the protection of the fundamental interests of the international community that it is recognized as a crime by that community.[47] Paragraph 3 provides four examples, inter alia, of what constitutes an international crime by a state. The commentary indicates that it is not exhaustive.[48] Finally, Paragraph 4 concluded that any internationally wrongful act not classified as a crime was a delict. What Article 19 did not include were the applicable regimes of responsibility and the consequences that followed the commission of a crime or delict. These rules were to be developed in the next section of the draft articles.

Ratio Legis of Draft Article 19

Article 19 would prove to be quite controversial,[49] but at the time the commission believed that emerging trends in international law supported, even demanded, a separate category of international crimes and a corresponding regime of responsibility.[50] The ILC admitted that laying out the concept for international crimes of States was a difficult task, but believed that it was of great importance to the international community.[51] They went so far as to assert 'it would be absolutely mistaken to believe that contemporary international law contains only one regime of responsibility applicable universally to every type of internationally

---

47 See *Id.*, at ¶ 59.

48 See *Id.*, at 64.

49 See for example, Joseph H.H. Weiler, 'On Prophets and Judges: Some Personal Reflections on State Responsibility and Crimes of State,' in *International Crimes of State: A Critical Analysis of the ILC's Draft Article 19 on State Responsibility*, 319, 320 (Joseph H.H. Weiler, Antonio Cassese & Marina Spinedi eds 1989) (noting that '[d]espite the fierceness with which opposition to, and support of, Article 19 is expressed it is difficult to identify any systematic commonality among those who support and those who oppose Article 19'). Debate within the Commission was centered around Article 19(4), whether or not it is essential and necessary to the definition of an international crime. Those who favor its inclusion argue that the provision is necessary and useful particularly in determining the regimes of responsibility applicable to the different types of internationally wrongful acts. In provisionally adopting the term 'international delicts', the Commission recognized that the term was used as a synonym for internationally wrongful acts in works on international law written in French, Italian, Spanish and German before the introduction of the category of 'international crimes' was contemplated. Further, the term 'international delicts' has been habitually employed in several systems of internal law to denote unlawful acts of lesser gravity than those called 'crimes.' However, the literal equivalent in English, 'international delict' is obsolete, and it is difficult to find terminology in the common law systems that corresponds to what is current in the systems of Roman origin. *See* Draft Articles on State Responsibility, Art. 19, in Report of the International Law Commission to the General Assembly, UN Doc. 1/31/10 (1976). I.L.C. Rep., [1976] 11 (Pt. 2), *International Law Commission Yearbook*, 95–122.

50 See generally *Id.* at 95–122.

51 See *Id.*

wrongful act.'[52] In their reasoning, the ILC looked to judicial decisions, state practice, the writings of various publicists, and the tenor of contemporary society. What they saw was an emerging multinational trend that began in part as a result of the atrocities of World War II. Society's memory of the war, the fear of its possible recurrence, the suffering and disappearance of large groups of people, and the proliferation of weapons of mass destruction all substantiated the need for an aggravated level of internationally wrongful act.[53]

The International Law Commission found little in international jurisprudence that explicitly supported or refuted state crimes. The ILC concluded that although international judicial and arbitral bodies had not directly examined different regimes, assumptions of their support for it could be gleaned from the decisions.[54] As a consequence, the Commission relied heavily on the *Barcelona Traction* case, where it interpreted specific endorsement for a 'fundamental distinction between international obligations' hence a distinction between the acts 'committed in breach of them.' The Commission relied on the following dicta:

> [A]n essential distinction should be drawn between the obligations of a State towards the international community as a whole, and those arising vis-à-vis another State in the field of diplomatic protection. In view of the importance of the rights involved, all States can be held to have a legal interest in their protection; they are obligations *erga omnes*.[55]

The ILC reviewed various cases and concluded that international tribunals were not denying the existence of two regimes of state responsibility, and in some instances seemed to support it.[56]

In the area of state practice, the ILC found state recognition of international crimes in treaties and in laws that reflected a heightened sense of collective interests. Various treaties had been executed during the period between the two world wars that were drafted incorporating the phrase 'international crimes,' although no separate regimes were designated.[57] In addition, new rules of international law appeared after World War II in response to an awareness of the need to protect humanity now and in the future. Also, existing laws that required states to respect obligations based on the interest of the entire international community had taken on greater significance.[58]

The focus on collective rights and interests was evident in three specific areas: 1) the establishment of peremptory norms of *jus cogens*, rules that are accepted by the international community of states to be of such importance that derogation by treaty is not allowed; 2) the principle of individual responsibility and punishment

---

52 *Id.*, at ¶ 53.

53 See generally *Id.*, at 95–122.

54 See *Id.*, at ¶ 8.

55 *Id.*, ¶ 10 (quoting Barcelona Traction, Light and Power Company, Limited judgment, 1970 ICJ 32 (February 5)).

56 See *Id.*, at ¶ 11.

57 *Id.*, at ¶ 14.

58 See *Id.*, at ¶ 15.

for those persons who have committed wrongful acts in their capacity as organs of the State; and 3) specific consequences that the United Nations Charter attached to the breach of certain international obligations, such as *apartheid* and racial discrimination, which threatened international peace and security.[59] These actions of the United Nations and its member states convinced the commission that acts such as *apartheid* had been distinguished from other breaches and consequently were of such seriousness that the state could be liable for more severe legal consequences than those of other breaches.[60]

Lastly, the ILC expounded on the history of jurists' opinions from the middle of the 19th century to the current time. They cited the writings following World War II of prominent jurists H. Lauterpact and D.B. Levin advocating a criminal element of state responsibility.[61] Lauterpact challenged the theory that state sovereignty precluded punishment.[62] He found it unjust that individuals who happened to form a state could have a level of immunity from certain criminal acts that they would not ordinarily have as individuals.[63] In 1946, Levin's dual regime of responsibility B international delicts, that is *narusheniya*, and international crimes, that is *prestupleniya* B was incorporated in Soviet doctrine.[64] Throughout the 1960s and 1970s Soviet authors continued to support the idea of international crimes.[65]

The ILC noted that other countries as well were positing various theories on collective obligations and international crimes. Some jurists incorporated the established concepts of *erga omnes* and *jus cogens*.[66] D. Schindler saw racial discrimination as an internationally wrongful act that gave rise to obligations *erga omnes*. Brownlie suggested that international crimes included the breach of an obligation flowing from *jus cogens*.[67] So in 1976 it was within the backdrop of what the ILC saw as clearly an emerging trend toward the recognition of two levels of wrongful acts in contemporary international law that Article 19 was drafted. And obligations *erga omnes* and norms *jus cogens* were the jurisprudential principles on which the ILC built its case.

Reactions to Draft Article 19

The Perspective of Publicists

The literature generated by Article 19 has been extensive, prompting even a book on the subject.[68] The opinions of publicists have been varied and covered virtually

---

59 See *Id.*, at ¶ 16.
60 See *Id.*, at ¶ 29.
61 See *Id.*, at ¶ 43.
62 See Nolte, *supra* note 1 at 1091.
63 See *Id.*
64 See Nolte, *supra* note 1 at 1095.
65 See *Id.*
66 See 1976 Yearbook, *supra* note 27 ¶ 48.
67 See *Id.*
68 Crawford, *supra* note 33, at 368 (selected bibliography on works published mainly

every position one might take. A brief overview of the literature merely draws one to the conclusion that no definitive conclusions can be drawn. The subject was very controversial and the authors served to add to that controversy. The controversy engendered by Article 19 revolves around three somewhat related issues. First, whether as a matter of positive law the concept of 'international crimes' constitutes a part of the corpus of contemporary international law?[69] Second, whether customary international law differentiates between various types of international wrongful acts and consequently between various regimes of international responsibility?[70] Put differently, whether customary law provides for a category of particularly serious wrongful acts to which it attaches a special and distinct regime of responsibility?[71] Finally, whether a relationship exists between international crimes (crimes of States) and crimes under international law (crimes by individuals) as defined in the ILC companion Draft Code on Crimes Against the Peace and Security of Mankind?

With respect to the first issue, proponents of Article 19 take the position that post-war legal developments point unswervingly in the direction of new protective norms with particular characteristics whose violations provoke graver legal consequences. It is the violation of this new category of norms that constitutes what has come to be called 'international crimes' or 'state crimes'. These super-norms, if you will, derive their *ratio legis* from the United Nations Charter, the several Geneva Conventions of 1949 and the regime of human rights instruments that have been adopted since 1945.[72]

As to whether customary international law differentiates between internationally wrongful acts reserving for the more egregious a separate regime of responsibility, the Commission has remained convinced that, despite the furor that its position seems to have aroused, such is the case. Marina Spinedi's excellent recount of the legislative history of Article 19 leaves no doubt that the Commission was fully convinced when it adopted the article that general international law has

---

since 1985 on state responsibility). *See* Weiler, Cassese & Spinedi, *supra* note 28, at 339 (bibliography 1946–1984).

[69] See Georges Abi-Saab, 'The Concept of 'International Crimes' and its Place in Contemporary International Law,' in *International Crimes of State: A Critical Analysis of the ILC's Draft Article 19 on State Responsibility*, 141 (Joseph H.H. Weiler, Antonio Cassese & Marina Spinedi eds, 1989).

[70] See Marina Spinedi, 'International Crimes of State: The Legislative History,' in *International Crimes of State: A Critical Analysis of the ILC's Draft Article 19 on State Responsibility*, 7, 115 ff (Joseph H.H. Weiler, Antonio Cassese & Marina Spinedi eds, 1989).

[71] *Id.*

[72] See Abi-Saab, *supra* note 69, at 142; but see Theodor Meron, 'Lex Lata: Is There Already a Differentiated Regime of State Responsibility in the Geneva Conventions?' in *International Crimes of State: A Critical Analysis of the ILC's Draft Article 19 on State Responsibility*, 225 (Joseph H.H. Weiler, Antonio Cassese & Marina Spinedi eds 1989) (noting that the 1949 Geneva Conventions are not good examples for the proposition that international law in force differentiates between 'crimes of States').

deliberately singled out from among the welter of international obligations a restricted set of obligations for discriminatory treatment.[73] She and others point out that the rules of international law in force have already recognized the existence of a special category of non-derogable peremptory norms or rules of *jus cogens* in the context of the law of treaties.[74] Article 19 merely provides a reasoned explanation for the distinction where gravity is determined by the degree to which the obligations are essential in safeguarding the fundamental interests of the international community as a whole. Thus, the enumeration of four exemplar crimes in paragraph 3 of Article 19 should properly be viewed as a reaffirmation of existing international law, no more, no less.

There have been several objections to the ILC's formulation of a differentiated regime of responsibility and this came through in a 1987 Conference on Crimes of State organized by the European University Institute and the University of Florence.[75] Sir Ian Sinclair, who as a member of the ILC must have participated in the drafting of Article 19, nonetheless takes issue with the assertion that existing international law, particularly the law of the Charter, supports 'a differentiation, in the context of the codification of the law of State responsibility, between different categories of internationally wrongful acts.'[76] The problem as he sees it is the tendency to confuse between differing consequences that may flow from the breach by a State of an internationally wrongful act and the nature of the obligation breached. As he argues, the consequences of an act of a particularly serious character may be different from the consequences of an 'ordinary' internationally wrongful act; but these differing consequences do not have to be punished by separate regimes of responsibility. They can easily be accommodated within a single one.[77]

---

[73] See Marina Spinedi, *supra* note 70, at 7; see also Manfred Mohr, 'The ILC's Distinction Between 'International Crimes' and 'International Delicts' and Its Implications,' in *United Nattons Codification of State Responsibility*, 115 (Marina Spinedi & Bruno Summa eds, 1987).

[74] *Id.*

[75] Among the participants at this conference were the President and several members of the International Court of Justice; several members of the International Law Commission, diplomats and academics representing all major trends in the international legal order. Also present and participating were two special Rapporteurs on the Draft Articles on State Responsibility: Judge Ago (the author of the concept of crimes in draft Article 19) and his successor Professor Riphagen, as well as the Rapporteur on the Draft Code on Crimes Against the Peace and Security of Mankind: Dr. Doudou Thiam. Their contributions were compiled into an anthology: *International Crimes of State: A Critical Analysis of the ILC's Draft Article 19 on State Responsibility* (Joseph H.H. Weiler, Antonio Cassese & Marina Spinedi eds, 1989).

[76] See Ian Sinclair, 'State Responsibility and the Concept of Crimes of States,' in *International Crimes of State: A Critical Analysis of the ILC's Draft Article 19 on State Responsibility*, 223, 225 (Joseph H.H. Weiler, Antonio Cassese & Marina Spinedi eds 1989).

[77] *Id.*

Another objection voiced by Professor Ted Stein to the ILC's approach in conceptualizing international crimes is on grounds that it operates to short-circuit the process through which international law norms are traditionally identified, that is, through 'the patient examination of State practice that is so much a part of the codification process as conventionally understood.'[78] Equally unsatisfactory for Professor Stein is the Commission's Orwellian approach of differentiating between international crimes and then designating certain types of international wrongful conduct as more wrongful than others hence belonging to the category of 'international crimes,' as lacking the precision necessary to 'discriminate between ordinary delicts and crimes on a systematic basis.'[79] In sum, not everyone, including members of the ILC, is in agreement that 'crimes of States' necessarily codify *existing* law.

Also the subject of much disagreement is the attribution of criminal responsibility to States which some commentators find inconsistent with the international reality of sovereign States. The concern here is with the misplaced attempt to draw parallels with national penal law. What this amounts to, according to Professor Bernhard Graefrath, is the burdening of international responsibility with the 'instruments and the dogmatic and sophisticated vocabulary of penal law ... [while] ignor[ing] that in international law we continue to have subjects with equal rights and that there exists no superior central power. It supposes that the violation of legal rules produces either civil or penal responsibility, which is not even the case in municipal law.'[80] His specific quarrel is with the obligations *erga omnes* (of which more will be said later) created as a result of characterizing an international wrongful act as a 'crime of States.' The pinning of this label on a wrongful act immediately transforms its violation into a breach of an obligation essential for the protection of the fundamental interests of the international community. Correspondingly, this triggers a response from the international community since it presumably has a strong interest in deterring the commission of such a crime and in bringing about the termination of the illegal conduct.[81] But because the international system is acephalous, lacking a superior central authority, obligations designed to be shouldered by the community as a whole are usually left to the 'decentralized, but multilateral sanctioning systems, that is, third-State sanctions'[82] for their implementation.

Reactions by Governments

The Commission would leave Draft Article 19 to percolate within the international community while it mapped out the dual regime of responsibility and

---

78 See Ted L. Stein, 'Observations on 'Crimes of States',' in *International Crimes of State: A Critical Analysis of the ILC's Draft Article 19 on State Responsibility*, 194, 196 (Joseph H.H. Weiler, Antonio Cassese & Marina Spinedi eds, 1989).

79 *Id.*

80 See Graefrath, *supra* note 28, at 163.

81 See Stein, *supra* note 78, at 195.

82 *Id.*, at 198.

consequences that would apply. What eventually came out of the debates with regard to responsibility was Article 40, Injured States.[83] The article covered three areas of responsibility B bilateral, multilateral, and multinational. Bilateral and multilateral responsibility arose within the context of treaties and other agreements among various state parties. Paragraph 3 addressed injured states within the universal context, where a state had not been directly injured. Paragraph 3 proposed that injured state meant if the internationally wrongful act constituted an international crime, all other States were injured. In other words, the breach of obligations that constitutes an international crime were obligations *erga omnes*. The content of these obligations affected and concerned the international community as a whole. *Ergo*, when a state breached a 'criminalized' obligation, all states had become injured by the act of the wrongdoing state. The commission had yet to determine the consequences of an international crime and the commentary noted that while all states are injured, Article 40(3) did not prejudice the extent of the legal consequences to be attached to international crimes. The ILC believed the legal consequences of Article 19 would require further explanations and distinction.[84]

Consequences of Draft Article 19

The drafting of the consequences of State crimes generated differences of opinion among the Commission members. Several proposals were put forward regarding what approach should be taken[85] One proposal was for a highly institutionalized procedure through existing international organs and new ones to be created. The process would start at the determination of a breach and then move through the system to the issue of consequences.[86] Some members envisaged a two-stage process of recognition of a crime and then arbitration, similar to that over disputes arising from norms of *jus cogens* in the ICJ. Others disagreed, finding the analogy to *jus cogens* misleading or needing further development.[87]

What eventually became the consequences for breaches of international obligations were set out in Part Two, Chapter II, Rights of the Injured State and Obligations of the State which has Committed an Internationally Wrongful Act. Rights included cessation of the wrongful conduct, reparations, restitution in kind, compensation, satisfaction, and assurances and guarantees of non-repetition.[88] Special Rapporteur Crawford called Article 40(3) the 'single most significant

---

83 See Crawford, *supra* note 33, at 357 (reprint of the 1996 draft articles).

84 See [1985] *International Law Commission Yearbook*, pt. 2 25–27 UN Doc.A/CN.4/SER.A/1985/Add.1 [hereinafter '1985 Yearbook'].

85 See http://www.cam.ac.uk/RCIL/ILCSR/stateresp.htm, *supra* note 45, (commentary to Art. 51).

86 See *Seventh Report on State Responsibility by Mr. Gaetano Arangio-Ruiz, Special Rapporteur*, 1995 *International Law Commission Yearbook*, pt. 2, ¶¶ 248–281, UN Doc. A/CN.4/SER.A/1995/Add.1 [hereinafter 'Arangio-Ruiz Report'].

87 See *Id.*

88 See Crawford *supra* note 33, at 358.

consequence of an international crime' because it pronounced that all states were injured states under international crimes and were therefore entitled to seek any of the remedies as the state that was directly injured.[89] It also implied that all states were entitled to take countermeasures under the provisions in articles 47–50.

For crimes, the commission carved out more severe consequences, given the seriousness of the acts. There were three specific provisions set out in Part Two, Chapter IV, International Crimes. Article 51, Consequences of International Crime states: 'An international crime entails all the legal consequences of any other internationally wrongful act and, in addition, such further consequences as are set out in Articles 52 and 53.'[90] The commentary notes the correlation to Article 40, which defined injured States as all states.[91]

The ILC set out two kinds of consequences related to crimes. The first, Article 52, addressed the relationship between the wrongdoing state and each injured state. The rights of the injured state are as follows:

> Where an internationally wrongful act of a State is an international crime:
>
> (a) an injured State's entitlement to obtain restitution in kind is not subject to the limitations set out in subparagraphs (c) and (d) of article 43; an injured State's entitlement to obtain satisfaction is not subject to the restriction in paragraph 3 of article 45.[92]

When a State had committed an international crime, the ILC believed certain limitations on the rights of the injured state should not apply.[93] Subsection (a) allowed restitution even if it was a burden out of proportion to the benefit to the injured State; and if it would jeopardize the political independence or economic stability of the State that committed the act. Subsection (b) entitled the injured State to satisfaction even though it might impair the dignity of a State.

The second particular consequence concerns what the ILC described as 'the minimum collective consequences of a crime.'[94] Article 53 States:

> An international crime committed by a State entails an obligation for every other State:
> (a) not to recognize as lawful the situation created by the crime;
> (b) not to render aid or assistance to the State which has committed the crime in maintaining the situation so created;

---

89 See *First Report on State Responsibility by Mr. James Crawford, Special Rapporteur*, UN GAOR International Law Commission, 50th Sess., ¶ 51, UN Doc. A/CN.4/490/Add.1 (1998) [hereinafter 'First Report Add.1'].

90 See Crawford *supra* note 33, at 361.

91 See http://www.cam.ac.uk/RCIL/ILCSR/stateresp.htm, *supra* note 45, (commentary to Art. 40).

92 Crawford, *supra* note 33, at 362.

93 See http://www.cam.ac.uk/RCIL/ILCSR/stateresp.htm, *supra* note 45, (commentary to Art. 52).

94 See http://www.cam.ac.uk/RCIL/ILCSR/stateresp.htm, *supra* note 45, (commentary to Art. 51 ¶ 14).

(c) to cooperate with other States in carrying out the obligations under subparagraphs (a) and (b); and
(d) to cooperate with other States in the application of measures designed to eliminate the consequences of the crime.[95]

The commentary noted that the provisions under subsections (a) and (b) were well-established international practice, illustrated in the Security Council Resolution on Rhodesia and on Kuwait.[96] Subsections (c) and (d) reflect the commission's view that a collective response by all States was 'necessary to counteract the effects of an international crime.'[97] State cooperation in non-recognition and assistance in the elimination of the consequences was what the Commission saw as a minimum requirement on the part of states. The Commission added, however, that in practice the response would be coordinated through the appropriate organs of the United Nations.[98]

With the completion of a first draft, the ILC provisionally adopted the draft in 1996. Special Rapporteur Arangio-Ruiz resigned and James Crawford was appointed to replace him. In 1997, the Commission adopted a provisional timetable to complete a second reading by 2001. In the interim, the General Assembly invited governments to comment on the 1996 draft, which was published at the 50th Session of the ILC on 25 March 1998.[99]

1998/1999 Government Comments

This was the first opportunity for governments to review a complete draft of the articles on state responsibility including the responsibility and consequences associated with international crimes. Many governments submitted written comments.[100] Although similarly small in number, the composition of the countries that provided written responses in 1998 and 1999 was quite different from those in the early 1980s. The dominating states of Western Europe and the US were significantly represented. Those states that supported draft Article 19

---

95 Crawford, *supra* note 33, at 362.

96 See http://www.cam.ac.uk/RCIL/ILCSR/stateresp.htm, *supra* note 45, (commentary to Art. 53(2)).

97 *Id.*, (commentary to Art. 53(3)).

98 *Id.*

99 *See State Responsibility Comments and Observations received from Governments*, UN GAOR International Law Commission, 50th Sess., UN Doc. A/CN.4/488 (1998) [hereinafter '1998 Comments'].

100 Asia: Japan and Mongolia; South America/Mexico: Argentina, Chile, and Mexico; Continental Western Europe: Austria, France, Germany, Greece, Spain, and Switzerland; Eastern/Central Europe: The Czech Republic and Uzbekistan; Nordic Countries: Denmark, Finland, Iceland, Norway, and Sweden; United Kingdom: England and Ireland, North America: The United States.

were very much absent. Countries also commented at the Sixth Committee meetings of the General Assembly.[101]

In general, there was a stronger B in intensity as well as quantity B rejection of the concept of international crimes. Most of the Western European countries B Austria, France, Germany, Ireland, Switzerland, and the United Kingdom B all argued, France quite strenuously, for the deletion of Articles 19, 40(3), 51, 52, and 53. The repeated criticism was that criminal responsibility attached to individuals, not states, and that the idea of State crimes had no support in international law. The United States echoed the view of most of Western Europe, finding no support in customary international law and finding the concept 'unworkable in practice.'[102] Mexico found an insufficient distinction between the concept of crimes and delicts.[103] Japan acknowledged the existence of an international community with shared interests, but the government did not find it necessary to incorporate the notion of international crimes into the draft articles.[104]

In support of draft Article 19, the Nordic countries suggested new terminology to replace 'crime' in an attempt to salvage a concept that was obviously in jeopardy.[105] The Czech Republic maintained its support as well, but found that the term 'crime' would Astand in the way of any progress on the draft as a whole.'[106] The Czech representative also expressed disappointment in the Commission's proposed consequences.[107] Greece, in a change from 1980, supported Article 19, which it felt made a 'considerable contribution to the establishment and strengthening of an international public order that the world sorely needs.'[108]

The consequences of an international crime garnered criticisms by virtually all states. The provisions were regarded as inadequate, unworkable, and difficult.[109] States commented that the international crimes described in Article 19 did not have equivalent consequences in articles 51–53, making the distinction between crimes and delicts meaningless.[110]

The dominating states were quite vigorous in their criticisms and Special Rapporteur Crawford took them seriously. Although states did comment in the Sixth Committee meetings, the countries that had submitted written comments received primary attention.

---

[101] Sixth Committee comments are taken from Crawford=s reports to the General Assembly.

[102] *Id.*, at 62.

[103] See *Id.*, at 59.

[104] See *State Responsibility Comments and Observations received from Governments*, UN GAOR International Law Commission, 51st Sess., 8–9, UN Doc. A/CN.4/492 (1999) [hereinafter '1999 Comments'].

[105] See 1998 Comments, *supra* note 99, at 53.

[106] *Id.*, at 52.

[107] *Id.*, at 137.

[108] 1999 Comments, *supra* note 104, at 8.

[109] See 1998 Comments, *supra* note 99, at 137–141.

[110] See *Id.*, at 139 (Switzerland).

The Undoing of Draft Article 19

An ill advised strategy The ILC may have made two missteps with draft Article 19, the terminology and its piecemeal approach to gaining support. Crime is not a neutral term. It already carried a regime of responsibility in domestic law that prejudiced some opinions from the start. Perhaps the commission should have considered this to a greater degree when deciding to use the term. Second, the ILC submitted draft Article 19 to governments in isolation, without its applicable regimes of responsibility and consequences because these rules were to be developed in the second part of the draft. There was discussion that states might be reluctant to express their opinions without the consequences, but Ago did not agree, which may have been a mistake.[111] Although it was doubtful that this was the intent, the ILC then left the States with their preconceived notions to ferment for another 20 years before presenting a completed set of draft articles.

In hindsight, the submission of a new concept in state responsibility called 'crimes' with details yet to be worked out proved to be an insurmountable obstacle. The ILC had 'left too much room for distortion and misinterpretation' with discussions that were burdened with 'misunderstandings and prejudices based on penal law.'[112] The Commission saw draft Article 19 as the codification of what they saw as a clearly developing trend in international law. The states saw it as *lege de ferenda*, or even worse an attempt to incorporate domestic law into an international 'criminal' concept. Some States assumed 'punishment' would be a natural consequence, imposing damages on the wrongdoing state. Other states came to contrary conclusions and supported draft Article 19 with the directive that there was no place for punishment in international law.[113]

The approach taken by the ILC was ill advised given the progressive nature of what they were asking the states to support and the controversial terminology. The states' preconceived notions may have colored their assessments in ways that could not be changed.

Never accepted An assessment of the demise of draft Article 19 might first lead one to ask whether *a priori* acceptance can be assumed in the first place. In 1989, the *travaux preparatoires* show that the 'great majority of States were in favour of Draft Article 19.'[114] However, the majority was mainly smaller countries, less developed countries, and socialist countries. Those states that were opposed may have been in the minority, but were 'States whose opinions can not be ignored when drafting a codification convention.'[115] Granted, acceptance among all states need not have been unanimous. But a cross-section of countries, including those more powerful, would have given the commission more confidence that a

---

111 See [1976] *International Law Commission Yearbook*, 78 UN Doc. A/CN.4/SER.A/1976 [hereinafter '1976 Yearbook'].

112 Graefrath, *supra* note 28, at 161.

113 See *Id.*, at 52.

114 *Id.*, at 48.

115 *Id.*, at 48.

convention could be supported with a regime of international crimes. For the less developed countries, their reasoning behind acceptance of Article 19 was fairly apparent. These smaller, less developed, countries are dependent on the United Nations and the oversight of the international community to protect them from exploitation and domination. As the countries most likely to be victims of international crimes, the harsher the breach in international law the greater the legal protection these countries would be afforded. The fact that no consequences were laid out was secondary to the recognition that states could commit crimes.

Changing World Order

Quite simply, the passage of time played a major role in draft Article 19's failure. As the Commission moved toward its completion of the second and third parts of the draft articles, the world changed. It appears that many of the original reasons for the need for international crimes were gone. While draft Article 19 remained the same, World War II had grown fainter in the mind of the international community. There had not been another conflict of its magnitude, which led the world to believe, perhaps wrongly, that such events could not happen again.

Treaties were signed to halt the proliferation of weapons of mass destruction. The Cold War had ended, and with it the USSR as the world knew it. The Soviet states declared their independence, severed their ties with Russia, and established democratic governments. Russia's economic collapse eliminated its status as a superpower and a military threat. Germany had been devastated by the war and East and West Germany were eventually reunited to form a democratic state when the Berlin Wall fell. Japan had retooled economically rather than militarily. These events left the US as the remaining dominant military power with a stable democratic government supporting it.

The environment became less of a focus as the world found it could continue to pollute and populate, creating social and economic problems for less developed countries, but not the threat to the world's existence as once thought. At least not within the time frame anticipated. In addition the UN drafted various treaties and other instruments to address the problems of environmental damage, human rights, and the rights of people to their land and resources. There were actions being taken that gave people a greater sense that something was being done.

Lack of State Practice and Judicial Decisions

The ILC had seen an emerging trend in favor of two levels of internationally wrongful acts and two regimes of responsibility. The idea of collective interests and multinational responsibility was not new and had gained some momentum in light of the atrocities of World War II. However, almost 20 years had passed and whatever 'trend' had been developing had not been put into practice by states. Governments had seen no evidence of state practice to support the notion of international crimes since draft Article 19 was originally approved in 1979.[116] Most countries viewed state practice as essential to the codification of state responsibility and were reluctant to accept it otherwise.[117] Although one of the roles of the ILC is the progressive development of international law, the mandate by the United Nations on state responsibility was only codification.[118] Some states regarded this as a clear evidence of the commission's limitations.

Beyond the *Barcelona Traction* case there had been little in the way of judicial decisions to support the commission's position. The ILC had looked more to what the courts had not said, that is, no rejection of the concept, rather than what they had said. Twenty years later, Special Rapporteur Crawford found little had changed. The judicial decisions since 1976 showed there was support for the idea of different kinds of *norms*, such as *jus cogens*. But, in Special Rapporteur Crawford's view, the acceptance of various principles that guide international law did not necessarily lead one to the conclusion that there should be different categories of breaches and regimes of responsibility.[119]

The New Regime of State Responsibility

The new Draft Articles on Responsibility of States for Internationally Wrongful Acts involves a unitary regime as opposed to the old dual regime of state responsibility under Article 19 of the 1996 Draft Articles. The 2001 Draft Articles opted for a compromise by deleting Article 19, which had so much baggage. First, Western European states and the United States strongly opposed the inclusion of Article 19 and its dual regime. While from a doctrinal standpoint state practice supporting this duality was evident, it was, however, still embryonic. Furthermore, there was no coherent system for dealing with criminal conduct of States, both from equally important procedural and substantive points of view. As a compromise, rather than a reintroduction, of Article 19, the new draft articles engaged in a development of the already accepted concepts of *erga omnes* and *jus cogens*. This compromise was satisfactory to Article 19's detractors and those that believed the notion of State crimes was an imperative in codifying international State responsibility. The result was embodied in articles 40 and 41 with one regime of responsibility based on obligations *erga omnes* and norms *jus cogens*.

Article 40 addresses serious breaches:

> The Chapter applies to the international responsibility which is entailed by a serious breach by a State of an obligation arising under a peremptory norm of general

---

116 See generally '1998 Comments,' *supra* note 99, at 51. See '1999 Comments,' *supra* note 104, at 19.

117 See *Id.*

118 GA Res. 799, UN GAOR, 8th Sess., 48th plen. mtg., UN Doc. A/RES/8/799 (1953).

119 See *First Report on State Responsibility by Mr. James Crawford, Special Rapporteur*, UN GAOR International Law Commission, 50th Sess., & 63, UN Doc. A/CN.4/490/Add.2 (1998) [hereinafter 'First Report Add.2'].

international law. A breach of such an obligation is serious if it involved a gross or systematic failure by the responsible State to fulfil the obligation.

Article 41 addresses consequences:

a. States shall cooperate to bring an end through lawful means any serious breach within the meaning of article 40.
b. No State shall recognize as lawful a situation created by a serious breach within the meaning of article 40, nor render aid or assistance in maintaining that situation.
c. This article is without prejudice to the other consequences referred to in this Part and to such further consequences that a breach to which this Chapter applies may entail under international law.[120]

According to Special Rapporteur Crawford, the new regime of state responsibility contained in the aforementioned articles reflects a better approach to international crimes, seeking 'to embody the values underlying the former Article [19], while avoiding the problematic terminology of "crime".'[121] Article 19 suffered from the same drafting defects that plagued most of the 1996 draft articles. Crawford was especially critical of this Article and found its paragraph 1 a statement of the obvious; Paragraph 2 circular; and Paragraph 3's definition illusory and wholly lacking in specificity.[122]

Although the language of current Article 40 has been called ambiguous, it does not, however, suffer from circularity nor is it illusory. Paragraph 1 establishes the character and scope of a breach of a certain type of obligation that entails state responsibility under international law. The breach must be serious and arise under a peremptory norm of general international law, that is, norms of *jus cogens*. Paragraph 2 defines serious as a gross or systematic failure to fulfill the obligation. This mirrors crimes against humanity in Article 18 of the Draft Code for the Peace and Security of Mankind, which defines crimes as systematic and large-scale.

Article 40 does not designate two categories of internationally wrongful acts, but clearly indicates that this is a distinct category of a breach that is more serious and is of concern to the international community as a whole. The commentary states that the breach of these obligations is intolerable because of the threat it presents to the survival of states and their peoples and the most basic human values.[123] This echoes Article 19's characterization of an international crime as essential for the fundamental interest of the international community.

In drafting Article 19 in 1976, the International Law Commission relied on Barcelona Traction case to support its belief that the international law recognized two separate regimes of international responsibility based on the subject matter of the obligation breached, hence two different types of wrongful acts.[124] In again recalling Barcelona Traction in 1998, the commission accepts the court's dicta that

120 See Crawford, *supra* note 33, at 69.
121 *Id*, at 38.
122 See First Report, *supra* note 119, ¶¶ 46–49.
123 Crawford, *supra* note 33, at 246.
124 1976 Yearbook, *supra* note 45.

in state responsibility there are certain obligations that are owed to the international community as a whole and that all states have an interest in their protection.[125] However, the commission stopped short of designating two regimes of responsibility.

Draft Article 19 included a list, though not exhaustive, of international crimes including aggression; the right of self-determination of peoples; human rights violations such as slavery, genocide, and apartheid; and environmental pollution. Although current Article 40 has no counterpart, the commentary includes basically the same non-exhaustive list of peremptory norms of general international law: aggression, slavery, genocide, racial discrimination, apartheid, torture, and the right of self-determination of peoples.[126]

The differences between the earlier draft Article 19 and current Article 40 are largely semantic. From a practical analysis, if a state commits genocide, under draft Article 19 the state has committed an internationally wrongful act called a crime because it has breached an obligation that is essential for the protection of the community as a whole, hence it is (impliedly) responsible. Under current Article 40 the state is (expressly) responsible for committing an act that is considered a serious breach, that is, gross or systematic, under a peremptory norm of general international law. And under both scenarios the international community has been engaged because of the seriousness of the obligation breached.

In a less clear-cut example, if a state commits a major act of terrorism under Article 19 it has committed an internationally wrongful act. In addition, the question is: Is it so essential for the protection of the fundamental interest of the international community that it should be a crime? Draft Article 19 does not answer, so we look to customary international law which indicates it is probably not a crime. Under current Article 40, the state has not committed a breach of a norm of *jus cogens* by current standards. However, if one looks to the commentary if the act presents a threat to the survival of states and their peoples, which is alternative protection of fundamental interests, it may still be a serious breach under Article 40. However, customary law has yet to elevate terrorism to the level of seriousness that engages the international community.

If crimes and serious breaches are merely 'twin brothers of horror,'[127] what is different about the new regime of state responsibility? The significant areas of divergence are found in the definition of injured state and the consequences of a breach. These rules are codified in articles 41, 42, and 48.

Article 41

> Particular consequences of a serious breach of an obligation under this Chapter States shall cooperate to bring to an end through lawful means any serious breach within the meaning of article 40.

---

[125] Crawford, *supra* note 33, at 246.

[126] *Id.*

[127] Eric Wyler, 'From 'State Crime' to Responsibility for 'Serious Breaches of Obligations under Peremptory Norms of General International Law',' 13 ELIJ 1147, 1159 (2002).

(a) No State shall recognize as lawful as situation created by a serious breach within the meaning of article 40, nor render aid or assistance in maintaining that situation.

The article is without prejudice to the other consequences referred to in this Part and to such further consequences that a breach to which the Chapter applies may entail under international law.[128]

Article 42

Invocation of responsibility by an injured state

A State is entitled as an injured State to invoke the responsibility of another State if the obligation breached is owed to:

(a) that State individually; or
(b) a group of States including that State, or the international community as a whole, and the breach of the obligation:

1. specifically affects that State; or
2. is of such character as radically to change the position of all other States to which the obligation is owed with respect to further performance of the obligation.[129]

Article 48

Invocation of responsibility by a State other than an injured state

ii. Any State other than an injured state is entitled to invoke the responsibility of another State in accordance with paragraph 2 if:
(a) the obligation breached is owed to a group of States including that State, and is established for the protection of a collective interest of the group; or
(b) the obligation breached is owed to the international community as a whole.
(b)a.1 Any State is entitled to invoke responsibility under paragraph 1 may claim from the responsible State:
(c) cessation of the internationally wrongful act, and assurances and guarantees of non-repetition in accordance with article 30; and
(d) performance of the obligation of reparation in accordance with the preceding articles, in the interest of the injured State or of the beneficiaries of the obligation breached.
(d)a.1.1.a The requirements for the invocation of responsibility by an injured State under articles 43, 44 and 45 apply to an invocation of responsibility by a State entitled to do so under paragraph 1.[130]

---

128 Crawford, *supra* note 33, at 249.
129 *Id.*, at 254
130 *Id.*, at 276.

Injured States

Current Articles 42 and 48 are reformulations of Article 40's definition of injured state. Current Article 42 addresses individual states or a small group and defines two conditions under which a state is considered injured, hence entitled to invoke the responsibility of another state. Paragraph (a) allows that a state may invoke responsibility if it is injured, that is, the obligation was owed to that state individually.[131] This situation may occur *inter alia* under a bilateral treaty, a unilateral commitment, or a general rule of international law. Paragraph (b) covers situations in which a group of states or the international community as a whole may be injured. Unlike Article 40, which declared that all states were injured in the event of a crime, Current Article 42 imposes certain conditions before states may be considered injured. First, under (b)(i) a state must be specially affected by the breach. Article 60(2) is modeled after the Vienna Convention.[132] For a state to be considered injured, it must be affected by the breach in a way that distinguishes it from the generality of other States to which the obligation is owed.[133] As in the convention, there is no definition of specially affected, with each situation assessed on a case-by-case basis.

The second provision, Paragraph (b)(ii) addresses an area not covered in the 1996 draft articles. It recognizes a special character of obligation, the breach of which radically changes the position of all the other states to which the obligation is owed with respect to the further performance of the obligation. This is what the commission refers to as an interdependent or integral obligation that is also taken from the Vienna Convention.[134] The commentary lists examples such as disarmament treaties, nuclear free zone treaties, and any treaty where each party's performance depends upon the performance of the others.

New Article 48 is the companion to new Article 42 in that it addresses the invocation of responsibility by a state other than an injured state. A state that is not injured may invoke the responsibility of another state under two conditions: 1) if the obligation is owed to a group of states and the obligation was created for the protection of a collective interest, that is, obligations *erga omnes partes*; or, 2) it is an obligation owed to the international community as a whole, that is, obligations *erga omnes*.[135] States that are entitled to invoke responsibility under this provision are limited to claiming cessation of the wrongful act, assurances of non-repetition, and reparations specifically in the interest of the injured state or other beneficiaries.[136] This provision differs from Article 40(3) in which a crime entitled all states to cessation and non-repetition, plus restitution, compensation, and satisfaction, as well as countermeasures.

While not totally eliminating certain rights of the international community, the

131 *Id.*, at 257.
132 *Id.*, at 259.
133 *Id.*
134 *Id.*
135 *Id.*, at 276.
136 *Id.* (emphasis added).

new articles have proscribed the rights of states that are not directly injured and limited what actions they may take.

Consequences and Obligations

As noted earlier, Article 51 prescribed the same consequences for crimes as those for delicts in articles 41–46. Article 52 expanded the consequences of an international crime in the areas of restitution and satisfaction. In seeking restitution, the injured states were allowed to burden the wrongdoing state even if it was out of proportion to the benefit to the injured state. Also, an injured state could jeopardize the political independence or economic stability of the wrongdoing state. In the area of satisfaction, an injured state was allowed satisfaction even if it would impair the dignity of the State.[137] Article 53 established four consequences in the form of obligations placed upon all states in the event of a crime. These were: 1) non-recognition of the act as lawful; 2) non- assistance to the wrongdoing state; 3) cooperation with other states in carrying out the obligations of 1 and 2; and 4) cooperation with other states in applying measures designed to eliminate the consequences of the crime.[138]

Current Article 41 imposes significantly less responsibility on those states not injured. They are to cooperate in bringing an end to the breach through lawful means and are not to recognize the situation created by the breach as lawful.

JURISPRUDENCE ON THE DRAFT ARTICLES ON STATE RESPONSIBILITY

Over the period 1996–2006, a number of international tribunals including the International Court of Justice have made reference to the draft articles in their jurisprudence.

International Court of Justice

In *Judgment on Preliminary Objections in Case Concerning Certain Phosphate Lands in Nauru,*[139] where the Republic of Nauru (Naura) claimed that Australia owed reparations for the rehabilitation of Nauru phosphate lands that were depleted by Australia during its trusteeship administration, the issue of state responsibility was vetted. Nauru had been placed under the joint trusteeship authority of Australia, New Zealand and the UK in 1947, which was terminated in 1967. The draft articles on state responsibility arose in the context of whether the three Governments were jointly liable, as Australia contended, or whether they were subject to joint and several liability, as Nauru contended. Australia argued that the ILC never adopted a position on the issue, but the court disagreed. The reference

137 *See* Crawford, *supra* note 33, at 358–360.

138 *Id.*, at 362

139 *Certain Phosphate Lands in Nauru* (Nauru v. Australia) 32 ILM 46, 1993 ICJ

was the commentary to Article 27, 'Aid or Assistance by a State to Another State for the Commission of an Internationally Wrongful Act' (Current Article 16).[140] The relevant portion of the commentary stated:

> According to the principles on which the articles of chapter II of the draft are based, the conduct of the common organ cannot be considered otherwise than as an act of each of the States whose common organ it is. If that conduct is not in conformity with an international obligation, then two or more States will concurrently have committed separate, although identical, internationally wrongful acts. It is self-evident that the parallel commission of identical offences by two or more States is altogether different from participation by one of those States in an internationally wrongful act committed by the other.[141]

The court held in favor of Nauru, finding that each State is separately answerable for the wrongful act of the common organ.[142]

The World Court again had occasion to revisit the subject of state responsibility as codified in the Draft Articles in the *Case Concerning the Gabcíkovo-Nagymaros Project.*[143] Here the dispute was over a treaty between Hungary and Czechoslovakia for the construction and operation of the Gabcíkovo-Nagymaros system of locks for the utilization of the natural resources of the Bratislava-Budapest section of the Danube River.[144] The project began in 1978 and in 1989 Hungary abandoned work on the project. Czechoslovakia proposed a solution and work resumed. However, in 1992, Hungary terminated the treaty. The parties submitted their dispute to the International Court of Justice in 1992. Slovakia entered the dispute when it became an independent state in 1993.

Hungary invoked the draft articles on state responsibility, claiming necessity as precluding the wrongfulness of their termination of the contract. The court relied on the Vienna Convention, which controls whether a convention is in force or has been denounced, and the draft articles on state responsibility. The court used the draft articles on state responsibility to determine the extent to which suspension of the treaty was incompatible with the law of treaties. The court evaluated Hungary's claim of necessity under Current Article 25, 'Necessity.'[145] The court held that the 'perils' Hungary claimed to support its defense of necessity was not sufficiently established or imminent, and Hungary was not entitled to suspend the contract.[146] The court then had to decide if Czech and the Slovak Federal Republic had committed an internationally wrongful act when it commenced unilateral work on the project. The court cited the draft articles

140 Article 27 stated: Aid or assistance by a State to another State, if it is established that it is rendered for the commission of an internationally wrongful act, even if, taken alone, such aid or assistance would not constitute the breach of an international obligation.

141 Nauru v. Australia, 32 ILM 46, at 70.

142 *Id.*

143 Gabcíkovo-Nagymaros Project, (Hungary v. Slovakia) 37 ILM 162, 1997 ICJ

144 *Id.*, at 174.

145 *Id.*, at 184–186.

146 *Id.*, at 187.

provisions on countermeasures in rejecting the Czech and Slovak claim that the acts constituted valid countermeasures.

Advisory Opinion: Difference Relating to Immunity from Legal Process of a Special Rapporteur of the Commission on Human Rights[147]

This was an advisory opinion by the International Court of Justice on the immunity from legal process of the United Nations Special Rapporteur on the Independence of Judges and Lawyers. The Special Rapporteur had been interviewed in his official capacity and had made comments to the press on litigation in Malaysia. The companies to which he had referred filed suit for defamation. The government of Malaysia had not informed the Malaysian court of the Secretary-General's finding that the Special Rapporteur had been acting in his official capacity and was immune from suit. The court refused to accept his defense of immunity.

In addition to the opinion regarding immunity, the court issued an opinion on Malaysia's liability in not informing the court of the Secretary-General's finding. The court cited the provisions on attribution in the draft articles and determined that the Malaysian government was responsible and had not complied with its obligation.

International Tribunal for the Law of the Sea

The M/V Saiga (No. 2) Case (Saint Vincent and the Grenadines v. Guinea)[148]

M/V Saiga involved Guinea's seizure of the Saiga, an oil tanker, and arrest of its crew in the exclusive economic zone of Sierra Leone. The cargo of gasoil was removed. Guinea claimed it lawfully exercised it right of hot pursuit to enforce its local law of controlling and suppressing the sale of gasoil.

The issue related to state responsibility involved a disagreement between the parties regarding the exhaustion of local remedies. Although the court found it unnecessary to decide this issue, it stated that the draft articles position would have controlled.[149]

International Centre for the Settlement of Investment Disputes (ICSID)

Maffezini v. Spain (Decision of the Tribunal on Objections to Jurisdiction)[150]

This case was between Emilio Agustín Maffezini, a national of Argentina, and the Kingdom of Spain regarding an investment dispute that had been submitted to

[147] Difference Relating to Immunity from Legal Process of a Special Rapporteur of the Commission on Human Rights, 38 ILM 873, 1999 ICJ.

[148] M/V Saiga (No.2) (Saint Vincent and the Grenadines v. Guinea) 38 ILM 1323, 1999 ITLS.

[149] *Id.*, at 1345.

[150] Maffezini v. Spain, 40 ILM 1129, 2001 ICSID.

ICSID for arbitration. One of the issues the court had to determine was whether or not Sociedad para el Desarrollo Industrial de Galicia (SODIGA) was an agent of the state of Spain for the purpose of jurisdiction. The court found that SODIGA was an agent of the state, citing attribution per Article 7 (Current Article 4, 'Conduct of Organs of a State').[151]

Metalclad Corp. v. United Mexican States[152]

This was a dispute between Metalclad, a US company, and the United Mexican States (Mexico). Metalclad claims that Mexico interfered with its development and operation of a landfill in San Luis Potosi in violation of the North American Free Trade Agreement (NAFTA). In deciding the threshold question of whether Mexico was internationally responsible for the governments of San Luis Potosi and Guadalcazar, the court cited Article 10 of the draft articles (Current Article 7, 'Excess of Authority or Contravention of Instructions'). The court found that Mexico was responsible even if the governments had exceeded their authority.[153] The court added that although the draft articles were still under consideration, they may be regarded as an accurate statement of the law.[154]

United Kingdom House of Lords

Regina v. Bartle and the Commissioner of Police for the Metropolis and Others Ex Parte Pinochet[155]

This case involved the extradition proceedings against Pinochet of Chile for charges of *inter alia* torture, murder and conspiracy to commit murder. Citing the Draft Code of the Peace and Security of Mankind, the court found he could not claim immunity. The court also clarified the distinction between Pinochet's individual culpability and Chile's responsibility under the Draft Articles on State Responsibility. The court stated:

> As the commission already emphasized in the commentary to article 19 of the draft articles on state responsibility, the punishment of individuals who are organs of the state 'certainly does not exhaust the prosecution of the international responsibility incumbent upon the state for internationally wrongful acts which are attributed to it in such cases by reason of the conduct of its organs.' The state may thus remain responsible and be unable to exonerate itself from responsibility by invoking the prosecution or punishment of the individuals who committed the crime.[156]

---

151 *Id.*, at 1142.

152 Metalclad Corp. v. United Mexican States, 40 I.L.M. 36, 2001 ICSID.

153 *Id.*, at 47.

154 *Id.*

155 Regina v. Bartle and the Commissioner of Police for the Metropolis and Others Ex Parte Pinochet, 38 ILM 581, 1999 HL.

156 *Id.*, at 641.

INDIVIDUAL RESPONSIBILITY

The one crucial difference between the Draft Articles on State Responsibility and the Draft Code of Crimes is that the former deals with serious breaches of international law for which responsibility to the injured State and the international community is placed on the breaching State. Under the Draft Articles concerning the commission of a State agent of an internationally wrongful act, it is the State not the agent that is liable to the international community. By implication, even if the agent was acting in a personal capacity, responsibility is still attributed to the State. The Draft Code of Crimes, on the other hand, shifts the responsibility for 'international crimes' away from States to private individuals since the primary focus is on crimes *by* individuals. To sustain this shift in emphasis, the Draft Code provides a different formula for determining what constitutes an internationally wrongful conduct.

In the absence of a definitive list of acts that would qualify as international crimes to which individual responsibility can be ascribed, the Code drafters took as their point of departure the three crimes listed in the Nuremberg Charter for which individual responsibility already attaches: crimes against peace, war crimes and crimes against humanity[157] together with the later post-Nuremberg crimes of genocide,[158] apartheid,[159] and torture.[160] The draft code of crimes includes these among others as crimes that engage individual responsibility.[161] The decision to expand the original list of international crimes contained in the Nuremberg Charter to include additional crimes such as drug trafficking, harm to the environment and mercenarism in earlier versions of the draft code of crimes, would support a strong inference that the enumerated crimes do not exhaust the list of possible

157 See Nuremberg Charter, Article 6; see also Draft Code of Offenses, Principle VI. See also Rome Statute for the International Criminal Court, arts. 6–8.

158 See Article IV, Convention on the Prevention and Punishment of the Crime of Genocide. Done at New York, 9 December 1948. Entered into force, 12 January 1951, 78 UNTS 277.

159 See Article III, International Convention on the Suppression and Punishment of the Crime of 'Apartheid.' Done at New York, 30 November 1973. Entered into force, 18 July 1976. UNGA Res. 3068 (XXVIII), 28 UN GAOR, Supp. (No. 30) 75, UN Doc. A/9030 (1974), reprinted in 13 ILM 50 (1974).

160 See Convention Against Torture and Other Cruel and Inhuman Or Degrading Treatment or Punishment. Done at New York, Dec. 10, 1984. Entered into force, June 26, 1987. UNGA Res. 39/46 Annex, 39 UN GAOR, Supp. (No. 51) 197, UN Doc. E/CN.4/1984/72, Annex (1984), reprinted in 23 ILM 1027 (1984).

161 The 1991 ILC Draft Code of Crimes lists as crimes against the peace and security of mankind: aggression (Art. 15); threats of aggression (Art. 16); intervention (Art. 17); colonial domination and other forms of alien domination (Art. 18); systematic or mass violations of human rights, for example, murder, torture, slavery, etc. (Art. 21); exceptionally serious war crimes (Art. 22); recruitment, use, financing and training of mercenaries (Art. 23); international terrorism (Art. 24); illicit traffic in narcotic drugs (Art. 25); and willful and severe damage to the environment (Art. 26).

international crimes that give rise to individual responsibility.[162] Pre- and post-Nuremberg practice suggest also that conduct that rises to the level of a draft code crime is one which by the nature of its seriousness undermines the very foundations of human society such that its proscription is made the business of the community of nations.

Characteristics of International Crimes by Individuals

Article 1 of the Draft Code of Crimes and the accompanying Commentary offer some useful guidelines in making the determination whether a particular conduct has risen to the level of an international crime. This article provides that '[t]he crimes [under international law] defined in this Code constitute crimes against the peace and security of mankind.' In deciding what these constitute, the ILC was torn between a conceptual definition that would establish the essential elements of such a crime and an enumerative definition incorporating a list of crimes defined *a priori* and individually in the draft code.[163] Several members of the Commission preferred the latter fearing that 'a conceptual definition might lead to a wide and subjective interpretation of the list of crimes against humanity, contrary to the fundamental principle of criminal law that every offence must be precisely characterized as to all its constituent elements.'[164] The ILC ultimately opted for a definition by enumeration.

While eschewing a broad conceptual definition, the Commission, nevertheless, identified 'seriousness' as the essential element of a crime against the peace and security of mankind.[165] Seriousness is to be 'gauged according to the public conscience … the disapproval it gives rise to, the shock it provokes, the degree of horror it arouses within the national or international community.'[166] Recognizing that seriousness can be established on the basis of subjective as well as objective factors, the ILC set forth three tests for establishing the subjective content of the seriousness of an offense: (1) the nature of the act, that is, its cruelty, monstrousness, and barbarity; (2) the extent of its effects, that is, the massiveness,

162 The *travaux preparatoires* of the 1991 LLC Draft Code of Crimes is replete with arguments to keep the list of offenses against peace and security open-ended. See Report of the International Law Commission on the work of its forty-first sess. (2 May–21 July 1989), 143, para. 122. GA Official Records Supp. No. 10 (A/44/10). In his Third Report to the General Assembly, the Special Rapporteur made a point of emphasizing that 'the field of application of Numberg has been broadened by the appearance of new transgressions, new international crimes which were not envisaged by the Charter of the Nurnberg Tribunal, but which are today reprehensible to the universal conscience.' See Third Report on the draft Code of Offences against the Peace and Security of Mankind, by Mr. Doudou Thiam, Special Rapporteur. [1985] *International Law Commission Yearbook*, 2, pt. 1 at 69. UN Doc. A/CNA/SER. A/1985/Add.1 Pt. l) (hereinafter 'Third Report').

163 1991 ILC Draft Code of Crimes, commentary to Article 1, para. 1.

164 *Id.*, at para. 3.

165 *Id.*, at para. l.

166 See Third Report, *supra* note 162.

the victims being peoples, populations or ethnic groups; and (3) the motive of the perpetrator. Alongside these, it also identified some of the objective factors that go into the definition of seriousness, basically they relate to violations of rights, physical persons or property: '[i]n respect to persons, what is at stake is the life and physical well-being of individuals and groups. As to property, public or private property, a cultural heritage, historical interests, etc., may be affected.'[167] In short, a serious offense that rises to the level of an international crime could be one that is directed against persons or property.

Mr. Doudou Thiam, the Special Rapporteur on the Draft Code, provided additional clarification on the criteria for establishing the seriousness of an offense for purposes of classifying it as a crime against the peace and security of mankind. In his Third Report to the General Assembly, he stated:

> *The more important the subject-matter, the more serious the transgression.* An offence against the peace and security of mankind covers transgressions arising from the breach of an obligation the subject-matter of which is of special importance to the international community. It is true that all international crimes are characterized by the breach of an international obligation that is essential for safeguarding the fundamental interests of mankind. But some interests should be placed at the top of the hierarchical list. These are international peace and security, the right of self-determination of peoples, the safeguarding of the human being and the preservation of the human environment. Those are the four cardinal points round which the most essential concerns revolve and these concerns constitute the summit of the pyramid on account of their primordial importance.[168]

Mr. Thiam's comments reflect the views of the other members of the Commission that crimes against the peace and security of mankind can be arranged on a scale of

---

[167] *Id.*

[168] *Id.*, at 70–71 (emphasis in original). As the Special Rapporteur noted in his Report, Article 19(3) (a–d) of the Draft Articles on State Responsibility lists these breaches as examples of the most serious violations of international law. The commentary to Article 19 elaborates:

> The four spheres mentioned respectively in subparagraphs (a), (b), (c) and (d) of paragraph 3 are those corresponding to the pursuit of the four fundamental aims of the maintenance of international peace and security, the safeguarding of the right of self-determination of peoples, the safeguarding of the human being, and the safeguarding and preservation of the human environment . . . The rules of international law which are now of greater importance than others for safeguarding the fundamental interests of the international community are to a large extent those which give rise to obligations comprised within the four main categories mentioned. It is mainly among them that are to be found the rules which the contemporary international legal order has elevated to the rank of *jus cogens*.

See [1976] *International Law Commission Yearbook*, 2, pt. 2, UN Doc. A/CN.4/Ser.A/1976/Add. 1 (Pt. 2) (Commentary to Art. 19).

seriousness beginning with the less serious gradually working up to the most serious.

POINTS OF CONTACT BETWEEN THE DRAFT ARTICLES, THE DRAFT CODE AND THE WRITINGS OF PUBLICISTS

The Draft Articles on State Responsibility and the Draft Code of Crimes Against the Peace and Security of Mankind address as well as seek to protect the infringement of certain interests that are of paramount importance to international society such as peace and security, order and stability, equality, justice and human dignity to mention just a few. In addition, both instruments seek to ensure that neither States nor private individuals operating under the canopy of the State should be allowed to infringe on these basic community-wide interests without incurring some punishment. Accordingly, both documents impose a regime of responsibility on the Member States of the international community to vindicate these public interests. The premise behind this thrust is the belief that the breach of an obligation with regard to any of these fundamental interests affects the rights of all the Member States regardless of whether the injured party is a State, a group of people or an individual. All States therefore have a duty, to borrow Professor Condorelli's fetching phrase, 'to stick their noses in'[169] cases involving these violations even though they may primarily concern only two States or occur within the territory of a single State.

In these two draft instruments, the ILC has given voice to a widespread and deep need felt in the international community that when '[f]aced with intolerable conduct by a State [and we may as well add private individuals], the international legal system ought not to leave the victim alone: other States – even if they have not personally and directly suffered any damage – ought to have their right recognized to react in order to help restore the situation.'[170] Thus, the ILC's position can be neatly summarized as follows: all international crimes whether *of* States or *by* private individuals injure all States and it is therefore up to them to right the wrong.

Bright-line Tests

The ILC paradigms offer a fairly elastic definition of international crime, whether of States or by individuals, which leaves ample room for the inclusion of new kinds of serious breaches of international obligations as they arise and are subsequently recognized by the international community as a whole. It is possible to extract from these paradigms four bright-line tests against which potential

169 See Luigi Condorelli, 'The Continuity between certain Principles of Humanitarian Law and the Concept of Crimes of States,' in *International Crimes of State: A Critical Analysis of the ILC's Draft Article 19 on State Responsibility*, 233 (Joseph H.H. Weiler, Antonio Cassese & Marina Spinedi eds, 1989).

170 *Id.*

candidates for inclusion among 'crimes of States' or 'crimes by individuals' can be evaluated. These are: the test of *essentialness*, the *trans-nationality* test, the *international community recognition test*, and the *erga omnes* obligations or *jus cogens* test.

The Test of Essentialness

For violation of a wrongful conduct to rise to the level of a responsibility for either States or individuals, it must be essential for the protection of fundamental interests of the world community. Both the Draft Articles on State Responsibility and the Draft Code on Crimes Against Peace contemplate grave breaches for the purpose of establishing the criminal liability of the perpetrators, be they States or individuals. They were not interested in the mundane, the prosaic or banal acts. Rather, their focus is on obligations that command *gravitas* and whose violation goes to the very heart of the collective existence of the members of the international community.

Under the Draft Articles State responsibility arises from breaches of obligations arising under peremptory norms of general international law. The obligations referred to arise from substantive rules of conduct that proscribe what has come to be seen as intolerable because of the threat it poses to the survival of the international community. The Commentary to the Draft Articles recognize the same group of essential obligations that were identified in previous drafts: maintenance of international peace and security; safeguarding the right of self-determination; safeguarding the human being; and safeguarding and preserving the human environment. The Draft Code also talks of obligations essential to fundamental 'community interests' defined as 'a consensus according to which respect for certain fundamental values is not to be left to the free disposition of States individually or *inter se* but is recognized and sanctioned by the law as a matter of concern to all States.'[171] Both the Draft Articles and the Draft Code include the range of prohibitions whose peremptory character has been confirmed by decisions of international and national courts and by consistent state practice. These include the prohibition against slavery and the slave trade, genocide, racial discrimination and apartheid, torture, and self-determination.

Trans-nationality of Effects

It is significant to note that a common thread running through the prohibited practices identified in the Draft Articles and the Draft Code is the presence of an international or transnational element. In fact this element is now recognized by publicists as the crucial basic in the transformation of a prohibited conduct to an

---

171 See Bruno Simma, 'International Crimes: Injury and Countermeasures. Comment on Part 2 of the ILC Work on State Responsibility,' in *International Crimes of State: A Critical Analysis of the ILC's Draft Article 19 on State Responsibility*, 283, 285 (Joseph H.H. Weiler, Antonio Cassese & Marina Spinedi eds, 1989) [hereinafter 'Simma'].

international crime.[172] According to Professor Cherif Bassiouni this element is supplied when the conduct 'can be defined by virtue of the impact of the conduct, in that it affects the collective security interests of the world community, or if by reason of the seriousness and magnitude of the violative conduct it constitutes a threat to the peace and security of humankind.'[173] The element of *trans-nationality of effects* is so essential to the definition of an international crime precisely because there are 'no common or specific doctrinal foundations that constitute the legal basis for including a given act in the category of international crimes.'[174] Bassiouni adopts this teleological approach in his definition of an international crime as 'any conduct which is designated as a crime in a multilateral convention with a significant number of State parties to it …'[175] and which meets one of ten penal characteristics.[176] Ultimately, what transforms a given conduct into the category of international crimes will depend on experiential or empirical observation, conventional and customary international law which implicitly or explicitly establishes that a given act is part of international criminal law.

International Community Recognition

The imprimatur of the international community is crucial in making the transition from a mundane breach to a sublime act that is worthy of a collective international response. A breach of an obligation is not wrongful in the international criminal law sense unless the international community as a whole declares it to be the case. In effect, it is this community that determines the *essentialness*, that is, the scope and content, of an international obligation for purposes of treating it as a crime of state or a crime by individuals. It makes eminently good sense to leave to the sovereign members of the international community the ultimate power of deciding what is acceptable international conduct and what is unacceptable and which among the latter can rise to the level of 'crimes of States' or 'crimes by individuals.' However, there has been some uneasiness expressed with respect to the notion of international community as a whole; primarily, that it is not sufficiently precise from the legal point of view. The Polish jurist, Henryk De Fiumel has asked what legal form this community will manifest itself, by what means and by what methods?[177]

---

172 See M. Cherif Bassiouni, 'Common Characteristics of Conventional International Criminal Law,' *Case Western Journal of International Law*, 15 (1983); see also M. Cherif Bassiouni, *International Criminal Law: A Draft International Criminal Code*, 40–44 (1980).

173 See M. Cherif Bassiouni, 'International Criminal Law and Human Rights,' in *International Criminal Law*, 15, 24 (M. Cherif Bassiouni ed., 1986) (emphasis added).

174 See M. Cherif Bassiouni, 'Characteristics of International Criminal Law Conventions,' in *International Criminal Law*, 1–2 (M. Cherif Bassiouni ed., 1986).

175 *Id.*, at 2.

176 *Id.*, at 3.

177 See Henryk De Fiumel, 'Critical Observations on Crimes of States and the Notion of 'International Community as a Whole',' in *International Crimes of State: A Critical Analysis of the ILC's Draft Article 19 on State Responsibility*, 251 (Joseph H.H. Weiler,

Judge Ago, who was the Special Rapporteur for Draft Article 19, has reassuringly stated that the notion of international community as a whole was never meant to suggest all members of the international community, as that would amount to giving each State a right of veto.[178] What the drafters had in mind was the test for the admission of a norm as *jus cogens* contained in the Vienna Convention on the Law of Treaties which is that *jus cogens* status is achieved when the norm is seen as such by the *opinio juris* of all the essential components of international society, that is, Western States, Eastern States, Third World States and so on.[179] While Judge Ago does not provide any clear answers on how this *opinio juris* can be verified, Professor De Fiumel, on the other hand, offers some very interesting suggestions on who the international ombudsman should be. The criterion of recognition by the international community as a whole could be met, according to De Fiumel, if it comes from multilateral treaties of a universal character or through some competent United Nations bodies.[180]

The Character of Erga Omnes Obligations or Jus Cogens

Obligations erga omnes *Jus cogens* and obligations *erga omnes* are 'but two sides of one and the same coin' according to Professor Bruno Simma.[181] He argues that if the international community as a whole considers observance of those rules of international law that are the concern of all States as essential, 'individual States cannot be allowed to contract out of them in their relations *inter se*, and the performance of such essential obligations for the common benefit is due to all members of this community, not just to one or more States engaged in a particular *quid pro quo*.'[182] As indicated above, the illustrative prohibited conduct listed in the Draft Articles on State Responsibility and the Draft Code of Crimes Against Peace suggest offenses of extreme gravity. Within the meaning and purpose of the Draft Articles, this would mean internationally wrongful conduct that produces obligations that are owed *erga omnes* and to which the international community as a whole has a right, nay a duty, to secure performance of the obligations. The responsibility of other States is engaged by the breach of this 'higher law,' to

---

Antonio Cassese & Marina Spinedi eds, 1989).

178 See Roberto Ago, 'The Concept of 'International Community as a Whole': A Guarantee to the Notion of State Crimes,' in *International Crimes of State: A Critical Analysis of the ILC's Draft Article 19 on State Responsibility*, 252, 252–253 (Joseph H.H. Weiler, Antonio Cassese & Marina Spinedi eds, 1989).

179 *Id.*

180 See De Fiumel, *supra* note 177, at 251; *see also* Santiago Torres Bernandez, 'Problems and Issues Raised by Crimes of States: An Overview,' in *International Crimes of State: A Critical Analysis of the ILC's Draft Article 19 on State Responsibility*, 271, 278 (Joseph H.H. Weiler, Antonio Cassese & Marina Spinedi eds, 1989) (favoring the United Nations as the appropriate body to verify on behalf of the international community as a whole).

181 See Simma, *supra* note 171, at 290.

182 *Id.*

borrow Professor Simma's apt terminology, and it arises not only in regard to the State which was the direct victim of the breach but also in regard to all other members of the international community.[183]

It may be useful at this juncture to recall briefly how the concept of obligations *erga omnes* entered the vocabulary of public international law. The concept owes its celebrity status to an *obiter dictum* by the International Court of Justice (ICJ) in its judgment in the *Barcelona Traction Case*[184] but its antecedents can be traced back to an earlier ICJ judgment in the *South West Africa Case, Second Phase*[185] where again by way of dictum the Court touched on this subject of fundamental community interests:

> [I]t may be said that a legal right or interest need not necessarily relate to anything material or 'tangible', and can be infringed even though no prejudice of a material kind has been suffered. In this connection, the provisions of certain treaties and other international instruments of a humanitarian character ... are cited as indicating that, for instance, States may be entitled to uphold some general principle even though the particular contravention of it alleged has not affected their own material interests; – that again, States may have a legal interest in vindicating a principle of international law, even though they have, in the given case, suffered no material prejudice, or ask only for token damages.[186]

However, it is in the *Barcelona Traction Case* that the ICJ fully expounded on the notion of an international duty to vindicate community interests. In the course of a very technical disquisition on *jus standi* of a State (Belgium) for purposes of extending diplomatic protection to shareholders who are its nationals, the Court digressed into a discussion on community-wide obligations. It framed the concept in this oft-quoted language:

> ... an essential distinction should be drawn between the obligations of a State towards the international community as a whole, and those arising vis-a-vis another State in the field of diplomatic protection. By their very nature the former are the concern of all States. In view of the importance of the rights involved, all States can be held to have a legal interest in their protection; they are obligations *erga omnes*.[187]

The Court then went on to illustrate with examples obligations of *erga omnes* character:

> ... Such obligations derive, for example, in contemporary international law, from the outlawing of acts of aggression, and of genocide, as also from the principles and rules concerning the basic rights of the human person, including protection from slavery and

---

183 See *International Law Commission Yearbook* 1976, vol. 2, pt. 2, at 99.

184 International Court of Justice, *Barcelona Traction, Light and Power Company, Limited, Second Phase,* 1980 ICJ Rep. 3 (Judgment of Feb. 5).

185 1966 ICJ Rep. 6.

186 *Id.*, at 32.

187 *Id.*

> racial discrimination. Some of the corresponding rights of protection have entered into the body of general international law … others are conferred by international instruments of a universal or quasi-universal character.[188]

The frequent complaints heard about the ICJ's discussion of *erga omnes* obligations are either that too much has been read into the dictum than the Court meant to convey[189] or that the case itself is weak authority for the notion of offenses with *erga omnes* effects.[190] When all is said and done, disagreements over the scope and content of obligations with *erga omnes* effect boil down to two core questions: How should these obligations be selected? How and who should enforce their violations? A collateral issue that has also been raised in these debates is the appropriateness of sanctions to be applied in the event of a breach of an *erga omnes* obligation.

Given a world legal order of sovereign States the issue of who gets to enforce serious breaches by one Member State of an international obligation is a very sensitive one. By definition violations of obligations that have the character of *erga omnes* entitles those States to which the norm containing the obligation is addressed, whether or not directly affected by the violation, to assert the responsibility of the State that is the author of the breach.[191] And *if* the breach is of obligations contained in rules of customary international law, it is *all* the Member States of the international community that are entitled to hold the guilty State responsible.[192] It would appear that the characteristic differentiating 'ordinary' internationally wrongful acts and the 'more serious' wrongs is the notion of entailment of a relationship of responsibility with all States. The commission of serious wrongs by a State entails a relationship of responsibility with all the Member States of the international community. Sir Ian Sinclair is on record arguing that if by this obligation to intervene is meant 'an unrestricted *actio popularis* available at the instance of any State,' it 'would lead to absurd results.'[193] Without spelling out what these absurd results could possibly be, Sir Ian expressed some skepticism nonetheless about how a right to intervene could possibly 'be

---

188 *Id.*

189 See Ian Sinclair, 'State Responsibility: Lex Ferenda and Crimes of State,' in *International Crimes of State: A Critical Analysis of the ILC's Draft Article 19 on State Responsibility*, 240, 242 (Joseph H.H. Weiler, Antonio Cassese & Marina Spinedi eds, 1989).

190 See Stephen McCaffrey, 'Lex Lata or the Continuum of State Responsibility,' in *International Crimes of State: A Critical Analysis of the ILC's Draft Article 19 on State Responsibility*, 242, 243 (Joseph H.H. Weiler, Antonio Cassese & Marina Spinedi eds, 1989) (complaining that the *erga omnes* dictum was uttered in the context of a case whose facts and legal issues hardly required such a pronouncement); but see Egon Schwelb, 'The Actio Popularis and International Law,' *Israel Yearbook of Human Rights*, 2, 46 (1972) (for a contrary view).

191 Spinedi, *supra* note 70, at 136.

192 *Id.*

193 See Sinclair, *supra* note 189, at 241.

regarded as vesting in the international community of States as whole' given the 'present disorganized and fragmented state of international society.'[194] In the event, the issue of enforcement of obligations *erga omnes* remains unresolved in the literature on state responsibility and suggestions range from leaving the task to some neutral international organization like the United Nations[195] to third party States not directly affected by the breach.[196]

Norms of jus cogens First and foremost, *jus cogens* is a rule of customary international law[197] and like all customs 'subject to both, growth, other change, and death, depending upon patterns of expectation and behavior that are recognizably generally conjoined in the ongoing social process.'[198] It is also a peremptory as well as a preemptive norm capable of preempting lesser norms whether treaty or custom-based.

It is in its capacity as a rule that cannot be invoked to invalidate a fundamental interest in international society that *jus cogens* and obligations *erga omnes* intersect. A rule designed to protect community-wide interests cannot be applied save in the context of a violation of an obligation *erga omnes*.[199] Commentators are in agreement that *jus cogens* and *erga omnes* obligations represent two forms of protection of matters of paramount importance to international society although, in the view of the ILC, the international obligations inherent in the latter are much narrower than those protected by the former.[200]

Indigenous Spoliation as an International Crime

In their conceptualization of what constitutes an international crime in which responsibility is assumed by the individual author, the drafters of the Draft Code of Crimes must have anticipated conduct along the lines of indigenous spoliation. If indigenous spoliation is understood as the deliberate and systematic plunder of the wealth and resources of a nation by officials in positions of public trust in violation of their fiduciary obligations to the larger community, then the practice satisfies in every respect the bright-line tests identified and discussed above.

---

194 *Id.*

195 Spinedi, *supra* note 70, at 62–71.

196 *Id.*, at 71–77.

197 See Ian Brownlie, *Principles of Public International Law*, 513 (3d ed. 1979); see also Anthony D'amato, *The Concept of Custom in International Law*, 111, 132 n. 73 (1971) (recognizing *jus cogens* as a very strong rule of customary international law).

198 See Jordan Paust, 'The Reality of Jus Cogens,' in *International Law Anthology*, 119 (Anthony D'Amato ed. 1994).

199 See Giorgio Gaja, 'Jus Cogens beyond the Vienna Convention,' *Recueil des Cours*, 172, 273, 281 (1981–III).

200 See Giorgio Gaja, 'Obligations Erga Omnes, International Crimes and Jus Cogens: A Tentative Analysis of Three Related Concepts,' in *International Crimes of State: A Critical Analysis of the ILC's Draft Article 19 on State Responsibility*, 151, 159 (Joseph H.H. Weiler, Antonio Cassese & Marina Spinedi eds, 1989).

Trans-nationality

There will be no difficulty in classifying indigenous spoliation as an international crime under the trans-nationality test. The conduct clearly rises to the level where 'it constitutes an offense against the world community *delicto jus gentium* [and its] commission ... affects the interests of more than one state'[201] looked at from any number of angles. Fraudulent enrichment by heads of state and other top State officials is an international crime: the sheer amounts of national wealth plundered is shocking to the conscience of mankind; the destruction of domestic economies and the political instability engendered in the wake; the displacement of large numbers of people and the resultant global economic refugee problem pose a direct or indirect threat to world peace and security; finally, the transfer of spoliated capital to 'tax haven' states involves the use of means and instrumentalities that transcend national boundaries.

Essentialness/Effects Test

It was earlier pointed out that in his Third Report to the General Assembly the Special Rapporteur for the Draft Code of Crimes placed the right to self-determination among the essential and fundamental community interests, the breach of which would amount to a serious violation of international law.[202] This right, which will be taken up in Chapter 3, subsumes the right of a people to freely dispose of their wealth and natural resources.[203] Therefore, a breach of the latter is tantamount to a violation of the former, and vice versa. So, on this basis alone, indigenous spoliation would qualify as an offense against the peace and security of mankind understood as a breach of an obligation essential for the protection of fundamental interests of the international community.

Even if this avenue is foreclosed, the *effects* test articulated in the Commentary to Article 1 of the Draft Code of Crimes provides another basis for treating indigenous spoliation as an international crime for which responsibility attaches to the individual. The test defines a crime against peace and security in terms of the extent of its effects, more particularly, whether it involves a large number of victims. If one thing is clear about indigenous spoliation, it is that whole populations are the direct and immediate victims. A practice whose effects are so widespread cannot be ignored particularly if it fully meets what can be considered an essential fundamental international interest as we have argued in the preceding chapter.

Character of Jus Cogens

The Draft Code of Crimes reflects the expectations of the international community with respect to the most serious international offenses committed by individuals

---

201 See Bassiouni, *supra* note 174, at 2.

202 *Id.*, at 70–71, para. 61.

203 See discussion in Chapter 3 *infra*.

that undermine the foundations of human society and for which they should be held individually responsible. The list of enumerated crimes in the code reflects, in the words of the Mongolian Representative, 'the realities and needs of the modern age.'[204] However, it was never intended to be viewed as exhaustive. That this could happen compelled one Commission member to place this concern on the table during the drafting of the code: '[e]veryone knew that the list of offences might get longer: the modern world was the scene of an increasing number of acts such as drug trafficking and terrorism, so it was not impossible that new types of crime might appear. That being so, how could the Commission be sure that the draft code would cover unforeseen circumstances?'[205] Anticipating precisely such 'unforeseen circumstances' the draft code makes it clear that the enumerated crimes 'could be supplemented at any time by new instruments of the same legal nature.'[206] Wanton acts of depredations carried out by high-ranking public officials, which have led to the financial and economic ruin of so many countries around the globe, belong to the category of serious offenses that the Draft Code of Crimes sets out to proscribe. That is, an offense that 'attack[s] the very foundations of human existence, injure[s] the vital interests of the international community and ought to be regarded as criminal by this community as a whole.'[207]

As a norm of *jus cogens* indigenous spoliation can stand on its own independent of a treaty.[208] The controlling factor in determining when a wrongful act can claim *jus cogens* status is the inherent wrongfulness of the conduct. International law recognizes certain crimes such as genocide, slavery, piracy, terrorism, and drug trafficking, as so egregious that their prohibition has now achieved broad acceptance among the community of nations. These crimes have become part of customary international law though a formal prohibition may not exist. Indigenous spoliation can also become part of international custom just as these other unconscionable crimes. Let us take as an example of an ordinary norm that a head of state is supreme and can do anything within his territory and is

---

204 *See* Observations of Member States received pursuant to General Assembly Resolution 411/75 on the Draft Code of Offences Against the Peace and Security of Mankind. UN Doc. A/CN.4/407, Add. 1 and 2, at 12, para. 4 (Remarks of Mongolia).

205 *See* Summary Records of the Meetings of the Thirty-Ninth Session, UN Doc. A/CNA/403, p. 12, para. 37 (Remarks by Mr. Tomuschat) (suggesting that the draft Article 1 be followed by a phrase such as '... without prejudice to any new characterizations that may be established by general rules recognized by the international community as a whole.').

206 *Id.*, at para. 4.

207 Summary Records of the Meetings of the Thirty-Ninth Session, at 12, para. 41 (Remarks by Mr. Barsegov) (arguing that the draft code's definition of crimes against peace and security should make clear that such acts attack the very foundations of human existence, injure the vital interests of the international community and are regarded as criminal by that community).

208 See Mark Janis, *An Introduction to International Law*, 53 (1988); Burns Weston, Richard Falk & Anthony D'amato, *International Law and World Order: A Problem Oriented Casebook*, 127,148 (1990).

immune from jurisdiction for any acts taken by him. This norm is clearly in conflict with the new *jus cogens* norm advanced here, to wit, that corrupt enrichment by a head of state and other top State officials violates an internationally-recognized fiduciary obligation inherent in the public trust reposed in these constitutionally responsible rulers. Following the doctrine of *jus cogens* the criminal culpability of a head of state who breaches this international obligation cannot set be set aside whether by the consent of the people who are victims of the breach or by an exoneration agreement among States.[209] Rather, the new elite norm promoting the fiduciary relation between leaders and the public should be allowed to trump the previous ordinary norm which validated the practice of corrupt enrichment by constitutionally responsible rulers.

International Community Recognition

The victims of indigenous spoliation – individuals and groups – representing countries from the major regions of the world have uniformly reacted with horror and outrage at the systematic destruction of their common patrimony as will be discussed in detail in Chapters 5 and 6. The criminalization of breaches of fiduciary obligations particularly in the context of fraudulent enrichment by top State officials is a practice that is both widespread and consistently followed by States. That this practice offends international sensibilities has been recognized by several important international and regional bodies and it is only a matter of time before the rest of the global community begins to translate these widespread expressions of communal disgust into a norm that imposes an obligation on public officials to protect and preserve their nations' natural resources and wealth. It is the challenge of the rest of the Members of this community to begin to reflect on these individual and societal forms of moral judgment in their State practice. Put differently, these moral judgments should now form the basis of an international law on economic crimes with particular reference to the crime of indigenous spoliation.

---

209 See Condorelli, *supra* note 169, at 234.

Chapter 3

Indigenous Spoliation as a Breach of Fundamental Human Rights Grounded in Customary Law

CUSTOMARY LAW DOCTRINE

There has been a noticeable and dramatic shift in international law in the last half of the 20th century from the historical preoccupation with sovereign-state rights to a concern for the well-being of the citizens of these states.[1] This concern has led to the recognition and subsequent elaboration of a corpus of rights that pertain to individuals *qua* individuals. Among the many rights that have been recognized are certain fundamental human rights, the right to certain minimum economic standards, basic rights to communications and information, the right to protection from pollution that is destructive of a healthy environment and so on. Because these rights, though 'dimly perceived,' are 'fundamental right[s] of a people,' *a fortiori* the international community has a duty to vindicate them.[2] While not all of the newly-minted rights have risen to the level of binding international law and quite a few are still mired in controversy,[3] the right of peoples to freely dispose of their national wealth and natural resources is not one of them. This is among the inalienable rights of all human beings. It is part of the doctrine of permanent

---

1 See C. Wilford Jenks, *The Common Law of Mankind*, 17 (1958); Wolfgang Friedmann, 'Human Welfare and International Law – A Reordering of Priorities,' in *Transnational Law in a Changing Society*, 113 (1972).

2 Panel Presentation 'Pursuing the Assets of Former Dictators,' at the *Proceedings of the 81st Annual Meeting of the American Society of International Law*, 394, 397 (1987) (Michael P. Malloy, ed., 1990).

3 See Philip Alston, 'A Third Generation of Solidarity Rights: Progressive Development or Obfuscation of International Human Rights Law?' *Netherlands International Law Review*, 29, 307 (1982); Philip Alston, 'Making Space for New Human Rights: The Case of the Right to Development,'*Harvard Human Rights Yearbook*, 1, 3 (1988); Stephen P. Marks, 'Emerging Human Rights: A New Generation for the 1980s?' in *International Law: A Contemporary Perspective*, 501 (Richard Falk et al. eds, 1985); Louis Sohn, 'The New International Law: Protection of the Rights of Individuals Rather than States,'*American University Law Review*, 32, 1 (1982); K. Vasak, For the Third Generation of Human Rights: The Rights of Solidarity, Inaugural Lecture to the Tenth Study Session of the International Institute of Human Rights, Strasbourg, France, 2–27 July 1979.

sovereignty. This chapter will trace the evolution of this doctrine through various United Nations bodies and then try to link it to the problem of indigenous spoliation. It will be argued that acts of indigenous spoliation by high-ranking government officials should be viewed as a violation of the doctrine of permanent sovereignty. More specifically, that these acts violate (1) customary law obligations imposing on States parties a duty to promote individual economic rights within their domestic spheres,[4] and (2) customary law obligations imposing on States parties a duty to promote and protect fundamental human rights and freedoms.

THE DOCTRINE OF PERMANENT SOVEREIGNTY: ITS ORIGINS, CONTENT AND RELATION TO INDIGENOUS SPOLIATION

Permanent Sovereignty and Self-Determination

The Draft Covenants on Human Rights

The concept of permanent sovereignty over natural resources had its genesis in the Eighth Session of the Human Rights Commission of the United Nations.[5] The issue arose as part of the preparation of the Draft International Covenants on Human Rights (the Covenant).[6] During the Commission meeting, the Afro-Asian members contended that since economic independence formed the basis of political independence, the right of the peoples to freely dispose of their own natural resources had to be recognized as an essential element of economic independence.[7]

A proposal by the Chilean representative ultimately defined the concept of permanent sovereignty over natural resources and was adopted as paragraph three of Article One of the Covenant.[8] The proposal read as follows: 'The right of peoples to self-determination should also include permanent sovereignty over

---

[4] See Article 2(1) of the International Covenant on Economic, Social and Cultural Rights which provides that a State party to the Convention '… undertakes to take steps … to the maximum of its available resources, with a view to achieving progressively the full realization of the rights recognized in the present Covenant by all appropriate means, including particularly the adoption of legislative measures'; Article 5 of the Fourth ACP-EEC Convention, *signed in Lome* on 15 December 1989 (Lome IV) '… the Parties reiterate their deep attachment to human dignity and human rights, which are the legitimate aspirations of individuals and peoples … [and] shall help abolish the obstacles preventing individuals and peoples from actually enjoying to the full their economic, social and cultural rights and this must be achieved through the development which is essential to their dignity, their well-being and their selffulfillment.'

[5] Somendu Kumar Banerjee, 'The Concept of Permanent Sovereignty Over Natural Resources – An Analysis,' *Indian Journal of International Law*, 8, 515, 517 (1968).

[6] *Id.*

[7] *Id.*, at 518.

[8] *Id.*

natural wealth and resources and that [sic] in no case might a people be deprived of its own means of subsistence on the grounds of any rights that might be claimed by other States.'[9] Thus, the concept of permanent sovereignty, early on, became inextricably linked with the concept of self-determination.

The concepts of permanent sovereignty and self-determination were again linked together in the General Assembly of the United Nations. In a 1952 Resolution, the General Assembly recognized 'that the underdeveloped countries have the right to determine freely the use of their natural resources in order to be in a better position to further the realization of their plans of economic development in accordance with their national interests … .'[10] The Resolution further recommended that,

> The Members of the United Nations, within the framework of their general economic policy, should ... consider the possibility of facilitating through commercial agreements ... the development of natural resources ... *provided that such commercial agreements shall not contain economic or Political conditions violating the sovereign rights of the under-developed countries including the right to determine their own plans for economic development …*[11]

In the Sixth Session of the General Assembly, the Assembly recognized 'the right of peoples and nations to self-determination as a fundamental right.'[12] Further, the General Assembly decided 'to include in the International Covenant or Covenants on Human Rights an article on the right of all peoples and nations to self-determination … .'[13]

Later that same year, the General Assembly passed a Resolution dealing with the right to exploit freely natural wealth and resources.[14] First, the General Assembly recognized 'that the right of peoples freely to use and exploit their natural wealth and resources is inherent in their sovereignty and is in accordance with the Purposes and Principles of the Charter of the United Nations … .'[15] Next, the Resolution recommended 'all Member States to refrain from acts, direct or indirect, designed to impede the exercise of the sovereignty of any State over its natural resources.'[16] Moreover, the Resolution recommended that all Member States, 'in the exercise of their right to freely use and exploit their natural resources … have due regard, consistently with their sovereignty, to the need for maintaining the flow of capital in conditions of security, mutual confidence and economic co-operation among nations.'[17] According to one international scholar, the Western

---

9 *Id.*

10 GA Res. 523 (VI) 12 January 1952.

11 *Id.* (emphasis added).

12 GA Res. 545 (VI) 5 February 1952 (citing GA Res. 421 D(V) 4 December 1950).

13 *Id.*

14 GA Res. 626 (VII) 21 December 1952.

15 *Id.*

16 *Id.*

17 *Id.*

Powers voted against the Resolution for fear that it 'would be interpreted by investors as a danger signal that they had better think twice before they placed their capital in the less developed countries.'[18]

Second committee debates: 1952 Also in 1952, the Second Committee of the United Nations General Assembly discussed the concept of permanent sovereignty in conjunction with discussions on the economic development of under-developed countries.[19] The representative from Uruguay, Mr. Cusano, said that 'the one problem directly connected with the financing of the economic development of under-developed countries was the free exploitation of their own wealth [and that] ... [t]he ideal for an under-developed country was to attain economic independence, [and] to dispose freely of its own resources ... .'[20] Thus, the delegate from Uruguay submitted a draft resolution affirming these principles.[21] He stressed that 'in submitting [the draft resolution], the Uruguayan delegation was not attempting to bring about a universal upheaval but simply wished to lay down standards assuring the welfare of peoples in a peaceful setting.'[22] He also emphasized that since Uruguay 'had never adopted legislation detrimental to foreign interests in the country … [t]he Uruguayan delegation therefore had the necessary moral authority to introduce its draft resolution.'[23] The Uruguayan representative noted that the purpose of the draft resolution 'was to affirm the need for protecting the population of under-developed countries and [to justify] their governments' desire to nationalize their natural resources.'[24] He cautioned, however, that 'the sovereign right of States to exploit what belonged to them should certainly not be confused with the manifestations of an aggressive and destructive ideology.'[25]

Interestingly, in support of the draft resolution, the Uruguayan representative recalled a recent statement by Mr. Hernan Santa Cruz, the Chilean representative to the United Nations,

> … in which Mr. Santa Cruz had depicted the miserable existence of populations of under-developed countries and had spoken of their catastrophic balances of trade. By way of contrast, he had described the under-developed countries' immense natural wealth and had stressed the fact that the industrialized countries were becoming

---

18 Banerjee, *supra* note 5, at 519 (citing United States Mission to the UN, Press Release 1624, Rev. 1, 21 December 1952 from Hyde, James N., at 854). For a discussion of subsequent developments indicating that Resolution did endanger capital in less developed countries, see *id.*, at 519 (discussing nationalization law passed in Iran relying on Resolution and expropriation in Guatemala also relying on Resolution).

19 7 UN GAOR, Second Comm. (231st Mtg) 253, UN Doc. A/C.2/S.R. 231, at 253 (1952) [hereinafter Second Committee Meeting].

20 *Id.*, at 253.

21 See UN Doc. A/C.2/L.165 and Corr. 1–3.

22 Second Committee Meeting, *supra* note 19, at 253.

23 *Id.*

24 *Id.*, at 254.

25 *Id.*

> increasingly dependent on them for industrial raw materials. Those were arguments in favor of revising the principles which governed the exploitation of natural resources in the underdeveloped countries.[26]

The Uruguayan delegate went on to strongly urge that 'if the economic and political liberation of peoples was sought, measures would have to be taken to enable them to exploit their natural resources themselves and for their own benefit.[27] Thus, the Uruguayan delegate emphasized the link between economic independence, self-determination and permanent sovereignty over natural resources.

The Mexican representative noted that

> [w]hile it approved of the ideas expressed in the Uruguayan draft resolution, the Mexican delegation was unable to accept the last paragraph, which recommended that Member States should 'recognize' the right of each country to nationalize and freely exploit its natural wealth. It was not for the United Nations to pass judgment on a principle of unquestionable validity.[28]

In that regard, the Haitian representative said that 'the adoption of a draft resolution like the one being considered by the Committee would weaken the right of sovereign States to nationalize and exploit their natural wealth.'[29]

The representative of the United Kingdom remarked that '[i]f the Uruguayan delegation was thinking of the right of governments of Member States to control the natural resources of their countries, then the resolution should stress that nationalization was merely one of the forms in which such control could be exercised.'[30] He went on to note that '[i]t was generally recognized that the control of resources was one of the attributes of government.'[31] The Iranian representative strongly expounded on the concept of permanent sovereignty by remarking that

> A State's right to dispose freely of its natural resources was derived from the very principle of sovereignty recognized in international law. That it was an inalienable right, and a disavowal of restriction of it would cause a State to lose sovereignty, without which it could not be a Member of the United Nations. Under the principle of sovereignty, every State had an unlimited right to dispose of its natural resources as it saw fit.[32]

The Iranian delegate went on to argue that the Committee should:

---

26 *Id.*
27 *Id.*
28 *Id.*
29 *Id.*, at 255.
30 *Id.*
31 *Id.*
32 *Id.*, at 256.

> ... make a recommendation dealing with the following ... aspects of the problem before it: first, that the right of under-developed countries freely to dispose of their natural resources was a very important factor in their economic development; [and] secondly, that the exercise of that right would safeguard the economic independence of the under-developed countries ... .[33]

Thus, once again, the notion of permanent sovereignty over natural resources was linked to self-determination and economic independence. The Iranian representative clearly warned that '[c]ertain industrialized countries would have to realize that in the modern world a policy of exploiting the resources of another country against the interests of that country's inhabitants could not be justified' and that '[a] States's right to nationalize its natural resources was the guarantee of its independence.'[34] The Iranian delegate recalled the era of concession agreements and noted that in its history certain transnational companies 'had aimed at drawing the maximum profits, but had given no consideration to the economic needs of Iran and had opposed any social reform. The concession regime had been an obstacle to the economic development of [Iran] ... .'[35] The Syrian representative concurred with the Iranian representative's analysis and pointed out that Syria 'considered that the right of States to nationalize and freely exploit their natural resources was of great importance for the economic development of the underdeveloped countries, all the more so because the exercise of that right by the under-developed countries often gave rise to disputes which had international repercussions.'[36]

The discourse of the representatives at the Second Committee Meeting emphasizes various attempts to define the parameters and scope of the concepts of economic independence and permanent sovereignty over natural resources. The capital-exporting countries resisted the notion of permanent sovereignty.[37] On the other hand, the capital-importing countries insisted that permanent sovereignty over natural resources lay at the heart of economic independence.[38]

The ninth session of the General Assembly debates: 1954 The controversy between capital-importing and capital-exporting countries continued in 1954 during the Ninth Session of the General Assembly.[39] During this Session the General Assembly considered the Draft International Covenants on Human Rights (the Covenant).[40] The capital-exporting countries raised objections to the inclusion of the term 'permanent sovereignty' in the discussion on self-determination contained in paragraph three of Article One of the Covenant.[41] These countries

---

33 *Id.*
34 *Id.*
35 *Id.* (citing *Review of Economic Conditions in the Middle East*, E/1910/Add.2/Rev.2).
36 *Id.*
37 *See supra* text accompanying notes 30–31.
38 *See supra* text accompanying notes 24–25, 32–36.
39 Banerjee, *supra* note 5, at 520.
40 *Id.*
41 *Id.*

voiced the concern that the concept of permanent sovereignty was dangerous in that it might sanction expropriation and confiscation of foreign-owned property.[42]

The capital-importing countries, on the other hand, insisted that the concept of self-determination necessarily included the concept that a nation or peoples should have control over their own natural resources.[43] These countries contended that recognition of permanent sovereignty was not intended to sanction abuses, nor to discourage foreign investment; it was intended to protect the economic and political independence of underdeveloped nations from exploitation by foreign investors.[44]

This debate in the Ninth Session culminated in a compromise Resolution intended to encourage a stable investment climate and to recognize some of the demands of the capital-importing countries with respect to permanent sovereignty.[45] Resolution 824 encouraged both capital-importing and capital-exporting countries to '(r]e-examine, wherever necessary, domestic policies, legislation and administrative practices ... .'[46] The Resolution did not directly tackle the concept of permanent sovereignty over natural resources, however.

The General Assembly did tackle the issue of permanent sovereignty over natural resources in the Ninth Session when it adopted a Resolution requesting:

> ... the Commission on Human Rights to complete its recommendations concerning the international respect for the right of peoples and nations to self-determination, including recommendations concerning their permanent sovereignty over their natural wealth and resources, having due regard to the rights and duties of States under international law and the importance of encouraging international co-operation in the economic development of under-developed countries.[47]

This Resolution was proposed by the representative from Afghanistan and amended by other representatives.[48]

The Human Rights Commission debates: 1955 Subsequently, the Human Rights Commission (the Commission) considered the General Assembly's Resolution in 1955.[49] A majority of members of the Commission welcomed the creation of a commission to survey the status of permanent sovereignty over natural resources, with an aim towards promoting self-determination.[50] The capital-exporting countries, however, questioned the validity of the concept of permanent

---

42 *Id.*

43 *Id.*

44 *Id.*

45 *See* GA Res. 824 (IX) 11 December 1954.

46 *Id.*

47 Banerjee, *supra* note 5, at 521.

48 *Id.*, at 520. India was one of the delegations to amend the Afghan representative's proposed resolution. *Id.*, at 520–21.

49 *Id.*, at 251.

50 *Id.*

sovereignty by questioning whether the concept was truly permanent and inalienable.[51] The Commission ultimately adopted a draft resolution recommending that 'in the conduct of the full survey of the status of permanent sovereignty of peoples and nations over their natural wealth and resources, due regard would be paid to the rights and duties of States under international law and to the importance of encouraging international cooperation in the economic development of under-developed countries.'[52] Thus, the Commission's draft resolution mirrored the language contained in the General Assembly's Resolution, requesting the Commission to consider the inter-relation between the concepts of self-determination and permanent sovereignty over natural resources.[53]

The Third Committee debates: 1955 In 1955, the Third Committee of the General Assembly conducted in-depth discussions on the concepts of economic independence, self-determination and permanent sovereignty. The discussion again centered around Article one, paragraph three of the Covenant.[54] During the Third Committee's debate, the issues of self-determination and permanent sovereignty deeply fractured the Committee.

The Brazilian representative proposed that Article One be deleted entirely or that the concepts contained therein be moved to the preamble.[55] The Yugoslav delegate insisted that 'the right of peoples to self-determination was of fundamental importance, and ... it should continue to appear in the operative part of the Covenants.'[56] The Afghan delegate expounded on the sharp division of the Committee with respect to the concept of self-determination:

> Two schools of thought had always been apparent with regard to self-determination, in discussions in the Third Committee, the Economic and Social Council and the Commission on Human Rights. One school of thought considered self-determination as

---

51 *Id.* These countries questioned how dependent territories could exercise permanent sovereignty over natural resources when they lacked independence. The capital-exporting countries also emphasized their reservations about the concept of permanent sovereignty, by bringing up examples of voluntary cessations of territory, where States had given up their sovereignty over these territories, in order to depict what capital-exporting countries viewed as the lack of permanence and inalienability which rendered the concept of permanent sovereignty of questionable validity.

52 *Id.*

53 Compare *supra* text accompanying note 47 with *supra* text accompanying note 53 (request of General Assembly virtually identical to draft resolution adopted by Human Rights Commission).

54 The draft before the Third Committee read: 'The right of people to self-determination shall also include permanent sovereignty over their natural wealth and resources in no case may a people be deprived of its own means of subsistence on the grounds of any rights that may be claimed by other States.' Banerjee, *supra* note 5, at 521–22 (citing ECOSOC 18th Session, Official Records, Supp. No. 7, Annex 1).

55 10 UN GAOR, Third Comm. (638th Mtg) 70, UN Doc. A/C.3/SR. 638, at 70 (1955) [hereinafter 638th Meeting] (Afghan representative discussing Brazilian proposals).

56 *Id.*, at 69.

> a principle, whereas the other regarded it as a right; those holding the first view wished the principle to be included in the preamble, while those holding the second view wished the right of self-determination to be stated in an article in the actual body of the covenants.[57]

The Greek representative emphasized the importance of Article one 'which acknowledged the right of self-determination of peoples and nations, [and which] constituted the cornerstone of the draft covenants.'[58] More importantly, '[t]he Greek delegation felt that right, upon which all the others were dependent, would not be safeguarded if it were only made the subject of a declaration of principle in the preamble to the covenants.'[59]

The representative from Denmark remarked that although 'Denmark attached the highest importance to the right of peoples to self-determination … the Danish Government did not favor the inclusion in the covenants of a provision such as the one set forth in article [one].'[60] The Danish representative proffered three reasons for its rejection of Article one: (1) it was 'vague and over general;'[61] (2) it was 'illogical to include in instruments dealing with individual rights a collective right such as the right of peoples to self-determination;'[62] and (3) 'the Committee would be acting unrealistically if it adopted an article on self-determination.'[63] Based upon those reasons, the Danish representative favored deletion of the article altogether.[64]

Several representatives voiced concern over the issue of colonialism implicitly raised by Article one.[65] While many representatives quarreled with the overall concept of self-determination embodied in draft Article one, some representatives expressly attacked the notion of permanent sovereignty contained in paragraph three of draft Article one.[66]

The delegate from Ecuador felt that the concept of permanent sovereignty was out of place and should not be contained in covenants on human rights because '[h]uman rights were essentially individual rights, whereas [paragraph three] referred to a right which could belong only to a people or to a nation ... [and] should therefore not be included in the draft covenants.'[67] Next, the Ecuadorian representative noted the warnings of the United States representative of possible

57 *Id.*, at 70–71.

58 *Id.*, at 71.

59 *Id.*

60 10 UN GAOR, Third Comm. (644th Mtg) 99, UN Doc. A/C.3/SR.644, at 99 (1955) [hereinafter 644th Meeting].

61 *Id.*

62 *Id.*

63 *Id.*

64 *Id.*

65 *See id.* at 100–102. *See also* 10 UN GAOR, Third Comm. (650th Mtg) 130–31, Doc. A/C.3/SR.650, at 130–31 (1955) (discussing colonialism issue) [hereinafter 650th Meeting].

66 For text of paragraph three of draft Article one, see *supra* note 54.

67 650th Meeting, *supra* note 65, at 131.

negative effects on international economic cooperation.[68] Finally, the Ecuadorian representative insisted that his delegation 'supported the right of peoples to their wealth, whether in the country itself, in the seas which bathed its coasts, or even in the depth of those seas, but felt that capital must be guaranteed against expropriation without prior compensation.'[69] Accordingly, he proposed the following addition to the end of paragraph three: 'It is understood that the said right, like all the rights inherent in sovereignty, shall not affect the principles of economic interdependence and international co-operation.'[70] The Ecuadorian delegate contended that his amendment made 'it possible to retain the reference to a right [permanent sovereignty] which was essential because it safeguarded the country's right to existence and guaranteed the security of the assets of the State that provided the capital.'[71] The Ecuadorian representative, in conclusion, recommended that the Committee divide itself into a small Working Party to consider the implications of Article one.[72]

The Panamanian representative emphasized that '[t]he peoples must ... be able freely to determine their political status; they must also be able to develop their economic resources and freely to direct [sic] their social and cultural development ... [and that] it was essential to recognize the right of every people to oppose all foreign interference … .'[73] In addition, the Panamanian representative again voiced the concern that paragraph three might adversely affect 'the economic development of countries which were obliged to import foreign capital.'[74] Therefore, the Panamanian delegate recommended a closer study of the provisions of the paragraph and supported the Ecuadorian representative's proposal that a working group be established to draft a final text for Article one.[75] The Cuban representative went several steps further, noting that the wording of paragraph three 'might be equivocal.'[76] She insisted that 'the principle of equity, which prohibited expropriation without prior compensation ... must be taken into account.'[77]

A Working Party was established by the Third Committee. Within the Working Party, the delegates were clearly divided, with the United States, Great Britain and the Netherlands opposing the inclusion of any article on self-determination and the Asian, African, and Arab groups favoring such an article.[78] The Working Party submitted a new proposed Article one. In it, the Working Party had switched paragraph three with paragraph two, and had redrafted the paragraph to contain no

---

68 *Id.*
69 *Id.*
70 *Id.*
71 *Id.*
72 *Id.*
73 *Id.*, at 132.
74 *Id.*
75 *Id.*
76 *Id.*
77 *Id.*
78 Banerjee, *supra* note 5, at 522.

express reference to permanent sovereignty over natural wealth and resources.[79] According to the Report of the Working Party,

> The new text had been preferred because the old one had roused strong opposition, and in addition because a reference to sovereignty seemed out of place when the article as a whole referred only to peoples; for sovereignty was an attribute of nations organized as States. The original idea [of paragraph three] was clearly expressed in the new wording, which had the added advantage of meeting the objections of the delegations which had feared that the paragraph might be invoked to justify expropriation without compensation.[80]

The Working Party's draft provoked a lengthy debate among the members of the Third Committee. The Argentine representative maintained that the right of self-determination in respect of natural wealth and the power to dispose of natural wealth 'constituted for the peoples and the nations a part of their sovereignty and were essential to the progress of human societies [and] should be set forth in the covenants.'[81] Ultimately, the Third Committee adopted the draft text proposed by the Working Party by a vote of thirty-three in favor, twelve against and thirteen abstentions.[82] The votes in favor were largely attributable to the under-developed nations and the Communist bloc.[83] The language the Committee adopted as paragraph two of Article one of the Draft Covenant read as follows:

> The people may for their own ends, freely dispose of their natural resources without prejudice to any obligations arising out of international economic cooperation, based on the principles of mutual benefit and international law. In no case may a people be deprived of its own means of subsistence.[84]

The deletion of any express reference of permanent sovereignty in conjunction with self-determination was clearly designed as a compromise measure, intended to eliminate as much opposition as possible. This was imperative in order to forge a strong consensus behind the Draft Covenant on Human Rights. Many delegates emphasized the importance of such a strong majority behind the Covenant to lend the document greater legitimacy.[85] The clear emphasis on permanent sovereignty

---

79 10 UN GAOR, Third Comm. (668th Mtg) 221, UN Doc. A/C.3/SR.668, at 221 (1955).

80 *Id.*

81 10 UN GAOR, Third Comm. (672nd Mtg) 239, UN Doc. A/C.3/SR.672, at 239 (1955) [hereinafter 672nd Meeting].

82 James N. Hyde, 'Permanent Sovereignty Over Natural Wealth And Resources,' *American Journal of International Law*, 50, 854, 857 (1956).

83 Banerjee, *supra* note 5, at 522.

84 *Id.* (citing UN document A/C.3/L.489).

85 See, for example, 650th Meeting, *supra* note 65, at 130 (Ecuadorian representative cautioning against weak majority); 638th Meeting, *supra* note 55, at 72 (Salvadoran representative emphasizing that it was 'essential that a large majority of the 60 nations represented on the Committee … support the covenants'); 644th Meeting, *supra* note 60, at

was compromised in order to forge a strong alliance behind the Covenant.

However, the language that the Third Committee ultimately adopted as paragraph two[86] did contain implicit reference to the concept of permanent sovereignty over natural resources. During the debate on the Working Party's Report, many delegations continued to interpret paragraph two as dealing with the concept. For instance, in interpreting the terms 'means of subsistence', the Saudi delegate contended that, contrary to the United Kingdom's characterization of the phrase as ambiguous, the terms had important meaning:

> It was intended to prevent a weak or penniless government from seriously compromising a country's future by granting concessions in the economic sphere – a frequent occurrence in the nineteenth century. The second sentence of paragraph two was intended to serve as a warning to all who might consider resorting to such unfair procedures.[87]

Responding to a proposed joint amendment to the Working Party's draft, made by Lebanon and Pakistan, proposing that paragraph two be deleted, the Saudi delegate argued that:

> [T]he Committee must adopt some text recognizing the right of peoples freely to dispose of their natural resources. If it were not to do so immediately it would have to do so later when the will of the peoples compelled the community of States to embody that essential right in an international instrument. The right of self-determination was of the utmost importance in the modern world … .[88]

The Greek delegate cautioned that she would not vote in favor of deleting paragraph two 'because political independence could be real only if it went with economic independence.'[89]

Thus, despite the fact that the concept of permanent sovereignty was not mentioned by name in the Third Committee's Draft Covenant, the concept was implicitly embodied within paragraph two of Article One. Clearly, numerous delegates continued to interpret the language of paragraph two as including

---

101 (Indonesian delegate insisting that 'every effort [must be made] to draw up the draft covenants in such a way as to ensure their ratification by the greatest possible number of States'); 644th Meeting, *supra* note 60, at 102 (Venezuelan representative urging a compromise solution to make the covenants acceptable to the greatest possible number of States by virtue of a more than substantial majority in the Committee); 650th Meeting, *supra* note 65, at 130 (representative of Denmark arguing for compromise 'which would enable delegations to reach agreement on a text acceptable to the greatest possible number of States … for the draft covenants would have no real meaning unless the majority of Governments were able to ratify them').

86 See *supra* text accompanying note 84.

87 672nd Meeting, *supra* note 81, at 240. For text of paragraph two, particularly the second sentence referred to by the Saudi delegate, see *supra* text accompanying note 84.

88 672nd Meeting, *supra* note 81, at 240.

89 *Id.*, at 241.

permanent sovereignty over natural resources, the right of peoples to exploit their own natural wealth.[90]

The Economic and Social Council Debate on Implementation: 1955

Also in 1955, the Economic and Social Council of the United Nations (the ECOSOC) continued the debate over the concept of permanent sovereignty.[91] When the ECOSOC convened it had an important draft resolution before it, submitted by the Human Rights Commission, to be transmitted to the General Assembly.[92] The draft resolution urged the establishment of a Commission to fully survey the status of the right to permanent sovereignty over natural wealth and resources and to recommend, if necessary, ways to strengthen that right.[93]

The United States' representative introduced an 'alternative' proposal urging that an Ad Hoc Commission be established to conduct a complete study of the concept of self-determination.[94] The Human Rights Commission had already rejected this proposal.[95] The ECOSOC ultimately agreed to transmit both the United States' proposal and the draft resolution of the Human Rights Commission to the General Assembly.[96] Vocal opposition to the United States' proposal stressed the importance of the concept of permanent sovereignty of peoples and nations over their natural resources.[97] The opposition emphasized that the Permanent Sovereignty Commission proposed by the Human Rights Commission would pay due regard to 'the rights and duties of States under international law.'[98]

The Commission on Permanent Sovereignty Over Natural Resources: 1959-61

A three-year moratorium on discussions of permanent sovereignty ended in 1958 at the Thirteenth Session of the General Assembly.[99] At the Thirteenth Session the

---

90 See *supra* text accompanying notes 86–89 (interpreting paragraph two as embodying concept of permanent sovereignty).

91 Banerjee, *supra* note 5, at 324.

92 Hyde, *supra* note 82, at 860.

93 *Id.*

94 *Id.* The Ad Hoc Commission was to contain five members appointed by the Secretary General.

95 *Id.* The US proposal was opposed by the Arab-Asian countries, the USSR, Czechoslovakia and Yugoslavia. Banerjee, *supra* note 5' at 525. The Afro-Asian countries argued that such an Ad Hoc Commission would afford no practical or immediate value. In emphasizing the utmost importance of the concept of permanent sovereignty' these countries continued to maintain that the proposed survey was not intended to oppose private foreign investment.

96 Hyde, *supra* note 82, at 860.

97 *Id.*, at 861. See also *supra* note 95 (further discussing opposition to US proposal).

98 *Id.* (citing 20th Session of ECOSOC, July–Aug. 1955' UN Docs. E/AC.7/ SR.324-28, E/SR.889-90).

99 Banerjee, *supra* note 5, at 525.

General Assembly resumed the debate as to whether the rights and obligations arising out of international law limited a country's permanent sovereignty over its natural wealth and resources.[100] The majority of the Members felt that the inclusion of the concept of permanent sovereignty in the Draft Covenants would aid in defining the concept as a fundamental and essential element of the right to self-determination.[101]

Ultimately, the General Assembly adopted Resolution 1314 (XIII) on 12 December 1958.[102] Resolution 1314 is entitled 'Recommendations concerning international respect for the right of peoples and nations to self-determination.'[103] The Resolution noted that 'the right of peoples and nations to self-determination as affirmed in the two draft Covenants completed by the Commission on Human Rights[104] includes permanent sovereignty over their natural wealth and resources.'[105] 'Believing it necessary to have full information at its disposal regarding the actual extent and character of this sovereignty,'[106] the Assembly decided,

> … to conduct a full survey of the status of this basic constituent of the right to self-determination, with recommendations, where necessary, for its strengthening, and further decide[d] that, in the conduct of the full survey of the status of permanent sovereignty of peoples and nations over their natural wealth and resources, due regard shall be paid to the rights and duties of States under international law and to the importance of encouraging international cooperation in the economic development of underdeveloped countries … .[107]

Thus, Resolution 1314 gave birth to the Commission on Permanent Sovereignty. The Commission was composed of delegates from Afghanistan, Chile, Guatemala, the Netherlands, the Philippines, Sweden, the Union of Soviet Socialist Republics, the United Arab Republic and the United States.[108] The monumental task facing the Commission consisted of 'determining the nature of the right of permanent sovereignty over natural resources; the manner in which that right should be exercised and what measures should be taken into account according to international law.'[109]

At its first meeting in May of 1959, the Commission directed the Secretariat of

---

[100] *Id.*

[101] *Id.* Capital-exporting countries still insisted that it was illogical to use the term 'sovereignty' simultaneously with the term 'peoples.'

[102] GA Res. 1314 (XIII) 12 December 1958.

[103] *Id.*

[104] *Id.* See also Official Records of ECOSOC, 18th Session, Supp. No. 7, annex I, UN doc. E/2573 (two draft Covenants completed by Commission on Human Rights).

[105] GAGA Res. 1314 (X111) 12 December 1958.

[106] *Id.*

[107] *Id.*

[108] *Id.*

[109] Banerjee, *supra* note 5, at 526 (quoting UN Document GA (XVII) A/C.2/SR.834, at 19).

the United Nations to prepare a study on the status of permanent sovereignty over natural wealth and resources.[110] The Secretariat's Preliminary Study over Natural Resources (the Secretariat's Report) was considered at the Commission's Second Session in February–March of 1960[111] and was found incomplete in many areas.[112] Because of the perception that the report was incomplete, the Commission adopted a Resolution requesting the Secretariat to revise the study and to submit such revision to the Commission by 15 March 1961.[113] The Secretariat submitted the revised study[114] at the Commission's third session, in May of 1961.[115]

Several delegations still found problems with the Secretariat's revised study.[116] The Soviet Union insisted that the study failed to reflect the actual situation of natural wealth and resources of the less-developed countries, in light of exploitation by foreigners and transnational companies.[117] In addition, the delegates from the United Arab Republic and from Afghanistan contended that the study failed to employ factual data to determine the methods of financing the exploitation of natural wealth and resources, the amount of foreign profits, and the extent of participation in such ventures by indigenous people.[118]

During this debate, Chile and the Soviet Union submitted draft resolutions.[119] The controversy over these two alternative resolutions focused around the issue of whether the right of permanent sovereignty over natural resources was an absolute right or whether it was a right limited by obligations and responsibilities imposed by international law.[120] Ultimately, the Chilean proposal was revised and amended and adopted by the Commission for submission to the Second Committee for their consideration.[121] The Commission also adopted other resolutions recommending that the Secretariat's study and the Commission's Report be transmitted to the ECOSOC for their consideration at their Thirty-second Session.[122]

During 1960, while the Commission on Permanent Sovereignty struggled to define the scope of permanent sovereignty, the General Assembly again emphasized its concern with the concept in a Resolution entitled 'Concerted action for economic development of economically less developed countries.'[123] In that Resolution, the General Assembly reiterated the link between economic

---

110 *Id.*

111 *Id.*

112 *Id.* (citing UN Doc. A/AC.97/5).

113 *Id.* (citing UN Doc. A/AC.97/5).

114 UN Doc. A/AC.97/5/Rev.l, Add.l, Corr. 1&2.

115 Banerjee, *supra* note 5, at 526.

116 *Id.*

117 *Id.*

118 *Id.*

119 *Id.*

120 *Id.*, at 527.

121 *Id.* The resolution was adopted by eight votes for, one vote against and no abstentions.

122 *Id.* (citing UN Doc. E/3511).

123 GA Res. 1515 (XV) 15 December 1960.

independence, self-determination, and permanent sovereignty, noting that 'a prime duty of the United Nations is to accelerate the economic and social advancement of developed countries of the world, thus contributing to safeguarding their independence … .'[124] In that regard, the Resolution recommended that 'the sovereign right of every State to dispose of its wealth and its natural resources should be respected in conformity with the rights and duties of States under international law … .'[125] In 1961, the General Assembly had before it the Secretariat's Report and the Commission on Permanent Sovereignty's Report, transmitted without consideration by the ECOSOC.[126] The General Assembly in Resolution 1720 (XVI) thanked the Secretariat for its report, requested that both reports be printed, and decided that 'the United Nations work on permanent sovereignty over … natural wealth and resources shall be continued … in the Second Committee at its next session.'[127]

Debates Preceding Resolution 1803

Debate ensued in the Permanent Sovereignty Commission and in the Second Committee, culminating in the General Assembly adopting Resolution 1803 dealing expressly with permanent sovereignty over natural resources.[128] This debate, predictably, highlighted the disparate viewpoints of capital-exporting and capital-importing countries.[129] Moreover, the debate shed light on the legislative intent behind the important Resolution.

Some nations, like Burma, argued that 'the principle of sovereign rights of nations over their own resources would seem so obvious as not to require elucidation.'[130] Ghana similarly felt that no need existed for a resolution on the subject of permanent sovereignty, that nothing should be done which might negatively impact the less-developed nations' economic development, and that these issues were best settled through bilateral negotiation.[131]

The issues of expropriation, compensation, and the binding nature of contracts between States and private investors caused the polarization between capital-exporting and capital-importing nations.[132] The United States, previously opposed to any resolution on permanent sovereignty, espoused the capital exporting nations' position that in the event of nationalization, prompt, adequate and

---

124 *Id.*

125 *Id.*

126 Banerjee, *supra* note 5, at 527 (citing UN Doc. 847 (XXXII)) (resolution by ECOSOC transmitting reports to General Assembly).

127 GA Res. 1720 (XVI) 19 December 1961.

128 Banerjee, *supra* note 5, at 528.

129 *Id.*

130 *Id.* at 529 (citing UN Doc. A/C.2/SR. 850, at p. 10).

131 *Id.* (citing UN Doc. A/C.2/SR. 840).

132 *Id.* For a discussion of the delegates' views regarding the binding nature of contracts between nations and private investors, see Banerjee, *supra* note 5, at 531–35.

effective compensation should be paid.[133] Capital-importing countries and the Communist bloc insisted that '[a]ny decisions relating to whether and how much compensation should be paid was essentially an internal affair of the State concerned … .'[134] The issue of compensation was resolved with a majority of the Commission's and the Committee's members insisting that States had a duty to pay compensation in cases of a taking, as a general principle of international law.[135] Views differed, however, with regard to which conditions require States to pay such compensation.[136]

Resolution 1803

Resolution 1803,[137] entitled 'Permanent Sovereignty Over Natural Resources,' constitutes the broadest, most explicit declaration from the United Nations on the subject.[138] This Resolution takes on added importance because it, in a sense, codifies the position of the United Nations on permanent sovereignty and signifies the foundation for the development of a new international economic order.

In Resolution 1803, the United Nations again links the concepts of permanent sovereignty, economic independence and self-determination.[139] For instance, the preamble attaches 'particular importance to the question of promoting the economic development of developing countries and securing their economic independence, [and notes that] the creation and strengthening of the inalienable sovereignty of States over their natural wealth and resources reinforces their economic independence … .'[140]

The Resolution declares that in sharing profits between investors and States, 'due care [must be] taken to ensure that there is no impairment, for any reason, of

133 Banerjee, *supra* note 5, at 529.

134 *Id.*, at 530 (citing UN Doc. A/C.2/SR. 864, at p. 4).

135 *Id.* (citing UN Doc. A/C.2/SR.850, at p. 7).

136 *Id.*, at 531.

137 GA Res. 1803 (XVII) 19 December 1962, reprinted in *International Law Materials*, 2, 223 (1963).

138 Resolution 1803, in its preamble, recalls other United Nation's Resolutions dealing with permanent sovereignty: GA Res. 523 (VI) 12 January 1952 (recognizing under-developed countries' right to freely determine the use of their natural resources); GA Res. 626 (VII) 12 December 1952 (dealing with the right to freely exploit natural wealth and resources); GA Res. 1314 (XIII) 12 December 1958 (establishing the Commission on Permanent Sovereignty over Natural Resources); GA Res. 1515 (XV) 15 December 1960 (recommending that the sovereign right of every state to dispose of wealth and natural resources should be respected). *See also supra* text accompanying notes 11–12, 16–20, 96–107, 123–125 (discussing the Resolutions cited in the preamble of Resolution 1803).

139 GA Res. 1803 (XVII) Dec. 19, 1962, reprinted in *International Law Materials*, 2, 223, 223–24 (1963).

140 *Id.*, at 224 (quoting preamble of GA Res. 1803). *Id.* at 225 (quoting paragraph 3 of GA Res. 1803).

that State's sovereignty over its natural wealth and resources.'[141] While authorizing nationalization, expropriation and requisitioning, Resolution 1803 emphasizes 'mutual respect of States based on their sovereign equality'[142] and goes on to declare that:

> International co-operation for the economic development of developing countries, whether in the form of public or private capital investments, exchange of goods and services, technical assistance, or exchange of scientific information, shall be such as to further their independent national development and shall be based upon respect for their sovereignty over their natural wealth and resources.[143]

Finally, the Resolution declares that violation of the people's and nations' right to sovereignty over natural wealth and resources is 'contrary to the spirit and principles of the Charter of the United Nations … .'[144]

The concepts expressed in Resolution 1803, like those expressed in other United Nations' Resolutions dealing with permanent sovereignty, are difficult to understand and apply. Nowhere is the term sovereignty defined. One international scholar suggests that sovereignty is synonymous with independence and involves a State's ability 'to control territories, persons and objects in disregard of any exterior authority.'[145] Clearly, the Resolution represents compromise; in the words of one international scholar, 'the resolution was a means of crystallizing prevailing views.'[146]

In evaluating Resolution 1803, an important inconsistency must be noted. First, the Resolution fails to clarify who possesses the right of permanent sovereignty. At various points the Resolution refers to it as a right of 'peoples and nations,' and at others it refers to the right as one of 'all States.'[147] This clouds one's ability to

---

[141] *Id.*, at 225 (quoting paragraph 3 of GA Res. 1803).

[142] *Id.* (quoting paragraph 4 of GA Res. 1803). The issues of nationalization and compensation, while highly controversial and of great import, are beyond the scope of this book. For in-depth discussions of these issues, see Karol N. Gess, *Permanent Sovereignty Over Natural Resources*, *International and Comparative Law Quarterly*, 13, 398, 420–35 (1964). See also P. J. O'Keefe, 'The United Nations and Permanent Sovereignty Over Natural Resources,' *Journal of World Trade Law*, 8, 239, 251–75 (1974) (discussing nationalization and compensation historically, and in context of Resolution 1803).

O'Keefe maintains that Resolution 1803 is important as it has been invoked by several nations, including Chile and Greece, to support various positions in the conflict over the control of natural resources. *Id.*, at 239–41.

[143] *International Law Materials*, 2, at 225 (quoting paragraph 6 of GAGA Res. 1803).
144 Id. at 226 (quoting paragraph 7 of GA Res. 1803).

[144] *Id.*, at 226 (quoting paragraph 7 of GA Res. 1803).

[145] O'Keefe, *supra* note 142, at 241 nn. 9–10 (citing Ian Brownlie, *Principles of Public International Law*, 80 (2d. Ed. 1973); Bin Cheng, 'The Rationale of Compensation for Expropriation,' *Transactions of the Grotius Society*, 44, 267, 274 (1958–59). For a full discussion of the notion of sovereignty, see O'Keefe, *supra* note 142, at 241–48.

[146] Gess, *supra* note 142, at 410.

[147] GA Res. 1803 (XVII) 19 December 1962, reprinted in *International Law Materials*,

define sovereignty, as it traditionally has been understood, to be a power of a State.[148] Because of this inconsistency, several scholars have argued that the concept of permanent sovereignty over natural resources is invalid as a legal principal,[149] 'representing an attempt to give legal force and validity to what is essentially a political goal.'[150] Regardless of its legal validity, the concept of permanent sovereignty embodied in Resolution 1803 seems to clarify the United Nations' opinion on the matter and paves the way for the establishment of the so-called new international economic order.

Other Developments: 1963–66

Secretary General's report: 1963 The last portion of Resolution 1803 requested the Secretary General of the United Nations to continue the study on permanent sovereignty over natural resources and to report to the ECOSOC and to the General Assembly at its 18th Session, if possible.[151] Pursuant to this request, the Secretariat issued its Report in November 1963.[152] Among other things, the Report examined national measures affecting ownership or the use of natural resources by foreigners, stressing the developing countries.[153] The Report also discussed State succession and arbitration/conciliation measures being employed.[154]

The ECOSOC's session: 1964 The ECOSOC considered the Secretary General's Report at its 37th Session in Geneva, in July-August of 1964.[155] The ECOSOC failed to adopt a Resolution dealing with the concept of permanent sovereignty, but submitted the Report and some general comments to the General Assembly.[156]

The Second Committee's session: 1965 The Second Committee briefly considered the issue of permanent sovereignty at its 20th Session in 1965.[157] During this consideration, Ceylon and Ecuador submitted a joint resolution; and Poland, Algeria, United Arab Republic and Tanzania submitted a second joint

---

2, 223 (1963).

148 See *supra* note 7 and accompanying text (discussing traditional definition of sovereignty). See also O'Keefe, *supra* note 142, at 244–48 (discussing the dichotomy between 'peoples' and 'state').

149 *See* O'Keefe, *supra* note 142, at 243–46; Gess, *supra* note 142, at 414 (noting that Japan and others expressed the view that the concept of permanent sovereignty over natural resources lacks legal validity).

150 O'Keefe, *supra* note 142, at 245.

151 GA Res. 1803 (XVII) 19 December 1962, reprinted in *International Law Materials*, 2, 223, 226 (1963) (quoting part III of GA Res. 1803).

152 Banerjee, *supra* note 5, at 535. See also Secretariat's Report, UN Doc. E /3840.

153 Banerjee, *supra* note 138, at 535.

154 *Id.*

155 *Id.*

156 *Id.* (citing ECOSOC, E/SR. 1135–37).

157 *Id.*, at 536.

resolution.[158] The Ceylon/Ecuador joint resolution requested the Secretary General to submit a report discussing the aspects necessary to be addressed as a prerequisite to formulating standards and procedures for the investment of foreign capital in less developed countries.[159] The joint resolution declared that these standards and procedures should promote the capital-importing countries' economic interests and should provide reasonable security for such investment.[160]

The second joint resolution, submitted by Algeria, Poland, Tanzania, and the United Arab Republic, was co-sponsored by Sudan.[161] This draft resolution called for the United Nations to provide maximum effort to ensure the permanent sovereignty of developing nations over their natural resources.[162] This draft resolution also emphasized the developing nations' right to increase their share of profits derived from the development and exploitation of their natural resources by foreigners.[163] Because of the sharp differences, raised by the United States and others,[164] the Second Committee adopted Chile and Poland's procedural suggestion to postpone further discussion on permanent sovereignty until the next session of the General Assembly.[165]

Special Committee debate: 1966 In 1966, the concept of permanent sovereignty was discussed by the Special Committee on Principles of International Law Concerning Friendly Relations and Cooperation among States (Special Committee).[166] The Special Committee, established by Resolution 1966 (XVIII) of the General Assembly,[167] debated the issue of whether or not permanent sovereignty over natural resources constituted a fundamental element of the sovereign equality of States.[168] During the Special Committee's First Session in Mexico City in 1964, the Czechoslovak delegate introduced a resolution affirming that, among other bases, 'the sovereignty of every State is based … [on its right] to dispose freely of its natural wealth and resources … .'[169] The Special Committee

---

158 *Id.*
159 *Id.*
160 *Id.*
161 *Id.* (citing UN Doc. A/C.2/L.828. Add. 1).
162 *Id.*
163 *Id.*, at 536–37.
164 The United States submitted an amendment to the Algeria, Poland, *et al.* draft joint resolution, emphasizing the right of *mutually satisfactory* arrangements to be concluded with foreign investors by developing countries, for the development of their natural resources. *Id.*, at 537. The 'mutually satisfactory' language conflicted with the joint resolution's call for an increased profit-share for developing countries. This amendment just emphasizes the sharp division in opinion between capital-importing countries and capital-exporting countries.
165 *Id.* at 537 (citing GA (XXI) Supp. A/6301, p. 159).
166 *Id.*, at 537.
167 *Id.*, at 535.
168 *Id.*, at 537.
169 *Id.* (citing UN Doc. A/5746, p. 148, 16 November 1964).

failed to resolve the debate surrounding this issue in its First Session, so Yugoslavia re-introduced the Czechoslovak proposal in 1966 at the Special Committee's next meeting.[170] Algeria supported the Yugoslav resolution, insisting that the concept of permanent sovereignty was a fundamental element of the sovereign equality of States.[171]

The capital-exporting nations opposed the Yugoslav proposal, arguing that the Special Committee lacked the competence to discuss the issue because Resolution 1803 vested that authority in the General Assembly.[172] Moreover, these nations contended that the concept of permanent sovereignty was irrelevant to the issue of equality of sovereigns that was before the Special Committee.[173] During the Special Committee's debate, the Committee struggled to reach a consensus over the applicability of the concept of permanent sovereignty. Kenya submitted a proposal stating that 'each State has the right to freely dispose of its natural wealth and resources. In the exercise of this right, due regard shall be paid to the applicable rules of international law and to the terms of agreements validly entered into.'[174] Although considerable support existed for the Kenyan proposal, the Special Committee failed to reach an agreement as to whether or not the right of nations to permanent sovereignty over natural resources was qualified by obligations and duties arising from international law.[175]

The Second Committee's session: 1966 In October to November of 1966, the Second Committee continued its discussions on permanent sovereignty, considering the Secretary General's Report and the relevant records of the ECOSOC.[176] The draft resolution ultimately adopted by the Second Committee largely was the product of the less-developed countries' efforts during the debate.[177]

During the debate, the delegates of several nations made statements as to the rights and obligations of the capital-exporting nations towards the less-developed

---

170 *Id.* The Yugoslav delegate also added that the position adopted in the Czechoslovak proposal was 'in keeping with the principles adopted by the United Nations Conference on Trade and Development and by the Cairo Conference of Non-Aligned countries' (citing UN Doc. A/ AC. 125/SR. 5, at p. 7). Preambular paragraph 8 or the Cairo Declaration of Developing Countries had insisted that full de-colonization was essential 'for the economic development of the dependent peoples and the exercise of their sovereign rights over their natural resources.'

Id., at 537 n. 75. The United Nations subsequently endorsed this by UN GA Res.1820 (XVII), UN Doc. A/5162. *Id.*

171 Banerjee, *supra* note 5, at 538 (citing UN Doc. A/AC. 125/SR. 6, pp. 10–11).

172 *Id.*, at 538.

173 *Id.*

174 *Id.* (citing UN Doc. A/AC.125/SR.5, at p. 15).

175 *Id.* (citing UN Doc. A/AC.125/L.33).

176 *Id.*

177 *Id.*, at 540.

countries.[178] For instance, the delegate from the United Arab Republic contended that developed nations, in return for the profits they derived from exploiting the less-developed countries' natural resources, owed an obligation to train the personnel in the less developed countries for work in developing natural resources.[179] The representative from Nigeria supported this position, emphasized the right of States to dispose of their own natural resources, and contended that all States possessed the right to alter existing economic agreements involving the development of natural resources in order to promote and secure their economic independence.[180] The delegate from Pakistan insisted that until developing countries were in a position to freely select the manner in which their natural resources would be exploited, the concept of permanent sovereignty would remain purely academic.[181] The Pakistani delegate further asserted that developing countries could develop technologically only if foreign investors trained national personnel and afforded nationals greater administrative duties in foreign enterprises.[182] The Committee ultimately adopted a draft resolution, following numerous amendments, by a vote of ninety-nine to none, with eight abstentions.[183]

Resolution 2158

Following the recommendation of the Second Committee,[184] the General Assembly adopted Resolution 2158 (XXI) entitled 'Permanent sovereignty over natural resources.'[185] As previously noted, the concepts embodied in this Resolution were derived largely from the less-developed countries' attempts to clarify and refine the concept of permanent sovereignty through debates in the Second Committee.[186] Thus, the provisions of Resolution 2158 strongly support the capital-importing countries' position. The primary focus of Resolution 2158 is accelerated economic and technological growth for the developing countries in the area of exploitation of natural resources. To this end, some of the significant provisions follow:

> (i) 'that the exploitation of natural resources in each country shall always be conducted in accordance with its national laws and regulations;'
> (ii) 'the right of all countries, and in particular developing countries, to secure and increase their share in the administration of enterprises which are fully or partly

---

[178] *Id.* at 539.
[179] *Id.* (citing UN Doc. A/C.2/SR.1050).
[180] *Id.*
[181] *Id.* (citing UN Doc.A/C.2/SR.1055).
[182] *Id.*
[183] *Id.*
[184] See *supra* notes 176–183 and accompanying text (discussion of Second Committee's debate and recommendation).
[185] GA Res. 2158 (XXI) 25 November 1966. The General Assembly adopted the Resolution by a vote of 104 in favor, none against, with six abstentions. Banerjee, *supra* note 5, at 540.
[186] See *supra* text accompanying note 177.

operated by foreign capital and to have a greater share in the advantages and profits derived therefrom on an equitable basis ...'
(iii) 'that, when natural resources of developing countries are exploited by foreign investors, the latter should undertake proper and accelerated training of national personnel at all levels and in all fields connected with such exploitation;'
(iv) 'the developed countries [should] make available to the developing countries . . . assistance, including capital goods and knowhow, for the exploitation and marketing of their natural resources in order to accelerate their economic development ... .'[187]

Thus, Resolution 2158 represents a strong statement against concession agreements of the past and affirms the new concept of permanent sovereignty as a method of increasing the economic and technological development of less-developed countries and ensuring their right to freely exploit their own natural resources. Although the Resolution recognizes the need for foreign capital in exploiting natural resources,[188] the Resolution clearly contemplates the move away from this type of exploitation of natural resources, towards having the less developed nations develop their own resources.[189]

PERMANENT SOVEREIGNTY AND THE CREATION OF A NEW ECONOMIC ORDER

With the concept of permanent sovereignty came other changes in the international arena. The less-developed countries' success in establishing this principle carried over into a push for a new world order. The United Nations seemed to adopt this goal as an extension of the concept of permanent sovereignty. For example, in 1970 the General Assembly passed Resolution 2626.[190] In its preamble, Resolution 2626 emphasized that '[e]very country has the right and duty to develop its human and natural resources, but the full benefit of its efforts can be realized only with concomitant and effective international action.'[191] Thus, the Resolution called for a

---

[187] GA Res. 2158 (XXI) 25 November 1966.

[188] *Id.* ('taking into account the fact that foreign capital ... can play an important role ... in the exploitation and development of natural resources, provided that there is government supervision over the activity ... .').

[189] See *id.* ('considering further that [the] aim [of securing the highest possible rate of growth of the developing countries] can better be achieved if the developing countries are in a position to undertake themselves the exploitation and marketing of their natural resources ... .'). See also *id.* (in an effort to enable all countries to exercise the right of permanent sovereignty fully, 'the maximum possible development of the natural resources of developing countries [should be achieved, along with] strengthening their ability to undertake this development themselves, so that they might effectively exercise their choice in deciding the manner in which the exploitation and marketing of their natural resources should be carried out').

[190] GA Res. 2626 (XXC) 24 October 1970.

[191] *Id.*, at 40 (paragraph (10)).

progression from theory to action, from an old world order to a new economic world order:

> Governments designated the 1970s as the Second United Nations Development Decade and pledge themselves, individually and collectively, to pursue policies designed to create a more just and rational world economic and social order in which equality of opportunities should be as much a prerogative of nations as of individuals within a nation. They subscribe to the goals and objectives of the Decade and resolve to take the measures to translate them into reality.[192]

The Resolution required, *inter alia*, that

> In particular, attention will be paid to overcoming their [the developing countries'] problem of the scarcity of indigenous technical and managerial cadres, to building the economic and social infrastructure, to the exploitation by these countries of their natural resources and to assisting them in the task of formulating and implementing national development plans.[193]

Emphasizing the thread of permanent sovereignty, Resolution 2626 heralded the push towards action and the creation of the new international order. At the heart of this push for change was the developing countries' claim that the structure and patterns of the current world trade and production system favored capital-exporting, industrial countries at the expense of capital-importing, raw material producing countries.[194] The new international order was foreshadowed by the passing of Resolution 3171 in 1973, strongly affirming the inalienable right of States to permanent sovereignty over natural resources.[195] This Resolution expressly supported developing nations 'in their struggle to regain control over their natural resources.'[196] Paragraph 3 of the Resolution signalled a new standard with respect to compensation for nationalization.[197] All of these developments, occurring since the 1960s, began to take on unforeseen momentum. The developing countries had begun to unite in the various United Nations organs and in the conferences of non-aligned countries, causing wide-spread debate about revising international economic relations.[198] At the institution of Algeria, the Secretary-General of the United Nations decided to convene a Special Session of the General Assembly to discuss economic relations generally, specifically

---

192 *Id.* (paragraph (12)).

193 *Id.*, at 45 (paragraph (57)).

194 Juha Kuusi, *The Host and the Transnational Corporation*, 129 (1979).

195 GA Res. 3171 (XXVIII) 17 December 1973.

196 *Id.*

197 *Id.* See also Algiers Summit Conference of Non-Aligned Countries, *Economic Declaration* (5–9 September 1973), reprinted in O. Jankowitxch & K. Sauvant, *Collected Documents of Non-Aligned Countries*, 214, 221 (1978) (containing provisions virtually identical to Resolution 3171, emphasizing the emerging consensus).

198 J. Kuusi, *supra* note 194, at 129.

focusing on the problems of raw materials and development of natural resources.[199]

Special Session of the General Assembly: 1974

In preparation for the Special Session, the Group of 77, which represents the developing countries, drafted two documents to present to the General Assembly: a Declaration on the Establishment of a New International Economic Order, and a Programme of Action.[200] The concept of permanent sovereignty over natural resources was one of the major topics.[201] The European Economic Community (now the European Union – EU) countries, the United States, Japan and Australia insisted upon linking the concept of permanent sovereignty with other rules of international law.[202] Debate ensued over whether the concepts should be linked in the draft documents.

The EU countries offered the following proposal for dealing with permanent sovereignty in the draft documents:

> The Sovereignty and rights in question shall be exercised in accordance with the applicable rules of international law, in particular with regard to the payment to the owners of prompt, adequate and effective compensation. The exercise of this sovereignty and these rights shall take account of the requirements and interdependence of the economies of all States and the necessity to contribute to the balanced expansion of the world economy.[203]

Peru rejected the EU proposal because it attempted to qualify the right of permanent sovereignty, subordinating it to international law.[204] Algeria emphasized that the EU countries:

> … began by admitting that it was inconceivable that true development could take place so long as the wealth of the developing countries remained under foreign control and was drained from the third world countries to the developed countries, but then they [the EU countries] immediately invoked international law. It must be borne in mind that international law had been first developed in the age of colonial domination to serve the interests of some 20 countries. The countries of the third world never had any voice in the matter, and it would hardly be realistic to suppose that international law could work in their favor.[205]

---

[199] *Id.* This special session came following the 1973 decision of the OPEC states to sharply raise the price of crude oil, causing widespread concern and repercussions world-wide.

[200] *Id.*, at 129. See also Report of Ad hoc Committee of the Sixth Session, UN GAOR, 6 Spec. Sess., Annexes, Agenda Item No. 7 (Doc. A/9556) (1974).

[201] *Id.*

[202] *Id.*

[203] *Id.* (citing UN Off. Record, GA Sess. VI, Ad Hoc Comm., 6th Mtg., para. 43).

[204] *Id.*, at 130 (citing UN off. Record, GA Sess. VI, Ad Hoc Comm., 6th Mtg., para. 44).

[205] *Id.* (citing UN Off. Record, GA Sess. VI, Ad Hoc Comm., 6th Mtg., para. 48.)

The preceding excerpts from the debate in the Special Session underscore the increasing vocalization by developing countries of the need for a new international economic order.

The New International Economic Order

The vocalizations culminated in the Declaration on the Establishment of a New International Economic Order (the Declaration)[206] and the Programme of Action on the Establishment of a New International Economic Order (the Programme).[207] The General Assembly adopted the Declaration without a vote.[208]

The impetus for the Declaration stemmed from the fact that 'the developing countries, which constitute 70 percent of the world's population account for only 30 percent of the world's income. It has proved impossible to achieve an even and balanced development of the international community under the existing international economic order.'[209] Thus, the Declaration called for the establishment of a new international economic order.[210] The Declaration contains twenty principles on which the new international order is to be founded, including:

> (e) Full permanent sovereignty of every State over its natural resources and all economic activities. In order to safeguard these resources, each State is entitled to exercise effective control over them and their exploitation with means suitable to its own situation, including the right to nationalization or transfer of ownership to its nationals, this right being an expression of the full permanent sovereignty of the State. No State may be subjected to economic, political or any other type of coercion to prevent the free and full exercise of this inalienable right;
> (g) Regulation and supervision of the activities of transnational corporations by taking measures in the interest of the national economies of the countries where such transnational corporations operate on the basis of the full sovereignty of those countries;
> (p) Giving to the developing countries access to the achievements of modern science and technology and the creation of indigenous technology for the benefit of the developing countries in forms and in accordance with procedures which are suited to their economies.[211]

The Programme attempts to specifically define the role of foreign investment in the new economic order.[212] The promotion of foreign investment, *inter alia*, is recommended in order to finance the development of less-developed countries.[213]

---

[206] GA Res. 3201 (S-VI) 1 May 1974, UN GAOR, 6 Spec. Sess., Supp. 1 (Doc. A/9559), at 3.

[207] GA Res. 3202 (S-VI) 1 May 1974, UN GAOR, 6 Spec. Sess., Supp. 1 (Doc. A/9559) at 6 (1974).

[208] GA Res. 3201 (S-VI) 1 May 1974.

[209] *Id.* (paragraph l).

[210] *Id.*

[211] *Id.* (paragraphs 4(e), (g) & (p)).

[212] GA Res. 3202 (S-VI) May l, 1974.

[213] *Id.* (Art. II).

Moreover, the Programme calls for developed countries to encourage investors to finance industrialization projects in less-developed countries.[214] Most significantly, the Programme establishes new guidelines for dealing with foreign investors, calling for 'an international code of conduct for the transfer of technology corresponding to the needs and conditions prevalent in developing countries'[215] and 'an international code of conduct for transnational corporations … .'[216] The goals of the code of conduct for transnational corporations are:

> (a) To prevent interference in the internal affairs of the countries where they operate … ;
> (b) To regulate their [the transnational corporations'] activities in host countries, to eliminate restrictive business practices and to conform to the national development plans and objectives of the developing countries, and in this context facilitate, as necessary, the review and revision of previously concluded arrangements;
> (c) To bring about assistance, transfer technology and management skills to developing countries on equitable and favorable terms;
> (d) To regulate the repatriation of the profits accruing from their operations taking into account the legitimate interests of all parties concerned;
> (e) To promote reinvestment of [transnational corporations'] profits in developing countries.[217]

Both the Declaration and the Programme attempt to establish a major structural change in, and to prescribe standards for, State behavior in the international economy.[218] The documents purport to cover the whole arena of international economic relations.

The Charter of Economic Rights and Duties of States

Along the lines of change in international economic relations, the General Assembly also adopted the Charter of Economic Rights and Duties of States (the Charter).[219] The Charter was drafted by a Working Group established by the United Nations Conference on Trade and Development (UNCTAD).[220] The Charter was

---

214 *Id.* (Art. III).

215 *Id.* (Art. IV(a)).

216 *Id.* (Art. V).

217 *Id.* (Art. V(a)-(e)).

218 Jonathan Dubitzky, 'The General Assembly's International Economics,' *Harvard International Law Journal*, 16, 670, 670 (1975).

219 GA Res. 3281 (XXIX) 12 December 1974, UN Doc. A/Res/3281 (XXIX) (1975). The Charter was adopted by a vote of 120 in favor, 6 against and 10 abstentions. White, 'A New International Economic Order,' *International and Comparative Law Quarterly*, 24, 542, 544 (1975). The US, Canada, Japan and the EEC countries all voted against the Charter or abstained. Dubitzky, *supra* note 218, at 674 (citing *International Law Materials*, 13, 746 (1974)).

220 UNCTAD Res. 45 (111), I Proceedings of UNCTAD Third Session, Reports and Annexes, Annex I.A., UN Pub. Sales No. E.73.11. D.4 (1972). GA Resolution 3082 (XXVIII) reaffirmed the decision for the Working Group to prepare a final draft of the

intended 'to establish or improve norms of universal application for the development of international economic relations on a just and equitable basis.'[221]

The Charter first lists sixteen principles that, *inter alia*, 'shall' govern international economic relations.[222] Article 2 of the Charter expressly addresses the concept of permanent sovereignty over natural resources and the regulation of transnational corporations.[223] Article 2 provides as follows:

> l. Every State has and shall freely exercise full permanent sovereignty, including possession, use and disposal, over all its wealth natural resources and economic activities.
>
> 2. Each State has the right:
>
> (a) To regulate and exercise authority over foreign investment within its national jurisdiction in accordance with its laws and regulations and in conformity with its national objectives and priorities.
> No State shall be compelled to grant preferential treatment to foreign investment;
> (b) To regulate and supervise the activities of transnational corporations within its national jurisdiction and take measures to ensure that such activities comply with its laws, rules and regulations and conform with its economic and social policies. Transnational corporations shall not intervene in the internal affairs of a host State. Every State should, with full regard for its sovereign right, co-operate with other States in the exercise of the right set forth in this subparagraph;
> (c) To nationalize, expropriate or transfer ownership of foreign property, in which case appropriate compensation should be paid by the State adopting such measures, taking into account its relevant laws and regulations and all circumstances that the State considers pertinent. In any case where the question of compensation gives rise to a controversy, it shall be settled under the domestic law of the nationalizing State and by its tribunals, unless it is freely and mutually agreed by all States concerned that other peaceful means be sought on the basis of the sovereign equality of States and in accordance with the principle of free choice of means.[224]

Article 17 also touches on the concept of permanent sovereignty, stressing the need to accelerate the economic development of developing countries while respecting

---

Charter for consideration of the General Assembly. The drafting of a Charter was originally proposed by the President of Mexico at the Third session of UNCTAD in 1972 when UNCTAD adopted its resolution establishing the Working Group. 29 UN GAOR, Second Comm. (1638th Mt.) 382, UN Doc. A/c.2/SR. 1638, at 382 (l974).

[221] GA Res. 3082 (XXVIII), 28 UN GAOR, Supp. 30 (UN Doc. A/ 9030), at 40 (1974).

[222] GA Res. 3281 (XXIX) 12 December 1974. The Working Group rejected a proposal utilizing the term 'should' instead of the mandatory term 'shall.' Dubitzky, *supra* note 218, at 672 (citing Report of the Working Group on the Charter of Economic Rights and Duties of States, UN Doc. TD/B/AS.12/4 (1974).

[223] GA Res. 3281 (XXIX) 12 December 1974.

[224] *Id.*

their sovereign equality.[225] Article 17 provides as follows:

> International co-operation for development is the shared goal and common duty of all States. *Every State should co-operate with the efforts of developing countries to accelerate their economic and social development by providing favorable external conditions and by extending active assistance to them, consistent with their development needs and objectives, with strict respect for the sovereign equality of States and free of any conditions derogating from their sovereignty.*[226]

The Charter purports to establish normative principles for international economic relations. The document certainly utilizes legalistic language[227] and while some commentators have criticized its dichotomous nature,[228] they are, nevertheless, fairly united in their recognition of the change in international economic relations brought about by this document as well as the companion Declaration and the Programme.[229] Through these instruments the developing nations were loudly declaring the advent of a new international economic order based upon independence, self-determination and permanent sovereignty over natural resources. It is therefore something of an irony that countries that championed this norm of indigenous control over national wealth and resources would turn out to be the victims of perhaps the most systematic spoliation of this wealth by their own rulers.

Link between Permanent Sovereignty and Indigenous Spoliation

In the debates and discussions leading to the inclusion of the principle of permanent sovereignty in a number of international human rights documents,[230] the focus was on two related rights: on the one hand, the right of states to exercise control over their natural wealth and resources; and on the other, the right of all peoples freely to use, exploit and dispose of their natural wealth and resources. Some publicists have, however, erroneously limited the application of the permanent sovereignty doctrine to foreign economic activities relating to natural

---

[225] GA Res. 3281 (XXIX) Dec. 12, 1974.

[226] *Id.* (emphasis added).

[227] See *supra* note 222 and accompanying text (discussing mandatory language of Charter provisions).

[228] For example, Dubitzky, *supra* note 218, at 672.

[229] See, for example, Kuusi, *supra* note 194, at 44 (noting that 'the period of unqualified investment promotion seems to be at an end and the era of reconciliation of private business interests with national development aspirations seems to have begun'); Dubitzky, *supra* note 218, at 670 (noting that Programme and Charter attempt to affect major structural change in world economy and in state behavior); White, *supra* note 219, at 543 ('these three documents [the Declaration, Programme and Charter] are clearly intended to be normative in character ... [and] are prime examples of the new militancy at the United Nations of the developing countries, which have so dramatically increased their political power over the last decade').

[230] *Supra* Part III.

resource exploitation.[231] It is of course true that the doctrine arose in the context of relations between host states and transnational enterprises engaged in the exploitation of natural resources in their territories. Hence the position that the doctrine was intended to safeguard primarily developing countries' interests in relation to the utilization of their natural resources by foreign corporations. As a result, the right of the state to legislate for the public good in respect of its natural resources and economic activities carried on its territory has become the most common construction given to the doctrine of permanent sovereignty. However, this focus is misplaced for several reasons. In the first place, in one of the human rights instruments there is an express reference to foreign transnational corporations which have historically exploited developing countries. Article 21(5) of the African Charter on Human and Peoples' Rights requires states to 'eliminate all forms of foreign economic exploitation particularly that practiced by international monopolies.' This article singles out for treatment foreign multinationals from among all the possible exploiters, including state governments – a clear indication that when the drafters' objective was the prevention of foreign exploitation of developing countries' resources, they made sure of this by including express language to that affect in the instrument. Where in fact such language is excluded it is fair to read an intention to treat the doctrine of permanent sovereignty as applying primarily to the right of nationals freely to use, exploit and dispose of their national wealth and resources for their collective benefit.

A second problem with limiting the interpretation of permanent sovereignty to host State-foreign investor relations is that it pins all the responsibility on foreigners for the exploitation of developing countries while providing the leaders of these countries with a ready excuse for their failure to fulfill their duty to dispose of wealth and natural resources for the benefit of the peoples. In short, this construction would permit the exploitation of finite Third World natural wealth and resources to continue unabated but this time by an indigenous class of exploiters.

---

[231] See for example Kamal Hossain, 'Introduction,' in *Permanent Sovereignty over Natural Resources in International Law*, ix (Kamal Hossain & Subrata Roy Chowdhury eds, 1984) (noting that the principle of permanent sovereignty must be understood in the context of the efforts of developing countries to restructure inequitable and onerous concession-type arrangements erected during the colonial period); *International Law Association, Report of the Sixtieth Conference*, Montreal, 1982, at 197 (noting that the principle underlines the domestic jurisdiction of states with regard to the natural resources within their national boundaries); Oscar Schachter, *Sharing the World's Resources*, 172 (1977) (noting that the 'principle of permanent sovereignty has become the focal normative conception used by States to justify their right to exercise control over production and distribution arrangements without being hampered by the international law of State responsibility as it had been traditionally interpreted by the capital-exporting countries …); but see Subrata Roy Chowdhury, 'Permanent Sovereignty and its Impact on Stabilization Clauses, standards of Compensation and Patterns of Development Co-operation,' in *Permanent Sovereignty over Natural Resources in International Law*, 42 (Kamal Hossain & Subrata Roy Chowdhury eds, 1984) (noting that the right of all peoples to use, exploit and dispose of their natural wealth and resources is an important component of the principle of permanent sovereignty).

This absurd result could hardly have been what the proponents of the doctrine of permanent sovereignty intended to achieve.

In the event, the tendency to focus on one branch of the permanent sovereignty doctrine means the other half, that is, the right of all peoples freely to use, exploit and dispose of their natural wealth and resources is usually given short shrift in scholarly commentaries. This is unfortunate because a review of the *travaux preparatoires* on the Civil and Political Rights Covenant as well as the Economic, Social and Cultural Rights Covenant reveals that representatives consistently spoke of the rights of peoples *and* nations over their wealth and natural resources. These and other instruments have incorporated specific provisions on the right of peoples. Article 13 of the Vienna Convention on Succession of States in Respect of Treaties,[232] Article 1(2) of both the Civil and Political Rights Covenant and the Economic, Social and Cultural Rights Covenant and Article 21(1) of the African Charter on Human and Peoples' Rights all guarantee a people's fundamental right to freely dispose of their wealth and natural resources. The African Charter takes this right one step farther by providing that it shall be exercised in the exclusive interest of the people. Furthermore, and this fact is frequently overlooked in the scholarly commentaries, all these provisions appear in instruments dealing with human rights suggesting that the rights mentioned attach to peoples *qua* human beings and not only to the States parties.[233]

Although these instruments incorporate 'people's' rights, they are, however, deliberately silent on the meaning of 'peoples' or 'nations.' For instance, the drafters of the African Charter decided it would be prudent not to attempt a definition of the former for fear they would 'end up in a difficult discussion'[234] and a possible impasse. But the definition of 'peoples' is critical to an appreciation of the full import of, say, Article 2(2) of the Civil and Political Rights Covenant which states: '[a]ll peoples may … freely dispose of their natural wealth and resources … .' Could peoples be referring to the State? Article 21(4) of the African Charter seems to think so. This article parallels Article 2(1) of the Charter of Economic Rights and Duties of States which also vests the right of permanent sovereignty over natural resources in the states.[235] Equating peoples with states

---

232 See *Vienna Convention on Succession of States in Respect of Treaties*. Done at Vienna, 22 August 1978. Opened for signature, 23 August 1978. UN Doc.A/CONF.80/31 as corrected by A/CONF.80/31 Corr.2 of 27 October 1978 at 1488 (1978), 72 AML 971 (1978).

233 See generally Louis Henkin, 'International Human Rights As 'Rights',' *Cardozo Law Review*, 1, 438 (1979) (arguing that while creating rights and duties for the states parties, international human rights agreements also give the individual rights against his society).

234 *See* Rapporteur's Report, OAU Doc.CM/1149 (XXXVII), Ann. l, at 4, para. 13 (1981), quoted in N.S. Rembe, *Africa and Regional Protection of Human Rights*, 112, n. 1 (1985).

235 See Article 2(l), *Charter of Economic Rights and Duties of States*. Adopted by the UN General Assembly, 12 December 1974. UNGA Res. 3281 (XXIX), 29 UN GAOR, Supp. (No. 31) 50, UNDoc. A/9631 (1975), reprinted in *International Law Materials*, 14,

makes sense inasmuch as people act through states and state-sponsored agencies. But 'peoples' could also mean all persons within the state in which case the power of the state to freely dispose natural wealth and resources would be subject to the consent of all persons within the state. This meaning of 'peoples' reflects the democratic ideal. Here people would exercise their collective right against the State to benefit from their wealth and natural resources.

> Article 1(2) [of the Covenant on Civil and Political Rights] ... is not merely a reaffirmation of the right of every state over its own natural resources; it clearly provides that the right over natural wealth belongs to *peoples*. This has two distinct consequences. For dependent peoples, the right implies that the governing authority is under the duty to use the economic resources of the territory in the interest of the dependent people. In a sovereign state, the government must utilize the natural resources so as to benefit the whole population. The right of the people over natural resources, and the corresponding duty of the government, are but a consequence, in economic matters, of the people's right to (internal) self-determination in the political field. Just as the people of every sovereign state have a permanent right to choose their own form of government ... so the people are entitled to insist that the natural resources of the nation be exploited in the interest of the people.[236]

Whether the state exercises the right of free disposal alone or subject to the consent of the people, two issues still have to be addressed. First, what rules will guide the disposal, if only to ensure that national resources are being utilized for the benefit of the people as a whole? Second, who constitutes the 'State'? Article 21(3) of the African Charter and Article 1(2) in both the Civil and Political Rights and the Economic and Social Rights Covenants define the parameters within which natural resources will be exploited: '[a]ll peoples may ... freely dispose of their natural wealth and resources without prejudice to any obligations arising out of international economic co-operation, based upon the principles of mutual benefit, and international law.' Aside from the 'without prejudice ...' clause, these instruments also contain specific rules that States are required to follow in their dealings with foreigners on matters pertaining to the exploitation of natural wealth and resources. For example: the requirement that nationalization or expropriation

---

251 (1975). The argument has been made that Article 2 subparagraph 1 of the Charter transforms the peoples' right into a duty of states; it 'replaces the right of peoples and nations to dispose by the state's duty to exercise freely permanent sovereignty, including possession, use and disposal.' See Paul Peters, Nico J. Schrijver & Paul J.I.M. De Waart, 'Permanent Sovereignty, Foreign Investment and State Practice,' in *Permanent Sovereignty over Natural Resources in International Law*, 88, 95–96 (Kamal Hossain & Subrata Roy Chowdhury eds, 1984) [hereinafter 'Foreign Investment and State Practice'].

[236] See Antonio Cassese, 'The Self-Determination of Peoples,' in *The International Bill of Human Rights: The Covenant on Civil and Political Rights*, 92, 103 (Louis Henkin ed., 1981). Other commentators agree with Cassese's formulation of Article l(2) of the Civil & Political Rights Covenant as imposing a duty on states to dispose of their wealth and resources on behalf of their peoples. See Foreign Investment and State Practice, *supra* note 235, at 96.

must be for public purpose[237] and that it must be accompanied by some compensation;[238] and the limitation of the scope of arbitrariness on the part of the host state in the determination of the quantum of compensation.[239] However, with respect to the relations between the State and the peoples, aside from the suggestion that the right to freely dispose wealth shall be exercised 'in the exclusive interest of the people', there is very little by way of concrete guidelines on how this can be accomplished.

Though we have some idea who disposes what and for whom, still to be clarified is how? In short, is the State accountable and to whom? To echo Juvenal: '*Sed quis custodiet ipsos Custodes*' ('But who is to guard the guards themselves')?[240] The answer to this question lies in how one conceptualizes the state. Rather than asking *what*, we should be asking *who*, is the state? Let me explain: if one were to suggest to a Equatoguinean subsistence farmer that it is the State's responsibility for ensuring that the wealth from Equatorial Guinea's vast petroleum deposits is put to use for his best interest, that suggestion is likely to elicit an incomprehensible stare. To him the State is President Teodoro Obiang Mbasogo, the tax collector or the principal in the local public elementary school. The State to this peasant farmer is not some legal abstraction but something that lives through its office holders. The office holder may be remote, literally and metaphorically, but at least he wears a human face. Therefore, in order for the statement – that the State exercises the right of free disposal – to make sense to this farmer and the millions of similarly situated compatriots, the focus ought to be on these human faces. That is, the men and women who run the governmental apparatus and the rules that guide their exploitation of the wealth and natural resources of their nations for the benefit of the entire population. What rules, if any, limit their power to dispose? More to the point, can these men and women be made accountable to the people? Whether they can be held personally responsible for conduct that undermines the right of permanent sovereignty is a subject that will be taken up in Part II.

---

237 See for example *Resolution on Permanent Sovereignty over Natural Resources*. Adopted by the UN General Assembly, 14 December 1962. UNGA Res. 1803 (XVII), 17 UN GAOR. Supp. (No. 17) 15, UN Doc. A/5217 (1963), reprinted in *International Law Materials*, 2, 223 (1963). ('Nationalization, expropriation or requisitioning shall be based on grounds or reasons of public utility, security or the national interest which are recognized as overriding purely individual or private interests, both domestic and foreign.')

238 See Charter of Economic Rights and Duties of States, Art. 2(2)(c).

239 *Id.*

240 See Juvenal, *Satires* no. 6, 1.347.

Chapter 4

Indigenous Spoliation as a Breach of International Customary Law of Fiduciary Relations

CUSTOM IN INTERNATIONAL LAW

By accepted convention, international law comes into being in one of three ways: through international treaties binding on the State parties or through international custom, as evidence of a general practice accepted as law, or through general principles of law recognized by the world's major legal systems.[1] Treaty law and customary international law are clearly the two major bodies of international law. Whereas the former represents the manifestation of the *express* consent of States, custom is the offspring of *implied* consent as can be established through the practice of states. That is, it is a rule of law whose widespread acceptance as legally binding can be inferred from 'official governmental conduct reflected in a variety of acts, including official statements at international conferences and in diplomatic exchanges, formal instructions to diplomatic agents, national court decisions, legislative measures or other actions taken by governments to deal with matters of international concern.'[2] The contemporary definition of customary international law as captured by the Restatement (Revised) of the Foreign Relations Law of the United States reflects this position. It defines international custom as law that 'results from a general and consistent practice of states followed by them from a sense of legal obligation.'[3] Any meaningful discussion of customary international law would require separating the norm or rule in question from the state acts that vest it with *opinio juris*.

Acts of indigenous spoliation are violative of international customary law. More specifically they violate the principle of a fiduciary duty owed to citizens of a State by their constitutionally responsible rulers. Although this duty is derived from general principles recognized by the world's major legal systems, it can

---

1 See *Statute of the International Court of Justice*, Art. 38(1); see also Mark Janis, *An Introduction to International Law*, 35–38 (1988).

2 See Thomas Buergenthal & Harold G. Maier, *Public International Law*, 23 (1985).

3 American Law Institute, Restatement of the Foreign Relations Law of the United States (Revised), §101, 102(2) (Tentative Draft No. 6,1985); see also *Statute of the International Court of Justice*, Art. 38(1)(b).

properly be said to have now ripened or matured into an international custom.[4] This chapter will trace the source of the principle of a fiduciary relation from the private law institution of 'trust', examine its development and elaboration as a rule of customary international law through the framework of the League of Nations Mandate System and the successor United Nations Trusteeship System, and then relate it to the problem of indigenous spoliation. The next chapter will be devoted to a detailed examination of state practice with respect to the principle of fiduciary duty. The widespread establishment, by States that have been victims of indigenous spoliation, of commissions of inquiry to investigate corrupt officials and the enactment of special laws making indigenous spoliation an economic crime reflect State practice expressing existing international legal expectation relative to the obligations of State officials in the promotion of individual economic rights. It will be shown that the reliance on commissions of inquiry as a vehicle for pursuing constitutionally-responsible rulers who have spoliated national wealth is a tacit admission that these high-ranking public servants have a fiduciary obligation to the public. This fiduciary relationship is breached when national wealth is diverted into the private accounts of political leaders.

THE DOCTRINE OF FIDUCIARY RELATIONS

The obligation arising from fiduciary relations has been described as one of the most elusive concepts in Anglo-American law.[5] Fiduciary obligation owes its elusive character in part to the diverse legal contexts from which it arises[6] and to the fact that it evolved through a jurisprudence of analogy rather than principle.[7] In

---

[4] Under the Statute of the International Court of Justice general principles of law recognized by 'civilized nations' constitute a residuary source of international law. See ICJ Statute, *supra* note 1, Art. 38(1)(c); *see also* Restatement (Revised), *supra* note 3, §102, Comment 10 which characterizes general principles as a 'secondary source of international law.' In the event, general principles are by far the most frequently relied upon non-treaty, non-customary source of international law. Hersch Lauterpacht has defined 'general principles' as 'those principles of law, private and public, which contemplation of the legal experience of civilized nations leads one to regard as obvious maxims of jurisprudence of a general and fundamental character.' See Hersch Lauterpacht, *International Law*, 1, 69–70 (1970). One such maxim of jurisprudence is the principle of fiduciary relationship that exists between one in a position of trust and the beneficiary of that trust. It is a principle that is widely recognized in the world's major legal systems: Anglo-American, Soviet, Islamic and civil law systems. It is the contention here that indigenous spoliation violates the principle of fiduciary relationship, an essential element in the relationship between leaders and citizens.

[5] See Deborah A. DeMott, 'Beyond Metaphor: An Analysis of Fiduciary Obligation,' 1988, *Duke Law Journal*, 879, 879.

[6] *Id.*, at 880; see also Tamar Frankel, 'Fiduciary Law,' *California Law Review*, 71, 795, 804 (1983); L.S. Sealy, 'Some Principles of Fiduciary Obligation,' 1962, *Cambridge Law Journal*, 69, 69–70.

[7] DeMott, *supra* note 5, at 879.

other words, rules for fiduciary relations evolved from judicial examination of existing prototypical fiduciary relations such as agency, trust, or bailment and then ascribing their characteristics to an emerging fiduciary relation.[8] The evolutionary process has been described as one in which as existing fiduciary relations multiplied, courts would 'analogize the new relations to the established fiduciary prototypes, and to apply the rules of the prototypes to the new relations. Corporate law, for example, frequently analogizes directors as trustees, agents, and managing partners.'[9] Rules for new fiduciary relationships have also been derived from analogies based on functional similarities between various fiduciary relations.[10] One of the most frequently given examples of this method of establishing a fiduciary relation is the attempt to draw a functional analogy between union officials and agency law with the former assigned the functional equivalence of an agent of the union members.[11] However, analogies based on functional similarity are useful only if a nexus can be established between the analogized functions and the problems posed by the fiduciary relations.

The process by which rules for brand new fiduciary relations have developed is of particular importance to this study for two reasons. It suggests that rules for new emerging fiduciary relations between office holders and the public can be created by drawing analogies from existing and established prototypes such as agency, trust, or bailment. Second, the history of the evolution of fiduciary law demonstrates a willingness by courts to impose fiduciary obligations in novel situations that went beyond the conventional categories.[12] Commentators are agreed that fiduciaries and fiduciary relations take on a variety of forms and are found in many areas. There is also fairly strong agreement that fiduciary law is a very dynamic body of rules capable of growth and expansion whose boundaries are flexible and elastic enough to allow for the incorporation of new or functionally equivalent kinds of relations. Being the product of a jurisprudence by analogy it offers ample room for constructing a framework for imposing fiduciary duties and obligations on public office holders by analogizing to preexisting relations in the law of trust. This private law institution is found in the world's major legal systems and has been incorporated into the international sphere. A brief discussion of the trust institution in municipal law will be undertaken followed by a more detailed analysis of its incorporation into the international law context.

---

[8] Frankel, *supra* note 6, at 804.

[9] *Id.*, at 805.

[10] DeMott, *supra* note 5, at 891.

[11] Frankel, *supra* note 6, at 807.

[12] *See* DeMott, *supra* note 5, at 909 (noting that courts have in recent years applied fiduciary relations to commercial franchises, distributorship arrangements, in the relationship between a bank, its borrowers and depositors, and that between holders of executive and non-executive interests in oil and gas estates); *see also* Frankel, *supra* note 6, at 796 (observing that newcomers to fiduciary relation status include physicians and psychiatrists and their patients and potential candidates would include the fiduciary relations between the state, parents, and children).

THE TRUST AS THE BASIS FOR FIDUCIARY RELATIONSHIPS

Anglo-American Common Law

At common law, the traditional notion of a trust is best defined by the Restatement of Trusts 2nd §2. 'A trust ... is a fiduciary relationship with respect to property, subjecting the person by whom the title to the property is held to equitable duties to deal with the property for the benefit of another person, which arises as a result of a manifestation of an intention to create it.'[13] Comment (b), of §2, defines a fiduciary as one with a duty to act for the benefit of the other as to matters within the scope of the relation.[14] He is under a duty not to profit at the expense of the beneficiary.[15] Furthermore, the duties of a trustee are more intensive than the duties of a normal fiduciary.[16]

The fiduciary duties of a common law trustee would be particularly suited served as a basis for the determination of a violation. The duties set out in the Restatement of Trusts 2nd can be analogized to the specific duties owed by leaders of national governments to their constituents.[17] As with a common law beneficiary, the citizen who is owed a duty by the principal, as trustee, should be allowed to maintain a cause of action against his leader upon discovery of the violation of the latter's fiduciary duty.

---

13 *Restatement (Second) of Trusts* §2 (1959).

14 *Id.* Comment (b).

15 *Id.*

16 *Id.*, at §§169–185 (some aspects that are particularly relevant are: (1) the trustee is under a duty to administer the trust [§169]; (2) solely in the beneficiaries interest and to deal with the beneficiary fairly by communicating all material facts [§170]; (3) not to delegate acts the trustee can reasonably perform [§171]; (4) to give at reasonable times accurate information as to matters under the trust [§173]; (5) to exercise such care and skill as a man of ordinary prudence or, if the trustee represents he has greater skill, then he is under a duty to exercise such skill [§174]; (6) to take and control trust property [§175]; (7) to preserve the trust property [§176]; (8) to enforce claims he may hold in trust [§177]; (9) to defend the trust from actions that may result in a loss to the trust estate; (10) to keep trust property separate and distinct [§179]).

17 For example, in the United States, the newly elected or appointed official can be viewed as a trustee for the American citizens. The scope of his duties depends on the branch of government. He may not profit from nor exploit the trust power. To do so would constitute a violation of his official obligation and therefore is akin to a violation of a trustee's fiduciary duty. Thus, where the late President Nixon may have violated his Presidential duties, he was all but forced to resign or face impeachment by the legislators (who in and of themselves are individual trustees) who could be viewed as a collection of 'beneficiaries' (who are free to remove the trustee by unanimous vote).

Trust Principle Under Civil Law[18]

The modern civil law is the product of three early legal systems: the law of the Roman empire (circa 753 BC to 533 AD); the folk laws of Germanic creation (circa the fifth century AD); and the canon law.[19] These three systems meshed to form the modern French and German legal systems.[20] However, though their origins are homogenous, French and German law differ on many points.[21] In analyzing the common law trust in terms of the civil legal system, it bears emphasizing that the trust is an English legal hybrid.[22] The civil system does not provide for a 'trust' per se.[23] Under French Law, there is no distinction between legal and equitable estates; a person cannot be an owner solely for management purposes.[24]

The obstacles to a civil law trust are numerous yet not sufficiently compelling to abandon the theory that the trust concept, for our purposes, cannot be embraced under the civil system. The first barrier is that the admission of the trust would infringe on the doctrine of the *numerus clausus*; that is, it is inconsistent with the civil property concept to accept a division of rights into managerial and beneficial ownership.[25] However, this obstacle has been generally regarded as academic in that a civil law system could very well decide to accept the fiduciary trust doctrine and several civil law systems have already adopted the concept.[26] Second is the idea that the trust would render meaningless the civil rule concerning real subrogation and restraints on alienation.[27] The trust's restraint on alienation is completely at odds with civil law concepts that prohibit the separation of the right to dispose of one's property.[28] The beneficial owner, at civil law, must be the property's owner and cannot be barred from disposing of it.[29] The justification for such a concept stems from the political unrest that occurred between 1792 and 1849, the fraudulent effect caused by the prolonged alienability of France's wealth in select few, and the abusive exploitation by 16th century fiduciaries as a result of the French fiduciary doctrine.[30] Thus, French law banned the fiduciary concept under the Act of 7 May 1894 and all property subject to a fiduciary relationship,

---

18 The most strict civil law countries are France and Germany.

19 K.W. Ryan, *An Introduction to the Civil Law*, 1 (1962).

20 *Id.*

21 *See id.*, at 15–22.

22 *Id.*, at 219.

23 *Id.*

24 See 'Comment, International Fiduciary Duty: Australia's Trusteeship Over Nauru,' *Boston University International Law Journal*, 8, 394, 411 (1990).

25 Ryan, *supra* note 19, at 221.

26 *Id.*

27 *Id.*, at 222.

28 *Id.*

29 *Id.*

30 G. Coquille, *Coutume de Nivernois*, XX ch. xxxiii, Art. 10.

but where the beneficiaries were not yet born, became freely alienable.[31]

The Roman law provided for a *fidei-commissum*, a method by which those incapable of holding property by law could take such under a Roman citizen's will.[32] The *fidei-commissum* was further broken down into the *fidei-commissum universale*, where the subject of the trust was the whole or part of the estate, and *fidei-commissum speciale*, where the subject was a single gift or sum of money. The 'trustee' was bound by the will of the testator to turn over the bequest or devise immediately upon accepting succession.[33] However, enforcement was problematic for under Roman law, direct heirs had the right to refuse succession and thus destroy his 'trustee' status.[34] Notwithstanding the resemblance to a trust, the Roman concept and civil law doctrine, as stated above, do not formally accept the law and equity dualism that is necessary to achieve the common-law trust.[35] However, that is not to suggest a complete exclusion of fiduciary principles.[36] In reality, the fiduciary functions which serve the common law system are performed by other institutions in civil law.[37] Indeed, several civil law jurisdictions have adopted the trust concept, including Scotland, Quebec, Sri Lanka, Louisiana, and the Netherlands.[38]

The civil law only bars an attempt to limit the power of disposition. Roman law and modern French civil law, in certain cases, allow the appointment of an administrator to limit an individual's rights concerning his property.[39] Specific cases where the civil system recognizes this need include where there is an executor, who manages the estate in which the heirs may have conflicting interests, and an administrator, for a bankrupt estate with numerous creditors who also, by the nature of the relationship, have conflicting interests.[40] Additionally, where the French system has, in form and substance, excluded the Roman *fiducia* concept, except as discussed above, the German legal system has created the *Treuhand*. The *Treuhand* is a German fiduciary relation that differs from the Roman *fiducia* in that the (Trustee) has extremely limited power that is specifically adapted for the special purpose of the relationship.[41] However, unlike the French system, the *Treuhand* can be created for virtually any purpose.

---

31 Verdelot, *Du Bien de Famille en Allemagne*, 614–634 (1899).

32 L. Mackenzie, *Studies in Roman Law*, 272 (1865).

33 *Id.*, at 273.

34 *Id.*

35 P. Eder, *A Comparative Survey of Anglo-American and Latin American Law*, 88 (1950).

36 Ryan, *supra* note 19, at 219; Amos & Walton, *Introduction to French Law*, 99 (1963).

37 *Id.*

38 *International Encyclopedia of Comparative Law*, 6, 90, 93–104 (1972).

39 *Id.*

40 *Id.* Impartiality and ease of administration seem to be the key reason why such individuals are needed.

41 *Id.*, at 226; citing Schultze, 'Treuhander im geltenden Burgerlichen Recht,' *Iherings Jahrbuch*, 43, 1.

The power is to be specifically tailored to the purpose for which the property was transferred; any exercise of power contrary to the prescribed purposes gives rise to a cause of action by the settlor and such exercise is ineffective *in rem*.[42] Thus, the restriction on a *Treuhander's* power is also effective as a limitation on the rights of subsequent purchasers even those with *bona fide* status; a significant deviation from the common law protection of the *bona fide* purchaser.[43] Therefore, where the settlor and beneficiary are one, the settlor would be more effectively protected under the *Treuhand* than the *fiducia* or even at common law.[44] Where the beneficiary and settlor are not the same, the beneficiary is protected by the reversionary rights in the trust property. However, in the absence of a specific assignment of rights by the settlor, the beneficiary's rights with regard to the *Treuhander* are strictly obligatory.[45]

Therefore, it may be said that the civil law provides for a general fiduciary relationship with regard to property where either the beneficiary's interests are in conflict or where the beneficiary's actions would be ineffective in terms of ability to actually control the property. The Germanic system provides for additional protection to the settlor and beneficiaries in that the power of the *Treuhander* is limited to the specific purpose for which the relationship was created. It has been suggested that the common law system has simply generalized the available uses of what could otherwise be described as a 'civil trust.'[46]

With the above discussion in mind, to what extent can the fiduciary doctrines found in these municipal systems be recruited to build an international norm of fiduciary relation between rulers and the ruled?

The French system provides for a fiduciary relationship where the status of the beneficiaries was such that their interests were in conflict and/or they lacked the power to administer the trust property.[47] Arguably, the citizens of a nation constitute just such a class of beneficiaries. Given the number of individuals who make up a nation, not surprisingly their desires and beliefs, their wants and needs will more often than not be at cross-purposes. As long as these basic interests are in conflict the responsibility for administering the nation's wealth and resources will have to be delegated to someone more neutral. These neutral arbiters could, under the French fiduciary doctrine, be analogized to the 'civil trustee.'

The German *Treuhand* relationship would also qualify. The *Treuhander*, as stated above, is limited in power to his specific duties under the trust.[48] Moreover, the concept of a *Treuhander* requires that he should exercise his own rights, that he should act in his own name for the benefit of others, and that his powers should not go beyond what is necessary for the fulfillment of his office.[49] The *Treuhand* has

---

42 *Id.*

43 *Id.*, at 229.

44 *Id.*, at 226.

45 *Id.*, at 229–30.

46 *Id.*, at 223.

47 Ryan, *supra* note 19, at 219; Amos & Walton, *supra* note 36.

48 *Id.*

49 *Id.*, at 230.

the effect of creating a multiplication of competencies or of capacities to exercise the rights over the property; not the diminution of the settlor's ability to administer it.[50] When applied to the conduct required of a constitutionally responsible ruler, the commonalties are numerous. An elected official acts as the principal, at least in the United States and other 'democratic' countries, in his own name. Through the unique governmental processes, the elected principal is able to affect the property interests of the nation's citizens without actually inhibiting the citizen's ability to convey such property.[51] Where an official ascends to power by means other than election, he may still be viewed as a *Treuhander* in the sense that the nation's citizens have consented to his ascension to power and for all practical purposes the official exhibits and functions as an elected official. Indeed such an individual may boast that he was elected or appointed by his people and is the center for national solidarity in his country.

Islamic Law

A Brief Overview of Islamic Shari'a

Islamic law, like most Western legal systems, recognizes trust and fiduciary obligation in various situations. The basis for the recognition of these duties and obligations is the Qur'an, and since all the Islamic schools adopt the Qur'an as the basic source of Islamic law, the law of fiduciary and trust does not differ substantially in the various Islamic schools. A word about Islamic law or Shari'a. The Shari'a is a comprehensive and preordained system of God's commands.[52] It has been described as a divine law and a jurist's law to reflect its twin sources: divine revelation and the human reasoning of jurists.[53]

Sources of Islamic Shari'a

The scholars of the *Science of Islamic Fiqh*[54] uniformly recognize four sources of Islamic Shari' a. These are, in order of importance: (1) the holy Qur'an, (2) the Sunna, (3) the ijima, and,(4) the qiyas. The holy Qur'an is the divine revelations of Allah (praise him) to Prophet Muhammed (peace upon him) and it is the primary source of Islamic law. The Qur'an contains the main principles of Shari'a,[55] for instance among more than its 6,000 verses only about 200 of these lay down any rules. The Sunna comprises what associates[56] of the Prophet reported about him in

---

50 *Id.*, at 230–31.

51 In the United States an example would be a proposed legislative tax bill that is signed into law by the President.

52 See Noel J. Coulson, *Conflicts and Tensions in Islamic Jurisprudence*, 3 (1969).

53 *Id.*

54 The translation commonly given of 'III U'sul al-Figh.'

55 With the exception of the inheritance rules which Allah laid down in detail, it is difficult to locate any comprehensive rules in the holy Qur'an.

56 An associate (Sahabi) is any Muslim, man or woman, who met the prophet.

one of three forms: a verbal form (hadith), a practice, or a ratification. The purpose of the Sunna is to clarify the rules of the Shari'a.[57] The hadith is a quotation of the Prophet Muhammed's words which together with his practices as recorded in the sira[58] books and the practices of the Prophet's associates subsequently ratified by him are all considered an integral part of the Sunna.

Ijima is a 'unanimous agreement among the qualified jurists on a given point' at any time in the past or in the future and is not limited to the points that have been agreed by the schools of Fiqh in the past. Finally, qiyas[59] is the fourth source of Shari'a law. Qiyas is a gapfiller used by jurists to arrive at an opinion on a matter for which there is no express rule in the Qur'an or Sunna and there is no prior ijima.[60] In addition, there are supplemental sources of Islamic Fiqh the legitimacy of which has been debated among jurists. One such source is istihsan ('seeking the most equitable solution').[61] However, the main sources of most present and, in all probability, future Shari'a rules are the ijima and the qiyas. However, the jurists' freedom to derive rules through these two sources is qualified to the degree that the derivations do not contradict the established rules in the Qur'an and/or the Sunna.

The Binding Effect of the Various Sources of Shari'a

Muslims believe that the Qur'an was, is, and will ever be preserved by Allah in exactly the same text it was revealed. Therefore the Qur'an has a binding and absolute authority over any other source of Shari'a. With respect to the Sunna, which was recorded several decades after the death of the Prophet, there are occasionally differences among some of its records. However, the uniformly recorded Sunna is binding and absolute authority to the extent that it is not in contradiction with any of the principles stated in the Qur'an. Ijima is binding so long as it too does not contradict principles established in the Qur'an or Sunna and is not superseded by a subsequent ijima. Qiyas receives the same treatment as ijima.

A final word, although in its classical form Muslim jurisprudence viewed Shari'a law as a single comprehensive, unitary code of behavior as prescribed by God, over time differences of opinion among jurists split this body into four

---

57 For example, it is believed that Allah instructed Muslims in the Qur'an to pray, however, there are no details as to the frequency or method of the prayers. This was subsequently clarified by the Sunna.

58 Sira is the Prophet's biography.

59 Strictly speaking, qiyas started as a *method* (as opposed to a source) for deducing the opinion of the Shari'a on a given point. With time the volume of rules deduced by this method became so numerous that qiyas was eventually recognized as a source.

60 The classic example often given in the Fiqh books is the forbidding of all intoxicating substances although all the Qur'an forbade are alcoholic drinks.

61 See Coulson, *supra* note 52, at 7.

distinct schools.[62] By the end of the ninth century, the four schools had converged around a common view of the theory of sources of Shari'a law. They 'mutually regarded their several bodies of doctrine as equally legitimate attempts to define Allah's law, equally authoritative versions of the Shari'a.'[63]

Trust, Fiduciary Relationship and Obligation

The Qur'an commands that one must fulfill one's contract and especially to return a trust or deposit to its owner. It forbids the consumption or appropriation for no good reason of the property of others.[64] Thus, when an owner hands over his property to another for safe keeping a fiduciary relationship (amana) is created. The custodian of the property guarantees the safe keeping and eventual return of the property. A subsequent refusal to return the property or deposit, or a denial of receipt of the deposit, or the confusion of the deposit with the personal property of the person in whose charge the property was placed is considered usurpation that ultimately engenders liability.[65] This is a tort (ta'addi) under Islamic law. The effect of this transgression in the case of a deposit of money ceases when the ta'addi ceases, or when the deposit is returned to its rightful owner.

Notions of obligations and responsibility also appear prominently in various Islamic economic formations and relationships. The Islamic approach to economics is to involve both citizens and the state in a pattern of partnership that inspires a deep sense of communal responsibility. Although Islam endorses and even demands individual liberty it, however, makes a clear distinction between economic liberty and greed. A hadith enjoins '[e]very person ... [to be] a responsible agent . . . [who] will be brought to account before God and be asked about his responsibility.'[66] But more particularly, Islam holds a ruler responsible for the well-being of his subjects and expects him to give account of how he discharges this responsibility.[67] This obligation is derived from a statement of the Prophet Muhammad: 'Anyone who has been given charge of people, but does not

62 These are: Hanafis, Malikis, Shafi'is and Hanbalis. Each school named after the founder-scholar and representing the legal tradition of a particular geographical locality. Hanafi law has traditionally been applied in Turkey, Syria, Lebanon, Iraq, Jordan, Egypt, the Sudan, and in the Indian subcontinent. Maliki law dominates in the Muslim populations of North, West, and Central Africa. Shafi'i law is used in East Africa, the southern part of the Arabian peninsula and in Southeast Asia. Hanbali law is the law of Saudi Arabia. *Id.*, at 21–24. All of these schools are within the Sunni community.

63 *Id.*, at 22.

64 Sura ii: 188; iv 29, 161; ix: 34. See also Joseph Schacht, *An Introduction to Islamic Law*, 12 (1964).

65 *Id.*, at 157.

66 Muhammad Ali & Muhammad Ibn Ismael Bukhari Sahih, *Manual of Hadith*, 4, 57 (1944).

67 Muhammed Abdul-raud, *A Muslim's Reflections on Democratic Capitalism*, 25 (1984).

live up to it with sincerity will not taste even the fragrance of paradise.'[68] Islam therefore imposes a fiduciary duty on *any person* who has been assigned a responsibility, be he a head of State, a cabinet minister, a member of Parliament, a public servant, a farmer, a doctor, or a teacher, and he shall be answerable before Allah for the discharge of that duty. So important is this obligation that Islamic law reserves the severest of penalties for its nonfulfillment: denial of entry to paradise!

Partnerships are recognized in Islamic economic systems and they share much the same characteristics as similar business forms in Anglo-American law. The Islamic partnership is based on mutual agency with each partner under the same fiduciary obligation to operate the partnership for the mutual benefit of all the co-partners and under the same duty of care expected of a partner when he is operating a business for his own benefit. Under Islamic law, partnerships can be organized in one of two juristic forms: Mudarabah and Shirikah. The former is called trust financing where the investor becomes the beneficial owner or sleeping partner and the agent-manager (mudarib) is the managing trustee or labor partner. Shirikah, on the other hand, is a business organization where two or more persons contribute to the financing and share equally or unequally in its management. They may also agree on a formula for sharing profits otherwise profits will be shared equitably but not necessarily equally.

Mudarabah and shirikah are treated as fiduciary relationships in fiqh and unblemished honesty and fairness are considered absolutely imperative in these relations. Each partner is expected to act in good faith for the benefit of the other partner and attempts by one partner to cheat and take an unfair share of the income would be treated as a violation of Islamic teaching. The Qur'an requires the honest fulfillment of all contracts, written or oral, express or implied.[69] It prohibits any betrayal of the trust relationship between partners[70] and considers it immoral to derive income through cheating, dishonesty or fraud.[71] Relying on the hadith 'Allah says I am third with two partners unless one betrays the other', Islamic fiqh[72] has interpreted as a breach of fiduciary duty in the partnership when one of the partners behaves in a way which brings harm to the other partners. A partner whose conduct results in injury to the partnership is under a duty to compensate for the resulting damage.[73]

The liability of a partner is unlimited except in mudarabah where the investor (beneficial owner) is only responsible for his share of the partnership liability regardless of the amount or by how much the indebtedness exceeds the value of his

[68] Quoted in M. Umer Chapra, *Towards a Just Monetary System*, 220 (1985).

[69] 5:1.

[70] 8:27.

[71] Chapra, *supra* note 68, at 248.

[72] The goal of Islamic jurisprudence was to reach an understanding (fiqh) of the Shari'a through the formulation of principles or sources from which one can arrive at an understanding. See Coulson, *supra* note 52, at 3.

[73] Nabil Saleh, *The General Principles of Saudi Arabian and Omani Company Laws*, 97 (1981).

own share of the partnership assets.[74] To protect investor interests, all schools of Islamic law place the same restrictions on the activities of agents. He is not permitted to commit the partnership to any sum greater than the capital at hand without prior authorization from the investors.[75]

THE FIDUCIARY RELATIONSHIP IN THE INTERNATIONAL SPHERE

Origin and Evolution of an International Fiduciary Duty

The principle of an international fiduciary duty can be traced to the League of Nations mandate system.[76] By the terms of Article 119 of the Treaty of Versailles Germany renounced in favor of the five Principal Allied and Associated Powers 'all her rights and titles over her overseas possessions.' In return, the Allied Powers through Article 22 of the League Covenant made provision for the future of these former enemy colonies and territories which were described as 'inhabited by peoples not yet able to stand by themselves under the strenuous conditions of the modern world.'[77] Article 22 went on to provide that for these colonies and territories 'there should be applied the principle that the well-being and development of such peoples form a sacred trust of civilisation and that securities for the performance of this trust should be embodied in this Covenant.'[78]

The tutelage of such peoples, Article 22 further laid down, should be entrusted to advanced nations, who, by reason of their resources, experience or geographical position, can best discharge this responsibility, and who are willing to accept it, and that this tutelage should be exercised by them as mandatories on behalf of the League of Nations.[79] Article 22 then went on to point out that the character of the mandates must 'differ according to the stage of the development of the people, the geographical situation of the territory, its economic conditions and other similar circumstances.'[80] It then proceeded to classify the mandates into three distinct types[81] which were subsequently allocated in each case by the Principal Allied Powers on terms approved by the League Council. The mandatory was placed

---

74 *Id.*

75 Nabil Saleh, *Unlawful Gain and Legitimate Profit in Islamic Law*, 109 (1986).

76 The genesis of the mandate system has in turn been traced to a pamphlet 'The League of Nations: A Practical Suggestion', published in 1918 by General Smuts, who later served as South Africa's representative at the Paris Peace Conference. The Smuts proposal was embraced by President Woodrow Wilson and it served as the point of departure for subsequent discussions on the mandate system. Smuts is also credited with the authorship of Article 22 of the Covenant of the League of Nations. See Aaron M. Margalith, *The International Mandates*, 21–22 (1930).

77 Covenant, Art. 22(1).

78 *Id.*

79 *Id.*, Art. 22(2).

80 *Id.*, Art. 22(3).

81 *Id.*, Art. 22, paras. 4–6.

under the obligation of rendering an annual report to the Council in reference to the territory committed to its charge.[82]

In interpreting the scope of the mandate system, that is, the authority conferred by the mandate, the rights and duties of the mandatory as well as those of the mandated peoples, learned commentators have focused on three key terms in Article 22: 'mandate,' 'tutelage' and 'trust.' The ensuing controversy over the wording of this article – the source of this inferred international fiduciary duty – has centered around the meaning they were intended to bear: (a) were they intended to bear technical legal meanings, by exact or close analogy to private law institutions of *trust, tutelage* and *mandatum* or (b) was the analogy, if any, intended to be of the broadest and most general nature only, and (c) whether the more detailed and technical aspects of these private law institutions were known to the drafters of the Covenant and therefore could fairly be presumed to have been intended to be incorporated in the mandate system?

It has been urged that the language in the opening paragraph of Article 22 where mention is made of a 'sacred trust' and 'tutelage' was simply a description of the 'idealistic or humanitarian objectives involved in the mandate system.'[83] Moreover, according to this view, the key terms in Article 22 were never intended to bear technical legal meanings either by exact or close analogy to municipal law institutions.[84] This was the position consistently taken by South African jurists in defense of that country's administration of South West Africa (later Namibia) throughout the mandate and trusteeship period.[85] However, in the view of a number of leading publicists of the League period, some, if not all, of the key terms in

---

82 *Id.*, Art. 22 para. 7.

83 See Counter-Memorial filed by the Government of the Republic of South Africa in *South West African Cases* (Ethiopia v. South Africa; Liberia v. South Africa) 104 [1966] ICJ Pleadings, South West Africa, Vol. II.

84 *Id.,* at 103–104.

85 For example, in oral arguments before the ICJ in 1970, Counsel for South Africa made the following argument with respect to the three institutions of private law to which reference was made in Article 22 of the Covenant, namely mandate, trust and tutelage:

> [T]he wording of Article 22 of the Covenant as a whole, as well as its historical background suggests strongly that the references to trust, tutelage and mandatories were not intended to bear technical legal meanings, by exact or close analogy to municipal law institutions of trust, tutelage and *mandatum*. This is also borne out by the fact that the English word 'trust', which is capable of a technical legal meaning as well as a more general ordinary meaning, was rendered in the French version by the word 'mission', meaning in this context task or undertaking. It is also significant that in the actual mandate instruments themselves, the words 'trust' and 'tutelage' did not appear at all. Even the words 'mandatory' and 'mandate' which were retained in the mandate instruments themselves, are, in our submission, not indicative of an intention to import into the mandate instruments the rules governing the *mandatum* of private law.

See The Legal Consequences for States for the Continued Presence of South Africa in Namibia (South West Africa) notwithstanding Security Council Resolution 276 (1970), Pleadings, ICJ Reports 1971, at 305–307 (Oral Statement by Mr. Van Heerden).

Article 22 were intended to assume the same characteristics they have in private law. Furthermore, it is their view that the drafters of that Article were not only familiar with these private law terms but intended to have the legal institutions designated by them applied by analogy to the international institution of the mandate and, later, trusteeship.[86] The positions taken by writers as well as decisions from some national courts and the International Court of Justice will be reviewed in this section.

The View of Publicists

While Article 22 may not have defined in very clear terms the relation that was to exist between the Mandatory and the mandated territory, and between the Mandatory and the League of Nations,[87] however, a persuasive argument can be mounted that as between the first pair a fiduciary relation was contemplated. Support for this argument comes not only from the three concepts that form the essence of the mandate system but also from the separate agreements between the Mandatories and the Council of the League of Nations.[88] Furthermore, of the many principles that followed logically from Article 22, for example, the principle of 'no annexation' or the principle of international supervision,[89] one – the principle of gratuity or 'no benefit'[90] – speaks directly to this notion of an international fiduciary duty. The principle of gratuity was to ensure that the work of the mandatory in administering the mandated territory had to be done gratuitously with no benefits allowed to accrue to it for discharging this voluntarily assumed obligation.[91] As one commentator observed the 'no benefit' principle 'follow[ed] from the concept of guardianship … and it [was] this feature … that [gave] the mandate the character of an obligation rather than a privilege. The Mandatory [was] not to be paid for its administration and must not pass any legislation

---

86 See Quincy Wright, *Mandates Under the League of Nations*, 375 ff (1930); J.L. Brierly, 'Trusts and Mandates,' [1929] *British Yearbook of International Law*, 217; Hersch Lauterpacht, *The Development of International Law by the International Court*, 214 (1958); H. Duncan Hall, *Mandates, Dependencies and Trusteeships*, 97–100 (1948); Aaron M. Margalith, *The International Mandates*, 36–45 (1930).

87 Margalith, *supra* note 86, at 30.

88 For instance, the Mandate for German South West Africa for which South Africa was the mandatory contained in its Articles 2 to 5 the mandatory's substantive obligations. Article 2 imposed the general obligation to 'promote to the utmost the material and moral well-being and the social progress of the inhabitants.' Article 6 in turn imposed the mandatory's procedural obligations among which was the obligation to render to the Council of the League, to its satisfaction, an annual report 'containing full information with regard to the territory, and indicating the measures taken to carry out the obligations assumed under Articles 2, 3, 4 and 5.' The duties imposed by these articles smack of the kind of obligations extant in a fiduciary relationship.

89 *Id.*, at 46–47.

90 *Id.*, at 47.

91 *Id.*, at 47.

favoring its own nationals … .'[92] The construction given to the key legal terms of Article 22 – mandate, tutelage and trust – by several publicists lends strong support for the view that it was in the contemplation of the drafters of the mandate system that a fiduciary relation would exist between the Mandatory and the mandated territory and its peoples.

Mandate We have it on the authority of Quincy Wright, perhaps the foremost authority of his time on the League of Nations' Mandate System, that the three terms – mandate, tutelage and trust – can be interpreted in light of private law institutions of the same name.[93] The term 'mandate', he points out found its way into the Covenant through the efforts of President Woodrow Wilson and General Smuts; and that the latter was undoubtedly 'familiar with the term in the technical sense attributed to it by the Roman Dutch law of South Africa.'[94] In addition to its technical formulation, the term 'mandate' was also, in popular usage, suggestive of 'command' or 'commission.' Wright, however, is insistent that it was as a *terminus technicus* that it was included in Article 22: 'as the word is a *terminus technicus* of both the civil law and the common law, writers have usually assumed that the treatydrafters had this usage in mind though many have doubted whether all the implications of the private law institution could be applied to the international law institution.'[95]

The term mandate is derived from the Latin *mandatum* which was a consensual contract in Roman law creating a gratuitous agency. Thus, the principal was the *mandans* or *mandator* and the agent the *mandatarius*. The *mandatum* had thirteen principal characteristics:

1 Its object must be *pro bono mores*;
2 It must be intended to benefit some one other than the *mandatarius*;
3 It terminates by death of either *mandatarius* or *mandans* and revocation by the latter before execution is begun;
4 The *mandans* must have accepted responsibility of the contract;
5 He may not revoke after execution has begun;
6 He is responsible within defined limits to third parties for acts of the *mandatarius*;
7 He is responsible to the *mandatarius* for expenses and losses under the contract and so is his estate in case execution had begun before his death or in ignorance of his death;
8 The *mandatarius* must have voluntarily accepted;

92 *Id.* The second paragraph of Article 22 described the best method of giving practical effect to the principle that 'the well-being and development of … [the inhabitants of the mandated territory] form a sacred trust of civilization …' would be to 'entrust' the 'tutelage' of the 'peoples' concerned to suitable 'advanced nations,' *willing to accept it.* Covenant, Art. 22(2).

93 Wright, *supra* note 86, at 375.

94 *Id.*, at 376.

95 *Id.*

9 His service must be gratuitous with exception of honoraria recognized by the later law;
10 He cannot renounce the contract except in extraordinary circumstances;
11 He is bound to keep within the terms of the *mandatum* and employ extraordinary diligence under penalty of infamy;
12 He is responsible to third parties for acts under the *mandatum*; and
13 He is responsible to the *mandans* for an accounting and for faithful execution and so is his estate if execution had begun before his death.[96]

The mandate is familiar to the civil law system and but for some few qualified exceptions the institution conforms quite closely to the Roman law *mandatum*.[97] Moreover, the Anglo-American law of agency also corresponds to a large extent to the civil law of mandate.[98] In both legal systems, the institution is understood to suggest a fiduciary relationship: 'The connotations of the Roman mandatum ... suggest that the real party at interest is the *mandans* and that the *mandatory has a fiduciary relation to him*.'[99] And under the League mandate system, the mandant, that is, the League, is 'logically and legally the principal, and from whom the authority of the mandatory is derived, no matter how nominal the authority of the mandant may be.'[100] Thus, a strict application of the Roman law *mandatum* by analogy to common law agency principles would result in a fiduciary relation between the League of Nations, as the principal, and its agent, the various mandatories, leaving out the mandated territories and their inhabitants of this relationship. Wright, however, was of the view that the latter qualify as beneficiaries under a type of *mandatum* recognized by Justinian where a third party was the beneficiary.[101] Viewed thus, the mandatory also had some fiduciary obligations to the mandated territory and its inhabitants.

Tutelage Quincy Wright concluded his examination of the use of the term 'mandate' in Article 22 claiming that there was ample evidence to suggest that its drafters used the word in its technical sense and seemed quite satisfied that the nexus between the accompanying private law institution and the international context was established.[102] But he was much more sanguine with respect to the evidence suggesting that the appropriation of the private law institutions of tutelage and, particularly, trust or their application *pari passu* to the institutions of the mandate was in their technical sense.[103] 'However, not every publicist who has commented on the mandate system shares this view.

Tutelage comes from *tutela* in Roman law meaning a guardianship of children

---

96 *Id.*, at 379.
97 *Id.*
98 *Id.*, at 380.
99 *Id.* at 382 (emphasis added).
100 *See* Lauterpacht, *supra* note 4, at 196 quoted in *id.*, at 381.
101 *Id.*, at 382.
102 *Id.*, at 377.
103 *Id.*

under fourteen.[104] It implied a fiduciary relation between tutor and pupil and revolved around eleven principal characteristics:

1 Its object is protection of the pupil or minor;
2 It may exist in one of five types, (a) tutelage over pupils 1–7, (b) tutelage over pupils 7–14 (12 for girls); (c) general curatorship over minors 14–25, (d) general curatorship over interdicted persons (insane, idiots, spendthrifts), (e) special curatorship for single transactions;
3 Tutors and curators are appointed by magistrates and tutors for children by will, or operation of law;
4 Tutelage or curatorship terminated by death or degradation of the tutor or curator, the pupil or minor, by the latter's coming of age, reduction to slavery, deportation, capture, ingratitude upon demand of patron, fulfillment of conditions or court removal;
5 A tutor or curator must be a man (or woman for her own children or grandchildren) over 25, not lunatic, spendthrift, deaf and dumb, bishop, monk, soldier, person guilty of corruption to obtain the office, Jew (for a Christian) and a qualified person must accept unless over 70, already burdened with three children or three pupils, holder of certain public offices, ill, illiterate or poor;
6 A tutor or curator has a right of action against anyone who interferes with his tutorship or curatorship and against pupil or minor for expenses and losses but by curator only after his mission has ceased;
7 A tutor or curator must submit to limited court supervision and give security in most cases and if the magistrate does not ask this or it proves insufficient the magistrate may be liable to action by the pupil;
8 A tutor can not alienate the pupil's property except with consent of the court. A curator of an interdicted person has full control of the estate. A curator of a minor can consent to alienations;
9 A tutor or curator is liable for fraud, neglect or waste of pupil's, minor's or interdicted person's property, to restitution, double fine, or removal by court. In such a case the pupil gets a curator *ad hoc* to sue the tutor. On termination of the relation the tutor or curator must give a full accounting. A tutor or curator removed for fraud is infamous;
10 A pupil must submit to the tutor both as to property and personal acts. A minor or interdicted must submit to the curator only as to property;
11 A pupil under 7 can perform no legal act even with the tutor's consent. The tutor acts in his own name for the pupil. The acts of a pupil under 14 and over 7are invalid unless the tutor acted also except for release from obligations, acquisitions or inheritance or succession and contracts for his own benefit. A minor could act legally without curator's consent but subject to restoration of previous conditions by the court if the act was to his disadvantage. Practically this had the effect of compelling minors to get curators as no one would

---

104 *Id.*, at 383.

transact with them alone. An interdicted person could not act. His curator acted for him.[105]

The institution of tutelage is found in all municipal systems of law and even retains the same appellation in modern civil law.[106] In the Anglo-American legal system it is known as the law of guardianship. Analogizing this institution to the international sphere, specifically to the mandate system, would mean that the drafters' intention was:

> [T]hat the mandated community would eventually acquire independence and sovereignty of its territory, that the mandatory must act for the benefit of that community, may be removed by the League for malfeasance, and may be held to an accounting by the mandated community on termination of the relation or even before. An action for the latter purpose could be brought by the pupil acting through a curator *ad hoc* ... in addition to the process of petition the community should be entitled to bring action in the Permanent Court through the mandatory *ad hoc* appointed by the League Council. The mandatory ... would be entitled to recoup expenses and losses and to object to any interference by outside states with the performance of his mission.[107]

There is reason to believe that the concept of tutelage or guardianship which is firmly rooted in the civil law of the European continent was brought into the mandate system to match the trusteeship concept which was the contribution of the Anglo-American common law.[108] In this sense then, the attributes of the civil law tutelage were presumed to be reflected in the common law institution of trust or trusteeship.

Trust Quincy Wright has acknowledged that lawyers from the Anglo-American common law tradition 'have found it natural to apply the doctrine of trusts to the mandates, which clearly indicate a relation of confidence between the mandatory and the mandated community.'[109] He also observed that in the French text of the Covenant, the terms 'trust' and 'intrusted' 'were used to emphasize the fiduciary character of the relations of both League and mandatory to the mandated peoples ... .'[110] On this point the majority of writers are agreed. According to Hersch Lauterpacht:

> [I]n the drafting of Article 22 an effort was made to lay stress on the fundamental purposes of the mandate. The terms employed ... evidence each in their own way the common character of the committal of a trust (*fides facta*) protective functions exercised by the international organization and on its behalf by the mandatory. The latter is bound by the mandate, like the organization with power of *offi cium*. It is for this reason, it

105 *Id.*, at 383–384.
106 *Id.*
107 *Id.*, at 385.
108 Margalith, *supra* note 76, at 41.
109 Wright, *supra* note 86, at 389.
110 *Id.*

> would seem, that the term 'tutelage' was chosen. One of the expressions to be found in paragraph 1 of Article 22 is practically the same as the standard definition of tutelage (*qui propter aetatem suam sponte se defendere naquit*; Digest, 26, 1, 1, pr.). This accords also with the nature of a trust, which mandates are also regarded as having. A guardian under the Common Law system is in the position of a trustee ('the relation of guardian and ward is strictly that of trustee and *cestui que trust*'). As these legal concepts essentially contemplate the protection of persons (in this case, peoples) who cannot govern themselves, the necessary consequence is the exercise of supervision over the person entrusted with guardianship 'supervision of the guardian', and in case of serious breaches of his duties (*fides fracta*) the loss or forfeiture of guardianship.[111]

Brierly also took the position that the language of Article 22 laid stress on the 'trust, and not to either of the other concepts as the governing principle' of the mandate system.[112] He was therefore insistent that only through an understanding of the nature of a trust would it be possible to resolve questions regarding issues of sovereignty and the actual powers of the mandatory. All that was necessary for there to be a trust; Brierly observed, is a 'res and an appropriation of that res to some aim.'[113] Not even the trustee, according to Brierly, is an essential element for the existence of a trust, although he may become necessary for its normal functioning.[114] For Brierly, echoing Lepaulle, the essential element present in trusts of all kinds is the 'segregation of assets from the *patrimonium* of individuals, and a devotion of such assets to a certain function, a certain end.'[115]

The private law institutions which were at the heart of the mandate system survived the dissolution of the League of Mandates. They became part of the United Nations Trusteeship System.[116] Chapter XII of the UN Charter, together with the various trusteeship agreements that grew out of it, provides the legal framework for analyzing this principle. Article 75 provides the authority for the trusteeship system: '[t]he United Nations shall establish under its authority an international trusteeship system for the administration and supervision of such territories as may be placed thereunder by subsequent individual agreements. These territories are hereinafter referred to as trust territories.' Article 76 then supplies the basic building blocks of this system: '[t]he basic objectives of the trusteeship system, in accordance with the Purposes of the United Nations laid down in Article 1 of the present Charter, shall be' and then follows a list of enumerated objectives the most pertinent of which is:

---

111 Lauterpacht, *supra* note 4, at 214.

112 Brierly, *supra* note 86, at 217.

113 *Id.*, at 218.

114 *Id.*

115 *Id.* quoting Pierre Lepaulle, 'An Outsider's View-point of the Nature of Trusts,' *Cornell Law Quarterly*, 14, 52 (19).

116 See International Status of South West Africa, Advisory Opinion, ICJ Reports 1950, at 137; see also United Nations General Assembly Resolution 2145 (XXI) of 27 October 1966 terminating the Mandate of South West Africa.

b. to promote the political, economic, social, and educational advancement of the inhabitants of the trust territories, and their progressive development towards self-government or independence as may be appropriate to the particular circumstances of each territory and its peoples and the freely expressed wishes of the peoples concerned, and as may be provided by the terms of each trusteeship agreement … .

Pursuant to Article 76(b) trusteeship agreements were approved by the General Assembly[117] in which a number of 'trust territories' were placed under the International Trusteeship System to be administered by hegemonic powers acting as the 'administering authority' or 'trustee.'[118] It has been pointed out that the choice of the term 'trusteeship' in describing the relationship between the administered territory and the administering authority was intended by the drafters of the UN Charter to make the administering power accountable for its actions in the non-self-governing territories. In theory at least, if not necessarily in practice, it was understood that the trustee countries assumed a fiduciary obligation to act in the non-self-governing territory's best interest.[119] For instance, the trusteeship agreement signed by Australia, New Zealand, and the United Kingdom which placed Naura under their trust contains an explicit listing of duties undertaken by the administering authority.[120] In Article 5(a), Australia agreed to 'take into consideration the customs and usages of the inhabitants of Nauru and respect the rights and safeguard the interests, both present and future, of the indigenous inhabitants of the Territory … .'[121] And in Article 5(b) Australia again undertook to '[p]romote … the economic, social, educational and cultural advancement of the inhabitants …' consistent with the obligations enumerated in Article 76 of the UN Charter.

The Nauru agreement was typical of the many other trusteeship agreements that

---

[117] Ten trusteeships were set up pursuant to agreements between the United Nations and various nations.

[118] Article 73 of the UN Charter captures this view. It provides:

Members of the United Nations which have or assume responsibilities for the administration of territories whose peoples have not yet attained a full measure of self-government recognize the principle that the interests of the inhabitants of these territories are paramount, and accept as a sacred trust the obligation to promote to the utmost, within the system of international peace and security established by the present Charter, the well-being of the inhabitants of these territories … .

[119] See International Fiduciary Duty, *supra* note 24, at 405–406, n. 74.

[120] See Trusteeship Agreement for the Territory of Nauru, Nov. 1, 1947, Australia-Great Britain-New Zealand, 10 UNTS 3, Art. 5. Under the terms of this agreement, the three countries agreed to place Nauru under their tutelage though they subsequently decided among themselves that Australia would act as the administering authority. See Certain Phosphate Lands in Nauru (Nauru v. Austl.), ICJ (Application of Nauru, unpublished, May 19, 1989) at 10 [hereinafter Case of Nauru, Application (Nauru v. Austl.), ICJ] cited in International Fiduciary Duty, *supra* note 24, at 406.

[121] *Id.*

came out of the UN system. By the clear and unambiguous terms of these trusteeship agreements, the administering powers assumed an explicit obligation to act in accordance with the best long-term interests of the indigenous peoples under their charge. As trustees, the administering authorities undertook a fiduciary duty in placing a territory under the International Trusteeship System.[122] In line with the preceding discussion on the mandate system, the trusteeship arrangement envisaged in Article 76 of the Charter suggests a trust, a trustee and a beneficiary. It must be presumed that the architects of the UN Trusteeship System, much like those of the predecessor mandate system, clearly knew what a trusteeship arrangement entailed and selected the term fully aware of its common usage.[123]

Judicial Decisions

The International Court of Justice Confirmation for the view that the mandate and successor trusteeship agreements were intended to give rise to a fiduciary relationship creating substantive rights and duties between the peoples of the non-self-governing territory and their administering authority can be found in judicial pronouncements by national and international courts. The few cases involving the international trusteeship system that have been argued before the International Court of Justice all involved South Africa's mandate over the former German South West Africa. In all, questions relating to the obligations of South Africa under the Mandate came before the ICJ on six different occasions.[124] These

---

[122] Nauru would later bring an action against Australia before the International Court of Justice alleging *inter alia* a breach of this fiduciary duty. The case was settled by a 'Compact Settlement' between the two countries on 10 August 1993. See Application Instituting Proceedings (Nauru v. Australia), at 14 (19 May 1989); Memorial of Nauru (Nauru v. Austl.), 1990 ICJ Pleadings (1 Certain Phosphate Lands in Nauru) 89 (April 1990); see also Antony Anghie, ''The Heart of My Home': Colonialism, Environmental Damage, and the Nauru Case,' *Harvard International Law Journal*, 34, 445 (1993).

[123] International Fiduciary Duty, *supra* note 24.

[124] See International Status of South West Africa, Advisory Opinion, ICJ Reports 1950 (held that South Africa continued to have the international obligations stated in Article 22 of the Covenant of the League of Nations and the Mandate for South West Africa, including the obligation to transmit petitions from the inhabitants of the Territory); Voting Procedure on Questions relating to Reports and Petitions concerning the Territory of South West Africa, Advisory Opinion, ICJ Reports 1955 (held that Rule F of the rules of procedure prepared by the General Assembly *Ad hoc* Committee on South West Africa was compatible with the language of the Court's 1950 Advisory Opinion that 'the supervision to be exercised by the General Assembly should conform as far as possible to the procedure followed in this respect by the Council of the League of Nations.'); Admissibility of Hearings of Petitioners by the Committee on South West Africa, Advisory Opinion, ICJ Reports 1956 (held that 'provided that the General Assembly was satisfied that such a course was necessary for the maintenance of effective international supervision for the administration of the Mandated Territory …' the grant of oral hearings to petitioners who had already submitted written petitions to the Committee on South West Africa would be

occasions provided the Court an opportunity to make some general comments about the nature of the trustee's obligations. In the first of the South West Africa cases the Court was asked by the General Assembly of the United Nations for an advisory opinion on the general status of the Territory and on a series of other questions relating to South Africa's obligations to the mandated territory of South West Africa.[125] In its Advisory Opinion the Court stated:

> The Mandate was created, in the general interest of the inhabitants of the territory, and of humanity in general, as an international institution with an international object – a sacred trust of civilization … . The international rules regulating the Mandate constituted an international status for the Territory … .[126]

However, in a separate opinion, Sir Arnold McNair took pains to describe this new international institution:

> The Mandate System (and the corresponding principles of the International Trusteeship System) is a new institution – a new relationship between territory and its inhabitants on the one hand and the government which represents them internationally on the other – a new species of international government, which does not fit into the old conception of sovereignty and which is alien to it … . What matters in considering this new institution is … what are the rights and duties of the mandatory in regard to the area of territory being administered by it. The answer to that question depends on the international agreements creating the system and the rules of law which they attract. Its essence is that the mandatory acquires only a limited title to the territory entrusted to it, and that the measures of its powers is what is necessary for the purpose of carrying out the mandate. 'The mandatory's rights, like the trustee's, have their foundation in his obligations; they are "tools given to him in order to achieve the work assigned to him"; he has "all the tools necessary for such end, but only those."'[127]

---

consistent with the Court's 1950 Advisory Opinion); South West Africa, Preliminary Objections, Judgment, ICJ Reports 1962 (held that Article 7 of the Mandate which conferred jurisdiction on the Court as to disputes between the mandatory and another member of the League was a 'treaty or convention still in force within the meaning of Article 37 of the Statute of the Court' and therefore the Court had jurisdiction to adjudicate upon the merits of the dispute); South West Africa, Second Phase, Judgment, ICJ Reports 1966 (held that Ethiopia and Liberia 'cannot be considered to have established any legal right or interest appertaining to them in the subject-matter of the present claims, and that, accordingly, the Court must decline to give effect to them'); and Legal Consequences for States of the Continued Presence of South Africa in Namibia (South West Africa) notwithstanding Security Council Resolution 276 (1970), Advisory Opinion, ICJ Reports 1971 (held that the continued presence of South Africa in Namibia was illegal; members of the United Nations were under an obligation to recognize the illegality of South Africa's presence and the invalidity of its acts on behalf of Namibia and must refrain from any dealings with the Government of South Africa; and that it is incumbent upon non-UN Members to assist in any UN action on Namibia).

125 See International Status of South West Africa, Advisory Opinion, ICJ Reports 1950.

126 *Id.*, at 128, 132.

127 *Id.*, at 150 (Separate Opinion of Judge McNair).

Judge McNair then offered his view of Article 22 of the Covenant:

> Article 22 proclaimed 'the principle that the well–being and development of such peoples form a sacred trust of civilization and that securities for the performance of this trust should be embodied in the Covenant.' A large part of the civilized world concurred in opening a new chapter in the life of between fifteen and twenty millions of people, and this article was the instrument adopted to give effect to their desire. In my opinion, the new regime established in pursuance of this 'principle' has more than a purely contractual basis and the territories subjected to it are impressed with a special legal status, designed to last until modified in the manner indicated by Article 22 … .[128]

The last of the South West Africa Cases to come before the ICJ for an advisory opinion also afforded a chance for several of the judges to explore in separate opinions the legal basis for an international fiduciary duty emanating from the new trusteeship system.[129] The need for an advisory opinion has its genesis in a 1966 United Nations Resolution 2145 (XXI) adopted by the General Assembly terminating South Africa's mandate over what had now become known as Namibia. South Africa, however, ignored the will of the General Assembly and so in 1970 the Security Council reaffirmed Resolution 2145 (XXI) and declared, *inter alia*, 'that the continued presence of the South African authorities in Namibia is illegal and that consequently all acts taken by the Government of South Africa on behalf of or concerning Namibia after the termination of the Mandate are illegal and invalid.'[130] In the face of South Africa's continued flouting of this and other UN resolutions, the Security Council, on 29 July 1970, adopted a resolution submitting to the ICJ for an advisory opinion the following question: 'What are the legal consequences for States of the continued presence of South Africa in Namibia, notwithstanding Security Council resolution 276 (1970)?'[131]

The Legal Consequences case[132] provided a platform for several judges to pronounce on the nature of the mandate system and the fiduciary relation that it established. Sir Arnold McNair began his separate opinion by noting, as he had done in the 1950 Advisory Opinion,[133] that the international trusteeship was a new institution with origins in municipal law. This being the case, the Judge rhetorically asked: '[w]hat is the duty of an international tribunal when confronted with a new legal institution the object and terminology of which are reminiscent of the rules and institutions of private law? To what extent is it useful or necessary to examine what may at first sight appear to be relevant analogies in private law systems and draw help and inspiration from them?'[134] Noting that the law of nations 'has

---

[128] *Id.*, at 154-155.

[129] See Legal Consequences for States of the Continued Presence of South Africa in Namibia (South West Africa) notwithstanding Security Council Resolution 276 (1970), ICJ Reports 1971.

[130] SC Res. 276, UN Doc. S/RES/276 (1970), at 1.

[131] SC Res. 284, UN Doc. S/RES/284 (1970), at 2.

[132] See ICJ Reports 1971, *supra* note 129.

[133] See *supra* notes 127–128 and accompanying text.

[134] *Id.*, at 148 (Separate Opinion by Sir Arnold McNair).

recruited and continues to recruit many of its rules and institutions from private systems of law', Judge McNair responded to his own question with the suggestion that the duty of the ICJ in resolving this issue is 'to regard any features or terminology which are reminiscent of the rules and institutions of private law as an indication of policy and principles rather than as directly importing these rules and institutions.'[135] Directing his attention to the legal terms employed in Article 22 of the Covenant – trust, tutelage and mandate – Judge McNair argued that they 'cannot be taken literally as expressing the definite conceptions for which they stand in law.'[136] Rather, they are reflective of the 'spirit in which the advanced nation who is honoured with a mandate should administer the territory entrusted to its care and discharge its duties to the inhabitants of the territory, more especially towards the indigenous populations.'[137] In any event, so long as the legal principles appropriated from private law are reasonably applicable to the international trusteeship system, Judge McNair, echoing the words of Judge de Villiers, of the South African Supreme Court, believed 'they should loyally be applied.'[138]

Adopting the view of Professor Brierly that the Anglo-American private law trust institution, along with its corresponding French Civil Law *tutelle*, was the governing principle of the mandate system, Judge McNair agreed that it closely mimics the trust institution in several ways beginning with the 'vesting of property in trustees, and its management by them in order that the public or some class of the public may derive benefit or that some public purpose may be served', to the use of the trust to protect the weak and the dependent in situations of unequal division of power.[139] Judge McNair went on to identify three general principles which are common to both the mandate system and the trust institution and which threw light on the international trusteeship system. These are:

1 that the control of the trustee, *tuteur* or *curateur* over the property is limited in one way or another; he is not in the position of the normal complete owner, who can do what he likes with his own, because he is precluded from administering the property for his own personal benefit;
2 that the trustee, *tuteur* or *curateur* is under some kind of legal obligation, based on confidence and conscience, to carry out the trust or mission confided to him for the benefit of some other person or for some public purpose;
3 that any attempt by one of these persons to absorb the property entrusted to him into his own patrimony would be illegal and would be prevented by the law.[140]

Judge De Castro appeared to approve these principles:

---

[135] *Id.*

[136] *Id.*, at 151.

[137] *Id.*

[138] *Id.* quoting Rex v. Christian, S.A. Law Reports [1923], Appellate Div., 101, 121 (Separate Opinion by De Villiers, J.A.).

[139] ICJ Reports, *supra* note 129, at 149.

[140] *Id.*

> The task which the mandatory States have to perform 'on behalf' of the League is qualified as a 'mandatory' function and consists in the exercise of 'tutelage.' It is characterized, as the same terms imply in municipal law, by absence of self-interest.[141]

Judge McNair concludes his review of the private law institutions that are the bedrock of the international trusteeship system with the observation that in the future development of this new institution the 'law governing the trust is a source from which much can be derived.'[142]

National courts Much like the International Court of Justice, few cases have come before national courts on the question of the precise scope of the mandatory's obligations toward the mandated territory. However, the ones that did provided national courts in Australia, South Africa and the United States a unique opportunity to pronounce on the mandate and subsequent trusteeship system. The High Court of Australia, for example, was asked to address the mandate issue only indirectly. The few cases on the mandate that were decided by the High Court were more concerned with defining the constitutional status of the mandatory power, whether or not it enjoyed sovereignty and the extent to which the laws of the commonwealth applied *mutatis mutandi* in the mandated territories administered by Australia. This became a problem for Australia because the country had assumed responsibility for some of the so-called Class 'C' Mandate Territories:

> … which owing to the sparseness of their population or their small size, or their remoteness from the centers of civilization, or their geographical contiguity to the territory of the Mandatory, and other circumstances, can be best administered under the laws of the Mandatory as integral portions of its territory, subject to the safeguards above mentioned in the interests of the indigenous population.[143]

A central theme running through the Australian mandate cases was the extent to which the language of paragraph 6 of Article 22 incorporated (or annexed) the mandated territory in that of the mandatory or preserved the mandated territory from becoming part of the other's territorial property. While attempting to resolve this question in the framework of specific legal disputes, individual judges opined in *obiter dicta* on the rights and duties of the mandatory in light of its international

---

[141] *Id.*, at 208 (Separate Opinion by Judge F. De Castro).

[142] *Id.* But see the dissenting opinion of Judge Alvarez who took the view that South Africa received not just an ordinary mandate, but a *sacred trust of civilization*, which is quite another thing. The act that has been created is not a *fedie-commissum*, a trust or a contract deriving from any similar national or international institution. The ordinary Mandate is a contract mainly in the interests of the principal, regulated by the rules of civil law, whereas the mission under consideration is an honorific and disinterested charge for the benefit of certain populations. It is an international function regulated by principles that conform to its nature. It is impossible therefore to apply, even by analogy, the national rules applicable to the Mandate or the other institutions that I have mentioned. *Id.*, at 179–180 (Dissenting Opinion by Judge Alvarez).

[143] Covenant, Art. 22(6).

responsibility under the League Covenant. Such was the case in Ffrost v. Stevenson[144] which came before the High Court of Australia on appeal from the Supreme Court of New South Wales.

Ffrost a onetime resident in New Guinea, a mandated territory under Australian administration, was implicated in a killing. Having relocated to New South Wales, a warrant was issued by the New Guinea authorities for his arrest and extradition to the territory to answer a charge of manslaughter. A magistrate in New South Wales issued a provisional warrant commanding that Ffrost be apprehended and brought before him. Ffrost moved to quash the order and the case worked its way up to the High Court of Australia where the Court was asked to decide whether the mandated territory of New Guinea was a 'part of His Majesty's dominions' or was a 'place out of His Majesty's dominions in which His Majesty has jurisdiction.'[145] The full Court held that the mandated territory of New Guinea was a place out of His Majesty's dominions in which the Crown had jurisdiction. But in separate opinions several judges raised and confronted the issue of the nature of the relation between the mandated territory and the mandatory.

In his concurring opinion Chief Justice Latham viewed the mandatory as a kind of international trustee who received the mandated territory subject to the provisions of the mandate which carefully circumscribed the exercise of the governmental powers of the mandatory.[146] In a similar vein, Mr. Justice Evatt stressed the trusteeship nature of the mandatory's relationship with the mandated territory. He cautioned the courts of the mandatory power never to 'overlook the supreme significance of the international duties and obligations which such power has assumed … .'[147] Mr. Justice Evatt quoted with approval a publicist's warning that if the words 'a sacred trust for civilization are to be ignored then the mandatory system was a fraud from beginning to end, merely a new method of imposing imperialistic will upon subject people.'[148] He also appeared to share Brierly's view that the trust is the governing principle of the new institution of the mandate,[149] while stressing the fact that 'the status of the Mandated Territory of New Guinea [was] very special in character, partaking of the nature of a trust … .'[150]

South Africa's mandate over South West Africa also raised serious legal issues that had to be resolved by the South African courts. In Rex v. Christian,[151] the Supreme Court of South Africa, on appeal from the High Court of South West Africa, had to decide on a matter of high treason, whether or not an inhabitant of South West Africa, Jacobus Christian, could legally be charged with *crimen laesae majestatis* against the Government of the mandatory. The Supreme Court answered in the affirmative. The decision involved a consideration of the scope of Article 22

---

144 58 CLR 528 (HC of A 1937).
145 58 CLR at 533.
146 58 CLR at 552–553 (Latham, C.J.)
147 58 CLR at 579 (Evatt J.).
148 *Id.* quoting Lee, *The Mandate for Mesopotamia*, 17 (1921).
149 *Id.*, at 584.
150 *Id.*, at 608.
151 South African Law Reports [1924], Appellate Division, 101.

of the Covenant and the Judges of Appeal were uniformly of the opinion that the mandate system could be analogized to such private law institutions like the trust even though the municipal law terms were probably employed not in their strict legal sense.[152] In his separate opinion, the Honorable J. de Villiers, Judge of Appeal, stated:

> South-West Africa is transferred to the people of the Union not by way of absolute property, but in the same way as a trustee is in possession of the property of the *cestui que trust* or a guardian of the property of his ward. The former has the administration and control of the property, but the property has to be administered exclusively in the interests of the latter. The legal terms employed in Article 22 - trust, tutelage, mandate, cannot be taken literally as expressing the definite conceptions for which they stand in law. They are to be understood as indicating rather the spirit in which the advanced nation who is honoured with a mandate should administer the territory entrusted to its care and discharge its duties to the inhabitants of the territory, more especially towards the indigenous populations. In how far the legal principles of these analogous municipal institutions should be applied in these international relations I shall not take upon myself to pronounce. But I may be permitted to say that in my opinion the use of the term shows that in so far as those legal principles are reasonably applicable to these novel institutions, they should loyally be applied.[153]

The rights and duties arising under the United Nations trusteeship system, the successor to the mandate system, have also been addressed by United States courts. In the case of People of Saipan v. United States Dep't of Interior,[154] the Ninth Circuit ruled that trusteeship agreements give rise to substantive rights and duties. Plaintiffs in Saipan, citizens of the Trust Territory of the Pacific Islands (known also as Micronesia), sued the US Department of Interior over a decision concerning land development. The Trust Territory government and the High Commissioner had approved and executed a lease agreement for construction of a hotel by a private developer on public land adjacent to an important historical, cultural, and recreational site for the people of the islands.[155] Plaintiffs argued that the action of the High Commissioner and the Trust Territory government in leasing public land against the expressed opposition of the elected representatives of the people of Saipan was a violation of their duties under the Trusteeship Agreement.[156] At issue was whether the Trusteeship Agreement created for the citizens of the Trust Territory any substantive rights that are judicially enforceable. The court ruled that it did:

> The preponderance of features in this Trusteeship Agreement suggests the intention to establish direct, affirmative, and judicially enforceable rights. The issue involves the

---

152 *Id.*, at 122 (Innes, C.J.).

153 Rex v. Christian, South African Law Reports [1924], Appellate Division, 101, 121 (De Villiers, J.A.).

154 502 F.2d. 90 (9th Cir. 1974), *cert. denied* 420 US 1003 (1975).

155 *Id.*, at 93–94.

156 *Id.*, at 96.

> local economy and environment, not security; the concern with natural resources and the concern with political development are explicit in the agreement and are general international concerns as well; the enforcement of these rights requires little legal or administrative innovation in the domestic fora; and the alternative forum, the Security Council, would present to the plaintiffs obstacles so great as to make their rights virtually unenforceable.[157]

Noting that the substantive rights guaranteed through the Trusteeship Agreement are not 'precisely defined,'[158] the court would go on to say that: '[h]owever, we do not believe that the agreement is too vague for judicial enforcement. Its language is no more general than such terms as 'due process,' 'seaworthiness,' 'equal protection of the law,' 'good faith,' or 'restraint of trade,' which courts interpret every day.'[159]

The origins of an international fiduciary duty and its link to private law institutions were thoroughly examined by jurists during the League of Nations period. In the view of the leading jurists the League mandate system, and by extension, the successor United Nations trusteeship system, contemplated a fiduciary relation between the mandatory and the mandated territories and its peoples. The regime of report, accountability, supervision and modification imposed on the mandatory clearly drew its inspiration from several private law institutions. These private law institutions were analogized to the new international institution in much the same way that we intend to analogize them to the fiduciary relation between national leaders and their citizens.

The jurisprudence of national and international tribunals and the writings of jurists appear to support the view that a fiduciary relation exists between national leaders and the citizens over whom they lead. The concept of an 'international trusteeship' established by the International Trusteeship System and which replaced the mandate system of the League of Nations was intended by the community of nations to call its more economically advanced members to a higher standard of care with regard to its administration of a non-self-governing territory.[160] At the most basic level 'this duty of care demands that the trustee act in a way *calculated to best serve the long term (sic) political, social, and economic interests of the indigenous people*, and to ensure that they are left with a reasonably developed nation and productive environment when the territory moves to full sovereignty' [emphasis added].[161] This argument rings true even in situations where indigenous leaders 'govern' territory 'owned' by indigenous people.[162] The principle is that in every nation, the leadership owes a duty to its citizens to protect

---

157 Saipan, 502 F.2d at 96–97.

158 *Id.*, at 99.

159 *Id.*

160 See International Fiduciary Duty, *supra* note 24, at 397.

161 *Id.*

162 *Id.* (applying the theory to Australian Government mining activities of lands owned by the Republic of Nauru which Australia administered under the UN and International Trusteeship System).

their political, social, and economic interests. This after all is the self-proclaimed goal of the United Nations, that is, to uphold such fundamental rights and freedoms.[163]

BASES FOR IMPOSING FIDUCIARY OBLIGATIONS ON PUBLIC OFFICIALS

A fiduciary relationship between office holders and the public they serve can arise in two ways. First, when a public official undertakes to exercise his constitutional powers to advance, promote, protect and defend the interests of the public at large. This relationship will be called the 'voluntary assumption' theory of public officials as fiduciaries. A fiduciary relationship between public officials and the public can also emerge out of a context where the latter entrusts the former with the responsibility of advancing and protecting its interests and well-being. I shall call this the 'entrusting' theory of the public official as a fiduciary. Under both theories, the public official in taking up a public appointment – whether voluntarily or by having it thrust upon him – undertakes or accepts a 'trust.' And as Sealy reminds us, a fiduciary relationship does not have to resemble a trust on all fours. All that is expected of it is that it approaches 'those situations which are in some respects trustlike but are not, strictly speaking trusts.'[164] As long as it conforms to a relationship 'in respect of which if a wrong arise, the same remedy exists against the wrongdoer on behalf of the principal as would against a trustee on behalf of the *cestui que trust*,'[165] then a fiduciary relation meets the trustlike characteristics requirements.

The Entrusting Theory

The entrusting theory of fiduciary obligation in its traditional formulation applies to relationships in which the fiduciary's role is that of a property-holder who holds and manages property 'entrusted' to him by, and on behalf of, the beneficiary.[166] In the context of the office holder, the entrusting theory is applicable in two ways. In the first, the Constitution of the state 'entrusts' certain defined responsibilities or undertakings to the office holder, from the head of state down to the lowly sanitation worker, to be performed on behalf of the public. In accepting this 'entrustment' the public official subjects himself to fiduciary constraints. Secondly, the entire corpus of the nation's wealth and natural resources are, under the public trust doctrine, entrusted to public officials to hold and manage on behalf of the people, the beneficiaries.

---

[163] Articles 1(3), 55, and 56 of the Charter of the United Nations; See also UN Center for Human Rights, *Human Rights: Status of International Instruments* (1985).

[164] See L.S. Sealy, 'Fiduciary Relations,' *Cambridge Law Journal* (1962) 69, 72.

[165] See Re West of England and South Wales District bank, ex p. Dale & Co. (1879) 11 Ch.D. 772, 778 quoted in Sealy, *supra* note 164, at 72.

[166] DeMott, *supra* note 5.

Constitutional Grant of Powers

The Constitutions of most States define in very clear and unambiguous language the duties of constitutionally-responsible rulers. For example, Article 5 of the Constitution of the Republic of Cameroon provides in its first paragraph that 'The President of the Republic ... shall ensure respect for the Constitution and the unity of the State, and shall be responsible for the conduct of the affairs of the Republic.' Paragraph 2 of the same article entrusts him with the task of 'defin[ing] the policy of the Nation.' To carry out these entrusted duties, the Constitution confers on him broad and extensive powers.[167] So extensive is this grant of constitutional powers that it allows the head of state to invade the other branches of government as well when carrying out his constitutional duties.[168] Among the broad powers enjoyed by

[167] See for example The Sierra Leone Constitution defines the powers of the President by stating that 'Notwithstanding any provisions of this Constitution or any other law to the contrary, the President shall, without prejudice to any such law as may for the time being be adopted by Parliament, be responsible, in addition to the functions conferred upon him in the Constitution, for-' then follows a list of enumerated responsibilities. *The Constitution of Sierra Leone*, 1991, section 40 (4); Under Article 4 of the Constitution of the Central African Republic (CAR) ('The President of the Republic is the Chief of State. He incarnates the unity of the Nation and watches over the continuity of the State and the integrity of its territory. He is the guardian of the institutions adopted by the people. He conducts the policies of the Nation, negotiates and ratifies treaties, promulgates the laws, exercises regulatory power, acts as commander in chief of the armies of the Nation, presides over the Superior Council of National Defense and appoints civil and military personnel. He accredits ambassadors abroad; ambassadors of foreign powers are accredited to him …') These powers must have convinced a former head of state, Jean-Bedel Bokassa, of CAR of his invincibility. In the late 1970s he made world headlines when he had CAR re-baptized the Central African Empire and declared himself the new Emperor, spending an estimated $22-$30 million – nearly 1/4 of the country's annual income – for his coronation in December 1976. Overthrown by a military coup three years later, Bokassa fled to Cote d'Ivoire where he was granted political asylum. The following year a court in Bangui tried him *in absentia* on charges of mass murder and embezzlement of $70 million of public funds. He was found guilty, sentenced to death, his property and assets forfeited to the State and an international warrant for his arrest issued by the Government of David Dacko. He returned voluntarily to CAR in October 1986. During his years in power, 'Emperor' Bokassa was very generous with CAR's wealth and natural resources: he bestowed a gift of 100 diamonds to President Giscard d'Estaing's wife, Anne Aymone, and for the President a gift of a hunting ground of nearly 1.4 million acres! See 'Bokassa Is Sentenced to Death in Absentia,' *New York Times*, 25 December 1980, p. 6, col. Al; Ronald Koven, 'French President Lines Up Forces to Dissipate the Scent of Scandal,' *The Washington Post*, 10 December 1980, pp. A23, A25, col, 1.

[168] For instance, Article 27 provides that 'matters not reserved for the legislature shall come under the jurisdiction of the authority empowered [President pursuant to Article 8(5)] to issue statutory rules and orders.' *Constitution of Cameroon*, Art. 27.

the Cameroon head of state are the powers of appointment,[169] to initiate laws jointly with the legislature,[170] make treaties[171] and rule by decree.[172]

With such extensive powers at their disposal the question naturally arises with respect to how these constitutionally responsible rulers can be made accountable to the people whom they ostensibly serve. The military junta in Nigeria must have wrestled with this question – the role of government and the personnel that run it, the expectations citizens have of their public holders, and the framework for holding them accountable to the people by whom they are elected or appointed to serve – when it seized power in 1984. As part of a national campaign to stamp out official corruption, the Federal Military Government headed by General Badamosi Babangida arrested and detained then investigated and punished many prominent office holders in previous civilian and military administrations under the State Security (Detention of Persons) Decree and the Recovery of Public Property (Special Military Tribunals) Decree.[173] In justifying why these measures were necessary, the Government explained that 'Public Office holding is a public trust' and:

> If anyone, elected or appointed into public office, corruptly enriches himself either by misappropriating public funds, receiving kickbacks and through such other abuse of office that public office holder must be compelled to disgorge such ill-gotten wealth … In addition, he must be disqualified from holding public office … firstly, to ensure that he does not have another opportunity for such mis-conduct and secondly, to serve as an object lesson to others who might be tempted in like manner.[174]

---

[169] Article 10(1) provides that 'the President of the Republic shall appoint the Prime Minister and, on the proposal of the latter, the other members of government. He shall define their duties … [and] terminate their appointment;' Articles 8(4) and 8(10), the President is empowered to '[a]ccredit ambassadors and envoys extraordinary to foreign powers' and '[a]ppoint to civil and military posts.'

[170] See *Constitution of Cameroon*, Art. 8(5) ['enact laws']. Article 36(1) authorizes the President of the Republic to go over the head of the National Assembly and 'submit to a referendum any reform bill which, *although normally reserved for the legislature*, could have profound repercussions on the future of the Nation and the national institutions' (emphasis supplied).

[171] Under Article 43 the President is empowered to '[n]egotiate and ratify agreements and treaties … .'

[172] *Constitution of Cameroon*, Art. 28(1) [subject to certain exceptions 'the National Assembly may empower the President of the Republic to legislate by way of Ordinance for a limited period and for given purposes.']; *see also* Article 11 of the National Charter of the Republic of Chad ('The President of the Republic has the power to make laws through Ordinances and to regulate by Decrees taken before the Council of Ministers.')

[173] See The Recovery of Public Property (Special Military Tribunals) Decree No. 3, 1984 (1986), para. 3(c) in *XXI Laws of the Federation of Nigeria (Revised)* ch. 389 (1990).

[174] See Federal Republic of Nigeria, Views and Decisions of the Federal Military Government on the Report and Recommendations of Justice Uwaifo Special Panel for the Investigation of Cases of Persons Conditionally Released from Detention and Persons Still in Detention Under the State Security (Detention of Persons) Decree no. 2, 1984 and the

The Nigerian government was expressing a view about the proper relationship between leaders and followers. While this position may have been revolutionary in the Nigerian context, it has an old and distinguished pedigree in political thought. The notion of public office holders as servants of the people and that government owes its citizens special duties of care or stewardship, is at the heart of democratic governance. They exercise this stewardship in their management of the resources of the State for the exclusive benefit of its citizens.

Public Trust Doctrine

Citizens have an indefeasible public interest in their national wealth and resources placed under the guardianship of their government. This is precisely what the Nigerian military junta had in mind though it was apparently restating an old and venerable doctrine – the public trust doctrine – in a different context. The doctrine has been around for so long[175] and is considered so fundamental that it is entrenched in the Constitutions of some countries.[176] It provides a context within which one can construct a framework for holding the guardians of the peoples' wealth accountable for their stewardship.

Basic to the public trust doctrine is the deceptively simple idea that the state owes its citizens special duties of care, or stewardship with respect to certain 'common property' public resources which comprise the wealth of the nation. These resources the state holds in trust for the public. The state must therefore act as a fiduciary in its management of the resources which constitute the corpus of this trust.[177] The beneficiaries of the trust are the citizens of the state, present and

---

Recovery of Public Property (Special Military Tribunals) Decree no. 3, 1984 (1986), para. 3(c) in *XXI Laws of the Federation of Nigeria (Revised)* ch. 389 (1990).

[175] The historical antecedents of the public trust doctrine have been traced back to the Roman empire. See Gregory F. Cook, 'The Public Trust Doctrine in Alaska,' *Journal of Environmental Law and Litigation*, 8, 2, 3 (1993) (hereinafter 'The Public Trust Doctrine').

[176] For instance, Article XII, Sec. 2 of the Constitution of the Philippines entrenches the public trust doctrine ('All agricultural, timber, and mineral lands of the public domain, waters, minerals, coal, petroleum, and other mineral oils, all forces of potential energy, and other natural resources of the Philippines belong to the State, and their disposition, exploitation, development, or utilization shall be limited to citizens of the Philippines …); see also *Political Constitution of Peru*, Art. 118; and *Constitution of the United States of Mexico*, Art. 27.

[177] Under the common law the trust is a device that allows a person known as a trustee to hold a property interest subject to a fiduciary duty to use the rights, privileges, powers and immunities which constitute the interest for the benefit of the beneficiary, be it a person or charity or a definite non-charitable purpose. *See* Restatement of Trusts 2d s. 3 comment d, s. 103 comment a, s. 113 comment b, s. 124 comment b, s. 396 comment a. The subject matter of the trustee's property interest is wide and diverse and may consist of land, buildings, tangible chattels, money, or intangibles (such as corporate shares, bonds, promissory notes, contract rights and undocumented choses in action), or any combination of these. *Id.* s. 74 comment b, s. 78 comment a, s. 82 comment b.

future generations. In the United States where this doctrine has held sway for at least a century,[178] it has been held to include *inter alia*: protection of navigational and commercial fishing rights over tidelands;[179] recreational fishing, boating, swimming, water skiing, and other related purposes;[180] protection of the public's right to hunt;[181] protection of fish and wildlife habitat;[182] recreational access to the ocean;[183] subathing, swimming, other shore activities, and access to and use of shorelands and upland dry sand beaches;[184] enjoyment of scenic beauty;[185] conservation of fishery resources;[186] conservation of wildlife resources;[187] waters and minerals;[188] and existing and future recreational uses.[189]

This list does not, however, exhaust the range of subjects that can be included among 'common property' public resources. Indeed, the public trust doctrine is adaptable and has been adapted to changing circumstances.[190] It applies not only to

---

[178] See 'The Public Trust Doctrine,' *supra* note 175, at 4.

[179] See Martin v. Waddell's Lessee, 41 US (16 Pet.) 367, 410 (1842).

[180] See Wilbour v. Gallagher, 462 P.2d 232 (Wash. 1969), cert. *denied*, 400 US 878 (1970); see also Act of 3 June 1985, ch. 82, s. 1(c), 1985 Alaska Temporary & Special Acts 30.

[181] See Bell v. Town of Wells, 557 A.2d 168 (Me. 1989); Opinion of Justices to Senate, 424 N.E.2d 1092 (Mass. 1981); Delmarva Power & Light Co. v. Eberhard, 230 A.2d 644 (Md. 1967); Hartford v. Gilmanton, 146 A.2d 851 (NH 1958); Swan Island Club Inc. v. White, 114 F.Supp. 95 (EDNC 1953), *aff'd sub nom*. Swan Island Club, Inc. v. Yarborough, 209 F.2d 698 (4th Cir. 1954).

[182] See Kootenai Envtl. Alliance, Inc. v. Panhandle Yacht Club, Inc., 671 P.2d 1085 (Idaho 1983); People of Smithtown v. Poveromo, 336 N.Y.S. 2d 764 (N.Y. Dist. Ct. 1972), *rev'd on other grounds*, 359 N.Y.S. 2d (N.Y. 1973); Just v. Marinette County, 201 N.W.2d 761 (Wis. 1972).

[183] See County of Haw. v. Sotomura, 517 P.2d 57 (Haw. 1973), *cert. denied*, 419 US 872 (1974).

[184] See Matthews v. Bay Head Improvement Ass'n, 471 A.2d 355, 365 (N.J.), *cert. denied*, 469 US 821 (1984).

[185] See City of Madison v. State, 83 N.W. 2d 674, 678 (Wis. 1957); Obrecht v. Nat'l Gypsum Co., 105 N.W. 2d 143, 149–51 (Mich. 1960).

[186] See Gilbert v. State Dep't of Fish & Game, Bd. of Fisheries, 803 P.2d 391, 398–99 (Alaska 1990); McDowell v. State, 785 P.2d 1, 12–18 (Alaska 1989); Owsichek v. State, Guide Licensing & Control Bd., 763 P.2d 488, 492–96 (Alaska 1988); Nathanson v. State, 554 P.2d 456, 458 n. 9 (Alaska 1976); Metlakatla Indian Community, Annette Island Reserve v. Egan, 362 P.2d 901 (Alaska 1961), *aff'd*, 369 US 45 (1962).

[187] See Herscher v. State, Dep't of Commerce, 568 P.2d 996, 1005 (Alaska 1977); Owsichek, 763 P.2d at 492–96; McDowell, 785 P.2d at 12–18; Gilbert, 803 P.2d at 398–399; Matthews, 471 A.2d at 361.

[188] See Herscher, 568 P.2d, at 1003.

[189] See 1985 Alaska Sess. Laws 82 s. 1(c).

[190] See Waarwick v. State, 548 P.2d 384, 391 (Alaska 1976) (Noting that public trust doctrine is 'not to be "fixed or static" but one to "be molded and extended to meet changing conditions and needs of the public it was created to benefit"').

unique and irreplaceable resources but to scarce resources that are replaceable though at tremendous cost. Thus the 'wealth' referred to in the various international covenants even if viewed as meaning all the property in existence at any given time which has money or an exchange value or economic utility would be included in an expanded list of 'common property' public resources governed by the public trust doctrine.

The notion of the fiduciary as a property-holder which is so central to the traditional formulation of the entrustment theory can be analogized to the public trust doctrine. First, that the wealth and natural resources of the nation constitutes 'common property' public resources representing the entire wealth of the nation. Second, that this wealth is held in constructive trust for the people by their constitutionally elected and appointed rulers. Third, that these public officials *in their role as* trustees are expected to act not as proprietors in their private capacity, but as the representatives and for the benefit of all the people in common. Finally, their stewardship must therefore be judged by fiduciary doctrine standards.

Voluntary Assumption Theory of Fiduciary Obligation

A Conscious and Voluntary Choice to Seek Public Office

When an individual runs for an elective office and eventually gets elected he by that action voluntarily assumes to discharge the duties of that public office. By the same token, when an individual applies to be considered for an appointive office and then accepts the position he also voluntarily assumes to carry out the functions of his office. Getting elected or appointed to a public office and agreeing to serve, the officeholder commits himself to act in the best interests and wellbeing of the public. This is particularly so since in both cases resignation is always a viable option for one who has a change of heart and feels he will not be able to fulfill the obligations of the office. Failing to exercise this option 'imposition of [a] fiduciary obligation is ... justified' because these public officials *qua* fiduciaries themselves 'undertook' to put themselves in positions that import such an obligation.[191] They chose to enter a fiduciary relation and cannot escape the legal duty such a choice carries.

Oath of Office

The justification for imposing a fiduciary obligation on a public official is based on his breach of a voluntarily assumed duty to act in the best interests of the general public. An important indicia of this voluntary assumption is in the oath taken before entering into public office. The taking of an oath constitutes an undertaking by the public official to place himself in a position that imparts a fiduciary obligation to the public he serves. Many national Constitutions require key office

---

[191] DeMott, *supra* note 5, at 910.

holders, elected or appointed, to take an oath[192] while others, in addition to the oath required of office holders to declare their assets[193] and pledge to abide by some code of ethics before taking office. The Constitution of the Federal Republic of Nigeria requires all elected officials beginning with the President[194] and including elected members of national[195] and state[196] legislatures as well as certain appointed holders of public office to take an oath, declare their assets and pledge to abide by a national Code of Conduct. The oath prescribed for the President is fairly typical and states:

> I, …, do solemnly swear/affirm that I will be faithful and bear true allegiance to the Federal Republic of Nigeria; that as President … I will discharge my duties to the best of my ability, faithfully and in accordance with the Constitution … and the law, and always in the interest of the sovereignty, integrity, solidarity, well-being and prosperity of … Nigeria; that I will strive to preserve the Fundamental Objectives and Directive Principles of State Policy contained in the Constitution … ; that I will not allow my personal interest to influence my official conduct or my official decisions; that I will to the best of my ability preserve, protect and defend the Constitution …; that I will abide by the Code of Conduct contained in the Fifth Schedule to the Constitution …; that in all circumstances, I will do right to all manner of people, according to law, without fear or favour, affection or ill-will; that I will not directly or indirectly communicate or reveal to any person any matter which shall be brought under my consideration or shall become known to me as President … except as may be required for the due discharge of my duties as President; and that I will devote myself to the service and well-being of the people of Nigeria.
>
> So help me God.

It is worth emphasizing the duties that an individual who seeks and is elected to the

---

[192] For example, Article 28 of the Constitution of Niger provides that before entering into office, the President of the Republic takes an oath before the 'Assemblée Nationale', in the following terms:

> I solemnly swear, before the people, to respect and to have the 'Charte Nationale', the Constitution and the Republic's laws respected; to respect and defend the State's republican system; to preserve territorial integrity and national unity; to protect the citizens' rights and liberties, to work without respite for the peoples' happiness; to work with all my strength to the realization of the ideals of peace, justice, freedom in the world. The 'Assemblee Nationale' is my witness.

See also *The Constitution of Sierra Leone*, 1991, section 46 (4), Second and Third Schedules.

[193] *See for example Political Constitution of Peru*, Art. 62 ('Officials and public servants who adjudicate the law or administer or handle funds of the State … must make a sworn declaration of their assets and income on taking office and on relinquishing their positions and periodically during their holding of same.').

[194] Constitution of Nigeria, Art. 137(1).

[195] *Id.*, Art. 50(1).

[196] *Id.*, Art. 92(1).

Presidency of Nigeria voluntarily undertakes to perform: (1) to devote himself to the service, well-being and prosperity of the people of Nigeria; (2) to preserve the Fundamental Objectives and Directive Principles of State Policy;[197] (3) to separate his personal interest from his presidential and to ensure that the former does not influence his official conduct or his official decisions; and finally, a pledge that these 'undertakings' will be carried out faithfully, with due diligence and to the best of his ability within the constraints of the Code of Conduct.

This Code to which all office-holders, from the level of local government councilors to the President himself, are expected to abide by contains the usual elements found in the prototypical fiduciary relationship. The Code begins with a clear prohibition against conflict of interest: '[a] public officer shall not put himself in a position where his personal interest conflicts with his duties and responsibilities,'[198] nor shall he 'engage or participate in the management or running of any private business, profession or trade … .'[199] This is consistent with the requirement under the common law of trusts that a trustee strictly separate trust property from his own property, and refrain from putting himself in a position where his personal interest may conflict with the interest of the beneficiary.[200] In an effort to eliminate the problem of commingling of assets, the Code identifies certain kinds of property transactions in which public servants are barred from participating. Public officials who come under the strictures of the ethics code are proscribed during their tenure of office to 'acquire or take any property of the State in which they exercise jurisdiction, sell such property or exchange it with any property belonging to them.'[201] Teeth to this prohibition is found in the requirement that office holders must declare in writing all their properties, assets and liabilities and those of their spouses and unmarried children under the age of

[197] Chapter 2 of the Nigerian Constitution contains the Fundamental Objectives and Directive Principles of State Policy which comprise 10 separate articles. Among the fundamental objectives that high-ranking public officials are pledged to promote and which are directly linked to the problem of indigenous spoliation are: the security and welfare of the Nigerian people [Art. 15(2)(b)]; the management and control of the national economy to ensure the maximum welfare, freedom and happiness of every citizen on the basis of social justice, equality of status and opportunity [Art. 17(1)(b)]; ensuring that the material resources of the commonwealth are harnessed and distributed in a manner that serves the common good of all Nigerians [Art. 17(2)(b)]; preventing the exploitation of Nigeria's human and natural resources for any reasons other than for the good of the community [Art. 18(2)(c)]; and the eradication of all corrupt practices and abuse of power [Art. 16(5)]. Finally, consistent with the belief that citizens have a responsibility to ensure that their national resources are not frittered away by a profligate leadership, the Constitution charges them with the duty of protecting and preserving public property, and to fight against misappropriation and squandering of public funds [Art. 24(b)].

[198] Code of Conduct, Fifth Schedule, Constitution of Nigeria, Sec. 1.

[199] *Id.*, Sec. 2 (b).

[200] See Corley v. Hecht Co., 530 F.Supp. 1155 (DCDC 1982).

[201] Code of Conduct, *supra* note 198, at Sec. 4.

18 years.[202] The declaration must be made immediately after taking office, quadrennially[203] and at the end of the office holder's term of office.[204] Any property or assets acquired after any of these written declarations and which cannot be fairly linked to income, gift or loan approved under the Code is presumptively treated as a breach of the Code of Conduct. False declarations are also a violation under the Code.

Under the Code loans and receipt of certain kinds of benefits are prohibited. Top ranking state officials may not accept 'a loan, except from government or its agencies, a bank, building society or other financial institution recognised by law,'[205] and 'any benefit of whatever nature from any company, contractor, or businessman, or nominee or agent of such person.'[206] Consistent with the notion that public office holding is a public trust voluntarily undertaken, the Code frowns on the public offering of bribes to office holders in exchange for their service. The Code peremptorily pronounces that '[n]o person shall offer a public officer any property, gifts or benefits of any kind as inducement or bribe for the granting of any favour or the discharge in his favour of the public officer's duties.'[207]

Fraudulently acquired State funds accounts for the extravagant lifestyles of public officials[208] and much of the capital flight that countries like Nigeria have experienced. The Code, therefore, admonishes all who fall under its proscriptions not to 'live above [their] legitimate income.'[209] In addition, and as part of a national desire to halt the illegal export of Nigerian capital, the Code prohibits the maintenance or operation of overseas bank accounts.[210]

All fiduciary relations inevitably give rise to the problem of abuse of power,[211] a fact recognized by the Nigerian Code which provides that '[a] public officer shall not do or direct to be done in abuse of his office any arbitrary act prejudicial to the rights of any other person knowing that such act is unlawful or contrary to any state policy or public morality.'[212]

The oath of office constitutionally required of top public officials in many States as well as the requirement in others to abide by some code of ethics taken

---

202 *Id.*, §12 (b).

203 *Id.*, §12 (a).

204 *Id.*, §12 (b).

205 *Id.*, §8 (a).

206 *Id.*, §8 (b).

207 *Id.*, §9.

208 See *infra* notes 220–232 and accompanying text.

209 Code of Conduct, *infra* note 198, Sec. 2 (c); see also Article XI, Sec. 1 of the Constitution of the Philippines ('Public office is a public trust, Public officers and employees must at all times be accountable to the people, serve them with utmost responsibility, integrity, loyalty, and efficiency, act with patriotism and justice and *lead modest lives*').

210 *Id.*. §3 Fifth Schedule.

211 See Frankel, *supra* note 6, at 807.

212 *Id.*, Sec. 10; see also Art. 16(5) of the Nigerian Constitution ('The State shall eradicate all corrupt practices and abuse of power.').

together suggest unmistakably a recognition of the fiduciary relation between office holders and the general public. Three things are discernible in these kinds of documents. First, the commitment, on the part of the office holder (fiduciary), to perform certain duties on behalf of the public (beneficiaries). This is followed by the delegation of constitutional powers or authority necessary for the office holder to carry out his duties. Finally, an expectation that the delegated powers will used by the office holder solely for the purpose of facilitating the performance of his constitutional functions.

The Fiduciary Relationship in Perspective

What is a fiduciary relationship in the context of public office holding? What duties a public official owe the general public? The general law of trusts to which this new fiduciary relation is analogized defines a fiduciary relationship as:

> [o]ne founded on trust or confidence reposed by one person in the integrity and fidelity of another. Such relationship arises whenever confidence is reposed on one side, and domination and influence result on the other .... Out of such a relation, the law raises the rule that neither party may exert influence or pressure upon the other, take selfish advantage of his trust, or deal with the subject-matter of the trust in such a way as to benefit himself or prejudice the other except in the exercise of the utmost good faith and with the full knowledge and consent of that other . . . .[213]

Among the many duties[214] a trustee owes to the beneficiaries of the trust are: duty of loyalty, that is, the duty not to engage in self-dealing; and a duty to preserve trust property.

The Duty of Loyalty

A trustee is under a duty to the beneficiary 'to administer the trust solely in the interest of the beneficiary.'[215] The fiduciary relationship between trustee and beneficiary imposes some limitations on the extent to which the former may personally benefit from the trust that he administers. When a trustee administers the trust in a manner that advances his personal interests at the expense of the beneficiary, he is in breach of his duty of fidelity.

The Duty to Preserve the Trust Property

In addition to the duty of loyalty, the trustee is also under a duty to the beneficiary

---

213 *Black's Law Dictionary*, 626 (6th ed. 1990).

214 Other duties owed the beneficiary of a trust include: a duty not to delegate; a duty to furnish information; a duty to deal impartially with beneficiaries; a duty to enforce the claims of beneficiaries; and a duty to make trust property productive.

215 *Restatement (Second) of Trusts* §170(1) (1959).

to 'use reasonable care and skill to preserve the trust property.'[216] Thus a certain obligation is placed upon each generation of political leadership to not only conserve the quality and quantity of the nation's wealth for future generations but to ensure access to this wealth on an equitable basis to all the members of the present generation. Implicit in this trust is the expectation that the political leadership in discharging its duty to present and future generations will not, even when tempted, divert the national wealth they hold in trust for their citizens, for their personal use. By the same token, it is also assumed that there will be some limits on the extent to which citizens can consume the fruits of their legacy.

Application of Fiduciary Duties in Spoliation Situations

Examples will be presented to show how public officials have breached their fiduciary duties through spoliation activities. The examples come from the findings of fact made by properly constituted commissions of inquiry appointed to investigate two former Presidents of Sierra Leone (Siaka Stevens and Joseph Momoh)[217] and other high-ranking cabinet ministers who served under

---

[216] *Id.* §176 (1959).

[217] Shortly after overthrowing the civilian government of President Joseph Momoh in April 1992, the National Provisional Ruling Council (NRCP) set as one of its principal objectives eradicating corruption, mismanagement and indiscipline in the affairs of government. It followed through on its promise, when by Public Notice No. 172 in the Extraordinary issue of the Sierra Leone Gazette dated Wednesday, 13 June 1992, it instituted the Justice Beccles-Davies Commission of Inquiry:

(i) to examine the Assets and other related matters of all persons who were Presidents, Vice-Presidents, Ministers, Ministers of State and Deputy Ministers within the period from the 1st day of June, 1986, to the 22nd day of September, 1991, and to inquire into and investigate whether such Assets were acquired lawfully or unlawfully;

(ii) to inquire into and investigate the activities of all persons who were Presidents, Vice-Presidents, Ministers, Ministers of State and Deputy Ministers within the period from the 1st day of June, 1986, to the 22nd day of September, 1991, and to ascertain as to:

(a) whether they maintained a standard of living above that which was commensurate with their past official emoluments;

(b) whether they were in control of pecuniary resources or property disproportionate to their past official emoluments;

(c) whether allegations of corruption, dishonesty, or abuse of office for private benefit by them, or in collaboration with any person or persons in respect of such corruption, dishonesty or abuse of office are established;

(d) whether they acted wilfully or corruptly in such manner as to cause financial loss or damage to the Government, a Local Authority, Corporation, a Statutory Corporation, or the University of Sierra Leone;

(iii) to inquire into and investigate any person or matters as may from time to time be referred to the Commission by the National Provisional Ruling Council.

See Sierra Leone Government, *White Paper on the Report of the Justice Beccles Davies Commission of Inquiry into the Assets and Other Related Matters of all Persons who were Presidents, Vice-Presidents, Ministers, Ministers of State and Deputy Ministers Within the*

them.[218] The inquiries focused on their performance while in office, in particular how well they discharged their duties as guardians of the nation's wealth and resources. One of the difficulties with allegations of high level corruption is that of proof. Accusations are hurled against individuals, sometimes with reckless abandon, and amounts of their reputed wealth obtained through illegal means paraded without any evidence actually linking the accused to the acts or the amounts. As a result, the actual amounts of national wealth spoliated by many of these Third World leaders remain unverified. The commissions of inquiry appointed by various governments have helped immensely in sifting through facts and fiction to provide some hard data. These commissions have sat as courts of law; applied standard rules of evidence, and ensured that all accused had a right to be represented by counsel whether or not they chose to exercise their right.[219] Thus, the findings of fact made by these tribunals are entitled to the same respect traditionally accorded such conclusions when reached by courts of first instance in this and other legal systems.

Period from the 1st Day of June, 1986, to the 22nd Day of September, 1991, and to Inquire Into and Investigate Whether Such Assets were Acquired Lawfully or Unlawfully (1993).

[218] See Sierra Leone Government, *White Paper on the Report of the Mrs. Justice Laura Marcus-Jones Commission of Inquiry into the Assets, Activities and Other Related Matters of Public Officers, Members of the Board and Employees of Parastatals, Ex-ministers of State, Paramount Chiefs and on Contractors – within the Period 1st Day of June, 1986 to the 22nd Day of September, 1991* (1993). The terms of reference of the Marcus-Jones Commission were couched as follows:

i. One of the objectives of the NPRC Government on taking over the reins of Government included the eradication of corruption, mismanagement and indiscipline in the Public Service, as well as the recovery of all State assets and properties improperly obtained, in order to create an efficient and corrupt-free Service as a foundation of good governance in the Public Administration of Sierra Leone, which is a necessary prerequisite for the establishment of a sound democratic system. Consequently, the Government instituted Commissions of inquiry in order to identify culpable ex-ministers, public officers and businessmen, who were largely responsible for the worst excesses of corruption, dishonesty, negligence and abuse of office for private benefit, as a first step towards the achievement of its desired objective.

[219] The Jiagge Commission made it clear that:

With regard to procedure generally, we tried as much as possible to stay close to the standards that are acceptable in a Court of Law. We sought corroboration in cases where allegations emanated from people who may with justification be regarded as accomplices. Persons against whom allegations were made, were invited as witnesses of the Commission to listen to, cross-examine either in person or by Counsel and state their case if they so desired.

See Republic of Ghana, *Report of the Ghana Jiagge Commission* (1967), para. 2. The Jiagge Commission like the over 70 other Commissions of Inquiry that were appointed to probe high level official corruption in Ghana were all appointed under the provisions of the Commissions of Enquiry Act, 1964 (Act 250), NLC Decree No. 72 dated 18 August 1966 and as amended by NLC Decrees Nos. 101 dated 1 November 1966 and 129 dated 24 January 1967.

The Stewardship of Siaka Stevens

The stewardship of Siaka Stevens and Joseph Momoh, two former Presidents of Sierra Leone was meticulously dissected by the Justice Marcus-Beccles Commission. The Commission found that in the discharge of their high office as guardian of the nation's wealth and resources, Stevens and Momoh put their personal interests above those of the people of Sierra Leone and failed to exercise the care and skill necessary to preserve the common public property of all Sierra Leoneans. In the case of Siaka Stevens, the Commission found that during his tenure of office (first as Prime Minister, 1968–80, then as President, 1980–88), his total income from the state was Le271,975.[220] Yet during this period Mr. Stevens was able to acquire an extensive portfolio of real estate holdings consisting of 16 houses including Kabassa Lodge which was valued at $5,850,000.[221] Findings of fact were made that Mr. Stevens 'applied undue pressure in acquiring certain real estate holdings,[222] and in some cases paid no consideration. He arranged to have furniture supplied to his Rest House by a State-owned company for free.[223] Finally, Mr. Stevens was found to have held shares in several local companies and cash deposits in several local and overseas banks.

The Stewardship of Joseph Momoh

In the case of Joseph Momoh, who was President from November 1985 to April 1992, the evidence adduced by the Commission paint a picture of a head of state who in the relatively short period he was in office became a millionaire several times over. He acquired during this seven year period a 'sizeable collection of real properties,[224] including homes, farms, a fleet of 23 expensive vehicles of various makes and descriptions, Le12,950,000 in Treasury Bills, cash deposits in various banks in Sierra Leone totalling Le45,613,870.22, cash deposits in various banks abroad totalling £128,478.73 and US$30,000, 110,000 shares in a local insurance company, and much more.[225] Of his many homes, one was valued by the Commission at Le383,218,180.[226] Gen. Momoh was able to make these acquisitions out of a 'total income in the form of emoluments and Overseas Travelling Allowances paid to him whilst in office ... [of] Le1,056,000 and Lel41,612,440 respectively.'[227] In addition to his income from the state, the former President succeeded in prying loose grants totalling Le25,150,000 from the National Aid Coordinating Secretariat for the execution of his farming projects![228]

220 White Paper, para. 8.
221 *Id.*
222 *Id.*, para. 4.
223 *Id.*, para. 11.
224 *Id.*, para. 2.
225 *Id.*
226 *Id.*
227 *Id.*
228 *Id.*, para. 3.

As Minister of Defense and Commander-in-Chief of the Armed Forces, Gen. Momoh presided over a War Cabinet that was assembled to review periodically the conduct of a border war between Sierra Leone and her neighbors. Evidence presented before the Commission established that between 4 April 1991 and 16 April 1992, the sum of Le5,280,001,393.79 (five billion, two hundred eighty million and one thousand, three hundred and ninety-three, leones seventy-nine cents) were paid to the Armed Forces as Emergency Defense Payments to prosecute the war.[229] Uncertainty as to how the funds were spent caused the NPRC to authorize an audit by external auditors to ascertain whether the funds were used for the purpose for which they were intended.[230] Suspecting that the funds might have been diverted into the personal accounts of the former President, the NPRC took the unusual step of freezing his assets pending the outcome of the external auditor's findings.[231]

Testifying before the Beccles-Davies Commission, Momoh's own Finance Minister, Hassan Gbassay Kanu, described his boss' conduct throughout his term as President of Sierra Leone as one that 'inflicted the severest mismanagement of the affairs of the people of this country.'[232] For its part, the Commission's final conclusions were that:

1 Dr. Momoh was in control of pecuniary resources and property disproportionate to his past official emoluments;
2 evidence of corruption, dishonesty and abuse of his office for private benefit by him and in collaboration with other persons has been established;
3 he acted wilfully and corruptly in a manner which resulted in loss and damage to Government.[233]

These two case studies exemplify how some heads of states have treated their countries like cash cows, exploiting their resources and using them as conduits to channel funds to their private accounts. They also demonstrate how the ruthless pursuit of self-interest can steadily impoverish the very people whom these leaders were elected to office to serve and protect. But the duty of loyalty demands unselfish and undivided attention to the interests of the nation as a whole. It admits to no conflict between that duty and self-interest. Above all, it imposes on public officials an affirmative duty to protect the interests of the people they serve and to refrain from doing anything that would work injury to them.

Other High-ranking State Officials

The disclosures from the inquiries confirmed the widely held view that high level corruption in Sierra Leone was systemic and engulfed the entire corps of top State

229 *Id.*
230 *Id.*, para. 7.
231 *Id.*
232 White Paper, para. 7.
233 White Paper, para. 4.

officials holding elective or appointive posts.[234] One of the first witnesses to appear before the Beccles-Davis Commission was the former Inspector-General of Police, Mr. James Bambay Kamara, who disclosed that he had substantial money in several local and overseas bank accounts and occasionally kept between Le10,000 and Le20,000 in his office which he used to help people. Kamara admitted that he owned over 30 pieces of property in the country including one that was bought for Le7.5 million less than two weeks before the coup that ejected him from office. The acquisitions were all made between 1974 and 1991 but at the time of the coup Mr. Kamara's monthly salary including allowances was Le18,042! It was also revealed that Kamara awarded Le96 million contract to an uncle of ex-president Momoh for the purchase of uniforms for the Security Services Division (SSD). A 50 percent deposit of the contract sum was paid into a local bank even though the contract for the supply of SSD uniforms was never performed. Another example of phantom contracts that was brought to the attention of the Lynton Nylander Commission of Inquiry was the award of a $20 million contract to Siemens for the rehabilitation of the Sierra Leone Broadcasting Service. The contract was never performed though the contractors were paid Le66 million on the instructions of the former minister of information and broadcasting.

Fake contracts, kickbacks, assets out of step with salaries, outright conversion of public funds were the order of the day in Sierra Leone. Take the case of Mr. Michael Abdulai, the former Minister of Transport and Communication, who also appeared before the Beccles-Davis Commission. His cabinet portfolio gave him jurisdiction over the country's sea and inland waters ports. In 1987 Abdulai executed a Memorandum of Understanding and Consultancy Agreement with Hamburg Ports Consultancy (HPC), the managers of the Sierra Leone Ports Authority (SLPA). The agreement provided that Abdulai would be paid in secret, a lump sum of $100,000 each year and that irrespective of change in status, profession or occupation or in the event of death or incapacitation, the money would be directed to his next of kin. In addition to all of this Abdulai also received a 10% commission on all purchases made overseas by the SLPA.

A former diplomat and government minister, Aiah M'bayo, told the Beccles-Davis Commission that the Algerian government had donated $4 million, 500 tons of fuel and a ship load of provisions, as Algeria's own contribution to the hosting of the Organization of African Unity (OAU) summit in Sierra Leone. But contrary to the intentions of the Algerian government, the money was distributed among some of Sierra Leone's ambassadors. M'bayo who negotiated for this OAU aid package and had the donation passed through him received for his efforts $25,000 and admitted before the commission that the package never benefitted Sierra Leone as a country! Other ministers and top public servants who testified before these commissions revealed huge assets that were out of step with their salaries. One senior official was found to own five homes and Le6m in two bank accounts but

---

[234] See for example Stephen Riley, ''The land of waving palms': political economy, corruption inquiries and politics in Sierra Leone,' in *Corruption: Causes, Consequences and Control*, 190, 202 (Michael Clarke ed., 1983) (noting that the only time high-ranking public servants are investigated is when there is a regime change).

could not account for the source of his wealth. Another with a salary of Le41,722 a month plus Le8500 allowance could boast two expensive foreign cars (a Mercedes Benz and a Volvo), a satellite dish costing Le2m, a house under construction on which he had already spent Le17m and shares in several local companies. He too could not tell the commission how he acquired his wealth. Former Foreign Minister, Alhaji Abdul Karim Koroma, owned a huge mansion in an exclusive Freetown suburb, a BMW car bought in 1988 for 25,000 pounds sterling and a satellite dish bought in 1991 for $8,000. He at least gave a glimpse into how he came by some of his wealth: selling food aid meant for starving Sierra Leonians and converting the money into his personal account. This is precisely what he did with the proceeds from the sale of Italian food aid! He was not alone in this practice. Other former ministers and some public servants close to former President Momoh acquired huge amounts from United States PL480 Fund for agricultural projects and community development and converted such monies to their own use.

Chapter 5

State Practice in International Fora with Respect to Acts of Fraudulent Enrichment

The preceding chapter traced the outlines of an emerging norm of international law that, drawing from private law institutions of trust and guardianship, imposes a fiduciary relation between high-ranking State officials and those whom they are elected or appointed to serve. This emerging fiduciary principle takes as its point of departure the proposition that public office holding is a public trust. Public servants who fraudulently enrich themselves at the expense of the public interest are in criminal breach of this public trust and therefore open to penal sanctions. There is evidence of a growing state practice in support of a norm which criminalizes corrupt practices by constitutionally-responsible rulers. Several resolutions adopted by key international human rights bodies bear witness to the emergence of this norm. It still remains the burden of its proponents to make the case that the extant state practice *per se* has created a new norm of general international law or changed existing customary law.

The notion that fraudulent enrichment of top State officials through acts of indigenous spoliation is prejudicial to the public interest and therefore a violation of the fiduciary obligation leaders owe to the citizens can be viewed in two ways. First, that even if this norm has not attained 'full normative stature,' to use Prosper Weil's felicitous phrase,[1] it is, at the very minimum, an embryonic norm. In this sense it is perhaps what Professor Schachter has called a 'formal normative conception' which can be used by the despoiled to justify sanctions directed against the despoilers.[2] On the other hand, a strong case can be made for viewing this norm as a corollary right of the fundamental principle of permanent sovereignty over national wealth and resources. This principle as was shown in Chapter 3 is the economic tributary of the *jus cogens* principle of political sovereignty. The people's right of permanent sovereignty over their national wealth and resources is a hollow right if (1) these resources are despoiled by top State officials, and (2) the despoiled themselves cannot hold the despoilers accountable. Thus the notion of fraudulent enrichment as a breach of a fiduciary obligation is merely the legal expression of the economic right of the people to

---

1 See Prosper Weil, 'Towards Relative Normativity in International Law,' *American Journal of International Law*, 77, 413 (1983).

2 Oscar Schachter, *Sharing the World's Resources*, 172 (1977).

control and dispose of their wealth and resources as they see fit and to seek redress against those who have despoiled this wealth.

The scope of this chapter is limited to consideration of State practice in recent years with regard to this emerging norm. The progressive development of an international legal regime to combat corruption has been pursued at two levels and in two stages. The first stage was at the level of the United Nations beginning with three key resolutions adopted in United Nations-sponsored international fora between 1990 and 1992, and finally culminating in the adoption almost twelve years later of a United Nations Convention Against Corruption. The decade following the adoption of these United Nations-sponsored resolutions marks the second phase in law-making at the international level on the subject of high level corruption. It is during this period that many of the leading international organizations, such as the United Nations, the World Bank, the IMF, the Council of Europe, the European Union, the Organization of American States (OAS), the Organization for Economic Co-operation and Development (OECD), the Global Coalition for Africa (GCA), and the International Chamber of Commerce have articulated anti-corruption policies and strategies. The concerted drive at the multilateral level to confront the problem of corruption has given birth to a number of anti-corruption instruments, which together make up the current international legal regime to combat corruption.

STATE PRACTICE AT THE INTERNATIONAL LEVEL

First Stage in the Law-Making Process

The first resolution on corruption in government was adopted in 1990 at the Eighth Quinquennial UN Congress on the Prevention of Crime and the Treatment of Offenders; the second a year later at a conference organized under the aegis of the United Nations Conference on Trade and Development (UNCTAD) and the most recent on the subject of fraudulent enrichment of high-ranking State officials and its deleterious effects on the despoiled countries as well as the international community as a whole was adopted by the United Nations Commission on Human Rights.

Background to the Resolutions on Fraudulent Enrichment

Eighth United Nations Congress on crime prevention The international community began to pay serious attention to the problem of corruption by public officials beginning with the Eighth United Nations Congress on the Prevention of Crime and the Treatment of Offenders (Eighth Congress) which met in Havana, Cuba in 1990.[3]

---

[3] See United Nations, *Eighth United Nations Congress on the Prevention of Crime and the Treatment of Offenders*, Havana, 27 August–7 September 1990, UN Doc.A/CONF.144/28/Rev. 1. The Eighth United Nations Congress was convened pursuant

This problem was addressed when the Eighth Congress considered the topic '[c]rime prevention and criminal justice in the context of development: realities and perspectives of international cooperation.'[4] A resolution on 'Corruption in government' was adopted at the close of these deliberations.[5] Although the focus of the resolution is on corruption in general, mention is also made of corruption among public officials. Corruption by this group is viewed as the single biggest impediment to achieving social and economic development in the victim countries. It has the potential of destroying the effectiveness of governmental programs, hindering development and victimizing individuals and groups. Thus, the resolution saw a connection between high level corruption, human rights and economic development on the one hand, and between corruption and other forms of economic crime such as drug trafficking and money laundering, on the other. It makes passing allusion to the transnational nature of official corruption in the recommendation to Member States to take the necessary steps to improve their banking and financial regulations and machinery so as to 'prevent capital flight of funds acquired through corrupt activities.'[6]

The resolution also includes two very important recommendations that are at the heart of the emerging norm. Recommendation 1(d) recognizes the principle of fiduciary obligation: Member States should adopt 'measures within government agencies to ensure accountability and effective disciplinary measures for public servants and remedial action.' The notion of accountability is a central tenet of the principle of fiduciary obligation. In addition, the resolution also recognizes the principle of restitution in insisting that despoilers must not be allowed to keep their ill-gotten wealth. Accordingly, Recommendation 3 urges Member States 'to create legal provisions for the forfeiture of funds and property from corrupt practices.'[7]

Finally, to underscore the seriousness of the problem and the determination to bring it under some form of international discipline, the resolution directs a request to the Crime Prevention and Criminal Justice Program of the Secretariat to 'develop a draft international code of conduct for public officials' for submission to the Ninth United Nations Congress on the Prevention of Crime and the Treatment of Offenders.[8] Furthermore, this unit is also charged with the task of soliciting the views of Governments, intergovernmental and non-governmental

---

to paragraph (d) of the annex to General Assembly resolution 415 (V) of 1 December 1950, which provided for the convening every five years of an international congress on crime prevention and the treatment of offenders. The first seven Congresses were held at Geneva in 1955, in London in 1960, at Stockholm in 1965, at Kyoto in 1970, at Geneva in 1975, at Caracas in 1980 and at Milan in 1985. A Congress is usually preceded by regional preparatory meetings and interregional meetings of experts who assist in the preparation of the necessary documentation for the Congress. *Id.*, at 200.

4 *Id.*, at 212.

5 *Id.*, at 136.

6 *Id.*, Recommendation 1(e).

7 *Id.*, Recommendation 3.

8 *Id.*, Recommendation 8.

organizations and professional associations as it prepares the draft code.[9]

The resolution on corruption represents an important step in the internationalization and criminalization of this practice. It is significant that its adoption was in the course of the United Nation's work in crime prevention and criminal justice.[10] In adopting the resolutions that they did, participants at the eighth congress were doing what earlier congresses in the past had done, that is, drafting instruments that set standards for States in the crime area. The Commission on Crime Prevention and Criminal Justice, the central policy-making organ of the UN Crime Prevention and Criminal Justice Program[11] has described these instruments as 'the most visible aspect' of the UN work in crime prevention. As the Commission noted in a recent report:

> [o]ther activities that the programme has carried out include the development of model agreements, surveys, research, the establishment of the United Nations Criminal Justice Information Network and the development of manuals on issues such as national criminal statistics, crime prevention measures, the prevention of corruption, and assistance to victims of crime. In addition, a broad range of activities involving, among other things, training courses, research and advisory services, are provided by the programme, including the network institutes.[12]

Resolutions approved at a congress usually return to the Commission for further possible consideration, before going on to the Economic and Social Council (ECOSOC) or the General Assembly for final action.[13] But these resolutions are not your usual hortatory declarations remembered more for the heat they generate than the light they shine. Congress resolutions have generally made a significant contribution to the formulation of normative instruments that have set international standards in crime prevention and criminal justice.[14] It is for precisely this reason

---

9 *Id.*, Recommendation 9.

10 *Eighth United Nations Congress on the Prevention of Crime and the Treatment of Offenders: Report Prepared by the Secretariat* 217, UN Doc. A/CONF.144/28/Rev. 1 (1991).

11 The Crime Prevention and Criminal Justice Program comprises the Commission on Crime Prevention and Criminal Justice, the UN Secretariat's Crime Prevention and Criminal Justice Branch, and five-yearly congresses on the Prevention of Crime and the Treatment of Offenders. The Commission consists of 40 member states of the UN elected for a 3-year term by the Economic and Social Council. For a comprehensive discussion of the UN crime prevention program, see Roger S. Clark, 'Stocktaking after Two Sessions of the Commission on Crime Prevention and Criminal Justice,' *Criminal Law Forum*, 4, 471 (1993).

12 See Report of the Commission on Crime Prevention and Criminal Justice on Its First Session, UN ESCOR, Supp. 10, UN Doc. E/1992/30 (1992), paragraphs 26-27.

13 See UN Congress on Crime Prevention, *supra* note 10, at 491.

14 See Compendium of United Nations Standards and Norms in Crime Prevention and Criminal Justice, UN Sales No. E.92.1V.1 (1992). The first congress in 1955 approved the text of the Standard Minimum Rules for the Treatment of Prisoners. See *First United Nations Congress on the Prevention of Crime and the Treatment of Offenders: Report*

that the Commission has interpreted its role as one of formulating standards and norms in the field. And at the Commission's urging, the ECOSOC has encouraged states to give effect at the national level to these evolving UN standards by institutionalizing them in their laws and practices.

Equally significant in the adoption of the resolution on corruption in government is the fact that when the subject was discussed by participants at the eighth congress, it was done in the same breadth that they discussed the more well-established crimes such as drug trafficking, terrorism and environmental destruction. And in their discussions on crime in general the stress was on its transnationality: '[a]ll participants stressed the seriousness of transnational crimes, which undermines the political and economic stability of nations and had adverse consequences on the well-being of large segments of the population.' Particular attention was directed at the economically weaker states who were easy prey to such transnational activities. And among the list of 'economic crimes' participants believed 'had a devastating effect on many nations' mention is made of 'large scale breaches of trust ... [and] corruption and various forms of abuse of power.'[15] It is a fair conclusion to draw that at this United Nations congress called to discuss the state of crime in the international community, the participants characterized corruption in government as among those crimes that have transnational effects deserving of serious and sustained attention by the international community as a whole.

Finally, the sponsorship of the draft resolution on corruption in government is also of some interest from the point of view of the trend in criminalizing this practice. It was sponsored by thirty-four countries including several that had been victims of indigenous spoliation, notably Nigeria, the Philippines and Zaire, and whose internal law make this activity punishable under the penal code.

Eighth UNCTAD conference The international concern over corruption in the public sector and the damage it inflicts on national economies did not end with the UN Congress resolution. In March of 1992, member states of UNCTAD met in Cartagena and adopted some broad policy statements that were included in the Final Act. Paragraph 27 of the policy statement called on all countries to 'increase their efforts to eradicate mismanagement of public and private affairs, including corruption, taking into account the factors responsible for, and agents involved in, this phenomenon.'[16] The statement recognized the growing importance of the

---

Prepared by the Secretariat 67, UN Doc. A/CONF.6/1 (1956). These were subsequently approved by ECOSOC in ESC Res. 663 (XXIV), UN ESCOR, 24th Sess., Supp. No. 1, at 11, UN Doc. E/3048 (1957), amended by ESC Res. 2076 (LXII), UN ESCOR, 62d Sess., Supp. No. 1, at 35, UN Doc. E/5988 (1977). A General Assembly resolution called the attention of member states to the Standard Minimum Rules. GA Res. 2858 (XXVI), UN GAOR, 26th Sess., Supp. No. 29, at 94, UN Doc. A/8429 (1972).

15 *Id.* The other economic crimes mentioned are illegal industrial and trade practices, illegal transactions and money laundering, tax evasion, customs and banking fraud, computer crimes and cultural theft.

16 See Report of the United Nations Conference on Trade and Development on its

market and the private sector for the 'efficient functioning of economies at all stages of development,' but noted that an effective functioning market requires conducive government policies and sound management. However, the prospects of good management are dramatically reduced when public institutions are snarled in the vortex of corruption. Therefore, it was urged, effective, efficient, honest, equitable and accountable public administration should be the objective of all governments.

The efforts just described to grapple with the problem of corruption in the public sector paved the way for the 1992 resolution on fraudulent enrichment adopted by the United Nations Human Rights Commission. The drafters of this resolution which is the subject of the next section specifically made reference to the aforementioned documents using them as basic building blocks in the final document.

Resolutions on Fraudulent Enrichment

During its fifty-second meeting on 3 March 1992, the United Nations Human Rights Commission adopted resolution 1992/50: 'Fraudulent enrichment of top State officials prejudicial to the public interest, the factors responsible for it, and the agents involved in all countries in such fraudulent enrichment,' and recommended it to the Economic and Social Council for adoption.[17] Before getting to the text of this very important resolution, it would be worthwhile to trace the preparatory steps taken that eventually lead to the adoption of Resolution 1992/50.

The preparatory work for Resolution 1992/50 The thirty-third meeting of the Sub-Commission on the Prevention of Discrimination and Protection of Minorities had on its agenda two items, among others, item 7 on 'The New International Economic Order and the Promotion of Human Rights' and item 8 on 'the Realization of Economic, Social and Cultural Rights.' In the course of the debate on these items, the problem of capital flight and fraudulent enrichment of high-ranking State officials was broached by several members.[18] It was noted that between $550 to $600 billion has been transferred from the developing Third World countries to the industrialized countries of Europe and North America and much of this was spoliated funds. This fraudulently obtained money was deposited in the 'tax havens' of Panama, the Cayman Islands, Switzerland and Luxembourg as 'life insurance for corrupt elites' as one member put it.[19]

There was widespread agreement that these spoliated funds were at the root of

---

Eighth Session, TD/364, 6 July 1992.

[17] Commission on Human Rights Resolution 1992/50, E/Cn.4/1992/8, Chap. 2, Sect. A. See *Commission on Human Rights, Report on the Forty-Eighth Session* (27 January–6 March 1992), E/CN.4/1992/84, at 118.

[18] See *Sub-Commission on Prevention of Discrimination and Protection of Minorities, Summary Record of the 33rd Meeting (Second Part)*, 28 August 1991, E/CN.4/Sub.2/199I/SR.33? Add. 1, at 2.

[19] *Id.*, at 4, paragraph 12 (Remarks of Mr. van der Weld).

the serious social and economic problems Third World countries are presently facing. This was accompanied by a general feeling that the funds spoliated by high-ranking officials could be used to partially offset the enormous foreign debts these countries have accumulated.[20] It was pointed out by Mrs. Graf of the International League for the Rights and Liberation of Peoples, that more than 40 per cent of the budget of Philippines or about $4 billion went for debt servicing; and then only 26 per cent of that amount was used to retire the principal while the bulk was used for paying off the interest.[21] The Philippines had to use up between 40 to 50 per cent of her export earnings to repay its $35 billion external debt.[22] While saddling the country with this crushing debt burden, the President (Ferdinand Marcos) used his 21 years in power to fraudulently amass a fortune estimated at between $10 to $12 billion which he deposited in Swiss banks under assumed names.[23] But Marcos was not the only Third World head of state who fraudulently enriched himself at the expense of the public interest. Mr. Dieng of the International Commission of Jurists mentioned the case of the former President of Mali who had transferred close to $2 billion to foreign banks with half of that amount going to Switzerland.[24]

Sub-Commission members called attention to the situation created in the majority of despoiled countries by the exigencies of illicit capital flight. In the case of the Philippines, it was duly noted that at the time President Marcos was transferring substantial amounts of state funds into his private bank accounts abroad, his country had the lowest nutritional standard in Asia save war torn Cambodia.[25] Furthermore, 40 per cent of the active population was unemployed or underemployed while 70 to 80 per cent of the population lived below the poverty line.[26] Mrs. Graf was able to put across the human dimensions of the consequences of indigenous spoliation:

> In Metro-Manila alone, there were 76,000 children living in the streets. It was easy to understand that debt-servicing led to serious shortcomings in the social services; consequently, many children died of diseases which could easily be prevented or cured. The hundreds of thousands of Filipino migrant workers abroad sent home amounts totalling approximately US$ 1 billion a year: however, those workers were not protected by the Government, which was anxious not to antagonize host countries.[27]

In summarizing the discussion on agenda items 7 and 8, it was the general sense that:

---

20 *Id.*

21 *Id.*, at 5, paragraph 18.

22 *Id.*, at 6, paragraph 23 (Remarks of Mr. Dieng).

23 *Id.*, at 5, paragraph 20 (Remarks of Mrs. Graf).

24 *Id.*, at 6, paragraph 23. The former President was overthrown by a military coup in March 1991.

25 *Id.*, at 6, paragraph 23 (Remarks of Mr. Dieng).

26 *Id.*

27 'Summit of the Americas: Declaration of Principles and Plan of Action,' *International Law Materials*, 34, 808, 818–819 (1995).

1 Illicit capital flight and the fraudulent enrichment of top State officials inhibited development in the affected countries and obstructed the realization of the economic, social and cultural rights proclaimed in the Universal Declaration of Human Rights and the International Covenant on Economic, Social and Cultural Rights;
2 Foreign banks as the direct beneficiaries of plundered Third World assets bore a heavy responsibility for the serious social and economic consequences created by these illicit transfers of wealth; and
3 An immediate response from the international community was imperative since what was at stake was not just a moral issue but, in a very real and frightening sense, one of survival.

It was in this spirit that Mr. van der Weld of the Centre Europe-Tiers Monde urged the Sub-Commission to take a more pragmatic approach to the problem of indigenous spoliation and to 'give some thought to the elaboration of an international convention which would compel the countries of the third world as well as the inter-national banks to face up to their responsibilities.'[28] And as a first step, Mr. Dieng on behalf of the International Commission of Jurists urged the Sub-Commission to adopt the draft resolution on the fraudulent enrichment of top State officials prejudicial to the public interest.[29]

35th meeting of the Sub-Commission At its 35th meeting on 29 August 1991, the Sub-Commission considered and adopted a draft resolution on 'Fraudulent Enrichment of Top State Officials Prejudicial to the Public Interest' (Draft Resolution 1991/36).[30] The resolution was later submitted to the Commission on Human Rights as Draft Resolution VIII.[31]

52nd meeting of the Commission on Human Rights At its fifty-second meeting held on 3 March 1992, the Commission took up for consideration Draft Resolution VIII.[32] Some concern was voiced that the draft resolution made no reference to the factors giving rise to, or the agents responsible for, indigenous spoliation. This aspect had to be addressed precisely because indigenous spoliation was not a

---

[28] *Id,*. at 4, paragraph 12.

[29] *Id.*, at 6, paragraph 24.

[30] See Resolution 1991/36 of the Sub-Commission on Prevention of Discrimination and Protection of Minorities in Report of the Sub-Commission on Prevention of Discrimination and Protection of Minorities on its Forty-Third Session, E/CN.4/Sub.2/1991/65, at 9–10, 80. The draft resolution was sponsored by Ms. Bautista, Mr. van Boven, Mr. Chernichenko, Mr. Despouy, Mr. Eide, Mr. Khalil, Mr. Ilkanahaf, Mr. Rivas Posada, Mr. Treat, Mr. Turk and Mr. Yimer. They were subsequently joined by Mr. Al-Khasawneh, Mr. Guisse, Ms. Ksentini, Mr. Maxim and Mr. Sachar. *Id.*, at 80, paragraph 225.

[31] The full text of the final resolution can be found later in this chapter.

[32] *Commission on Human Rights, Summary Record of the 52nd Meeting (First Part)*, E/CN.4/1992/SR.52.

purely local affair. As the Representative of India explained, given 'the multinational nature of the complicity that encouraged the phenomenon ... it was unrealistic to hope to stem the tide of corruption without acknowledging that aspect.'[33] Accordingly, he proposed an amendment – which was endorsed by his Colombian and Sri Lankan counterparts[34] and subsequently adopted by the whole body – to include the words 'the factors responsible for it and the agents involved in all countries in such fraudulent enrichment' to come immediately after the phrase 'fraudulent enrichment of top State officials prejudicial to the public interest' wherever it appeared in the title or in the text of the draft resolution.[35]

The Representative of Colombia explained his support for the draft resolution as a whole together with the amendment proposed by India because it was of interest to his country both from the point of view of substance and from a basic conviction that a 'practice as disturbing and reprehensible as the fraudulent enrichment of top State officials, *all those responsible, from the top downwards, should be identified.*'[36] Mrs. Dewaraja, the Representative of Sri Lanka, was of the view that 'corruption must be condemned in all countries and the factors which encouraged it must be recognized.'[37] Clearly with an eye toward the elaboration and progressive development of a rule of law on fraudulent enrichment of top State officials, she like Mr. Shah wanted to align the language of the draft resolution with the text of the Final Act of the eighth United Nations Conference on Trade and Development adopted in Cartagena.[38]

While the severe damage wrought on nations and economies as a result of indigenous spoliation and the pressing need for a concerted global response were widely acknowledged, the Representative of Japan took exception to any hint or suggestion that the developed countries are 'responsible for the restitution to despoiled peoples of the funds which their leaders had extorted from them.'[39] Like the Pakistani counterpart,[40] the Japanese Representative was of the view that responsibility for despoliation should attach to the individual leaders not the developed States. State responsibility, if any, could only be engaged 'in accordance with specific agreements between countries.'[41]

At the close of the discussion, the draft resolution submitted by the Sub-Commission to the parent body was adopted with amendments by 49 votes to none, with 2 abstentions.[42] The final text reads:

---

[33] *Id.*, at 9, paragraph 52 (Remarks of Mr. Shah).

[34] *Id.*, at 9, paragraphs 53–54.

[35] *Id.*, at 9, paragraph 52.

[36] *Id.*, at 9, paragraph 53 (Remarks of Mr. Grillo) (emphasis added).

[37] *Id.*, at 9, paragraph 54.

[38] *Id.*

[39] *Id.*, at 9, paragraph 56 (Remarks of Mr. Sezaki).

[40] *Id.*, at 10, paragraph 57 (Remarks of Mr. Kamal) (noting that the money from fraudulent enrichment originated with and circulated through agents therefore special attention should be paid to despoilers).

[41] *Id.*

[42] *Id.*, at 10, paragraph 62.

1992/50. *Fraudulent enrichment of top State officials prejudicial to the public interest, the factors responsible for it, and the agents involved in all countries in such fraudulent enrichment*

The Commission on Human Rights,

Recalling the resolution on corruption in government adopted by the Eighth United Nations Congress on the Prevention of Crime and the Treatment of Offenders (Havana, 27 August—7 September 1990), in which the Congress noted that the problems of corruption in public administration were universal and that, although they had particularly deleterious effects on nations with vulnerable economies, those effects were felt throughout the world, and stated its conviction that corrupt activities of public officials could destroy the potential effectiveness of all types of governmental programmes, hinder development and victimize individuals and groups (*see* A/CONF.144/28/Rev. 1, Chap. 1, Sect. C),

Considering the necessity for determined action to combat the fraudulent or illicit enrichment of top state officials and the transfer abroad of the assets thus diverted, as well as to prevent those practices which undermine the democratic system in countries throughout the world and constitute an obstacle to the economies of the countries concerned,

Considering also that, in some countries, corruption has become systematic,

Noting with anxiety that corruption has further acquired a transnational character, in particular as a result of the illicit arms trade, international drug trafficking and money laundering,

Convinced that the solution of these problems calls not only for resolute political will on the part of national authorities, but also for close international cooperation, notably in the form of mutual legal assistance,

Noting with regret that, although international law does not regard the misappropriation of public funds as a political offence but accords it the character of a common law offence, the law and judicial practice of most States do not allow the extradition of persons guilty of such misappropriation,

Considering that, for many peoples who have been the victims of institutionalized corruption and who, at present, are seeking to strengthen their democratic system, a satisfactory solution to these problems is necessary not only from a moral point of view, but above all in order to ensure reparation of damage caused to their economic interests as a result of the illicit removal of these resources,

Considering that all countries have an obligation to take steps to prevent fraudulently acquired funds from entering their territory,

Convinced that developed countries have a special responsibility to contribute diligently to the restitution to despoiled peoples of the funds which their leaders have extorted from them, with a view to contributing to their economic, social and cultural development,

> *Recalling* its resolution 1991/18 of 1 March 1991, in which it expressed its awareness that, despite progress achieved by the international community with respect to the setting of standards for the realization of economic, social and cultural rights contained in the International Covenant on Economic, Social and Cultural Rights, the implementation and promotion of those rights and the problems of their realization had not yet received sufficient attention within the framework of the United Nations system,
>
> *Recalling also* General Assembly resolution 45/155 of 18 December 1990, in which the General Assembly decided, *inter alia*, that one of the objectives of the 1993 World Conference on Human Rights should be to examine the relationship between development and the enjoyment by everyone of economic, social and cultural rights, as well as of civil and political rights,
>
> 1. *Decides* to keep in mind the question of the fraudulent enrichment of top State officials prejudicial to the public interest, the factors responsible for, and the agents involved in all countries in such fraudulent enrichment when discussing the question of the realization in all countries of the economic, social and cultural rights proclaimed in the Universal Declaration of Human Rights and the International Covenant on Economic, Social and Cultural Rights;
>
> 2. *Requests* the Secretary-General to bring the present resolution to the attention of the Commission on Crime Prevention and Criminal Justice.

An overview of resolution 1992/50 The resolution regards fraudulent enrichment of top State officials and the illicit transfer abroad of spoliated assets as first and foremost a human rights problem. It places such acts and practices squarely within the human rights framework established by the United Nations. Indigenous spoliation is seen to have a direct impact on the fundamental rights guaranteed in a number of international human rights instruments. The resolution beams forth a clear and unmistakable message, to wit, that there is a link between these despicable acts of depredations and the human rights of groups as well as individuals. To allow such practices to go unchecked would be to hold back the realization in all countries of the economic, social and cultural rights promised them in the Universal Declaration of Human Rights and the International Covenant on Economic, Social and Cultural Rights. It follows therefore that progress toward the attainment of these guaranteed rights depends to a great extent on the prevention of acts of indigenous spoliation.

Resolution 1992/50 explodes the myth that indigenous spoliation is a localized problem. Rather, it recognizes that it is global and its effects are no longer confined exclusively within national borders, if they ever were, but are felt throughout the world. The transnational nature of this problem therefore calls for a transnational solution. The resolution laments the fact that contemporary international law has proved unable to bring the problem of fraudulent enrichment of top State officials under some kind of international discipline. It blames this failure on the fact that international law treats these acts not as an international crime but merely as a common law offense. Consequently, States where the authors of this crime have sought and been given asylum are under no obligation to extradite them back to their home states to answer to charges of fraudulent enrichment. Noting the destructive effects of indigenous spoliation on human lives as well as societies, Resolution 1992/50 insists that international law must step in by imposing some kind of obligation *erga omnes* on all States to 'take steps to prevent fraudulently acquired funds from entering their territory.'[43]

The resolution recognizes that the victims of spoliation are entitled to some form of redress and compensation. Accordingly, a special responsibility is placed on developed countries to contribute diligently to the restitution to despoiled peoples of the funds which their leaders have extorted from them. It is clear that what the Commission has in mind are reparations; that much is acknowledged in the seventh preambular paragraph where it talks of the need to find a 'satisfactory solution to these problems ... in order to ensure reparation of damage caused to [the victims'] economic interests as a result of the illicit removal of [their] resources.' Moreover, in the debate on the draft resolution during the Commission's 52nd meeting, this was precisely the construction given to the draft ninth preambular paragraph which retained the same position and wording in the final text. It will be recalled that at this meeting the representative of Japan objected to the inclusion of this preambular paragraph and requested a separate vote. However, he lost on the vote and the paragraph was retained by 31 votes to 4 (Australia, Canada, Japan and the United States of America), with 17 abstentions.[44] The Commission's resolution is in line with the discussions during the Sub-Commission's meetings where it was acknowledged that developed countries were the direct beneficiaries of the plundered wealth of the developing countries.[45] It was noted that a number of developed countries had become tax havens where private fortunes were deposited and had no compunctions in using their complex network of bank secrecy laws to frustrate efforts by the despoiled victims to capture and repatriate some of these stolen assets. Banks in the developed countries were also singled out as coconspirators with top State officials in the despoliation of developing world resources. Surely, the records of the Sub-Commission meetings were readily available to the Commission when it was debating the draft resolution submitted to it by the former.

Finally, a request is directed to the Secretary General to bring the resolution to the attention of the Commission on Crime Prevention which lists among its objectives the protection of human rights in the administration of justice and the prevention and control of crime.[46] Here is ground for an inference of an intention to see fraudulent enrichment of top State officials as an offense that can be transformed into a crime with transnational implications.

---

[43] Resolution 1992/50, paragraph 6.

[44] See Summary Record (First Part), *supra* note 32, at 10, paragraphs 58–60. It is also worthwhile to note that it was the representative of Japan who at the close of the debate called the question on Draft Resolution VIII including the objectionable ninth paragraph that was adopted by 49 votes to none, with only 2 abstentions! *Id.*

[45] See generally Summary Record of the 33rd Meeting (Second Part), *supra* note 18, at 4–6.

[46] See GA Res. 46/152, UN GAOR, 46th Sess., Supp. No. 49, UN Doc. A/46/49 (1992), Annex, para. 21.

The Legal Basis of Commission Resolution 1992/50

What importance should be accorded a resolution adopted by the Commission and to the views expressed? To what extent were the representatives, whether in taking part in the debates or voting for the resolution on Fraudulent Enrichment of Top State Officials, intended to express themselves as a matter of *de lege lata* rather than *de lege ferenda*? What about the Commission, as the sum of the disparate parts, was it expressing itself *de lege lata* or *de lege ferenda*? It is entirely possible that these questions are somewhat premature since resolution 1992/50 is not framed as a law-declaring or law-affirming resolution. It merely requests the Secretary-General of the General Assembly to bring the text to the attention of the Commission on Crime Prevention and Criminal Justice.

Although the resolution does not purport to express international law does it, nevertheless, imply a general legal prescription for States ('all countries have an obligation …', 'developed countries have a responsibility …') on the issue of fraudulent enrichment of top State officials? Can the significance of this resolution be divorced from any claims it makes to legality? It is possible to separate and identify the importance of this document independent of any legal claims because the resolution is discussed here as evidence of state practice at the international level with regard to the problem of indigenous spoliation.

The importance of resolution 1992/50 as evidence of state practice derives from the stature of the Commission and its historic role in the drafting of major standard-setting human rights instruments over the last five decades. It might therefore be necessary to place the work of the Commission in some perspective.

Role of the Commission The Commission's terms of reference as articulated by the Economic and Social Council (ECOSOC) are to submit proposal, recommendations and reports to ECOSOC regarding:

1 An international bill of rights;
2 International declarations or conventions on civil liberties, the status of women, freedom of information and similar matters;
3 The protection of minorities;
4 The prevention of discrimination on grounds of race, sex, language or religion;
5 Any other matters concerning human rights not covered by items (a), (b), (c) and (d);
6 The coordination of activities concerning human rights in the United Nations system.[47]

From its inception the Commission was viewed as the principal institution for the elaboration and progressive development of human rights law under the United

[47] See Egon Schwelb and Philip Alston, 'The Principal Institutions and Other Bodies Founded Under the Charter,' in *The International Dimensions of Human Rights*, 1, 231, 241 (Karel Kasak ed., 1982).

Nations system. Bearing witness to this role is an impressive list of human rights conventions and declarations in which the Commission played a significant role in their drafting and subsequent adoption by the UN, from the Universal Declaration of Human Rights to the standard setting International Covenants on Civil and Political Rights and the companion one on Economic, Social and Cultural Rights.[48]

Debating and then recommending action on the problem of fraudulent enrichment of top State officials are the within the charge of the Commission.

Composition of the Commission The Commission consists of 53 members who are elected by the Economic and Social Council (ECOSOC). They are all government representatives. When the Commission was initially established in 1946, a proposal to have all its members serve as non-governmental representatives was turned down by the ECOSOC.[49] From its inception the intention was to allow the Commission representatives function as their counterparts in the United Nations General Assembly. Therefore, when representatives to the Commission make statements and vote on proposed resolutions and decisions, they do so on behalf of the governments of the States they represent.[50] These representatives are instructed diplomats who speak and vote within the carefully circumscribed policy of the governments they represent: '[s]ome governments may give their representatives broad discretion or strict instructions. The more sensitive the issue, the more likely that members will be obliged to seek instructions from their capitals.'[51] So unlike the members of the Commission's Sub-Commission on Prevention and Protection of Minorities[52] who serve in their individual capacity as experts and not as representatives of their Governments, Commission members are not independent, freelance experts but diplomats with portfolios. And while the Sub-Commission can be expected to act purely on the merits of human rights issues, representatives to the Commission are expected to examine these same issues in the light of their Governments' overall human rights policies. Consequently the views expressed by these representatives and pronouncements they make are reflective of the policy-positions their Governments have embraced. It is therefore entirely proper to treat these statements as evidence of state practice on a particular subject.

---

48 *Id.*, at 245 ff.

49 Schwelb & Alston, *supra* note 47, at 243.

50 Most other UN members not represented on the Commission are allowed to, and often do, send observer delegations to the Commission deliberations. They are allowed to make statements but have no right to vote. See Nigel S. Rodley, 'United Nations Non-Treaty Procedures for Dealing with Human Rights Violations,' in *Guide to International Human Rights Practice*, 60, 61 (Hurst Annum ed. 2d ed. 1992).

51 *Id.*

52 The Sub-Commission is composed of 26 individual experts who are nominated by their governments and elected by the Commission. They are free to express views and position independent of government policy. However, in practice some Sub-Commission members have official positions or serve in their governments' delegations to the Commission. *Id.*

The vote to adopt Resolution 1992/50 The vote to adopt the resolution on fraudulent enrichment was 49 in favor with only 2 abstentions. This is a very significant endorsement coming as it does from delegates representing countries from all the major regions of the world, that is, Africa,[53] Asia and the Middle East,[54] Latin America,[55] and Europe and North America.[56] Equally significant is the fact that among the countries voting in favor of the resolution were some with a long and well-documented history of indigenous spoliation (for example, Argentine, Ghana, Nigeria, Mexico, Peru and the Philippines) as well as States that have a tradition of offering sanctuary to fleeing dictators including those who fraudulently enriched themselves (such as France, United Kingdom and Venezuela).

On 16 December 1996, the United Nations General Assembly, acting on an earlier recommendation of the Economic and Social Commission, adopted the United Nations Declaration against Corruption and Bribery in International Commercial Transactions. The Declaration highlights the economic costs of corruption and bribery, and points out that a stable and transparent environment for international commercial transactions in all countries is essential for the mobilization of investment, finance, technology, skills and other resources across national borders. Member States pledge in the Declaration to criminalize bribery of foreign public officials in an effective and coordinated manner and to deny the tax deductibility of bribes paid by any private or public corporation or individual of a Member State to any public official or elected representative of another country. Corruption was also the subject of a 1997 United Nations General Assembly Resolution entitled Action Against Corruption. The resolution underscored the General Assembly's concern about the serious problems posed by corrupt practices to the stability and security of societies, the values of democracy and morality, and to social, economic and political development.[57] The resolution also drew a link between corruption and organized crime, including money laundering. Interestingly enough, the preamble of the Inter-American Convention called attention to the 'steadily increasing links between corruption and the proceeds generated by illicit narcotics trafficking … which undermine and threaten

---

53 Angola, Burundi, Gabon, Gambia, Ghana, Kenya, Lesotho, Libya, Madagascar, Mauritania, Nigeria, Senegal, Somalia, Tunisia and Zambia.

54 Australia, Bangladesh, China, India, Indonesia, Iran, Iraq, Pakistan, Philippines, Sri Lanka and Syria.

55 Argentina, Brazil, Chile, Colombia, Costa Rica, Cuba, Mexico, Peru, Uruguay and Venezula.

56 Austria, Bulgaria, Canada, Czech and Slovak Federal Republic, Cyprus, France, Germany, Hungary, Italy, Netherlands, Portugal, Russian Federation, the United Kingdom and Yugoslavia.

57 See United Nations Ad Hoc Committee for the Negotiation of a Convention against Corruption, *Global Study on the Transfer of Funds of Illicit Origin, Especially Funds Derived from Acts of Corruption,* UN Doc. A/AC.261/12, ¶¶ 7-11.

legitimate commercial and financial activities, and society, at all levels.'[58] Acknowledging that corruption now has trans-border effects, the General Assembly's anti-corruption resolution recommends a multilateral approach to combat it.

The Second Stage in the Law-Making Process

Pronouncements by States in recent years also evidence a universal condemnation of corrupt practices by public officials and a general interest in cooperating to suppress them. This widespread condemnation of acts of corruption is reflected in the preambles of a number of multilateral anti-corruption conventions and resolutions of international organizations.[59] Reading through them leaves one in no doubt as to the seriousness with which the international community as a whole attaches to the problem of corruption. The burst of law making energy began with the 1995 European Union Convention on the Protection of the European Communities' Financial Interests and its two additional Protocols,[60] followed by the 1996 Inter-American Convention Against Corruption (Inter-American Convention) and the 1997 OECD Convention on Combating Bribery of Foreign Public Officials in International Business Transactions, ending with the 1999 Council of Europe Criminal Law Convention on Corruption. As important as these developments have been, much is still to be done in combating the problem of official corruption.[61]

THE EUROPEAN UNION ANTI-CORRUPTION CONVENTION

---

[58] In the same vein, a 1995 Resolution on Combating Corruption in Europe adopted by the European Parliament also stressed the ties between corruption and organized crime while expressing the view that combating the latter can help to curb the former. *See* European Parliament, Report of the Committee on Civil Liberties and Internal Affairs on Combating Corruption in Europe, DOC.EN\RR\287\287701 (1 December 1995) [hereinafter European Parliament Resolution].

[59] In interpreting a treaty, the preamble and annexes are included as part of the text of the treaty. *See generally,* Vienna Convention on the Law of Treaties (with annexes). Concluded at Vienna, 23 May 1969. Entered into force, 27 January 1988. 1155 UNTS 331; 1969 UNJYB 140; 1980 UKTS 58, Cmnd. 7964; reprinted in *International Law Materials*, 8, 679 (1969), Art. 31, paragraph 1.

[60] See Convention on the Protection of the European Communities' Financial Interests, 1995 OJ (C316/49) [hereinafter Convention]. *See also* Protocol to the Convention, 1996 OJ (C313/2) as well as the Second Protocol to the Convention, 1997 OJ (C221/12).

[61] In a 1995 Resolution on combating corruption in Europe, the European Parliament called for stronger measures to be taken by Member States of the European Union to combat corruption. The resolution raised concern about the current anti-corruption measures, noting that the agreements concluded between the Member States on this subject are inadequate. *See* European Parliament Resolution, *supra* note 58.

Specific provisions in the three European Community Treaties had earlier anticipated the need to combat acts of fraud: the Treaty establishing the European Community (EC Treaty), the Treaty establishing the European Atomic Energy Community (Euratom Treaty) and the Treaty establishing the European Coal and Steel Community (Eurocoal Treaty) within the so-called first pillar of the institutional structure of the European Union (articles 209a EC Treaty, 183a Euratom Treaty and 78i Eurocoal Treaty). These provisions articulate the Member States' obligation to take the same measures to counter fraud affecting the financial interests of the Community as they take to counter fraud affecting their own financial interests. To fulfill this mission Member States are required to coordinate their action aimed at protecting the financial interests of the Community against fraud. To this end they shall organize, with the help of the Commission, close and regular cooperation between the competent departments of their administrations. To reduce the inconsistencies between laws on fraud in several Member States that make it possible for international fraud to flourish, it became necessary to draft a Convention with a common definition of fraud to protect the Community's financial interests on the basis of article K.3.2. Under Title VI of the Treaty of the European Union, article K.3 authorizes the Council to draw up conventions that it recommends to the Member States for adoption in accordance with their respective constitutional arrangements. On 13 June 1995, the President of the European Parliament authorized the Committee on Civil Liberties and Internal Affairs (Committee) to draw up a report on combating corruption in Europe with Mrs. Heinke Salish as the Rapporteur. The Committee's report on Combating Corruption in Europe was considered by the European Parliament on December 1995, and it became the basis of a resolution.

The Resolution on Combating Corruption in Europe states, *inter alia*, that 'corruption, particularly in conjunction with organized crime, poses a threat to the functioning of the democratic system and thus destroys public confidence in the integrity of the democratic State' as well as that 'combating corruption nationally and internationally concerns all Member States and that the agreements concluded between the Member States on this subject are inadequate [and] that legal provisions and stiffer penalties for crimes of corruption are not enough on their own and that success will be achieved primarily through society's resolute condemnation of corruption and the determination of the responsible authorities to combat it.'[62] The 1995 Convention on the Protection of European Communities' Financial Interests builds on this earlier effort. It was drawn up under the terms of article 209a of the Maastricht Treaty, which requires every Member State of the European Union to take the same measures to counter fraud on the Community budget as they do on their own financial interests. The convention tries to harmonize the various national legal instruments for the criminal prosecution of fraudulent conduct endangering the Communities' financial interests. In addition to adopting a common definition of fraud,[63] the convention also contains provisions

---

[62] *Id.*

[63] Article 1(1) of the Convention defines the type of fraud that affects the European Communities' financial interests as consisting of: (a) in respect of expenditure, any

requiring the Member States to incorporate the definition of fraud into their own body of criminal law. The 1995 Convention also includes the usual provisions for jurisdiction,[64] extradition and prosecution,[65] as well as mutual cooperation in the investigation, prosecution and punishment of individuals accused of committing fraud affecting the Communities' financial interests.[66]

The following year the First Protocol to the Convention on the Protection of the Communities' Financial Interests was signed. The Protocol deals with corruption of public officials that endangers the Communities' financial interests. It fills in the gaps in existing criminal law on corruption having a link with protection of the Communities' financial interests that involve Community and/or national officials. As a consequence, the Protocol extends to offenses committed not just by national officials within each Member State but by members of the Commission, Parliament, the Court of Justice, and the Court of Auditors in the exercise of their functions. The Second Protocol followed on the heels of the first and incorporates certain areas that were left out of the Convention itself. In this sense, it complements the provisions of the 1995 Convention. The main purpose of the Second Protocol is the criminalization of money laundering and the confiscation of the fruits of fraud, and for cooperation between the Commission and the national prosecuting authorities in the Member States with respect to fraud, corruption and money laundering.[67]

---

intentional act or omission relating to: the use or presentation of false, incorrect or incomplete statements or documents, which has as its effect the misappropriation or wrongful retention of funds from the general budget of the European Communities or budgets managed by, or on behalf of the European Communities, non-disclosure of information in violation of a specific obligation, with the same purposes other than those for which they were originally granted; (b) in respect of revenue, any intentional act or omission relating to: the use or presentation of false, incorrect or incomplete statements or documents, which has as its effect the illegal diminution of the resources of the general budget of the European Communities or budgets managed by, or on behalf of the European Communities, nondisclosure of information in violation of a specific obligation, with the same effect, misapplication of a legally obtained benefit, with the same effect. Until this broad definition of fraud was formulated in the Convention, considerable differences could be observed in the substantive law of Member States as to the type of offenses covered under fraud. Most of the criminal offenses of fraud in the Member States covered either only expenditure fraud (subsidy fraud) or revenue fraud. The Convention definition of fraud applies equally to revenue and expenditure. See Lothar Kuhl, 'The Criminal Law Protection of the Communities' Financial Interests Against Fraud-Part 1,' 1998, *Criminal Law Review*, 259, 264–65 (1998) [hereinafter Kuhl Part 1]; Lothar Kuhl, 'The Criminal Law Protection of the Communities' Financial Interests Against Fraud-Part 2,' 1998, *Criminal Law Review*, 323, 324-25 (1998) [hereinafter Kuhl Part 2].

64 See Convention, *supra* note 60, Art. 4.

65 *Id.*, Art. 5.

66 *Id.*, Art. 6.

67 See Kuhl Part 1, *supra* note 63, at 259; see also Kuhl Part 2, *supra* note 63, at 323.

THE OECD CONVENTION ON COMBATING BRIBERY OF PUBLIC OFFICIALS

In 1997, the European countries were able to secure a comprehensive anti-corruption instrument that went beyond the limited goal of protecting only the Communities' financial interests when they adopted the OECD Convention on Combating Bribery of Public Officials in International Business Transactions (OECD Convention).[68] Like the new generation of anti-corruption conventions, the OECD Convention differentiates between demand-side and supply-side bribery. That is, the side that took the initiative that led to bribery and then ascribes sanctions accordingly. The OECD Convention is a supply-side-oriented, anti-bribery instrument and, as such, it only proscribes what, in the law of some countries, is called active corruption or active bribery, meaning the offense committed by the person who promises or gives the bribe, as contrasted with passive bribery, the offense committed by the public official who receives the bribe. Bribery is defined in Article 1, paragraph 1, of the OECD Convention as the direct or indirect intentional offer or provision of 'any undue pecuniary or other advantage … to [or for] a foreign public official' in violation of the official's legal duties 'in order to obtain or retain business or other improper advantage.'[69] Bribery is the offer of payments to induce a breach of the official's duty.

The crime of bribery as defined in paragraph 1 also includes 'any use of the public official's position, whether or not within the official's authorised competence. The Commentaries to the Convention appear to suggest that the paragraph 4.c offence is closer to the misuse of influence by an official to affect another public official's decision. The Commentaries state:

> One case of bribery which has been contemplated under the definition of paragraph 4.c is where an executive of a company gives a bribe to a senior official of government, in order that this official use his office – though acting outside his competence – to make another official award a contract to that company.

While influence-peddling with a view to affecting a desired outcome is not *per se* corruption, at least not in the traditional sense, and is an accepted practice in some countries, the conduct has all 'the hallmarks of a corrupt transaction that involves an illicit transfer resulting in a questionable exercise of governmental power.'[70]

---

68 See OECD Convention on Combating Bribery of Foreign Public Officials in International Business Transactions, 18 December 1997, *International Law Materials*, 37, 1 (1998) [hereinafter OECD Convention]. The OECD was established in 1961 to promote economic growth and free trade and to expand and improve development aid to the developing countries. It is made up of fifteen EU countries, Japan, Canada, Australia, the United States and a number of Central European countries.

69 *Id.* Art. 1, para. 1.

70 See Peter J. Henning, 'Public Corruption: A Comparative Analysis of International

This more expansive interpretation of the crime of bribery only applies to "*foreign* public officials"' not office holders in the host country.

In addition, by limiting its scope to active bribery, the OECD Convention only targets the bribe giver and *not* the receiver. Furthermore, by excluding 'small facilitation payments'[71] from Article 1's broad proscription against providing 'any undue pecuniary or other advantage' to an office holder, but without defining what constitutes a small facilitation payment,[72] the Convention leaves open a door through which unscrupulous public officials engaged in illicit enrichment can avoid criminal liability. This exclusion of petty corruption from the definition of bribery appears to contradict the drafters' desire to define corruption in culturally-neutral language by treating it as an offence 'irrespective of ... perceptions of local custom, the tolerance of such payments by local authorities, or the alleged necessity of the payment in order to obtain or retain business or other improper advantages.'[73]

THE COUNCIL OF EUROPE'S 1999 CRIMINAL LAW CONVENTION ON CORRUPTION

The Council of Europe's 1999 Criminal Law Convention on Corruption (Criminal Law Convention)[74] sets outs in its preamble a concise outline of the serious and varied forms of damage caused by corruption and the urgent need to combat it through a multi-disciplinary national and international approach. The Parties to the Criminal Law Convention expressly acknowledge that 'corruption threatens the rule of law, democracy and human rights, undermines good governance, fairness and social justice, distorts competition, hinders economic development and endangers the stability of democratic institutions and the moral foundations of society.'[75]

Corruption Conventions and United States Law,' *Arizona Journal of International and Comparative Law*, 18, 818 (2001) [hereinafter 'Henning'].

[71] OECD Convention Commentaries, para. 9.

[72] The justification advanced for exempting this form of payment from the reach of the Convention is that '[o]ther countries can and should address this corrosive phenomenon by such means as support for programmes of good governance. However, criminalisation by other countries does not seem a practical or effective complementary action.' *Id.*

[73] *Id.*, at para. 7.

[74] In May 2003, the Council of Europe adopted the Additional Protocol to the Criminal Law Convention on Corruption which complements the Criminal Law Convention. The Additional Protocol requires Parties to provide, in their domestic law, for criminal responsibility in the fields of arbitration and jury service for offenses already covered in the Criminal Law Convention, that is, active and passive bribery of domestic and foreign arbitrators (Articles 3 and 4) as well as domestic and foreign jurors (Articles 5 and 6). Adopted in Strasbourg, 15 May 2003, ETS No. 191 (2003).

[75] Council of Europe, *Preamble to the Criminal Law Convention on Corruption* (visited 26 February 2000) <http://www.coe.fr/eng/legaltxt/173e.htm>; reprinted in

The Criminal Law Convention is different from the OECD Convention in that it attacks corruption from both the supply and demand sides. The instrument was actually designed as a framework convention that: (i) enumerates the principles that States Parties would undertake to respect in their national legislation and practice against corruption; and (ii) provides a basic structure that stands to be completed by various additional instruments. Although the Criminal Law Convention has corruption as part of its title, that is the only place the word is mentioned in the instrument; throughout the document the reference is to bribery. The crime of bribery is defined under two separate provisions to reflect the duality of the offense, that is, its passive and active attributes. For instance, under article 2, which deals only with passive bribery, this offense is defined as the intentional 'promising, offering or giving by any person, directly or indirectly, of any undue advantage to any of its public officials, for himself or for herself or for anyone else, for him to act or refrain from acting in the exercise of his or her functions.'[76] Article 3, the active bribery provision, on the other hand, concerns itself with the intentional act of requesting or receiving, or accepting an offer or a promise by a public official, either directly or indirectly, of any undue advantage aimed at compromising him in the exercise of his functions.

With articles 2 and 3 as predicate provisions, the convention then enumerates an exhaustive list of acts that it directs the States Parties to criminalize in their domestic legislation. These are: active and passive bribery of foreign officials;[77] active and passive bribery in the business sector;[78] trading in influence involving national and foreign public officials;[79] bribery of international officials and other persons who carry out functions in international organizations;[80] bribery of high officials of international organizations;[81] bribery in money laundering;[82] and bribery in accounting.[83] Within each of these enumerated acts, reference is then made to either article 2 or 3 for the definition of the criminal offense of bribery that is appropriate.

The Criminal Law Convention contains a number of innovations not found in other anti-corruption regimes. First, it extends the reach of its bribery provisions to cover not only government officials at the international and national levels but also private sector transactions that do not involve any misuse of public authority.

Second, the Convention explicitly incorporates 'Trading in Influence' as a crime, which it defines as:

> [Internationally] promising, giving or offering, directly or indirectly, of any undue

---

International Law Materials, 38, 505 (1999).

76 *Id.* Art. 2.

77 *Id.* Arts. 4, 6.

78 *Id.* Arts. 7, 8.

79 *Id.* Art. 12.

80 *Id.* Arts. 9-11.

81 *Id.*

82 *Id.* Art. 13.

83 *Id.* Art. 14.

advantage to anyone who asserts or confirms that he or she is able to exert an improper influence over the decision-making of any person referred to in Articles 2, 4 to 6 and 9 to 11 in consideration thereof, whether the undue advantage is for himself or herself or for anyone else, as well as the request, receipt or the acceptance of the offer or the promise of such an advantage in consideration of that influence, whether or not the influence is exerted or whether or not the supposed influence leads to the intended result.[84]

As the Exploratory Report explains, the goal of the article 12 prohibition is to reach misconduct by those 'who are in the neighborhood of power,' to address a type of 'background corruption.'[85] In order for this type of misconduct to be punished, it 'must contain a corrupt intent by the influence peddler.'[86] Regrettably, this term is not defined in either the Convention or its Explanatory Report.

THE COUNCIL OF EUROPE'S CIVIL LAW CONVENTION ON CORRUPTION

The Council of Europe opened a second front in the war against corruption when it adopted the Civil Law Convention on Corruption in 1999 ('Civil Law Convention').[87] The convention, which complements the earlier Criminal Law Convention, is part of the Council's multi-disciplinary plan of action to combat corruption. It is a bold attempt by the Europeans to define common international rules in the field of civil of civil law and corruption. The basic idea behind the approach taken by the Council to tackle corruption from a civil law perspective was the realization that, in certain cases, such as in competition situations, the party who has suffered damage as a result of an act of corruption, might be more interested in recovering the money lost, than to see the other party, the presumed briber, in prison.[88]

The Civil Law Convention grew out of a meeting of a Committee of European Ministers held in November 1997 during which they adopted Resolution (97) 24 on the 20 Guiding Principles for the fight against corruption. Principle 17 specifically calls on States to 'ensure that civil law takes into account the need to fight corruption and in particular provides for effective remedies for those whose rights and interests are affected by corruption.'[89] At their 22nd Conference in Chisinau in June 1999, the European Ministers of Justice adopted yet another resolution on the

---

[84] Criminal Law Convention, Art. 12.

[85] Explanatory Report, Criminal Law Convention on Corruption para. 64 (1998) [hereinafter Council Convention Exploratory Report], available at http://conventions coe.intlTreaty/en/Reports/Html/173.htm.

[86] *Id.*, para. 65

[87] CETS No. 174 Entered into force in November 2003.

[88] See Peter Csonka, Civil Law and Corruption, Paper presented at the 9th International Anti-Corruption Conference [hereinafter 'Csonka'].

[89] See Resolution (97) 24.

fight against corruption. Resolution No. 3 urged the Committee of Ministers to adopt the draft convention on civil aspects of corruption and open it for signature before the end of 1999. Following the adoption of the Criminal Law Convention in 1997, the Council of Europe finalized an international legal instrument to fight corruption through civil law remedies.

Definition of Corruption for the Purpose of Civil Law

At the beginning of its work the drafters initially adopted a definition of corruption[90] that was later abandoned in favor of the one that is now included in Article 2. The word 'corruption' as used in the Civil Law Convention means 'requesting, offering, giving or accepting directly or indirectly a bribe or any other undue advantage or the prospect thereof, which distorts the proper performance of any duty or behavior required of the recipient of the bribe, the undue advantage of the prospect thereof.'[91] This definition is intended to reflect the Council's comprehensive approach to the fight against corruption as a threat not only to international business or to financial interests but to democratic values, the rule of law and social and economic progress.[92] While Parties are free to do so, they do not necessarily have to adopt this definition of corruption in their domestic law. The drafters' aims in proposing this definition are two-fold: (1) to clarify the meaning of the term 'corruption' in the context of this Convention; and (2) to provide a proper legal framework within which the other obligations arising out of the Convention operate.[93] The definition also has the added advantage of laying the foundation for any future work in the field of civil law and corruption, both at the national and international level, and serves as a precondition for any agreement that can be reached at an international level in this area.[94]

Victim's Right to Compensation

Article 3, paragraph 1 embodies the main purpose of the Convention which is to provide a right of action, in accordance with each State's domestic law, to compensation for damages resulting from an act of corruption. Paragraph 2 specifies the extent of damages to be granted by the court and distinguishes between 'material damages' or *damnum emergens* and 'loss of profits' or *lucrum*

---

90 The original definition of corruption was 'bribery and any other behavior in relation to persons entrusted with responsibilities in the public or private sector, which violates the duties that follow from their status as a public official, private employee, independent agent or other relationship of that kind and is aimed at obtaining undue advantage of any kind for themselves or for others.' It was felt that this definition would not match the legal definition of corruption in most member States. See Explanatory Report to the Civil Law Convention on Corruption, para. 29 (1999) [(hereinafter cited as 'Explanatory Report'].

91 Art. 2.

92 Explanatory Report, *supra* note 90, at para. 33.

93 *Id.*

94 Csonka, *supra* note 88, at 4.

cessans. The former represents the actual, effective material damages suffered by the victim while the latter represents the profits which could be reasonably have been expected but that were not obtained as a result of corruption. Finally, 'non-pecuniary loss' refers to those losses that do not amount to a tangible or material economic loss and cannot therefore be immediately calculated. This would include loss of reputation that may be compensated financially or by the publication of the judgment at the costs of the defendant. The Convention leaves it to the Parties to decide, again in accordance with their domestic law, the nature of non-pecuniary losses that will be covered, as well as the nature of compensation that will be given. Conceivably, a Party would be in full compliance with its obligations under this provision, if its domestic law recognizes compensation of loss of reputation only under compensation for non-pecuniary loss.

Burden of Proof

Article 4, paragraph 1 sets forth the elements of a claim for damages which the plaintiff must prove. In order to obtain compensation, the plaintiff must prove that (1) an act of corruption has occurred, (2) that the defendant is responsible for this act of corruption, (3) that the plaintiff has suffered damage, and (4) that there is a causal link between the act of corruption and the damages. The Explanatory Report has clarified the drafters' intent with respect to these elements of proof. First, as to unlawful and culpable behavior on the part of the defendant, it states:

> Those who directly and knowingly participate in the corruption are primarily liable for the damage and, above all, the giver and the recipient of the bribe, as well as those who incited or aided the corruption. Moreover, those who failed to take the appropriate steps, in the light of the responsibilities which lie on them, to prevent corruption would also be liable for damage. This means that employers are responsible for the corrupt behavior of their employees if, for example, they neglect to organize their company adequately or fail to exert appropriate control over their employees.[95]

The Explanatory Report also points out that the damage referred to in Article 4, paragraph 1 (ii) can only give rise to a right to compensation if it is 'sufficiently characterized,' particularly as regards the connection with the victim himself. Moreover, this provision does not prevent Parties to the Convention from allowing a person other than the one who suffered damage to bring a claim for its compensation.[96]

To constitute an adequate causal link between the act and the damage, the latter need not be an 'extraordinary consequence' of corruption. An 'ordinary' damage is all that is required as in the following example included in the Explanatory Report:

> 'Loss of profits' by an unsuccessful competitor, who would have obtained the contract if an act of corruption had not been committed, is an ordinary consequence of corruption

---

95 See Explanatory Report, *supra* note 90, at para. 38.

96 *Id.*, at para 43.

> and should normally be compensated. On the other hand, there would be no adequate connection if, for example, an unsuccessful competitor, in his or her anger and disappointment over the loss of business fell down the stairs and broke his leg.[97]

Paragraph 2 of Article 4 provides for joint and several liabilities of several joint defendants, regardless of whether they knowingly co-operated or whether one of them is simply liable through his own negligent behavior. The term 'jointly and severally liable' as used in the Convention means that anyone who has suffered damages as a result of an act of corruption, for which several defendants are liable, may seek full compensation from any one or more of these defendants.[98]

Victims Contributory Negligence

The behavior of the victim of an act of corruption may also have some bearing on his right to compensation. Accordingly, Article 6 provides for an exception to the victim's right to full compensation of the damage suffered contained in Article 3, which allows for a reduction or disallowance of compensation, if the victim through his own culpable behavior 'contributed to the damage or to its aggravation.'[99] The operative words here are the 'culpable behavior' of the victim since not everything will disturb his right to compensation. 'Culpable behavior' are also the watch words in assessing the victim's contribution to damage suffered and its aggravation.[100] The Convention leaves it up to the judge to decide, in light of the circumstances surrounding the act of corruption, what constitutes 'culpable conduct' for purposes of reducing the compensation to the victim.

Evidence Gathering

To assist the victim of an act of corruption in establishing his claim for compensation in a civil proceeding, the Convention includes a provision requiring each state Party to put in place 'effective procedure for the acquisition of evidence in civil proceedings arising from an act of corruption.'[101] The gathering of evidence to substantiate a claim for compensation could prove to be an insurmountable hurdle for most victims to overcome since corruption, by its nature, is secretive.[102] Although Article 11 does not address it, there are a number of methods of confronting this problem. For instance, some legal systems (common law jurisdictions, in the main) allow the plaintiff to apply for an order of discovery while in other legal systems, typically civil law jurisdictions, a judge can appoint a specific person to obtain the information required.

It is worthy of note that the drafters chose not to follow the path taken by the

---

97 *Id.*, at para. 45.
98 *Id.*, at para. 46.
99 Art. 6.
100 See Explanatory Report, *supra* note 90, at para. 55.
101 Art. 11.
102 See Explanatory Report, note 90 *supra*, at para. 77.

African Union anti-corruption convention of reversing the burden of proof in civil proceedings relating to corruption cases. This is because the Convention aims at encouraging those Parties which do not have any effective procedures for the acquisition of evidence, to adopt such procedures in particular in order to deal with corruption cases.[103]

Protecting the Rights of Plaintiff-Victims and the Accused

It is usually the case that attempts by victims of acts of corruption to recover damages through civil actions are frustrated by the dilatory tactics of the alleged offenders. Unscrupulous debtors will spare no efforts at concealing or dissipating their illicitly acquired assets in anticipation of an adverse judgment. To protect innocent plaintiffs seeking to vindicate their rights under this Convention, Article 12 provides for interim measures to enable these victims to apply to court for such interim orders as are necessary to preserve their rights and interests (for example, for the preservation or the custody of property during the course of civil proceedings).[104] The goal of these interim measures is to preserve the position of both the plaintiff and defendant pending a final judgment on the matter. It is up to the parties to decide how this objective can be accomplished. For instance, they can agree between themselves to provide for the possibility of adopting interim measures before the proceedings have formally started, at the beginning or during or a combination of these.[105]

With a view to ensuring that the goals of the civil justice system are not defeated, Article 12 aims at accomplishing two things. First, providing preliminary means of securing assets out of which a final judgment may be satisfied; and second, maintaining the status quo pending determination of the issues at stake.[106]

To demonstrate its concern for the rights of defendants in civil proceedings for compensation, the drafters provide in Article 7 a statute of limitations. The idea behind this time limitation is to provide a degree of certainty for both plaintiffs and defendants about the risks of obligation. Limitation rules generally requires a plaintiff to commence an action within a fixed period when he becomes aware of the act which gives rise to the claim or of the damage. Because limitation periods vary from country to country and even between types of cases, Article 7 shies away from prescribing a fixed period to be applied to all corruption cases. Rather, Article 7 provides that proceedings for the recovery of damages are subject to a limitation period of 3 years from the date the plaintiff becomes aware or should have become aware that damages occurred or that an act of corruption has taken place, and of the identity of the responsible person. The Explanatory Report explains that in the interest of balance and fairness the absolute bar on commencing civil actions should not come into effect before the expiry of 10 years

103 *Id.*, at para. 78.
104 Art. 12.
105 See Explanatory Report, *supra* note 90, at para. 81.
106 *Id.*, at para. 83.

of the corrupt act.[107]

Recognizing that rules regulating suspension or interruption of limitation periods also vary from country to country, and are also bound with other aspects of domestic procedures for the administration of justice, Article 7, paragraph 2 does not prescribe a uniform approach for corruption cases.

Whistle-blower Protection

The Convention includes a provision to protect employees, who in good faith and on the basis of reasonable grounds, report their suspicions on corrupt practices or behaviors, against any 'unjustified sanction.'[108] The appropriateness of the protection against unwarranted sanction is a matter left to the domestic law of the Parties. That said, the appropriate protection the drafters' have in mind is the kind that 'encourages employees to report their suspicions to the responsible person or authority' without fear of possible reprisals.[109] By the same token, any disciplinary action taken against an employee for reporting an act of corruption to his superiors will be deemed an unjustified sanction. For example, a dismissal or demotion of a whistle-blowing employee or any action taken that has the effect of limiting the employee's career advancement would constitute an 'unjustified sanction' within the meaning of this Convention.[110]

International Cooperation and Monitoring of Implementation

The Civil Law Convention in its Article 13 requires Parties to co-operate, whenever possible, in accordance with existing and relevant international legal instruments, in matters relating to civil proceedings in cases of corruption. Co-operation is encouraged in areas such as the service of documents, obtaining evidence abroad, jurisdiction, recognition and enforcement of foreign judgments and litigation costs. Monitoring the implementation of the Convention is in the capable hands of the 'Group of States against Corruption – GRECO.'[111] The drafters recognized from the outset that the establishment of an efficient and appropriate mechanism to monitor the implementation of international legal instruments against corruption was an essential element for the effectiveness and credibility of the Council of Europe's initiative in this area.[112]

---

107 *Id.*, at para. 60.

108 Art. 9.

109 See Explanatory Report, *supra* note 90, at para. 71.

110 *Id.* at para. 69.

111 Art. 14. GRECO was established by the Council of Europe following the adoption of the Criminal Law Convention in 1997. GRECO's aim is 'to improve the capacity of its members to fight corruption by following up, through a dynamic process of mutual evaluation and peer pressure, compliance with their undertakings in this field.' See Explanatory Report, *supra* note 90, at para. 93.

112 *Id.*, at para. 92.

THE INTER-AMERICAN CONVENTION AGAINST CORRUPTION

Of all the first generation multilateral instruments that make up the international anti-corruption regime, only the Inter-American Convention[113] attempts to give a broader meaning to the term corruption or bribery. The Inter-American Convention was the first anti-corruption treaty in the world resulting from the December 1994 Summit of the Americas Declaration of Principles and Plan of Action that called for the elaboration 'within the OAS,'

> [W]ith due regard to applicable treaties and national legislation, [of] a hemispheric approach to acts of corruption in both the public and private sectors that would include extradition and prosecution of individuals so charged, through negotiation of a new hemispheric agreement or new arrangements within the existing framework for international cooperation.[114]

In the 1994 Summit of the Americas Declaration of Principles and Plan of Action, the Heads of State of thirty-four nations of the southern hemisphere pointedly linked the survival of democracy to the eradication of corruption. 'Effective democracy,' they declared, 'requires a comprehensive attack on corruption as a factor of social disintegration and distortion of the economic system that undermines the legitimacy of political institutions.'[115] In the preamble to the Inter-American Convention that followed the 1994 summit, again the leaders of the OAS came back to the theme of corruption as a phenomenon that undermines the legitimacy of public institutions and strikes at society, moral order and justice, as well as the comprehensive development of peoples. Acknowledging that corruption has international dimensions, the signatories of the Convention agreed on the need for prompt adoption of an international instrument to promote and facilitate international cooperation in fighting corruption and the responsibility of States to hold corrupt persons accountable. The instrument that came out of this summit has been widely acclaimed as perhaps the most far-reaching multilateral agreement to combat corruption.[116]

---

113 See Inter-American Convention Against Corruption, *opened for signature* 29 March 1996, reprinted in *International Law Materials*, 35, 724 (1996) [hereinafter Inter-American Convention].

114 An unprecedented 21 countries signed the Convention immediately upon the conclusion of negotiations. They were later joined by the United States and Guatemala. To date, 26 States have signed and 17 have deposited instruments of ratification. Inter-American Convention, at B-58. Available at http://www.oas.org/En/prog/juridico/english/Sigs/B-58.html> (last visited 29 February 2000).

115 See Summit of the Americas: Declaration of Principles and Plan of Action, 11 December 1994, *International Law Materials*, 35, 808, 811.

116 See Henning, *supra* note 70, at 793, 807; see also David A. Gantz, 'Globalizing Sanctions Against Foreign Bribery: The Emergence of an International Legal Consensus,' *Northwestern Journal of International Law and Business*, 18, 457, 478 (1998) (The Inter-American Convention 'went much further than any other actual or proposed international agreement in seeking not only to make bribery of foreign officials a crime in the country of

Like the Criminal Law Convention, the OAS anti-corruption treaty attacks the problem of corruption from both the supply and demand sides.[117] But then it goes one step farther than the other instruments examined thus far; it expressly proscribes 'illicit enrichment' – defined as 'a significant increase in the assets of a government official that he cannot reasonably explain in relation to his lawful earnings during the performance of his functions.'[118] The focus on illicit enrichment as an integral part of the definition of corruption in the Inter-American Convention is not shared by the other multilateral anti-bribery conventions. They, on the other hand, are focused exclusively on two varieties of corruption: either active or passive or both.

Article VI(1) defines three principal 'acts of corruption':

> a. The solicitation or acceptance, directly or indirectly, by a government official or a person who performs public functions, of any article of monetary value, or other benefit, such as a gift, favor, promise or advantage for himself or for another person or entity, in exchange for any act or omission in the performance of his public functions.
>
> b. The offering or granting, directly or indirectly, to a government official or a person who performs public functions, of any article of monetary value, or other benefit, such as a gift, favor, promise or advantage for himself or for another person or entity, in exchange for any act or omission in the performance of his public functions; and
>
> c. Any act or omission in the discharge of his duties by a government official or a person who performs public functions for the purpose of illicitly obtaining benefits for himself or for a third party...

The first two acts of corruption, Article VI(a)-(b) reflect the traditional crime of bribery, that is, a payment involving a *quid pro quo* between the offeror and the public official where each party acts with the intent that the exchange influence the exercise of governmental authority. The Inter-American Convention's broad view of corruption is evident in the third form of corruption in Article VI(1), which makes it a crime when a public official acts or fails to act 'for the purpose of illicitly obtaining benefits for himself or for a third party.' This form of corruption does not involve a two-party transaction, as such there is no *quid pro quo* linking the receipt of the benefit to the official's conduct. Article VI(1) makes the act of corruption the *illicit* receipt or appropriation of a benefit that results from the performance of one's official duties.

In addition to Article VI, the Inter-American Convention also contains specific prohibitions on the misuse of one's office for personal enrichment. These provisions, as one publicist acknowledges, 'expand the definition of corruption by identifying more subtle forms of misconduct that, while resulting in the personal enrichment of the official, fall outside the traditional two-party exchange of a

---

the exporting firm or individuals, but also in encouraging local governments to deal more effectively with the problem of domestic corruption').

117 See Inter-American Convention, *supra* note 113, Art. VI.

118 *Id.* Art. IX.

bribe.'[119] A separate provision, Article IX, defines 'Illicit Enrichment,' as '... a significant increase in the assets of a government official that he cannot reasonably explain in relation to his lawful earnings during the performance of his functions.'[120] The intent behind this provision is 'to make proof of corruption much easier by removing any requirement to demonstrate a nexus between a benefit gained by an official and a particular governmental action.'[121] The burden of proof is on the office holder to explain the disproportionate increase in his assets. This reversal of the burden of proof became a stumbling block in the application of this provision in the United States and Canada. The governments of these two countries objected to this provision on the ground that it violated their constitutional presumption of innocence. Canada attached to its ratification of the Inter-American Convention a 'Statement of Understanding,' which reads as follows:

> Article IX provides that the obligation of a State Party to establish the offence of illicit enrichment shall be 'Subject to its Constitution and the fundamental principles of its legal system.' As the offence contemplated by Article IX would be contrary to the presumption of innocence guaranteed by Canada's Constitution, Canada will not implement Article IX, as provided for by this provision.[122]

The United States also attached a reservation to Article IX by way of the following 'understanding':

> ILLICIT ENRICHMENT. The United States of America intends to assist and cooperate with other States Parties pursuant to paragraph 3 of Article IX of the Convention to the extent permitted by its domestic law. The United States recognizes the importance of combating improper financial gains by public officials, and has criminal statutes to deter or punish such conduct. These statutes obligate senior-level officials in the federal government to file truthful disclosure statements, subject to criminal penalties. They also permit prosecution of federal public officials who evade taxes on wealth that is acquired illicitly. The offense of illicit enrichment as set forth in Article IX of the Convention, however, places the burden of proof on the defendant, which is inconsistent with the United States constitution and fundamental principles of the United States legal system. Therefore, the United States understands that it is not obligated to establish a new criminal offense of illicit enrichment under Article IX of the Convention.[123]

Aside from the Canadian and American reservations there has been no other reservation or understanding to Article IX. Despite the constitutional presumption

---

[119] Henning, *supra* note 70, at 813.

[120] Inter-American Convention, Article IX.

[121] Henning, *supra* note 70, at 814.

[122] OAS, Reservations to the Inter-American Convention Against Corruption, 29 March 1996, *International Law Materials*, 5 (1960), available at http://www.oas.org/juridico/english/sigs/b-58.html (last visited on 2 February 2005).

[123] S. Res. of 27 July 2000, 106th Cong. (2000), available at www.usdoj.gov/criminal/fraud/fcpa/OAS.htm (last visited 2 February 2005).

of innocence in some OAS member states, the crime of illicit enrichment has been added to the penal codes of some signatories of the Inter-American Convention.[124] Moreover, the more recent African Union Convention on Preventing and Combating and the United Nations Convention Against Corruption (discussed below) contain provisions on the crime of illicit enrichment that were clearly influenced by Article IX of the Inter-American Convention.

THE AFRICAN UNION CONVENTION ON PREVENTING AND COMBATING CORRUPTION

Sensitive to the havoc that corruption has caused in many African countries, African leaders resolved during the Thirty-fourth Ordinary Session of the Assembly of Heads of State and Government of the Organization of African Unity ('OAU') in June 1998 in Ouagadougou, Burkina Faso, to convene a high level meeting of experts 'to consider ways and means of removing obstacles to the enjoyment of economic, social and cultural rights, including the fight against corruption and impunity.'[125] The African leaders were further spurred on by a follow-up decision of the Thirty-seventh Ordinary Session of the Assembly of Heads of State and Government of the OAU held in Lusaka, Zambia, in July 2001 as well as the July 2002 Declaration of the Assembly of the African Union[126] relating to the New Partnership for Africa's Development calling for the setting up of a coordinated mechanism to combat corruption effectively. In signing on to the African Union Convention on Preventing and Combating Corruption (AU Corruption Convention), the continent's leaders agreed 'to formulate and pursue, as a matter of priority, a common penal policy aimed at protecting society against corruption.'[127]

Objectives of the Convention

The AU Corruption Convention that was adopted by the 2nd Ordinary Session of the Assembly of the Union in July 2003 and opened for signature immediately thereafter[128] is a relatively compact document of 28 articles. Its core objectives are

---

124 See generally Peter W. Schroth, 'The United States and the International Bribery Convention,' *American Journal of Comparative Law*, 50 (supp.), 593 (2000) [hereinafter 'Schroth']. It also appears as Section 10 of the Hong Kong Prevention of Bribery Ordinance; and Article 34 of the Botswana Corruption and Economic Act discussed in chapter 4 *supra*.

125 Resolution AHG-Dec 126 (XXXIV) 1998.

126 In July 2000, the African Union replaced the OAU. See Constitutive Act of the African Union, 11 July 2000, OAU Doc. CAB/LEG/23.15 (entered into force 26 May 2001), available at http://www.africa-union.org/About_AU/Constitutive_Act.htm. (last visited on 20 January 2005).

127 See Preamble to AU Corruption Convention.

128 The Convention will enter into force when 15 countries have ratified or acceded to it. Article 23(3). As of 31 January 2005, 34 countries have signed the convention but as of

listed in Article 2 as (1) the promotion and strengthening the development of national mechanisms aimed at preventing, detecting, punishing and eradicating corruption in the public and private sectors; (2) to promote, facilitate and regulate cooperation among States Parties to ensure that the measures adopted to fight against corruption are effective; (3) coordinating and harmonizing continental-wide policies and strategies for the prevention, detection, punishment and eradication of corruption; and (4) establishing an enabling environment that fosters transparency and accountability in the management of public affairs.[129] While most of the articles in the convention commence with a mandatory general principle, the manner of its implementation is left to the discretion of each State Party.[130]

Prohibited Practices

The convention proscribes outright five categories of corrupt activities: bribery of public officials,[131] bribery in the private sector,[132] abuse of office,[133] the diversion of State property by a public official who received it in his official capacity[134] and the use or concealment of the proceeds of bribery.[135] The AU convention prohibits both active and passive bribery, that is, the offeror and recipient of the payment may be subject to prosecution. It defines active bribery of public officials as 'the offering or granting, directly or indirectly, to a public official ... of any goods of monetary value, or other benefit, such as a gift, favor, promise or advantage for himself … in exchange for any act or omission in the performance of his public functions.' Passive bribery is defined as 'the solicitation or acceptance, directly or indirectly, by a public official … of any goods of monetary value, or other benefit, such as a gift, favor, promise or advantage for himself … in exchange for any act or omission in the performance of his public functions.' Interestingly, unlike the European and Latin American anti-corruption conventions, the AU Corruption Convention does not cover corruption as it relates to *foreign* public officials or officials of international organizations. Presumably these officials are free to engage in the acts prohibited in Article 4 without fear of sanctions. This would be an unfortunate and unintended consequence of the drafter's failure to address this aspect of corruption. As one commentator laments, 'the offering of bribes to foreign public officials, including officials of public international organizations, is at the root of many corrupt administrations in Africa.'[136]

---

writing only six (Comoros, Libya, Lesotho, Namibia, Niger and Uganda) have ratified it.

129 Art. 2.

130 Each State Party shall 'adopt legislative and other measures to proscribe ....'

131 Art. 4(1)(a) and (b).

132 Art. 4(1)e) and (f).

133 Art. 4(1)(c).

134 Art. 4(1)(d).

135 Art. 4(h).

136 See Nsongurua J. Udombana, 'Fighting Corruption Seriously? Africa's Anti-Corruption Convention,'*Singapore Journal of International and Comparative Law*, 7, 447, 464 (2003) [hereinafter 'Fighting Corruption Seriously.']

While the bribery provisions dealing with public officials do not require proof of a breach of duty, those relating to the private sector require proof that the bribe induced the employee to breach a duty owed to the employer. Article 4(1)(e) defines private sector bribery as 'the offering or giving, promising, solicitation or acceptance, directly or indirectly, of any undue advantage to or by any person who directs or works for, in any capacity, a private sector entity, for himself or herself or for anyone else, *for him or her to act, or refrain from acting, in breach of his or her duties.*' The AU Corruption Convention acknowledges the laundering of the proceeds of corruption[137] and includes the crime of 'illicit enrichment'[138] as one of the prohibited acts of corruption but leaves it to the States Parties, following their own domestic law, to adopt necessary legislation to criminalize such conduct. The definition of illicit enrichment as 'the significant increase in the assets of a public official or any other person which he or she cannot reasonably explain in relation to his or her income' might prove to be problematic from a due process point of view. This definition shifts the common law burden of proof away from the prosecution to the accused who under normal circumstances enjoys the right to a presumption of innocence until proven guilty by a competent court or tribunal.[139] As a matter of fact, presumptions of innocence are entrenched in the constitutions of many African countries. For instance, section 35(2) of the South African Constitution guarantees to the accused the right 'to be presumed innocent, to remain silent, and not to testify during the proceedings.'[140] Similarly the Constitution of Kenya also includes a presumption of innocence provision in paragraph 77(2)(a): 'Every person who is charged with a criminal offence ... shall be presumed to be innocent until he is proved or pleaded guilty.'[141] However, it would appear that this presumption in the Kenya Constitution which is found in the Nigerian Constitution,[142] is qualified with a view to saving the illicit enrichment reversal of the burden of proof. Paragraph 77(12)(a) of the Constitution of Kenya demonstrates this qualification with the language: 'Nothing contained in or done under authority of any law shall be held to be inconsistent with or in contravention

[137] Money-laundering within the meaning of the convention is defined as (a) 'the conversion, transfer or disposal of property, knowing that such property is the proceeds of corruption or related offenses for the purpose of concealing or disguising the illicit origin of the property or of helping any person who is involved in the commission of the offense to evade the legal consequences of his or her action; (b) the concealment or disguise of the true nature, source, location, disposition, movement or ownership of or rights with respect to property which is the proceeds of corruption or related offenses; and (c) the acquisition, possession or use of property with the knowledge at the time of receipt, that such property is the proceeds of corruption or related offenses.'

[138] Article 8 enjoins States Parties that have not yet criminalized illicit enrichment in their domestic law to do so by enacting the necessary legislation.

[139] See Article IX of the Inter-American Convention, notes 120-24 *supra* and accompanying discussion.

[140] S. Afr. Const. §35(2).

[141] Kenya Const. §§77(2)(a).

[142] Nig. Const. §36(5).

of ... subsection (2)(a) to the extent that the law in question imposes upon a person charged with a criminal offence the burden of proving particular facts.'[143]

This reverse onus provision is also at odds with Article 14 of the convention which guarantees anyone accused of committing acts of corruption the right to 'a fair trial in criminal proceedings in accordance with the minimum guarantees contained in the African Charter on Human and Peoples' Rights and any other relevant international human rights instrument recognized by the concerned States Parties.' Included among these 'minimum guarantees' is the unqualified 'right to be presumed innocent until proved guilty by a competent court or tribunal' found in Article 7(1)(b). The International Covenant on Civil and Political Rights, which has been ratified by over 40 African States, also guarantees to the accused the right to be presumed innocent until proven guilty.[144] Restrictions on the right to presumption of innocence are usually justified on the ground that the rights set out in these human rights instruments are qualified rights, subject to a rational limitation and require some balancing between two competing sets of public interests: the wider interests of society as a whole, such as national security, public order and public safety, as against the rights of particular individuals. Restrictions on the latter are justified provided they pursue a legitimate goal and are proportionate to that goal. Differently put, the restriction on individual rights that are guaranteed must be a proportional response to the social problem being addressed, for example, corruption, and should go no further than is reasonably necessary to safeguard the relevant public interest. This principle was deftly handled in a number of landmark cases in which Hong Kong's anti-corruption legislation, specifically Section 10 on illicit enrichment, was challenged on due process grounds.[145]

Prevention and Eradication

The focus of the AU Corruption is two-fold: prevention and eradication of corruption. Towards this end, the convention contains several provisions dealing with the preventive aspects or the front-end, so to speak, of the trans-continental fight against corruption. The convention includes an assets declaration provision requiring all or designated public officials 'to declare their assets at the time of assumption of office, during and after their term of office in the public service.'[146]

---

[143] Kenya Const. §77(12)(a).

[144] Art. 14.

[145] See for example, Sin Yap Ming: Presumption of Innocence and Rationality/Proportionality Tests (1991) HKPLR, 1, 88; Attorney General v. Lee Kwon Kut: Presumption of Innocence and Rationality/Proportionality Tests (1993) HKPLR, 3, 72; and Attorney General v. Hui Kin-hong: Presumption of Innocence versus Eradication of Corruption [1995] HKCLR, 1, 227. The courts in these cases sought to strike a balance between the concerns of law enforcement on the one hand and the right to presumption of innocence on the other by recognizing that the latter can be limited provided such limitations were rational and proportional.

[146] Art. 7(1). A similar provision can be found in the Cameroon Constitution but it has

Other preventive measures contained in the convention include the establishment of a code of conduct for public officials, sensitizing and training these public servants on ethical matters;[147] promoting the education and sensitization of the population to respect the public good and public interest;[148] setting up independent national anti-corruption agencies;[149] developing disciplinary measures and up-to-date investigative techniques and procedures;[150] and guaranteeing a right of access to any information required to assist in the fight against corruption.[151]

Provision is made for relaxing bank secrecy laws to permit greater access to hidden assets. This is an important provision in the Convention. All too often efforts to trace and recover the proceeds of corruption are thwarted by the wall of silence that private banks around the world erect to shield their clients from investigations. This banker's instinct to valorize client's confidentiality over society's interest, this reflexive respect for secrecy have also proved to be tools for money laundering.[152] Under Article 17 of the AU Convention, States Parties are not allowed to invoke banking secrecy to justify their refusal to cooperate in the

---

never be followed. See Article 66 of Law No. 96-06 of 18 January 1996 to amend the Constitution of 2 June 1972.

[147] Art. 7(2).

[148] Art. 5(8).

[149] Arts. 5(3) and 20. Frequently mentioned as the necessary conditions for the success of these anti-corruption monitoring bodies in the fight against corruption are the following: (i) Political independence – Benin's anti-corruption agency was found to have low credibility and a poor record of anti-corruption investigations because it operates under the jurisdiction of the executive branch; See US General Accounting Office, *Foreign Assistance: US Anti-corruption Programs in Sub-Saharan Africa Will Require Time and Commitment*, GAO-04-506 (Washington, D.C.: April 2004, p. 28, note 20 [hereinafter 'GAO Report'] (ii) Sufficient funding and human resource capacity – according to a 2000 United States Agency for International Development assessment of a number of anti-corruption commissions in Africa, Uganda's was unable to undertake its work because it lacked sufficient funding; [*Id.* Note 21] . In contrast, the very successful and much admired Hong Kong Independent Commission Against Corruption (ICAC) had a total staff of 1,286 members in 2001 and a budget of HK$686.7 million (US$88 million). Similarly, Singapore's Corrupt Practices Investigation Bureau ('CPIB') had a total staff of 80 members and a budget of S$10.7 million (US$6.3 million) in 2001. Hong Kong's per capital expenditure of US$12.57 for fighting corruption is much higher than Singapore's US$1.54 per capita expenditure because the ICAC's three-pronged strategy of investigation, education, and prevention has required more manpower and funds than the CPIB's emphasis on investigation. See John S.T. Quah, 'Best Practices for Curbing Corruption in Asia,' *The Governance Brief* (Issue 11-2004)] . (iii) Political will of leadership. (iv) An adequate legal framework. Add to these effective partners, such as law enforcement, an independent and competent judiciary, and free and effective media, to name a few. See GAO Report.

[150] Art. 7(3).

[151] Art. 9.

[152] See Richard C. Morais, 'Private Banking: R.I.P.,' Forbes Magazine, 11 Deecmber 2001. Available at http://www.forbes.com/forbes/2001/1112/080_print.html (last visited on 9 February 2005).

tracing and detecting of the proceeds of corruption. Concomitantly, States Parties are expected to waive bank secrecy laws on 'doubtful accounts' in order to permit 'competent authorities the right to obtain from banks and financial institutions, under judicial cover, any evidence in their possession.'[153] The provisions on bank secrecy together with those on the funding of political parties[154] are significant innovations. In the same vein, the commitment of States Parties to ensure that any immunity granted to public officials shall not be an obstacle to the investigation of allegations against and the prosecution of such officials is equally noteworthy.[155] The grant of immunity from investigation and prosecution of high-ranking officials for corruption has always been a stumbling block in the fight against corruption.[156] While Article 7(5) does not entirely lift the immunity from investigation and prosecution enjoyed by certain high-level state officials, it does at least open that door a little wider by serving notice to corrupt officials that they cannot count on their immunity to shield them from criminal investigation and prosecution.

Engaging Civil Society

The AU Corruption Convention includes an open invitation to society at large to become fully engaged in the fight against corruption. A special role is reserved for the media and civil society in popularizing the convention. States Parties have also agreed to create an enabling environment that would permit the media and civil society to perform their watch-dog role.[157] The convention also provides whistle-blower protection so that citizens can 'report instances of corruption without fear of consequent reprisals'[158] or risk having their identities revealed.[159] To guard against possible abuse by disgruntled citizens who may wish to settle old scores by pointing accusing fingers at their enemies, a provision is included to punish those who falsely and maliciously accuse innocent citizens of engaging in corrupt activities.[160]

Assets Recovery

The assets recovery provisions of the AU Corruption Convention are perhaps the first of their kind in a multilateral anti-corruption instrument and for good reason. The African continent has been weakened by the steady hemorrhaging of its national wealth and resources through acts of corruption. According to the Nyanga Declaration on the Recovery and Repatriation of Africa's Wealth: '[a]n estimated

153 Art. 17(4).

154 Article 10 proscribes the use of 'funds acquired through illegal and corrupt practices to finance political parties.'

155 Art. 7(5).

156 See Fighting Corruption Seriously, *supra* note 136, at 468.

157 Art. 12(2),(3),(4).

158 Art. 5(6).

159 Art. 5(5).

160 Art. 5(7).

US $20-40 billion has over the decades been illegally and corruptly appropriated from some of the world's poorest countries, most of them in Africa, by politicians, soldiers, businesspersons and other leaders, and kept abroad in the form of cash, stocks, real estate and other assets.'[161] Indeed, Africa's modern history of statehood is littered with unimaginable acts of indigenous spoliation. The continent has watched helplessly over the last four decades or so as an estimated $400 billion or more of its scarce development resources have been looted by its *own* leaders, elected as well as appointed, and stashed away in foreign countries.[162] Perhaps a few examples will suffice to make the point. There can be no better example to begin with than with the case of Field Marshall Mobutu Sese Seko, whose years as head of state remain the example *par excellence* of kleptocracy.[163] In the thirty-two years that he was the incontestable ruler of the former Republic of Zaire (now the Democratic Republic of the Congo), Mobutu succeeded in embezzling some four billion[164] dollars of his nation's wealth. If Mobutu's conduct was outrageous, that of the late General Sani Abacha of Nigeria, who seized power in a *coup d'état* in 1993 and ruled Nigeria with an iron fist until his sudden death in 1998, would require the suspension of disbelief. His tenure as head of a post-colonial African State is perhaps one of the most egregious cases of corruption by a public official in the 20th century. Based on credible estimates by the respectable *Times of London*, Abacha is believed to have stashed in European banks more than 3.6 billion pounds sterling (approximately $5.4 billion)[165] during his five-year tenure as Nigeria's Head of State.[166] Yet, he was not done. Over a two-year period and

---

[161] The Nyanga Declaration was signed on 4 March 2001 by representatives of Transparency International and the Governments of Botswana, Cameroon, Ethiopia, Ghana, Kenya, Malawi, Nigeria, South Africa, Uganda, Zambia, and Zimbabwe (for the full text, see http://www.transparency.org.

[162] *Id.*

[163] For an excellent account of how Mobutu systematically and methodically pillaged from his nation's resources, see Colette Braeckman, *Le Dinosaure: Le Zaire De Mobutu* (1990). Mobutu was ousted from power by Laurent Kabila and his band of loyal guerilla fighters in May 1997, and in September of the same year he died in exile in Morocco.

[164] See Seidi Mulero, *Nigeria: Use Stolen Billions to Pay the Debt,* IPS, 10 August 1998, available in WESTLAW, INTERPS File.

[165] *Id.*

[166] Several months after his death, General Abacha's widow was intercepted at the Kano International Airport with 38 suitcases stuffed with foreign currency. One of her sons who was accompanying her also had with him about $100 million in cash, while between $2 to $3 billion is believed in the safe-keeping of the late General's foreign front men. His security adviser returned $250 million to the Nigerian government, funds that had been set aside for distribution to African heads of state attending the 1998 summit of the Organization of African Unity holding at Ouagadougou, Burkina Faso. Ironically, General Abacha, who was expected at that summit, suffered a heart attack literally on the eve of the first plenary session. See Cameron Duodu, 'How the Grand Lootocracy Beggared Nigeria's People,' *The Observer* (UK), 22 November 1998, at 25. But General Abacha was not alone among Nigeria's former military rulers to raid the national coffers. Abacha's predecessor,

acting under the instructions of General Abacha, his national security adviser withdrew close to $2.45 billion from the Nigerian Central Bank ostensibly to pay back debts owed to Russian contractors for the construction of the giant Ajaokuta Steel plant.[167] The debts owed to the Russians were grossly overvalued allowing the Abacha family to pocket the difference. The fraud was uncovered by the successor government who eventually recovered some of the stolen money.[168] But the outrage continues. According to a Government White Paper, the Nigerian government earned $12.225 billion from sales of surplus petroleum during the 1990–1991 Gulf War. Of this amount the military generals made away with $12 billion and only $225 million trickled back into the national treasury.

As is typical of stolen national wealth, much of it is banked in offshore safe havens[169] and hardly ever invested in economically productive enterprises at home. To this extent, the victim country loses twice as the exported national wealth contributes to the problem of flight capital. Additionally, it is also typical in these cases that individuals involved usually skip town to avoid prosecution in their national courts. Again, the victim state loses a third time as its citizens are denied the opportunity to bring these individuals to justice. To be worthy of its name, it was imperative that a pan-African anti-corruption convention would include strong provisions on the repatriation of illicitly acquired and exported national wealth.

The provisions of the AU Corruption Convention on asset recovery cover the traditional water-front. They allow for the search, identification, tracing, administering and freezing or seizure of the 'instrumentalities and proceeds of corruption,' the confiscation of property whose value corresponds to that stolen by

---

General Ibrahim Babanguida, who was head of state from 1985-1993, is reputed to have placed in overseas accounts about 30 billion French Francs or roughly $5 billion. See Mulero, *supra* note 165.

167 See '$4 Billion Missing: Abacha Aide Held,' *Reuters*, 8 June 1998, available in WESTLAW, RTRLWIRES File. Ajaokuta has been described as one of Africa's disastrous development projects. It was budgeted at $1.4 billion but ended up costing the Nigerian taxpayer $4 billion. Construction began in the late 1970s and has dragged on at enormous cost for two decades. Yet, it has never produced a single piece of steel! *See Nigeria Alleges Huge Abacha Fraud*, BBC, 3 December 1998, available in WESTLAW, BBCWM File; Global Coalition for Africa, Corruption and Development in Africa, GCA/PF/N.2/11/1997, 12 (1997) .

168 The government of General Abdulsalami Abubakar recovered about $750 million of this money in various currency denominations from General Abacha's family. Apparently, the Abachas had no confidence in the Nigerian banks. The amount recovered included $625 million in dollar notes and another $125 million in pounds sterling. See *Nigeria Alleges Huge Abacha Fraud*, *supra* note 168, at 2.

169 General Abacha's illicitly acquired wealth was split up in various countries (Switzerland, Britain, Luxembourg, Liechtenstein and Jersey) in banks with an international network of branches. In Switzerland alone the general's funds were stashed in over a hundred accounts in 19 different banks – from the venerable Credit Suisse to M.M. Warburg Bank. See Swiss Federal Banking Commission, Abacha's Funds at Swiss Banks; Report of the Swiss Federal Banking Commission, 4 September 2000, at 3.

a public official, and the repatriation of these assets to the victim State.[170] Assets can be frozen or seized pending a final court judgment or[171] confiscated and handed over to the Requesting State even when criminal proceedings are pending ongoing on condition that the assets are returned to the Requested State.[172] At the request of a State Party, the Requested State Party is under an obligation, in so far as its law permits, to surrender any object which may be required as evidence in the Requested State or that can be used to support a request for extradition. The Requesting State gets to keep the returned evidence even if its extradition is denied.[173]

International Cooperation

Convinced that the fight against corruption can only be won through collaborative effort, the AU Corruption Convention includes provisions for its signatories to engage in mutual legal assistance through bilateral or multilateral treaty arrangements. States Parties are enjoined to provide each other with technical cooperation and assistance in the prevention, detection, investigation and punishment of acts of corruption;[174] to exchange studies, researches and technical expertise on how to prevent and combat corruption.[175] In the spirit of international

[170] Art. 16. The problems of recovery and repatriation of illicitly acquired assets are immense as the Nigerian government's efforts to repatriate late General Abacha's wealth banked abroad. After two years of trying, the government with the help of the Swiss Federal Office of Justice agreed to an out-of-court settlement with banks in Switzerland, Luxembourg, Liechtenstein and Britain. In return for the repatriation of about $1 billion in frozen assets stolen by the late military dictator and his family, the Nigerian authorities would drop all criminal charges for corruption and fraud against Abacha's son Mohammed Sani Abacha and businessman Bagudu Abubakar, a family friend. Furthermore, the Abacha family would be allowed to keep $100 million, a sum the Nigerians and the Swiss authorities agreed to treat as assets 'acquired prior to Abacha's term of office and which ... demonstrably do not derive from criminal acts.' *See* Cameron Duodu, 'Nigeria Retrieves Part of Stolen Billions,' D+C Development and Cooperation (No. 4, July/August 2002, p.29). The deal effectively brought to a close all proceedings in the Abacha case. See 'Swiss banks to return $1 billion in funds allegedly embezzled from Nigerian government,' Available in http://www.findarticles.com/p/ articles/mi_m1355/is (last visited on 9 February 2005.) In opting for a pragmatic solution to the recovery of its stolen assets, the Nigerian government had to engage in some trade-offs that resulted in rewarding the Abacha family with a $100 million windfall. It would be difficult to justify how on a general's salary in the Nigeria army, Abacha could have acquired $100 million prior to assuming the presidency of his country! On balance, the $1billion recovered, provided it is used for the social and economic development of the people of Nigeria, far outweighs the $100 million the Abachas were allowed to keep.

[171] Art. 16(1)(a).

[172] Art. 16(4).

[173] Art. 16(3).

[174] Art. 18(1).

[175] Art. 18(3).

cooperation, States Parties agree to work with other regional and international groupings to eradicate corruption in development aid[176] and in preventing corrupt practices in international trade transactions.[177]

The AU anti-corruption convention defines corruption as an extraditable offense and States Parties. In the absence of any extradition agreements in force between and among the States Parties the convention operates by default as an extradition treaty. Pursuant to Article 15 of the convention a State Party is under an obligation to extradite or to prosecute anyone charged with or convicted of offenses of corruption committed in the territory of another State Party.[178] This principle of *aut dedere aut judicare* is present in almost all the anti-corruption treaties examined. The inclusion of such a provision in the AU Corruption Convention provides the legal basis for extradition in the absence of a bilateral treaty. Its fundamental purpose is to 'ensure that individuals who are responsible for particularly serious crimes are brought to justice by providing for the effective prosecution and punishment of such individuals by a competent jurisdiction.'[179] The obligation of the custodial state to prosecute or extradite a fleeing felon is a major deterrent to high-ranking public officials who loot with impunity while in office, and hope that when thrown out they can seek asylum in safe haven states without ever having to answer for their outrageous conduct.

Jurisdiction

The Convention's jurisdictional provision breaks no new ground; subject to any other criminal jurisdiction exercised by a State Party in accordance with its domestic law,[180] the Convention vests each State with jurisdiction over acts of corruption when:

1 the breach is committed wholly or partially inside its territory;
2 the offence is committed by one of its nationals outside its territory or by a

---

[176] The focus on protecting development aid from the clammy fingers of corrupt public officials is understandable. Between 1995 and 2002, Sub-Saharan Africa received an estimated $114 billion in bilateral and multilateral development assistance. Yet these African countries have consistently being ranked at the bottom of the United Nations Development Program's Human Development report, which measures life expectancy, gross domestic product per capita, and literacy. A ranking that suggests that much of this money was looted by senior level state officials. This brazen diversion of overseas development assistance to the private bank accounts of African leaders has provoked a donor backlash. It is reported that some donors, such as DANIDA (Danish International Development Agency) cut off aid to Malawi and Kenya as a consequence of blatant corruption. See Susan Dicklitch, *African corruption is a crime against humanity*, Christian Science Monitor, 8 September 2004.

[177] Art. 19.

[178] Art. 15(3).

[179] Art. 15.

[180] Art. 13(2).

person who resides in its territory;

3 the alleged criminal is present in its territory and it does not extradite such person to another country; and

4 when the offence, although committed outside its jurisdiction, affects, in the view of the State concerned, its vital interests or the deleterious or harmful consequences or effects of such offences impact on the State Party.[181]

Monitoring and Follow-up

Finally, to ensure that the AU anti-corruption convention is respected in the observation and not in its breach, an oversight mechanism is built into the instrument. First, each State Party on signing or ratifying the convention is expected to designate an independent and autonomous 'national authority or agency' to oversee the fight against corruption at the national level.[182] In addition, the convention sets up a high-level Advisory Board on Corruption whose eleven members are elected by the Executive Council of the African Union from a list of experts of the 'highest integrity, impartiality, and recognized competence in matters relating to preventing and combating corruption ... .'[183] The board is required to submit regular reports to the executive council on the progress made by each State Party in complying with its obligations under the convention. This board also receives annual reports from the Article 20 national anti-corruption authorities on their work in supervising the fight against corruption. Its duties include *inter alia* the promotion and adoption of continent-wide anti-corruption measures; working to harmonize the codes of conduct for public officials established by States Parties; the collection and documentation of information on the nature and scope of corruption in Africa; sensitizing the African public on the negative effects of corruption.[184]

THE UNITED NATIONS CONVENTION AGAINST CORRUPTION

As the first globally binding anti-corruption instrument, the 2004 United Nations Convention against Corruption ('UN Convention') represents a transition to the second generation of multilateral instruments that is not regional in scope and designed to operate in a more restricted environment. The UN Convention is truly a global instrument, 113 countries have signed, while twelve have already ratified, the instrument. The convention was adopted in Mexico in December 2004 but its genesis can be traced to a General Assembly resolution[185] of 4 December 2000 recognizing the need for an effective international legal instrument against corruption, independent of the United Nations Convention against Transnational

---

181 Art. 13(1).
182 Art. 20.
183 Art. 22(2).
184 Art. 22(5).
185 Resolution 55/61.

Organized Crime.[186] Resolution 55/61 set up an Ad Hoc Committee for the Negotiation of a Convention against Corruption ('Ad Hoc Committee').[187] In two subsequent resolutions[188] the General Assembly directed the Ad Hoc Committee to negotiate a broad and effective convention and urged the committee to complete its work by the end of 2003. The text of the convention was negotiated during seven sessions of the Ad Hoc Committee between January 2002 and October 2003. At the fifty-eighth session of the General Assembly, the committee submitted its final report[189] together with a draft convention. On 31 October 2003 the General Assembly adopted the draft convention[190] and opened it for signature by Member States. The Convention will enter into force when 30 countries have ratified it.[191]

The Preamble to the UN Convention draws attention to the serious problems and threats posed by corruption to the stability and security of the international community, undermining democratic institutions and values, ethical values and justice and jeopardizing sustainable development and the rule of law. The Preamble also points to cases of corruption that involve vast quantities of assets that constitute a substantial proportion of the resources of States and the threat high-level corruption poses to the political stability and sustainable development of the victim States. Recognizing that corruption is no longer a local matter but a phenomenon that cuts across national borders affecting all societies and economies, the States Parties stressed the need for international cooperation as the only effective means to prevent and combat corruption. Preventing and eradicating corruption is 'a responsibility of all States and … they must cooperate with one another' in order to succeed in the global fight against corruption.

---

186 See Resolution 55/25 annex.

187 The first session of the Ad Hoc Committee which was held in Vienna from 21 January to 1 February 2002, was attended by representatives of 97 States as well as observers for the United Nations Secretariat units, other UN bodies, and intergovernmental and non-governmental organizations. The bureau of the Ad Hoc Committee elected by acclamation was made up as follows: Chairman: Hector Charry Samper (Colombia); Vice-Chairmen: Thomas Stelzer (Australia); Istvan Horvath (Hungary); Muhyieddeen Touq (Jordan); Ivan Leslie Collendavelloo (Mauritius); Abdulkadir Bin Rimdap (Nigeria); Victor G. Garcia III (Philippines); Javier Paulinich (Peru) and Peter Redmond (United Kingdom). The rapporteur was Anna Grupinska (Poland). See *Report of the Ad Hoc Committee for the Negotiation of a Convention Against Corruption on the Work of Its First to Seventh Sessions*, UNGA A/58/422, pp. 1-2] [herein after '*Report of the Ad Hoc Committee*'].

188 56/260 of 31 January 2002 and 57/169 of 18 December 2002.

189 *Report of the Ad Hoc Committee*, supra note 188.

190 Resolution 58/4.

191 Art. 38(1). This numerical threshold for entry into force represents a compromise between two opposing groups: delegations that advocated for 20 ratifications, on the one hand, and those that preferred 40. See Transparency International, 2004 *Global Report on Corruption*, 114 (2004).

Preventive Measures

The UN Convention breaks new ground with its provisions on prevention, criminalization, asset recovery and international cooperation. Prevention takes up an entire chapter of the convention with separate provisions directed at both the public[192] and private[193] sectors. The convention includes model preventive strategies, such as the establishment of anti-corruption bodies[194] and practices,[195] adoption of codes of conduct for public officials,[196] and tough requirements for financial and other disclosures,[197] and appropriate disciplinary measures against these officials.[198] The convention directs States Parties to ensure that their public services are subject to safeguards that promote efficiency, transparency and recruitment based on merit.[199] States Parties are under an obligation to promote transparency and accountability in matters of public finance[200] as well as in the financing of political parties.[201] The convention also imposes specific requirements on its signatories for the prevention of corruption in such particularly critical areas of the public sector like the judiciary[202] and public procurement.[203] In an effort to include everyone in this fight, the convention contains specific provisions that actively involve non-governmental and community-based organizations, as well as other sectors of civil society, in the prevention and fight against corruption; and to work through them to raise public awareness of corruption and what has to be done to eradicate it.[204] Provisions to protect witnesses[205] and whistle blowers[206] are included in the regime of civil society involvement in the fight against corruption.

Offenses

Individual States are responsible for criminalizing a wide range of corrupt activities, if these are not already crimes under domestic law.[207] In some cases, States Parties are legally obliged to criminalize certain acts of corruption, such as

---

192 Arts. 5,6, and 7.
193 Art. 12.
194 Art. 6.
195 Art. 5.
196 Art. 8.
197 Art. 8(5).
198 Art. 8(6).
199 Art. 7(1)(a).
200 Art. 9.
201 Art. 7(3).
202 Art. 11.
203 Art. 9.
204 Art. 13.
205 Art. 32.
206 Art. 33.
207 Arts. 15-24.

bribery of national and/or foreign officials,[208] embezzlement and misappropriation of public funds,[209] and laundering of the proceeds of corruption.[210] In other cases, given the differences in domestic law, States Parties are only required 'to consider adopting' legislation to criminalize such corrupt practices as influence trading,[211] abuse of office,[212] illicit enrichment,[213] private sector bribery[214] and embezzlement.[215] . The provision of 'illicit enrichment,' which is modeled after similar provisions in the Inter-American Convention and the AU Corruption Convention, deserves a brief comment. At the drafting stage, this provision drew objections from the delegations of the Russian Federation and the member States of the European Union who expressed a strong wish to have it deleted from the final text.[216]

It would appear that the UN Convention goes beyond previous anti-corruption instruments in criminalizing not only the classical types of corruption such as bribery and embezzlement (in both the public and private[217] sectors) but also influence trading[218] and the concealment and laundering of the proceeds of corruption.[219] The connection between corruption and money laundering was ably demonstrated in the Riggs Bank scandal.[220] A United States Senate investigation uncovered some unsavory ties between Riggs Bank and the former President of Chile, Augusto Pinochet Ugarte, and the Government of Equatorial Guinea. Senate investigators found that Riggs Bank managed more than 60 accounts and certificates of deposit for Equatorial Guinea, its officials, and their family members, accounts that held hundreds of millions of dollars of revenue obtained from oil companies doing business in this tiny central African country. They were managed with little or no attention to the bank's anti-money laundering obligations, turned a blind eye to evidence suggesting that the bank was handling the proceeds of foreign corruption, and allowed numerous transactions to take

---

208 Arts. 15-16.

209 Art. 17.

210 Art. 23.

211 Art. 18.

212 Art. 19.

213 Art. 20.

214 Art. 21.

215 Art. 22.

216 See Revised Draft UN Convention Against Corruption, Ad Hoc Committee for the Negotiation of a Convention against Corruption, 6th Sess., Agenda Item 3, Art. 25, note 135, UN Doc. A/AC.261/3/Rev.

217 Art. 22.

218 Art. 18.

219 Arts. 23 and 24.

220 See United States Senate, Money Laundering and Foreign Corruption: Enforcement and Effectiveness of the Patriot Act. Case Study Involving Riggs Bank, 14 July 2004. By the time the dust had cleared in what would become the most extensive money-laundering scandal in modern banking, Riggs would be fined $25 million and damaged so severely that it was forced into a merger with PNC Financial Services Group Inc.

place without notifying law enforcement authorities. In the case of Pinochet who was the subject of a world-wide attachment order in Spain seeking to freeze his bank accounts, Riggs Bank helped this fugitive from justice to evade court orders attempting to freeze his accounts with the bank. It failed to file any suspicious activity reports that would have alerted law enforcement in the countries where Pinochet was wanted to the existence of these funds; willfully altered official names on the personal account controlled by Pinochet in the US to prevent any manual or electronic search for the name 'Pinochet' from identifying any accounts at the bank.[221] Officials in Riggs Bank engaged in frequent movement of funds while Pinochet was under investigation to evade detection and actively concealed the existence of certain accounts from bank examiners and resisted requests for information. When they were concealing Pinochet's bank accounts from the prying eye of US bank auditors, Riggs Bank was busy helping its client in setting up offshore corporations in the Bahamas to transfer some of his assets.

Senate investigators also found deficiencies in Riggs' due diligence investigation of its moneyed clients, paying little or no attention to its 'Know Your Customer' obligation of compiling and verifying background information on its clients as a safeguard against money laundering. The bank failed to compile information on all accounts related to its clients; the information it maintained on its clients background and the source of the wealth in their accounts was inadequate; failed to identify high risk accounts; its monitoring of client transactions and its systems for reporting suspicious activity were also found inadequate. The revelations from the Riggs Bank case underscore the relevance of the Convention's money laundering provisions, all of which address the specific deficiencies uncovered in Riggs Bank's handling of both the Pinochet and Equatorial Guinea accounts.

The Convention also addresses predicate offenses, defined in Article 2(h) as 'any offence as a result of which proceeds have been generated that may become the subject of an offence as defined in article 23 of the Convention.' In other words, offenses such as money-laundering[222] and obstruction of justice[223] committed in the furtherance of corruption. It is also the only multilateral anti-corruption instrument that mandates the disallowance of tax deduction of bribes of either foreign or national officials.[224] In contrast, the Inter-American Convention only calls upon States Parties to 'consider' denying favorable tax treatment for expenditures in violation of their anti-corruption laws.[225]

Assets Recovery

Any meaningful solution to the problem of corruption must make provisions for

[221] For instance, accounts in the name of 'Augusto Pinochet Ugarte and Lucia Hiriart de Pinochet' were altered to read 'L. Hiriart &/or A. Ugarte.'

[222] Art. 23.

[223] Art. 25.

[224] Art. 12(4).

[225] *Cf.* Inter-American Convention, *supra* note 113.

cross-border recovery and repatriation of assets derived from corruption.[226] It is in this vein that asset recovery takes a whole chapter in the UN Convention comprising eight articles, some quite detailed such as Articles 52, 55 and 57 dealing, respectively, with prevention and detection of transfers of the proceeds of corruption, international cooperation in the confiscation of the proceeds of corruption and the return and disposal of assets. Asset recovery is of particular importance to many developing countries where high-level corruption has plundered the national wealth, and where new governments badly need resources for reconstruction and rehabilitation of broken-down infrastructure.[227] For these victim-States, an effective asset-recovery regime was crucial to support their efforts to recover purloined national wealth while at the same time sending a powerful message to corrupt public officials that there will be no place to hide their ill-gotten wealth. This would explain why the opening article in Chapter 5 views the repatriation of purloined assets as a 'fundamental principle of [the] Convention.'

Given the sensitivity of the subject, it is hardly surprising that it took intensive negotiations before agreement could be reached on the provisions covering asset recovery. Common ground had to be established between developing countries seeking repatriation of their stolen assets and the developed countries where these funds are usually placed for safe-keeping. It was necessary to reconcile the needs of the former with the legal and procedural safeguards of the latter.[228] The result is Chapter V which sets forth a regime for cooperation and assistance in the recovery of assets derived from corrupt activities.

Article 53 outlines different measures for direct recovery through the courts of a State Party on an action to recover stolen national wealth initiated by another State Party. Articles 54 and 55, on the other hand, identify mechanisms for recovery through international cooperation including outright confiscation. Specific provisions spell out where recovered assets can be returned. For instance, public funds that are embezzled public funds would be confiscated and returned to the requesting State Party.[229] Where the confiscated funds represent the proceeds from any other offense covered by the Convention, they would be returned to the requesting State Party once the state reasonably establishes its prior ownership of the property or when the requested State recognizes damage to the requesting State as a basis for returning the confiscated property.[230] In all other cases, priority consideration would be given to the return of confiscated property to the requesting State returning such property to its prior legitimate owners or to compensating the

---

[226] See Ad Hoc Committee for the Negotiation of a Convention against Corruption, *Global Study on the Transfer of Funds of Illicit Origin, Especially Funds Derived from Acts of Corruption*, A/AC.261/10 28 November 2002, at 3.

[227] See *United Nations Office on Drugs and Crime: United Nations Convention Against Corruption*, Mon. 13 September 2004, p. 3.

[228] *Id.*

[229] Art. 57(3)(a).

[230] Art. 57(3)(b).

victims.[231] Article 43 obliges States Parties to extend the widest possible cooperation to each other in the investigation and prosecution of offences defined in the Convention. With regard to asset-recovery in particular, Article 43 provides in pertinent part that 'In matters of international cooperation, whenever dual criminality is considered a requirement, it shall be deemed fulfilled irrespective of whether the laws of the requested State Party place the offence within the same category of offence or denominate the offence by the same terminology as the requesting State Party, if the conduct underlying the offence for which assistance is sought is a criminal offence under the laws of both States Parties.'[232]

Article 43 is just one of several provisions in the Convention devoted to international cooperation. The thrust of these provisions is the pledge by the States Parties to cooperate with one another in every aspect of the global war against corruption. This commitment of mutual cooperation extends to law enforcement cooperation[233] and includes investigation[234] and even the prosecution of alleged offenders.[235] The States Parties agree also to extend to each 'to the fullest extent possible' mutual legal assistance in the gathering and transferring of evidence for use in court as well as the extradition of alleged offenders.[236]

Liability, Statute of Limitations and Immunities

The Convention provides for a private right of action and subjects persons held liable for violating any of the enumerated offenses to 'effective, proportionate and dissuasive criminal or non-criminal sanctions, including monetary sanctions.'[237] Provision for compensation is included in Article 35 for those ' who have suffered damages as a result of an act of corruption …'[238] States Parties are required to maintain an appropriate balance between immunities and jurisdictional privileges that may shield public officials from criminal prosecution or civil suit so as not to obstruct the effective investigation, prosecution and adjudicating of Convention offenses.[239] Finally, the convention mandates a long statute of limitation period in which to commence proceedings for any offense under the Convention and provides for its suspension where the alleged offender becomes a fugitive from justice.[240]

---

231 Art. 57(4).
232 Art. 43(2).
233 Art. 48.
234 Arts. 49 and 50.
235 Art. 47.
236 Art. 44.
237 Art. 26.
238 Art. 35.
239 Art. 30.
240 Art. 29.

International Cooperation

As if to underscore its significance, Article 46 on Mutual Legal Assistance is the longest article in the convention with 30 separate sub-paragraphs covering a wide range of subjects from assistance in the taking of evidence to recovery of illicitly acquired assets; the form in which requests for mutual legal assistance are to be drafted and the circumstances under which mutual legal assistance can be refused. To facilitate the task of providing legal assistance in investigations, prosecutions and judicial proceedings, the Convention requires each State Party to designate a central authority to receive requests for mutual legal assistance and to either execute them or transmit them to the competent authorities for execution.[241] The central authority ensures the speedy and proper execution or transmission of any requests received. Requests for mutual legal assistance can also be addressed to a State Party through diplomatic channels and where time is of the essence through the International Criminal Police Organization, provided the States Parties agree.[242] Requests for legal assistance must be in writing and in a language acceptable to the requested State Party.[243] The requested State Party may postpone the execution of a request if it interferes with an ongoing investigation, prosecution or judicial proceeding. Alternatively, the requested State Party may refuse to execute a request for mutual legal assistance that it considers to be prejudicial to its sovereignty, security, *ordre public* or other overriding national interests.[244] A request for legal assistance not in conformity with the provisions of Article 46 may also be refused. Reasons must be given for any refusal of mutual legal assistance.[245]

In addition to the formalities associated with requests for mutual legal assistance, the States Parties agree to undertake measures which will support the tracing, freezing, seizure and confiscation of the proceeds of corruption[246] as well as the sharing of intelligence with respect to suspicious financial movements[247] and the sharing of information and analytical expertise concerning corruption with a view to developing common definitions, standards and methodologies to prevent and combat corruption.[248] The Convention also contains a set of provisions on technical cooperation aimed at strengthening the capacity of developing countries

---

241 Art. 46(13).

242 *Id.*

243 Art. 46(14).

244 Art. 46(21)(b).

245 Art. 46(23).

246 Art. 46(3)(j) and (k). When the Nigerian government formally requested Swiss authorities for, and received, legal assistance in recovering General Sani Abacha's funds, it was informed by the investigating judge that the general's frozen assets were scattered in 140 accounts in 13 banks in Geneva and Zurich. Without the help of the Swiss authorities, it would have taken the Nigerian government years of investigation and millions of dollars to trace these funds.

247 Art. 58.

248 Art. 61.

in implementing the provisions of the Convention. A separate provision is included for the implementation of the Convention through economic development and technical assistance. Article 62 invites States Parties to give special support to developing countries and countries with economies in transition in their fight against corruption by providing technical assistance and enhancing their 'financial and material assistance.' Provisions for training and technical assistance also oblige all the States Parties, irrespective of level of economic development, to 'initiate, develop or improve' training programs for officials in the front-line of the fight to prevent and combat corruption.[249] States Parties are encouraged to develop training programs in detection, evidence-gathering as well as investigative techniques.[250]

Monitoring Mechanism

Finally a mechanism for monitoring of convention implementation is found in Chapter 7. Article 63 establishes a Conference of States Parties to improve the capacity of and cooperation between the States Parties in achieving the objectives set out in the Convention and to promote and review its implementation.

This brief survey of the steps the community of nations as a whole has taken to design an international legal regime to combat official corruption amply demonstrate that corruption is now a subject of global concern. This progressive development of an international anti-corruption regime has produced an impressive array of instruments at the regional and global levels to combat this menace. In the following chapter, attention will shift to a discussion of what States themselves have been doing to make corruption a punishable offense under their domestic laws.

---

[249] Art. 60.
[250] Art. 60(1)(a).

Chapter 6

State Practice at the Domestic Level Criminalizing Acts of Fraudulent Enrichment by Top State Officials

Chapter 5 examined a number of resolutions and conventions adopted in various international fora that point to an emerging international norm that considers fraudulent enrichment by constitutionally responsible rulers as wrongful criminal conduct with far reaching consequences for domestic as well as global peace and security. In this chapter the focus shifts to the domestic context to find support from state practice for this embryonic norm. It will be shown that here too consistent, long standing and widespread state practice has viewed acts of pillaging, pilfering, plundering and purloining by presidents and other high-ranking State officials as punishable criminal conduct. This state practice reflects not only the views of national elites but the sentiments of the masses also. There is a general sense that acts of corrupt enrichment and abuse of the public trust attack the very foundations of collective national existence, injure the vital interests of the nation and should be regarded as criminal by that national community. Evidence for this position will be drawn from national legislation, especially constitutional provisions, laws, judicial decisions and reports of commissions of inquiry established to investigate allegations of fraudulent enrichment of high-ranking State officials in a representative sample of victim states.

CONSTITUTIONAL PROHIBITIONS

Haiti, Paraguay and Peru

Immediately following Jean-Claude Duvalier's departure from Haiti, the government on 18 February 1986, nationalized all properties belonging to the deposed president and ordered all Haitian and foreign nationals to disclose within two weeks assets they might be holding in Duvalier's name.[1] In the spring of 1987, the Constitutional Assembly, finally completed a draft Constitution that was subsequently presented at a nation-wide referendum for approval.[2] In the hope of

---

1 See Haitian Cabinet Named; Asylum Sought for Duvalier; Issue Causes French US Tensions, *Facts on File World News Digest*, 21 February 1986, p. A2.

2 See *Constitution of the Republic of Haiti*, 1987.

curbing rampant corruption by both elected and appointed officials, the 1987 Haitian Constitution broadens the definition of treason to include economic crimes and misuse of public funds.[3]

Haiti is among a growing number of countries that has included a prohibition against indigenous spoliation in its fundamental law. Several provisions of the Haitian Constitution specifically address the problem of 'unjust gain' as it applies to civil servants.[4] For instance:

> *Art. 241*: The law punishes violations committed against the treasury and unjust gain. Officials who have knowledge of such actions have the duty to report them to the competent authorities.
>
> *Art. 242*: Unjust gain may be determined by all types of evidence, particularly presumption of a sharp disproportion between the official's means acquired after his entry into service and the accumulated amount of salaries and emoluments to which the post he has occupied entitles him.

Although Article 240 clearly states that holders of public office or positions including 'Ministers and Secretaries of State, officers of the Public Prosecutor's Office, Delegates and Vice Delegates, ambassadors, private secretaries of the President of the Republic, members of the Cabinet of Ministers, the Director Generals of the Ministerial Department of autonomous agencies, and members of the Administrative Council' are not civil servants for purposes of Articles 241 and 242, there is a provision in another section of the Constitution that would support the application of these articles to top State officials including the President of the Republic himself. Article 279 requires *inter alia* that:

> Thirty days after his election, the President of the Republic must deposit with the Clerk of the Court of First Instance of his domicile a notarized inventory of all his movable and immovable goods, and he shall do the same at the end of his term.[5]

This inventory is also required of the Prime Minister, the Ministers and Secretaries of State under Article 279-1 and also of civil servants under Article 238 of Title VIII. Clearly this inventory is meant to serve as evidence of unjust gain should such charges arise in the future. It must follow then that by requiring the President and his Ministers to file a similar, yet more detailed, declaration of assets, the Constitution contemplates the possibility of these high officials facing charges

---

[3] *Id.*, Art. 21 ('The crime of high treason consists in bearing arms in a foreign army against the Republic, serving a foreign nation in a conflict with the Republic, *in any official's stealing State property entrusted to his management*, or any violation of the Constitution by those responsible for enforcing it.') (emphasis added); see also John C. Metaxas, Stroock Is Trailing Baby Doc's Millions, *The National Law Journal*, 9 June 1986, p. 2.

[4] See *Constitution of the Republic of Haiti*, Title VIII. 'The Civil Service,' Arts. 234–244.

[5] *Id.* Title X11, 'General Provisions,' Art. 279.

equal to those which can be leveled against a civil servant, that is, violations against the treasury and unjust gain. But even without Article 238, these constitutional officers are still indictable for acts of fraudulent enrichment. Article 186 underscores this possibility by providing that:

> [t]he House of Deputies, by a majority of two-thirds (2/3) of its members, shall indict: a) The President of the Republic for the crime of high treason or any other crime or offense committed in the discharge of his duties; b) The Prime Minister, the Ministers and the Secretaries of State for crimes of high treason and embezzlement or abuse of power or any other crimes or offenses committed in the discharge of their duties.[6]

It should be pointed out that fraudulent enrichment under the new Haitian Constitution is *crimen laesae majestatis*. These constitutional provisions suggest nonetheless that under Haitian law, the imposition of a fiduciary obligation, particularly on public servants entrusted with financial duties, for the misappropriation of those funds can be justified. The same can be said for Paraguay and Peru, two Latin American countries that have also been scarred by wanton acts of indigenous spoliation.[7]

The Paraguayan Constitution contains provisions which allow for the imposition of liability on public officials guilty of embezzling public funds. Article 41 provides that '[h]igher government authorities, officials, and employees shall at all times act in accordance with the provisions of this Constitution and the laws. These persons shall exercise the duties within their competence in conformity with the latter and shall be personally responsible for the violations, crimes or misdemeanors they commit in the performance of their duties, without prejudice to

---

6 *Id.*, Art. 186 (a) and (b).

7 Since its independence in 1811, Paraguay has been ruled almost continuously by authoritarian regimes. Among the more recent is Alfredo Stroessner who ruled Paraguay for 34 years until he was deposed in 1989. As Latin America's longest surviving dictator, Stroessner is believed to have salted away a fortune in foreign banks. Much of the corruption that went on in Paraguay during Stroessner's tenure only began to be exposed by his successor, President Andres Rodriguez whose government is committed to recapturing as much of that stolen wealth as possible. The amount of funds spoliated have been quite spectacular. Take the case of a former roving ambassador Gustavo Gramont Berres, who fled to Europe when Stroessner was overthrown, and is alleged to have embezzled $60 million in public funds and was wanted in Paraguay to stand trial. Or, the case of 36 former officials of the Stroessner regime whose assets, the combined worth of which was estimated at $550 million, equivalent to one quarter of Paraguay's foreign debt! See 'US Judge orders former Paraguayan ambassador held without bond,' *Reuters*, Tuesday, 4 June 1991, AM cycle; 'Municipal elections again postponed; Delay in compiling electoral rolls as voters unresponsive,' *Latin American Regional Reports: Southern Cone*, 18 October 1990, p. 7. Of the total, $12 million were recouped in cash, properties and cattle from three high-ranking military officers: Gen. Hugo Dejesus Araujo, former social welfare director; Gen. Roberto Knopfelmacher, former president of the state oil company, Petropar; and Gen. Alcebiades Britez, former director of the national police. *Id.*

the responsibility of the state, which shall be regulated by law.'[8] Article 177 is even more specific. It provides that the President of the Republic 'shall be entitled to a salary, which may not be changed during his term of office, and during that term he may not engage in any other employment, nor devote himself to his profession, business or industry, nor receive any other emolument from the republic.'[9] The Peruvian Constitution tackles the problem of fraudulent enrichment by authorizing the prosecution of public officials suspected of such practices: '[o]n the basis of a complaint by any individual or office, the State's public prosecutor proffers charges in court when unlawful enrichment is suspected.'[10] This provision in effect transforms every Peruvian citizen into an ombudsman of sorts responsible for monitoring the performance of constitutional officers and to cause criminal charges to be brought against those suspected of fraudulent enrichment.

Nigeria and Sierra Leone

Under the Constitution of Sierra Leone, the ban against fraudulent enrichment appears to apply only to members of Parliament who are directed to 'regard themselves as representatives of the people of Sierra Leone and *desist from any conduct by which they seek improperly to enrich themselves*' (emphasis supplied).[11] However, the Constitution also contains an accountability provision which subjects the public accounts of the State and of all public offices to periodic audits by an independent Auditor-General. This must have been intended by the drafters to serve as a mechanism for ferreting out corrupt public officials.[12]

The Constitution of the Federal Republic of Nigeria requires all elected officials beginning with the President[13] and including elected members of national[14] and state[15] legislatures as well as certain appointed holders of public office to take an oath, declare their assets and pledge to abide by a national Code of Conduct. In addition, the Constitution includes a separate Chapter under the Fundamental Objectives and Directive Principles of State Policy that comprise 10 separate articles. High-ranking public officials are bound by the Constitution to promote these fundamental objectives and to tailor their public stewardship to reflect the directive principles of the Nigerian State. Several of these are directly

---

8 See *Constitution of Paraguay*, Chapter IV, General Provisions, Art. 41.

9 *Id.* Chapter VIII, The Executive Power, Art. 177.

10 *Political Constitution of Peru*, Art. 62.

11 *The Constitution of Sierra Leone*, 1991, Sec. 97(b).

12 *Id.*, Sec. 119(2) ('The public accounts of Sierra Leone and of all public offices ... shall be audited and reported on by or on behalf of the Auditor-General, and for that purpose the Auditor-General or any person authorized or appointed in that behalf by the Auditor-General shall have access to all books, records, returns and other documents relating or relevant to those accounts.'). Section 119(1) provides for the appointment of an Auditor-General and subsections 6 and 8 recognize and protect his independence.

13 *Constitution of Nigeria*, Art. 137(1).

14 *Id.*, Art. 50(1).

15 *Id.*, Art. 92(1).

linked to the problem of indigenous spoliation. All public officials who come under Chapter 2 are under a constitutional duty to promote the security and welfare of the Nigerian people;[16] diligently manage and control the national economy to ensure the maximum welfare, freedom and happiness of every citizen on the basis of social justice, equality of status and opportunity;[17] ensure that the material resources of the commonwealth are harnessed and distributed in a manner that serves the common good of all Nigerians;[18] prevent the exploitation of Nigeria's human and natural resources for any reasons other than for the good of the community;[19] and eradicate all corrupt practices and abuse of power.[20] Finally, consistent with the belief that citizens have a responsibility to ensure that their national resources are not frittered away by a profligate leadership, the Constitution charges them with a watch-dog duty of protecting and preserving public property, and to fight against misappropriation and squandering of public funds.[21]

The Philippines

The Constitution of the Philippines proclaims public office as a public trust. Those privileged to be called to serve the Philippine nation are reminded that they 'must at all times be accountable to the people, serve them with utmost responsibility, integrity, loyalty and efficiency, act with patriotism and justice, and lead modest lives.'[22] The top constitutional officers risk being cashiered from office 'on impeachment for and conviction of culpable violation of the Constitution, treason, bribery, graft and corruption, other high crimes, or betrayal of public trust. All other public officers and employees may be removed from office as provided by law, but not by impeachment.'[23] To ensure that these public officials do not exploit their positions for personal gain, the Constitution bans the granting to them of loans, guaranties, or other forms of financial accommodation for any business purpose 'directly or indirectly by any government-owned or controlled bank or financial institution.'[24] The ban is comprehensive and it extends to the President of the Republic, the Vice-President, the Members of the Cabinet, the Congress, the Supreme Court Justices, and the Constitutional Commissions, the Ombudsman 'or to any firm or entity in which they have controlling interest, during their tenure.'[25]

16 *Id.*, Art. 15(2)(b).
17 *Id.*, Art. 17(1)(b).
18 *Id.*, Art. 17(2)(b).
19 *Id.*, Art. 18(2)(c).
20 *Id.*, Art. 16(5).
21 *Id.*, Art. 24(b).
22 *Constitution of the Republic of the Philippines*, Art. XI, Sec. 1.
23 *Id.*, Art. XI, Sec. 2.
24 *Id.*, Art. XI, Sec. 16.
25 *Id.*

NATIONAL LEGISLATION

Prohibitions against misuse of public funds by elected and appointed officials have been enacted into law in several countries that have themselves been victims of indigenous spoliation. Under the civilian government of Kwame Nkrumah, the Ghanaian Parliament enacted into law the Public Property (Protection) and Corrupt Practices (Prevention) Act in 1962. This law was subsequently amended by decree by the National Liberation Council[26] (NLC): the Public Property (Protection) and Corrupt Practices (Prevention) Act, 1962 (Amendment) Decree, 1967. The NLC also enacted the Investigation and Forfeiture of Assets Decree in 1966. When the National Redemption Council (NRC) replaced the NLC in 1972 it repealed all prior NLC decrees on investigation and forfeiture of assets[27] and enacted its own Investigation and Forfeiture of Assets Decree.[28]

Nigeria's State Security (Detention of Persons) Decree 1984 and the Recovery

---

[26] Ghana was granted full independence from Great Britain on 6 March 1957. Kwame Nkrumah who had led the nationalist movement for independence became Ghana's first prime minister and became President on 1 July 1960 when Ghana was declared a republic. Nkrumah was overthrown on 24 February 1966 by the police and military who established the National Liberation Council under Lt. Gen. Joseph A. Ankrah. He was forced to resign on 2 April 1969 and replaced by Brig. Akwasi A. Afrifa who organized civilian elections that led to election of Dr. Kofi A. Busia as prime minister and head of government and the appointment of Akufo-Addo as President. Ghana's second civilian government was toppled on 13 January 1972 in a military coup led by Col. (later General) Ignatius Acheampong who then established the National Redemption Council (NRC), later expanded and renamed the Supreme Military Council (SMC). Four years later Acheampong was arrested and deposed by his chief of staff, Lt. Gen. Frederick Akuffo. The Akuffo-led SMC was overthrown on 4 June 1979 by junior officers of the armed forces led by Flight Lt. Jerry John Rawlings who set up the Armed Forces Revolutionary Council (AFRC) and became its first and only chairman. The AFRC quickly organized parliamentary elections the very month it seized power and then presided over the transfer of power to a civilian government headed by Dr. Hilla Limann in September of 1979. The members of the AFRC did not remain long in the barracks as they under Rawlings' leadership removed in December 1981 the civilian government they had earlier installed. They renamed their group the Provisional National Defense Council (PNDC). Rawlings and the PNDC ruled Ghana for twelve years until 1993 when Rawlings was elected President. See Kwasi Ohene-Bekoe, GLOBAGRAM: REPUBLIC OF GHANA (1993–1994).

[27] Repealed were: National Liberation Council (Investigation and Forfeiture of Assets) Decree, 1966 (NLCD 72); National Liberation Council (Investigation and Forfeiture of Assets) (Amendment) Decree, 1966 (NLCD 101); National Liberation Council (Investigation and Forfeiture of Assets) (Amendment) (No. 2) Decree, 1967 (NLCD 174); National Liberation Council (Investigation and Forfeiture of Assets) (Amendment) Decree, 1968 (NLCD 253); National Liberation Council (Investigation and Forfeiture of Assets) (Amendment) (No. 2) Decree, 1968 (NLCD 266); National Liberation Council (Investigation and Forfeiture of Assets) (Amendment) Decree, 1968 (NLCD 297).

[28] National Redemption Council, Investigation and Forfeiture of Assets Decree, 1972 (NRCD 19).

of Public Property (Special Military Tribunals) Decree[29] also contain prohibitions against fraudulent enrichment by public servants. Section 1 (c) of the Detention of Persons Decree gave the Federal Military Government special power to detain persons who had committed acts prejudicial to State security or by their actions have contributed to the economic adversity of the nation. When asked to explain why offenders were subjected to very harsh penalties, it was explained that:

> Public Office holding is a public trust ... If anyone, elected or appointed into public office, corruptly enriches himself either by misappropriating public funds, receiving kickbacks and through such other abuse of office that public office holder must be compelled to disgorge such ill-gotten wealth ... In addition, he must be disqualified from holding public office ... firstly, to ensure that he does not have another opportunity for such mis-conduct and secondly, to serve as an object lesson to others who might be tempted in like manner.[30]

This and several other decrees from prior military governments were the basis for a new Code of Conduct. The Code is incorporated to the Nigerian Constitution as a Fifth Schedule and is specifically mentioned in all the constitutional provisions dealing with oaths of office and declaration of assets and property.[31] In June 2000 the first civilian government following the overthrow of the Abacha military regime in 1998, adopted a new anti-corruption legislation, the Corrupt Practices

---

[29] See The Recovery of Public Property (Special Military Tribunals) Decree No. 3, 1984 (1986), para. 3(c) in XXI LAWS OF THE FEDERATION OF NIGERIA (REVISED) ch. 389 (1990). *Failed Banks (Recovery of Debts and Financial Malpractices)* Decree No 18, 1994 and the *Bank Employees, Etc. (Declaration of Assets) Decree* 1986. The first two were designed to try mainly public officers, while the two latter laws focused principally on corrupt practices involving private businesses and employees in the banking sector. The *Recovery of Public Property (Special Military Tribunals) Act, 1984* was impliedly displaced by a latter decree by the same regime when it was made punishable to allege corruption against former or serving public officers. *See, Public Officers (Protection Against False Accusation) Decree No 4 1984*. The decree gained notoriety after two journalists were sentenced to long terms of imprisonment for publishing what was substantially true, but not true in 'all material particular.'

[30] See *Federal Republic of Nigeria, Views and Decisions of the Federal Military Government on the Report and Recommendations of Justice Uwaifo Special Panel for the Investigation of Cases of Persons Conditionally Released from Detention and Persons still in Detention under the State Security (Detention of Persons) Decree No. 2*, 1984 and the *Recovery of Public Property (Special Military Tribunals) Decree No. 3*, 1984 (1986), para. 3(c) in XXI Laws of the Federation of Nigeria (revised) ch. 389 (1990) (hereinafter 'Federal Military Government Decisions').

[31] In addition, Nigeria's principal statutes contain provisions penalizing corruption and these antedate the period of military rule. Among these are the Criminal Code (CC) and Criminal Procedure Act (CPA) which apply in southern states. The Penal Code and Criminal Procedure Code apply in northern states. These pieces of legislation were introduced by the British colonial authorities. Different sections applied to corruption. See generally, §§ 98, 99, 100 and 494 CC.

and Other Related Offences Act 2000. A Nigerian scholar describes the salient features of this 'exceptional piece of legislation'[32] as follows:

> First, it is a federal legislation having national effect. Second, it is a statute that creates and must be interpreted as a fundamental public policy of Nigeria. Third, it covers not only corrupt dealings relating to public officers and public institutions, but also strictly private dealings between private businesses. Fourth, it has an extra-territorial effect in relation to investigation and liability for enumerated offences. Fifth, it imposes a duty of disclosure and assistance on all persons who may be subject to the Act and who are required to provide information .... Sixth, it is not acceptable to use corruption as a tool of commerce or trade or a basis of social and cultural norms. Seventh, the abridgment of standard human rights norms, relating to fair hearing, privacy, and property rights may be deemed constitutionally reasonable and necessary where investigation procedures of corruption in public or private office are at issue. Finally, the administrative apparatus of the Act, the Commission, is a powerful body operating independently of any other organ and superior to any other law enforcement agency in matters within its subject matter jurisdiction.[33]

Haiti

In addition to the provisions of the Haitian Constitution already discussed there are other regulatory laws available from which a fiduciary obligation can be held to apply to the President of the Republic and other high-ranking elected and appointed officials. The Commercial Code of Haiti, for example, imposes criminal penalties in the following cases:

1. Managers who in bad faith have misused or utilized the funds of the corporation or its credit in some manner contrary to the interest of the company, in their favor or in favor of certain shareholders or third parties;

2. Managers who may have prepared or authorized the publication of false balance-sheets.[34] On the concept of fiduciary duty, the Commercial Laws of Paraguay are

---

32 See Olakunle O. Olagoke, The Extra-Territorial Scope of the Anti-Corruption in Nigeria, *International Law*, 38, 71, 78 (Spring 2004) [hereinafter 'Extra-Territorial Scope'].

33 *Id.*

34 See Commercial Laws of Haiti. *Digest of the Commercial Laws of the World*. chap. 18, 'Partnerships and Corporations;' (C) Elements of a Corporation (prepared by Tallerand & Talleyrand, April 1983). This section incorporates language from Article 337 of the Criminal Code: 'Quiconque soit en faisant usage de faux noms ou de fausses qualites, soit en employant des manoeuvres frauduleuses, pour persuader l'existence de fausses entreprises, d'un pouvoir ou d'un credit imaginaire, ou pour faire naitre l'esperance ou la crainte d'un succes, d'un accident, et de tout autre evenement chimerique, se sera fait remettre ou delivrer des fonds des meubles, ou des obligations, dispositions, billets, promesses, quittances ou decharges, et aura, par un de ces moyens, escroque ou tents d'escroquer la totalite ou partie de la fortune d'autrui, sera puni d'un emprisonnement d'un an au moins et de trois ans au plus.'

simple and direct. Article 337, for instance, provides that '[d]irectors are jointly and severally liable to the corporation, shareholders, and third parties for negligence or bad faith in the carrying out of the mandate, whether by violation of the law or bylaws or by any other prejudice caused by indolence, abuse of authority, or criminal act.'[35]

Perhaps one of the more detailed national legislation against government corruption is the Philippine Anti-Graft and Corrupt Practices Act. Long plagued by persistent acts of government corruption and determined to curtail and minimize 'the opportunities for official corruption and maintaining a standard of honesty ... [and] to promote morality in the public service',[36] the Filipino people acting through their National Assembly passed an anti-graft statute, Republic Act No. 1379, in 1955 which was supplemented five years later by another act, Republic Act No. 3019 (1960). The anti-graft statute targets not only public officials in elective and appointive offices but also private individuals who have family or close personal relation with any public official as well as relatives. Section 5 makes it unlawful for the 'spouse or for any relative, by consanguinity or affinity, within the third civil degree of the President of the Philippines, the Vice-President of the Philippines, the President of the Senate, or the Speaker of the House of Representatives, to intervene ... in any business, transaction, contract or application, with the Government.'[37] During the term for which they have been elected, Members of Congress are prohibited under the anti-graft statute from acquiring or receiving any 'personal pecuniary interest in any specific business enterprise which will be directly and particularly favored or benefitted by any law or resolution authored by him previously approved or adopted by Congress during the same term.'[38] Anyone coming within the statute is required within thirty days of assuming office to file a sworn declaration of his assets and liabilities with the appropriate government agency. Thereafter, the filing is to be done once a year as well as upon the expiration of his term of office, or upon his resignation or separation from office.[39] Penalties for violations of the anti-graft statute range from imprisonment, permanent disqualification from public office, and confiscation and forfeiture to the State of 'any prohibited interest and unexplained wealth manifestly out of proportion to [one's] salary and other lawful income.'[40] A public official is presumptively in violation of the statute if he is found to have 'acquired during his incumbency, whether in his name or in the name of other persons, an amount of property and/or money manifestly out of proportion to his salary and to his other

---

35 See Commercial Laws of Paraguay: Section IV; Administration and Inspection; Art. 337.

36 Nunez vs. Sandiganbayan, SCRA 111, 433, 442 (1982).

37 Significantly, the statute does not cover the very top elective offices in the country: the President and Vice-President of the Republic, the President of the Senate, or the Speaker of the House of Representatives.

38 Republic Act, Sec. 6.

39 *Id.*, Sec. 7.

40 *Id.*, Sec. 8.

lawful income.'[41] The presence of unexplained wealth is ground for dismissal or removal from office.[42]

SPECIAL CONSTITUTIONAL STRUCTURES TO COMBAT SPOLIATION

A majority of the constitutions examined in this study make provision for special judicial bodies empowered to investigate allegations on corruption and to hear and decide cases brought against high-level ranking officials suspected of acts of fraudulent enrichment. These bodies may go by different names, Anti-graft courts or Ombudsman in the Philippines, Office of Citizen Protection in Haiti,[43] Commissions of Inquiry in Sierra Leone and Panama or Code of Conduct Tribunals in the case of Nigeria, but their composition, powers, functions and duties are fairly similar.

Commissions of Inquiry

The Constitution of Panama contains a provision for the setting up of a judicial commission to investigate '[a]ccusations or charges against the President and Vice-President of the Republic, Magistrates of the Supreme Court of Justice, the Attorney General of the Republic, the Commander in Chief of the National Guard and the Solicitor General . . . .'[44] This constitutional provision also provides that '[i]f there are grounds therefore, the Judicial Commission shall try them for acts in violation of the Constitution and laws committed in the performance of their duties.'[45] Furthermore, Article 171 of the Constitution defines the acts which can give rise to an Article 142 inquiry. It provides that '[t]he President and Vice-President of the Republic' are held accountable only in the following cases:

1. For exceeding their constitutional powers;

2. For impeding the meeting of the National Assembly or for obstructing it or any other public body or authority established by the Constitution, in the exercise of its functions; and

3. For crimes against the Nation or against the public order. In the first two cases the penalty shall be removal from office and disqualification to hold public office

---

41 *Id.*, Sec. 8.

42 *Id.*

43 *The Constitution of Haiti*, 1987, chap. IV.

44 *Constitution of the Republic of Panama*. Title V, the Legislative Organ. Chap. II Art. 142. The Judicial Commission shall be 'composed of the officers of the National Assembly and three representatives from each province and one for the District of San Blas, elected by the full Assembly . . .' *Id.*

45 *Id.*, Art. 142.

for the period fixed by law. In the third case ordinary law shall apply.[46]

Corruption, embezzlement and misappropriation involving constitutionally elected and appointed leaders are 'crimes against the Nation' within the meaning of Article 171. Indeed, one of the first actions taken by the Government of Panama following the arrest and subsequent removal of General Manuel Noriega to the United States was to seize the assets of former pro-Noriega legislators who allegedly stole $1.8 million from Panama's national treasury during the Noriega regime. The seizure followed investigations conducted by the controller general's office which later submitted a report of its findings to the attorney general's office for possible prosecution of these individuals.[47]

Unlike the Panamanian constitutional commission of inquiry, that of Sierra Leone leaves out the President from its investigatory reach.[48] The Sierra Leone Constitution instead authorizes the President to appoint *ad hoc* Commissions of Inquiry into any matter of public interest provided it is certified as such by the Cabinet or Parliament.[49] A Commission established under this provision is required to:

1 make a full, faithful and an impartial inquiry into any matter specified in the commission of appointment;
2 report in writing the result of the inquiry; and

---

[46] *Constitution of the Republic of Panama*. Title VI, the Executive Organ. Chap. 1, Art. 171.

[47] 'Panama Moves to Seize Assets of Former Noriega Allies,' *Reuters*, Thursday, 21 November 1991. Barely a month after the US invasion, Panamanian investigators had prepared over 300 cases of corruption against former officials accused of bleeding the country through padded payrolls, illegal procurements and other embezzlement schemes. See Richard Boudreaux, Scale of Panama corruption huge; Investigation: New regime targets 300 ex-officials. Records indicate 20% of the budget went to graft, *Los Angeles Times*, 7 January 1990, part A, p. 1. The Endara government also sought to have the assets of Noriega frozen worldwide. See 'British Government Continues Freeze on Noriega Accounts,' *The Reuter Library Report*, Monday, 22 April 1991, BC Cycle.

[48] The Constitution also provides for the office of Ombudsman to be established by an Act of Parliament. Presumably this office could investigate Presidential acts of fraudulent enrichment. However, upon closer examination it becomes quite evident that the intended targets of the Ombudsman are public officials several levels below that of the President. The Constitution states that the Act of Parliament setting up this office will 'define the functions and duties of the Ombudsman, which shall include the investigation of any action taken or omitted to be taken by or on behalf of - (a) any department or Ministry of Government; (b) any statutory corporation or institutions of higher learning or education, set up entirely or partly out of public funds; (c) any member of the Public Service, being an action taken or omitted to be taken in the exercise of the administrative functions of that department, ministry, statutory corporation, institution or person.' See *Constitution of Sierra Leone*, 1991, Sec. 146(2).

[49] *Constitution of Sierra Leone*, 1991, Sec. 147(1).

3 furnish in the report the reasons leading to the conclusions arrived at or reported.[50]

A section 147 Commission of Inquiry enjoys the same powers, rights and privileges as are vested in the High Court of Justice or a Judge. In that capacity the Commission can call and examine witnesses, even those living outside Sierra Leone, under oath and to compel the production of documents.[51] Commission findings carry the weight of High Court judgments and can be appealed as of right to the Court of Appeal at the instance of the party against whom an adverse judgment was rendered.[52] The penalty for any public official found guilty by the Commission is either forfeiture of property and assets, presumably to the State, or loss of status.[53] Finally, as would be expected of any High Court in Sierra Leone, the proceedings of a Commission of Inquiry are held in public though *in camera* sittings are permitted 'in the interest of public safety or public order.'[54]

Code of Conduct Tribunal

An innovation in the 1979 Nigerian Constitution is the provision for the establishment of a permanent structure – the Code of Conduct Tribunal (Tribunal) – to deal with acts of fraudulent enrichment by top ranking State officials and entrenching this institution within the Constitution. Actually, any fruitful discussion of the Tribunal has to be done in the context of the Code of Conduct and the Code of Conduct Bureau.

Section 13 of the Fifth Schedule to the Nigerian Constitution provides that '[a]ny allegation that a public officer has committed a breach of or has not complied with the provisions of … [the Code of Conduct] shall be made to the Code of Conduct Bureau.' Section 1 of the Third Schedule establishes a Code of Conduct Bureau whose function it is to receive and examine *inter alia* all declarations of assets by top State officials, ensure compliance and where appropriate enforce the provisions of the Code of Conduct.[55] In addition, the Bureau is authorized to 'receive complaints about non-compliance with or breach of the Code of Conduct … investigate the complaint and, where appropriate, refer such matters to the Code of Conduct Tribunal.'[56]

The Code of Conduct Tribunal was set up under Section 16 of the Fifth Schedule to the Constitution as the exclusive judicial forum to try cases on the non-compliance with or breach of any of the provisions of the Code of Conduct by a

50 *Id.*, Sec. 149(1).
51 *Id.*, Sec. 148(1).
52 *Id.*
53 *Id.*, Sec. 149(4).
54 *Id.*, Sec. 148(3).
55 *The Constitution of the Federal Republic of Nigeria*, 1989, Third Schedule, Sec. 3(a).
56 *Id.*, Third Schedule, Sec. 3(e).

public officer.[57] The powers of the Tribunal are set out in Section 19 of the Fifth Schedule and are:

1 where the Code of Conduct finds a public officer guilty of contravention of any of the provisions of this Code it shall impose upon that officer any of the punishment specified under sub-paragraph (2) of this paragraph and such other punishment as may be prescribed by an Act of the National Assembly.
2 The punishment which the ... Tribunal may impose shall include any of the following – (a) vacation of office or seat in any legislative house; (b) disqualification from membership of a legislative house and from holding any public office for a period not exceeding 10 years; and (c) seizure and forfeiture to the State of any property acquired in abuse or corruption of office.

Subsection 19 (4) gives a right of appeal to the Federal Court of Appeal:

> Where the Code of Conduct Tribunal gives a decision as to whether or not a person is guilty of a contravention of any of the provisions of this Code, an appeal shall lie as of right from such decision or from any punishment imposed on such person to the Court of Appeal at the instance of any party to the proceedings.

Anti-Graft Courts and Office of the Ombudsman

There are two separate constitutional bodies responsible for policing corruption among public officials in the Philippines. These are the anti-graft court known as the *Sandiganbayan* which is mentioned fleetingly in the Constitution[58] and the independent office of the Ombudsman or *Tanodbayan.*

Office of the Ombudsman or Tanodbayan

Section 5 of Article XI of the Constitution creates the Office of the Ombudsman, to be known as *Tanodbayan*, which shall 'determine the causes of ... mismanagement, fraud, and corruption in the Government and make recommendations for their elimination and the observance of high standards of ethics and efficiency.' The Philippine Supreme Court has held in the case of Inting v. Tanod-Bayan,[59] that the *Tanodbayan* is conceived as an administrative body and was purposely created to 'give effect to the constitutional right of the people to petition the government for redress of grievances and to promote higher standards of integrity and efficiency in government services.'[60]

---

57 See for example Dr. Ifeoma Ogbuagu v. Dr. Geoffrey Ogbuagu, [1981] 2 NCLR 680 (Held that Code of Conduct Tribunal not the High Court is the proper forum under the Constitution for a complaint that a public official has breached the Code of Conduct).

58 *Constitution of the Republic of the Philippines*, Art. XI, Sec. 4.

59 97 SCRA 495, 499 (1980).

60 Article XI Sec. 13(7).

The powers of the *Tanodbayan* are prescribed in Section 10 of Presidential Decree No. 1607:

> (a) He may investigate, on complaint by any person or on his own motion or initiative, any administrative act whether amounting to any criminal offense or not of any administrative agency including any government-owned or controlled corporation;
>
> * * *
>
> (f) He may file and prosecute civil and administrative cases involving graft and corrupt practices and such other offenses committed by public officers and employees, including those in government-owned or controlled corporations, in relation to their office.

Under P.D. 1607 section 10 the *Tanodbayan* clearly functions as an ombudsman, but he also has prosecutorial powers. And as a prosecutor, his authority is plenary and without exceptions. These powers are defined in Sections 17 and 19 as follows:

> Sec. 17. Office of the Chief Special Prosecutor. – There is hereby created in the Office of the *Tanodbayan* an Office of the Chief Special Prosecutor composed of a Chief Special Prosecutor, an Assistant Chief Special Prosecutor, and nine (9) Special Prosecutors, who shall have the same qualifications as provincial and city fiscals and who shall be appointed by the President;
>
> * * *
>
> The Chief Special Prosecutor, the Assistant Chief Special Prosecutor, and the Special Prosecutors shall have the exclusive authority to conduct preliminary investigation of all cases cognizable by the *Sandiganbayan*; to file informations therefor and to direct and control the prosecution of said cases therein; Provided, however, that the *Tanodbayan* may, upon recommendation of the Chief Special Prosecutor, designate any fiscal, state prosecutor or lawyer in the government service to act as Special Prosecutor to assist in the investigation and prosecution of all cases cognizable by the *Sandiganbayan* who shall not receive any additional compensation except such allowances, per diems and travelling expenses as the *Tanodbayan* may determine in accordance with existing laws, rules and regulations.
>
> * * *
>
> Sec. 19. Prosecution of Public Personnel or Other Person. – If the *Tanodbayan* has reason to believe that any public official, employee, or other person has acted in a manner warranting criminal or disciplinary action or proceedings, he shall cause him to be investigated by the Office of the Chief Special Prosecutor who shall file and prosecute the corresponding criminal or administrative case before the *Sandiganbayan* or the proper court or before the proper administrative agency. In case of failure of justice, the *Tanodbayan* shall make the appropriate recommendations to the administrative agency concerned.

Section 17 thus confers upon the *Tanodbayan*, through the Chief Special Prosecutor and his assistants, the exclusive authority to 'conduct preliminary investigation of all cases cognizable by the *Sandiganbayan*, to file informations therefor, and to direct and control the prosecution of said cases therein.'

Anti-Graft Court or Sandiganbayan

Although the Constitution of the Philippines specifically provided for but did not create a special court, the *Sandiganbayan*, with specific jurisdiction over graft and corruption committed by officers and employees of the government, government instrumentalities and government-owned and -controlled corporations. The *Sandiganbayan* came into existence with the promulgation in 1978 of a Presidential Decree No. 1606.[61] Its establishment was authorized 'precisely in response to a problem, the urgency of which cannot be denied, namely, dishonesty in the public service.'[62] Presidential Decree No. 1606, which took effect on December 10, 1978, provides that:

> Sec. 4. *Jurisdiction* – The *Sandiganbayan* shall have jurisdiction over:
>
> a) Violations of Republic Act No. 3019, as amended, otherwise known as the Anti-Graft and Corrupt Practices Act, and Republic Act No. 1379;
>
> b) Crimes committed by public officers and employees, including those employed in government-owned or controlled corporations, embraced in Title VII of the Revised Penal Code, whether simple or complexed with other crimes; and
>
> c) Other crimes or offenses committed by public officers or employees, including those employed in government-owned or controlled corporations, in relation to their office.

The jurisdiction conferred on the *Sandiganbayan* by Presidential Decree No. 1606 is original and exclusive 'if the offense charged is punishable by a penalty higher than *prision correccional*, or its equivalent, except as herein provided; in other offenses, it shall be concurrent with regular courts. To further strengthen the functional and structural organization of the Sandiganbayan, several amendments have been introduced to the original law creating it, the latest of which are Republic Acts No. 7975 and No. 8249.[63] Under these new laws, the jurisdiction of

---

[61] PD 1606 repealed Presidential Decree No. 1486, the original charter of the *Sandiganbayan* issued on 11 June 1978.

[62] Nunez v. *Sandiganbayan*, 111 SCRA 433, 434 (1982).

[63] See Republic Act No. 8249 (further defining the jurisdiction of the *Sandiganbayan*, amending PD 1606, as amended). For a statutory history of this anti-corruption court, See Presidential Decree No. 1486 – Creating a Special Court to Be Known as '*Sandiganbayan*' and for Other Purposes – Promulgated 11 June 1978; Presidential Decree No. 1606 – Revising Presidential Decree No. 1486 Creating a Special Court to Be Known as '*Sandiganbayan*' and for Other Purposes – Promulgated 10 December 1978; Presidential Decree No. 1629 – Amending Presidential Decree No. 1486 Creating a Special Court to Be

the *Sandiganbayan* is now confined to cases involving public officials occupying positions classified as salary grade '27' and higher.

The *Sandiganbayan* is placed on the same level as the Court of Appeals[64] so its decisions can only be reviewed by the Supreme Court through a writ of *certiorari*.[65] The *Sandiganbayan* is a 'collegiate trial court'[66] composed of a presiding Justice and 8 associate Justices, sitting in three divisions of three Justices each.[67] Under Section 5 the unanimous vote of three Justices in a division is necessary for the pronouncement of a judgment. However, in the event that the three Justices do not reach a unanimous vote, the Presiding Justice shall designate two other Justices from among the members of the *Sandiganbayan* to sit

---

Known as '*Sandiganbayan*', as Revised by Presidential Decree No. 1606 – Promulgated 18 July 1979; Presidential Decree No. 1822 – Providing for the Trial by Courts-martial of Members of the Armed Forces Charged with Offenses Related to the Performance of Their Duties – Promulgated 16 January 1981; Presidential Decree No. 22-a – Amending Section 1, PD No. 1822, Providing for Trial by Courts-martial of Members of the Armed Forces Charged with Offenses Related to the Performance of Their Duties – Promulgated 16 January 1981; Batas Pambansa Blg. 129 – the Judiciary Reorganization Act of 1980 – Promulgated 14 August 1981; Presidential Decree No. 1850 – Providing for the Trial by Courts-martial of Members of the Integrated National Police and Further Defining the Jurisdiction of Courts-martial over Members of the Armed Forces of the Philippines – Promulgated 4 October 1982; Presidential Decree No. 1860 – Amending the Pertinent Provisions of Presidential Decree No. 1606 and Batas Pambansa Blg. 129 Relative to the Jurisdiction of the *Sandiganbayan* and for Other Purposes – Promulgated 14 January 1983; Presidential Decree No. 1861 – Amending the Pertinent Provisions of Presidential Decree No. 1606 and Batas Pambansa Blg. 129 Relative to the Jurisdiction of the *Sandiganbayan* and for Other Purposes – Promulgated 23 March 1983; Presidential Decree No. 1952 – Amending Section One of Presidential Decree No. 1850, Entitled 'Providing for the Trial by Courts-martial of Members of the Integrated National Police and Further Defining the Jurisdiction of Courts-martial over Members of the Armed Forces of the Philippines' – Promulgated 9 September 1984; Executive Order No. 14 – Defining the Jurisdiction over Cases Involving the Ill-gotten Wealth of Former President Ferdinand E. Marcos, Mrs. Imelda R. Marcos, Members of Their Immediate Family, Close Relatives, Subordinates, Close And/or Business Associates, Dummies, Agents and Nominees – Promulgated 7 May 1986; Executive Order No. 14-a – Amending Executive Order No. 14 – Promulgated 18 August 1986; Executive Order No. 101 – Further Amending Presidential Decree No. 1486, as Amended by Presidential Decree No. 1606 Creating a Special Court to Be Known as '*Sandiganbayan*' – Promulgated 24 December 1986; and Executive Order No. 184 – Amending Section 3 of Presidential Decree No. 1606 – Promulgated 5 June 1987.

64 *Id.*, Sec. 1.

65 PD No. 1606, Sec. 7, para. 3.

66 Nunez v. *Sandiganbayan*, 111 SCRA 433, 456 (1982) (Barredo, J. concurring).

67 PD No. 1606, Sec. 3. Following the amendments to the original law setting up the anti-graft court, the restructured *Sandiganbayan* is presently composed of a Presiding Justice and fourteen (14) Associate Justices who sit in five (5) Divisions of three Justices each in the trial and determination of cases.

temporarily with them to form a division of five Justices. The concurrence of the majority of this enlarged division is necessary for rendering a judgment.

Relationship between Sandiganbayan and Tanodbayan

Both institutions were created to complement each other and to work in tandem in carrying out the constitutional and statutory prohibitions against graft and corrupt practices in Government. Presidential Decree No. 1607 provides:

> Sec. 18. *Prosecution of Public Personnel or Other Person.* If the *Tanodbayan* has reason to believe that any public official, employee, or other person has acted in a manner warranting criminal or disciplinary action or proceedings, he shall conduct the necessary investigation and shall file and prosecute the corresponding criminal or administrative case before the *Sandiganbayan* or the proper court or before the proper administrative agency.

The *Tanodbayan* conducts the preliminary investigation and then refers the matter to the *Sandiganbayan* which has exclusive jurisdiction over graft and corruption committed by public officers.

Special Military Tribunals

These deserve separate treatment as they have been a favorite mechanism employed by successive military governments in Nigeria to deal with cases of fraudulent enrichment and abuse of office.

Investigation Panels

Under the Recovery of Public Property (Special Military Tribunals) Act the President is empowered to constitute a panel to conduct an investigation into any matter with which the officer has been concerned in the performance of his duties or to conduct an investigation into the assets of any such public officer. Section 1 provides that any public officer who:

1 has engaged in corrupt practices or has corruptly enriched himself or any other person;
2 has by virtue of abuse of his office contributed to the economic adversity of the Federal Republic of Nigeria;
3 has in any other way been in breach of the Code of Conduct; or
4 has attempted, aided, counselled, procured or conspired with any person to commit any of the offences set out in this section, at any time after 30th September, 1979 shall be guilty of an offence under this Act and upon conviction shall, apart from any other penalty prescribed by or pursuant to any other provision of this Act, forfeit the assets, whether movable or immovable property connected with the commission of the offence, to the Federal Government.

An investigation panel constituted under this Act is authorized to issue a notice compelling a public officer to declare his assets within thirty days after receipt of the notice.[68] The declaration is checked by the panel for accuracy and a public official who, without reasonable excuse, refuses, or neglects to declare his assets in the prescribed manner or *knowingly* makes a false declaration of his assets is guilty of an offence under this Act, and liable on conviction to imprisonment for a term of not less than five years without the option of a fine; and any undeclared assets whether or not they are in his name or under his control, shall be forfeited to the State.[69] The investigation panel may also investigate relatives of public officers who appear to have acquired assets far in excess of any income from their known or ostensible means of livelihood and to apply the provisions of the Recovery Act with necessary modifications to these non-public servants.[70]

Special Military Tribunals

Investigation panels[71] are required under the Recovery of Public Property Act to send their reports to the President who after reviewing them may decide to appoint a special military tribunal to try the public officers accused of fraudulent enrichment.[72] A tribunal appointed under this authority is usually comprised of a chairman who shall be a serving or retired Judge of a High Court or of any court of like jurisdiction and three officers of the Armed Forces not below the rank of Lieutenant Colonel or its equivalent.[73] The tribunal has jurisdiction to try any public officer or other person charged with any offence under the Act and to award any of a number of specified penalties including reparations[74] and:

> [I]mprisonment for a term not exceeding twenty-one years; or
>
> [I]n cases where the tribunal arrives at a finding that undeclared assets (whether in Nigeria or elsewhere) of such person have a value of or amount to not less than N, 1,000,000 or its equivalent in any other currency or combination of currencies, a sentence of life imprisonment.[75]

There is a presumption of unlawfulness and the accused has the onus of proving at

---

68 Recovery of Public Property (Special Military Tribunals) Act, Sec. 2(1)(a).

69 *Id.*, Sec. 3.

70 *Id.*, Sec. 3(5).

71 The military *junta* that replaced that of General Buhari in August 1985 appointed a special panel to investigate the cases of persons who had been detained under the provisions of Decrees Nos. 2 and 3 of 1984. The Special Panel of four was headed by Mr. Justice S.O. Uwaifo. It reviewed a total of 689 cases involving 1,017 persons and submitted recommendations on each of them. See Federal Military Government Decisions, *supra* note 30, at 2.

72 *Id.*, Sec. 5(1).

73 *Id.*, Sec. 5(2).

74 *Id.*, Sec. 6(4).

75 *Id.*, Sec. 13(1).

trial that enrichment was lawful.[76] The rules of procedure to be adopted in prosecutions for offenses before a tribunal allow an accused to defend himself in person or by a person of his own choice who is an attorney resident in Nigeria.[77] However, if an accused charged with an offense punishable with life imprisonment cannot afford legal Counsel, a tribunal will assign Counsel for his defense.[78]

A tribunal has the power to summon witnesses, issue warrants authorizing any police officer or any member of the armed forces or any security agencies to enter, if necessary by force, any building or other place where spoliated funds are hidden, and to search for, seize and remove any evidence found in the course of the search.[79] The Chairman of the tribunal may by order prohibit any disposition of property movable or immovable by or on behalf of a party appearing before the tribunal whether or not the property is owned or held by that person or by any other person on his behalf.[80] Since justice delayed is justice denied, the special military tribunal is required to deliver its judgment not later than twenty working days from the day the charge is read to the accused person.[81] Its decision will not be set aside or treated as a nullity solely on the ground of non-compliance with the provisions of this section unless the Special Appeal Tribunal exercising jurisdiction by way of appeal from or review of that decision is satisfied that there has been a miscarriage of justice.[82]

A person convicted by the tribunal shall have the right of appeal to the special Appeal Tribunal established under the Recovery of Public Property Act.[83] The appeal like the trial is heard in public except where it is in the interest of public security that the trial or appeal shall be held in camera.[84]

Special Appeal Tribunal

An appeal from a special military tribunal goes directly to the Special Appeal Tribunal composed of:

1 two serving or retired Justices of the Court of Appeal, one of whom shall be the Chairman;
2 three military officers not below the rank of Colonel or its equivalent.[85]

The Appeal Tribunal has six weeks from the date an appeal is lodged to render a judgment. The Tribunal can be disposed in one of several ways:

---

76 *Id.*, Sec. 6(3).
77 *Id.*, Sec. 7(3).
78 *Id.*
79 *Id.*, Sec. 9.
80 *Id.*, Sec. 10(1).
81 *Id.*, Sec. 12(1).
82 *Id.*, Sec. 12(2).
83 *Id.*, Sec. 14(1).
84 *Id.*, Sec. 14(2).
85 *Id.*, Sec. 15(2).

1 confirm, vary or set aside the judgment or order of the tribunal; or
2 maintain and uphold the conviction and dismiss the appeal; or
3 allow the appeal and set aside the conviction if it appears to the Appeal Tribunal that the conviction should be set aside on the ground that it was, having regard to the evidence adduced, unreasonable, or that the conviction should be set aside on the ground of a wrong decision on any question of law, or on the ground that there was a substantial miscarriage of justice; or
4 set aside the conviction and convict the appellant of any offence of which he might lawfully have been convicted by the tribunal upon the evidence adduced thereat and sentence him accordingly; or
5 set aside the conviction and order that the appellant be re-tried in a tribunal or court of competent jurisdiction; or
6 order the forfeiture of additional assets of the appellant to the Federal Government or the State Government.[86]

However a sentence meted out by a tribunal or Appeal Tribunal cannot be enforced until it has been confirmed by the Armed Forces Ruling Council.[87] Confirmation is not automatic and it can be withheld.[88] In confirming the sentence of a tribunal or Appeal Tribunal the confirming authority may either remit the sentence below or substitute it for a less severe penalty.[89]

Corrupt Enrichment Under Romanian Law

The fall of Nicolae Ceausescu in 1989 exposed to a wider audience the extent of official corruption in this former communist State. Yet Romanian law made provisions for such wrongful conduct. It set up a two-step process in investigating corrupt enrichment of public officials ('illicit acquisition') under Law 18 of 1968 as amended.[90] Law 18 establishes a two-track system for dealing with corruption by public office holders; one track reserved exclusively for 'dignitaries' and a second for subordinate State officials. Articles 4 and 5 provide for the establishment of a commission of inquiry operating from the district court to

---

86 *Id.*, Sec. 17.
87 *Id.*, Sec. 20(2).
88 *Id.*, Sec. 20(3).
89 *Id.*, Sec. 20(4).
90 See Law 18 of 1968, Regarding the Control of Acquisition of Goods by Physical Persons Through Illicit Means, as amended and modified by the Law of 30 April 1979, Art. 9. The purpose and effect of the 1979 amendment was to immunize high officials of the Romanian Communist Party (RCP) from Law of 1968. Chapter VII dealing with Guidance and Control makes the entire administration of this law subject to the final control of the Central Committee of the RCP. Ceausescu pushed through the 1979 amendment in order to protect himself from its reach since he controlled both the RCP and the Central Committee. The amendment coincided with the period when Ceausescu was already fully engaged in his plunder of the Communist patrimonium and rightly felt that the 1968 law could be used against him.

investigate persons suspected of having acquired property by illicit means. A commission set up under this provision is composed of a district court judge, a state prosecutor, a representative from the taxing authority, a member nominated by the county police, a representative from the city council and 4 workers. If the accused is a dignitary, the composition of the commission of inquiry will include two judges from the Supreme Court nominated by the President of that Court, a prosecutor from the Office of the Procurator General, a representative from the Superior Court of Financial Control, a representative of the Minister of Finance, two deputies from the Great National Assembly and four workers.[91]

A commission of inquiry is empowered to investigate officials suspected of corrupt enrichment and determine within 45 days whether a prima facie case can be made against the accused. The commission has one of three options: send the file to the courts if there is evidence of illicit acquisition or send it to the prosecutor if there was a crime involved in the acquisition of the property or close the file for lack of evidence of illicit acquisition.[92] Commission proceedings and documents are closed to the public.[93] Persons appearing before an inquiry commission have the burden of proving that property was acquired legally.[94] Witnesses can be called and the Commission is empowered to summon expert witnesses to evaluate the value of property allegedly spoliated as well as the suspect's income and expenses.[95] To ensure that spoliated assets are not dissipated, the Commission has the power to order their sequestration until its investigation is completed.[96]

Low level office holders suspected of illicit acquisition of property by a commission of inquiry have their cases referred to a tribunal of first instance composed of two judges and three workers.[97] Jurisdiction over cases involving dignitaries is vested in the civil bench of the Supreme Court which in turn delegates its power to a special tribunal comprised of three Judges and four workers.[98] Persons found guilty of illicit acquisition of wealth have a right of appeal within 15 days from the date of the judgment. Appeals from the tribunals of first instance go to the Court of Appeals comprised of three judges and two workers.[99] Cases involving dignitaries can be appealed to a special nine member appeals tribunal consisting of five judges and four deputies from the Great National Assembly.[100]

An official adjudged guilty of fraudulent acquisition will be disqualified from

---

91 *Id.*, Art. 15.
92 *Id.*, Art. 9.
93 *Id.*, Art. 6.
94 *Id.*, Art. 2.
95 *Id.*, Arts. 7–8.
96 *Id.*
97 *Id.*, Art. 10.
98 *Id.*, Art. 17.
99 *Id.*, Arts. 12–14.
100 *Id.*, Art. 17.

holding any position of financial responsibility[101] and required to forfeit any illicitly acquired property to the State.[102]

COMMISSIONS OF INQUIRY IN ACTION

When in 1970 President Suharto of Indonesia responded to nationwide demonstrations protesting widespread corruption in his government by appointing a special Commission of Four to review the problem and make concrete suggestions for change,[103] he was merely falling back on a tried and proven technique for dealing with corruption among public servants. The use of an official inquiry to investigate allegations of corrupt practices by public officials is widespread. Usually appointed by the head of state, holding public sittings and using quasi-judicial procedures, these commissions have been a common feature of post-independence politics in Africa and Asia. As 'dramatic political events they have had an impact upon the politics of current regimes, or have acted as apologias for new ones,' according to one seasoned observer.[104] Corruption inquiries can be of two types: internal inquiries, which are usually instituted by departments, ministries or public bodies and conduct their work usually *in camera*; and public inquiries, which are formally announced and operate in the open, with witnesses and Counsel. This distinction might be useful for analytical neatness but in practice it is academic since the internal and supposedly closed inquiries tend to be leaked while reports of the open and public inquiries are routinely suppressed[105] or allowed to release only sanitized portions to the public.[106]

---

[101] *Id.*, Art. 26.

[102] *Id.*, Art. 2, para. 1.

[103] The 1970 protests were led by students and are believed to be the strongest anti-corruption outburst in Indonesia's first 25 years as an independent State. See Theodore M. Smith, 'Corruption, Tradition, and Change in Indonesia,' in *Political Corruption: A Handbook*, 423 (Arnold J. Heidenheimer, Michael Johnson & Victor T. Le Vine eds, 1989).

[104] See Stephen Riley, '*The land of waving palms': political economy, corruption inquiries and politics in Sierra Leone,* in CORRUPTION: CAUSES, CONSEQUENCES AND CONTROL 190, 193 (Michael Clarke ed. 1983). Much cynicism has been attached to these probes. In coup-prone Africa, for example, corruption inquiries have been dismissed by some as post-coup rationalizations. See Joseph S. Nye, 'Corruption and Political Development: a cost-benefit analysis,' *American Political Science Review*, 61, 417 (1967).

[105] In his highly controversial book*: The Rise and Fall of Kwame Nkrumah: A Study of Personal Rule in Africa* (1966), Henry Bretton makes the claim that the Abraham Commission on Trade Malpractices' 1965 Report was heavily censored by the Ghanaian government before publication. *Id.*, at 214 no. 42 citing Kweku Akwei's article which appeared in the Evening News, 25 March 1966. For corroboration of this view, see Victor T. Le Vine, *Political Corruption: The Ghana Case*, 26 (1975).

[106] For instance, in 1964 and again in 1967, the Ghana government appointed a commission to inquire into allegations of corruption in connection with the granting of import licenses. The first commission chaired by Justice Akainyah issued a report which

Grave social ills provide the justification for the appointment of commissions of inquiry. In coup-prone Africa, the pattern has been unmistakable. A government, usually civilian and authoritarian but oftentimes military, considered to be very corrupt is overthrown and the successor government now clothed with virtue announces a 'drive to eradicate corruption, mismanagement and indiscipline in the affairs of government' and its desire to 'restore morality, accountability, transparency and good government in the body politic of the Nation once more.'[107] Towards these ends, it appoints a Commission or several Commissions of Inquiry to examine the assets of a defined class of State officials and to inquire and investigate whether such assets were acquired lawfully or unlawfully. Few successor governments bent on sweeping clean the Augean stables have strayed from this mould.

This section will examine some of these commissions paying particular attention to their composition, terms of reference, methodology, procedure, findings, recommendations (penalties) and expressions of *de lege ferenda*. The sample for analysis includes the published reports of roughly 40 inquiry commissions from four countries with a long history of indigenous spoliation (Ghana, Nigeria, Philippines and Sierra Leone) covering a span of three decades. The sample is fairly representative of state practice with respect to this problem.

Composition

The authority to appoint a commission comes from one of several instruments: the Constitution,[108] a statute[109] or a special decree.[110] To underscore their importance

---

suggested that the amount of money involved was not substantial. However, a subsequent report by the second commission chaired by Justice Ollenu revealed not only that portions of the Akainyah Commission report were never published but also that the import licensing corruption was widespread. See Ollenu, *Report of the Commission of Enquiry into Irregularities and Malpractices in the Grant of Import Licenses*. White Paper: WP No. 4/67 (1967), para. 146.

[107] See Government of Sierra Leone, *White Paper on the Report of the Justice Beccles Davies Commission of Inquiry into the Assets and Other Related Matters of All Persons who were Presidents, Vice-Presidents, Ministers, Ministers of State and Deputy Ministers Within the Period From the 1st Day of June, 1986, to the 22nd Day of September 1991, and to Inquire Into and Investigate Whether Such Assets were Acquired Lawfully or Unlawfully* (1993).

[108] *Constitution of the Republic of Sierra Leone*, 1991, §147 (1); *Constitution of the Republic of Panama*, Art. 142; *Constitution of the Republic of Haiti*, 1987, chap. IV; *Constitution of the Federal Republic of Nigeria*, §16 Fifth Schedule.

[109] Ghana's Commissions of Enquiry Act, 1964 (Act 250); Philippines Republic Act No. 3019 (1960).

[110] See Ghana's National Liberation Council (Investigation and Forfeiture of Assets) Decree, 1966 (NCLD 72); Sierra Leone's Public Notice N. 172; Nigeria's State Security (Detention of Persons) Decree No. 2, 1984 and the Recovery of Public Property (Special Military Tribunal) Decree No. 3, 1984; Philippines' Presidential Decree No. 1606.

and as an affirmation of the government's firm belief in the rule of law, nearly all commissions are chaired by a High Court Judge or a Justice of the Supreme Court. Other members may or may not be all law officers or trained in law but they are usually people of substance in the nation. Even the Special Military Tribunals set up in Nigeria were headed by, and comprised mainly judicial legal officers.[111] Given the ubiquity of military governments, particularly in Africa, it is not surprising that a ranking military officer is usually included in the membership of most commissions of inquiry. The size of these commissions varies but it stays roughly between three and five members including the chairperson.

Terms of Reference

The terms of reference of these corruption inquiries are fairly standard and uniform and can be summed up in three words: investigate, ascertain and report. They are appointed to investigate the existence, nature, extent and method by which assets were acquired by persons specified in the executive instrument appointing the Commission. Some terms of reference are stated in such a way as to shape the direction of the inquiry. A good example is the 1991 Beccles Davies Commission which was specifically instructed by the National Provisional Ruling Council that appointed it to find out whether former Presidents, Vice-Presidents, Ministers, Ministers of State and Deputy Ministers of Sierra Leone within a given period: '(a) maintained a standard of living above that which was commensurate with their past official emoluments; (b) were in control of pecuniary resources or property disproportionate to their past official emoluments; (c) [can withstand] allegations of corruption, dishonesty, or abuse of office for private benefit by them, or in collaboration with any person or persons in respect of such corruption, dishonesty or abuse of office … [and] they acted wilfully or corruptly in such a manner as to cause financial loss or damage to the Government ….'[112]

These terms of reference almost always identify the individuals who are to be investigated and increasingly they include former heads of state and other top level constitutionally responsible leaders.

Proceedings

The proceedings of most Commissions are held in public and only a few are held in private with the public not entitled to be present in the room or place where they are held.[113] With regard to procedure, Commissions generally strive to adhere to the standards that are acceptable in a Court of Law. Persons against whom allegations are made are allowed to listen, to examine and cross-examine witnesses (under oath) either in person or by Counsel and state their case, if they so desire.

---

[111] See *supra* notes 63–80 and accompanying text.

[112] *Id.*

[113] See *Republic of Ghana, Report of the Commission of Enquiry on the Commercial Activities of the Erstwhile Publicity Secretariat*, 52 (1966).

Exhibits are allowed to be tendered and admitted into evidence and corroboration is usually sought for submitted testimony.

Almost all the executive instruments setting up the Commission of Inquiry cross-nationally have introduced some procedural innovations that depart markedly from generally accepted standards. To take one example, Ghana's National Liberation Council (Investigation and Forfeiture of Assets) Decree 1966 (NLCD 1972) which was the legal basis for over forty Commissions of Inquiry appointed during a long period of military rule, contains a provision commonly found in other legal texts setting up inquiry commissions in other countries that all properties of persons under investigation are deemed unlawful unless the contrary is proved.[114] When first introduced this provision was so unique that a Ghanaian inquiry panel described it as 'revolutionary in the history of the statute laws' of Ghana where the common law presumption of lawfulness governs.[115] To their credit, many of the Ghanaian commissions chose not to have their hands tied by this decreed presumption of unlawful acquisition, electing instead to moderate the oppressive effects of this provision by subjecting its application 'in all cases to an overriding consideration of fairness and justice.'[116] However, other Commissions opted for a literal interpretation of the same Decree and took the position that since all the facts or matters to be investigated were within the exclusive knowledge of the person being investigated, he carried the burden of proving that his assets were acquired lawfully.[117] This burden was generally met when the accused was able 'to establish by preponderance of evidence or by tilting the balance of probabilities in his favour that his properties were acquired lawfully.'[118] But any doubts as to the manner of acquisition of any properties were to be resolved in favor of the accused.

Recommendations

In all cases where adverse findings were made against the accused, the penalties usually were: seizure and forfeiture of all unlawfully acquired assets and properties to the State; disqualification from holding public office or participation in party politics either for a specified period of time or for the rest of the guilty person's life; being stripped of all titles, national honors and awards bestowed on him by the State; a ban for life or a specified period of time from doing any business with the government, government agencies and corporations either alone or in association with any other business or individuals. In addition to these civil sanctions, an adverse finding more often than not was also the basis of a criminal action. Usually

---

114 See NCLD 72, Sec. 8(3). A similar provision is found in the Recovery of Public Property (Special Military Tribunals) Act promulgated by the Federal Military Government in Nigeria. See Recovery of Public Property Act, Sec. 6(3).

115 See Republic of Ghana, *Report of the Taylor Assets Committee – Assets of Scheduled Persons*, Vol. 1, ii (1974).

116 *Id.*, at iv.

117 See Republic of Ghana, *Report of the Sowah Commission – Assets of Specified Persons*, Vol. 1, 4 (1968).

118 *Id.*

when criminal liability is ascertained the culpable public official would be sent for trial within the normal judicial system or disciplined departmentally. However, in the exceptional cases involving 'public servants who have been engaged in perhaps unprecedented massive fraud, corruption and personal enrichment over so short a time,' a special Judicial Tribunal can be created to try them.[119]

STATUTORY ANTI-CORRUPTION BODIES

The general trend in the last fifteen years (1990–2005) has been to entrust the investigation of corruption to independent anti-corruption agencies or commissions. These bodies go under various names, such as independent anti-corruption commission (Hong Kong) inspectorate of government (Uganda) directorates on corruption and economic crime (Botswana) high authority for coordinating the fight against corruption (Burkina Faso) special investigating units and tribunal (South Africa) corrupt practices investigation bureau (Singapore) anti-corruption agency (Malaysia) or ombudsman (Papua New Guinea). They enjoy different kinds of legal authority and different missions. Whatever the name they go by, these organizations typically perform at least one or more three core functions. Some are structured to operate as enforcement bodies with responsibility for enforcing the criminal law on corruption through the investigation of persons suspected of violating anti-corruption statutes, and the assembling of evidence for use in prosecution, either by the anti-corruption body itself of by the Attorney General, Director of Public Prosecutions or some other appropriate state agency. Others perform a range of functions that are non-legal but largely preventive. In this role these commissions may or may not be vested with investigative or prosecutorial powers. Some may combine either or both of the two preceding roles with that of raising public awareness of corruption. This educative role will usually but not necessarily involve direct communication with the public through the use of the mass media as well as involving itself formally in the public education system.[120] A representative sample of this new generation of anti-corruption bodies is discussed briefly below.

Nigeria's Independent Corrupt Practices and Other Related Offences Commission

Nigeria passed the Corrupt Practices and Other Related Offences Act, a new anti-

---

[119] That is the route the Federal Military Government in Nigeria followed. See Federal Republic of Nigeria, *Views and Decisions of the Federal Military Government on the Report and Recommendations of Justice Uwaifo Special Panel for the Investigation of Cases of Persons Conditionally Released from Detention and Persons Still in Detention under the State Security (Detention of Persons)* Decree no. 2, 1984 and *The Recovery of Public Property (Special Military Tribunals)* Decree no. 3, 1984, 5, 6 (1986).

[120] *See* African Anti-corruption Commissions – First Report: Overview and Issues. Available at http://www.u4.no/document/aacc/main.cfm (last visited on 7 February 2005).

corruption legislation in 2000.[121] Section 3 of the Corrupt Practices Act establishes the Independent Corrupt Practices and Other Related Offences Commission. The Commission is an independent agency whose duties and powers are set out in various sections of the statute.[122] As a body corporate, the Commission can sue or be sued in its corporate name. The Commission is comprised of 13 members headed by a Chairman[123] who must be a person qualified to hold the office of judge

---

[121] In 2002 the Nigerian Government established the Economic and Financial Crimes Commission (EFCC) and charged it with the enforcement and administration of the provisions of the Economic and Financial Crimes Commission (Establishment) Act of 2002. The scope of EFCC's activities is quite broad. The EFCC is empowered to prevent, investigate, prosecute and penalize economic and financial crimes and is charged with the responsibility of enforcing the provisions of other laws and regulations relating to economic and financial crimes, including: Economic and Financial Crimes Commission Establishment Act (2004); The Money Laundering Act 1995; The Advance Fee Fraud and Other Related Offences Act 1995; The Failed Banks (Recovery of Debts) and Financial Malpractices in Bank Act 1994; The Banks and Other Financial Institutions Act 1991; and Miscellaneous Offences Act.

The EFCC is made up of a Chairman (who must be a serving or retired member of any government security or law enforcement agency) who acts as the chief executive and accounting officer of the Commission; a Director-General who is the head of the administration; the Governor of the Central Bank or his representative; a representative of the Federal Ministry of Foreign Affairs; a representative of the Federal Ministry of Finance; a representative of the Federal Ministry of Justice, all of whom should not be below the rank of a Director; the Chairman of the National Drug Law Enforcement Agency; the Director General of the National Intelligence Agency; the Director General of the Department of State Security Services; the Director-General Securities and Exchange Commission; the Commissioner for Insurance; the Postmaster-General of the Nigerian Postal Services; the Chairman, Nigerian Communications Commission; the Comptroller-General, Nigeria Customs Services; the Comptroller-General Nigerian Immigration Services; a representative of the Nigerian Police Force not below the rank of an Assistant Inspector-General of Police; four eminent Nigerians with cognate experience in any of the following – finance, banking or accounting.

The EFCC appears to be very serious about its mission. In the first half of 2004, it caused the arrest of more than 500 Nigerians for e-mail, fax and letter frauds that spread around the world, the so-called '419 scams' named for the section of the Nigerian penal code that outlaws them. A member of Parliament was arrested and held without bail (he died in prison) and several prominent Nigerians were charged in a fraud trial involving a Brazilian banker whose institution was destroyed by a $242 million '419' scam. The brain behind the scam, Mrs. Amaka Anajemba received a 2½ year prison sentence and was ordered to give up $25.5 million in cash and assets – including houses in Nigeria, the United States, Britain and Switzerland – to help repay the bank, Sao Paulo's Banco Noroestre. See 'Five Nigerians charged in $242 million '419' fraud trial,' Available at http://www.cnn.com/2004/WORLD/africa/02/05/nigeria.419.trial.ap (last visited on 19 August 2005).

[122] §3(14).

[123] According to one commentator, the powers of the Commission Chairman 'generated

of a superior court of record.[124] Commissioners enjoy all the powers and immunities of a police officer.[125]

The Philippines Presidential Anti-Graft Commission

By Executive Order No. 268 of 18 July 2000, the Presidential Commission Against Graft and Corruption (PCAGC) was abolished and replaced with the National Anti-corruption Commission. A year later, on 16 April 2001, President Gloria Macapagal-Aroyo signed Executive Order No. 12 creating the Presidential Anti-Graft Commission and providing for its powers, duties, and other purposes.[126] This new Commission is placed under the Office of the President, pursuant to Article VII, Section 17 of the Constitution which provides that the President shall have control of all executive departments, bureaus, and offices. It is composed of a Chairman and two Commissioners appointed by the President, all of whom serve on a full-time basis and a majority of whom must be members of the Philippine Bar.[127] Section 4 of the Executive Order sets out the jurisdiction, powers and functions of the Commission which include *inter alia* the power to investigate or hear administrative cases or complaints involving the possible violation of the 'Anti-graft and Corrupt Practices Act' and Related Offences;[128] and to investigate or hear administrative cases or complaints against all presidential appointees in the government and any of its agencies or instrumentalities (including members of the governing board of any instrumentality, regulatory agency, chartered institution and directors or officers appointed or nominated by the President to government-owned or controlled corporations or corporations where the government has a minority interest or who otherwise represent the interests of the government), occupying the positions of assistant regional director, or an equivalent rank, and higher, otherwise classified as Salary Grade '26' and higher, of the Compensation and Position Classification Act of 1989 (Republic Act No. 6758).[129] The Commission's jurisdiction also includes the investigation of a non-presidential

fear and suspicion from the federal legislature causing severe political crisis in the first term of the Obasanjo government.' See Extra-Territorial Scope, *supra* note 32, at 78, note 41.

[124] §3(4).

[125] §§5(1) and 65.

[126] See The Order Repeals Executive Order Nos. 151 and 151-a, dated 11 January 1994 and respectively, which established the PCAGC as well as Executive Order No. 268 of 24 January 1994 which set up the National Anti-corruption Commission.

[127] Section 2.

[128] Sec. 4(a). These would include offenses codified in Republic Act No. 1379 on the Unlawful Acquisition of Property by a Public Officer or Employee; Republic Act No. 6713, otherwise known as the 'Code of Conduct and Ethical Standards for Public Officials and Employees;' Presidential Decree No. 46, making it punishable for public officials and employees to receive gifts on any occasion, including Christmas; any provision under Title Seven, Book Two of the Revised Penal Code; and rules and regulations duly promulgated by competent authority to implement any of the foregoing laws or issuances.

[129] Sec. 4(b).

appointee who may have acted in conspiracy or may have been involved with a presidential appointee or ranking officer mentioned in this subsection. Interestingly, members of the Armed Forces of the Philippines and the Philippine National Police are exempt from the jurisdiction of the presidential anti-graft commission.[130]

A special procedure is reserved for investigations and hearings involving presidential appointees with the rank of Undersecretary or higher. Any enquiry involving this category of public officer is conducted by the Commission sitting *en banc*. For lower ranking presidential appointees, the investigation or hearing can be safely entrusted to a Commissioner or panel of hearing officers duly designated by the Chairman.[131] However, the report or recommendations issuing from this panel investigation has to be deliberated and reviewed by the Commission *en banc* before a final report and recommendations are submitted to the President.

To facilitate its work, the Commission is vested with the power to administer oaths and issue *subpoena ad testificandum* and *duces tecum* as well as the power to call upon and secure the assistance of any office, committee, commission, bureau, agency, department or instrumentality in the Executive Branch, including government-owned or controlled corporations.[132] Failure to comply with a subpoena issued by the Commission or by its authority without adequate cause may result in a Commission recommendation to the President, after formal charge and hearing, to suspend or dismiss the non-complying government personnel from the service.[133]

On the completion of its investigation or hearing, the Commission submits a report and recommendations to the President which include, among others, the factual findings and legal conclusions, as well as the penalty recommend to be imposed or such other action that may be taken.[134]

Hong Kong's Independent Commission Against Corruption

Hong Kong's much admired and talked about Independent Commission Against Corruption (ICAC) was established under the Independent Commission Against Corruption Ordinance in February 1974 when Hong Kong was still a British Crown Colony. This Commission survived China's resumption of the exercise of sovereignty over Hong Kong on 1 July 1997 and answers directly to the Chief Executive of the Hong Kong Special Administrative Region under Article 57 of the Basic Law.[135] The success of the ICAC has been such that a former chairman

---

130 *Id.*

131 Sec. 4(e).

132 Sec. 5.

133 Sec. 6.

134 Sec. 8.

135 See The Basic Law of the Hong Kong Special Administrative Region of the People's Republic of China, Adopted on 4 April 1990 by the Seventh National People's Congress of the People's Republic of China at its Third Session. Available at http://www.constitution.org/cons/hongkong.txt (last visited on 5 February 2005).

would openly boast that Hong Kong now has 'a fundamentally clean public service, a private sector that is vigilant against corruption, and a community which no longer accepts corruption as a way of life.'[136] Since its inception, the Commission has waged war against corruption[137] with the three-pronged approach

---

[136] See Daniel R. Fung, Anti-Corruption and Human Rights Protection: Hong Kong's Jurisprudential Experience, *Paper prepared for presentation at the 8th International Anti-Corruption Conference*, Lima Peru, 7-11 September 1997; see also Julie Mu Fee-Man, 'Hong Kong, China's Anticorruption Strategy,' in *Developing Anticorruption Strategies* [hereinafter 'Anti-Corruption Strategy'] (thanks to the ICAC, Hong Kong can now boast of being one of the world's least corrupt places; with one of the cleanest civil services; having succeeded in bringing about a fundamental change in public attitude toward corruption, from acceptance to revulsion, and from passive acquiescence to positive identification with the ICAC's goals and mission). Available at http://unpan1.un.org/intradoc/groups/public/documents/APCITY/UNPANO (last visited on 7 February 2005).

[137] The law of Hong Kong on corruption is to be found in the Elections (Corrupt and Illegal Conduct) Ordinance (Cap. 554), the Prevention of Bribery Ordinance (Cap. 201) and the Independent Commission against Corruption Ordinance (Cap. 204).

Section 4 (2) of the Hong Kong Prevention of Bribery Ordinance provides –

(2) Any public servant who, whether in Hong Kong or elsewhere, without lawful authority or reasonable excuse, solicits or accepts any advantage as an inducement to or reward for or otherwise on account of his –

(a) performing or abstaining from performing, or having performed or abstained from performing, any act in his capacity as a public servant;

(b) expediting, delaying, hindering or preventing, or having expedited, delayed, hindered or prevented, the performance of an act, whether by himself or by any other public servant in his or that other public servant's capacity as a public servant; or

(c) assisting, favouring, hindering or delaying, or having assisted, favoured, hindered or delayed, any person in the transaction of any business with a public body, shall be guilty of an offence.

As we can see, this subsection deals with 'passive corruption,' that is public servants who take a bribe for performing an act of their functions.

'Active' corruption is dealt with in Section 4 (1) of the same Ordinance which provides –

Any person who, whether in Hong Kong or elsewhere, without lawful authority or reasonable excuse, offers any advantage to a public servant as an inducement to or reward for or otherwise on account of that public servant's –

(a) performing or abstaining from performing, or having performed or abstained from performing, any act in his capacity as a public servant;

(b) expediting, delaying, hindering or preventing, or having expedited, delayed, hindered or prevented, the performance of an act, whether by that public servant or by any other public servant in his or that other public servant's capacity as a public servant; or

(c) assisting, favouring, hindering or delaying, or having assisted, favoured, hindered or delayed, any person in the transaction of any business with a public body, shall be guilty of an offence.

It is worth noting that, in Hong Kong, –

it is an offence for a public servant to solicit or accept any advantage offered as an

of investigation, prevention and education. In tackling corruption, the ICAC has sought to forge a partnership with civil society in general and the private sector in particular. Through creative use of the media, the ICAC has successfully kept corruption at the forefront of public minds. To effectively enforce anti-corruption laws, the Commission maintains close ties with the civil service, public service organizations, regulatory bodies, trade associations, and professional institutions.[138]

A string of successful court cases where corrupt public officials and prominent members of the business community, including the Chairman of the Stock Exchange, were brought to justice has helped in gaining public trust in and support for the ICAC.[139] The Commission is a corporate body whose sole purpose is to fight corruption. It is composed of one Commissioner, one Deputy Commissioner and such officers as may be appointed. The Commissioner and his deputy are appointed by the Chief Executive, and the former is under the sole direction of the Chief Executive. The ICAC enjoys immense powers of arrest, search, seizure, fingerprinting and photographing.[140] As a safeguard against the vast powers it enjoys, the ICAC is accountable to Government and to Parliament and the Commissioner may be summoned to attend meetings in the Legislative Council to

---

inducement to or reward in connection with the performance of his official duty;

it is also an offence to offer such an advantage to a public servant in connection with the performance of his official duty;

the gift must still have been made or received for consideration relating to the officer's functions;

the purpose for the gift must be corrupt;

the offence is committed even where the gift is received ex post facto;

It is useful to note that Section 4(3) and (4) of the Ordinance provides that a public officer may receive a gift if he obtains prior permission from his superior officer.

[138] See generally, 'Anti-Corruption Strategy,' *supra* note 136.

[139] The first important task of the Commission was to bring Godber to justice. Peter Fitzroy Godber was the Police Chief Superintendent accused of corruption who succeeded in escaping to England. Acting on intelligence received alleging that Godber was habitually remitting considerable sums of money abroad, the Anti-Corruption Agency, predecessor to the ICAC, launched a large scale investigation into Godber's financial dealings. Initial investigations revealed that Godber had close to HK $330,000 in various Hong Kong banks and his remittances abroad, mainly to Australia, Canada and Singapore, amounted to more than HK$624,000. Further investigations revealed that Godber's total net worth was in excess of HK$4,370,000 – six times his total official income since he joined the Police Force! In early 1975, Godber was extradited from England to stand trial. The charges were a conspiracy offence and one of accepting bribes. Godber was found guilty on both counts and sentenced to four years imprisonment. Godber's extradition and prosecution were demonstrative of the ICAC's determination and resolution to eradicate corruption. It was this landmark case that kicked off a quiet revolution – a new start against corruption. To read more on the Godber story, see http://www.icac.org.hk/text/eng/cases/godber/index.html (last visited 6 February 2005)

[140] §§10, 10D, Independent Commission against Corruption Ordinance, Cap. 210. Available at http://www.icac.org.hk/eng/power/powe_acct_3.html (last visited 6 February 2005).

answer questions.

Built into the structure of the ICAC is another oversight mechanism. There are a number of advisory committees composed of citizens which act in a purely advisory capacity and constitute the ICAC's umbrella.[141] For instance, the immense powers of the Commission to dismiss members of its staff will be tempered by the necessity to seek advice from any of the following advisory committees which ICAC would be foolish to disregard save in exceptional circumstances:

(a) The *Advisory Committee on Corruption* has the following terms of reference, viz.–

1 To advise the Commissioner of the Independent Commission Against Corruption on any aspect of the problem of corruption in Hong Kong, and, to this end:
(a) to keep the operational, staffing and administrative policies of the Commission under review;
(b) to advise on action being considered by the Commissioner under section 8(2) of the Independent Commission Against Corruption Ordinance;
(c) to receive reports by the Commissioner on disciplinary action taken;
(d) to consider the annual estimates of expenditure of the Commission to scrutinize the annual report of the Commission before its submission to the Chief Executive; and
(e) to submit an annual report to the Chief Executive on the work of the Committee.
2 To draw to the Chief Executive's attention, as it considers necessary, any aspect of the work of the Commission or any problem encountered by it.
The Commissioner and the Chairpersons of the other committees are ex officio members. The Committee is composed also of six other members appointed by the Chief Executive.

(b) The *Operations Review Committee* has the following terms of reference:

1 To receive from the Commissioner information about all complaints of corruption made to the Commission and the manner in which the Commission is dealing with them.
2 To receive from the Commissioner progress reports on all investigations lasting over a year or requiring substantial resources.
3 To receive from the Commissioner reports on the number of, and justifications for, search warrants authorised by the Commissioner, and explanations as to the need for urgency, as soon afterwards as practical.
4 To receive from the Commissioner reports on all cases where suspects have

[141] *Id.*

been bailed by ICAC for more than six months.

5 To receive from the Commissioner reports on the investigations the Commission has completed and to advise on how those cases that on legal advice are not being subject to prosecution or caution, should be pursued.

6 To receive from the Commissioner reports on the results of prosecutions of offences within the Commission's jurisdiction and of any subsequent appeals.

7 To advise the Commissioner on what information revealed by investigations into offences within its jurisdiction shall be passed to government departments or public bodies, or other organizations and individuals, or, where in exceptional cases, it has been necessary to pass such information in advance of a Committee meeting, to review such action at the first meeting thereafter.

8 To advise on such other matters as the Commissioner may refer to the Committee or on which the Committee may wish to advise.

9 To draw to the Chief Executive's attention any aspect of the work of the Operations Department or any problems encountered by the Committee.

10 To submit annual reports to the Chief Executive which should be published.

It is composed of the Secretary for Justice or her representative (ex officio) Commissioner of Police or his representative (ex officio) Director of Administration (ex officio) Commissioner, Independent Commission Against Corruption (ex officio) and some 12 other members appointed by the Chief Executive.

(c) The *Corruption Prevention Advisory Committee* receives and calls for reports from the Commission about practices and procedures of Government Departments, public bodies and the private sector which may be conducive to corruption and advises the Commissioner what areas should be examined and the degree of priority to be accorded to each. It also monitors action taken to implement recommendations. It is composed of the Commissioner of Police or his representative (ex officio), Director of Administration or his representative (ex officio) and Commissioner, Independent Commission Against Corruption (ex officio).

(d) Lastly, the *Citizens Advisory Committee on Community Relations* advises the ICAC on the strategy to educate the public and enlist their support.

Botswana's Directorate on Corruption and Economic Crime

Following a flurry of scandals involving government purchases, land distribution and housing management, the Government of Botswana set up three separate commissions of inquiry which unearthed the depth of corruption in that country. This led to the passing of the Corruption and Economic Crime Act of 1994 which established the Directorate on Corruption and Economic Crime (DCEC), inspired by Hong Kong's ICAC.

The Directorate is an autonomous body under the Office of the President. It consists of a Director, Deputy Director and such other officers of the Directorate as may be appointed. The Director is formally and directly responsible to the President.

Section 6 of the Corruption and Economic Crime Act provides that the functions of the Directorate shall be to:

1 to receive and investigate any complaints alleging corruption in any public body;
2 to investigate any alleged or suspected offences under this Act, or any other offence disclosed during such an investigation;
3 to investigate any alleged or suspected contravention of any of the provisions of the fiscal and revenue laws of the country;
4 to investigate any conduct of any person, which in the opinion of the Director, may be connected with or conducive to corruption;
5 to assist any law enforcement agency of the Government in the investigation of offences involving dishonesty or cheating of the public revenue;
6 to examine the practices and procedures of public bodies in order to facilitate the discovery of corrupt practices and to secure the revision of methods of work or procedures which, in the opinion of the Director, may be conducive to corrupt practices;
7 to instruct, advise and assist any person, on the latter's request, on ways in which corrupt practices may be eliminated by such person;
8 to advise heads of public bodies of changes in practices or procedures compatible with the effective discharge of the duties of such public bodies which the Director thinks necessary to reduce the likelihood of the occurrence of corrupt practices;
9 to educate the public against the evils of corruption; and
10 to enlist and foster public support in combating corruption.

The powers of the Director are quite extensive. He may request for information, require any person to give an account of his belongings, ask for information on bank accounts, arrest any person without warrant, search premises, seize property or documents, apply *ex parte* for the surrender of travel documents. The Directorate has also adopted the three-pronged strategy of investigation, prevention and education pioneered by the Hong Kong ICAC from which it drew inspiration. It is composed of five departments: (1) a Prosecutions and Training department responsible for prosecutions, liaisons with the Attorney General's Chambers and staff training; (2) an Investigations department consisting of the four investigation groups; (3) the Intelligence department responsible for the information gathering functions of the intelligence group, the surveillance group, the technical support unit and a report center which receives reports from the public; (4) the Corruption Prevention and Public Education department is responsible for: examining the operational systems of Government Departments and private companies with the objectives of reducing or eliminating corrupt practices, education the public against the evils of corruption and enlisting and fostering public support in combating corruption; and (5) lastly, an administrative department for general administration and support.[142]

JURISPRUDENCE

According to a report prepared by the US General Accounting Office, the fight against corruption is a long-term project but in some cases, visible, early 'wins' (such as successful prosecution of a high-level official) may be critical for building credibility and generating sustained pressure for reform.[143] The cases examined below though few in number have had far reaching consequences in the global fight against high-level corruption for a number of reasons. In the first place, they are not the usual run of the mill cases targeting low level rent seeking public officials but involved some of the most prominent politicians and business figures in the countries covered. In the case of the Philippines and Zambia, respectively, a sitting and a former head of state were indicted and prosecuted for the crime of corruption and fraud. The prosecution of Joseph Estrada and Frederick Chiluba mark a major turning point for these heretofore 'constitutional untouchables' who have historically dodged legal attempts to hold them to account. The cases are important also for the substantial sanctions that were meted out to the defendants; substantial enough to serve notice on public officials and private businessmen that in the long run corruption does not pay.

Acres International Limited

In July 2004, the World Bank sanctioned Acres International Limited ('Acres'), a Canadian corporation, and declared it ineligible to receive any World Bank contracts for the next three years.[144] This decision may also lead to periods of debarment for other construction companies involved in the corruption trials in Lesotho, sparked by Acres' corrupt activities related to the Bank-financed hydro-electric contracts on the Lesotho Highlands Water Project.[145] The debarment followed a finding by the Bank's sanctions committee that Acres had engaged in corrupt activities for the purpose of influencing the decisions of the then chief

---

[142] The DCEC has an establishment of over 100 officers. By the end of 1999 it had received 5250 reports, since inception, from which it has launched 1565 investigations, 1018 of which have been completed. Thus far 197 persons have been prosecuted with a conviction rate of 84%.

[143] See United States General Accounting Office, *Foreign Assistance: US Anticorruption Programs in Sub-Saharan Africa Will Require Time and Commitment*. GAO Report No. GAO-04-506, Washington, DC: 17 May 2004.

[144] See 'World Bank gives Acres three-year debarment as company sells out to Canadian partner,' 27 July 2004. Available at http://www.ciob.org.uk (last visited 8 February 2005).

[145] *Id.*

executive of the water authority, activities which violated the Bank's procurement standards.

The Acres case is notable for a number of reasons. First, it was one of the largest debarment proceedings in World Bank history.[146] Second, as a result of the

[146] Debarment is a step through which the World Bank delists – that is, bars from World Bank work contractors that it concludes have not conformed to World Bank contracting standards. Since the names of parties it has debarred are usually made public, the consequences of a debarment can be devastating, both in terms of lost business and damage to reputation. To date, 72 companies or persons have been debarred, according to the World Bank's website.

'In 1996, the World Bank initiated a program against corruption and fraud in development projects financed through World Bank funds. Since 1997, the World Bank has debarred 72 firms and individuals from participating in future Bank-financed projects; 66 of these firms and individuals have been debarred permanently, while the remaining six have been debarred for no less than three years. Of the 72 debarments, 11 are for fraud, 19 for corruption, and 42 for both fraud and corruption. According to the World Bank's Guidelines: Selection and Employment of Consultants by World Bank Borrowers, contractors who work on a World Bank funded project are expected to "observe the highest standard of ethics" during the execution of their contracts. Where the Bank finds that a contractor has engaged in "corrupt or fraudulent practices in competing for, or in executing, a Bank-financed contract," it will "declare a Consultant ineligible, either indefinitely or for a stated period of time, to be awarded a Bank-financed contract." The World Bank also may demand disgorgement of any fees it paid the contractor from World Bank funds. The World Bank normally initiates a debarment proceeding against a firm after receiving a tip from an outside source, such as a disappointed bidder or a disgruntled employee. All tips are reviewed by the Bank's Legal Adviser for Procurement and Consultant Services who, upon "sufficient" evidence, assigns the complaint to further investigation. The Legal Adviser's decision to proceed with an investigation may be subject to a Bank-imposed three-year statute of limitations, and requisite approval by the Bank's General Counsel. If the complaint is assigned for further investigation, the Department of Institutional Integrity's Investigations Unit (formerly known as the Corruption and Fraud Investigations Unit) conducts it. This Department is an independent body within the Bank that reports directly to the Bank's President. The investigation can take weeks or months, and is supposedly designed to protect the privacy of the accuser and the accused.

After concluding the investigation, the results are transmitted to the World Bank's Sanctions Committee, which decides whether to issue a formal notice of debarment ('notice') to the targeted firm. The Sanctions Committee has five members, all of whom are senior officials in the Bank. The notice summarizes the allegations and provides the accused contractor with an opportunity to respond in writing within a set period of time, usually 30 days. It also allows the accused contractor to deliver an oral presentation. Following that, if the Sanctions Committee determines that the evidence is "reasonably sufficient" to show that the firm has engaged in corrupt or fraudulent practices, the Committee recommends formal debarment to the President for final approval. The President of the Bank then has two weeks to make his decision.' *See* John Oberdorfer, Harold Kim and Vince Martinez, Contractors Beware: The Pitfalls of a World Bank Debarment Proceeding. Available at http://www.ciob.org.uk (last visited 8 February 2005).

parallel litigation in Lesotho,[147] it made news as one of the first instances of a criminal prosecution of a major multinational is among the few corruption cases involving prominent citizens in a developing country. As the Court of Appeal of Lesotho itself recognized the prosecution and the conviction of the defendants were 'milestones on the road ... to greater morality in the initiation and management of development activity.' The *Acres* is also of interest because of the support Lesotho's prosecutors received from the World Bank. Having identified corruption as perhaps the greatest single obstacle to economic and social development, the Bank has in the last decade or so taken it as its duty to ensure that the loans and credits it extends are used for their intended purposes. Not surprisingly, therefore, when the indictments against Acres were published by the Government of Lesotho in mid-1999, the World Bank's Department of Institutional Integrity initiated an investigation into the allegations, seeking to discover whether it was true that the consultants had indeed engaged in corrupt practices. At that time the Bank concluded that the evidence was not sufficient to show that this was so and as a result refrained from sanctioning Acres.[148] Nevertheless, it provided extensive evidentiary support to the Lesotho prosecutors and made Bank staff available for interview. Later the Bank assisted the Lesotho Government by bringing the prosecutors together with the various project funding agencies and anti-fraud officials from the European Union.[149] This is precisely the kind of international cooperation and mutual legal assistance that most multilateral anti-corruption instruments advocate.

The events which gave rise to the World Bank disbarment of Acres arise out of illicit payments Acres made to the Swiss bank accounts of its Lesotho agent, Z.M. Bam, and his wife, Margaret Bam, between 1991 and 1999. More than half of the $500,000 in payments was forwarded to the Swiss bank accounts of Mustapha E. Sole, the CEO of the Lesotho Highlands Water Project. Acres made these payments to secure a leg up in its bid for and negotiation of contracts related to a nearly $4 billion project, consisting of a series of dams to which the World Bank had committed $110 million in funding for Phase 1-A. Following an independent investigation commissioned by the World Bank that found sufficient evidence of corruption by Acres, the World Bank sanctions committee found the evidence insufficient and did not debar Acres from bank projects. However, in March 2004, some six months after the Lesotho appellate court upheld a $2 million criminal penalty imposed on Acres for bribery in the Lesotho project, the World Bank reopened its investigation of Acres.[150] In July 2004 Acres was sanctioned by the World Bank.[151]

---

[147] See Acres International Limited and the Crown, C of A (CRI) of 2002, CRI/T/144/02.

[148] The investigation was re-opened following the bribery conviction of 2002, upheld by the Court of Appeal on one of the two counts. See 'World Bank gives Acres three-year debarment as company sells out to Canadian partner,' 27 July 2004. Available at http://www.ciob.org.uk (last visited on 8 February 2005).

[149] *Id.*

[150] Acres was fined a total of $2.2 million on conviction in September 2002 but this was

Elf-Aquitaine S.A.

The core of the Elf-Aquitaine ('Elf')[152] case were a series of allegations that between 1989 and 1993 senior officials of Elf, an oil concern formerly owned by the French government and then the largest company in France, had embezzled some $350 million in funds from the company. In the course of investigating the embezzlement allegations, French investigators reportedly considered whether some of these funds were kept by the defendants or were used to secure Elf business in Germany, Spain, Russia, and countries in southern Africa and South America. Eventually, the *juge d'instruction*[153] (the prosecuting magistrate), Mme. Eva Joly,[154] brought charges against some thirty-seven defendants in one of the largest criminal trials in French history.

In the course of the proceedings, a former German diplomat and a French spy were accused of pocketing more than $40 million in 'commissions' in 1992 for arranging the purchase and rebuilding by Elf of the Leuna oil refinery in former East Germany. According to news reports, the payments may have been effected through a Liechtenstein bank account titled in the name of a third party. Some reports suggested that the German businessman may have acted as an intermediary and forwarded some of these funds to former Chancellor Helmut Kohl's political party, the Christian Democratic Union, to secure approval of the sale of the refinery complex and some $1 billion in subsidies to rebuild the refinery.

Other allegations raised in the press relate to kickbacks[155] allegedly paid to

---

reduced on appeal to about two-thirds of that sum. The chief prosecutor in the case, Guido Penzhorn, told the Canadian press recently that the High Court in Lesotho considers Acres delinquent on its fine and is taking action to recover the outstanding balance through the Canadian courts. *Id.*

[151] It has been observed that the fate of Acres however is a warning to the international construction industry that when the judiciary in client countries is prepared to act impartially and according to law, companies cannot expect to get clean away with time-honored practices which purchase favors in the award of contracts and the settlement of claims. *Id.*

[152] Elf was founded in 1965 by General Charles de Gaulle as a state-owned company and was then called *Société Nationale des Pétroles d'Aquitaine.* The company was privatized in 1999 and taken over by another French giant, TotalFina.

[153] The post of *juge d'instruction* was formally created in France in 1808 and today there are approximately 660 *juges d'instruction.* A *juge* has the power to gather evidence, witnesses, and direct the work of the *police judiciare* (judicial police) assigned to him.

[154] In 1995, Mme. Joly was appointed to investigate the charges against Elf. Despite death threats, intense pressure and constant manipulation, she uncovered several cases of fraud in the company. In May 2001, she concluded the largest financial investigation ever conducted in Europe.

[155] In an interview he gave to *Le Monde* Tarallo explained the system of bonuses handed out to African heads of state: 'In the petroleum field we talk of bonuses. There are official bonuses, which are anticipated in the contracts....; the petroleum company which wants an exploration permit agrees, for example, to finance the construction of a hospital, a school or a road, or to pay a sum of money, which may be a considerable amount if the

African leaders and their families, notably Presidents Sassou-Nguesso of the Republic of Congo, Paul Biya of Cameroon, Dos Santos of Angola and Omar Bongo of Gabon. It is believed that these payments were motivated by a desire to block competitors in oil deals and secure continued loyalty to Elf. This alleged scheme involved the use of shell corporation accounts managed through a New York bank. Additional bribes were paid in Angola, Cameroon, and Congo. Some of the funds cited may have been generated from oil revenues and paid into bank accounts in Liechtenstein, according to a Transparency International report of statements made by André Tarallo, former head of the Elf hydrocarbons division and called by some 'Mr. Africa' for his friendships with a number of African leaders.

In late 2003 criminal sentences and fines were imposed on many of the defendants, including the German businessman (15 months in jail and a fine of $1.5 million) and *'Monsieur Afrique'* André Tarallo (four years in jail and $2 million fine). Jail sentences totaled sixty years while fines totaled some 35 million Euro. The role of the French press in the Elf case was instrumental in prompting the French 1 National Assembly to act. As a consequence in 2000 a law implementing France's international obligation to ban bribery in connection with commercial contracts was passed. Other corporate casualties from the Elf scandal include Technip, one of the companies investigated as part of the Elf probe. Technip was in the TSKJ consortium for a Nigerian energy project that included Halliburton subsidiary Kellogg, Brown & Root. Investigation of Technip revealed a TSKJ slush fund, triggering an ongoing inquiry into the consortium partners. The investigation of Halliburton was the first under the 2000 French law and it was handled by the same magistrate, Reynaud van Ruymbeke, who handled the Elf case.

Baker Hughes Incorporated

The Baker Hughes Incorporated ('Baker Hughes') litigation was the first prosecution under the Foreign Corrupt Practices Act ('FCPA') that was jointly conducted by the Securities and Exchange Commission ('SEC') and the US Department of Justice ('DOJ'). The case raised two important issues. First, whether payments made to reduce taxes constitute payments made to 'obtain or retain business' or secure an improper advantage? Second, what measures must parent companies take to prevent seeming strict liability under the FCPA accounting provisions?

In February 1999, the Indonesian Tax Ministry levied a $3.2 million tax assessment on an Indonesian subsidiary controlled by Baker Hughes, a publicly traded US oilfield services concern. After a tax official requested Baker Hughes to make a $75,000 'goodwill' payment to him in exchange for his reducing the assessment to $270,000, the CFO and controller of Baker Hughes authorized a

---

interest in an area is justified.... This practice has always been used by Elf as well as numerous other companies.' See *Le Monde*, 25 October 1999.

$140,000 payment to the subsidiary's accounting firm, KPMG-SSH, 'knowing or aware' that some $75,000 of that payment would be passed on to the tax official. The payment was recorded on the consolidated books of the Baker Hughes subsidiary for 'professional services rendered' by KPMG-SSH.

Allegedly, in violation of the FCPA accounting provisions, the management of Baker Hughes also authorized payments to intermediaries in India in 1998 and Brazil in 1995 without making adequate inquiry as to whether these agents might give all or part of the payments to foreign government officials in violation of the FCPA. When the general counsel for Baker Hughes and the FCPA advisor discovered the Indonesian payment, they took investigative and remedial action.

Baker Hughes, KPMG-SSH, and KPMG-SSH partner Sonny Harsono all agreed to consent decrees that, interestingly, prohibited violations of the FCPA but imposed no fine. The Securities and Exchange Commission justified the lack of fines on the aggressive internal investigation and remedial action by Baker Hughes. But both the CFO of Baker Hughes and the controller litigated the SEC charges that they violated the FCPA anti-bribery provision and assisted in violation of the FCPA accounting provisions. The two were able to persuade the US District Court for the Southern District of Texas to dismiss the charges, but the government appealed. The SEC then sought a reversal and remand of that dismissal, based on the February 2004 decision in US v. Kay, which held that payments to reduce customs duties could satisfy the 'obtain or retain business' prong of the FCPA.

The Estrada Impeachment

Under pressure from big business to rapidly end the country's political impasse,[156] the Philippines House of Representatives in November 2000 impeached President Joseph Estrada on four counts of corruption, bribery, betrayal of public trust and culpable violation of the constitution.[157] The impeachment – the first in the

---

[156] See Peter Symond, 'Philippines Congress rushes through impeachment of President Estrada.' [hereinafter 'Symond']. Available at http://www.legalaffairs.org/issues/May-June-2002/story_ignatius (last visited on 8 February 2005).

[157] As an insurance against abuse of power and committing of crimes by the high officials of the country, the 1987 Constitution provides in its Article XI, Section 2 for the removal of the President by impeachment. The bill of particulars submitted to the Senate by the House of Representatives read as follows:

This complaint for impeachment is based on the following grounds:

I. THAT RESPONDENT COMMITTED BRIBERY;
II. THAT RESPONDENT COMMITTED GRAFT AND CORRUPT PRACTICES;
III. THAT RESPONDENT BETRAYED THE PUBLIC TRUST;
IV. THAT RESPONDENT CULPABLY VIOLATED THE CONSTITUTION.

Pursuant to the Constitution which provides:

Section 2. The President, the Vice President, the members of the Supreme Court, the

members of the constitutional commission, and the Ombudsman may be removed from office, on impeachment for and conviction of, culpable violation of the Constitution, treason, bribery, graft, and corruption, other higher crimes or betrayal of public trust. (Article XI)

DISCUSSION

I. That respondent committed bribery

Complaints accuse respondent of committing bribery as follows: That from November 1998 to August 2000, respondent has received P10 million a month as bribery from jueteng lords as protection money channeled through Luis C. Singson, provincial governor of Ilocos Sur as may be seen from his affidavit dated September 14, 2000 (Annex 'A' hereof).

Pursuant to the Constitution which provides:

II. That respondent committed graft and corrupt practices

President Joseph E. Estrada violated the Constitution and stands guilty of graft and corruption when he directly requested or received for his personal benefit P130 million out of the P200 million released by Secretary Benjamin Diokno of the Department of Budget and Management allocated under R.A. 7171 in violation of Section 3(c) of R.A. 3019, as may be seen from the affidavit of Luis C. Singson, provincial governor of Ilocos Sur, dated September 25, 2000 (Annex 'B' hereof).

President Joseph E. Estrada violated the Constitution and stands guilty of graft and corruption when he participated directly in the real estate business thru family-controlled corporation which constructed 36 townhouses in Vermont Park, Executive Village, Antipolo City, as shown in the PCIJ in the article on President Joseph E. Estrada's family and financial interest. He also violated the Anti-Graft Law he is sworn to uphold. He filed his Statement of Assets and Liabilities for the year 1999, stating therein that he and his wife and children have business interests in only three (3) corporations. The President by that sworn statement also committed perjury and the offense of unexplained wealth because records show that he and his wife and mistresses and their children have other interests in other companies outside of the firms listed in his Statement of Assets and Liabilities (Annex 'C' hereof).

III. That respondent betrayed the public trust

President Joseph E. Estrada betrayed public trust and violated his own oath of office when he unduly intervened in the Securities and Exchange Commission on behalf of a presidential crony.

Barely two months after assuming office in 1998, the President referred to the Philippine Gaming and Amusement Board (Pagcor) the application for an online bingo of Best World Gaming and Entertainment Corp. Despite absence of any bidding or notice to the public, Pagcor acted expeditiously and granted said corporation an exclusive franchise to operate online bingo nationwide on December 3, 1998 (Annex 'D' hereof).

Therefore, in view of alleged stock manipulation on BW shares, the Securities and

Exchange Commission started an investigation.

On or about November 1999, President Estrada called Chairman Perfecto Yasay Jr. of the Securities and Exchange Commission to intercede for BW, claiming that its principal and majority stockholder Dante Tan was not a manipulator but a victim of transactions which resulted in the rise and fall of BW shares, as shown by the affidavit of former Securities and Exchange Commissioner Perfecto Yasay Jr., which is hereto attached as Annex 'E'.

The President called Chairman Yasay not once but five times. The act of the President violated his solemn oath of office to execute the law. He obstructed justice because he intervened with the duties of a public servant who was investigating transactions as a quasi judicial officer pursuant to the mandate of the law.

President Estrada betrayed public trust when he wantonly violated his official pronouncement during his inaugural speech, when he solemnly declared, 'sa aking administrasyon, walang kamag-anak, walang kumpadre, walang kaibigan.'

The majority of the people cheered. They believed in him. They trusted him after having voted him into office the highest plurality in the election of May 1998.

He betrayed the people's trust. When his son Jinggoy Estrada got into trouble with some doctors and personnel at the Cardinal Santos Memorial Hospital in July 30, 1999, the President defended him instead of letting the law take its course (Annex 'F' hereof). As a result, no one pursued the complaint. When another son, Jude Estrada, flew government plane to Cagayan de Oro at government expense, he also got into trouble, leaving the hotel where he stayed without paying the bills worth more than P60,000. Again, the President defended him instead of letting the law take its course.

He appointed Cecilia de Castro, a cousin, as presidential assistant, although he disclaimed knowing her in the wake of the textbooks scam in 1998 (Annex 'G' hereof). He appointed a brother-in-law, Captain Rufino F. Pimentel, as director of Pagcor (Annex 'H' hereof). He appointed another brother-in-law, Raul de Guzman, as member of the board of Regents of the University of the Philippines (Annex 'I' hereof), and a nephew-in-law, the son of Mr. de Guzman, as presidential consultant on environment and water (Annex 'J' hereof).

He appointed more than a hundred kumpadres and kaibigans as presidential assistants/consultants, extended franchises and favors such as the ones specified in Annex 'K' hereof.

President Estrada has often proclaimed that his main program is to uplift the poor. But records show that during his tenure as President, he focused mainly on the participation in business for himself, his family and friends. The Philippine Center for Investigative Journalism has revealed that there exist 66 corporate records wherein Estrada, his wife, mistresses and children are listed as incorporators or board members. Thirty-one of these companies were set up during Estrada's vice-presidential tenure and one (1) since he assumed the presidency. Altogether they had an authorized capital of P893.4 million when they were registered.

The President and his family had shares of P121.5 million with a paid-up capital of P58 million when the companies were formed. Based on available 1998 and 1999 financial statements – 14 of the 66 companies alone have assets of over P600 million. He abetted gambling, tolerated excessive imports and smuggling to favor friends and relatives, to the prejudice of farmers, fishermen, and businessmen, as shown in the latest report of the

Philippine Center for Investigative Journalism (Annexes 'L,' 'L-1' and 'L-2' hereof).

President Estrada betrayed the public trust and his oath of office when he disobeyed the strict mandate of the Constitution that he sternly avoid conflict of interest in the conduct of his office.

On October 15, 1998, the First Lady, Mrs. Loi Ejercito, registered with the Securities and Exchange Commission her private foundation – the Partnership for the Poor Foundation, Inc. (Annex 'M' hereof). Its primary purpose was to provide relief and livelihood to the poor. SEC records list its address at No. 1 Polk Street, Greenhills, San Juan, Metro Manila, which is also the legal residence of President Estrada.

The First lady signed the articles of incorporation and by-laws as one of its five incorporating directors, another one being Ramon Cardenas, deputy executive secretary in Malacañang.

A few months after its incorporation, the Foundation received a P100 million donation from the Philippine Charity Sweepstakes Office to fund its projects (Annex 'N' hereof). Said donation exceeded the PCSO's combined donation of P65 million to regular PCSO beneficiaries like orphanages and hospitals throughout the country.

The Constitution under Section 13, Article VII, expressly prohibits conflict of interest in the conduct of his office. When the President approves a P100 million donation of government funds to private foundation organized by his wife, deliverable to his address at No. 1 Polk Street, Greenhills, San Juan, Metro Manila, where the approving authority himself lives – that transaction violates the no-conflict rule mandated by the nation's fundamental law.

IV. That respondent culpably violated the Constitution

President Estrada violated the law and his own oath of office when he ordered the Commissioner of Customs to turn over 52 luxury vehicles to Malacañang for distribution to Cabinet members and other senior officials to give them more prestige and financial help – contrary to his oath to execute the law faithfully because said acts clearly contravened Section 3, Paragraph A of R.A. 3015, Anti-Graft Law, Section 2535, 2536, 2601, 2604 and 2610 of the Customs and Tariff Code.

President Estrada willfully violated the Constitution when he appointed certain members of his Cabinet, their deputies or assistants to another office or employment in direct contravention of Section 13, Article VII of the Constitution.

Said provision is a strict prohibition that has been interpreted no less by the Supreme Court in Civil Liberties vs. Executive Secretary, 94 SCRA 320, which declared that the prohibition stands, save only when the concerned official holds the other portion in ex-officio capacity or is otherwise allowed by the Constitution to do so. The reason for the prohibition, according to the Supreme Court, is to make the concerned officials give full attention to their jobs to maximize public benefit.

Despite said constitutional prohibition positively interpreted by the Supreme Court, President Estrada appointed the following to other offices or employment.

1. Senior Deputy Executive Secretary Ramon Cardenas as director of Manila economic and Cultural Office (MECO), chairman of the Philippine Coordinating Committee in the Asian Development Bank, chairman of Philippine Retirement Authority, and member of the

country's history – 'was rushed through the House without debate, or a vote, in eight minutes flat.'[158] The House Speaker Manual Villar, who until the impeachment was a loyal supporter of Estrada, asserted that no vote was necessary as the impeachment petition already had the necessary signatures of more than one third of the House. The articles of impeachment were then forwarded to the Senate where Estrada's trial was to take place.[159]

A Senate impeachment trial then followed in January 2001. But after six weeks it was aborted when senators voted against opening a sealed envelope that prosecutors claimed would tie Estrada to a multimillion-dollar bank account. The vote sparked huge protests demanding his resignation, and he left the palace through the back door on 20 January 2001. In April, the Philippines Supreme Court ruled that Estrada had effectively resigned as President on 20 January and proceeded to strip him of presidential immunity. This paved the way for the *Sandiganbayan*, the anti-graft court, to indict Estrada on accusations that he pocketed $82 million in kickbacks and payoffs during 31 months in office. On 16 April 2001, Estrada turned himself in and posted bond after the anti-graft court had issued a warrant for his arrest; a fortnight later, the former President was arrested on warrant for non-bailable offense issued by the *Sandiganbayan*.

Four months after the Office of the Ombudsman filed criminal charges against Estrada and his associates, prosecutors sought a court order to freeze Estrada's

---

Movie and Television Review and Classification Board.

2. Chief Legal Presidential Counsel Magdangal Elma, who holds Cabinet rank – chairman of the Presidential Commission on Good Government.

3. Robert Aventajado, Secretary for Flagship Projects, garbage czar, head of solid waste management, and chief negotiator for hostages of the Abu Sayyaf.

4. Deputy Executive Secretary for Finance and Administration Ric Tan Legada – director of PNOC Shipping and Transport Corp. and director of United Coconut Chemicals, Inc.

5. Asst. Executive Secretary for Legal Affairs Gaudencio A. Mendoza, Jr. – director of Food Terminal, Inc. and director of Subic Bay Metropolitan Authority.

6. Presidential Adviser on Development Administration Raul de Guzman – director of San Miguel Corporation, regent of the University of the Philippines, and director of Philippine Long Distance Telephone Company.

Conclusion

Public office is a public trust. When a teacher or government clerk commits a dishonest act, he or she is removed from the service. When the President no less commits bribery, commits graft and corruption and other high crimes, betrays the public trust, and culpably violates the Constitution and his own oath of office, he should also be removed.' The impeachment complaint is available at http://www.philsol.nl/A00b/Erap-Complaint.htm (last visited on 8 February 2005).

[158] Symond, *supra* note 156.

[159] Under Senate rules, a vote of two-thirds or 15 out of the 22 senators are needed to remove the president from office.

bank deposits. The *Sandiganbayan* anti-graft court granted the prosecution's motion and ordered a freeze on bank deposits believed to have been illegally amassed by the ousted president. The court also ordered a freeze on the property of two of Estrada's co-accused, Charlie 'Atong' Ang and Yolanda Ricaforte, in a four-billion-peso plunder case. In addition, it placed under its custody assets registered under the name of 'Jose Velarde,' the alias Estrada used in signing bank documents purportedly to facilitate a loan of 500 million pesos to his businessman-friend William Gatchalian in February 2000.[160] The *Sandiganbayan* freeze order was intended to prevent these assets from being lost, transferred or reduced in value should the accused be found guilty and ordered to pay the State for damages. In a 10-page resolution, dated 23 August 2001 the special division granted the prosecution's motion for the issuance of a writ of preliminary attachment to Estrada et al.'s 'properties whether real and personal ... sufficient to secure the amount of the alleged ill-gotten wealth' cited in the case. The *Sandiganbayan* ruling covered four specific items prosecutors initially wanted frozen pending their determination of Estrada's other alleged ill-gotten assets.[161]

---

[160] Records contained in an envelope that the Senate opened on 14 February 2001, a month after the impeachment trial of Estrada was aborted, showed that the Velarde account with Equitable PCI Bank contained a total of 3.2 billion pesos in deposits. See 'Estrada Bank Deposits Frozen,' *Philippine Star*, 25 September 2002. Available at http://www.philsol.nl/news/02/Erap04-aug02.htm (last visited on 8 February 2005).

[161] Of the four, two were said to belong not to Estrada himself but to his co-accused. These were:

- A house and lot at 25 Freedom Avenue, Area I, Veterans Village, Barangay Pasong Tamo, Quezon City, owned by Ricaforte, Estrada's alleged 'auditor' for 540 million pesos in protection money from the ousted president allegedly collected from the operators of the 'jueteng' an illegal numbers game.
- A house and lot at 18 Manansala Street, Corinthian Gardens, Quezon City, belonging to Ang, an Estrada associate who allegedly helped put up the gambling payola network. Ang also allegedly diverted 130 million pesos in tobacco tax revenues into Estrada's pockets.
- Deposits made by Ricaforte in six branches of Equitable PCI Bank totaling 11.13 million pesos, believed to be part of Estrada's jueteng payola collections (Ang and Ricaforte are in the United States and have been fighting extradition efforts by the Philippines).
- Bank deposits under the name of the Erap Muslim Youth Foundation amounting to 201.4 million pesos as of September 2000. The foundation was allegedly a dummy corporation put up by Estrada with the help of his then legal adviser Edward Serapio, another co-accused, to launder jueteng money.

The court did not grant the prosecution's bid to include another 10 million pesos deposited in two accounts of the Erap Muslim Youth Foundation at the United Coconut Planters Bank (UCPB) branch on Makati Avenue in Makati City. 'There is so far no evidence with respect to the source of the amount (in UCPB),' the ruling said. Asked about the 'Boracay mansion' and other houses Estrada built for his mistresses, Solicitor General Simeon Marcelo spoke of another complaint for forfeiture initiated by civil society groups,

The Corruption Trial of Frederick Chiluba

On 16 July 2002, the Zambian Parliament voted unanimously to lift former President Frederick Chiluba's immunity from criminal prosecution. This paved the way for the government to proceed with the trial of the man who was President of Zambia for ten years (1991–2001) on allegations of corruption and abuse of office. Mr. Chiluba was charged, along with his former intelligence chief, Xavier Chungu, several former ministers and senior officials[162] and the former Zambian ambassador to the United States, Atan Shansonga, with 168 counts of theft totaling more than $40 million. In a separate trial, Mr. Chiluba and Mr. Chungu faced another 65 charges of state theft totaling $4 million. It is alleged that during his tenure in office, Mr. Chiluba presided over a 'permissive culture of corruption' which contributed to making Zambia one of the poorest countries in the world.[163] Two of the accused, Chungu and Shansonga, fled Zambia before the trial began. In an initial setback, the charges were dropped against Chiluba and four co-accused when the prosecution asked for leave of the court to review the indictment in a bid to re-organize the cases with a view to expediting the trial. Thereafter, Chiluba was re-arrested and charged with only eight counts of embezzling one million dollars. In the meanwhile, the Zambian government sought and was granted permission to freeze properties owned by the former president and his co-accused in Britain and other countries pending the outcome of the trial.

REPRISE

What general conclusions can be drawn from this examination of the history, text and general purpose of constitutional provisions, national laws and statutes setting up inquiry commissions, special tribunals and various anti-graft bodies to deal with corrupt enrichment by constitutional responsible rulers and the various criminal prosecutions of high-ranking individuals accused of engaging in acts of corruption? What expressions of *de lege ferenda* can be discerned from the activities of these

---

which, according to him, already covered the controversial houses. Acting Ombudsman Margarito Gervacio said prosecutors had 'not yet identified the owners (of the Boracay mansion), how it was acquired, and the source of the money used to purchase it.' See 'Estrada Bank Deposits Frozen,' *Philippine Star*, 25 September 2002. Available at http://www.philsol.nl/news/02/Erap04-aug02.htm (last visited on 8 February 2005).

[162] They included the Foreign Affairs minister, Katele Kalumba, former auditor-general, Fred Siame, former permanent secretary in the ministry of finance, Stella Chibanda, and the former chief economist in the finance ministry, Bede Mpande. See 'Dr. Frederick Chiluba's lawyers cry foul,' Wednesday, 9 February 2005. Available at www.zamnet.zm/newsys/news/viewnews.cgi?category (last visited on 21 February 2005).

[163] Zambia's external debt stood at $5.4 billion in December 2002. Debt servicing accounted for an astonishing 20% of domestic revenue and over 80 per cent of the population live on less than a dollar a day with a life expectancy of just under 40 years.

institutions? A fair reading of the findings and recommendations of inquiry commissions and tribunals points directly to a state practice which views public office, elective or appointive, as a public trust which imposes a fiduciary obligation on public holders. This widespread state practice examined against the historical background of the reasons that led to the establishment of commissions of inquiry in the first place supplies the necessary justification for the existence of an implied, if not express, fiduciary duty to which public holders are held.

The basic elements of this leadership fiduciary duty are: political accountability, criminal liability and forfeiture and restitution. With respect to the first element, widespread state practice has consistently mandated that any individual elected or appointed into public office and who thereafter enriches himself by misappropriating public funds and/or through abuse of his office must be held publicly answerable for his conduct. The principle advanced here is that one who has abused the public trust should not only be made to account for his stewardship but, more importantly, should never be allowed to hold public office again or until a considerable amount of time has lapsed. Disqualification from holding public office not only denies the disgraced public servant another opportunity for such misconduct but it also serves as a stern warning to others who might be tempted to follow in his footsteps.

A constitutionally responsible leader who corruptly enriches himself at the expense of the public interest must also forfeit to the victims what he has improperly appropriated for himself. This principle of restitution ensures that public officials who have demonstrated an extraordinary indifference to, or difficulty in understanding, the conventional separations between state and personal financial interests are not rewarded. This sentiment was captured by Nigeria's Federal Military Government in this pithy statement: 'It is imperative that no one should be left in doubt, whether now or in future, that whoever steals public funds would be compelled not only to return the loot but also be made to revert to his original economic status. In other words, no one would be allowed to retain for his use, improperly acquired wealth at the public expense.'[164]

Fraudulent enrichment is not simply a civil offense the effects of which can be extirpated through the simple act of disgorgement. State practice, as evidenced in the types of sanctions meted out by courts, inquiry commissions and tribunals, uniformly treat corrupt enrichment and breach of public trust by top State officials as crimes for which criminal liability attaches to the authors. It is worth noting that the frequent and widespread use of criminal sanctions, in addition to other measures such as forfeiture, confiscation and disqualification from public office holding, to punish acts of fraudulent enrichment is in line with the position adopted by the International Law Commission (ILC or Commission) in its work on the Draft Code of Crimes Against the Peace and Security of Mankind.

Of the many issues that the ILC agonized over perhaps none was more important than the issue of penalties for the serious crimes identified in the Draft

---

[164] See Federal Military Government Decisions, *supra* note 30, at 3.

Code.[165] ILC members searched for penalties that would not only fit the gravity of the dangers posed but also that would prevent a recurrence of the prohibited conduct. Discussions on the criteria for selecting a penalty for a particular Draft Code crime centered on the expressed desire for something that would be exemplary in nature and would serve as a deterrent for the commission of the very serious crimes listed in the Draft Code.[166] But the Commission also wanted to set out a regime that could be contained within the bounds of customary international law principles.[167] A consensus appeared to have emerged on the death penalty as an inappropriate penalty for the violation of any of the Draft Code crimes given the worldwide trend which makes it obsolete on moral, constitutional and conventional law grounds.[168] Several international instruments provide for the abolition of the death penalty or for a prohibition on its reintroduction. Moreover, the Constitutions of many countries have also abolished the death penalty. Life imprisonment with no chance for commutation was accepted as a substitute for the death penalty in addition to temporary imprisonment for terms ranging from 10 to 40 years.[169]

Discussion in the Commission also focused on the appropriate sanctions in situations where the commission of any of the Draft Code crimes involved the illegal acquisition of property, particularly in drug trafficking crimes. It was decided that in such instances confiscation for the purposes of restitution was the appropriate penalty.[170] The choice of this form of sanction was intended to make clear that neither the offender nor his family members should be allowed to benefit from any misappropriated property.[171] To drive home this point, confiscated property was to be forfeited to the victims of the crime in question or to the injured State. Finally, in addition to imprisonment and confiscation, Commission members were also in agreement that 'accessory penalties of total legal incapacity and deprivation of civil rights' would be quite appropriate to punish violations of the Draft Code crimes.[172]

It could be objected that the repeated occurrence of outrageous cases of fraudulent enrichment at the highest levels of Government vitiate any claims that state practice evidences expressions of *de lege ferenda* for viewing of this conduct as a crime under international law. After all, virtually every State discussed above has been the victim of indigenous spoliation despite the constitutional provisions and national laws prohibiting such practices. To the objection that the concept of 'international crimes' in the ILC Draft Articles on State Responsibility was

---

[165] The discussion in this section draws on the Commission's Report on the work of its 43rd session. See *Report of the International Law Commission on the Work of its Forty-third Session 29 April-19 July 1991, Official Records: Forty-sixth Session*, Supplement No. 10 (A/46/10).

[166] *Id.*, para. 86, at 208.

[167] *Id.*, para. 84, at 207.

[168] *Id.*

[169] *Id.*, para. 89, at 209.

[170] *Id.*, para. 96, at 210.

[171] *Id.*, para. 97, at 211.

[172] *Id.*, para. 98, at 211–212.

ineffective, one of its supporters, Professor Abi-Saab has conceded that most States frequently pay lip service to values they do not uphold or respect and one should therefore be circumspect in taking their verbal affirmations at face value.[173] But the focus, Abi-Saab argues, ought to be on what States practice. To be sure, the national laws examined above proscribing acts of fraudulent enrichment by constitutionally responsible rulers have been honored more by breach than by respect. But this is no reason to jump to quick conclusions that these laws have fallen into desuetude. If one focused on the practice of states particularly in the reports of commissions of inquiry and the judgments of special tribunals, a different conclusion will be reached.

Moreover, even if these laws have not worked in the past, they at least provide a context and an institutional framework which can now be reactivated and made to function more effectively, given the current international predisposition to criminalize this behavior. And the fact that violations of national laws proscribing indigenous spoliation continue to occur is no reason for denying the emergence of an international norm in favor of treating these violations as criminal breaches of public trust. As Professor Abi-Saab argued in his defense of the effectiveness of the concept of 'international crimes', that few or even many violations of a norm of international law occur is no reason for jettisoning it. If a system (the reference here was the system of maintenance of peace and security under the UN Charter) reveals loopholes scuttling it is not the answer, Professor Abi-Saab argued, rather the goal should be to 'try to fill these loop-holes and to bring it to a more perfect state … .'[174]

The view of indigenous spoliation as conduct that seriously undermines the fundamental interests of the international community and therefore qualifies as a crime under international law is firmly rooted in state practice at both the domestic and international levels. The measures employed by States to bring back corrupt office holders to the observance of their fiduciary obligations to the public are in accord with international practice. In this respect the legislation on expropriation of the enterprises and assets of war criminals and Nazi criminals enacted after World War II offers an interesting precedent.[175] Against this backdrop, we believe the

---

[173] See George Abi-Saab, 'The Concept of 'International Crimes' and its Place in Contemporary International Law,' in *International Crimes of State: A Critical Analysis of the ILC's Draft Article 19 on State Responsibility*, 141, 145 (Joseph H.H. Weiler, Antonio Cassese and Marina Spinedi eds, 1989).

[174] *Id.*, at 146.

[175] See generally Bernhard Graefrath, 'The Crime of Apartheid: Responsibilities and Reparations,' *1981 Review of Contemporary Law*, 31, 36; see also *Die Wiedergutmachung Nationalsozialistischuen Unrechts Durch die Bundersrepublik Deutschland*, Vols. 1–VI (Walter Schwarz ed., 1974–1987) (describing dozens of laws and hundreds of amendments enacted by the Federal Republic of Germany to compensate some of those who were persecuted and plundered by the Third Reich); Detlev Vagts & Benjamin B. Ferencz, Book Review, *American Journal of International Law*, 84, 1 (1990) (noting that the term 'Wiedergutmachung means 'to make good' [and] [i]t encompasses 'Entschadigung,' which means 'to wipe away injury' and 'Ruckerstattung,' which means 'to restore what has been

case has now been made that (1) fundamental community interests are undermined by acts of fraudulent enrichment by high-ranking State officials; (2) the international community must work to bring this conduct under some kind of international discipline; and (3) States are under some legal obligation to judge and punish authors of this crime, on the basis of their internal law, waiving in the process the ordinary rules of jurisdiction, extradition, and so forth.

---

taken away'); Benjamin B. Ferencz, 'Book Review,' *American Journal of International Law*, 69, 707 (1975); *Convention on the Settlement of Matters Arising Out of the War and the Occupation*, 6 UST 4411, TIAS 3425 (1954), Chapter 3 (covering restitution of identifiable property to victims of Nazi oppression); Chapter 4 (compensation for victims of Nazi persecution); Chapter 5 (providing for an administrative agency to search for, recover and restitute jewelry, silverware and antique furniture as well as cultural property spoliated during the Third Reich).

PART II

RESPONSIBILITY AND ACCOUNTABILITY FOR THE CRIME OF INDIGENOUS SPOLIATION

Chapter 7

The Cult of Sovereignty as an Obstacle to the Principle of Leadership Responsibility for International Economic Crimes

The peoples' right to exercise permanent sovereignty over their wealth and natural resources has risen to the level of international customary law and some have even claimed for it *jus cogens* status.[1] Article 1 paragraph 2 of the International Covenants on Civil and Political Rights[2] and Economic, Social and Cultural Rights[3] provide that:

> All peoples may, for their own ends, freely dispose of their natural wealth and resources without prejudice to any obligations arising out of international economic co-operation, based upon the principle of mutual benefit and international law. *In no case may a people be deprived of its own means of subsistence* (Emphasis supplied).

Along the same lines, the African Charter on Human and Peoples Rights[4] in its Article 21 first paragraph states that '[a]ll peoples shall freely dispose of their

---

1 See Subrata Roy Chowdhury, 'Permanent Sovereignty Over Natural Resources,' in *Permanent Sovereignty Over Natural Resources in International Law*, 1, 8 (Kamal Hossain & Subrata Roy Chowdhury eds, 1984) (noting that the principle of permanent sovereignty enjoys *jus cogens* status because it emanates from the right of self-determination which unquestionably has that status); Ian Brownlie, *Principles of Public International Law*, 3rd ed. 513 (1979) (observing that the principle of permanent sovereignty is one of the 'candidate rules' which may have the special status of *jus cogens*).

2 See *International Covenant on Civil and Political Rights*. Done at New York, 16 December 1966. Entered into force, 23 March 1976. UNGA Res. 2200 (XXI), 21 UN GAOR, Supp. (No. 16) 52, UN Doc. A/6316 (1967), reprinted in *International Law Materials*, 368 (1967).

3 See *International Covenant on Economic, Social and Cultural Rights*. Done at New York, 16 December 1966. Entered into force, 3 January 1976. UNGA Res. 2200 (XXI), 21 UN GAOR, Supp. (No. 16) 49, UN Doc. A/6316 (1967), reprinted in *International Law Materials*, 6, 360 (1967).

4 See *African Charter on Human and Peoples' Rights*. Done at Banjul, 26 June 1981. Entered into force, 21 October 1986. OAU Doc. CAB/LEG/67/3 Rev. 5, reproduced in *International Law Materials*, 21, 59 (1982).

wealth and natural resources. This right shall be exercised in the exclusive interest of the people.' And in its second paragraph, the same Article provides that '[i]n case of spoliation the dispossessed people shall have the right to the lawful recovery of its property as well as an adequate compensation.' These provisions notwithstanding, African as well as other Third World countries continue to experience acts of indigenous spoliation as heads of states as well as other high-ranking State officials openly and fraudulently divert national wealth and resources into their private accounts. And each time the victims of despoliation have sought judicial redress they have run into serious obstacles[5] such as where to locate the assets allegedly spoliated; linking them to inappropriate use of public funds; restraining the assets; and then actually retrieving them.[6] Success in overcoming any one of these has also required getting past the financial privacy laws of 'tax haven' States, and the various devices available to conceal the true identity of the beneficial interest or owner of banked assets. While many of these obstacles are not necessarily insurmountable,[7] perhaps the single most formidable obstacle to recovery of spoliated assets is the Western paradigm of the State and the collateral doctrines of sovereignty, leadership infallibility, and sovereign immunity that are its direct progeny.

THE CULT OF STATE SOVEREIGNTY

Over the last several centuries the European concept of the State has taken on the

---

5 The Marcos's plunder of the Philippine economy is one of the best documented examples of fraudulent enrichment by a head of state and high-ranking officials working for his administration. That after years of protracted litigation the successor Government was able to recover only a fraction of Philippine assets despoiled by the Marcos's underscores the inadequacy of current municipal law in dealing with this problem and the need for international law to step in. Mobutu of Zaire also presents another well documented case of fraudulent enrichment by a modern head of state. See *Political and Economic Situation in Zaire – Fall 1981, Hearing before the Subcommittee on Africa of the Committee on Foreign Affairs House of Representatives*, 97th Cong., 1st Sess. 1 (1981); see also *The Situation in Zaire – Fall 1991, Hearing before the Subcommittee on African Affairs of the Committee on Foreign Relations United States Senate*, 102nd Cong., 1st Sess. 1 (1991); *Assistance to Zaire, Hearings before the Foreign Operations Subcommittee of the House Appropriations Committee* doc. No. Y4.Ap6/1:F76/6/991/pt. 5. The Government of Corazon Aquino, after years of pursuing the Marcos's assets, succeeded in recovering only $125 million of an estimated $2 to $10 billion of spoliated assets! See Drogin, 'Corruption; Manila Under Fire for its Deals on Marco' Assets,' *The Los Angeles Times*, 24 November 1990, at A3, Col. 1.

6 See D. Edelman, Remarks during the panel presentation 'Pursuing the Assets of Former Dictators,' at the *Proceedings of the 81st Annual Meeting of the American Society of International Law*, 394, 399–400 (1987) (Michael P. Malloy ed., 1990).

7 For instance, Swiss banks under intense international pressure to change their secrecy laws have buckled and recently added new anti-money laundering provisions to the penal code. This subject is covered in detail in Chapter 8 *infra*.

trappings of a legal cult, which the legal order appears unwilling or unable to deviate from lest, perhaps, it fall under suspicions for apostasy. This concept together with the immunity doctrines it has engendered – act of state and sovereign immunity – has become the instrument through which corrupt oligarchies justify the plunder of national wealth and resources. In this sense, as Chapter 8 demonstrates, it operates as a sword for cutting loose the purse strings to the State coffers so that looters can go in and remove however much they can without any hindrance. Equally noteworthy is the fact that the idea of state sovereignty has made it difficult for courts to exercise jurisdiction over top state officials involved in acts of spoliation. Here the concept has been turned into a protective shield to keep perpetrators of acts of spoliation beyond the jurisdictional reach of domestic as well as foreign courts. In both formulations, victims of spoliation are rendered helpless, unable to rely on the legal order for vindication of the rights promised to them in the international human rights instruments cited earlier. It is the thesis of this chapter that the cult of state sovereignty is inconsistent with the doctrine of leadership responsibility and the time has come for international law and the legal order to reassess its continued viability in light of the contemporary problem of indigenous spoliation.

Of the many outrages that the Duvalier family name has come to be associated with in recent times, none quite approaches the following statement attributed to its patriarch: '*Je suis le drapeau Haitien, Uni et Indivisible, François Duvalier*'.[8] As absurd as this claim may strike some, Duvalier was merely giving expression to a belief shared by this generation of Third World heads of states, in the main, who like him see their nations as their personal estates writ large.[9] In any event, as

---

[8] See Graham Greene, *The Comedians*, 109 (1965). Not satisfied with being the Haitian flag, Francois Duvalier also declared himself 'an immaterial being' shortly after he became 'President-for-Life', and issued a *Catechisme de la Révolution* to the faithful containing the following version of the Lord's Prayer:

> Our Doc, who art in the National Palace for Life, hallowed be Thy name by present and future generations. Thy will be done in Port-au-Prince as it is in the provinces. Give us this day our new Haiti and forgive not the trespasses of those antipatriots who daily spit upon our country; lead them into temptation, and, poisoned by their own venom, deliver them from no evil…

Quoted in J. DeWind & D.H. Kinley III, *Aiding Migration: The Impact of International Development Assistance on Haiti*, 18 (1988). The comment is reminiscent of the maxim upon which Benito Mussolini based his rule: 'Il Duce ha sempre ragione' ('The leader is always right'). quoted in Henry L. Bretton, *The Rise and Fall of Kwame Nkrumah: A Study of Personal Rule in Africa*, 53 (1966); Article 54 of the Constitution of Zaire provides: 'The person of the President of the Republic shall be inviolable. Except in the case of high treason, the President of the Republic is not criminally responsible for his acts accomplished in the exercise of his official functions.'

[9] Duvalier's claim appears modest in comparison to the conduct of other heads of states. Take the case of Macias Nguema who after being named President-for-Life of

Haiti's flag Francois 'Papa Doc' Duvalier saw himself as the incarnation of the Haitian State. The implications of this claim are fairly obvious. Duvalier as the emanation of the Haitian State could do no wrong neither could he steal from the State since the State could not steal from itself. That would be like taking from one pocket and putting it in the other. That he together with his family looted the Haitian treasury with impunity[10] was, from a strict absolutist view of sovereignty,

---

Equatorial Guinea arranged the following year to have a new constitution approved by the sole and ruling party (Partido Unico Nacional de Trabajadores – PUNT) and ratified by referendum. A document under which Macias Nguema was not bound by any constitutional considerations. In the meantime, his Party Congress had Fernando Poo, one of three constituent provinces of the Republic, renamed Macias Nguema after the President. A third of a country's territory named after a living head of state! See Ibrahim K. Sundiata, *Equatorial Guinea: Colonialism, State Terror and the Search for Stability*, 67 (1990); and Max Liniger-Goumaz, *Small is Not Always Beautiful*, 56–57 (1989) (John Wood trans.). PUNT must have borrowed a page from a book written almost two decades before Equatorial Guinea became a modern State. Kwame Nkrumah, the first President of Ghana, chose as the title of his autobiography: *Ghana: The Autobiography of Kwame Nkrumah*, (1957) to underscore the fact that the two were like Siamese twins and the country's destiny was inextricably tied to that of its maximum leader. Nearly all the Third World leaders implicated in indigenous spoliation activities had been elevated to the exalted status of *de jure* President-for-Life: Ceausescu of Romania, the Duvaliers, pere et fils of Haiti, Ferdinand Marcos of the Philippines, Mobutu Sese Seko of Zaire, self-proclaimed Emperor Bokassa of the Central African [Empire] Republic while others by their sheer longevity in office act or acted as *de facto* life Presidents: Biya of Cameroon, Siaka Stevens of Sierra Leone, Stroessner of Paraguay, and so on.

[10] In his book *Peasants and Poverty: A Study of Haiti*, (1979), Lundahl describes the relentless despoliation of the Haitian environment and people by a small class on a scale never before seen in the Western hemisphere since the Spanish Conquest. See also DeWind & Kinley, *supra* note 8, at 16. One estimate puts this class at between 1 and 2 percent of the population, roughly 24,000 people in a population of 5.9 million. See Alex Dupuy, *Haiti in the World Economy: Class, Race and Underdevelopment Since 1700*, at 184 (1988). This class has appropriated 44 percent of the national income and owns 40 percent of the country's wealth. *Id.* Lundahl and others contend that Haitian rulers under successive regimes but most notably under those of the Duvaliers (pere et fils), established a predatory relation with the Haitian economy. They devised numerous strategies and deployed the entire machinery of the state, including all its repressive apparatus, to extract wealth from the economy: 'The treasury has continued to be legitimate prey for the cliques in power, and power is viewed as a means to reach the prey.' Lundahl, *supra* at 399. As a result of this predatory relationship, it is estimated that between 1960 and 1967 as much as 87 percent of the government's expenditures were paid out directly or indirectly to Francois Duvalier's supporters. DeWind & Kinley, *supra* note 8, at 20.

While in power from 1957 to 1971, Papa Doc Duvalier officially received a modest presidential salary of only $20,000 per annum. Yet, during the first few years in office, he was able to purchase two mansions for $575,000, amassed some $400,000 and stashed another $1.5 million in a Swiss bank account. Lundahl, *supra* at 345. In 1963, according to estimates by the International Commission of Jurists, Duvalier and his close collaborators mulcted the Haitian treasury of about $10 million per year. The august group concluded that the only reason for this pillage was 'to place the country under tribute in order to ensure the future affluence of those in power.' Quoted in B. Diederich & A. Burt, *Papa Doc: Haiti and its Dictator*, 257 (1969), cited in Lundahl, *supra* at 345. The plunder of the Haitian economy continued unabated under the regime of Duvalier (fils). Nothing was spared, no funds were sacred, even foreign aid. International development assistance earmarked for economic development was systematically diverted away from the genuinely needy. *See* DeWind & Kinley, *supra* note 8, at 40. From 1973 through 1983, $477 million of international aid went to Haiti, of which amount the United States contributed $213.6 million. In an extensive review of United States AID programs undertaken in Haiti during the period 1973-1981, the US General Accounting Office somberly concluded that: 'The AID program to date has had a limited impact on Haiti's dire poverty.' See *US General Accounting Office, Assistance to Haiti: Barriers, Recent Program Changes, and Future Options*, Report ID-82–13, 22 February 1982, at 6–7, cited in DeWind & Kinley, *supra* note 8, at 46. During the first four years of Jean-Claude Duvalier's rule, official aid increased more than tenfold, reaching $59.3 million in 1975. By the early 1980s, this amount had almost doubled again, in excess of $100 million per year. See World Bank, *Country Program Paper, Haiti (Review Draft)*, 20 May 1983, at 21–22, cited in DeWind & Kinley, *supra* note 8, at 41–42.

But true to its predatory character, Haiti's ruling class pocketed close to one-third of all foreign aid and as much as 80 percent of the US-provided aid in the years preceding Jean-Claude's rise to power. During 1977–78 alone, $69 million, an amount equal to 63 percent of all recorded central government revenues in 1978, were misappropriated by the Haitian government. See P.E. English, *Canadian Development Assistance to Haiti*, 24–26 (1984). However, as studies show the wealth extracted from the national economy has never been used to finance public services or economic development programs likely to benefit the masses of Haitians. Accumulated wealth was invested instead to maintain the opulent lifestyle of the ruling class and to 'feed the ravenous appetite of the repressive state security apparatus.' See DeWind & Kinley, *supra* note 8, at 20. During the three decades the Duvaliers were in power, the standard of living of the majority of Haitians declined significantly. The per capita GDP declined from about $80 in 1950–51 to $74 in 1967–1968 while the per capita income went down from $67 in 1962 to $62 in 1967. In 1967, Haiti had the highest infant mortality rate in the Americas (147 per 1000) with 50 percent of children dying before the age of 5; the lowest life expectancy (47.5 years); a generalized malnutrition and the lowest per capita consumption of calories and protein (1700/40); a total of 332 medical doctors or 0.68 doctors per 10,000 inhabitants (in contrast to 1 per 6700 persons in Guatemala, the next lowest); 0.67 hospital beds for every 1,000 people (compared with 1.9 per 1,000 in the Dominican Republic). Only 2.6 percent of all houses (12.1 percent in Guatemala) and 21 percent of all urban residences (43 percent in Guatemala) had pipe-borne water, and only 0.1 percent had indoor sanitation. There were 17.4 kilowatt-hours of electricity per capita (compared with 164 for the Dominican Republic); 1 telephone per 1,000 inhabitants (compared with 63 in Barbados), almost all of them in the capital of Port-au-Prince; and 200 miles of paved roads and 2,000 miles of unpaved roads in a country the size of Maryland. See Dupuy, *supra* at 185 ff.

Some two decades after these grim statistics were recorded, the situation has become much worse. When compared to her Caribbean neighbors in 1985, Haiti's infant mortality rate of 123 per 1,000 remained the highest and was lowest in life expectancy (53 years),

of no consequence since those actions were sovereign acts. And so long as Duvalier wrapped himself with the mantle of a Sovereign Prince he had no cause to fear that any court in the world could find him guilty of fraudulent enrichment and for good reason: *par in parem imperium non habet* (an equal has no dominion over an equal). Thus, the legality of Duvalier's actions could not be called into question in the courts of another State. And if he were actually named as a defendant in a civil suit for recovery of spoliated Haitian assets, Duvalier could simply plead defense of immunity from the suit since only with his consent could he, the very embodiment of the Haitian State, be sued in a foreign court.

This view of leadership infallibility is a throwback to sixteenth century European doctrines of state sovereignty and the divine right of kings. When he reaffirmed these doctrines in his famous statement, Francois Duvalier was merely bearing witness to their pervasive influence on Western thought and, equally important, the dominance of the latter on the world stage. These essentially Western concepts have served as the reigning paradigm, shaping and organizing the universal discourse on fundamental questions regarding the nature and derivation of political authority and political obligation, in the last four centuries. They have also been absorbed into Western jurisprudence and have influenced the development of legal doctrines with respect to the designation of international legal personality, the attribution of responsibility under international law for economic injuries to aliens, the territorial reach of domestic courts and so forth.

Because these European-derived concepts have become so ubiquitous in daily discourse and because as tools they have proved quite convenient for courts that wish to avoid passing judgments on the activities, no matter how sordid, of foreign sovereigns, it is easy to forget that they were expounded to deal with problems of a different age. An age when sovereigns could theoretically do no wrong and when the exercise of authority by one sovereign over another could very well be interpreted as *casus belli* by the more sensitive of sovereigns. It is proposed here that these concepts have now lost some of their Delphic quality. They have instead

---

literacy rate (23 percent), in ratio of access of population to pipe-borne water (21 and 3 percent, respectively) and in per capita income ($310). See DeWind & Kinley, *supra* note 8, at 18. Students of Haiti see a direct connection between the predatory state and Haiti's poverty. *See* English, *supra* at 10, cited in DeWind & Kinley, *supra* note 8, at 50. By 1985, Haitians as a whole were consuming 20 percent fewer calories and 30 percent less protein (40 percent and 50 percent, respectively, in the rural areas) than the daily recommended amounts. One-third of all children under five years old were chronically malnourished and 90 percent of child deaths were attributed to malnutrition and gastroenteritis. See R.I. Rotberg & C.K. Clague, *Haiti: The Politics of Squalor*, 6–11 (1971), cited in Dupuy, *supra* at 165.

Although in the 1980's 90 percent of the Haitian population earned less than $150, and fewer than 20 percent of the workers employed full time received the official minimum wage of $3 per day, their President Jean-Claude Duvalier, his wife Michele, and their close associates were estimated to have filched over $505 million from the public treasury. For a flattering view of Jean-Claude's father, Papa Doc Duvalier, see D. Nicholls, *From Dessalines to Duvalier. Race, Colour and National Independence in Haiti*, 237, 246 (1979).

become excess baggage weighing down on the search for meaningful solutions to the problems of this epoch of which the fraudulent enrichment of heads of state and other high-ranking officials prejudicial to the public interest is one. It is appropriate at this juncture to pause and inquire whether the historical context in which these doctrines arose bears any resemblance to the contemporary setting in which they are now being applied. Answering this question would require going back, if only briefly, to the history of Western political thought in order to track the evolution of the concepts of 'state' and 'sovereignty'. This retreat into history is for purposes of identifying the particular problems which these concepts were intended to resolve and discovering whether any parallels can be drawn between those problems of yore and the contemporary problem of indigenous spoliation.

Historical review is important for another reason. Michael Reisman has taken international lawyers to task for not paying enough attention to the historical incidents from which political advisers infer their normative universe.[11] The result is that judges tend to gloss over the historical background to a dispute and selectively pick the 'relevant' facts they consider necessary for disposing the matter. However, what is left out of the recital of facts contained in judicial opinions is precisely the material that is needed to provide a perspective to the problem. Reisman cites the example of the Schooner Exchange v. MacFaddon[12] judgment to show how key facts were carefully left out of the record in order to reach a desired result:

> Somehow the judgment never states the extraordinary fact that the case was being decided against the background of the War of 1812, in which the British had set fire to Washington. France, the real defendant, was the only ally of the United States. It seems most unlikely under these circumstances that any United States court would have risked imperiling that relationship.[13]

Yet, *The Exchange* is widely acknowledged as the case which firmly implanted foreign sovereign immunity in American law.[14] Were the defendant an enemy State would the United States Supreme Court have passed up the opportunity to decide on who had title to the schooner Exchange? Of course not. This being the case, it would appear that unspecified and unstated normative factors influence the decision whether or not to grant jurisdictional immunity to a Sovereign State claiming it. But these factors evidently have very little to do with abstract legal reasoning as The Exchange case so dramatically illustrates. A case which successfully peels back some of the mystique which judicial decisions have been wrapped exposing them to be no different from other kinds of human decisions; they all arise from, and are shaped by, socio-historical conditions.

---

11 See W. Michael Reisman, 'Incidents,' in *International Law Anthology*, 53 (Anthony D'Amato ed., 1994).

12 11 US (7 Cranch) 116, 3 L.Ed. 287 (1812).

13 *Id.*, at 57.

14 See Comment, 'The Jurisdictional Immunity of Foreign Sovereigns,' *Yale Law Journal*, 63, 1148 (1954) [hereinafter 'Jurisdictional Immunity'].

Finally, the resort to historical reconstruction is central to resolving the broader question with respect to the continuing viability of the Western cult of the state and the sovereign immunity doctrines it has engendered; doctrines which restrain foreign courts from inquiring into the legality of certain activities of public officials designated as sovereign acts. The historical review provides a context for judging the implications flowing from a claim such as the one made by Francois Duvalier that he embodied the Haitian State.

But the backdrop to any discussion of the concept of sovereignty is our changing world; one that has increasingly become a global village in which sovereignty claims are routinely tempered with the realization that few States have the resources to live off themselves. As a result States have turned to each other for basic economic survival and with this has come the implicit waiver or surrender by the more economically vulnerable States of 'some' of their sovereignty claims to the more powerful States or the most critical international organizations. The vast majority of States in Africa, Asia, the Caribbean, Latin America and now Central and Eastern Europe can hardly survive without financial hand-outs from the major economic powers (United States, European Economic Community and Japan) and loans on very favorable terms from the leading multilateral lending agencies such as the International Bank for Reconstruction and Development (World Bank) and the International Monetary Fund (IMF). Donor countries and lending agencies are increasingly using their enormous financial leverage in the receiving countries to legislate in areas previously regarded as the exclusive domain of the sovereign even to the point of rewriting their constitutions![15] When officials from the World Bank or a donor country are allowed to rewrite a borrowing country's trade policy, its fiscal policies, labor laws, civil regulations, budgetary policy, and to dictate its economic policies, can such a country claim to be sovereign? Is not sovereignty in this instance a fiction that is conceded only as a matter of international courtesy?

Consider this: in an article appropriately titled 'Aid, Debt, and the End of Sovereignty: Mozambique and Its Donors',[16] Dr. David Plank meticulously examines the impact of World Bank and IMF programs of structural adjustment and sectoral policy reform on Mozambique. His thesis is that these kinds of external 'interventions have thoroughly discredited traditional notions of sovereignty in many parts of Africa.'[17] He goes on to argue that Mozambique's embrace of the World Bank/IMF prescribed approach to development has led to a pattern of 'overt and extensive instructions by outside agencies into what had once been viewed as the exclusive purview of sovereign governments....'[18] How did the leaders of Mozambique get themselves in this predicament? Plank is careful to

---

[15] See for example, Jonathan Cahn, 'Challenging the New Imperial Authority: The World Bank and the Democratization of Development,' *Harvard Human Rights Journal*, 6, 159 (the World Bank continues to use its power through its financial leverage to legislate entire legal regimes including altering the constitutional structure of borrowing nations).

[16] See David N. Plank, 'Aid, Debt, and the End of Sovereignty: Mozambique and Its Donors,' *Journal of Modern Africa Studies*, 31, 407 (1993).

[17] *Id.*, at 409.

[18] *Id.*

point out that they were faced with Hobson's choice; trapped, as it were, between the rock of Scylla and the whirlpool of Charybdis. The choice was between retaining control over domestic political arrangements and policy choices and lose foreign aid or ceding substantial control over the levers of power to external agencies and sustain the flow of aid and avert economic collapse. They chose the latter; understandably so. Mozambique, it must be pointed out, is the poorest country in the world, with a Gross Domestic Product (GDP) per capita of approximately $80 in 1990. It is a country that cannot survive without foreign assistance, which accounts for two-thirds of measured GDP. It is also, relatively speaking, the most heavily-indebted country in the world with a total stock of external debt that is more than four times the annual Gross National Product (GNP), and almost 20 times larger than annual export earnings, requiring for its servicing in excess of $500 million per year or approximately 40 per cent of GDP.[19] These are some of the factors that have conspired to undermine Mozambique's claim to sovereignty and left its economy at the mercy of principal aid donors.

And such has been the extent of external interventions in the developing countries that Plank bluntly concludes that as far as much of Africa is concerned 'traditional notions of sovereignty are now virtually meaningless ...'[20] Neo-colonial vassalage, he warns, will likely move in to fill the vacuum left behind by the loss of sovereignty. In which event, Africa would come under the direct and open-ended control of Western powers who will takeover the running of the 'administration, security, and economic policies of 'deteriorated' States under the banner of the UN and various donors.'[21] If, as the empirical evidence suggests, traditional notions of sovereignty have become virtually meaningless in many economically vulnerable countries, why then should their constitutionally responsible leaders be allowed to hide behind the immunity doctrines derived from this notion? Why should not a head of state, whose diversions of State funds and whose mismanagement of the economy make inevitable the foreign invasion of aid accompanied by a retinue of aid handlers to rescue that economy, be stripped of the sovereign immunity defense and made to answer for the economic injuries to his people brought about by his depredations?

Voltaire is reputed to have said somewhere that the view of a tree is different from the branches than from the roots. Few leaders of developing countries would contest Plank's assessment of the state of sovereignty in their countries[22] even as

---

19 *Id.*, at 407–412; see also World Bank, *World Development Report* (1993).

20 *Id.*, at 429.

21 *Id.*, at 430.

22 See *Challenges of Leadership in African Development* (Olusegun Obasanjo & Hans D'Orville eds, 1990), a book that brings together 18 statements and papers presented at the inaugural program of the African Leadership Forum held in Ota, Nigeria in 1988. In his keynote address, a former Head of State of Nigeria, General Olusegun Obasanjo, acknowledged the erosion of sovereignty in many African States when he noted that Washington-based financial institutions 'have installed their own men in commanding positions in key sectors of our economies, in central banks, in customs departments, and in

they continue to exploit its immunity doctrines for reasons of expediency and self-preservation. Regrettably, the international legal order has not been able to see through this subterfuge. Courts that apply international law in real cases involving high-ranking officials who have been implicated in the spoliation of national wealth continue to parade the fiction of sovereignty and to allow these leaders to hide behind its protective doctrines.

Fortunately, the absolutist theory of the state that Francois Duvalier espoused has not remained static. It has undergone some profound changes since its inception and along the way it has been augmented by several competing theories of the state such as the constitutional, the ethical (Hegelian), the class (Marxian), and the pluralist (Dewey) theories of the State.[23] In a parallel development, legal doctrine has also moved away from some of the collateral doctrines of the absolutist State.[24] For instance, the absolute theory of sovereign immunity has been abandoned in favor of a restrictive theory that allows for exceptions in two categories of activities. The first exception allows for acts of state that consist of commercial transactions and the second allows for cases in which the Executive Branch of government has represented that it has no objection to denying validity to the foreign sovereign act. As the discussion in Chapter 8 demonstrates these derogations from the absolute theory of sovereign immunity have been formulated through case law, codified in statutory law and negotiated into multilateral treaties. These exceptions have been applied in cases involving the nationalization and expropriation of foreign assets, the issuance of public debt instruments, disputes over state-private party contracts and so forth. A foreign sovereign's invocation of immunity from jurisdiction in situations such as these is understandable. They are precisely the kinds of situations where, arguably, the nation as a whole is the intended beneficiary and therefore nothing good could be achieved in having the decisions of its leaders called to question in a court of law, and a foreign one, at that. But in the specific context of indigenous spoliation activities involving heads of state and other high-ranking public officials, the motivations and consequences are dramatically different. These activities contribute absolutely nothing to the common interest of the national community since they are directed solely toward the build up of private individual fortunes at the expense of the public good. Consequently, the invocation and subsequent judicial grant of jurisdictional immunity of the person of the Sovereign risks being interpreted as a validation of the plunder of Third World assets.

Fraudulent enrichment of top State officials, under current law, is not one of the

---

ministries of finance and planning.' And in candor quite remarkable for a head of state, Obasanjo admitted that 'no major decision or initiative on the economy can be taken without their acquiescence at the very least' concluding that '[t]he defeat of this new colonialism will not be easy.' *Id.*, at 28–29.

[23] For a discussion of these competing theories, see Andrew Vincent, *Theories of the State* (1987).

[24] See Jurisdictional Immunity, *supra* note 14, at 1169; see also Hersch Lauterpacht, 'The Problem of Jurisdictional Immunities of Foreign States,' *1952 British Yearbook of International Law*, 220, 226 *et seq.*

prototypical cases for which the modified immunity doctrines were intended to cover, as a result they have not been all that helpful either in disciplining the perpetrators of such activities or in helping in the recovery of spoliated assets. But these doctrines can be further reformed to make them more responsive to the problem of indigenous spoliation. One approach would require treating the problem as an extension of the commercial exception to sovereign immunity by placing it under the omnibus 'acts of a private nature' category. Alternatively, rather than trying to squeeze spoliation activities into one of the already recognized exceptions, a separate judicial exception could be carved specifically for fraudulent enrichment of top state officials prejudicial to the public interest. Under either formulae, a constitutionally responsible ruler who is named as a defendant in an action to recover spoliated assets would not count on an automatic entry into the protective sanctuary of sovereign immunity. This will balance the equities somewhat by allowing victims of despoliation their day in court to prove the link between the spoliation of their national assets and the resultant economic injury suffered. As one commentator put it 'the vice of immunity is ... the permanent refusal to hear an injured party's complaint when it is doubtful that he will be otherwise compensated.'[25] Victims of indigenous spoliation do not see the fine legal distinction between the absolute theory or the restrictive theory of sovereign immunity and granting either to a sovereign defendant produces the same effect, from a victim's point of view. What the despoiled victims need is their day in court. To deny them this much would amount to a judicial preference for a policy of avoiding any affront to sovereign prestige over one of promoting fundamental human rights including the economic right to exercise permanent sovereignty over national wealth and resources.

STATE AND SOVEREIGNTY IN HISTORICAL PERSPECTIVE

The Doctrine of Absolute Sovereignty

The story of State sovereignty as a juridical concept begins from about the middle of the sixteenth century with the writings of the French lawyer, Jean Bodin (1530–96), who is generally acknowledged as the pioneer in the formulation of the doctrine of sovereignty.[26] The Bodinian State is an association of families recognizing a sovereign power: 'La République est un droit gouvernement de

---

[25] See Jurisdictional Immunity, *supra* note 14, at 1164.

[26] Bodin's theory of sovereignty was fully developed in his work *Les Six Livres de la Republique* (translated as *The Six Books of a Commonwealth*). See J.W. Allen, *A History of Political Thought in the Sixteenth Century*, 410 (1928); see also Andrew Vincent, *Theories of the State*, 34 (1987) (noting that the first real conscious and systematic use of the word sovereignty was by Bodin who also associated it with the State). Other influential 16th century theorists of sovereignty were Hobbes and Machiavelli. They were joined in the succeeding centuries by William Blackstone, Jeremy Bentham, John Austin and Albert Dicey.

plusieurs ménages et de ce qui leur est commun avec puissance souveraine.'[27] 'Puissance souveraine,' essentially an unlimited power of making law for itself, was for Bodin the hallmark of the fully-formed State: 'La souveraineté est la puissance absolue et perpetuelle de la République'[28] – an absolute and perpetual power upon which is founded the authority to make law. Here Bodin is identifying the sovereign with the State where the former 'encapsulates the entire body of authority necessary to bring a State into full existence.'[29] Hobbes would later expand on this notion of the sovereign/State identity in his discussion of the representative sovereign: '[a] Multitude of men are made *One* Person, when they are by one man, or one Person, Represented ... it is the *Unity* of the Representer not the *Unity* of the Represented, that maketh the Person *One*.'[30] The State exists, can only exist by virtue of one who represents them in the fictional person of the sovereign.[31] It is in the representative sovereign that the State exists.[32]

If the sovereign was the *suprema potestatis* from whence did he derive his authority, from man or conferred by God? Bodin's contemporary Pierre de Belloy, who is credited with being the first in France to expound with any fullness the theory of the Divine Right of Kings, saw the sovereign Prince as the Viceroy of God responsible only to Him.[33] As the very image of God, Belloy found it inconceivable that the king's authority to command, implying obligation to obey, could possibly be created by man.[34] But Bodin, who also believed in the divine right of kings, did not, however, share the view that the Prince received his sovereignty by virtue of a special divine commission.[35] He does, however, concede that de Belloy's sovereign Prince may even be called God's vicar: '*[p]uisqu'il n'y a rien de plus grand en terre aprés Dieu que les princes souverains, et qu'ils sont établis de lui comme ses lieutenants ... qui méprise son prince souverain, il méprise Dieu duquel it est l'image*.'[36] Notwithstanding this concession, Bodin maintained that sovereignty was man's creation, arising from the nature of man and of human needs and aspirations.[37]

---

27 See Jean Bodin, *Les Six Livres de la Republique* [*The Six Books of a Commonwealth*] (Richard Knolles, trans. 1606, Kenneth D. McRae ed., 1962) Bk. 1, Chap. 8 (1593), at 125, quoted in Allen, *supra* note 26, at 413.

28 *Id.*, at 125.

29 Vincent, *supra* note 23, at 57.

30 See Thomas Hobbes, *The Leviathan*, 220 (1968) quoted in Vincent, *supra* note 23, at 57.

31 Vincent, *supra* note 23, at 57.

32 *Id.*

33 Allen, *supra* note 26, at 383.

34 *Id.*, at 384–385.

35 *Id.*, at 415.

36 'Since there is nothing greater on earth, after God, than sovereign princes, and since they have been established by Him as His lieutenants ... Contempt for one's sovereign prince is contempt toward God, of whom he is the earthly image.' See Republic, Bk. 1, ch. 10, at 211 quoted in Allen, *supra* note 26, at 415.

37 Allen, *supra* note 26, at 415.

Regardless of its origin, sovereignty involves more than the power to make law; it must be permanent and subject to no limitation in time, in function or in law. Sovereignty consists in a right always to do anything and as such is incapable of limitation. While the sovereign may feel morally bound to honor the promises he makes, that is wholly a matter between himself and God. But as *legibus solutus*, he can never be bound legally.[38] That would simply be inconceivable for a sovereign to be bound by his own will, 'a thing by nature altogether impossible,' Bodin wrote.[39] The sovereign makes law and as such he embodied the ultimate and supreme right and authority to command over all the subjects of his realm. Since sovereignty was supreme and the source of law, then law was the will of the sovereign and it would have been inconceivable to subject the sovereign to *his* command. For a sovereign subject to law would no longer be its source *a fortiori* not sovereign. But Bodin's sovereignty is also the recognized and unlimited authority to make law and by definition it is indivisible. An unlimited law-making authority involves and includes all other powers and is not ideally suited for separation. The idea of multiple or divided sovereignties struck Bodin as nonsensical.

The Historical Background

Sixteenth century European political thought drew inspiration from two sources: first, the basic philosophical assumptions which informed on the writings of Bodin and the other major thinkers of this period; and second, some pragmatic considerations compelled by concrete political realities for which accommodations had to be made.

Some Basic Philosophical Assumptions

An historian of this period has argued that much of the political thought of the sixteenth century was the product of old wine in new wine bottles. That is, old questions were simply restated in new terms.[40] The basic assumptions made by period thinkers were essentially the same that had been made by their medieval predecessors. These assumptions, which influenced the development of the political thought of this period, were basically four: (1) the primacy of the Scriptures as the word of God; (2) the existence of a 'natural' moral law, recognized by all men alike and binding absolutely; (3) an acknowledgement that goodness in action was in conformity with the Eternal law, that is with God's Purpose in creation therefore, and by extension, 'right' is something which cannot be denied without defiance of God; and (4) every conceivable 'right' is an expression of Divine Will and real authority, whether conferred on a king or some lesser mortal, is a right to demand obedience as a duty to God.[41]

---

38 See Republic, Bk. VI, Chap. 4, at 965.

39 *Id.*

40 Allen, *supra* note 26, at xiv.

41 *Id.*, at xiv–xv.

Political Realities

Sixteenth century political thought was directed to answer the central *political* problems of the period. The Peace of Westphalia (October 1648) is generally viewed as a watershed in modern state history. It ostensibly brought to an end the Wars of Religion and the assorted divisive theological controversies that had rent Europe asunder during the century 1559–1659. In the wake of Westphalia Europe witnessed the rise of a new national State centered in, and represented by, the king. The contours of what would become, for the next couple of centuries, the paradigmatic State were captured in Louis XIV famous aphorism 'L'état ç'est moi'! The overriding challenge for the national State was that of political consolidation or, to use a more contemporary term, nation-building. The preoccupation was in reconstituting or rediscovering effective central governments capable of generating and sustaining widespread loyalty from the governed. There was a crying need to build strong governments that would serve as a bulwark for political stability and prevent any sudden lurch toward anarchy.

The establishment of order and security called for new institutional forms and in response to this need 'there arose not only strong monarchical sentiments, but a tendency towards formation of theories of unlimited sovereignty in the monarch,' particularly in England and France.[42] The new theory of state sovereignty, which sustained the 'monarchical' state drew from the 14th century doctrine of Divine Right of Kings:[43]

> … [which] had been first developed … as a support for the Germanised Emperor Lewis IV in his controversy with the Gallicised Pope John XXII. But it had been taken up by national kings such as Henry VIII of England and Henry III of France, and had been used by them as a defence not only against Papalist, but also against Calvinistic rebels, common lawyers, recalcitrant Parliaments, and social revolutionaries.[44]

The central theme in Bodin's theory of state sovereignty is the need, suggested by the disorders of his time, for complete concentration and centralization of political authority. Coming through his writings is the overriding concern for stability.[45] It explains his belief that in every stable commonwealth there must exist a supreme sovereign authority – 'puissance souveraine' – vested in some single individual or group whose power is 'absolute and perpetual.'[46] Power concentrated in a central institution, a supreme law-making authority whose decisions are final was the best

42 *Id.*, at xv.

43 Fossey John Cobb Hearnshaw, *The Social and Political Ideas of Some Great Thinkers of the Sixteenth and Seventeenth Centuries*, 36 (1926).

44 *Id.*

45 See Julian H. Franklin, 'Bodin, Jean,' in *International Encyclopedia of the Social Sciences*, 15, 111 (David L. Sills ed., 1968); see also Jean Bodin, *On Sovereignty* (Julian H. Franklin, trans. & ed. 1992) [hereinafter 'Franklin 1992'].

46 *Id.*

antidote to the chronic disorders that Bodin's France had suffered.[47] On this point, the late Professor Allen of the University of London wrote: '[i]t was the civil wars and the prospect of civil war interminable that made France royalist.'[48]The answer to this was to formulate a theory which made obedience to the Sovereign the highest form of duty for the subjects;[49] a theory designed as a universal recipe for political stability.

With the rise of strong 'monarchical' States, the international relations among them became a preoccupation. It is not beyond the pale to assume that statesmen of the period were quite concerned about the contact of these sovereign states with one another, or that they must have pondered over the appropriate framework that would best accommodate these strong monarchies. And jurists must have shuddered at the thought of subjecting the acts of one sovereign to the scrutiny of the judicial authorities of another sovereign. One can imagine them scurrying around trying to formulate and elaborate legal rules to prevent this from happening. Is it any wonder that doctrines to immunize sovereign activities such as act of state and sovereign immunity began to take shape during this period?

Certainly not as the history of the nascent first new nation[50] in the New World attests. Hersch Lauterpacht, after trawling through early American judicial decisions, concluded that the doctrine of absolute immunity held sway in the formative years of the United States[51] and for good reason. The American sovereign state was an unusual one comprising thirteen sovereign states held together at the center by one overarching Sovereign, acting somewhat as a *primus inter pares*. The doctrine of immunity of foreign states from jurisdiction embraced by these jurists evolved from two related considerations: first, considerations of the dignity of the sovereign state; and secondly, the traditional claim of privilege, now transposed into the international context, which placed the sovereign state above the law and to claim before its own courts.[52] Both factors influenced court decisions in the formative years of the American republic. Lauterpacht was struck by the ubiquity of the theme of the dignity of states in these decisions: 'it was by reference to dignity of states of the union that their immunity from suit was urged insistently and repetitiously.'[53] The concern about the indignity inflicted upon any state in the Union by making it a defendant in an action was unsettling to some of America's Founding Fathers.[54] Thus, the peculiar problems created by the mutual

---

[47] See Frederick M. Watkins, 'State: The Concept,' in 15 *International Encyclopedia of the Social Sciences*, 15, 150, 152 (David L. Sills ed., 1968).

[48] Allen, *supra* note 26, at 367.

[49] Watkins, *supra* note 47, at 150.

[50] The words are borrowed from an American political scientist's study on national integration in the United States which he called the first 'new nation.' See Seymour Martin Lipset, THE FIRST NEW NATION (1963)

[51] *See* Lauterpacht, *supra* note 24, at 229 *et seq.*

[52] *Id.*, at 230–231.

[53] *Id.*, at 230.

[54] See *The Debates in the Several State Conventions of the Adoption of the Federal Constitution*, 3, 533 (J. Elliot ed., Philadelphia 1866 & photo. reprint 1941) ('[J]urisdiction

relations of the United States and its constituent sovereign units made necessary the adoption and extension of the traditional prerogative immunity of sovereign from suits to the States that made up the Federal Union.

Lauterpacht attributes this compelling need to immunize the constituent units from suits both in the domestic and international spheres as one of the major reasons for the adoption of the Eleventh Amendment to the United States Constitution which states: 'The judicial power of the United States shall not be construed to extend to any suit in law or equity commenced or presented against one of the United States by citizens of another State or by citizens or subjects of any foreign State.' The amendment was enacted to overrule Chilsom v. Georgia[55] wherein the United States Supreme Court held that it had jurisdiction to hear a suit brought against the state of Georgia by a citizen of South Carolina, in effect denying Georgia the protection of sovereign immunity. In a subsequent case, Hans v. Louisiana[56] the Court read the amendment to grant a broad right of sovereign immunity upon the states, arguing that the amendment merely restored the original understanding that the constituent states would be immune from suit in all circumstances and that Article III, Section 2 of the US Constitution was never intended to authorize such suits in federal courts.[57]

---

in controversies between a state and citizens of another state is much objected to, and perhaps without reason. It is not in the power of individuals to call any state into court. The only operation it can have, is that, if a state should wish to bring a suit against a citizen, it must be brought before the federal courts. It appears to me that this can have no operation but this – to give a citizen a right to be heard in the federal courts; and if a state should condescend to be a party, this court may take cognizance of it.'); see also The Federalist No. 81, at 511–512 (A. Hamilton) (B. Wright ed., 1961) (Arguing that '[i]t is inherent in the nature of sovereignty not to be amenable to suit of an individual *without its consent.* This is the general sense, and the general practice of mankind; and the exemption, as one of the attributes of sovereignty, is now enjoyed by the government of every State in the Union') (emphasis in original).

55 2. US (2 Dall.) 16 (1973).

56 134 US 1 (1890).

57 This interpretation of the historical background of the amendment has come under some fire. In a reasoned article Judge Gibbons of the United States Court of Appeals for the Third Circuit dismisses as erroneous the orthodox interpretation of the eleventh amendment as the embodiment of a sweeping doctrine of state sovereign immunity from federal jurisdiction. He argues that at the time of its adoption the commonly held understanding of sovereign immunity was that it was personal to the monarch but was not enjoyed by other government officers or by corporate bodies, all of whom were subject to ordinary legal process. And that while in theory the King could do no wrong, the petition of right, the writ by which suit could be brought against the monarch, was entertained routinely so that for all practical purposes the wrongs of the King could always be set right. See John J. Gibbons, 'The Eleventh Amendment and State Sovereign Immunity: A Reinterpretation,' *Columbian Law Review*, 83, 1889 (1983).

The Contemporary Application of the Absolutist Doctrine

Bodin and the Modern Presidential Regimes

Bodinian notions of the sovereign as the embodiment of the State and of sovereignty as representing absolute and, in the language of Bentham, 'indefinite law-making power,'[58] have had a profound influence on contemporary Third World Sovereign Presidencies. They have interpreted Bodin's absolutism to mean that the boundaries of the State were coterminous with those of the Presidency and that the President as the embodiment of the State exercises sovereign power and is generally above the law.[59] This has frequently meant that the Sovereign President can pass any law on any subject he chooses and such law will be regarded as valid, in the sense that the courts of the State will enforce it. The Sovereign President 'can do everything but make a woman a man, and a man a woman,' to borrow DeLolme's pithy description of the far-reaching consequences flowing from the legal absolutism inherent in the concept of sovereignty. One cannot be sovereign if he can legislate only on a limited range of subjects since the quintessential attribute of sovereignty is that its scope as well as its law-making power is unlimited. Only the sovereign can determine the limits of its own competence as such he can, if he so chooses, derogate from the rights set forth in the State's Constitution, or even suspend constitutional guarantees and rule by decree. He may strip the judiciary of all its powers and arrogate these to himself. Alternatively, he may combine the executive, legislative, and judicial powers under his control. Nothing stops him from taking any of these actions given the fact that, from a strictly juristic viewpoint, there will be no body or person in the realm legally superior to the Sovereign.

But it is often overlooked that Bodin's concept of the State and his formulation of the doctrine of absolute sovereignty were intended as a radical remedy for the political disorders of his own France; a universal recipe for political stability. Undivided sovereignty was seen therefore as what gave the State its ideal unity. The destruction of sovereign power was tantamount to a death sentence for the State, a fate he did not wish for France.

The Continued Vitality of Sovereign Immunity Doctrines

That the protective doctrines built around the Sovereigns of the sixteenth and

---

[58] See Jeremy Bentham, *A Fragment on Government*, 1st Ed. c. iv, par xxiii (1776).

[59] In the Francophone African States and some Latin American countries, the Presidency is traditionally referred to as 'la magistrature supreme' implying its supreme law-making role. The authoritative Grand Larousse describes the President of the Republic as 'le prémier magistrat de la République,' the first magistrate of the republic. *Grand Larousse de la Langue Francaise*, 4, 3157, col. 3 (Louis Guilbert et al. eds, 1975). See for example *The Constitution of Colombia*, Art. 189 (describing the President as 'chief of State, head of government, and supreme administrative authority …').

seventeenth centuries continue to serve a useful purpose in the twentieth century[60] is not the quarrel. Rather, the concern is the attempt to reproduce ancient institutions without reference to the historical factors that shaped them. We need to be clear what institutions we are talking about when reference is made to the doctrine of sovereign immunity. Do we mean the immunity of foreign states and their property or immunity with regard to the person of the foreign sovereign, from the jurisdiction of courts of foreign states? Trawling through judicial decisions and relying on a long and distinguished group of authorities – Grotius, Bynkershoek and Vattel – Lauterpacht reached the very interesting conclusion that the former formulation had no support in classical international law.[61] He went on to argue that there was no binding rule of international law on the subject and questioned the misplaced reliance on The Exchange case as authority for the doctrine of immunity of foreign states:[62] 'It is doubtful,' Lauterpacht wrote,

> [W]hether that decision can accurately be quoted as an authority in favour of the rigid principle of jurisprudential immunity of foreign states. It is clear from the language of that decision that the governing, the basic, principle is not the immunity of the foreign state but the full jurisdiction of the territorial state and that any immunity of the foreign state must be traced to a waiver – express or implied – of its jurisdiction on the part of the territorial state. Any derogation from that jurisdiction is an impairment of the sovereignty of the territorial state....[63]

If the doctrine of immunity of foreign state rests on a questionable jurisprudential base, such is not the case with regard to the person of the foreign sovereign which Lauterpacht found to have a more secure place in international law. It would seem to me that when the doctrine is raised by modern Sovereign Presidents, it is in the context of immunity to their person as Sovereign. This latter formulation is closely tied to the issue of the dignity and prestige of the sovereign.

Against this backdrop, the question must be asked: when a twentieth century Head of State enriches himself at the expense of the nation and then tries to justify the plunder as an act of state is he not using a doctrine that, stripped of its context, bears no resemblance to its historical prototype? Even for Bodin, the guru of the

---

[60] Two policy justifications have been advanced for the continued vitality of the doctrine of sovereign immunity: judicial fear of offending sovereign dignity or avoiding any affront to sovereign prestige and causing any embarrassment to foreign relations. See 'Jurisdictional Immunity,' *supra* note 14, at 1153 *et seq*; see also Lauterpacht, *supra* note 24, at 221–224 *et seq.*

[61] See 'Jurisdictional Immunities,' *supra* note 24, at 228. Lauterpacht had a very strong aversion to jurisdictional immunity of foreign states – either in its absolute or modified restrictive form – and this may partly explain this conclusion. He believed that foreign immunity, like the jurisdictional immunity of the domestic state, is 'contrary to the wider principle which postulates the submission of the instrumentalities of the state to the ordinary operation of law as administered by courts.' *Id.*, at 237. The law is supreme and not even the Sovereign Prince is above it.

[62] *Id.*, at 229.

[63] *Id.*

absolutist State, sovereignty was created by need. In his discussion of the different kinds of monarchical sovereignty, Bodin recognized a specie which he called '*monarchie seigneuriale*' or '*dominates*.'[64] This was a 'sovereignty absolutely unlimited save by that law of nature which can never be abrogated.'[65] The seigneurial monarch was regarded in law as sole proprietor in his dominion, all property was his and he governed his subjects as slaves.[66] While Bodin recognized the legality of this specie of sovereignty, he nonetheless dismissed it as primitive.[67] At best, it was a proto-State, a State-in-formation but hardly the paradigmatic State: the 'république bien ordonnée' (the 'well-ordered State'), which is the *mére idée* of Bodin's theory of sovereignty.

Bodin did not conceive of sovereignty as an unlimited right or as unconditioned or as involving a right to do anything. Sovereignty 'existed only to subserve the ends for which the State existed; and only in relation to those ends could it be conceived as existing at all.'[68] Thus, the clumsy attempts by some modern sovereign Presidents to appeal to Bodinian notions of absolutism to justify greed and avarice ignore the broad national interests that Bodin's doctrines were intended to serve. But this construction of sovereignty also ignores the fact that Bodin imposed some restraints on his Sovereign Prince.[69] The Bodinian Sovereign was restrained in three different ways. First, he was bound always by the constraints of natural and divine law; secondly, he was required to perform within the bounds of certain 'fundamental' laws or '*leges imperii*' concerning the form and nature of government;[70] and thirdly, he was bound always to respect the sanctity of property and of the family, which together form the foundations of the State.[71] Bodin was most emphatic and uncompromising in the view that 'tons les princes de la terre y sont sujets et nest pas en leur puissance d'y contrevenir, si'ils ne veulent être coupables de lèse-majesté divine … Et par ainsi la puissance absolue des princes et seigneuries souveraines ne s'étend aucunement aux lois de Dieu et de nature.'[72] The sovereign was absolute, but within clearly defined legal parameters.

These legal and institutional constraints that acted as restraints on Bodin's sovereign Prince are absent in the modern day sovereign Presidents. Bodin himself had already disabused any notions that his absolute kingship was designed to favor despots such as the likes of Duvalier, Mobutu, and Marcos to name just a few.

---

64 Allen, *supra* note 26, at 424.

65 *Id.*, at 424.

66 Republic, Bk. 2, ch. 2, at 273.

67 *Id.*

68 Allen, *supra* note 26, at 422.

69 See Franklin 1992, *supra* note 45, at xiii, xxi.

70 These were the law prescribing the rule of succession to the throne, and the law forbidding alienation of the royal domain without consent. *Id.*, at xxv.

71 *Id.*, at 416.

72 Republic, Bk. 1, ch. 8, at 133. ['But as for divine and natural laws, every prince on earth is subject to them, and it is not in their power to contravene them unless they wish to be guilty of treason against God … Thus, the absolute power of princes and other sovereign lordships does not in any way extend to the laws of God and of nature.']

Accused by one of his many critics that he favored despotism Bodin angrily replied in this passage that deserves to be quoted *in extenso:*

> I am amazed by those who believe that I have given more power to one man than is becoming to an honest citizen. For specifically in Book 1, Chapter 8 of my *Republique,* and in other passages as well, I was the very first, even in these dangerous times, unhesitatingly to refute the opinions of those who would expand the right of the treasury and the regalian prerogatives, on the grounds that they give kings unlimited power beyond the laws of God and nature. And what would be more public-spirited than what I have dared to write – that even kings are not allowed to levy taxes without the fullest consent of the citizens? Of what importance is it that I have also held that princes are more strictly bound by divine and natural law than those who are subject to their rule? Or that they are obligated by their contracts like any other citizen? Yet almost all the masters of juristic science have taught the opposite?[73]

This ringing endorsement of limits on sovereignty provides the jurisprudential compass for navigating around the contemporary shoals of sovereign immunity defenses whenever these are raised by modern sovereign Presidents in the context of spoliation disputes.

But there is more. Lauterpacht found the notion of granting immunity from jurisdiction, in order to avoid any affront to a foreign sovereign's prestige, offensive and archaic and recommended that it be abandoned. Since this aspect of immunity remains of interest to modern sovereign Presidents, the choice before foreign courts hearing spoliation claims is clear. In deciding whether to grant or deny immunity, foreign courts must ask whether the 'dignity' of the person of the foreign sovereign claiming immunity outweighs the economic injury to the claimant? The operative word is 'outweigh' not 'impair' – the concern should not be on whether delicate sensibilities would be impaired or offended by subjecting the person of the foreign sovereign to the law. Rather, it should be one of balancing the indignity the person of a foreign sovereign President *may* suffer from a denial of immunity to the harm that *will be* inflicted on victims of spoliation from a grant of sovereign immunity.

REPRISE

This chapter has tried to clear away the debris standing in the way of a full understanding of the nature of the State in an effort to show that its cognate doctrines – Act of State and Sovereign Immunity – arose in specific circumstances to address specific needs of a particular historical epoch. Having absorbed these doctrines into the jurisprudence of modern international law, it is important that their application in the contemporary context be done with an eye toward the needs they were originally intended to satisfy. While it is recognized that the historical conditions that gave rise to these doctrines cannot be reproduced, lock, stock and

---

73 See Jean Bodin, *Les Six Livres de la Republique, Epistola* (1961), quoted in Franklin 1992, *supra* note 45, at xxv–xxvi.

barrel, nevertheless, the acts for which sovereign immunity has been and continues to be sought should, at the very minimum, advance the public interest in one form or another.

The overall aim of this second part of the book is to attempt a *ratio legis* for an international law for *individual* responsibility for economic injuries to nationals arising from acts of fraudulent enrichment committed by Heads of States and other constitutionally responsible officials. Chapter 8 will examine in detail immunity doctrines as an obstacle to the concept of leadership liability. Chapter 9 will present a normative framework for holding constitutionally responsible leaders individually liable for acts of indigenous spoliation, noting in passing the classical law of responsibility for economic injuries, the rights and responsibilities of individuals in international law, the traditional crimes for which international law has attached individual responsibility. Finally, in Chapter 10, the basis for exercising jurisdiction will be discussed.

Chapter 8

Judicial Barriers to Holding Heads of State Individually Liable for Acts of Indigenous Spoliation

Going back to the hypothetical in Chapter One. Suppose that after much soul-searching, the financially-strapped Candide Government decides to go after the assets of Pangloss and his henchmen in multiple jurisdictions. Through independent investigations, Government is able to establish that a sizeable chunk of the former President's considerable personal wealth is invested in the United States. A suit is filed in the appropriate federal district court alleging that Pangloss and his closest associates misappropriated, embezzled or converted billions of dollars in Colony funds; and the successor Government now seeks the return of all wrongfully acquired funds, exemplary damages, imposition of a constructive trust on the defendants' worldwide assets, and an accounting of all money and property spoliated from the government of Colony. Pangloss moves to dismiss and invokes the common law doctrine of *forum non conveniens* and the act of state as defenses. What result? Unless Colony can persuade the court that defendants' activities violate the law of nations, defendants will, under existing US case law, prevail.

THE CASE LAW

The Defense of Forum Non Conveniens

The doctrine of *forum non conveniens* allows a court to decline jurisdiction, even when jurisdiction is authorized by a general venue statute. For a defendant to prevail on a motion to dismiss on *forum non conveniens* ground, he must establish that the foreign forum is adequate and that the private and public factors set out in Gulf Oil Corp. v. Gilbert[1] weigh in favor of dismissal. In Piper Aircraft Co. v.

---

1 Gulf Oil Corp. v. Gilbert, 330 US 501, 508–509 (1947). Private factors include: the relative ease of access to sources of proof; the availability of compulsory process for attendance of unwilling witnesses; the cost of obtaining attendance of willing witness; the possibility of viewing subject premises (if appropriate to the action); and other practical concerns making trial easy, expeditious and inexpensive (for example, the ability to implead third-party defendants, the enforceability of judgment if one is obtained, etc.). Public interest factors include: the administrative difficulties flowing from a court congestion; the

Hartzell Propeller, Inc.,[2] the United States Supreme Court further streamlined the criteria to be utilized in a *forum non conveniens* determination. Under Piper, a suit will be dismissed under this theory after taking into account the following circumstances: (1) any alternative forum for plaintiff's action; (2) the private interest factors affecting the interests of the litigants; and (3) the public interest factors affecting how convenient the present forum is. Although parts one and three of the three-pronged analysis are relatively simple in their application, part two – the private interest concerns – requires a more in-depth analysis. This second factor was subsequently subdivided into: (1) sources of proof; and (2) access to witnesses by the court in Union Carbide Corp. Gas Plant Disaster at Bhopal,[3] with each regulated by the proper procedure for obtaining evidence located abroad.

Application of Forum Non Conveniens in Spoliation Cases

The defense of *forum non conveniens* has been used successfully to foreclose litigation in a foreign jurisdiction to recover allegedly spoliated funds. In Islamic Republic of Iran v. Pahlavi,[4] Iran alleged 'that defendants accepted bribes and misappropriated, embezzled or converted 35 billion dollars in Iranian funds.' Iran sought the return of all wrongfully acquired funds, exemplary damages, imposition of a constructive trust on the defendant's worldwide assets, and an accounting of all money and property received from the government of Iran. The Court of Appeals of New York upheld the dismissal of the suit based on *forum non conveniens* despite the fact that Iran did not have a suitable alternate forum.

> In sum, the record does not demonstrate a substantial nexus between this State and plaintiff's cause of the [sic] action. That being so the courts below could, in the exercise of their discretion, dismiss the action on grounds of *forum non conveniens* notwithstanding the fact that the record does not establish an alternate forum where the action may be maintained and they could do so without conditioning their dismissal on defendant's acceptance of process in another jurisdiction.[5]

Thus, under the common law doctrine of *forum non conveniens*, a court must exercise its discretion and weigh the Piper and Bhopal factors which include: the potential hardship to the defendant, the burden on the courts, the availability of a suitable alternative forum, and whether the chosen forum could afford the parties appropriate relief. The court, however, can dismiss the action even if that effectively forecloses relief.

---

unfairness of burdening citizens in an unrelated forum with jury duty; the local interest in having localized controversies decided at home; the trial in a forum familiar with governing law; and the avoidance of unnecessary problems in conflicts of law. See Piper Aircraft Co. v. Hartzell Propeller, Inc., 454 US 235, 254 n. 22 (1981).

2 454 US 235 (1981).

3 634 F. Supp. 842 (SDNY 1986).

4 62 NY2d 474, 478 NYS2d 597 (Ct. App. 1984), *cert. denied,* 469 US 1108 (1985).

5 62 NY2d at 478.

Foreign Sovereign Immunity and the Act of State Defense

The Foreign Sovereign Immunities Act (FSIA) is the sole basis for asserting US jurisdiction over a foreign state and its agencies and instrumentalities.[6] Under the FSIA, the foreign state will be presumptively immune from jurisdiction unless it can be shown that a statutory exception applies.[7] The FSIA is, however, silent as to

---

6 See The Foreign Sovereign Immunities Act of 1976 (FSIA) 90 Stat. 2891, 28 USC §§1330, 1332, 1391, 1441, 1602–1611, as amended by Pub.L. 100–640, 102 Stat. 3333 (1988), codified the restrictions on absolute sovereign immunity which had been announced in 1952 by the Department of State and transferred the decision on jurisdiction from the executive branch to the courts. See also Verlinden B.V. v. Central Bank of Nigeria, 461 US 480 (1983). In that year the State Department decided that it would henceforth operate under the 'restrictive' theory of sovereign immunity, recommending immunity only where the adjudication involved the public acts of a foreign sovereign *(jure imperii)*, not when it involved commercial acts that could be carried on by private parties *(jure gestionis)*. The State Department decision was communicated to the Department of Justice in a letter from the Legal Advisor's Office, The Tate Letter, 26 State Dept. Bull. 984 (1952). Until the Tate Letter, initial responsibility for deciding questions of sovereign immunity fell primarily on the Executive branch acting through the State Department. It was the State Department that determined whether or not immunity should be granted, and not the result of an independent judicial inquiry. The restrictive theory of immunity is followed in Canada, see Act to Provide for State Immunity, 29, 30 & 31 Eliz. 2, Ch. 93, 21 ILM 798 (1982); the United Kingdom, State Immunity Act, 26 & 27 Eliz. 2, Ch. 33, 17 ILM 1123 (1978); the European Economic Community, European Convention on State Immunity of 1972, 74 ETS, 11 ILM 470 (1972); Australia, Foreign States Immunities Act 1985, 25 ILM 715 (1986). For a discussion on recent developments in State immunity doctrines, see Christoph H. Schreuer, *State Immunity: Some Recent Developments* (1988).

7 See 28 USC §1604. These are (1) the *waiver exception* under which a foreign sovereign is not immune from suit in actions where the sovereign explicitly or implicitly waives its immunity. Implicit waivers of immunity have been found in only three circumstances: where the foreign sovereign agrees to arbitration in another country; where it agrees that a contract is governed by the laws of a particular country; and where the foreign sovereign files a responsive pleading without raising the immunity defense; see for example, Elixir Shipping, Ltd. v. Perusuahaan Pertambangan Minyak Dan Gas Bumi Negara, 267 F. Supp. 2d 659 (SD Tex. 2003), Corzo v. Banco Central De Reserva del Peru, 243 F.3d 519 (9th Cir. 2001), Atlantic Tele-Network Inc. v. Inter-American Development Bank, 251 F. Supp. 2d 126 (DDC 2003), Gulf Resources America v. Republic of Congo, 276 F. Supp. 2d 20 (DDC 2003), Anderman v. Federal Republic of Austria, 256 F. Supp. 2d 1098 (CD Cal. 2003), Blaxland v. Commonwealth Director of Public Prosecutions, 323 F. 3d 1198 (9th Cir. 2003), and Siderman de Blake v. Republic of Argentina, 965 F.2d. 699 (9th Cir. 1992); (2) the *commercial activity exception* which permits federal courts to exercise jurisdiction over foreign sovereigns in circumstances where the claim is based on a commercial activity carried on in the United States by the foreign state or where the claim is based upon an act performed in the US in connection with a commercial activity of the foreign state or where the claim is based upon acts outside the US in connection with a commercial activity of the foreign state elsewhere and that causes direct effects in the United States, see for example,

the issue of what sovereign immunity, if any, should be afforded a sitting head of state. Among the few cases that have explored this question is Tachiona v. Mugabe,[8] where a federal district court examined whether the FSIA may be used to breach Head of State immunity in respect of a head of state who is individually named in the suit. Plaintiffs in Tachiona were Zimbabwean citizens who alleged that the President of Zimbabwe, Robert Mugabe,[9] other Government officials and Zimbabwe's ruling party, had waged a campaign of violence against them. Plaintiffs claimed that this campaign included murder, torture, terrorism, rape, beatings, and destruction of property.[10] These acts were committed, plaintiffs alleged, with a view to suppressing political opposition groups prior to Zimbabwe's June 2000 parliamentary elections. Relying on a federal Court of Appeals decision in the case of Chuidian v. Philippine Nat'l Bank[11] and its

---

Beg v. Islamic Republic of Pakistan, 353 F.3d 1323 (11th Cir. 2003), Fuller v. Hanvit Bank, 247 F. Supp. 2d 425 (SDNY 2003), Gulf Resources America v. Republic of Congo, 276 F. Supp. 2d 20 (DDC 2003), BPA International, Inc. v. Kingdom of Sweden, 281 F. Supp. 2d 73 (DDC 2003), and Global Index, Inc. v. Mkapa, 290 F. Supp. 2d 108 (DDC 2003); (3) the *expropriation exception* where federal courts have jurisdiction over cases in 'which rights in property taken in violation of international law are in issue and that property or any property exchanged for such property is present in the United States in connection with a commercial activity carried on in the United States by the foreign state; or that property or any property exchanged for such property is owned or operated by an agency or instrumentality of the foreign state and that agency or instrumentality is engaged in a commercial activity in the United States.' See 28 USC §1605(a)(3); see also Anderman v. Federal republic of Austria, 256 F. Supp. 2d 1098 (CD Cal. 2003); (4) the *immovable property exception* for 'any case in which ... rights in immovable property situated in the United States are at issue.' See 28 USC. §1605(a)(4); see also Fagot Rodriguez v. Republic of Costa Rica, 297 F.3rd 1 (1st Cir. 2002) (5) the *tortious activity exception,* under this exception federal courts have jurisdiction over claims in which 'money damages are sought against a foreign state for personal injury or death, or damage to or loss of property, occurring in the United States and caused by the tortious act or omission of that foreign state or of any official or employee of that foreign state while acting within the scope of his office or employment.' See 28 USC §1605(a)(5)(A)(2003); see also Simons v. Lycée Française de New York, No. 03 Civ. 4972 (LAK), 2003 WL 22295360 (SDNY 7 October 2003); and (6) the *terrorism exception* was added in 1996 when Congress amended the FSIA by creating an exception for foreign sovereign immunity for countries designated by the State Department under section 6(j) of the Export Administration Act of 1970 as sponsors of terrorism, if the countries in question either committed a terrorist act resulting in the death or personal injury of a US national, or provided material support and resources to an individual or entity that committed such a terrorist act. See 28 USC §1605(a)(7) (2004); see also Roeder v. Islamic Republic of Iran, 333 F.3d 228 (DC Cir. 2003).

[8] Tachiona v. Mugabe, 169 F.Supp. 2d 259 (SDNY 2001).

[9] Mugabe was sued in his capacity as president of the ruling party, ZANU-PF and was served notice whilst in the US to attend a meeting at the United Nations.

[10] These claims were brought under the Alien Tort Claims Act, 28 USC §1350 (1998), and Torture Victim Protection Act, 28 USC §1350 (1998).

[11] Chuidian v. Philippine Nat'l Bank, 912 F.2d 1095 (9th Cir. 1990).

progeny, plaintiffs urged that the FSIA applies to claims against individuals as agents or instrumentalities of the foreign state, and that sovereign immunity ceases when such individuals act beyond the scope of their authority.[12] The US State Department, following its pre-FSIA practice, entered a 'suggestion' of immunity on behalf of Mr. Mugabe and the other Government officials. The court deferred to the State Department's suggestion of immunity, as had been the practice prior to the FSIA, and ruled that the Government officials – not the ruling political party over whom it found jurisdiction – retained immunity.[13] The court side-stepped the issue on how it would have ruled on a Suggestion of Immunity by the State Department if the head of state's conduct fell under one of the commercial activity exceptions of the FSIA.[14]

Unlike the FSIA, the act of state doctrine is not jurisdictional.[15] Instead it is a 'prudential doctrine designed to avoid judicial action in sensitive areas.'[16] The doctrine is a binding rule of decision and not one of abstention and it comes into play when US courts are called to assess the validity of an official act of a foreign

---

12 See Tachiona, 169 F. Supp. 2d at 281–84.

13 See *id.*, at 296–297. Although Mugabe, as a sitting head of state, was immune from the jurisdiction of US courts, service to ZANU-PF, as a non-immune entity, could be effected through him. *Id.*, at 296. The court was of the view that service to effect jurisdiction over matters collateral to a head of state's official status is possible since the head of state will not have to appear in court nor be subject to the court's compulsory powers 'in a manner that could be deemed an assertion of territorial authority over the foreign dignitary.' *Id.*, at 309. The district court held that service could be effected where a 'head-of-state or diplomat would not be subjected to a foreign court's jurisdiction nor exposed to liability in that court.' *Id.*, at 308. In a Memorandum of Law in Support of the United States' Motion for Reconsideration, the US government challenged the court's decision to effect service through an inviolable individual as it risked giving 'rise to vexatious and embarrassing assaults on the dignity of foreign leaders and diplomats, as individuals who wish to protest or humiliate such officials will be able through simple artifice to plead a complaint against a nongovernmental entity with which an official allegedly is affiliated, and then to publicize and stage a highly-visible service of process on the visiting dignitary.' The government's motion for reconsideration was subsequently denied by the federal district court, see Tachiona v. Mugabe, ZANU-PF, Mudenge et al., 186 F. Supp. 2d 383 (2002). In a case decided after Tachiona the International Court of Justice held that the functions of a foreign minister in respect of their states are similar to heads of state and as such an incumbent foreign minister is inviolable against any act of authority of another state, such as the service of process. See Case Concerning the Arrest Warrant of 11 April 2000 (Democratic Republic of Congo v. Belgium), 2002 ICJ (14 February 2002), ¶¶ 1, 53–54. See also Annex: Arrest Warrant of 11 April 2000 (Democratic Republic of Congo v. Belgium), *Annual Survey of International and Comparative Law*, 8, 151 (2002) (summarizing the judgment of Democratic Republic of Congo v. Belgium).

14 See Tachiona, *supra* note 12, at 296.

15 See Argentine Republic v. Amerdera Hess Shipping Corp., 109 S.Ct. 683 (1989) Bicaud v. American Metal Co., 246 US 304, 309, 38 S.Ct. 312, 313, 62 L.Ed. 733 (1918).

16 See Int'l Assoc. of Machinists & Aerospace Workers v. The Organization of the Petroleum Exporting Countries, 649 F.2d 1353, 1357 (9th Cir. 1981) (IAM v. OPEC).

state. A successful assertion of the act of state doctrine precludes a litigant from bringing action against a foreign state, regardless of the litigant's jurisdictional arguments. Once invoked, a court must treat the act of a foreign court within its own boundaries as valid in US courts.[17] The burden of proof of the applicability of the Act of State Doctrine rests with the party attempting to invoke it as a basis for dismissing the action.[18]

The doctrine was first articulated by the United States Supreme Court in the case of Underhill v. Hernandez,[19] where the Court held that 'every sovereign State is bound to respect the independence of every other sovereign State, and the courts of one country will not sit in judgment on the acts of the government of another done within its own territory.'[20] While the act of state doctrine has remained essentially the same since Underhill, it has been narrowed in recent years beginning with the exception created based on the separation of powers doctrine in Bernstein v. N.V. Nederlandsche-Amerikannsche Stoomvaart-Maatschappij.[21] Bernstein involved a Second Circuit review of a case involving the confiscation of property in Germany by the Nazi government. After the US State Department informed the court that United States' foreign relations did not demand judicial abstention in cases involving Nazi confiscations, the Court of Appeals for the Second Circuit proceeded to determine the validity of the acts of the German state. This case has come to represent the so-called 'Bernstein exception' to the act of state doctrine and through it the State Department can explicitly indicate that the conduct of American foreign relations does not require application of the act of state doctrine in a given case.

In Banco Nacionale de Cuba v. Sabbatino,[22] the US Supreme Court held that '[w]hile historic notions of sovereign authority do bear upon the wisdom of employing the act of state doctrine, they do not dictate its existence' and that the doctrine had 'constitutional underpinnings' requiring the judiciary to refrain from interfering with the executive's conduct of foreign relations. Sabbatino involved the use of the act of state doctrine by the Supreme Court to refuse to adjudicate the validity of an uncompensated confiscation of American-owned property in Cuba by the Cuban government. The Court found that since the American government had already taken a position on the Cuban taking, further adjudication would risk

---

[17] W.S. Kirkpatrick & Co. v. Envtl. Technotics Corp., 493 US 400, 404 (1990) (quoting Sabbatino, 376 US, at 423); see also Trugman-Nash, Inc. v. New Zealand Dairy Bd., 942 F. Supp. 905 (SDNY 1996), on reargument, 954 F. Supp. 733 (SDNY 1977); Credit Suisse v. US Dist. Court for Cent. Dist. of Cal., 130 F.3d 1342 (9th Cir. 1997).

[18] See Presbyterian Church of Sudan v. Talisman Energy, 244 F. Supp. 2d 289, 344–45 (SDNY 2003).

[19] 168 US 250, 252, 18 S.Ct. 83, 84, 42 L.Ed. 456 (1897). The case involved a Venezuelan general who was accused of assaulting a US citizen in Venezuela. The Supreme Court refused to uphold Underhill's claim that he was unlawfully detained by the Venezuelan government and dismissed the suit on the basis of the act of state doctrine.

[20] *Id.*

[21] 210 F.2d 375 (2nd Cir. 1954).

[22] 376 US 423 (1964).

embarrassment to the executive branch.

In Alfred Dunhill of London, Inc. v. Republic of Cuba,[23] the Supreme Court again faced the issue of the act of state doctrine. Dunhill involved former owners of several expropriated Cuban cigar companies who brought an action against Dunhill to recover payments made by Dunhill for cigar shipments made before and after their property was confiscated by the Cuban government. The Court held that the proprietary acts of the government of Cuba did not warrant the application of the act of state doctrine. The Court in effect created a commercial exception to the act of state doctrine. As a consequence, an essential element of the application of the act of state doctrine is the characterization of the action as the public, not private or commercial, act of a sovereign. In order to establish an act of state defense, a State must show that the act in question was accomplished by the sovereign and that the purpose of the sovereign act was in the public interest. In addition, courts must consider that judicial interference with the act may 'touch sharply on national nerves.'[24] The burden of establishing an act of state defense is with the defendant foreign state.[25]

In the years since Dunhill was decided, the act of state doctrine has undergone some further tightening. Following the US Supreme Court's decision in *W.S.* Kirkpatrick & Co. v. Environmental Techtonics Corp.,[26] which set out the parameters of the modern act of state doctrine, domestic courts are barred from considering cases involving foreign states where resolution of those claims turn on the legality or illegality of official actions by foreign sovereigns on their own territory. A District of Columbia district court has applied this modern version of the act of doctrine in World Wide Minerals Ltd. v. The Republic of Kazakhstan[27] by declining to consider claims against Kazakhstan that would have required a determination of the validity of official acts. World Wide Minerals involved a contract dispute between a Canadian company, World Wide Minerals, and the government of Kazakhstan for the mining and exporting of uranium. In 1996 and 1997, World Wide signed a number of agreements with Kazakhstan relating to the management of a northern mines complex in Kazakhstan. World Wide was never able to sell the uranium it extracted from the mines because Kazakhstan could not provide an export license having entered into a prior confidential agreement with an American company for the exclusive marketing of the uranium. In response to World Wide's suit, Kazakhstan raised the act of state doctrine as a defense. The district upheld the defense, stating that under the test set out in *Kirkpatrick*, no relief was available to World Wide. The court's reasoning was that it was not in a position to assess the legality of Kazakhstan's denial of the export license since to do so would require an assessment of the validity of regulations enacted for

---

[23] 425 US 682 (1976).

[24] AM v. OPEC, 649 F.2d at 1356–1357.

[25] Dunhill, 425 US at 694.

[26] W.S. Kirkpatrick & Co. v. Environmental Techtonics Corp., 493 US 400, 406 (1990).

[27] World Wide Minerals Ltd. v. The Republic of Kazakhstan, 116 F. Supp. 2d 98 (DDC 2000).

national and international security that are matters of foreign sovereign activity.[28]

The Act of State Doctrine as a Defense in Spoliation Cases

The act of state doctrine was the centerpiece of the Marcoses' defense during their legal skirmishes with the Aquino government that succeeded Ferdinand Marcos. In two noteworthy cases, two Courts of Appeals were asked to consider whether the doctrine prevented US courts from adjudicating the claims of the Aquino government because they involved acts of a former foreign sovereign. While the Aquino government alleged that Ferdinand Marcos abused his position as President of the Philippines for 20 years, and went beyond his scope of authority in acquiring vast amounts of property and wealth belonging to the Filipino people, Marcos (and his wife, Imelda) claimed that the act of state doctrine prevented American courts from adjudicating the acts of a sovereign state. Thus, the question the Second and Ninth Circuits had to answer was whether the Marcoses' actions would be considered acts of the sovereign state or private acts for personal gain.

(i) In Republic of Philippines v. Marcos,[29] the Second Circuit found a number of weaknesses in the defendant's act of state defense. The Justice Department, with the concurrence of the State Department's Office of the Legal Advisor, argued before the Court that 'with respect to the act of state doctrine the burden is on the party asserting the applicability of the doctrine, that [the] defendants [Marcoses] have to date not discharged their burden of proving acts of state, and that, as to the allegation of head of state immunity, the defendants do not have standing to invoke the doctrine.'[30] Applying Dunhill, the Court found that the defendants had failed to show that their acts were public acts protected under the doctrine, but the Court also questioned whether the act of state doctrine was applicable in the present case.[31] A typical act of state defense involves a foreign government defending a suit in United States courts but in this case the Philippine government was the plaintiff and the defendant was the former president of the country.[32] Because these unusual circumstances weighed against the application of the doctrine the court allowed the assets of the Marcoses to be frozen.

(ii) When this same defense was raised in another case involving the Philippine government and Ferdinand and Imelda Marcos, the outcome was different. In Republic of Philippine v. Marcos,[33] the Ninth Circuit Court of Appeals denied the application of the act of state defense in upholding a district court preliminary injunction barring the Marcoses from transferring their assets, allegedly purchased with money stolen from the Philippine government, anywhere in the world. The Court found that the Marcoses' activities were public actions, therefore, the act of

---

[28] *Id.*, at 104 (citing Mol. Inc. v. Peoples Republic of Bangladesh, 572 F. Supp. 79, 85 (D. Or. 1983).

[29] 806 F.2d 344 (2d Cir. 1987) (*Marcos 1*).

[30] 806 F.2d at 356–357.

[31] 806 F.2d at 359.

[32] *Id.*

[33] 818 F.2d 1473 (9th Cir. 1988) (*Marcos II*).

state doctrine precluded judicial review. The Court rejected the view that the Marcos's activities were private and asserted that governmental actions fall under the act of state doctrine even if illegal and regardless of whether the ruling power is lawful and recognized.[34] The acts of governmental officials that display sovereign power are inherently public and, therefore, any challenge to them in an American court necessarily falls within the act of state doctrine.[35] In addition to the Marcos's acts being found public, the Court also concluded that Marcos could invoke the act of state doctrine as a defense because a United States pronouncement of the legality of his actions could interfere with foreign relations with the Philippines.[36]

Unlike the Second Circuit action, the Ninth Circuit suit did not seek the recovery of specific property but rather of all wealth allegedly obtained by the Marcos's through theft, fraud, expropriation, and an enterprise engaged in a pattern of racketeering activity in violation of the Racketeer Influenced and Corrupt Organizations Act (RICO).[37] While the Second Circuit action sought to freeze New York property exclusively, the Ninth Circuit case sought to freeze and return property located throughout the world.[38] And although the district court granted plaintiffs' request for a preliminary injunction to freeze the property, this was quickly overruled by the Ninth Circuit on the ground that the act of state doctrine precluded plaintiffs' claim.[39]

The Ninth Circuit opinion was widely criticized by reviewers many of whom felt that the two cases were virtually indistinguishable and could not understand why the Court did not follow the path charted by the Second Circuit by disallowing defendant Marcos from invoking the act of state doctrine as a defense.[40] It has even been suggested that the Ninth Circuit's application of the act of state doctrine is indicative of the Court's confused view of the issue.[41] This confusion is no more apparent than in the following statement:

---

[34] *Id.*, at 1483 (citing Banco de Espana v. Federal Reserve Bank, 114 F.2d 438, 444 (2d Cir. 1940).

[35] See J. Meagher, 'Act of State and Sovereign Immunity: The Marcos Cases,' *Harv. Int'l L.J.*, 29, 129 (1988).

[36] 818 F.2d at 1485.

[37] 818 F.2d at 1475–1477.

[38] *Id.*, at 1476.

[39] *Id.*, at 1490.

[40] See A Robitaille, 'The Marcos Cases: A Consideration of the Act of State Doctrine and the Pursuit of the Assets of Disposed Dictators,' *B.C. Third World L.J.*, 9, 83, 85 (1986); see also T. Sundack, 'Republic of Philippines v. Marcos: The Ninth Circuit Allows a Former Ruler to Invoke the Act of State Doctrine Against a Resisting Sovereign,' *Am.U.L.Rev.*, 38, 247 (1988); W. Ritter, 'International Relations-Act of State Doctrine-Marcos' Assets as Act of Philippine State,' *Suffolk Trans.L.J.*, 11, 510 (1988); D. Chu, 'Marcos Mania: The Crusade to Return Marcos' Billions to the Philippines Through the Federal Courts,' *Rutgers L.J.*, 18, 217 (1988).

[41] Robitaille, *supra* note 40.

> We cannot shut our eyes to the political realities that give rise to this litigation, nor to the potential effects of its conduct and resolution. Mr. Marcos and President Aquino represent only two of the competing political factions engaged in a struggle for control of the Philippines. While the struggle seems to be resolving itself in favor of President Aquino, this may not be the end of the matter. Only four years ago, the tables were turned, with Mr. Marcos in power and Mrs. Aquino and her husband in exile in the United States. While we are in no position to judge these things, we cannot rule out the possibility that the pendulum will swing again, or that some third force will prevail. What we can say with some certainty is that a pronouncement by our courts along the lines suggested by plaintiff would have a substantial effect on what may be a delicate political balance, as would a contrary pronouncement exonerating Mr. Marcos.[42]

The Court of Appeals appeared to have overlooked the fact that President Aquino had already been recognized by the United States as the head of state and government of the Philippines.[43] Second, although the Philippines was experiencing some internecine strife, there was no 'struggle' in the sense of a state of belligerency in which one faction was pitted against the other making the outcome uncertain. Third, as Judge Nelson pointed out in her dissent, 'it is not clear why the majority believes that such potential embarrassment in our relations with the [then] Philippine government if our courts were to shut the door to the Philippine's government request for adjudication of the claims.'[44] The majority chose to overlook the extant relationship between the Philippines and the United States speculating instead on future Philippine political conditions.

These criticisms aside, the Court's opinion also goes against established precedent, in particular the basic policies underlying the act of state doctrine. First, the Court of Appeals erroneously concluded that Marcos' illegal governmental activities were public and therefore beyond United States jurisdiction.[45] But United States courts have long recognized the distinction between a foreign official's public and private acts and that the act of state doctrine only protects official public actions.[46] The line between public and private acts was earlier demarcated in the case of Jimenez v. Aristeguieta, where the Fifth Circuit Court of Appeals recognized that a dictator is capable of engaging in private, unofficial acts.[47] The Jimenez Court held that former Venezuelan President Jimenez's crimes were acts committed for his private financial benefit, and were therefore not sovereign acts shielded by the act of state doctrine.[48] The acts complained of – embezzlement, fraud, and receipt of unlawfully obtained money – 'constituted common crimes committed by the Chief of State done in violation of his position and not in pursuance of it … They are as far from being an act of state as rape which

---

42 818 F.2d at 1486.

43 Robitaille, *supra* note 40, at 99.

44 *Id.*, at 100 (citing Marcos, 818 F.2d at 1496).

45 See Sundack, *supra* note 40, at 247.

46 *Id.*, at 248 (citing Marcos, 806 F.2d at 359).

47 *Id.*, at 249 (citing Jimenez v. Aristeguieta, 311 F.2d 547 (5th Cir. 1962)).

48 Jimenez, 311 F.2d at 557–558.

appellant concedes would not be an "Act of State."'[49] The Court implicitly articulated a benefit test by emphasizing that acts done for 'private financial benefit' are not immunized from judicial review by the act of state doctrine.[50] Furthermore, a sovereign's illegal activities are not public actions simply because they are related to governmental activities. Following Jimenez, it could be argued that Marcos was acting in furtherance of his own private interests when he expropriated property through official decrees and received commissions on government contracts.[51] He was therefore not entitled to the protection of the act of state defense.

Even if the Ninth Circuit was correct in holding that Marcos's crimes were public acts, the act of state doctrine would still have been inapplicable since Marcos's activities were not fully executed in the Philippines as some were carried out in the United States in violation of US law and public policy.[52] Marcos, for instance, attempted to hide the money he spoliated from the Philippines by purchasing real estate in the United States under an assumed name in violation of US law. Clearly, these illegal activities were reviewable by the Ninth Circuit. By refusing to adjudicate the legality of Marcos's activities, the Court of Appeals unwittingly validated his illegal actions. This position is inconsistent with precedent that requires a court to invalidate shocking acts of foreign governments affecting United States property.[53]

Finally, the Court of Appeals' statement that allowing Marcos to invoke the act of state doctrine prevents embarrassment to the United States executive branch and that tension between the Philippines and the United States may result from adjudication are *non sequitur*. In the first place, it was the Philippines government that brought the action against Marcos.[54] Second, it did not require a particular stretch of the imagination to divine that the Court's insistence on applying the act of state doctrine to protect Marcos would have been offensive to the Philippine government. It is difficult to see where the Court would have gone wrong had it ruled that adjudication of the validity of Marcos's illegal practices, such as the taking of bribes which is widely recognized as corrupt, was proper and would not interfere with US foreign relations.[55]

Reprise

In light of the foregoing analysis of case law, it would appear unlikely that even the most compassionate US court would be willing to serve as a forum to adjudicate

---

49 *Id.*, at 558.

50 *Id.*; see also Robitaille, *supra* note 40, at 92.

51 Sundack, *supra* note 40, at 249.

52 *Id.* at 250 (citing Marcos, 818 F.2d at 1476).

53 *Id.*, at 251 (citing Republic of Iraq v. First Nat'l City Bank, 353 F.2d 47 (2nd Cir. 1965).

54 Marcos, 818 F.2d at 1485–1486.

55 See Note, 'Prohibiting Foreign Bribes: Criminal Sanctions For Corporate Payments Abroad,' *Cornell Int'l L.J.*, 10, 122, 138 (1922).

Colony's attempts to recapture its wealth spoliated by Pangloss and his close associates. Under current practice, their actions do not conform to those that courts have exempted from the act of state's protection.[56] In sum: 1) The activities of a sitting or former sovereign that qualify as public acts are, regardless of their legality under the law of the State, protected under the act of state doctrine and, therefore, beyond the reach of US courts; 2) But if the activities are considered private acts for personal gain, the defense of act of state is no longer available; 3) A review of case law alleging spoliation of state wealth by high-ranking government officials reveals a very fine line between what courts will characterize as public or private activities. This increases the uncertainty in the outcome of any legal efforts to recover spoliated wealth, at least in US courts; and 4) To make acts of spoliation adjudicable and redressable in domestic US courts would require treating them as a violation of the law of nations. If treated as internationally prohibited conduct, States will therefore be under a duty to lend assistance in the recovery of spoliated funds anywhere in the world.

OTHER OBSTACLES TO RECOVERY OF ASSETS

The four primary steps in recovering spoliated assets are: 1) locating the assets; 2) linking those assets to inappropriate use of public funds; 3) restraining the assets; 4) actively retrieving them for repatriation.[57] The financial privacy laws of many

---

[56] War crimes and crimes against humanity have now been added to the list of acts for which the act of state doctrine is no longer available to bar claims. This development bodes well for the acts of indigenous spoliation that we argue should be given the same status as crimes against humanity as defined in the Draft Code of Crimes, the Rome Statute, and the Statutes of the International Tribunals for the former Yugoslavia and Rwanda. In Sarei v. Rio Tinto PLC, 221 F.Supp. 2d 1116 (C.D. Cal. 2002), the District Court for the Central District of California held that the act of state doctrine did not bar claims asserting war crimes and crimes against humanity based on the conduct of the Papua New Guinean military during a civil war. Plaintiffs were a class of Papua New Guineans permanent US residents who brought claims against Rio Tinto, PLC, a multinational mining consortium. Plaintiffs alleged that Rio Tinto's mining operations destroyed the environment, harmed the health of Papua New Guineans and was at the root of a ten-year civil war. The court held that orders given by military commanders that do not involve legitimate warfare are illegal acts committed during wartime and do not qualify as official acts of state.

[57] See D. Edelman, Remarks during the panel presentation 'Pursuing the Assets of Former Dictators,' at the *Proceedings of the 81st Annual Meeting of the American Society of International Law*, 394, 399–400 (1987) (Michael P. Malloy ed., 1990) [hereinafter 'Pursuing the Assets']. Ms. Edelman was a member of the legal team that represented the Haitian government in its attempt to recover the illegally acquired assets of the deposed President Jean-Claude Duvalier who was forced to flee Haiti on 7 February 1986.

Haiti is another impoverished country that managed to make its leader rich. Deposed dictator Jean-Claude 'Baby Doc' Duvalier and his wife fled to France in 1986, where they still flaunt an extravagant lifestyle. They reside in a rented villa on the sunny Riviera and

countries, and the various devices available to conceal the true identity of the beneficial interest or owner of the assets block efforts to locate assets in various foreign jurisdictions. The bank secrecy laws of 'safe havens,' principally Switzerland have been employed to effectively forestall any probing into spoliated funds.

Devices used to prevent identification of the true owner of assets include corporate veils, shell corporations, Liechtenstein foundations,[58] trusts, agents, and the attorney-client privilege. Even if assets can be located and legally restrained before they are dissipated, often difficulty arises in linking them to spoliated funds. Other obstacles to recovery of assets include a despoiled country's lack of funds to pursue protracted litigation in jurisdictions scattered all over the globe, the management of multiple cases in various jurisdictions, and obtaining jurisdiction and service over defendants that reside abroad. The focus here, however, is on bank secrecy laws.

Bank Secrecy Laws

While bank secrecy laws have been under intense international pressure to change,[59] they still remain the primary means for dictators and other high-ranking officials to hide spoliated assets. Banking secrecy simply means that the 'banks must keep secret any information about their clients regarding privacy and property, which they receive by practicing their business. This discretion applies to the banks' officers, employees and any other persons with a direct relation to the bank.'[60] These laws are firmly rooted in respect for an individual's privacy rights

---

tool about in a $121,000 Ferrari Testarossa. No one can say just how much wealth Baby Doc has to comfort him in exile. It is thought to be as high as $1 billion, though the 15 court cases filed up to now – forming a 17-volume dossier of 9,000 documents – accuse him of embezzling a mere $120 million. 'That's what can be proven so far,' says a lawyer for Strook & Strook & Lavan, the Haitian government's legal counsel.

See Hetzer, 'The Pols & Pariahs; Wealth That Leaves No Tracks,' *Fortune*, 12 October 1987, at 189.

[58] A Liechtenstein foundation provides almost absolute secrecy. The name of their beneficial owner (which may be an individual or a foreign corporation) appears only in the fiduciary agreement with a Liechtenstein lawyer, who protects the secrecy of his clients with his professional privilege. The foundation becomes a legal entity upon depositing the articles of foundation, which are not open to the public. The foundation is also exempt from publishing financial statements.

See Hoets & Zward, 'Swiss Bank Secrecy and the Marcos Affair,' *N.Y.L. Sch. J. Int'l & Comp. L.*, 9, 75, 82, n. 36 (1980) (citations omitted).

[59] See 'Swiss Banks Could Give Up Secrets,' *The Times*, 7 July 1990, at 23, col. 2; Tempest, 'Ex-Despots Can't Bank on the Swiss,' *The Los Angeles Times*, 31 January 1990, at 1, col. 1; and Zanker, 'Days Numbered for Secret Swiss Accounts?' *US News & World Report*, 21 May 1984, at 40.

[60] Honegger, 'Demystification of the Swiss Banking Secrecy and Illumination of the United States-Swiss Memorandum of Understanding,' *N.C.J. Int'l L. & Com. Reg.*, 9, 1, 1–2

and a belief in individual freedom. In Switzerland, as in other civil law countries, protection of privacy is deemed legally fundamental.[61]

Swiss Bank Secrecy Laws

Since Switzerland has historically been one of the most popular destinations for flight capital, an understanding of its bank secrecy regime will promote an understanding of how bank secrecy can be an obstacle to the recovery of spoliated wealth. Accordingly, we shall: 1) review the history of Swiss bank secrecy laws; 2) identify the sources of bank secrecy and any exceptions and limits to these laws; and 3) discuss recent legislation and how this has affected the Swiss banking tradition of secrecy.

History of Swiss bank secrecy laws Swiss law expresses a general commitment to the preservation and protection of the individual's right of privacy. This right of privacy is viewed as encompassing economic as well as purely personal affairs. Thus, Swiss concepts of personal property extend not only to such personal matters as relationships with physicians and lawyers, but also to personal economic affairs, such as relationships with bankers. The formal adoption of Article 47 of the Swiss Banking Act in 1934 and adoption of the predecessor of Swiss Penal Code Article 273 in 1935 emphasized the importance of these privacy rights by providing criminal sanctions for privacy violations.[62]

Both of these provisions were also adopted in order to protect individuals against the efforts of neighboring countries, particularly Nazi Germany, at finding out information that could be used against their own citizens and Swiss residents. It is important to remember that in the year the Banking Act was adopted – 1934 – foreign nations were attempting to confiscate Jewish property. Foreign agents were sent into Switzerland to find bank accounts of Jews and other dissidents. Jews facing expropriation by the Nazis hid assets in Swiss banks in the 1930s, as did Hungarians faced with the Soviet takeover a decade later.[63]

While banking, money changing, and finance are as old as civilization, the practice of bank secrecy developed in recent centuries. Modern bank secrecy evolved after World War I when hyperinflation and exchange controls forced prudent individuals to hold assets outside of their home nations. Other nations attempted to control their economies with restrictive monetary practices that enhanced the appeal of other more stable and salubrious banking climes. The first

(1983).

61 See for example, Meyer, 'Swiss Banking Secrecy and Its Legal Implications in the United States,' *New Eng. L. Rev.*, 4, 18, 20–21 (1978) (noting that personality rights also include a person's physical and intellectual integrity, his liberty of action, his legal capacity, and his own name).

62 Lutz Krauskopf, 'Regents Lectures Comments on Switzerland's Insider Trading, Money Laundering, and Banking Secrecy Laws,' *Int. Tax and Bus. Law.*, 9, 277, 293 (1990) Schweizerisches Bankengesetz [Bankg] Art. 47 (Switz.) & STGB Art. 273.

63 *Id.*

major challenge to the new bank secrecy order occurred during this post-war economic upheaval when in 1933, the Nazis published regulations requiring all German nationals to declare assets held outside of Germany. The penalty for noncompliance was the death sentence. The execution of three Germans one year later prompted the Swiss government to codify what until then had only been an unofficial secrecy practice among Swiss bankers. The new law provided for strong criminal penalties for violations.[64]

The first international counter-attack against the Swiss law, however, came not from Germany but from the United States. When the Germans invaded Poland, the Swiss kept their bank assets in US financial institutions. After the fall of France, the Swiss, fearing an invasion, physically moved their national gold supply to New York. In mid 1941, US government officials became convinced that Nazis were hiding their wealth in Swiss deposit accounts. Based on the personal jurisdiction over the Swiss branches located in the United States, the government attempted to obtain account holder names from the branches, only to discover that the holdings were in the names of the banks and not the clients. In response, the US government blocked the expatriation of all Swiss assets and gold reserves. This plenary use of personal jurisdiction over both persons and property would later be repeated to obtain the secret bank information the United States desired.[65]

After World War II, the reasons for bank secrecy expanded. Currency and other government economic controls remained after the war while the expansion of socialism and, concomitantly, heavy income taxes drove money to secrecy havens. Criminal tax statutes, a new prosecutorial weapon, increased investors' desires for secret locales to hide assets from the prying eyes of their governments. The growth of international crime also facilitated the growth of banking centers that protected bank customers' identities and assets. Many other small nations in addition to Switzerland, given this currency flight and their own lack of hard currency, catered to such customers with favorable bank secrecy laws.[66]

While media articles on topics like insider trading, or the laundering of drug money, claim or at least give the impression that the inviolability of banking secrecy and the protection it provides is being undermined, the fact of the matter is that the legal basis for banking secrecy in Switzerland has remained virtually unchanged since World War II. It is and will remain the protection of privacy as part of an individual's rights. In Switzerland, it is an especially important tradition that the private sphere, which is to be safeguarded, also covers financial transactions and matters relating to personal wealth. Unfortunately, it is because of this tradition that Switzerland has been made the financial home of tax evaders,

---

[64] C. Todd Jones, 'Compulsion Over Comity: The United States' Assault on Foreign Bank Secrecy,' *Nw. J. Int. Law & Bus.*, 12, 454, 455 (1992).

[65] *Id.*, at 455–456, See also Chambost, *Bank Accounts*, 5, 6–7 (1983). See for example, In re Sealed Case, 825 F.2d 494, 495 (D.C. Cir.), *cert. denied sub. nom.*, 484 US 963 (1987).

In Re Marc Rich & Co., 707 F.2d 663 (2d Cir.), *cert. denied*, 463 US 1215 (1983); In Re Grand Jury Proceedings, United States v. Field, 532 F. 2d 404, 405 (5th Cir.) *cert. denied*, 429 US 940 (1976).

[66] *Id.*, at 456.

money launderers and corrupt dictators ranging from Haiti's Jean-Claude 'Baby Doc' Duvalier to Ferdinand Marcos of the Philippines.[67]

A BIRD'S-EYE VIEW OF SWISS BANKING SECRECY

Bank Secrecy Statutes

Swiss Banking Law of 1934 – Article 47 of the Swiss Penal Code

Switzerland's banking secrecy is protected by the Swiss Penal code. The Swiss Banking Law of 1934 codified and reinforced the bank secrecy requirement. Article 47 of the 1934 Banking Law states:

> (1) Anyone who, in his capacity as an officer or employee of a bank, or an auditor or his employee, or as a member of the Banking Commission or as an officer or employee of its Board, violates his duty of confidentiality or his professional rule of conduct of confidentiality, or anyone who induces or attempts to induce a person to commit any such offense, shall be subject to a fine of up to 50,000 Swiss francs [approximately US $35,000] or to imprisonment for up to six months.
> (2) If an offender of section (1) acted negligently, he shall be subject to a fine of up to 30,000 Swiss francs [approximately US $35,000].
> (3) The violation of the obligation of confidentiality remains punishable even after the assignment or employment of the violator has terminated, or where the person charged with the obligation of confidentiality no longer engages in his profession.
> (4) The provisions of federal and cantonal law providing for the obligation to report to the authorities and to give evidence in legal proceedings are reserved.[68]

This Article establishes specific duties and provides severe penal sanctions for bankers, their employees, and government inspectors who disclose any information obtained in the course of a professional relationship of a client without the customer's consent or without a decision order disclosure by a Swiss cantonal or federal authority. Secret information required by foreign authorities also falls within the scope of Article 47. Thus, bank officials would have to violate the Swiss Banking Act and be subject to prosecution in order to disclose the information requested, unless they first obtain customer consent or an official order requiring disclosure.[69] Furthermore, under Article 47, the banker's duty of confidentiality is defined very broadly. The duty includes the confidentiality of the customer's name; the fact of the banker's relationship with the customer; the type of account and transactions; any information given by the customer concerning his financial situation, including his relationship with other banks; and any information

---

[67] Steven Mufson, 'Swiss to End Anonymous Bank Accounts 57 Year Tradition Provided Haven for Dictators and Drug Dealers,' *Washington Post*, 4 May 1991.

[68] Krauskopf, *supra* note 62, at 294. See also Banking Art. 47.

[69] *Id.*

concerning the bank's own transactions with the customer.[70] It is also clear that Article 47 protects the privacy interests of any bank customer, whether or not he is a Swiss citizen or resident. In addition, Article 47 is an *ex officio* offense, which means that prosecution may take place without there being a complaint filed by an injured party. The *ex officio* nature of the offense indicates the broad purpose of the statute, which is the protection of banking secrecy against any kind of intrusion. So too, the seriousness of purpose is reinforced by the fact that Article 47 provides that even negligent disclosures are punishable.[71]

In sum, Article 47 of the Swiss Banking Law of 1934 while setting forth the specific duties for bankers, their employees, and government inspectors also criminalizes any disclosure of information obtained in the course of a professional relationship with the bank except as provided by law. However, absolute secrecy does not exist because banks must furnish pertinent information when the higher interest of the public or the state is involved, particularly in cases defined as crimes under Swiss law.[72]

Article 273: Economic Information in the Interest of a Foreign Country

Disclosure of confidential information could also involve the provisions of Article 273 of the Swiss Penal Code, which makes it a crime for anyone to make available secret business information to a foreign authority or to its agents. This Article also takes the form of a blanket rule against disclosure, subject only to the consent and official direction exceptions. Article 273 reads as follows:

> Any person who seeks to discover a manufacturing or business secret with a view to making it available to a foreign official or private organization or to a foreign private enterprise or to the agents thereof or any person who makes available a manufacturing or business secret to a foreign official or private enterprise or to the agents thereof shall be punished by imprisonment or in serious cases to reclusion. The judge may, in addition, impose a fine.[73]

Interpreting this statute as early as 1959, the Swiss Federal Supreme Court, in the Blunier case, stated that the Article does not protect private interests alone, but also protects the interest of the state in defending persons under its territorial sovereignty. Thus, for purposes of the Article, it does not matter by what means the defendant acquires knowledge of the secret; Article 273 is triggered in any event.[74]

Much like Article 47, Article 273 establishes an *ex officio* offense. Again the *ex*

---

70 *Id.*

71 *Id.*

72 Jones, *supra* note 64, at 562. See also Bundesgesetz uber die Banken and Sparkasses of 8 November 1934 (Banking Law of 1934) implemented in Verordnung of 17 May 1972 (Ordinance) and Vollziehungsverordnung of 30 August 1961 (Implementing Ordinance).

73 Krauskopf, *supra* note 62, at 295. See STGB Art. 273.

74 *Id.* See also Judgment of 3 July 1959, Bundesgericht, Switz., 85 Entscheidungen des Schweizerischen Bundesgerichts [BGE] IV 139 (Highest Court, Criminal Case).

officio nature of the offense indicates its serious purpose, namely the protection of Swiss sovereignty against intrusions by foreign agencies seeking to get secret information. Reinforcing this point, Article 273 is part of the thirteenth title of the Swiss Penal Code, entitled 'Crimes Against the State and National Defense.'[75] Closely following the article's language and purpose, the Federal Supreme Court in the Brugger case held that Article 273 prohibited false reports of investments in Switzerland given to German foreign exchange control agents. The court held that this disclosure not only violated privacy interests but was a violation of Swiss territorial sovereignty as well.[76]

In the Bodmer case, the Federal Supreme Court went on to define a 'secret' within the meaning of the predecessor of Article 273 of the Penal Code. According to the Federal Supreme Court,

> The term 'business secret,' in this connection, is not understood in a narrow sense, merely as an operating secret of an economic enterprise; but it includes any data of economic life, provided there is a legitimate interest in keeping the secret. Consequently, the term may also include relations and transactions of private economy concerning property and income.[77]

It is well established in Swiss law that banking information is regarded as a business secret within the meaning of Article 273. The article thus prohibits anyone from transmitting confidential banking information to a private or official foreign organization. The penalty is severe – imprisonment for a period up to twenty years.[78]

Civil Tort and Contract Liability

Violations of a client's confidences by a bank would also subject it and its officials to civil liability under tort and contract theories. Both of these theories involve the violation of the client's privacy rights. The two theories do differ, however, with reference to some specifics of the right and the remedy.[79] Swiss tort law recognizes an individual's right to privacy, which includes an intangible property right in the secrecy of financial affairs. Under Article 28 of the Swiss Civil Code, anyone wrongfully injured in his personal affairs may sue for injunctive relief, as well as for monetary damages. Article 28 provides that '[w]hoever suffers unlawful harm in his personal interests may bring an action for an injunction. An action for damages or for payment of a sum of money as compensation may be brought only in the cases stated in the statute.' The statutes referred to in Article 28, on which an

---

75 Krauskopf, *supra* note 62, at 295.

76 *Id.* See also Judgment of 6 July 1945, Bundesgericht, Switz., 71 BGE IV 217 (Highest Court, Criminal Case).

77 *Id.* See also, Judgment of 20 November 1939, Bundesgericht, Switz., 65 BGE 1 330 (Highest Court, Administrative and Constitutional Case).

78 *Id.*, at 296.

79 *Id.*

action for damages or monetary compensation could be based, are Articles 41 and 49 of the Swiss Code of Obligations. Article 41 allows any person to sue for damages another who, either intentionally or negligently, causes him harm. Article 49 gives a person wrongfully injured in his personal affairs the general right to sue for damages.[80]

In addition to the above forms of tort liability, a Swiss bank's breach of customer confidentiality also establishes a claim for monetary damages based on contract theory. Under Swiss law, an agency relationship arises between the bank and the customer. This relationship is governed by the Swiss Code of Obligations, particularly Article 97. In order to meet the requirements of the Code, the banker must maintain secrecy in order to fulfill his 'contract' with the customer. Otherwise, the banker would be liable to the customer under contract theory for monetary damages resulting from the contractual breach.[81]

Therefore, a bank customer whose secrets have been revealed can sue the bank for civil damages under Article 28 of the Swiss Civil Code and under Articles 41, 49, and 97 of the Swiss Code of Obligations. These sections encompass both contract and tort theories of liability and differ to some degree in the right and remedy afforded to the customer. They all reflect, however, the seriousness with which the Swiss approach the topic of banking secrecy.[82]

Administrative Sanctions

In addition to criminal and civil sanctions, disclosures of a customer's confidences would expose a bank to administrative sanctions imposed by the Federal Banking Commission. Under the Swiss Banking Act, particularly Articles 2, 23(3), and 23(5), the sanctions could include a possible revocation of the bank's authority to do business. Thus, a knowledge of the administrative sanctions is important to an understanding of the overall framework of Swiss bank secrecy.[83]

Article 23(3) of the Swiss Banking Act authorizes the Federal Banking Commission to take a number of actions that may seem appropriate in light of the particular circumstances at hand. Revocation of banking authority is specifically provided for by Article 23(5), paragraph 1, of the Swiss Banking Act, which provides that 'the Banking Commission shall withdraw a bank's permit to do business in Switzerland when the conditions required for the business are not met or a serious violation of its legal obligations has been committed by the bank.'[84] The 'obligation' of preserving confidences is one of the important legal duties of a bank as defined by Article 47 of the Swiss Banking Act. Thus, the Federal Banking Commission may withdraw the authority to do business from any bank that fails to preserve its customers secrets, particularly if disclosure constitutes a 'serious

---

80 *Id.* See also ZGB Art. 28; Schweizerisches Obligationenrecht [OR] Art. 41, 49 (Switz.).

81 *Id.* OR Art. 97.

82 *Id.* See also Banking Art. 2, 23(3), 23(5).

83 *Id.*, at 297; See also Banking Art. 23(5).

84 *Id.* See also Banking Art. 47.

violation' of the bank's obligations.[85]

The Federal Banking Commission could also impose other administrative sanctions for violation of bank secrecy obligations. For example, it could order a Bank to replace or suspend an executive convicted of violating banking secrecy. Thus, the Federal Banking Commission enjoys great flexibility in imposing sanctions designed to enforce the Swiss banking regime. The Federal Banking Commission, with these extraordinary powers and the will to use them, reinforces the criminal and civil mechanisms for the enforcement of Swiss banking secrecy.[86]

Exceptions to Swiss Banking Secrecy

The secrecy of bank accounts is not absolute. It can be lifted. There are a number of cases when banking secrets can be disclosed. Such exceptions to the general secrecy rule include client waiver or criminal proceedings against the client or a third party, when a Swiss magistrate or other official issues an order to this effect. Generally, such an order will not be given in civil proceedings. Under Swiss law, the following circumstances may relieve a bank of its obligation to preserve customer confidences as is protected by the foregoing statutes.

Customer Consent

Consent to disclosure by the customer generally relieves a bank of its secrecy obligation. Since secrecy is a right of the customer, not the bank; it is, in that respect, similar to the attorney-client privilege. Banks have no discretion as to whether to keep or disclose the secret. This is true because the secret is seen under Swiss law as belonging to the customer, not to the bank. Consent therefore, relieves a bank of both civil and criminal liability for disclosure. However, while a customer's written consent to disclosure will protect a bank against criminal penalties under Article 47 of the Swiss Penal Code and against private civil liability, it is not clear that consent will relieve the obligation of secrecy imposed by Article 273 of the Swiss Penal Code. To reiterate, Article 273 is aimed at the protection of Swiss sovereign interests from foreign encroachments, rather than the mere protection of individual interests. It is, therefore, unclear whether an individual can and should be able to consent to a waiver of these structural interests as well as his individual interests.[87] Finally, customer consent must be evidenced by an affirmative act. In the absence of an affirmative act, like a written waiver, the confidentiality of the customer's affairs must be respected and maintained.[88]

Disclosure Required by Certain Swiss Authorities

In the absence of affirmative consent, a bank may generally disclose the

85 *Id.*
86 *Id.*
87 *Id.*, at 298.
88 *Id.*

customer's secrets only pursuant to an order by proper Swiss authorities. This requirement is codified in the fourth paragraph of Article 47 of the Swiss Penal Code, which subjects a bank's obligation to preserve secrets to 'the provision of federal and cantonal law providing for the obligation to report to its authorities and give evidence in legal proceedings.'[89] The proper way for a foreign court or agency to request evidence located in Switzerland is by sending a request for mutual assistance in the form of 'letters rogatory' to the competent Swiss authority. Swiss law regards any compulsory attempt to secure evidence without pursuing official Swiss assistance as an intrusion upon Swiss sovereignty. Still, this exception to the general rule of confidentiality in banking relationships is limited and emphasizes again the importance of the policy reflected in the general rule.[90]

In criminal proceedings, the banking secrecy does not apply. The federal and cantonal penal procedures do not provide secrecy. This obligation to disclose the banking secrecy exists towards judges, prosecutors, attorneys, but not the police. On the other hand, the banking secrecy will not generally be disclosed in most civil proceedings. In fact, Swiss law regarding civil disclosure is, at best, mixed. In Switzerland's federal domain, judges decide on a case-by-case basis whether or not to set aside banking secrecy. Generally, secrecy is preserved by the federal judiciary. Moreover, in six cantons, the rules are similar to the federal civil procedures. Beyond this, eight cantons protect banking secrecy absolutely, while twelve other cantons do not recognize the banker's right to refuse disclosure at all.[91]

BILATERAL AND MULTILATERAL AGREEMENTS

Treaty for Mutual Assistance in Criminal Matters

The Origins of Mutual Assistance and Organized Crime

There have been tremendous efforts between the Swiss and the United States to achieve a method for increased cooperation in securing the disclosure of financial information, including the identity of investors and bank reports. The Swiss system, drawn from civil law origins, differs dramatically in its approach to these issues, from the Anglo-American common law tradition. For instance, under the Swiss model, the gathering of evidence is always an official act to be undertaken by the proper authorities. Also, plea bargaining does not fit neatly into the Swiss notion of the rule of law ('Rechstaatlichkeit').[92] Therefore, the United States and Switzerland started negotiating bilateral treaties that were designed to effectuate a better system of obtaining evidence and piercing bank secrecy.

Historically, extradition has been the most dramatic aspect of mutual

---

89 *Id.* See also Banking Art. 47.

90 *Id.*

91 *Id.*, at 298–299.

92 *Id.*, at 291.

assistance, even though the process involves other elements, such as transfer of proceedings and prisoner exchanges. Interestingly, extradition was originally regarded as a neutral form of foreign policy and mainly involved the extradition of political offenders, adventurers, or opponents back to the requesting state. Similarly, the opposite of extradition, political asylum, was regarded as an additional means of foreign policy. Residuals of these ideas can be found today in many countries, whose governments may deny extraditions or other forms of cooperation for political reasons. Mutual assistance was originally regarded as merely involving extradition and not until after World War II did it evolve into a separate field of international cooperation. The Treaty between Switzerland and the United States in 1973 and Swiss Law on Mutual Assistance in Criminal Matters in 1981 are examples of this evolution.

Today, mutual assistance has become more important than extradition in total cases as well as in the effect of specific cases. The reason for this may be found in the continually expanding globalization of trade and markets of all types, including the illegal markets for drugs, weapons, and dubious money transactions. Since much of this trade is undertaken by organized groups, mutual assistance efforts often involve special provisions against organized crime. For example, Switzerland and the US agreed to assist each other in the fight against organized crime. Therefore, as a consequence, their first treaty contained a complete chapter of provisions dealing only with organized crime. However, since organized crime and insider trading are the main focus of such agreements, they have not been very successful in penetrating Swiss bank secrecy laws.[93]

Treaty for Mutual Assistance in Criminal Matters

In 1977, the Treaty for Mutual Legal Assistance in Criminal Matters (MLAT) between the United States and Switzerland became effective.[94] The MLAT provides for 'cooperation between the law enforcement authorities of the United States and Switzerland in connection with investigations or court proceedings involving criminal offenses.' This cooperation includes the '[p]roduc[tion] and authentica[tion] of [bank] records.' Because the MLAT is a binding international agreement, the United States and Switzerland each have an obligation to furnish each other 'mutual assistance' in investigations and the return of property obtained through crimes when all disclosure requirements of the MLAT are met.[95] The

---

[93] *Id.*

[94] Jill Elizabeth Asch, 'Comment Bank Secrecy: A Barrier To The Prosecution of Insider Trading,' *Emory Int'l L.Rev.*, 4, 185 (1990). See also 25 May 1973, United States-Switzerland 27 UST 2019, TIAS 8302 (entered into force 23 January 1977).

[95] Singh, 'Nowhere to Hide: Judicial Assistance In Piercing the Veil of Swiss Banking Secrecy,' *Boston U.L.Rev.*, 71, 847 (1991); Breaches of bank secrecy are prohibited under both Swiss civil and criminal law. *Schweizerisches Strafgesetzbuch*, Code Penal Suisse, Codice Penal Svizerro, Art. 47, 273; see also Catherine F. Donohue, 'Swiss Law Prohibiting Insider Trading: Its Impact on Switzerland and the United States,' *Brooklyn J. Int'l L.*, 16, 379, 380–385 (1990).

MLAT establishes general guidelines to promote increased cooperation between the Swiss and the United States in securing the disclosure of financial information, including the identity of investors and bank reports. Although a duty to disclose information under a treaty should provide an effective method for penetrating Swiss bank secrecy laws, the treaty does not specifically include provisions mitigating bank secrecy. Instead, the treaty is designed to provide bilateral assistance in obtaining information in criminal matters. The MLAT establishes a procedure to provide information on request. The bodies that handle the requests are the United States Department of Justice and the Swiss Department of Justice and Police.

However, there are limitations on the effectiveness of the MLAT. For example, the MLAT is not applicable where the offense prosecuted is of a political, military, tax or antitrust nature. Furthermore, when the request for assistance implies measures of coercion, Switzerland will assist the United States only if the acts described in the request contain the elements of an offense that would be punishable under the law in Switzerland if the offense were committed within its jurisdiction and if it is listed in the schedule annexed to the treaty or is described in item 26 of the schedule. A schedule of the offenses for which measures of coercion may be taken is annexed to the treaty. Previously, the Securities and Exchange Commission (SEC) and the United States courts had to persuade the Swiss government that insider trading involved one of the activities enumerated in the Schedule of Offenses attached to the MLAT. It is worth noting that Switzerland did not have a general law prohibiting insider trading until 1987. Although insider trading is not included in the Schedule of Offenses, fraud is included, and information has been disclosed by claiming fraudulent violations.[96]

However, in the case of an offense not listed in the schedule, the central authority of the requested state (in Switzerland the Federal Police Department) shall determine whether the importance of the offense justifies the use of compulsory measures. Furthermore, differences in technical designation and constituent elements added to establish jurisdiction can be ignored. If any of the conditions mentioned above have not been met, assistance can still be granted but without the use of compulsory measures. The MLAT is designed to provide broad bilateral assistance in obtaining information in criminal matters, but does not specifically include provisions mitigating bank secrecy. Instead, nations limit the use of information to the purpose in the assistance request in order to prevent circumvention of the dual criminality requirement. Another limitation on the effectiveness of the MLAT is that the granting state may refuse to provide assistance if it will prejudice essential interests of the requesting state.

Furthermore, in practice MLAT has proved ineffective in obtaining evidence. For instance, in SEC v. Banca Della Svizzera Italiana the SEC had to invoke judicial intervention. In that case, Banca Della Svizzera Italiana (BSI) purchased call options for the common stock as well as the underlying common stock of St. Joe Minerals for its principals. These purchases were made the day before the

---

96 Asch, *supra* note 94, at 186.

announcement of Seagrams' proposed tender offer for all the outstanding shares of St. Joe Minerals and resulted in a profit just short of two million dollars. Because of the undue activity in the options market the SEC investigated, and as a result of its findings, brought suit. After eight months of unsuccessfully trying to obtain the identity of the persons involved in the purchases, the SEC moved for an appropriate order while the bank argued in defense that disclosure would violate Swiss bank secrecy laws and civil and criminal liability could be imposed against the bank. The federal district court rejected the bank's defense and granted the SEC's motion and ordered the bank to disclose the identity of the customer or suffer substantial monetary sanctions. The bank obtained a waiver from its customers, then complied with the judicial order and produced the requested information. In reaching the decision to grant the order to compel discovery, Judge Pollack balanced the interests at stake and considered the resisting party's purported good faith.

The case of Unknown Purchasers of the Common Stock and Call Options of Santa Fe is a further example of the Treaty's inadequacy. In that case, documents and testimony pertaining to 3,000 option contracts and 27,000 shares of underlying stock of Santa Fe International Corporation were requested under the 1977 Treaty. The initial request for assistance was filed on 22 March 1982, and denied by the Swiss Federal Tribunal on 26 May 1984. However, the SEC only received the names of the unknown purchasers because the request granted by the Swiss Federal Tribunal was appealed to several political bodies with jurisdiction over the matter and they prevented the Commission from obtaining further documentary evidence with respect to the purchaser.[97]

Swiss Memorandum of Understanding

As a result of SEC frustration and Swiss complaints, the United States and Switzerland negotiated another bilateral agreement following negotiations between the Swiss Bankers Association ('SBA') and the SEC. On 31 August 1982, the United States and Switzerland signed the Swiss Memorandum of Understanding to Establish Mutually Acceptable Means for Improving International Law Enforcement Cooperation in the field of Insider Trading ('MOU'). The 1982 MOU demonstrated the recognition by both countries of the need for a consensus on bank secrecy laws and insider trading investigations.[98] MOU was created to facilitate the use of the 1977 treaty through creation of a procedure for assistance when investigations are not covered by the MLAT. The first section contains an 'Exchange of Opinions' regarding the MLAT, in which parties agree that insider trading could constitute fraud, unfaithful management or violations of business

---

97 *Id.* See also SEC v. Banca Della Svizzera Italiana 92 FRD 111 (SDNY 1981).; The sanctions were a $550,000 per day fine and a ban on trading in the United States securities market; see also Unknown Purchasers of the Common Stock and Call Options of Santa Fe 81 Civ 6533 (SDNY 1981).

98 *Id.* See also 22 ILM at 1 (1983) and 14 Sec. Reg. & L. Rep. (BNA) 1737 (8 October 1982).

secrets under the Swiss Penal Code therefore making assistance under the treaty possible. The second part of MOU was a private agreement among the SBA, which recognized that the SEC might not always be able to prove violations of the Swiss Penal Code, and thus they created the Commission of Enquiry to determine whether the SEC's requests are reasonable.[99]

When the 1982 MOU was signed, it was agreed that once insider trading became illegal in Switzerland, the MOU would cease operation. In November of 1987, the United States and Switzerland exchanged Diplomatic Notes to provide that, in insider trading cases, the MLAT would be utilized. There were limitations to the 1982 MOU particularly because it is not legally binding on either government and therefore subject to breach at any time. Also, the 1982 MOU only applied to those banks that signed the agreement. Another restriction of the 1982 MOU was that it only applied to securities fraud in connection with acquisitions and business combinations.[100] Consequently, a second Memorandum of Understanding was exchanged in 1987, which was designed to improve the exchange of information in investigations of insider trading, money laundering and other crimes. This 1987 Memorandum provides procedures for collecting information utilizing the MLAT treaty rather than the use of unilateral measures by the United States. The agreement commits Switzerland to quicker response in its handling of requests by the United States and establishes a notification system for requests.[101]

Federal Law on Mutual Legal Assistance in Criminal Matters

On 1 January 1983, the Swiss Federal Law on Mutual Legal Assistance in Criminal Matters (MLACM) entered into force.[102] The main feature of the law was to spell out for the first time that international assistance is to be made available in cases of tax fraud offenses. All countries, including those that have entered into a treaty with Switzerland, may request the assistance of the Swiss authorities through the

---

99 *Id.* See also Senate Report of the Committee on Banking, Housing, and Urban Affairs Rep. No. 100–461 regarding S. 2544 (8 August 1988) at 5 reprinted in *Fed. Sec. L. Rep. (CCH)* #1300 (24 August 1988).

100 *Id.*

101 *Id.*

102 The MLACM was amended on 1 February 1997 to expedite proceedings on requests for legal assistance and to simplify conflicting cantonal procedural laws. Three major changes have resulted from the 1997 revisions. First, the number of legal remedies originally offered in the old version, and which contributed in protracting proceedings, has now been reduced. Second, the revised law contains a nationwide standardized procedural law regarding legal assistance procedures. Finally, it has identified a centralized competent authority for the execution of requests for Swiss legal assistance. See MLACM, Arts. 78, para. 2 to 79; see also Mark Pieth, Working Paper: Switzerland's International Mutual Legal Assistance in Criminal Matters. Available at http://www.transparency.org/working_papers (last visited 4 April 2005) [hereinafter 'Pieth'].

Act. However, Swiss cooperation is discretionary.[103] The Act also incorporates another fundamental principle derived from Switzerland's internal laws: the refusal to provide any assistance when the acts prosecuted constitute a tax evasion offense or a violation of the regulation concerning the monetary, commercial, or economic policy of the foreign state.[104]

MLACM contains various provisions on the delicate issue of the protection of the private sphere. Article 9 of the Act refers to the Swiss provisions concerning the right to refuse to testify. Accordingly, in a criminal pursuit, priests, lawyers, and doctors have the right to refuse to testify. Other persons, bankers for example, are obliged to testify and to produce documents if required. Lastly, Switzerland has always required that the use of the evidence and information obtained through the procedure of cooperation be limited to the prosecution of the offense upon which the assistance was granted.[105]

Four different kinds of mutual legal assistance are available to a requesting state under the MLACM. These are: (1) extradition of the accused to the requesting state for the purpose of prosecution or execution in respect of a criminal offense under jurisdiction in both the requesting state and Switzerland;[106] (2) transmission of information to foreign authorities as well as several procedural and other official acts thought to be of importance to the foreign proceedings or the production of criminal profits (for example, delivery of documents, taking of evidence, search of persons and places, release of objects and values for the purpose of seizure in the requesting state, etc.);[107] (3) substitutional administration of criminal justice on behalf of the requesting state;[108] and (4) the recognition and enforcement of foreign judgments.[109]

The Swiss Federal law is available to any states that ask for it even if there is no bilateral treaty on mutual legal assistance in force between Switzerland and the state requesting Swiss assistance. Unilateral legal assistance will be provided only if the facts subject to the foreign criminal procedure satisfy the requirement of dual criminality, that is, the offense qualifies as a crime in both the requesting state and under Swiss law. The principle of dual criminality is of particular importance in the context of indigenous spoliation because Swiss penal law provides no sanctions for the bribery of foreign public officials. Until this situation changes, probably when Switzerland ratifies the OECD Convention on Combating Bribery of Foreign Public Officials in International Business Transactions, an expert on the Swiss legal assistance law has advised that 'if third countries file requests for legal assistance in the scope of criminal procedures dealing with the bribery of foreign public officials, the demanded acts must not include compulsory measures since

---

103 Nicolas Pierard & Nicolas Killen, 'Switzerland,' *Int'l. Law*, 26, 545, 556 (1992). See also Federal Act on Assistance in Criminal Matters, RS 351.1 (1981).

104 *Id.*

105 *Id.*, at 556–557.

106 MLACM, Part 2, Arts. 32–62.

107 *Id.*, Part 3, Arts. 63–80q.

108 *Id.*, Part 4, Arts. 85–93.

109 *Id.*, Part 5, Arts. 94–108.

the requirement of dual criminality is not met.'[110] In addition to satisfying the principle of dual criminality, the offense for which legal assistance is being sought must also satisfy the principle of speciality as well as the *non bis in idem* rule. These two principles protect the due process rights of the accused.

The principle of speciality guarantees to the accused for whom legal assistance is sought, usually by way of extradition, that he will be prosecuted in the requesting state, with the aid of mutual legal assistance provided by Swiss authorities, only for the exact offense referred to in the request for assistance.[111] An accused can, however, waive the protection provided by the principle of speciality.[112] To protect an accused from being prosecuted or punished twice for the same offense in violation of the non bis in idem rule, Swiss authorities can refuse a request for legal assistance if the accused remains in Switzerland and if there is already a procedure against him pending in Switzerland involving the same acts referred to in the request for legal assistance.[113]

The Swiss law on mutual judicial assistance was put to the test in December 1999 when the successor government in Nigeria filed a formal request with the Swiss Federal Office for Police Matters (FOP)[114] in connection with the former head of state, Sani Abacha, and his close associates. These individuals were suspected of having systematically plundered the Nigerian Central Bank over a period of years and depositing some of the funds with several Swiss banks. The Nigerian government request was for the surrender of bank documents, the freezing of the Abacha assets and their eventual repatriation to Nigeria. About $500 million of these assets were frozen after preliminary investigations by the FOP; $450 million of which was subsequently ruled to be the proceeds of crime and therefore subject to repatriation to Nigeria.[115]

---

110 See Pieth, *supra* note 102, at ¶33.

111 MLACM, Art. 67.

112 *Id.*, Art. 38, para. 2 lit.

113 *Id.*, Art. 66.

114 Under the MLACM, requests for judicial assistance in criminal matters first go to the FOP where a summary evaluation is made. If a request passes this preliminary hurdle, it is then forwarded to the competent federal or cantonal (there are 26 cantons) authority for a second screening on the merits of the material requirements. The screening is followed by a summary decision on the opening of a requested legal assistance procedure. The next stage is the final determination deciding on the admissibility and the extent of the legal assistance act is pronounced. It is at this stage only that appeal can be heard. See MLACM, Art. 78, para. 2; see also Pieth, *supra* note 102.

115 For a chronology of the Abacha case as it worked its way through the Swiss judicial system, see the various press releases put out by the Federal office of Justice. Available at http://www.ofj.admin.ch/themen/presscom (last visited 4 April 2005).

Recent Regulatory Developments

New Anti-Money Laundering Provisions

Although not part of the European Union (EU), Switzerland has taken the lead in combating money laundering. Swiss financial institutions were notorious havens for criminals and dictators to safely conceal the source of their funds by hiding behind Swiss bank secrecy laws. Swiss banks have been implicated frequently in international money-laundering operations. In an effort to break from its past, the Swiss government in conjunction with Swiss financial institutions recently enacted two anti-money laundering provisions supplementing the Swiss Penal or Criminal Code.[116]

The enactment of the new criminal provisions was undoubtedly caused by various factors, some of which were not internal to Switzerland. First, the FBC as well as various groups repeatedly claimed that the Original Agreement and the 1987 New Agreement were inadequate in fighting money laundering. Second, prior to the enactment of the new provisions, money laundering was not expressly illegal in Switzerland. Thus, mutual assistance in criminal matters could not be granted failing the double incrimination requirement. The Swiss authorities were pressured by various foreign governments, particularly the United States, into adopting provisions that would enable them to pierce Swiss banking secrecy.[117] Due to all of these factors, finally on 1 August 1990, the Swiss Penal Code was amended by the addition of two new money laundering provisions: Article 305 bis and 305 ter.[118] Article 305 bis prohibits the concealment of criminal proceeds and provides a statutory definition of money laundering while Article 305 ter deals with the lack of due diligence in financial transactions.[119]

Article 305 bis, entitled Money Laundering states:

> Money Laundering
>
> 1. Any person carrying out an act appropriate to prevent the investigation of the origin, the discovery, or the confiscation of assets that, as he knows or must assume, result

---

[116] Scott E. Mortman, 'Putting Starch in European Efforts To Combat Money Laundering,' *Fordham L.Rev.*, 60, 429, 441 (1992). In acting to prevent money laundering, Switzerland was motivated to reform by strong pressure from the United States and by internal scandals. See Bates, 'Swiss Phasing Out Secret Bank Accounts,' *L.A. Times*, 4 May 1991 at D1, col. 2. See Art. 305 bis Swiss Penal Code. Knowledge under 305 bis may be proven directly by actual or constructive knowledge or indirectly by reckless disregard or willful blindness. Under 305 bis, the Swiss prosecutor must prove the illegal origin of the assets or property in question.

[117] *Id.* See also New, Proposed Swiss Laws Seen Tougher Yet Against Money Laundering, Reuter Libr. Rep. 7 May 1991, available in Lexis, world library, ALLWLD file.

[118] Franco Taisch, 'Swiss Statutes Concerning Money Laundering,' *INT LAW*, 26, 695 (1992).

[119] *Id.*

from a crime shall be punished by imprisonment or fine.
2. In severe cases, the punishment shall be penal servitude for up to five years or imprisonment. A fine amounting up to SF 1 million shall be combined with the sentence of imprisonment or penal servitude, respectively. A case is severe, particularly if the perpetrator:

> a. acts as a member of a criminal organization;
> b. acts as a member of a gang, formed with the purpose of continued money laundering;
> c. obtains a high turnover or makes considerable profits from professional money laundering;

3. The perpetrator shall also be punished if the principal offense has been committed abroad and is punishable as well in the country where the act has been perpetrated.[120]

Article 305 ter of the Swiss Penal Code states:

> Lack of Due Diligence in Financial Transactions
>
> Any person who professionally accepts, keeps on deposit, manages, or transfers assets belonging to a third party, and fails to establish with all due diligence the identity of the beneficial owner, shall be punished by imprisonment up to one year, detention, or fine.[121]

Article 305 bis proscribes any act 'tending to defeat the determination of the origin, the finding or the seizure of [illegal] assets.' Because the statute was enacted recently, there are no definitive interpretations of the phrase 'tending to defeat.' Nevertheless, it appears that a criminal's actions need not actually 'defeat the determination of the origin' of illegal assets. At least one commentator has interpreted the statute as proscribing all acts 'likely to frustrate the identification of the origin, discovery, or the confiscation of ... assets.'[122] Under this article, a defendant who commits any act 'tending to thwart the identification of the origin, [or] the [finding or seizure] of assets which ... he knows, or must assume stem from a crime' is guilty of a felony. The *mens rea* for this crime requires that a defendant 'know' that assets originate from a crime. Nevertheless, this standard can be satisfied by demonstrating actual or constructive knowledge, or by showing reckless disregard or willful blindness.[123] Therefore, this provision penalizes acts that tend to impede the investigation and prevent the discovery of the source and the confiscation of assets that the committer knows or should have known were derived from a crime.[124]

The statute also requires that the assets stem from either an act committed in Switzerland that constitutes a felony, or from an act committed outside of

---

[120] *Id.*
[121] *Id.*
[122] Singh, *supra* note 95, at 848.
[123] *Id.*
[124] Pierard and Killen, *supra* note 103, at 549.

Switzerland that is regarded as a felony in Switzerland.[125] Generally, Swiss jurisdiction applies to offenses perpetrated in the territory of Switzerland only. However, pursuant to a special provision, money laundering activities are punishable under Swiss law even if the prior offense has been committed abroad. In addition, the legislation covers the laundering of proceeds of a felony but not proceeds of a misdemeanor.[126]

Article 305 ter has an even greater impact on an institution engaged in the financial sector by requiring financial intermediaries to implement internal procedures in order to identify the beneficial owner of the assets with which they are entrusted. Under this disposition, an individual who, in the conduct of his profession, accepts, keeps on deposit, helps to transfer, or invests assets belonging to a third party, and who omits to verify with the vigilance commanded by the circumstances the identity of the beneficial owner, will be punished by imprisonment for up to one year, or fined, or both. In contrast to the New Agreement, the new criminal provision applies to all members of the Swiss financial community such as money changers, fiduciary institutions, asset managers, finance companies, and lawyers, among others. The punishable act is the failure to exercise the degree of care required under the specific circumstances in verifying the identity of the beneficial owner of the funds. A violation of the obligation to identify the beneficial owner constitutes an offense under Article 305 ter even though the funds deposited are not the result of a crime.[127]

Any person who professionally deals with funds and other financial assets and who fails to ascertain the identity of the actual beneficial owner is susceptible to prosecution. Professionals have to establish with all due diligence the identity of the beneficiary. Because the line is still unclear on how far financial institutions have to go in determining such identity, the Swiss Federal Banking Commission has recently established closer guidelines that provide a helpful tool for making banks and bank-like institutions deal sensibly with the new provision.[128]

Effect of the New Law

These two provisions reflect the Swiss Government's reaction to the accelerated expansion in recent years of crime organized on an international scale, more particularly in the context of drug trafficking. Thus, it has emerged that the financing of such activities on the one hand, and the process of recycling the illegal profits flowing from such activities, on the other hand, were vital aspects and aspects in respect of which criminal organizations are particularly vulnerable.[129] Unfortunately, this new law fails to address concerns with retrieving assets from corrupt dictators' spoliations of the countries they once ruled. The law instead is

---

[125] Singh, *supra* note 95, at 849.

[126] Taisch, *supra* note 118, at 713.

[127] Pierard and Killen, *supra* note 103, at 549.

[128] Taisch, *supra* note 118, at 713.

[129] Shelby R. du Pasquier & Dr. Andreas von Planta, 'Money Laundering in Switzerland,' *Int'l Bus. Law*., 394 (1990).

targeted primarily at prohibiting criminal organizations in the financing of their drug related activities or drug trafficking. Although Switzerland had already criminalized certain acts of money laundering in connection with drugs pursuant to the Federal Narcotics Law, it had no general answer to organized crime. By the adoption of the new money laundering provisions, Switzerland has joined the international fight against organized crime.[130]

Furthermore, the new money laundering provisions do not destroy traditional Swiss rules of banking secrecy; the preexisting general limits to the banking secrecy rules remain the same. Due to the new provisions supplementing the Swiss Penal Code, however, criminal proceedings with respect to money laundering activities and lack of due diligence can now be brought upon reasonable suspicion.[131]

THE RESPONSE OF THE BANKING INDUSTRY

Due Diligence Convention and Form B Accounts

Swiss banks have also exhibited initiative in combatting money laundering. One significant effort is an agreement between the Swiss Bankers' Association and the signatory Swiss banks to identify actual owners of deposits. This agreement – *la Convention relative a l'obligation de diligence des banques* (CDB) – is a privately sponsored code of conduct contained in an agreement among Swiss banks and administered by the Swiss Bankers Association. The CDB obligates signatory banks 'to verify the identity of their contracting partners and, in cases of doubt, to obtain from the contracting partner a declaration setting forth the identity of the beneficial owner. In establishing business relations, if the bank has any doubt that the contracting partner may not be the beneficial owner, the bank agrees to exercise due diligence in obtaining a written statement known as a 'Form A.' The Form A contains a certification by the contracting partner that the partner is the beneficial owner or, if not, discloses the identity of the beneficial owner. If a bank has 'serious doubts' about the accuracy of this information that can not be resolved through further inquiry, the bank agrees to terminate its relationship with the customer.[132]

Pursuant to the CDB, persons prohibited from identifying beneficial owners due to rules regarding professional confidentiality are required to provide the banks with a different type of written statement, known as a 'Form B.' Third-party representatives of beneficial owners are required to certify that they know the beneficial owners and that, having exercised due diligence, they were not aware of any fact indicating that the owners were abusing bank secrecy laws or concealing criminally derived proceeds,[133] These Form B accounts preserve anonymity by

---

130 *Id.*

131 Taisch, *supra* note 118, at 714.

132 Mortman, *supra* note 116, at 444–445.

133 *Id.*, at 446.

permitting professionals to open accounts for customers on a fiduciary basis without giving the names of the beneficiary owners. However, the CDB requires Swiss bankers to identify the ultimate beneficial owner of an account before opening it. This includes not only physical persons, but also any shell company without premises or employees of its own. The CDB 'know-your-customer' procedures require banks to identify the beneficial ownership of account-holders by completing a document called Form A.[134]

The CDB explicitly requires identification of the beneficial owner of what it calls 'domiciliary companies' – *sociétés de domicile* – commonly called 'shell entities,' 'screen companies,' 'letterbox companies.' Usually, such corporate entities that are set up principally to serve as a screen for a family or an individual have neither staff nor premises of their own, but rather rely on the employees and the offices of outside lawyers for these purposes. Information about the account's beneficial owner is recorded on Form A.[135] A cautious banker will also monitor account activity, even after the Form A has been completed, in order to check for suspicious transactions that are either unusual or oddly complex, including large cash deposits, wire transfers made in a quick 'in/out' turnaround fashion, and commercially unjustifiable letters of credit, guarantees or back-to-back loans. In their annual report to the Federal Banking Commission, a bank's external auditors are asked to indicate any instances in which the audited bank has violated the CDB.[136]

Until recently, the CDB know-your-customer rules have had a significant escape hatch. Lawyers could substitute themselves for the real account owner by signing another document – the Form B – which stated that the lawyer knew the identity of the account's beneficial owner, but could not disclose this identity because of the attorney-client privilege. The signer of Form B was required to declare absence of any suspicion that the assets were acquired through criminal activity.[137] In the original version of the CDB, the lawyer signing Form B had to state only that he knew of no illegal transaction being carried on by the owner of the account. Some lawyers reportedly marketed themselves as signers of Form B. A potential customer with an unsavory reputation might be sent by the banker to an equally unsavory attorney down the street. The attorney, of course, could sign the declaration stating no knowledge of the customer's illegal activity, precisely because the lawyer usually knew nothing at all about the customer's activity, legal or illegal.[138]

To prevent money launderers from continuing to abuse this Form B loophole, the Swiss Federal Banking Commission, in its supervisory capacity, issued a regulation to the effect that attorneys, notaries, trust administrators, and money managers were no longer permitted to use the so-called Form B when opening a

---

[134] William Park, 'Anonymous Bank Accounts: NarcoDollar, Fiscal Fraud, and Lawyers,' *Fordham Int'l L.J.*, 15, 652, 654 (1991/1992).

[135] *Id.*

[136] *Id.*

[137] *Id.*

[138] *Id.*

bank account on a fiduciary basis. Until then, these professionals were entitled to open accounts for their customers on a fiduciary basis, that is without revealing the identity of the beneficial owner of the funds, mostly in the name of an offshore corporation or trust.[139] The latest decision by the Federal Banking Commission was an effort to weed out attorney-client relationships that were transitory and superficial in nature.[140]

Switzerland has been under pressure to cooperate with authorities from the United States and the European Union who seek access to information on the accounts of suspected criminals. The latest ruling comes on the heels of legislation designed to curb money laundering. And it reflects a change in attitude that can be traced in part to a heightened awareness by the Swiss of the importance of their long-term relationship with the countries in the European Union.[141]

It is nearly impossible to gauge the amount of deposits held in Form B accounts though there has been some speculation that the change could cause vast deposits to be moved to other countries by customers concerned about their identities being revealed.[142] Despite the potential loss, officials at Swiss banks remain optimistic that the abolition of Form B accounts will not hurt their institutions or Switzerland's reputation for bank secrecy. Anticipating the change, several Switzerland-based institutions – including Bank Julius Baer and Credit Suisse – stopped accepting Form B accounts two years before the new rule was passed.[143]

However, bankers insist that privacy and discretion will remain a key aspect of private banking in Switzerland. To counter possible concern about bank secrecy, the Swiss Bankers Association issued a press release shortly after regulators abolished Form B accounts, saying that the decision by the supervisory authorities to abolish the 'Form B' accounts 'has not in any way changed the contents and significance of Swiss banking secrecy.' Any revision to banking secrecy would require either a national referendum or a parliamentary decree.[144] And it is equally doubtful that confidentiality will ever be sacrificed, given that 'It's very fundamental to the Swiss mentality ... the privacy of the individual.'[145]

Gauging the Effect of the Bankers' Response

The FBC's decision to abolish the so-called Form B accounts has, however, neither abolished nor narrowed the protection provided by Swiss banking secrecy. Any revision to banking secrecy would require either a national referendum or a parliamentary decree. A bank's legal obligation to preserve the confidentiality of its customer remains unchanged. Swiss banks are prohibited from disclosing any

---

[139] Pierard & Killen, *supra* note 103, at 546.

[140] Park, *supra* note 134, at 654.

[141] David R. Sands, 'Swiss accounts no longer discreet,' *The Washington Times* (28 June 1991).

[142] *Id.*

[143] *Id.*

[144] *Id.*, at 19.

[145] *Id.*

information about the identity or the affairs of a customer to any person, agency, or administration, whether it be the tax administration, an administrative agency, or other inquirer. Exceptions to this rule are only possible in the event of criminal proceedings by the Swiss authorities or in the context of international mutual assistance, mainly in criminal matters. Thus, the decision was only meant to abolish the possibility, for certain professionals, to open bank accounts in a fiduciary capacity without disclosing the identity of the beneficial owner, except in specific circumstances listed in the decision.[146]

Effect of These Changes on Spoliated Funds

Bilateral agreements are useful in enforcing federal securities laws or in fighting international organized crime. However, they are of limited usefulness in our situation. Further measures need to be taken to ensure that dictators will be unsuccessful in depositing their funds. In the meantime, they continue to find secrecy havens.

Swiss banks were widely known as offering Form B accounts, which lawyers and trust administrators could open on behalf of clients by saying that they knew a client's identity and that his anonymity is not being used to hide criminal activity. As a consequence, some of these secret accounts were used by dictators to keep their money as safely guarded as their identities. For example, Ferdinand Marcos of the Philippines is alleged to have resorted to Form B accounts to deposit the billions of dollars of plundered state funds. Partly in response to this abuse of Swiss banking regulations, the Swiss Federal Banking Commission decided that as from 1 July 1991, Swiss banks would no longer be allowed to accept 'anonymous accounts' and beneficiaries of existing accounts had to be identified by 30 September 1992.[147] Some commentators believe that these developments have created a means of piercing the Swiss veil of secrecy. They also believe the Swiss government is making an effort to prevent criminals from abusing Swiss bank secrecy, by passing the anti-money laundering provisions and even going as far as freezing the accounts of several ousted dictators, including those of Jean-Claude Duvalier of Haiti, Ferdinand Marcos of the Philippines, Manuel Antonio Noriega of Panama and Nicolae Ceausescu of Romania.[148]

However, other commentators remain skeptical about how far the Swiss are willing to change their bank secrecy laws. They believe that Swiss banking secrecy has not changed in essence since it first came into effect in 1935. Instead, the new legislation contains clearly defined limitations in criminal cases and where international mutual legal assistance is requested. For many banking experts, the recent efforts to combat money laundering were aimed mainly at discouraging the entry of drug money or tax dodgers who use Form B accounts. In short, recent changes in Swiss law have simply provided a vehicle with which to fight securities

[146] Pierard & Killen, *supra* note 103, at 546.

[147] Ellen Braitman, 'Private Banking: Swiss Expect to Weather Curbs on Account Secrecy,' *The American Banker*, 6 (15 May 1991).

[148] D. Schorttense, 'Swiss banks keep secret,' *The Jerusalem Post*, 2 January 1992.

swindlers, criminals, tax evaders, but not corrupt dictators. And while it can be said that Swiss banking secrecy laws have become less absolute in recent years, nevertheless they remain intact and any major revision would require an amendment of the Federal Banking Act by parliament or by national referendum. Therefore news of the death of bank secrecy in Switzerland is at best exaggerated.[149]

[149] In the Agreement on the Swiss Banks' Code of Conduct with regard to the Exercise of Due Diligence made between the Swiss Bankers' Association and the signatory banks, it specifically states that the agreement does not in any way alter the obligation to maintain bank secrecy. Furthermore, the Swiss Bankers' Association issued a press release shortly after regulators abolished Form B accounts, saying the decision 'has not in any way changed the contents and significance of Swiss banking secrecy.' See Braitman, *supra* note 147, at 6. Yet, some US newspapers carried exaggerated reports of the death of bank secrecy in Switzerland. However, the new regulations were not designed to narrow the scope and extent of banking secrecy and have not produced that result. It is simply a question of what information the bank must demand when an account is opened. All information which comes to the knowledge of the bank and its employees in this way still enjoys the protection of Swiss banking secrecy, which itself is firmly protected by the Swiss Penal Code.

Chapter 9

Toward a Framework for Holding Constitutionally Responsible Rulers Individually Liable for Acts of Indigenous Spoliation

THE DOCTRINE OF INDIVIDUAL RESPONSIBILITY

Acts of spoliation are usually committed by those who occupy leadership positions that give them direct access to their country's wealth and resources. They are able to use these strategic positions to appropriate national wealth for personal use. To the extent that spoliation is preeminently a leadership activity, responsibility for its commission must be shouldered by these same leaders. Holding high-ranking public officials individually responsible for their acts taken while in office is no longer the novel idea that it was some five decades ago. The War Crimes Tribunals played a central role in affirming the principle of individual culpability. Article 6 of the Charter of the International Military Tribunal was unequivocal in its view that 'persons who, acting in the interests of the European Axis countries, whether as *individuals* or as members of organizations, committed' any war crimes will be tried and punished.[1]

This principle of individual responsibility for crimes under international law is the enduring legacy of the Nuremberg Charter and Judgment. In confirming the direct applicability of international law with respect to the responsibility and punishment of individuals for violations of international criminal law, the Nuremberg Tribunal stated: 'It was submitted that international law is concerned with the actions of sovereign States, and provides no punishment for individuals ... In the opinion of the Tribunal, [this submission] must be rejected. That international law imposes duties and liabilities upon individuals as well as upon States has long been recognized.'[2] This principle of individual responsibility and punishment for crimes under international law recognized at Nuremberg as the cornerstone of international criminal law has been reaffirmed

---

[1] See Agreement for the Prosecution and Punishment of the Major War Criminals of the European Axis Powers and Charter of the International Military Tribunal, Done at London, 8 August 1945, entered into force, 8 August 1945, 59 Stat. 1544, 82 UNTS 279 (hereinafter 'Charter of the Nuremberg Military Tribunal') (emphasis added).

[2] See Nuremberg Judgment, p. 53. See also Commentary to the 1996 Draft Code of Crimes Against the Peace and Security of Mankind ('commentary'), Art. 2, para. 1.

expressly in the Statutes of the International Criminal Tribunal for the former Yugoslavia[3] and Rwanda[4] and implicitly in the Rome Statute of the International Criminal Court.[5]

Following Nuremberg and its progeny individuals can be held responsible *qua* individuals for conduct that violates the law of nations law: '[c]rimes against international law are committed by men, not by abstract entities, and only by punishing individuals who commit such crimes can the provisions of international law be enforced.'[6] The Nuremberg Principles received further boost when they were affirmed by the United Nations General Assembly on 11 December 1946[7] which subsequently directed the International Law Commission (ILC) to '[f]ormulate the principles of international law recognized in the Charter of the Nurnberg Tribunal and in the judgment of the Tribunal, and [p]repare a draft code of offenses against the peace and security of mankind, indicating clearly the place to be accorded' to the Nuremberg Principles.[8] In 1996 the ILC brought this process of formulation, codification, and progressive development of international law to closure when it submitted the final version of the Draft Code of Crimes Against the Peace and Security of Mankind

---

[3] *Statute of the International Tribunal (for the Prosecution of Persons Responsible for Serious Violations of Humanitarian Law Committed in the Territory of the Former Yugoslavia)*. UN Doc. S/25704 (3 May 1993); reprinted in *International Law Materials*, 1159 (1993), Art. 7, para. 1 and Art. 23, para. 1.

[4] *United Nations Security Council Resolution 827 on Establishing an International Tribunal for Rwanda (with Annexed Statute)*. Adopted 8 November 1994. SC Res. 955, UN SCOR, 49th Sess., 343rd mtg., at 15, UN Doc. S/RES/955 (1994), Art. 6, para. 1 and Art. 22, para. 1.

[5] Adopted by the United Nations Diplomatic Conference of Plenipotentiaries on the Establishment of an International Criminal Court, 17 July 1998. Entered into force, 1 July 2002. 2187 UNTS 3.

[6] See *Nazi Conspiracy and Aggression, Opinion and Judgment*, 66 (1947) (hereinafter 'Judgment at Nuremberg').

[7] See Affirmation of the Principles of International Law Recognized by the Charter of Nuremberg Tribunal. Adopted by the UN General Assembly, 11 December 1946. UNGA Res. 95(I), UN Doc. A/236 (1946), at 1144.

[8] See Resolution 177 (II) on the formulation of the Nuremberg Principles and the legislation of international criminal law, 21 November 1947. The ILC submitted a first draft code to the General Assembly in 1951, a second draft in 1954. Thereafter, work on the Commission was suspended. After a 27 year hiatus, the General Assembly invited the ILC to resume its work on the Draft Code. By 1991, the ILC was ready with another draft and, in 1996, it submitted a final version to the General Assembly. See *Draft Code of Crimes Against the Peace and Security of Mankind*. Adopted by the UN International Law Commission in 1954, *Y.B. Int'l L. Comm.*, 2, 150 (1954); revised in 1987, 1988, 1989 and 1991, UN Doc. A/42/420 (1987), UN Doc. A/CN.4/404 (1987), UN Doc. A/43/539 (1988), UN Doc. A/CN.4/419 (1989), UN Doc. A/44/150 (1989), UN Doc. A/CN.4/L.464/Add.4 (1991); see also Draft Report of the International Law Commission on the work of its forty-third session, UN Doc. A/CN.4/L.464/Add.4 (1991). See also Rosemary Rayfuse, 'The Draft Code of Crimes Against the Peace and Security of Mankind: Eating Disorders at the ILC,' *Crim. L. Rev.*, 8, 43 (1997).

('Draft Code of Crimes') to the General Assembly.[9]

Article 3 of the Draft Code of Crimes states that '[a]n individual who is responsible for a crime against the peace and security of mankind shall be liable to punishment.'[10] This article reflects the first paragraph of Article 6 of the Nuremberg Charter which contains the most important provisions on personal punishability for particular offenses under international law.[11] Article 3 also reaffirms the position taken by the International Military Tribunal that international law imposes human duties directly on both public and private authors of an international crime. This position was again reinforced in the Judgment in the Flick Trial, also based on the provisions of law as formulated in the Nuremberg Charter, wherein it was stated:

> [that] the International Military Tribunal was dealing with officials and agencies of the State and it is argued that individuals holding no public offices and not representing the State, do not, and should not, come within the class of persons criminally responsible for a breach of international law. It is asserted that international law is a matter wholly outside the work, interest and knowledge of private individuals. The distinction is unsound. International law as such binds every citizen just as does ordinary municipal law. Acts judged criminal when done by an officer of the Government are criminal also when done by a private individual. The guilt differs only in magnitude, not in quality. The offender in either case is charged with personal wrong and punishment falls on the offender in *propria persona*.[12]

The noose for individual responsibility is tied so tightly that even heads of states are not spared, as it should be. Crimes against the peace and security of mankind often require the involvement of persons in positions of governmental authority who are capable of formulating plans or policies involving acts of exceptional gravity and magnitude. These crimes require the power to use or to authorize the use of the essential means of destruction and to mobilize the personnel required for carrying out these crimes. A government official who plans, instigates, authorizes or orders such

---

9 See 'Draft Code of Crimes Against the Peace and Security of Mankind' (hereinafter 'Draft Code of Crimes').

10 *Id.*

11 See Charter of the Nuremberg Tribunal, *supra* note l. It appears as Article 3 of the Draft Code of Crimes:

1. An individual who commits a crime against the peace and security of mankind is responsible therefor and is liable to punishment.

2. An individual who aids, abets or provides the means for the commission of a crime against the peace and security of mankind or conspires in or directly incites the commission of such a crime is responsible therefor and is liable to punishment.

3. An individual who commits an act constituting an attempt to commit a crime against the peace and security of mankind [as set out in article ... 1] is responsible therefor and is liable to punishment. Attempt means any commencement of execution of a crime that failed or was halted only because of circumstances independent of the perpetrator's intention.

12 See *United Nations War Commission, 15 Law Reports of Trials of War Criminals*, 59–60 (1949).

crimes not only provides the means and the personnel required to commit the crime, but also abuses the authority and power entrusted to him. He may, therefore, be considered to be even more culpable than the subordinate who actually commits the criminal act. It would be paradoxical to allow the individuals who are, in some respects, the most responsible for the crimes covered by the Code to invoke the sovereignty of the State and to hide behind the immunity that is conferred on them by virtue of their positions particularly since these heinous crimes shock the conscience of mankind, violate some of the most fundamental rules of international law and threaten international peace and security.[13]

The Draft Code of Crimes has addressed the paradox of holding subordinates acting on orders of their superior responsible while leaving untouched those who planned, instigated, authorized or order the commission of crimes against international law. Article 7 provides that an individual's official position does not relieve him of personal responsibility for committing a crime against the peace and security of mankind. The article singles out chief executives, making it clear that the 'official position of an individual who commits a crime against the peace and security of mankind, even if he acted as head of State or Government, does not relieve him of criminal responsibility or mitigate punishment.' Much like the Draft Articles on State Responsibility, the principle of leadership responsibility proclaimed in draft Article 7 also owes its doctrinal pedigree partially to the provisions on the Charter of the Nuremberg Tribunal, the Judgment of the Tribunal which was adopted by the Commission in 1950 and in the 1954 Draft Code of Offences against the Peace and Security of Mankind as well as the charters of the International Military Tribunals established in the wake of the Second World War. Article 7 of the Nuremberg Charter states that 'the official position of defendants, whether as Heads of State or responsible officials in government departments, shall not be considered as freeing them from responsibility or mitigating punishment.' A similar provision – Article 6 – was included in the Charter of the International Military Tribunal for the Far-East and can be found in Principle III of the Principles of International Law Recognized in the Charter of the Nuremberg Tribunal which reads: 'The fact that a person who committed an act which constitutes a crime under international law acted as Head of State or responsible government official does not relieve him from responsibility under international law.'[14] More recently, an individual's official position has also been excluded as a possible defense to crimes under international law in the Statutes of the International Criminal Tribunals for the former Yugoslavia (article 7) and Rwanda (article 6).

The Nuremberg Tribunal rejected the plea of act of State and that of immunity which were submitted by several defendants as a valid defense or ground for immunity:

It was submitted that ... where the act in question is an act of State, those who carry it out

---

13 Commentary, Art. 7, para. 1

14 See Affirmation of Principles of International Law, *supra* note 7.

> are not personally responsible, but are protected by the doctrine of the sovereignty of the State. In the opinion of the Tribunal, [this submission] must be rejected. ... The principle of international law, which under certain circumstances, protects the representative of a State, cannot be applied to acts which are condemned as criminal by international law. The authors of these acts cannot shelter themselves behind their official position in order to be freed from punishment in appropriate proceedings. ... [T]he very essence of the Charter is that individuals have international duties which transcend the national obligations of obedience imposed by the individual State. He who violates the laws of war cannot obtain immunity while acting in pursuance of the authority of the State if the State in authorizing action moves outside its competence under international law.[15]

The express reference to Heads of State to the exclusion of other constitutionally responsible rulers such as vice-presidents, ministers, judges and so on was merely to underscore their enormous decision-making power in most constitutional schemes. It was never the intent of the drafters to apply draft Article 7 exclusively to heads of state as the words 'the official position of an individual ... and particularly' clearly suggest a contrary intention. The Commentary takes the position that the intended effect of this provision is to stress the fact that an individual who commits a crime against the peace and security of mankind cannot invoke his official position to escape personal responsibility or immunize himself from such an act; nor can he use his official position to avoid punishment:

> The absence of any procedural immunity with respect to prosecution or punishment in appropriate judicial proceedings is an essential corollary of the absence of any substantive immunity or defence. It would be paradoxical to prevent an individual from invoking his official position to avoid responsibility for a crime only to permit him to invoke this same consideration to avoid the consequences of this responsibility.[16]

Responsibility attaches even when the individual claims that the acts constituting the crime were performed in the exercise of his official functions. Equally, a person masquerading as a Head of State or Government or as some other constitutionally responsible officer would incur criminal responsibility just as much, if the acts he committed were criminal acts under the Draft Code of Crime. In short, the words 'that he acts' apply to the exercise of both legal powers and factual powers. Equally noteworthy is the fact that Article 7 also excludes an individual's official position as a mitigating factor in determining the commensurate punishment for crimes under international law.

Although the scope of application of the Draft Code of Crimes is limited to 'individuals' and culpability for crimes under international law is personal, the doctrine of state responsibility is nevertheless retained in the code. For instance, the Commentary to Article 2 points out that the 'act for which an individual is responsible might also be attributable to a State if the individual acted as an 'agent of the State,' 'on behalf of the State,' 'in name of the state' or as a de facto agent, without any legal

15 See Commentary, Art. 7, para. 3.

16 *Id.* Art. 7, para. 6.

power.'[17] Consistent with this reasoning, Article 4 makes clear that criminal responsibility of individuals is 'without prejudice to any question of the responsibility of States under international law.'[18] Thus, the Code is without prejudice to any question of the responsibility of a State under international law for a crime committed by one of its agents. Article 2 must be read together with Article 19 of the Draft Articles on State Responsibility. The Commentary to Article 19 makes the point that the punishment of individuals who are organs of the State 'certainly does not exhaust the prosecution of the international responsibility incumbent upon the State for internationally wrongful acts which are attributed to it in such cases by reason of the conduct of its organs.' The State may thus remain responsible and be unable to exonerate itself from responsibility by invoking the prosecution or punishment of the individuals who committed the crime.

An individual who stands accused of committing a crime under international law cannot absolve himself by trying to shift the blame to someone else, be he a superior or a subordinate. Draft Article 5 denies such an individual the defense of superior orders. This defense, as the Commentary to the Code points out, has been consistently excluded in the relevant legal instruments adopted since the Nuremberg Charter, including the Tokyo Tribunal Charter (article 6), Control Council Law No. 10 (article 4) and, more recently, the Statutes of the International Criminal Tribunals for the former Yugoslavia (article 7) and Rwanda (article 6).[19] The fact that he acted pursuant to 'an order of a Government or a superior does not relieve him of criminal responsibility.'[20] While rejecting any defense based on superior orders, Article 7 recognizes it as a possible mitigating factor when invoked by a subordinate who committed a crime while acting pursuant to an order of his superior.[21] But superior orders as a plea in mitigation, will be considered in determining the appropriate punishment, only 'if justice [so] requires.' In making this determination, a court must weigh a number of factors: (1) whether the individual entering the plea was justified in carrying out an order to commit a crime to avoid the consequences resulting from a failure to obey a directive; (2) the seriousness of the consequences flowing from the order having been carried out; (3) the seriousness of the likely consequences had the subordinate failed to carry out the order. It is on the basis of these factors that a court

---

[17] See Commentary, Art. 2.

[18] Draft Code of Crimes, *supra* note 9, Art. 4.

[19] See Commentary, Art. 5, para. 4. See also The Commission in the Nuremberg Principles (Principle IV) and the 1954 draft Code (Article 4).

[20] Earlier drafts allowed for the defense of superior orders 'if, in the circumstances of the time, it was possible for him [subordinate] not to comply with that order.' *See* Article 11 of the 1991 Draft Code of Crimes against the Peace and Security of Mankind. But if a moral choice was possible and a genuine possibility of not complying with that order was present, then the subordinate cannot escape personal responsibility. Possible defenses would include situations of 'irresistible moral or physical coercion, state of necessity and obvious and acceptable error.' See Commentary to Draft Article 11, paragraph 3.

[21] *Id.* Art. 5, para. 5.

will decide the kind of punishment justice requires to be imposed.[22]

The Draft Code in its Article 6 recognizes the doctrine of *respondeat superior:* the criminal acts of a subordinate can be imputed to his master and the master cannot relieve himself of criminal responsibility by blaming his servant for the commission of the prohibited conduct. If the superior had prior knowledge or information that would have led him to believe 'in the circumstances at the time' that a crime under international law was about to be or had been committed by the subordinate and he failed to take 'all necessary measures within his power' to forestall its commission, then he is just as responsible as the actual perpetrator.[23]

Nuremberg also established conclusively the bases for personal punishability under international law independently of any provisions of national law. Individual responsibility attaches when: (1) the wrongful conduct does not constitute a crime under municipal law, and/or (2) the act constitutes an international crime but its commission was compelled under municipal law.[24] Article 1 of the Draft Code of Crimes reaffirms this doctrine of the supremacy of international law over municipal law:

> Crimes against the peace and security of mankind are crimes under international law and punishable as such, *whether or not they are punishable under national law.*[25]

This article tracks the language of sub-paragraph (c) of Article 6 of the Nuremberg Charter defining as crimes against humanity certain acts committed 'whether or not in violation of domestic law of the country where perpetrated.' The International Military Tribunal had earlier staked out the primacy of international law when it said: '[o]n the other hand the very essence of the Charter is that individuals have international duties which transcend the national obligations of obedience imposed by the individual State.'[26] The concluding clause of paragraph 2 of Article 1 suggests that 'the characterization, or the absence of characterization, of a particular type of behaviour as criminal under national law has no effect on the characterization of that type of behaviour as criminal under international law.' Thus, it is conceivable that 'a particular type of behaviour characterized as a crime against the peace and security of mankind ... might not be prohibited or might even be imposed by national law.' By the same token such behavior might be characterized merely as a crime under national law, rather than as a crime under international law.[27]

Taking place in the last three decades or so in countries around the globe has been the planned, organized and deliberate looting of national wealth and resources on a scale so massive as never before seen in history. This pillage and plunder is usually accomplished by forcible, questionable and dishonest means. Usually such acts of

---

22 *Id.*

23 *Id.* Art. 12.

24 See Peter Drost, *The Crime of State: Genocide*, 2, 152 (1959).

25 See Draft Code of Crimes, *supra* note 9, Art. 1, para. 2. Emphasis added.

26 See Judgment at Nuremberg, *supra* note 2, at 53.

27 See Commentary, Art. 1, para. 10.

sacking are committed by an enemy but what makes this genre of spoliation so different is that it is practiced by people indigenous to the countries. Worse, those responsible are the men and women who eagerly sought and obtained public office or had it thrust on them. These are not some marauding horde of armed bandits who have no stake in the conquered territory and therefore have no scruples about sacking and destroying property belonging to the enemy. Furthermore, the looting is directed at all the wealth-generating sectors of the economy, with long-lasting consequences on society as a whole. It is only fair and just that these constitutionally responsible rulers are held individually accountable before the law of nations for their acts of economic sabotage. In Prosecutor v. Erdemovic, the tribunal captured the essence of a crime against humanity as '... inhumane acts that by their very extent and gravity go beyond the limits tolerable to the international community, which must per force demand their punishment. But crimes against humanity also transcend the individual because when the individual is assaulted, humanity comes under attack and is negated. It is therefore the concept of humanity as victim which essentially characterises crimes against humanity.'[28] When a head of state takes for his private use state resources that are sufficient to retire his country's external debt, such conduct goes beyond the pale and deserves to be punished.

In a fascinating article on inter-generational equity, Professor Edith Brown Weiss of Georgetown University Law School sets forth a theory of justice between generations that she reduces into a set of obligations and rights enforceable in international law.[29] According to Professor Weiss, each generation receives a natural and cultural legacy in trust from previous generations that it holds in trust for succeeding generations. This obligation of environmental stewardship entails a duty on mankind to pass on to succeeding generations a planet at least as healthy as the one it inherited, 'so that all generations will be able to enjoy its fruits.' Weiss' formulation of this obligation borrows from Edmund Burke's view of the state as a partnership between the living, the dead, and the unborn.[30] Since, according to her, the 'welfare and well-being' of each generation is the *raison d'être* of society, the environment, 'society's life-support system' must be kept both healthy and decent.[31] This task can be achieved through three basic principles of inter-generational equity. First, the 'conservation of options' by which each generation must conserve the diversity of natural and cultural resources, so as not to restrict unduly the options available to future generations. Second, the 'conservation of quality' on the strength of which each generation must maintain the quality of the planet, so that it is passed on in no worse condition than that in which it was received. Finally, the 'conservation of access,' which obligates each generation to provide equal rights of access to the legacy of

---

[28] Prosecutor v. Erdemovic, Sentencing Judgment, Case No. IT–96–22-T, Trial Chamber I, 29 November 1996, reprinted in 108 ILR 180 (1996).

[29] Edith Brown Weiss, 'Our Rights and Obligations to Future Generations for the Environment,' *Am. J. Int'l L.*, 84, 198 (1990) [hereinafter 'Weiss 1990'].

[30] See Weiss 1990, *supra* note 29, at 199–200 citing Edmund Burke, *Reflections on the Revolution in France.*

[31] *Id.*, at 200.

previous generations to all of its members.[32]

Weiss is convinced that mankind is now capable of changing the global environment irreversibly unless the human species intervenes. They 'alone among all living creatures have the capacity to shape significantly our relationship to the environment' being 'the most sentient of living creatures.'[33] But in discharging their special obligation as global ombudsmen, the human species must not lose sight of the central vision of the principles of inter-generational equity: 'First, the principles should encourage equality among generations, neither authorizing the present generation to exploit resources to the exclusion of future generations nor imposing unreasonable burdens on the present generations to meet indeterminate future needs. Second, they should not require one generation to predict the values of future generations. Third, they should be reasonably clear when applied to foreseeable situations. Fourth, they must be shared generally by different cultural traditions and be acceptable to different economic and political systems.'[34]

All in all Weiss makes a compelling case for viewing each generation as under some moral, if not legal, obligation to preserve the planet's natural and cultural heritage and to pass this on to future generations in no worse condition than it is received.[35] We believe that her theory of inter-generational equity provides a provocative starting point in the search for a framework within which to develop a 'normative' theory of leadership responsibility for international economic crimes, one that identifies legal norms that the international community can use to prevent and punish the crime of indigenous spoliation. A normative explanation of behavior presupposes not only the existence of a norm or norms but also conformity to them. The approach taken here is to ask two fundamental questions: Are there any legal norms to condition the behavior of constitutionally responsible rulers with respect to the problem of indigenous spoliation? Second, what is the international legal order prepared to do when responsible rulers fail to conform to these norms?

Legal norms, like norms in general, are rules for conduct, that is, they prescribe and proscribe standards by reference to which behavior is judged and approved or disapproved.[36] A norm, according to Professor Williams,

> … calls for 'right action' and implies a generalizable reason for the rightness of the indicated conduct. Ultimately this propriety or rightness traces back to some standard of

---

32 *Id.*, at 202.

33 *Id.*, at 199.

34 Weiss, 1990, *supra* note 29, at 129.

35 *See* Edith Brown Weiss, 'The Planetary Trust: Conservation and Intergenerational Equity,' *ECOLOGY L.Q.*, 11, 495, 499 (1984) [hereinafter 'Weiss, Planetary Trust].

36 See Williams, 'The Concept of Norms,' in *International Encyclopaedia of the Social Sciences*, 11, 204 (D. Sills ed. 1968). The Dictionary of Philosophy defines a norm as a term that 'is closely related to the terms criterion and standard.' Criterion applies, however, more definitely to the process of judgment; it is the rule or mode of control as employed to assist judgment in making proper discriminations; see also J.M. Baldwin, *Dictionary of Philosophy and Psychology, Vol. II*, 182 (1911).

value that is taken without further justification as valid by the individual or group in question.[37]

A normative theory of individual responsibility with respect to international economic crimes must set forth and rationally defend a system of legal norms with respect to the crimes that the international community chooses to enforce.

Nonetheless, some clarification is called for in our resort to Weiss' theory of justice between generations. First, her theory focuses on the much grander planetary rights of access to mankind's common heritage – the undifferentiated resources of planet earth. The heritage Weiss has in mind is the natural heritage, which 'includes the atmosphere, the oceans, plants and animal life, water, soils, and other natural resources, both renewable and exhaustible'[38] and the cultural heritage, which 'includes the intellectual, artistic, social, and historical record of mankind.'[39] Our interest is narrower concerned as we are only with the rights of access to, and the guardianship of, material wealth and resources within particular geopolitical contexts, that is, within specific nations. Second, Weiss' theory embraces the entire human species within a given generational time-span, that is, mankind temporally and spatially defined, undifferentiated into classes, rank, occupation, and so on, and the relationship between generations across time and space. In other words, her concern is with the obligations generations owe one another. We, on the other hand, wish to focus on the relationship between a small handful of public officials and their close collaborators and the larger mass of the population within certain countries. More specifically, the obligations owed the latter by the former. Finally, unlike Weiss, our interest is not the planet earth as such and the ecosystem that all mankind feeds from. Rather, our interest is in the wealth of a nation, more narrowly defined to mean the capital and valuable natural resources such as petroleum, minerals, fauna, etc. that run the engine of economic development and provide the crucial basics for the dignified survival of individuals and groups in societies across the globe.

Distinction between Leaders and Citizens

An important distinction can be drawn between leaders holding public office and the citizens they serve. Public officials are obliged to pursue the public interest; to use the powers and resources of their offices to accomplish public purposes efficiently and effectively. In part this duty derives from normal obligations that attach to administrative offices in which an agent works with the authority and resources of others to accomplish their purposes. But the duty also partakes of a general duty of beneficence – to do what one can to help others.[40]

In *The Warriors*, J. Glenn Gray's sensitive memoir of World War II, the author

---

37 See Williams, *supra* note 36, at 205.

38 See Weiss, Planetary Trust, *supra* note 35, at 495.

39 *Id.*

40 M. Moore, 'Realms of Obligations and Virtue,' in *Public Duties: The Moral Obligations of Government Officials*, 3, 9 (J. Fleishman, L. Liebman & M. Moore eds, 1981).

proposes a principle for fixing responsibility for collective acts by suggesting that: '[t]he greater the possibility of free action in the communal sphere, the greater the degree of fault for evil deeds done in the name of everyone.'[41] It would appear that what the philosopher has in mind is moral, not merely legal, responsibility; and his overriding concern, as Michael Joseph Smith sees it, is with conscience, not strict liability.[42] For both Gray and Smith, the conception of moral responsibility extends well beyond the provisions of the legal code. What determines one's responsibility in the moral sense is the degree of freedom to act or 'free action' that one enjoys in a given sphere.[43] Responsibility must be defined or fixed within the limits of one's freedom to act.

If Gray's notion of freedom to alter things is central to the fixing of moral responsibility, then an important distinction can be made between leaders and citizens. Regardless of how free citizens are to act in the communal sphere, the acts of their leaders carry far greater consequences. Because leaders *qua* leaders assume far greater power, they also bear far greater moral responsibility.[44] A second proposition that flows logically from Gray's principle of free action is that political leaders act not as personal agents but as trustees for their States. Since they act on behalf of the entire community, it is incumbent on them to consider the consequences of their actions not simply from the point-of-view of their narrow self-interest but, perhaps more important, from the view of the State and its collective interests.[45] This is consistent with Max Weber's injunction that true leaders must adopt an ethic of consequence and responsibility.[46]

Political leaders hold greater power and therefore bear far greater moral responsibility than ordinary citizens.[47] A nation's wealth and resources are passed down to the citizens and political leaders as the natural legacy from previous generations. But this legacy is held by the leaders in trust for the present generation of citizens and for those yet unborn. Thus a certain obligation is placed upon each generation of political leadership to not only conserve the quality and quantity of the nation's wealth for future generations but to ensure access to this wealth on an equitable basis to all the members of the present generation. Implicit in this trust is the expectation that the political leadership in discharging its duty to present and future generations will not, even when tempted, divert for their own private use the national

---

41 J. Glenn Gray, *The Warriors: Reflections on Men in Battle*, 199 (1959).

42 See Michael Joseph Smith, 'Moral Reasoning and Moral Responsibility,' in *Ethics and International Affairs and International Relations*, 33 (Kenneth Thompson ed., 1985).

43 See *The Warriors*, *supra* note 41, at 199.

44 *Id.*

45 *Id.*, at 34. Gray also makes the point that a leader's moral responsibility is dictated by the context of uncertainty wherein he operates. Although leaders seek and hold greater power and greater responsibility than the citizens they rule, nevertheless 'they operate under circumstances that make purely ethical action quite difficult.' *Id.*, at 35.

46 *Id.* See also Weber, 'Politics as a Vocation,' in *From Max Weber*, 122 (H. Gerth & C. Wright Mills, 1948).

47 See Smith, *supra* note 42, at 33.

wealth they hold in trust for their citizens, the living as well as the unborn.

As we tried to show in the first chapter, wanton acts of depredation carried out by high-ranking public officials have succeeded in bankrupting the economies of many nations. In country after country where these acts have occurred they have been uniformly greeted with widespread horror, revulsion and indignation by the public whose fundamental interests have been undermined. Increasingly, the world community is beginning to take notice; important international organizations have adopted resolutions condemning this conduct. It is only a matter of time before modern international law begins to reflect these individual and societal forms of moral judgment and use them as the basis of an international law on economic crimes. Accordingly, we advance the thesis that an international norm which views public office as a public trust and the political leader as a fiduciary who must be held personally accountable for his stewardship is finally emerging. The norm imposes certain obligations on constitutionally responsible rulers and confers certain powers, rights and privileges on the public they have sworn to serve. However, since the precise contours of these powers, privileges, rights and duties, their respective holders and bearers have yet to be clarified, we shall in this chapter explore their interplay in the context of the problem of indigenous spoliation.

Rights and duties exist within a framework of some rule or system of rules regulating the behavior of individuals or groups towards each other.[48] Legal positivists would argue that rights and duties follow from law and that law is the command of the 'sovereign.' Consistent with this view, whatever there is to say about the jural relations between citizens and their leaders must be grounded in judicial decisions or in rules originating in customs or in agreements between states. By insisting that the expressed moral indignation of members of a society over the conduct of some public officials should be accepted as reflective of an emerging international norm opposed to indigenous spoliation, we take sides with the view that law does not exist apart from public recognition. Thus, in contrast to the imperative theory of law, we take the position that law is a juridical norm expressing the social consciousness of the group or, as Kant would have it, that it expresses the 'legislation' of the individual moral will. That is, in 'making a moral judgment the individual performs essentially the same operation as does a legislature or court in making or declaring law.'[49] If law is not exclusively the command of the 'sovereign' then the moral judgments of individuals on the subject of indigenous spoliation, particularly the ones who have been and are the victims, should suffice as their 'legislation' of what ought or ought not to be the appropriate and acceptable behavior of their constitutionally elected and appointed leaders.

ON RIGHTS AND DUTIES

In attempting to trace the outlines of a normative theory of rights and duties as they

---

[48] William Dawson Lamont, 'Rights,' *Aristotelian Society*, 24, 83, 94 (1950).

[49] *Id.*, at 87.

pertain to the problem of indigenous spoliation, it would be necessary to articulate a system of rules that would form the basis of international regulation of the behavior of leaders towards their citizens with respect to their guardianship over the wealth and natural resources of their nations. The analysis that follows will hopefully shed some light on some critical questions. Do citizens have any rights to their national wealth and resources? Do these rights generate any corresponding obligations/duties on others? Do these duties fall on the constitutionally elected and appointed leaders exclusively or do others share in the burdens? If so, what is the nature, scope and content of these rights and duties? What is the juridical base of these rights and duties? Are they the products of sovereign command or of a principled conscience?

Scholarly discourse on rights fall basically into three categories: (1) the moral or logical correlativity theory of rights; (2) the 'essential element' theories of rights; and (3) the functional or Neo-Hohfeldian theory of rights. This division, it must be emphasized, is purely for analytical neatness since there is a degree of overlap among these theoretical formulations.

The Logical or Moral Correlativity Theory of Rights

At one time the dominant theory of rights among philosophers, this school views rights and duties as correlatives.[50] That is, rights and duties are opposite sides of the same coin. Richard Brandt captured the common view when he suggested that rights can be defined in terms of obligations, that the difference between A's right against B and B's duty to A is mainly the difference between the passive and the active voice.[51] Accordingly, 'when one person has a moral right, some other person or persons have corresponding obligations.'[52] In other words, a right is just a duty seen from another perspective, therefore, every duty entails a right and every right entails a duty.[53] Or, as Braybrooke puts it, a right which does not entail a corresponding duty is no right at all; it is a right without meaning.[54]

A more extreme view, generally associated with Jeremy Bentham, equates having a right with being the beneficiary of an obligation. Bentham describes this 'beneficiary theory' of rights in the following language: 'to assure to individuals the possession of a

---

[50] Leading proponents of this school would include Francis Herbert Bradley, *Ethical Studies*, 1, 207–213 (2nd ed. 1927); Stanley I. Benn & Robert Stanley Peters, *The Principles of Political Thought* (1965); William David Ross, *The Right and the Good*, 1, 48–56,59–62 (1930).

[51] See Richard B. Brandt, *Ethical Theory*, 436 (1959).

[52] *Id.*, at 433–444.

[53] See Rex Martin & James W. Nickel, '1 Recent Work on the Concept of Rights,' *American Philosophical Quarterly*, 17, 165, 166 (1980) (hereinafter cited as 'Martin & Nickel').

[54] See David Braybrooke, 'The Firm But Untidy Correlativity of Rights and Obligations,' *Canadian J. of Philosophy*, 1, 351, 361 (1972); see also Lamont, *supra* note 42, at 94 (a duty is what is demanded in the creation of a right, it is correlative to and logically consequent upon the notion of 'right').

certain good, is to confer a *right* upon them.'[55]

The 'Essential Element' Theories of Rights

Not all writers share the view that all duties entail rights of other people, even though they will concede that such a correlation might exist for many, but not all, duties.[56] Criticism and rejection of the correlative rights theory gave rise to theories that seek to characterize rights by focusing on the kind of normative element that all rights contain. Subsumed under the 'essential element' theories are two distinct formulations of the essential basis of rights: the rights-as-claims formulations and the rights-as-entitlements formulation.

Rights-as-Claims

Under this approach, rights are characterized as valid claims: 'To have a right is to have a claim *to* something and *against* someone, the recognition of which is called for by legal rules or, in the case of moral rights, by the principles of an enlightened conscience.'[57] According to its proponents, a right always has two principal elements: a valid claim-to-something and a valid claim-against someone.[58] A claim is something which people demand as their due, not as a matter of the giver's generosity.[59] However, a claim must fulfill certain requirements before it ripens a full-fledged right.[60] In the Feinberg scheme for a person to *have a claim* and be in a position to *make a claim*, that claim must, among other things, be fully validated.[61] That is, to qualify as a right, a claim must undergo a validation check. Central to this validation

---

[55] See Jeremy Bentham, *Works*, 111, 159 (Bowring ed., 1843) (emphasis in original) quoted in Martin & Nickel, *supra* note 53, 166, note 3. For a critique of the beneficiary theory, see Herbert L.A. Hart, 'Are There Any Natural Rights?' *Philosophical Rev*., 64, 175 (1955); 'Bentham Lecture on a Mastermind Series,' *Proceedings of the British Academy*, 48, 297, 313–317 (1962); 'Bentham on Legal Rights,' in *Oxford Essays in Jurisprudence*, 2nd Series, 171 (Alfred William Brian Simpson ed., 1973); Thomas R. Kearns, 'Rights, Benefits and Normative Systems,' *Archiv fur Rechts-Und Sozial Phiosophie*, 61, 465 (1975); See also David Lyons, 'Rights, Claimants, and Beneficiaries,' *American Philosophical Quarterly*, 6, 173 (1969).

[56] See Joel Feinberg, 'Duties, Rights and Claims,' *American Philosophical Quarterly*, 3, 137, 142 (1966) (hereinafter cited as 'Feinberg on Duties'); Hart, Bentham on Legal Rights, *supra* note 55, at 190.

[57] See Joel Feinberg, 'The Rights of Animals and Unborn Generations,' in *Philosophy and Environmental Crisis*, 43, 43–44 (William T. Blackstone ed., 1974).

[58] See Joel Feinberg, The Nature and Value of Rights, *J. Value Inquiry*, 4, 243, 256 (1970).

[59] *Id.*, at 249–252.

[60] This view of rights-as-claims is in sharp contrast to the one embraced by Bernard Mayo who sees a right as simply a claim, no more, no less. See Bernard Mayo, 'What are Human Rights?' in *Political Theory and the Rights of Man*, 68, 75 (David Daiches Raphael ed., 1967).

[61] See Feinberg on Duties, *supra* note 56, at 253–255; see also Joel Feinberg, *Social Philosophy*, 64–67 (1973).

process is the distinction Feinberg draws between a valid claim-to-something and a valid claim-against someone as the principal elements a right always has. Feinberg then distinguishes his rights-as-claims theory from the rights-and-duties-as-correlatives theory when he suggests that one can speak meaningfully of someone having a claim-to without advance knowledge about whom that claim-to might be against: 'Imagine a hungry, sickly, fatherless infant ... in a squalid Mexican slum. Doesn't this child have a *claim* to be fed, to be given medical care, to be taught to read? Can't we know this before we have any idea where correlative duties lie?'[62] Feinberg is careful that his formulation of rights do not lead him into the correlativity trap which posits that all rights generate corresponding closely-related second-party duties. He does this in two ways. First, by requiring that all claims satisfy a validation test before they become full-fledged rights in the legal sense, that is, rights that can be asserted against someone. Second, by not insisting that a valid claim does not necessarily and logically entail an obligation on someone to act in such a way as would satisfy it.[63]

Rights-as-Entitlements

Proponents of this formulation see entitlement rather than claim or duty as the basic normative element of a right.[64] Rights, according to H.J. McCloskey, are best 'explained positively as entitlements to do, have, enjoy, or have done, and not negatively as something against others, or as something one ought to have.'[65]

Functional Theories of Rights

Functional theories of rights have been described as an alternative to the 'essential elements' approach.[66] Whereas the latter approach seeks to characterize rights by focusing on a single normative element – a valid claim or an entitlement – underlying the concept of rights, the functionalists in contrast view rights as constellations of groups of elements.[67] Two branches of functional theorizing have emerged over the years: one represented by Wellman's neo-Hohfeldian 'Dominion-if-Respected' model and the other by Robert Dworkin's rights-as-trumps model.

Wellman's 'Dominion-If-Respected' Model

Heavily influenced by the writings of Wesley Hohfeld functionalists, like Carl Wellman, believe that every right is a complex normative structure which typically

62 See Feinberg on Duties, *supra* note 56, at 142.

63 See Martin & Nickel, *supra* note 53, at 168.

64 See Richard Wasserstrom, 'Rights, Human Rights, and Racial Discrimination,' *J. of Philosophy*, 61, 628, 630 (1964); Robert Nozick, *Anarchy, State, and Utopia* (1974).

65 See Henry John McCloskey, 'Rights-Some Conceptual Issues,' *Australian J. Philosophy*, 54, 99 (1976) (hereinafter cited as 'McCloskey on Rights').

66 See Martin & Nickel, *supra* note 53, at 170.

67 See Carl Wellman, *A Theory of Rights* (1985).

involves the four Hohfeldian elements or 'fundamental legal conceptions' in a variety of combinations: a claim, a liberty, a power, or an immunity. For every right there is a *defining core* that is fundamental to the existence of the right as well as the *associated* elements that contribute to the satisfaction of the core. Thus when rights are classified as 'liberty-, claim-, power-, or immunity-rights, it is to their defining cores that we refer, whatever other legal elements may be contained in any rights, they belong to this right because of their relation to its core.'[68]

It has been said that Wesley Newcomb Hohfeld's great contribution to the legal profession was in removing analytical jurisprudence from its misty heights of intellectual abstraction and to ground it squarely within the everyday world of the lawyer and judge.[69] In two celebrated essays published in 1913 and 1917, respectively, in the Yale Law Journal, Hohfeld dramatically changed the direction of the debate on legal rights and legal duties. In these essays Hohfeld sought to remove the ambiguity and inadequacy of terminology surrounding the words 'rights' and 'duties.' He lamented the fact that '[o]ne of the greatest hindrances to clear understanding, the incisive statement, and the true solution of legal problems frequently arises from express or tacit assumption that legal relations may be reduced to 'rights' and 'duties', and that these latter categories are therefore adequate for the purpose of analyzing even the most complex legal' problems.[70] Hohfeld thought it unfortunate that the words 'rights' and 'duties' are used loosely to apply to instances where other terminology might be more appropriate.[71] He points to the indiscriminate use of the word 'rights' to 'cover what in a given case may be a privilege, a power, or an immunity, rather than a right in the strictest sense.'[72]

To provide greater clarity and precision and to remove the persistent ambiguities in the language of rights and duties, Hohfeld proposed a scheme of eight fundamental conceptions in which he believed all legal problems could be analyzed. These concepts are conveniently arranged in a scheme of 'opposites' and 'correlatives':

Opposites:	right/claim[73]	privilege	power	immunity
	no-right/no-claim	duty	disability	liability
Correlatives:	right/claim	privilege	power	immunity
	no-right/no-claim	no-right	liability	disability

68 See Carl Wellman, 'A New Conception of Human Rights,' in *Human Rights*, 48, 53 (E. Kamenka & A.E.S. Tay eds, 1978); see also Wellman, *supra* note 67, at 81–95.

69 See Walter Wheeler Cook, 'Introduction: Hohfeld's Contributions to the Science of Law,' in *Fundamental Legal Conceptions*, 3 (W.W. Cook ed., 1923); see also Wellman, *supra* note 67, at 17.

70 Wesley Newcomb Hohfeld, *Fundamental Legal Conceptions*, 35 (W.W. Cook ed., 1923).

71 *Id.*, at 36.

72 *Id.*

73 Hohfeld uses the term 'claim' as a synonym for 'right.' *Id.*, at 38.

In his scheme, claims, privileges, powers and immunities constitute a comprehensive general classification of legal 'rights' in the generic sense. The four correlative terms – duty, no-claim, liability and disability – represent the legal burdens that correspond to the legal benefits. Together, these eight fundamental conceptions describe generically the legal relations of persons and represent the lowest common denominator of the law,[74] in his own words, 'the lowest generic conceptions to which any and all legal quantities may be reduced .'[75] Hohfeld saw every single legal relation as involving two persons. Thus to say that A has a right to X is to suggest that A has a complex aggregate of claims, privileges, powers and immunities against one or more persons, all of which claims, etc. naturally have to do with X. By the same token the person or persons against whom A is asserting this right also bear a correlative duty, no-claim, liability, and disability toward A with respect to X.

Hohfeld distinguishes sharply between these fundamental legal concepts.

Rights and Duties

To avoid the confusion surrounding the word 'right', Hohfeld twins it with the correlative 'duty', for as he explains, '… it is certain that even those who use the word and the conception 'right' in the broadest possible way are accustomed to thinking of 'duty' as the invariable correlative.'[76] For '[a] duty or legal obligation is that which one ought or ought not to do. 'Duty' and 'right' are correlative terms. When a right is invaded, a duty is violated.'[77] For instance, If A has a right/claim to X against B, the correlative is that B is under a duty toward A with respect to X.

Privileges and 'No-Rights' or 'No-Claims'

In Hohfeld's scheme, a privilege is the opposite of a duty, and the correlative of a 'no-right' or 'no-claim.' Right/claim and privilege have been used interchangeably, as if they are synonymous: '… it is very common to use the term 'right' indiscriminately, even when the relation designated is really that of privilege.'[78] Hohfeld distinguishes clearly between these two concepts. A right signifies one's affirmative claim against another, as distinguished from 'privilege,'[79] one's freedom from the right or claim of another; the absence of duty, so to speak. For example, if A has a *right* or *claim* that B should stay off his land, B has a duty to stay off, whereas A himself has the *privilege* of entering on the land; or, conversely, A does not have a duty to stay off. In other words, the privilege of entering on the land negatives the duty to stay off it.

The correlative of a privileged legal relation is a 'no-right.' For example, whereas the correlative of A's right that B shall not enter his farm is B's duty not to enter; the

---

74 *Id.*, at 38.

75 *Id.*

76 *Id.*, at 38.

77 See Lake Shore & M.S.R. Co. v. Kurtz, 10 Ind. App. 60, 37 N.E. 303, 304 (1894).

78 See Hohfeld, *supra* note 70, at 38.

79 In the scheme 'privilege' is synonymous with liberty or freedom. *Id.*, at 47.

correlative of A's privilege of entering himself is B's 'no-right' that A shall not enter. Hohfeld was at pains to point out that two classes of distinct relations are subsumed under this example. First, A's privilege against B and others in relation to entering the farm, or, correlatively, the 'no-rights' of B and others that A should stay off the farm. Second, A's rights or claims as against B and others that they should not interfere with the physical act of entering the property, or, correlatively, the duty of B and others that they should not interfere. Hohfeld suggests in the above example that privileges could be present even though the rights mentioned are absent. That is, if B and others, being the owners of the farm, said to A 'Hey fella, you can enter our farm; you have our license to do so, but we don't agree not to interfere with you.' In such an outcome, Hohfeld argues, A's privilege of entering the farm exists, so that if he does exercise it, he has violated no rights of B or the others. Equally true is that if B were to barricade the entrance to the farm so that A could not gain access, no right of A would have been violated.[80]

The central point here is that previous writers had found a conflict or antinomy to exist between two rights when in reality they were confusing rights and privileges.[81] The two cannot be in conflict with each other as Hohfeld stressed, since to the extent that one party, in a legal relation, has privileges the other party has no rights; and, conversely, to the extent the latter has rights, the former has no legal privileges.[82]

Powers and Liabilities

In his conceptual scheme, Hohfeld treats legal power as the opposite of legal disability, and the correlative of legal liability.[83] Power is the ability to produce change in legal relations. Liability is the opposite of immunity (exemption).

Immunities and Disabilities

Immunity is the correlative of disability, that is, 'no-power' and the opposite, or negation, of liability:

> … a power bears the same general contrast to an immunity that a right does to a privilege. A right is one's affirmative claim against another, and a privilege is one's freedom from the right or claim of another. Similarly, a power is one's affirmative 'control' over a given legal relation as against another; whereas an immunity is one's freedom from the legal power or 'control' of another as regards some legal relation.[84]

Our interest is in an analytical scheme that can be applied to the legal resolution of the

---

80 *Id.*, at 41.

81 *Id.*, at 43.

82 *Id.*, at 43–44.

83 Hohfeld does not treat the term as exclusively an onerous relation of one party to another; but sees it also in its agreeable form. *Id.*, at 60 n. 90.

84 *Id.*, at 60.

concrete problem of indigenous spoliation. However, its resolution within the framework of litigation requires answers to several questions: to whom does the spoliated wealth belong? The State or the People? Who has standing to sue to recover these funds? Any member State of the international community or only the victim State? Any citizen of the world? What and, perhaps, whose legal interests are harmed? Should spoliated funds be repatriated to their countries of origin or allowed to remain in foreign banks? The answers to these questions call for an analysis of the legal relations between victims and spoliators in terms of their respective claims and duties, privileges and no-claims, powers and liabilities, immunities and disabilities with respect to national wealth and resources.

The legal relation we seek to explore here is fundamentally between the citizens and their leaders; between the members of the public and their public officials, that is those persons engaged in a 'public calling.' Professor Wyman has described the duty placed upon anyone exercising a public calling as 'primarily *a duty* to serve every man who is a member of the public.'[85] Wyman sees this duty as exceptional and difficult to locate in the legal system precisely because 'the obligation resting upon one who has undertaken the performance of a public duty is *sui generis*.'[86] The Hohfeldian bifurcation of legal relations into jural opposites and jural correlates and its subsequent reformulation and expansion by several other philosophers but most notably Carl Wellman provides a workable framework for examining the interplay of rights and duties between leaders and the led with respect to a nation's wealth and resources.

In the Hohfeldian scheme duties and rights are correlative such that for each legal advantage there is, and logically must be, a correlative legal disadvantage or burden. For instance, a national of a State (X) has a legal claim against his constitutionally-responsible rulers (Y) that Y hold and protect the nation's wealth and resources (Z), if and only if Y has a legal duty to X to protect Z. X has a legal privilege in face of Y to exploit his nation's wealth if and only if Y has no legal claim against X that X not do the action. X has a legal power over Y to change some legal relation of Y, for instance, not re-electing Y to office, if and only if Y has a legal liability of having this legal relation of Y changed by some voluntary action of X. X has a legal immunity from Y with respect to some legal relation of X if and only if Y has a legal disability of changing this legal relation of X by any action of Y.

Another reason for the appeal of the Hohfeldian vocabulary of rights and duties is that it strikes a responsive chord in jurists because it takes account of the adversarial context of assertions and denials of rights. It recognizes that much of the technical vocabulary of law consists of words that describe bilateral legal relations, such as 'masterservant,' 'principal-agent,' 'trustee-beneficiary,' 'assignor- assignee' and so forth. Each of Hohfeld's eight fundamental conceptions refers to a legal relation between two persons (or parties) and when Hohfeld speaks of these conceptions as jural relations, he means legal relations. And ultimately for Hohfeld every jural relation is a legal relation between two natural persons regarding some specific human

---

85 Wyman, Public Service Companies, §§330–333, cited in Hohfeld, *supra* note 70, at 57.

86 *Id.*

action.[87] Because of Hohfeld's stated bias that law should be understood primarily in terms of its application in courts of law, his focus never wavered from the relational aspects of legal positions in the context of a confrontation between plaintiff and defendant. Wellman offers the following example to flesh out this point:

> [T]o say that I have a legal liberty in face of my neighbor of barbecuing in my back yard is to say that my legal position is such that if my neighbor were to go to court and attempt to obtain a court order that I cease and desist from thus producing noxious smoke and odors that invade his property, he would probably lose his case. *In the absence of any possible application to some such courtroom confrontation between legal adversaries, the language of legal rights – the very conceptions of legal claims, liberties, powers and immunities – would lose its meaning* … (emphasis added).[88]

Following Hohfeld, any serious discussion of legal rights and duties with respect to the issue of a nation's wealth and resources makes sense only in the context of some possible legal confrontation between two parties: those who have clear and unambiguous rights over the use and enjoyment of these resources – the right-holder(s) and putative plaintiff(s) who could initiate a legal action – and those who have clear duties to hold and protect these same resources in trust for the people – the duty-bearers and defendants in a potential legal action. We are persuaded by the argument that the language of rights is essentially adversarial and as a consequence rights are asserted or denied only when two parties are, or at least could be imagined to be, in conflict.[89]

Adopting the Hohfeldian scheme helps to avoid the persistent conceptual confusion over the language of rights and duties since the focus is on the legal relations between leaders who spoliate the wealth of their nations and the nationals who are the victims of such spoliation. This way of looking at things forces the analyst not to lose sight of the fact that these two parties are potential legal adversaries. Thus, the Marcoses, the Mobutus, the Duvaliers, the Abachas, the Macias Nguemas and the Ceausescus of the world and the citizens over whom they preside stand on opposite sides of the jural fence.

Finally, Hohfeld's fundamental legal conceptions provide a useful vocabulary for the analysis of complex legal positions, particularly those relating to property and ownership rights. Wellman has argued that if legal property rights are thought of in terms of Hohfeld's fundamental legal conceptions, the underlying philosophical and legal problems would be much easier to resolve.[90] This is important for our purposes here because any discussion of indigenous spoliation is really about property (a nation's wealth and natural resources) and ownership rights in the broad sense of the term. It is fundamentally a discussion which attempts (i) to untangle the underlying

---

87 *See* Wellman, *supra* note 67, at 19.

88 *Id.*, at 10; see also H.L.A. Hart, 'Are There Any Natural Rights,' *Philosophical Rev.*, 64, 175, 183 (1955).

89 Wellman, *supra* note 67, at 10.

90 *Id.*, at 11.

legal web that binds citizens and leaders; (ii) simplify the complexities of their respective legal positions vis-a-vis these natural resources and wealth; and (iii) to disaggregate the many and varied legal consequences of this relationship. The following example by Hohfeld captures the complexity of this analysis and exposes the inadequacy of the traditional language of rights and duties:

> Suppose, for example, that A is fee-simple owner of Blackacre. His 'legal interest' or 'property' relating to the tangible object that we call *land* consists of a complex aggregate of rights (or claims), privileges, powers, and immunities. First, A has multiple legal rights, or claims that *others*, respectively, shall *not* enter on the land, that they shall not cause physical harm to the land, etc., such others being under respective correlative legal duties. Second, A has an indefinite number of legal privileges of entering on the land, using the land, harming the land, etc.; that is, within limits fixed by law on grounds of social and economic policy, he has the privileges of doing on or to the land what he pleases; and correlative to all such legal privileges are the respective legal no-rights of other persons. Third, A has the legal power to alienate his legal interest to another, that is, to extinguish his complex aggregate of jural relations and create a new and similar aggregate in the other person; also the legal power to create a privilege of entrance in any other person by giving 'leave and license'; and so on indefinitely. Correlative to all such legal powers are the legal liabilities in other persons – this meaning that the latter are subject *nolens volens* to the changes of jural relations involved in the exercise of A's powers. Fourth, A has an indefinite number of legal immunities, using the term immunity in the very specific sense of non-liability or non-subjection to a power on the part of another person. Thus A has the immunity that ordinary person can alienate A's legal interest or aggregate of jural relations to another person; the immunity that no ordinary person can extinguish A's own privileges of using the land; the immunity that no ordinary person can extinguish A's right that another person X shall not enter on the land or, in other words, create X a privilege of entering on the land. Correlative to all these immunities are the respective legal disabilities of other persons in general.[91]

This example carried over to the subject of this study would suggest that the simple assertion that a people have rights over their wealth and natural resources encompasses a complex aggregate of claims, privileges, powers and immunities. Therefore in the interest of accurate analysis and exposition but, more particularly, in order to bring out the economic significance of this position these rights or claims need to be sharply differentiated from privileges.

Notwithstanding its obvious appeal, the Hohfeldian scheme is not without its weakness as Carl Wellman and others have so ably demonstrated. At issue is the reductionism inherent in Hohfeld's fundamental legal conceptions.[92] Wellman takes issue with the notion that all legal positions are necessarily relational and as a consequence every application of fundamental legal concepts occurs within an adversarial legal process.[93] He is equally ill at ease with the companion Hohfeldian view that every legal action involves a confrontation between two legal adversaries, a

---

91 Hohfeld, *supra* note 70, at 96–97.

92 See J.W. Harris, *Legal Philosophies*, 84 (1980).

93 See Wellman, *supra* note 67, at 22.

plaintiff and a defendant and that their respective legal position is defined in relation to some potential legal contest.[94]

It is not always the case, Wellman argues, that the law is applied to those subject to it only in the courtroom context. While admitting that 'court cases may well provide paradigm examples of the application of the law,' empirically, Wellman points out, the overwhelming majority of instances when the law is applied occur outside the courtroom.[95]

Also coming up for criticism is the Hohfeldian view of a simple legal duty as entailing a legal relation between two and only two natural persons, one duty-bearer (read: putative defendant) and one second party (the plaintiff who could initiate a legal action). To this binary relation, Wellman asks: must the potential plaintiff ultimately be a single individual? Without a doubt, he observes,

> … the potential plaintiff has the legal power to set the process of legal enforcement in motion, but can the plaintiff be said to impose any legal constraint all by himself or herself? … Any constraint he or she can impose is obviously *via* a judicial holding against the defendant. Nor does any decision of the court enforce itself. In the end, force is applied to the individual subject to the law by police officers, officers of the court, or officials in our penal institutions.[96]

Wellman's point is that the power of legal constraint vested in the plaintiff in the Hohfeldian scheme is not inherently one that can be applied only in a courtroom against someone else. It can and is frequently applied against oneself, that is, as self-restraint:

> [A]n individual can, and often does, apply the law to himself or herself. Motorists often stop at a red light when there is no policeman waiting to arrest them; most of us send in our monthly payments on our mortgages before the bank threatens to foreclose; and many taxpayers fill out their income tax returns in strict accordance with the law.[97]

In short, there is a tradition of auto-compliance with the law out of a sense of duty independent of any threat of enforcement through the courts. Moreover, legal constraint, to the extent that it is imposed by an external agent, does not have to be a monopoly of a single plaintiff, as Hohfeld posits. There can be just as many and diverse legal constrainers all capable of initiating legal action against a putative dutybearer. After all, the breach of a legal action could harm not just a single individual but even an entire nation of people. Thus an expansion of Hohfeld's scheme to include legal relations between groups and classes of people would make room for many more persons to assume the role of legal constrainers-cum-potential plaintiffs able to impose constraints upon the duty-bearer(s).

---

94 *Id.*, at 21.

95 *Id.* See also Harris, *supra* note 92, at 84.

96 *Id.*, at 22; see also Carl Wellman, 'Upholding Legal Rights,' *Ethics*, 86, 49, 51 (1975).

97 *Id.*, at 22–23.

RIGHTS AND DUTIES WITH RESPECT TO NATIONAL WEALTH

When we talk of an individual having a legal right to his nation's wealth and natural resources, the term 'legal right' should be understood as a complex cluster of legal liberties/privileges, claim-rights, powers and immunities. It may mean any one of four possible alternatives.

First, it may mean that if A (a citizen of a State) has a right that B (a high-ranking State official) should not spoliate the nation's wealth and resources (X) for his private use, he himself has the privilege of using these resources; or, A does not have a duty not to use the nation's resources. Second, to say A has a right to the use and enjoyment of his nation's wealth and resources may be intended to indicate that B, his constitutionally elected or appointed leader (or everyone) has a duty to let A enjoy X. The existence of such a duty gives A something of a claim against B, or what Wellman in his reformulation of Hohfeld calls a *claim-right*. But this claim-right may involve either a purely negative duty not to impede A's actions or a positive requirement[98] on B to do what he can to make it possible for A to enjoy X. That is, claim-rights include rights to active assistance as well as rights to negative freedom,[99] on the one hand, and claim-rights *in personam* and claim-rights *in rem*, on the other. A's right *in personam* to the use and enjoyment of his nation's wealth and resources is correlative to a duty peculiarly incumbent on an assignable person or group of persons.[100] Put differently, A's right *in personam* is availing against a few definite persons such as the nation's constitutionally-responsible rulers. His claim-rights *in rem*, on the other hand, are correlative in principle incumbent on everyone.[101] In other words, A's *in rem* claim-rights to his nation's wealth means everyone – nationals and foreigners included – have a duty to refrain from using these resources to A's detriment.

Thirdly, we use 'right to' mean A's ability or *power* to alter existing legal arrangements. A can extinguish his own legal interests (claim-rights, powers, immunities) in X or transfer them to B or to someone else for that matter and in the process create new and corresponding interest.[102] A has a right to exploit his nation's wealth and natural resources or enter into a contract, say, with foreign transnational corporations to do so for their mutual benefit. In so doing, A brings about a change in legal relations with a third-party; the foreign company now acquires all the rights (privileges/liberties, claim-rights, and powers) that ownership bestows while A in turn acquires the duties, liabilities, and disabilities correlative to these rights. Since in the Hohfeldian scheme powers are correlative to liabilities, if A has a legal power to X, then someone (or everyone) is liable to have his legal position changed in response to an exercise of A's will.

Finally, we use the term 'right' to describe the correlate of *disability*, the lack of a

---

98 See Hohfeld, *supra* note 70, at 73.

99 See Jeremy Waldron, 'Introduction,' in *Theories of Rights*, 1, 6 (Jeremy Waldron ed.).

100 See Hohfeld, *supra* note 70, at 72.

101 Hohfeld talks of *in rem* rights availing 'against persons constituting a very large and indefinite class of people.' *Id.*

102 *Id.*, at 51.

power – an *immunity* from legal change. When we say A has an immunity with regard to X, then B (or everyone) lacks the power to alter his legal position in regard to X.

Rights are not only complex normative structures but create normative relations involving more than two parties:

> … the first party who possesses the right, second parties against whom the right holds, third parties who might intervene either to aid the possessor of the right or the violator, and various officials whose diverse activities make up the legal system under which first, second and third parties have their respective legal liberties, claims, powers, and immunities and whose official activities are in turn regulated by the legal system itself.[103]

Any adequate analysis of rights must distinguish among these different parties, identify and assign their respective roles and legal positions *vis-a-vis* one another. Applying this formulation to the problem of indigenous spoliation, it becomes quickly evident that the old rights versus duties on second party approach is inadequate in isolating the multiple parties, roles, and legal positions and relations contained in this complex problem. In addition to the right-holders and primary addressees of the right to the use and enjoyment of their nation's wealth and resources, that is, the nationals, other parties involved include the constitutionally elected and appointed leaders who have spoliated these resources with impunity, their closest associates who aid and abet them in this undesirable conduct, successor governments that seek to capture and repatriate these funds, the many foreign nations that offer refuge to both spoliated funds and the fugitive spoliators, foreign courts where victim States and victim nationals can initiate legal action to recover and repatriate this stolen wealth, nationals of third party States whose tax dollars provide foreign aid to these countries, which in turn is diverted into private bank accounts or used to underwrite the profligate lifestyles of the spoliators, commercial banks who advanced loans to these countries and cannot now collect on them, and so forth.

This formulation allows us to look beyond the single political leader who might have spoliated national wealth and the individual citizens who have been denied the use of these funds. It forces an analysis which must include a focus on the liberties, and sometimes powers and duties of third parties who *can* aid the possessors of the right and who *can* refrain from helping second parties who threaten to violate this right.

Finally, we view rights and duties in the context of this study as a complex normative structure conferring autonomy to the holder, assigning legal advantage to some and legal disadvantage to others. The notion of the autonomy of rights is particularly well-developed in the writings of Carl Wellman[104] and H.J. McCloskey. For the latter, rights are entitlements 'intrinsic to their possessors' and held

---

[103] Wellman, *supra* note 96, at 51.

[104] See Carl Wellman, 'Legal Rights,' *Uppsalaskolan-Och Efterat*, 213, 220–221 (1978) cited in Martins & Nickel, *supra* note 53, at 171; see also Carl Wellman, 'A New Conception of Human Rights,' in *Human Rights*, 48, 55–56 (Eugene Kamenka & Ann Erh Sooh Tay eds, 1978).

'independently of other people and … of what else ought to be.'[105] An entitlement need not depend on the will of anyone, including the rightholder. It rests, rather, on objective moral considerations – on a moral authority to act in a certain way – on 'the nature of autonomous existence.'[106] As a term that confers a legal advantage on someone, such an assignment can occur even prior to knowing who would or should bear the corresponding legal disadvantage.[107] Following this formulation, the right to the wealth and resources of a nation are intrinsic to the citizens of that nation. It is their entitlement whether or not it is recognized as such by some external agency. As we explore in the subsequent chapter these rightholders can press for the legal advantages flowing from these entitlements by initiating legal action against their constitutionally responsible rulers.

---

[105] See McCloskey, *supra* note 65, at 99.

[106] See Henry John McCloskey, 'Rights,' *Philosophical Quarterly*, 15, 115, 120 (1965); Henry John McCloskey, 'The Right to Life,' *Mind*, 84, 403, 417, 413–416 (1975) (developing the view of rights as autonomous in defense of the right to life).

[107] See David Lyons, 'The Correlativity of Rights and Duties,' *Nous*, 4, 45, 51 (1970); see also Feinberg on Duties, *supra* note 56, at 142.

Chapter 10

Legal Basis of Jurisdiction over Crimes of Indigenous Spoliation

EXTRA-TERRITORIAL JURISDICTION IN INTERNATIONAL LAW

If indigenous spoliation is a crime committed by nationals in their own States, upon what basis therefore can the courts of another State prosecute and punish this conduct? The issue of jurisdiction is relevant for two reasons. First, spoliated assets are usually sent abroad, particularly to 'safe haven' States, for safe keeping, and secondly, the majority of high-ranking officials, including heads of States, who have been implicated in such activities traditionally flee to other States to escape prosecution from their domestic courts. Given these facts victims of spoliation who seek to recover stolen assets are left with no alternative but to bring civil actions against the involved public officials in the foreign jurisdictions where they or their assets are located. Usually when this happens the defendants have responded by asserting that these actions are property suits against a sovereign and they are therefore entitled to immunity from jurisdiction.

It has already been pointed out in earlier chapters that immunity doctrines were developed precisely to foreclose the prospect of subjecting Sovereigns and their agents to jurisdiction, *in personam* or *in rem*, of foreign courts. This is in keeping with traditional principles of jurisdiction found in customary international law.[1]

The activities associated with indigenous spoliation take place outside the territory where suit is usually brought. However, under the territorial principle, a State's absolute power to prescribe, adjudicate and enforce rules of law extends only to conduct that occurs within its own territory.[2] This limitation on a State's jurisdictional competence would normally pose a serious problem to spoliation cases except that it admits to one exception. The principle of territoriality allows the exercise of jurisdiction even for acts that occur outside the State but which have effects within its territory.[3]

---

1 See S.S. Lotus (France v. Turkey), 1927 PCIJ, ser. A, No. 10; see also 'Harvard Research in International Law, Jurisdiction With Respect to Crime,' *Am. J. Int'l L. Supp.*, 29, 435 (1935) [hereinafter 'Draft Convention on Jurisdiction'].

2 See S.S. Lotus, *id.*

3 This is the so-called 'objective territoriality' principle which was recognized in the S.S. Lotus Case. The principle is also the basis for the elaboration of an international nuisance doctrine under which a state incurs responsibility to another if it permits its territory to be used

In the event, the dialectics between prospective plaintiffs and defendants in spoliation cases over the proper application of sovereign immunity raises a very intriguing question: at what point does the immunity of the person of the Sovereign yield to the needs of an injured private party plaintiff? Differently stated, does a private party plaintiff deserve a day in court to have his claim heard on the merits, the doctrine of sovereign immunity notwithstanding? This question is particularly pertinent in spoliation cases where the economic injury is usually so profound and felt across the entire national community and the injustice of allowing immunity particularly apparent. The consequences of indigenous spoliation are ubiquitous: destruction of economies, diminution of national wealth and resources, damage to lives and property and so on. All of these follow on the heels of the fraudulent activities of constitutionally-responsible rulers. It would be stretching it beyond acceptable limits of belief to suggest that the victims voluntarily assumed the risk of the resulting economic injuries. Under these circumstances, their right to sue as well as to a hearing on the merits of their claim should not be barred by the doctrine of sovereign immunity. On the other hand, a deposed head of State living in exile in a foreign country, arguably, assumed voluntarily the risk of being haled into a foreign court. To the degree that he enjoys the benefits and protections of the foreign State's law by electing to reside within the territory and have his assets safely ensconced in forum banks protected by forum's laws including their bank secrecy regulations, he cannot claim otherwise. The equities cry out for the denial of sovereign immunity to such a defendant while also raising a fundamental question so central to the disposition of indigenous spoliation cases in foreign courts. Assuming *arguendo* that defendants in these actions qualify as sovereigns under classical international law doctrines, whose conception of sovereign immunity should govern in foreign courts? The defendant's, the plaintiff's or the foreign court's definition?

The Universality Principle

Customary international law recognizes that one of the methods by which extra-territorial jurisdiction can be exercised is through the *universality principle*.[4] The principle applies to universal crimes 'over which all states could exercise jurisdiction regardless of the alleged offender's nationality.'[5] According to Section 404 of the Restatement (Third) of the Foreign Relations Law of the United States: '[a] state has jurisdiction to define and prescribe punishment for certain offenses recognized by the community of nations as of universal concern … .' Under this principle member States of the international community are empowered to punish crimes deemed universally dangerous to States and their subjects. Jurisdiction is exercised over the authors of such crimes wherever they occur without any regard to their link between the State and

---

in such a way as to create harm in the latter's territory. See The Trail Smelter Arbitration (US v. Canada), 3 UN Rep. Int. Arb. Awards 1911 (1941).

4 See Draft Convention on Jurisdiction, *supra* note 1, 443.

5 Rebecca Wallace, *International Law: A Student Introduction*, 104 (1986).

the parties or the crimes in question.[6] The most frequently mentioned example of such a universal crime is piracy in international law – piracy *jure gentium* – as opposed to piracy in municipal law, defined as 'any illegal act of violence or depredation which is committed for private ends either on the high seas or without the territorial control of any state.'[7] The applicability of the universal jurisdiction principle to piracy cases as customary law was reaffirmed in Article 19 of the 1958 Convention on the High Seas and Article 105 of the 1982 Convention on the Law of the Seas.[8] The universality principle was one of the bases for the assertion of Israeli jurisdiction in the celebrated Eichmann case.[9] The court held that 'a universal source (pertaining to the whole of mankind), which vests the right to prosecute and punish crimes of this order in every state within the family of nations; and a specific or national source, which gives the victim nation the right to try any who assault its existence.'[10] It also provided the basis upon which a Spanish magistrate sought extradition to Spain of General Augusto Pinochet in October 1998, while he was on a private visit to England,[11] for crimes

6 Principle 1 of the Princeton Principles on Universal Jurisdiction provides that 'universal jurisdiction is criminal jurisdiction based solely on the nature of the crime, without regard to where the crime was committed, the nationality of the alleged or convicted perpetrator, the nationality of the victim, or any other connection to the state exercising such jurisdiction.' Princeton Project on Universal Jurisdiction, *The Princeton Principles on Universal Jurisdiction* (2001). The Pinochet case is emblematic of the application of the universality principle: the Spanish judge, Garzon, who ordered the arrest of Pinochet arrest for crimes committed primarily in Chile and primarily against Chileans did so under Spanish law; there was no traditional jurisdictional nexus linking the alleged perpetrator and the prosecuting state; the alleged crimes had not been committed in Spain; Pinochet was not a Spanish national; and he was not in Spain at the time of his arrest; the alleged victims were not Spanish citizens, and, ostensibly, there were no protected Spanish economic interests at stake. Thus the legal rationale and authority for the actions of the Spanish judge were on the basis of a universal interest. In other words, through Judge Garzon, Spain was acting in the universal interest of the international community insofar as the basis of Spain's jurisdiction was exclusively the nature of the alleged crime of torture.

7 Article 15 of the 1958 Geneva Convention on the High Seas; Article 101 of the 1982 Geneva Convention on the Law of the Sea; Wallace, *supra* note 5, at 104.

8 *Id.*

9 Attorney-General of the Government of Israel v. Eichmann (1961) 36 ILR 18 (Isr. Dist. Ct.-Jerusalem 1961), aff'd, 36 ILR 277 (Isr. Sup. Ct. 1962).

10 Attorney-General v. Eichmann, at 50. On appeal, the Israeli Supreme Court reached the same conclusion: '[T]here is full justification for applying here the principle of universal jurisdiction since the international character of 'crimes against humanity'... dealt with in this case is no longer in doubt....' See Attorney-General v. Eichmann, 36 ILR 277, 299 (Isr. Sup. Ct. 1962).

11 General Pinochet entered the United Kingdom in September 1997 for medical treatment. After undergoing surgery and shortly before his return to Chile, the general was arrested on the strength of two provisional arrest warrants issued by two stipendiary magistrates (respectively, Nicholas Evans and Ronald Bartle), following a request for extradition from Spanish courts, pursuant to the 1957 European Convention on Extradition (incorporated in the

allegedly committed, not in Spain, but in Chile. The Law Lords ruled that Pinochet, as former head of state, could not claim immunity for torture, as it does not constitute an official act, and they upheld the possibility of Pinochet's extradition to Spain. In the end, the British Home Secretary, Jack Straw, had Pinochet extradited to Chile on grounds of age and illness. In the event, for the first time, the House of Lords, Britain's highest court, ruled that in certain circumstances, English law too might uphold a claim of universal jurisdiction.

Under this doctrine, it is the universal character of the crime that vests in every State the authority to try and punish those who participated in its commission. That is, each State is viewed as a guardian of international law and an agent for its enforcement.[12] In this role, the State has a duty to either extradite or, in the absence of extradition, bring legal proceedings against an alleged perpetrator who is present on its

---

United Kingdom by the European Convention on Extradition Order 1990 (SI 1507 of 1990) as amended). Pinochet's counsel immediately moved to have the two arrest warrants quashed by the High Court of Justice, Queen's Bench Division in *In the Matter of an Application for a Writ of Habeas Corpus ad Subjicendum. Re: Augusto Pinochet Duarte*, 28 October 1998 (reprinted in 38 ILM 68 (1999)). The high court ruled in Pinochet's favor with respect to the first warrant on the ground that the crimes for which Spain was requesting extradition were not extraditable crimes under the UK Extradition Act. As regards the second arrest warrant, the Lord Chief Justice held that under section 20 of the UKState Immunity Act – which grants to heads of states the same privileges and immunities as those enjoyed by heads of diplomatic missions under the 1961 Vienna Convention on Diplomatic Protection – Pinochet was immune from jurisdiction as the acts that he was alleged to have committed were official acts performed in the exercise of his functions of head of state.. The Court granted leave for the Crown to appeal to the House of Lords, certifying as a point of law of general public importance 'the proper interpretation and scope of the immunity enjoyed by a former head of state from arrest and extradition proceedings in the United Kingdom in respect of acts committed while he was head of state.' On appeal, the House of Lords reversed the lower court's ruling and held, by a narrow three to two decision, that a former head of state is not entitled to immunity for such acts as torture, hostage taking and crimes against humanity, committed while he was performing the duties of head of state. See Regina v. Bartle and the Commissioner of Police for the Metropolis and Other (Appellants), Ex Parte Pinochet (Respondent) (On Appeal from a Divisional Court of the Queen's Bench (Division); Regina v. Evans and Another and the Commissioner of Police for the Metropolis and Others (Appellants), Ex Parte Pinochet (Respondent) (On Appeal from a Divisional Court of the Queen's Bench Division), Judgment of 25 November 1998, 37 ILM 1302 (1998).

[12] See for example, Matter of Barbie, [1983] Gaz.Pal.Jur. 710 (Cass.Crim. 6 October 1983) (holding that the charges against Barbie transcended internal French rules of procedure in as much as they involved crimes against all humanity as defined by conventional and customary international law); see also Matter of Demjanjuk, 603 F. Supp. 1468 (N.D. Ohio), *affirmed*, 776 F.2d 571 (6th Cir. 1985), *certiorari denied*, 457 US 1016, 106 S. Ct. 1198, 89 L.Ed.2d 312 (1986) (commenting on request for the extradition of the accused to stand trial in Israel: '[i]nternational law provides that certain offenses may be punished by any state because the offenders are "common enemies of all mankind and all nations have an equal interest in their apprehension and punishment."').

territory. This principle of *aut dedere aut judicare* (or *prosequi*) together with the fact that statutes of limitations or other forms of prescription do not apply to crimes under international law[13] add to the attraction of the universality principle as a basis for exercising jurisdiction over crimes of indigenous spoliation. Equally of importance, the class of offenses for which universal jurisdiction is applicable is an expansible one[14] and the criteria for inclusion being universal opprobrium with which the conduct

---

[13] See Article 29 of the Rome Statute of the International Criminal Court which provides that genocide, crimes against humanity and war crimes 'shall not be subject to any statutes of limitations'; United Nations Convention on the Non-Applicability of Statutory Limitations to War Crimes and Crimes Against Humanity (1968) (crimes under international law are not subject to any statutes of limitation regardless when they were committed); United Nations Principles on the Effective Prevention and Punishment of Extra-legal, Arbitrary and Summary Executions; Convention against Torture (exempts states from the duty to bring to justice those responsible for such crimes through statutes of limitations); Convention on the Non-Applicability of Statutory Limitations to War Crimes and Crimes Against Humanity, 26 November 1968, 754 UNTS 73; European Convention on Non-Applicability of Statutory Limitations to Crimes Against Humanity and War Crimes (Inter-European), 25 January 1974, Europ. T.S. No. 82.

[14] The first crimes under international law over which States could exercise universal jurisdiction were brigandage, war crimes, piracy, slavery and the slave trade. By the end of the Second World War the scope of universal jurisdiction had expanded to include trafficking in women and children, terrorism, use of submarines and asphyxiating gases during time of war, white slavery, etc. These new crimes were added in treaties, state practice and national legislation authorizing the exercise of jurisdiction over crimes against humanity. A sizeable and representative number of States drawn from the world's major legal systems have enacted legislation permitting their courts to exercise universal jurisdiction over crimes against humanity, war crimes or other crimes *under* international law. These states include: • **Belgium** Under *the Loi du 16 juin 1993 relative à la répression des infractions graves aux Conventions internationales de Genève du 12 août 1949 et aux Protocoles I et II du 8 juin 1977, additionnels à ces Conventions* (Moniteur Belge, 5 août 1993), Belgian courts have universal jurisdiction over violations of the four Geneva Conventions of 1949 and their Protocols. In addition, Belgian courts are considered to have jurisdiction over crimes against humanity under customary law. *See* Luc Reydams, '*De Belgische wet ter bestraffing van inbreuken op het internationaal humanitair recht: een papieren tijger?*', 7 Zoeklicht (1998) p. 4. In addition, *Loi 13 avril 1995, Art. 8, loi relative aux abus sexuels à l'égard des mineurs* provides for universal jurisdiction over crimes against minors. • **Bolivia** The Bolivian Penal Code (Article 1 (7)) provides that national courts have jurisdiction to try those crimes that were committed abroad, independently of the nationality of the person presumed responsible and that of the victim, when the state, through international treaties or conventions, has pledged to punish them. • **Brazil** The Brazilian Penal Code (Article 7) provides that national courts have jurisdiction to try those crimes that were committed abroad, independently of the nationality of the person presumed responsible and that of the victim, when the state, through international treaties or conventions, has pledged to punish them. • **Canada** Section 7 (3.71) of the Canadian Criminal Code provides for universal jurisdiction over non-Canadians found in Canada for conduct outside Canada that constitutes a crime against humanity or a war crime if the conduct would have constituted an offence in Canada had it been committed in Canada. • **Chile** Article 5 of the

Chilean Constitution recognizes as limits on sovereignty the respect for law which is inherent in the person and provides that the authorities have the duty to promote and respect rights guaranteed by treaties ratified by Chile which are in force. The Supreme Court of Justice of Chile has recognized under Article 5 the possibility of the direct application of the provisions of international treaties to which Chile is a party and which are in force (Judgment of 10 September 1988, Pedro Enrique Poblete Cordoba, paras 9 & 10). Chile is a party to the Inter-American Convention to Prevent and Punish Torture, which it ratified on 30 September of 1988. Article 12 of that treaty provides for universal jurisdiction over persons suspected of torture. Chile has also signed the Inter-American Convention on Forced Disappearance of Persons on 10 June 1994. Article IV provides for universal jurisdiction over this crime under international law and Chile is obliged under international law to refrain from acts that would defeat the object and purpose of the Convention pending a decision on ratification (Vienna Convention on the Law of Treaties, Art. 18). Chile has also ratified the Convention against Torture on 23 September 1989, which provides for universal jurisdiction in Article 5. • **Columbia** The Colombian Penal Code (Article 15 (6)) provides that Colombian courts have jurisdiction over crimes committed abroad by foreigners against other foreigners, when the person presumed responsible is within Colombian territory. • **Costa Rica** The Costa Rican Penal Code (Article 7) states that national courts, independently of the place of the event and the nationality of the person presumed responsible, have jurisdiction to judge according to national law the crime of genocide and any crimes against human rights according to treaties accepted by Costa Rica or by its Penal Code. • **Denmark** Article 8 (5) of the Danish Penal Code gives the courts jurisdiction to try those responsible for certain crimes when Denmark is bound to do so by treaty (see Marianne Holdgaard Bukh, 'Prosecution before Danish Courts of Foreigners Suspected of Serious Violations of Human Rights or Humanitarian Law,' *Eur. Rev. Pub. L.*, 6, 339 (1994). • **Ecuador** The Ecuadorean Penal Code (Article 5) provides that national courts have jurisdiction to try those crimes that were committed abroad, independently of the nationality of the person presumed responsible and that of the victim, when international treaties or conventions establish this jurisdiction. • **El Salvador** The Penal Code of El Salvador (Article 9) provides the competence of national courts to exercise jurisdiction over crimes committed abroad, when they are considered crimes of international significance according to international treaties or conventions. • **France** On 6 January 1998, the Cour de Cassation held in the *Weceslas Munyeshyaka* case that France has universal jurisdiction under the French Law 96-432 of 22 May 1996 over genocide and crimes against humanity. • **Germany** Article 6 (1) of the German Penal Code provides that German criminal law applies to acts of genocide committed abroad. Article 6 (9) of the German Penal Code provides that German criminal law applies to conduct, including conduct abroad, which Germany is obliged to prosecute under a treaty to which it is a party. • **Guatemala** The Guatemala Penal Code (Article 5 (5)) provides that national courts have jurisdiction to try those crimes that were committed abroad, independently of the nationality of the person presumed responsible and that of the victim, when the state, through international treaties or conventions, has pledged to punish them. • **Honduras** The Honduran Penal Code (Article 5 (5)) provides that courts have jurisdiction to try those crimes that were committed abroad, independently of the nationality of the person presumed responsible and that of the victim, when the state, through international treaties or conventions, has pledged to punish them, or when principles of international permit courts to exercise such jurisdiction. • **Israel** The Israeli Nazi and Nazi Collaborators (Punishment) Law, 5710/1950, Sections 1 and 3, which prohibit certain crimes, including crimes against humanity, have been interpreted as applying to acts committed outside Israel by non-Israeli citizens. See Attorney-General of the Government of Israel v. Eichmann, *Int'l L. Rep.*, 36, 18, 50 (Isr. Dist. Ct. - Jerusalem), aff'd, *Int'l L. Rep.*, 36, 277, 299 (Isr. Sup. Ct. 1962). • **Mexico** Mexican Penal Code (*Código Penal para el Distrito Federal en materia de Fuero Común y para toda la República en materia de Fuero Federal*, Art. 6) provides that courts have jurisdiction to try those crimes under international treaties imposing this obligation on Mexico. • **Nicaragua** The Penal Code of Nicaragua (Article 16 (3) (f)) provides for universal jurisdiction, inter alia, over crimes of piracy, slave commerce, racial discrimination and genocide. • **Norway** Section 12 (4) of the Norwegian Criminal Code provides that, 'Unless it is otherwise specially provided or accepted in an agreement with a foreign State, Norwegian criminal law shall be applicable to acts committed: … (4) abroad by a foreigner when the act either' (a) constitutes murder, assault and certain other crimes under Norwegian law or (b) 'is a felony also punishable according to the law of the country in which it is committed, and the offender is resident in the realm or is staying therein'. • **Panama** Article 10 of the Panamanian Penal Code provides that courts have jurisdiction to try those crimes that were committed abroad, independently of the nationality of the person presumed responsible and that of the victim, when the offence was established by international treaties or conventions ratified by Panama. • **Peru** Article 2 of the Peruvian Penal Code provides that courts have jurisdiction to try those crimes that were committed abroad, independently of the nationality of the presumed responsible and that of the victim, when the state, through international treaties or conventions, has pledged to punish them. • **Spain** Article 65 of the 1985 Judicial Power Organic Law (*Ley Orgánica del Poder Judicial, Ley orgánica* 6/1985) gives Spanish courts jurisdiction over acts committed outside Spain where the conduct would violate Spanish law if committed in Spain or violates obligations under international treaties. Article 23 (4) of this law gives Spanish courts jurisdiction over other offences that international treaties require Spain to prosecute, including genocide, terrorism and where treaties require Spain to prosecute such crimes; *see* 'The Criminal Procedures against Chilean and Argentinian Repressors in Spain: A Short Summary' (Revision One), 11 November 1998, Derechos Human Rights, http://www.derechos.org). • **Switzerland** Article 6 bis of the Code pénal suisse gives the courts universal jurisdiction over crimes committed outside the territory that Switzerland is obliged to prosecute under a treaty, such as torture. See Switzerland's Initial Report to the UN Committee against Torture, UN Doc. CAT/C/5/Add.17, para. 52. Article 109 of the *Code pénale militaire* (Violations of the Laws of War) provides that it is a crime for anyone to act 'contrary to the provisions of any international agreement governing the laws or the protection of persons and property, or … in violation of any other recognized law or custom of war.' Article 2 (9) extends the application of the Code to civilians and members of foreign armed forces, even if they commit the crimes abroad during an international armed conflict and have no link to Switzerland. Article 108 (1) provides for the application of Articles 109 to 114 to international armed conflict; Article 108 (2) extends their application to non-international armed conflict. See Andreas R. Zeigler, 'In re G. ,' *Am. J. Int'l L.*, 92, 78, 79 (1998). • **Uruguay** Article 10(7) of the Uruguayan Penal Code provides that courts have jurisdiction to try those crimes that were committed abroad, independently of the nationality of the person presumed responsible and that of the victim, when the state, through international treaties or conventions, has pledged to punish them. • **Venezuela** Article 4(9) of the Venezuelan Penal Code provides that courts have jurisdiction to try and punish crimes against humanity committed abroad, by nationals or foreigners, when they are in Venezuelan territory.

See Amnesty International, Universal Jurisdiction and Absence of Immunity for Crimes

is received and the general interest in cooperating in its suppression 'as reflected in widely-accepted international agreements and resolutions of international organizations.'[15]

DUTY OF ALL STATES TO PROSECUTE ACTS OF INDIGENOUS SPOLIATION

We have argued in the preceding chapters that indigenous spoliation is wrongful conduct that properly belongs to the category of an international economic crime. It was also argued that in view of the fundamental rights involved 'all States can be held to have a legal interest in their protection [since] they are obligations *erga omnes*.'[16] Since these obligations are the concern of all States, any member State of the international community has both a duty and a right to take legal action in the form of an *actio popularis* to vindicate the broad community-wide interests implicated. The *actio popularis* is perhaps the most appropriate vehicle for accomplishing this task because it permits jurisdiction to be exercised in the form of criminal law while not precluding the application of non-criminal law principles such as providing a remedy in tort or restitution for victims of spoliation.

The *actio popularis* can be traced back to Roman law of obligations under which an action could be brought by any member of the public (*quivis ex populo*) to vindicate a public interest. Its origins in the law of obligations notwithstanding, the two most well known *actiones populares* contained 'a certain penal and policing element'[17] and it is in this sense that it is being recruited into international law by analogy. These were the *actio de delectus vel effusis* and the *actio de posito et suspenso*. The former was an action brought against a homeowner from whose house things had been thrown or liquids poured resulting in injury to passers-by. The latter was an action that could be brought by any member of the public by leave of the Roman *praetor* when things were located or suspended on the outside of a house or in a window in such a way as to endanger the lives of people on the street.[18] Since both types of actions were classified as *quasi ex delicto*, they created obligations similar to those arising from a delict, that is, the liability to pay damages and, where appropriate, criminal responsibility.[19]

Until 1970 when the International Court of Justice resolved the issue in the Barcelona Traction judgment, there was some uncertainty whether 'the equivalent of

---

Against Humanity (1 January 1999). Available on http://web.amnesty.org/library (last visited 25 February 2005).

[15] See Restatement (Third) of the Foreign Relations Law of the United States, '404 comment a.

[16] See Case Concerning the Barcelona Traction, Light and Power Co., Ltd. (Belgium v. Spain), [1970] ICJ Rep. 3, 32.

[17] See Egon Schwelb, 'The Actio Popularis and International Law,' *Israel Y.B. Hum. Rts.*, 2, 46, 47 n. 6 (1972).

[18] *Id.*

[19] *Id.*

an "*actio popularis*" or right resident in any member of a community to take legal action in vindication of a public interest'[20] was known to international law.[21] The Restatement (Third) of the Foreign Relations Law of the United States appears to endorse this view. Section 902 of the Restatement provides that:

> (1) A state may bring a claim against another state for a violation of an international obligation owed to the claimant state or to states generally, either through diplomatic channels or through any procedure to which the two states have agreed.
>
> (2) Under Subsection (1), a state may bring claims, *inter alia*, for violations of international obligations resulting in injury to its nationals or to other persons on whose behalf it is entitled to make a claim under international law.

This provision is fleshed out in the accompanying commentary which carefully points out that '[w]hen a state has violated an obligation owed to the international community as a whole, *any state may bring a claim* in accordance with this section *without showing that it has suffered any particular injury.* Thus, any state may call on the violating state to terminate a significant injury to the general environment … or pursue a remedy for a denial of human rights in violation of customary international law …' (emphasis added).[22] Aside from the legal, and perhaps moral, duty that conventional and customary international law may impose on States, there are also some compelling pragmatic reasons for obligating the international community to police the type of wrongful conduct associated with indigenous spoliation.

Although acts of spoliation are carried out by an indigenous elite, success depends on the assistance, direct or indirect, it receives from the rest of the international community. The consequences that ineluctably follow from these fraudulent activities can therefore be attributed not only to the indigenous elites who treat their national treasuries as their personal accounts but also to their foreign backers and aid donors who overlook their excesses for one reason or another. The silence or inaction by these foreign friends completely changes the character of these acts from a purely local problem to one with global implications. In hearings conducted by a subcommittee of the United States House of Representatives on the investments by the Marcoses in the US, Congressman Torricelli of New Jersey directed his remarks to the problem of Western complicity. After reviewing the assets of the Marcoses in America, the representative from New Jersey then concluded with the following words: '… one day

---

[20] See South West Africa Cases (Second Phase) (Ethiopia and Liberia v. South Africa), [1966] ICJ Rep. 6, 47.

[21] In the South West Africa Cases, the International Court of Justice denied the existence of *actiones populares* in international law. *Id.* However, Egon Schwelb in a reasoned analysis challenged the correctness of the Court's statement and proceeded to demonstrate through a canvass of authorities that an equivalent to an *actio popularis* was, indeed, known to international law 'in 1919/20, in 1962 and in 1966, and is "known" today.' See Schwelb, *supra* note 17, at 55.

[22] See *Restatement (Third) of the Foreign Relations Law of the United States*, §902 comment a.

America will be held accountable, accountable to whether we were complicitous, whether we stood silent while the Philippine people went further into debt, while Mr. Marcos and his family feathered their American nest in preparation for their eventual departure.'[23]

The Conspiracy of Silence

As the American lawmaker's remarks reveal, Western complicity has been in the form of a studied silence in the face of brazen acts of spoliation by ruling elites around the world; a silence that has been maintained even when these elites have used force to get their way. It is no secret that repression has been one of the favorite and most effective tools employed by dictators to plunder the economy. Each of the dictators mentioned in this study was quite successful in the way he used repressive government apparatus to extract wealth from the national economy. Francois Duvalier, for instance, set out early in his presidency to establish his own praetorian guard, the dreaded and infamous *Tontons Macoutes*.[24] Duvalier's *Macoutes* operated as a paramilitary and mercenary force with arbitrary powers which were used 'widely and wantonly to terrorize the population, deprive them of their most elementary civil rights, and engage in all sorts of extortionary and corrupt practices.'[25] Francois Duvalier skillfully manipulated and exploited the United States' fear of the specter of Communism and Haiti's proximity to Cuba to wring badly needed aid from the United States.[26] It is estimated that between 1958 to 1962, Haiti received a total of $70 million in gifts and loans from the United States 'despite the knowledge that the money would be used by the regime to reinforce the Macoutes and/or stolen by government officials.'[27] Though President Kennedy suspended all US economic and military aid to Haiti in 1963 to protest Duvalier's deplorable human rights record,[28] President Nixon would barely six years later restore full aid to the country.[29] Following the death of Francois Duvalier, the US in 1972 established new development assistance programs for Haiti, an example that was quickly copied by other major west European nations such as France, Belgium and Canada. Throughout the long Haiti-US relationship, the United States 'assumed the responsibility for financing the Haitian government through foreign aid, despite the

---

[23] *Investigation of the Philippine Investments in the United States, Hearings before the Subcommittee on Asian and Pacific Affairs of the Committee on Foreign Affairs, House of Representatives*, 99th Cong., 1st & 2nd Sess. (1985–1986), at 264.

[24] See Josh DeWind & David Kinley 111, *Aiding Migration: The Impact of International Development Assistance on Haiti*, 16–17 (1988); Alex Dupuy, *Haiti in the World Economy: Class, Race, and Underdevelopment since 1700*, 160 (1988).

[25] See Dupuy, *id.*, at 160–161; DeWind & Kinley, *id.*, at 17. When Jean-Claude Duvalier succeeded his father in 1972, he too quickly created his own elite military force, the Leopards, 'equipped and trained by the United States in counterinsurgency tactics.' Dupuy, *id.*, at 170.

[26] *Id.*, at 166.

[27] *Id.*

[28] *Id.*

[29] *Id.*, at 167.

knowledge of widespread fraudulent practices and misappropriation of public and aid monies by government officials.'[30] Misappropriations were possible because the Duvaliers enjoyed absolute control over the state apparatuses and the repressive forces. Ministerial appointments were made with an eye toward pleasing Washington, though it was generally understood that Ministers were not to take their responsibilities seriously lest they jeopardize or expose government corruption.[31]

It was not only in Haiti that the instruments and weapons of repression financed by Western friends were pressed into service by ruling elites around the globe to assist in the pillage of their economies. In the twenty years Marcos was President of the Philippines, his country was tied to the United States by a web of treaty arrangements dating back to the 1940s.[32] During his presidency the United States pumped hundreds of millions of dollars annually in military assistance grants and credits.[33] Filipino military students were allowed to attend professional military-education and technical training courses in the United States.[34] Under Ferdinand Marcos, the Philippines was viewed as a longstanding treaty ally and a special friend of the United States.[35] Marcos

---

30 *Id.*, at 169.

31 *Id.*, at 171.

32 The Agreement Between the United States of America and the Republic of the Philippines Concerning Military Bases, *signed at* Manila, 14 March 1947, *entered into force 26* March 1947, as amended. 61 Stat. 4019, TIAS 1775; The Agreement Between the United States of America and the Republic of the Philippines on Military Assistance to the Philippines, *signed at* Manila, 21 March 1947, as amended; The Mutual Defense Treaty Between the United States of America and the Republic of the Philippines, *signed at* Washington, DC, 30 August 1951; and The Southeast Asia Collective Defense Treaty (Manila Pact), *signed at* Manila, 8 September 1954. The close relationship between the Philippines and the United States is underscored by the fact that the 1951 Mutual Defense Treaty between the two countries was the only one signed by the US with any Southeast Asian nation. See P.M. Kattenburg, 'The Case For Ending the Special Relationship and Leaving the United States Bases in the Philippines,' in *Rebuilding a Nation: Philippine Challenges and American Policy*, 547, 549 (C.H. Landes ed., 1987).

33 *Id.*

34 See A.M. Bowen, Jr., 'The Philippine-American Defense Partnership,' in *Rebuilding a Nation*, 449, 450 (C.H. Landes ed., 1987).

35 See W.M. Wise, 'The Philippine Military After Marcos,' in *Rebuilding a Nation*, 435, 447 ff (C.H. Landes ed., 1987). Successive US Presidents went out of their way to reaffirm this special relationship with the Philippines. In a 4 January 1979 letter to President Marcos, President Jimmy Carter pledged that his administration 'will during the next five fiscal years, make its best effort to obtain appropriations for the Philippines of the following amounts of security assistance': Military Assistance – $50 million, Foreign Military Sales credits – $250 million, Security Supporting Assistance – $200 million. 'In addition,' the letter continued, 'the United States will give prompt and sympathetic consideration to requests for specific items of military equipment to be provided under these programs, and to requests for the sale of other military equipment which your Government may wish to purchase through the US Government or commercial channels, consistent with the worldwide policies of this Government with respect to the transfer of conventional arms,' quoted in Bowen, *supra* note 34, at 479–480.

used this 'special friendship' to milk the United States for funds to combat communist and other insurgencies that were plaguing his administration. American military aid went to the equipment and training of Philippine counterinsurgency forces.[36] In addition to this overt official military assistance, an estimated $500 million from wages and other expenses related to operation of US naval and air force bases at Subic Bay and Clark Air Base were pumped annually to the Philippines economy.[37] Much of the aid was misused and even stolen[38] while the insurgencies grew because, as most Filipinos knew, the insurgencies were 'stimulated by economic hardship, exacerbated by tyrannies of the Marcos government …'[39]

Like Marcos, Mobutu of Zaire (now the Democratic Republic of the Congo) looted his country's treasury with the knowledge and apparent approval of his Western allies. For the thirty-two years that he presided over the declining fortunes of Zaire,[40] Mobutu's excesses were overlooked because he was seen as a valuable Western ally on an unstable continent.[41] During the cold war, Mobutu was America's 'man in Kinshasa' who allowed his country to become the 'great American counterweight to Soviet adventurism in Africa.'[42] The US was responsible for his ascent to power three decades ago and American money, intelligence information and political support helped keep him there.[43] Other Western friends, notably Belgium and France, also provided Mobutu with crucial financial and military backing that has sustained him in power for this long. Mr. Herman Cohen, the Assistant Secretary of State for African Affairs during the Bush administration, described the historical role of the US in Zaire

---

A similar letter from Jimmy Carter's successor, President Reagan, dated 31 May 1983, contained the same pledge except this time some of the amounts promised had increased exponentially: Military assistance $125 million – a 500 per cent increase, FMS credits $300 million – a 20 per cent increase and Economic Support Fund Assistance $475 million. *Id.*, at 485–486.

[36] See L. Stull, 'Moments of Truth in Philippine-American Relations: The Carter Years,' in *Rebuilding a Nation*, 517, 520 (C.H. Landes ed., 1987); see also Bowen, *supra* note 30, at 453.

[37] *Id.*

[38] *Id.*, at 524.

[39] Bowen, *supra* note 34, at 453; see also L.G. Noble, 'Muslim Grievances and the Muslim Rebellion,' in *Rebuilding a Nation*, 417 (C.H. Landes ed., 1987).

[40] For an excellent account of how Mobutu systematically and methodically pillaged from his nation's resources, see Colette Braeckman, *Le Dinosaure: Le Zaire de Mobutu* (1990). Mobutu was ousted from power by Laurent Kabila and his band of loyal guerilla fighters in May 1997, and in September of the same year he died in exile in Morocco.

[41] See K.B. Richburg, 'Despite Enormous Potential, Zaire's Economy Left to Wither,' *The Dallas Morning News*, Sunday, 12 April 1992, at 22A col. 1.

[42] See Louise Lief & Douglas Paternak, 'Payback time: Our man in Kinshasa,' *US News & World Report*, 2 August 1993, pp. 36–37.

[43] *Id.*, at 36, col. 2. Now that the cold war has ended, the United States government has been distancing itself from Mobutu and has called for him to resign and turn the reigns of power to a democratically elected government. *Id.*

dating back to the 1960s as 'proconsular;'[44] a term that is usually applied to a governor of a modern dependency, colony or conquered territory[45] but definitely inappropriate when applied to an independent country! But Mr. Cohen should know the limits of Zaire's sovereignty for he served in that country during those early years and would later oversee the US government's overall policy on Africa.[46] So close was the US-Zaire relationship that 'for 26 years the US has poured over $1 billion of overt aid into Zaire for the support of Mobutu and his regime.'[47] To which, Professor Weiss adds that 'apart from Liberia, nowhere in Africa has US influence and involvement been greater than in Zaire.'[48] To those who may doubt how the Western nations could have backed Mobutu with full knowledge of the extent to which he has systematically plundered the Zairian economy, these doubts were laid to rest by none other than Nguza Karl-I-Bond, Mobutu's onetime foreign minister and prime minister![49]

Privileged Treatment for Heads of State Guilty of Spoliation

Western complicity in these acts of depredations is also evidenced in the treatment deposed dictators receive from their allies in the West. When the end finally came for Duvalier and Marcos,[50] for instance, both were flown out of their respective countries on US air force planes together with their family members, close associates and, in the case of Jean-Claude Duvalier, even bodyguards.[51] Duvalier and his entourage were flown to France while the Marcoses had a presidential invitation to come and live in

---

44 *See The Situation in Zaire – Fall 1991, Hearing Before the Subcommittee on African Affairs of the Committee on Foreign Relations United States Senate,* 102nd Cong., 1st Sess. 11 (1991) (Statement of Herman J. Cohen, Assistant Secretary of State for African Affairs) [hereinafter '1991 Congressional Hearings'].

45 Oxford Dictionary, p. 553.

46 *Id.*

47 See 1991 Congressional Hearings, *supra* note 44, at 29 (Prepared Statement of Nancy W. Warlick).

48 See 1991 Congressional Hearings, *supra* note 44, at 20 (Testimony of Herbert F. Weiss).

49 See Nguza Karl-I-Bond, *Mobutu Ou L'Incarnation du Mal Zairois*, 125, 145, 150 ff (1982). For several years, as one of Mobutu's closest collaborators, Karl-I-Bond held some of the most important and sensitive posts in Zaire: 1972–74, foreign minister; 1974–77, secretary-general of the M.P.R. (*mouvement populaire de la revolution*) Zaire's only party at that time and member of its powerful political bureau; 1977, 1979–80, 1980–81 prime minister. In between offices he was convicted and jailed for some time for treason and was on exile in Belgium before returning to Zaire in the early 1980s. *Id.*, at 138.

50 At nine o'clock in the evening of 27 February 1986, Ferdinand Marcos fled the presidential palace of Malacanang in Manila, crossed the Pasig River at its rear, and from the opposite shore took a United States air force helicopter to Clark Field. See *Crisis in the Philippines: The Marcos Era and Beyond*, xi (J. Bresnan ed., 1986) [hereinafter *Crisis in the Philippines*].

51 See DeWind & Kinley, *supra* note 24; see also *Crisis in the Philippines*, *supra* note 50, Preface.

the United States.[52] Neither of these disgraced leaders were forced to endure an odyssey of Homerian proportions in their search for a safe harbor to take refuge. Western friends were waiting with open arms to welcome these prodigal sons and grant them asylum. Contrast this reception with the treatment routinely meted out to the so-called Haitian 'boat people' heading for US shores or Filipino 'economic refugees' in Kuwait. The latter, fleeing the wrenching poverty and hardship that Marcos had inflicted on them eagerly accept the most menial jobs anywhere these can be found even as they stoically endure physical and psychological abuse at the hands of their hosts.

The Problem of Jurisdiction Over Non-Resident Spoliators

The special treatment reserved for fleeing dictators demand some type of concerted international response. It is more the case than not that indigenous elites who engage in acts of fraudulent enrichment usually flee their countries and seek refuge in other States placing them well beyond the jurisdictional reach of their national courts. As we have already indicated, Haiti's Jean-Claude Duvalier fled to France,[53] Imelda and Ferdinand Marcos headed for the United States while Paraguay's strongman, Alfredo Stroessner, took refuge in Brazil following his overthrow in a February 1989 coup.[54] As long as these fugitives are on the run, extradition or abduction remain the only available avenues for repatriating them so they can stand trial. But both methods have proved difficult to accomplish in the past.[55] Several factors account for the inadequacy

[52] See S. Solarz, 'A New Era: An Auspicious Beginning,' in *Rebuilding a Nation*, 57, 58 (C.H. Landes ed., 1987).

[53] See Picton, Most ousted, exiled dictators now living high on the hog, *The Toronto Star*, 10 March 1991, page A12.

[54] *Id.*

[55] Countries harboring these fugitives have been very reluctant to extradite them and have routinely refused such requests from other governments. Brazil rejected Paraguay's request to extradite Gustavo Stroessner Mora, son of the deposed dictator, on the ground that there was insufficient evidence of the charges brought against him to warrant extradition to Paraguay where he faces charges of administrative corruption, extortion, and enriching himself illicitly. See Brazilian High Court Rejects Paraguay Extradition Request, *Chicago Tribune*, 1 November 1990, p. 4. Britain has routinely refused to extradite individuals accused of indigenous spoliation back to their countries of origin to face charges. Such was the case in 1966 when the National Liberation Council which had in February of that year deposed Kwame Nkrumah's civilian government in Ghana, requested the British government to extradite a former official in that administration to answer charges in Ghana. Mr. Kwesi Armah, a former Trade Minister and High Commissioner to London, applied for political asylum in England in 1966. The NLC sought to have him extradited to face corruption charges. Mr. Armah was alleged to have irregularly received #20,000 from an Accra businessman and to have been offered a further #40,000 by the same individual. A warrant was issued in the Supreme Court of Ghana on 26 May 1966 and was subsequently endorsed by Sir Robert Blundell, the Chief Metropolitan Magistrate. It was on the basis of this warrant that Mr. Armah appeared before a Bow Street Magistrate's court in London on 27 July. The court subsequently ruled that there was a *prima*

of these two methods: (i) the absence of an extradition treaty between victim-state and asylum-state, and since under international law a state is under no duty to extradite in the absence of a treaty,[56] these fugitives have no cause to worry; (ii) even if an extradition treaty exists, the crime of indigenous spoliation is most likely not one of the enumerated extraditable offenses;[57] and (iii) the international doctrines of sovereign immunity and act of state continue to provide a convenient wall for chief executives involved in indigenous spoliation to hide behind and thus avoid answering

---

facie case for Mr. Armah to answer in Ghana for extortion and corruption and ordered him held in detention. Mr. Armah appealed the ruling in the High Court (Queen's Bench Division) in London asking for relief under the Fugitive Offenders Act from being returned to Ghana. The Queen's Bench Divisional Court refused to grant a writ of habeas corpus, but gave leave to appeal to the House of Lords. The appeal was upheld by the Lords. See *The Guardian*, 9 June 1966, 27 July 1966, 28 July 1966; *The Times*, 29 April 1966. Some twenty years later, it was the turn of the Nigerian government to request the extradition of former public officials who it was alleged had embezzled large sums of money and fled to England. Again, the British government refused the Nigerian government's extradition requests of fugitives Akinloye, Makele, Umaru Dikko and others.

In desperation some governments have even tried to abduct these wanted persons. Such was the case with the attempted kidnapping of Umaru Dikko in 1984 even though the Nigerian government never admitted involvement. Dikko, an *eminence grise* in the civilian government of Shehu Shagari that was overthrown by the military in December 1983, fled Nigeria three days after the coup and took up residence in Britain. As transport minister, Dikko effectively controlled the disbursement of Nigeria's vast oil income. It is believed that it was Dikko who masterminded 500 million naira of imports in President Shagari's efforts to cut prices and end chronic shortages of basic consumer goods. Dikko is believed to have embezzled over #1 billion and the military junta declared him their 'most wanted man' and talked of attempting to extradite him and several others to face charges of corruption. On 4 July 1984, Dikko was snatched at gunpoint in a London street and later found drugged in a crate labeled 'Diplomatic Baggage' at Stansted Airport, on the night of 5 July. The crate was scheduled for loading on a Lagos-bound Nigerian Boeing 747 aircraft when its human cargo was discovered. For more on the Dikko affair, see Martin Wainwright, Stephen Cook & Michael Smith, 'Mercenary team held for Dikko abduction,' *The Guardian*, Saturday, 7 July 1984, p. 1; Patrick Smith, 'Nigerians amused by kidnapping attempt,' *The Guardian*, Saturday, 7 July 1984, p. 2; Editorial, 'To Lagos by special delivery,' *The Guardian*, Saturday, 7 July 1984, p. 12; David Pallister & Ad'Obe, 'Twenty one reasons why Nigeria wants Dikko,' *The Guardian*, Saturday, 7 July 1984, p. 17.

[56] See for example, Factor v. Laubenheimer, 290 US 276, 287, 54 S.Ct. 191, 193, 78 L.Ed. 315 (1933) (where the Supreme Court noted that '[t]he principles of international law recognize no right to extradition apart from treaty'); see also A.P. O'Connell, *International Law*, 2, 793–794 (1970).

[57] Alternatively, it may be punishable in the requesting state but not punishable in the asylum state either because it is not defined as an offense or it is defined differently. Under the requirement of 'double criminality' spoliation must be characterized as an offense punishable under the law of both states. See generally Harvard Research in International Law, 'Draft Convention on Extradition,' *Am. J. Int'l L.*, 29, Spec. Supp. 81–86 (1935); *Oppenheim's International Law: A Treatise*, 958 (H. Lauterpacht, vol. 1, 8th ed., 1955).

to their crimes. Secure in the belief that they can never be brought before the courts of their hosts, many of the ousted heads of state have simply resumed their normal life in exile living quite comfortably off the funds stolen from their national treasuries.

If these stolen funds stand any chance of being recaptured and repatriated, some basis must be found for piercing the veil of sovereign immunity and act of state doctrines. This way courts can reach the assets of foreign heads of state taking refuge in their jurisdictions. In this regard traditional notions of sovereignty[58] must give way when human lives are at stake as in this case. As Elie Wiesel so eloquently put it,

> [s]ometimes, we must interfere when human lives are endangered, when human dignity is in jeopardy, national borders and sensitivities become irrelevant. Wherever men or women are persecuted ... that place must – at that moment – become the center of the universe.[59]

Because the consequences of indigenous spoliation are so dire, national sensitivities must not be allowed to stand in the way of efforts to capture and punish those guilty of such acts. While the traditional doctrines of sovereign immunity and act of state should be entitled to some deference, in compelling circumstances courts should be free to treat them as flimsy veils and not impenetrable barriers.[60] As we point out in Chapter

---

58 There is pressing need for a reassessment of the concept of sovereignty in a world that has increasingly become a global village. In an implicit recognition that we are all 'thy brother's keeper,' states have implicitly waived or surrendered part of their sovereignty to others: the vast majority of states in Africa, Asia, the Caribbean, Latin America and now Central and Eastern Europe can hardly survive without economic hand-outs from the major economic powers (United States, European Economic Community and Japan) and loans from the leading multilateral lending agencies (World Bank, International Monetary Fund, etc.). Donor countries and lending agencies are increasingly using their enormous financial leverage in the receiving countries to legislate in areas previously regarded as the exclusive domain of the sovereign even to the point of rewriting their constitutions! See for example, Jonathan Cahn, 'Challenging the New Imperial Authority: The World Bank and the Democratization of Development,' *Harv. Hum. Rts. J.*, 6, 159 (the World Bank continues to use its power through its financial leverage to legislate entire legal regimes including altering the constitutional structure of borrowing nations). When officials from the Bank or a donor country are allowed to rewrite a borrowing country's trade policy, its fiscal policies, labor laws, civil regulations, budgetary policy, and to dictate its economic policies, can such a country claim to be sovereign? Is not sovereignty in this instance a fiction?

59 Nobel Peace Prize Acceptance Speech by Elie Wiesel in Oslo, Norway.

60 Scholars confronting such fundamental problems as indigenous spoliation must take particular care, as Professor D'Amato warns, not to get trapped by 'the statist conception of international law that they [become] unable to see through the abstraction that we call the "state" to the reality of human beings struggling to achieve basic freedoms.' See Anthony D'Amato, 'The Invasion of Panama Was a Lawful Response to Tyranny,' *Am. J. Int'l L.*, 84, 516 (1990). Indigenous spoliation touches on the fundamental right of a people to exercise sovereignty over their natural resources and economic output and their right to be the principal beneficiaries of their national wealth. When these fundamental human rights are trampled upon then legal formalisms must not be used to deny the victims an opportunity to seek redress. In

7, the doctrine has become a fig leaf behind which dictators hide their obscene acts of plunder and pillage. A redefinition of the concept of sovereignty is an imperative and is already under way, as Chapter 8 makes clear. Evidence culled from reports of commissions of inquiries worldwide paint a picture of heads of states and other high-ranking officials as nothing more than politicians-turned-businessmen.[61] Consider Professor Le Vine's observation in connection with political corruption in Ghana:

> A … point that emerges from the assets inquiries is that the politicians showed great enterprise in maximizing the new income opportunities to which their positions gave them access. A good many were small businessmen and contractors before they went into politics … [and they] simply continued and expanded their business activities while in public office. In addition, many who came to government from the civil service and professional ranks started businesses while they were in office … [Many] also held stock and directorships in large private businesses, some maintained businesses through third parties (most often relatives) …[62]

In Latin America, just as in Africa, heads of state have routinely used state resources to build an economic base and to operate in the marketplace as entrepreneurs. President Trujillo of the Dominican Republic (1930–61), took over the country's only shoe factory and then proceeded to issue a decree forbidding anyone in the capital from going barefoot![63] Trujillo's business interests were not confined to shoe manufacturing but included oligopolies in sugar production, cement, paper, paint, cigarettes, milk,

---

this vein, when the doctrine of sovereign immunity is placed in its proper historical perspective it turns out to be a doctrine of expediency promoted by a court to protect some very definite state interests. Consider Professor W. Michael Reisman's description of the historical context of this rule:

> The Schooner Exchange judgment of Chief Justice Marshall ... usually cited as the cornerstone for the doctrine that the public acts of foreign governments will not be reviewed by the courts of another state even if the effects of the act are felt in that other state. Somehow the judgment never states the extraordinary fact that the case was being decided against the background of the War of 1812, in which the British had set fire to Washington. France, the real defendant, was the only ally of the United States. It seems most unlikely under these circumstances that any United States court would have risked imperiling that relationship.

See W. Michael Reisman, 'Incidents,' in *International Law Anthology*, 53, 57 (Anthony D'Amato ed., 1994).

[61] See Ruth First, *Power in Africa*, 96 (1970).

[62] See Victor T. Le Vine, POLITICAL CORRUPTION: THE GHANA CASE 63–64, 73–74 (1970).

[63] See Laurence Whitehead, 'On presidential graft: the Latin American evidence,' in *Corruption: Causes, Consequences and Control*, 146, 148 (Michael Clarke ed., 1983). The shoe business also attracted Chief Festus Okotie-Eboh, Finance Minister in Nigeria's First Republic (1960–1966) who also opened a shoe factory 'but not before he had legislated tax relief for local industry and a tax on imported shoes.' See Power in Africa, *supra* note 61, at 103.

wheat and flour, plus the nation's only airline, its leading newspapers, and the three principal radio and television stations, among other commercial ventures.[64] Neighboring Cuba's onetime President, Gomez (1910–1935), is reputed to have run his country as 'the private preserve of his own family and the army. Through various kinds of graft, particularly speculation in dealing with oil concessions, and through confiscating the property of his opponents, he became the nation's largest landholder. His accumulated fortune in cattle, coffee plantations, industrial plant, and real estate was estimated as over $200 million.'[65]

The Somoza dynasty that presided over the shifting political fortunes of Nicaragua for 40 years had business interests that in 1972 were 'variously estimated to be worth between 150 and 200 million dollars, stretch[ed] into the national airlines, LANICA, the country's only shipping line, MAMENIC, cattle and meat packing, fishing, rum and beer, hotels, banking, cement, radio, television and newspapers,' as well as a local Mercedes Benz dealership.[66] Testifying before the United States Congress on official corruption in the Philippines, many witnesses revealed that the Marcoses owned directly or through proxies properties in the United States worth more than $400 million. The First Family of the Philippines was involved in a variety of business ventures including real estate speculation, development and management of a shopping mall, hotels, luxury condominiums, office buildings as well as banks in California and New York.[67]

As long as heads of state and other high-ranking officials involved in indigenous spoliation use the stolen wealth in running commercial ventures, they ought to be treated as politicians-turned-businessmen and therefore not eligible for protection under the various immunity doctrines.

Spoliated Capital Invested in Western Economies

Involving the international community in the difficult but necessary task of apprehending, prosecuting and punishing persons who commit acts of spoliation is dictated also by one simple fact. Much of the spoliated wealth is banked or invested in countries that have been all too willing to grant asylum to the authors of these acts. These states are just as much a part of the problem since their gain is the loss of the victim-states.[68] But viewed from a broader perspective, the gains from the investments

---

64 *Id.*, at 161, n. 12.

65 See Edwin Lieuwen, *Venezuela*, 49 (1961) quoted in Whitehead, *supra* note 63, at 152.

66 *Id.*, at 155.

67 See *Congressional Record-Senate*, 7 November 1985, p. 31160 ff.

68 In what Susan George describes as the practice of having one's cake *and* eating it too: 'Money spirited out of the South in huge quantities has allowed Northern commercial banks to defy the adage about cake. It turns out the banks *can* both have and eat it because they control both ends of the financial system. First, they make the loan. Almost instantaneously, a large proportion of it returns to their coffers as deposits because corrupt government officials may transfer it directly. National companies, heavy borrowers who governments have guaranteed their debt, may also feel that the money they were supposed to invest at home will be happier

from the stolen wealth are short term. Taxpayers in the asylum states end up paying far more to bail out countries that are the victims of indigenous spoliation. Considerable sums of money go into the interdiction in the high seas of economic refugees trying to make it to American and West European shores; processing their asylum applications; and providing them with temporary quarters pending a final decision on their asylum requests.[69] And even when these refugees are finally admitted into the industrialized countries, the cost of maintaining each on a per capita basis far exceeds what it would take to maintain that same refugee in his or her country of origin. Furthermore, the benefits resulting from investing these spoliated funds in the host economy – employment generation, infrastructural development, provision of social services – are also short term. As capital flees the developing countries it leaves behind impoverished consumers who cannot afford to buy the goods produced in the industrialized countries. Without markets for their products, it is only a matter of time before these developed country economies begin to feel the full impact of what was originally viewed as a Third World problem.

The Absence of Independent Judiciaries in Victim States

Finally, international action is the only way out because no court in the victim-state would want to take on the risk of adjudicating a claim of indigenous spoliation as long as the defendants/officials are still in office wielding enormous powers. Where is that impartial court and the equally brave judge who would agree to sit in judgment over a sitting president or his closest associates?[70] The attitude of Haitian courts with respect

---

abroad. This capital, which in fact left the debtor country long ago, will still, unfortunately, appear on the banks' books as loans on which interest is due. The banks are thus paid back twice for a single commitment – first in deposits from foreigners, then in interest.' See Susan George, A Fate Worse Than Debt, 19–20 (1990). In the same vein, an American economist has remarked that '[t]he most aggressive banks, such as Citibank, have probably accumulated almost as much in assets from poor countries as they have loaned to them. Their real role has been to take funds that Third World elites have stolen from their governments and to loan them back, earning a nice spread each way.' See James S. Henry, 'Where the Money Went,' *New Republic*, 14 April 1986.

[69] An editorial in the Sunday, 10 October 1993 edition of *The Dallas Morning News* laments the fact that special agents of the federal immigration service devote up to a third of their time trying to deport foreign-born offenders. The editorial points out that nationwide close to 100,000 prisoners are currently deportable; in 1991 13,000 alien criminals were deported compared to 1,900 in 1986. See Editorials, 'Immigration: Congress must confront criminal impact,' *The Dallas Morning News*, Sunday, 10 October 1993, at 2J.

[70] The issue of an appropriate tribunal to try crimes involving heads of states and their close collaborators was also raised in the debates leading to the adoption of the Genocide Convention. In the General Assembly debate on the draft convention on genocide, the Egyptian delegate (Mr. Rafat) noted that 'the punishment of a crime such as genocide could be effective and serve as a warning only if the most dangerous culprits were convinced that, while they might easily escape under the timid or indulgent judgment of national courts, they would not escape the judgment of the free, impartial and independent international tribunal.' See

to the *ancien regime* is emblematic. While legal actions were proceeding in France and the United States against members of the Duvalier regime to recover the millions of dollars of Haitian wealth they were alleged to have stolen, the judiciary was doing everything within its power to protect the remnants of a discredited *ancien* regime. For instance, two Haitian judges and two law clerks forged judicial orders dismissing all charges of embezzlement against several powerful supporters of Jean-Claude Duvalier. The orders released their assets from judicial attachment and suspended fraud charges against them.[71] An African participant at the 13th session of the African Commission on Human and People's Rights reacted with some incredulity to the naive suggestion that victims of human rights violations must first exhaust all local remedies before bringing suit in an international forum: 'You taking an African head of state to court in your country and you would be signing your death warrant.'[72] The only answer to combating the problem of spoliation by chief executives and high-ranking officials is concerted international action.

The wisdom of establishing a universal duty to prosecute international crimes that could likely be committed by high-ranking State officials has long been recognized. In the discussion of the Secretary General's Report on the Draft Code of Offenses Against the Peace and Security of Mankind in the Sixth Committee of the United Nations several UN members were opposed to the idea of relying on national judicial systems to judge offenses committed under the Code. The Representative of Zaire expressed his reservations in this manner:

> … if the acts concerned had been committed by a State itself or one of its organs, the matter would be more complicated, since the national judicial authorities called on to prosecute and try the offences might not have sufficient independence to ensure their impartiality. Moreover, if States themselves urged or ordered certain persons to undertake actions that were forbidden in the proposed Code, it was unlikely that they would be prosecuted. That would lead to the same situation, in which offences under the Code could be committed with impunity.[73]

Continuation of the discussion on the draft convention on genocide: reports of the Economic and Social Council and of the Sixth Committee (A/760 and A/760/Cory. 2,), 195th Plenary Mtg. Thursday, 9 December 1948, at 3:30 pm, at 810 (Remarks of Mr. Rafat). It is safe to presume that national tribunals will be powerless or too timid to punish powerful friends of a sitting president proved to have spoliated national funds.

[71] See *Lawyers Committee for Human Rights, Paper Laws, Steel Bayonets*, 27 (1990). A Haitian priest would only say that 'The rule of law presents a revolutionary act in Haiti; everything is corrupt. People want to make money and you cannot make money fast out in the open. It must be done under the table and this is why corruption is rampant.' *Id.,* at 29.

[72] See G. Gyan-Apenteng, 'Defining the terrain in Banjul,' *West Africa*, 19–25 April 1993, pp. 634, 635.

[73] UN, GAOR, Sixth Comm. (36th Sess.) 2, UN Doc. A/C.6/36/SR.60, at 6 (1984) (Mr. Balanda Mikwim, Zaire).

ISSUES OF PROCEDURAL CAPACITY FOR OTHER TYPES OF PLAINTIFFS

The Question of Locus Standi to Bring Suit[74]

Other than member States of the international community, who else can sue to recover spoliated assets? It was pointed out in Chapter 9 that rights enjoyed by multiple constituencies are implicated when a nation's wealth and resources are diverted into the private accounts of constitutionally-responsible rulers. In addition to the governments and citizens of the victim-States, taxpayers from donor States also have some claim to spoliated funds. Whether these various and diverse interests can rise to a justiciable legal claim will be explored in this section.

Article III of the United States Constitution, for instance, requires that there be a 'case' or 'controversy' before a court can resolve a dispute.[75] The Supreme Court has interpreted this language to mean that an issue must 'be presented in an adversary context and in a form historically viewed as capable of judicial resolution,'[76] in other words, 'justiciable.'[77] Accordingly, the Court has developed six doctrines of justiciability: no advisory opinions, no collusive suits, ripeness, mootness, political questions, and standing.[78] While the first five of these doctrines concern themselves with the issues in dispute,[79] the doctrine of standing concentrates on the litigants themselves: whether or not the individual litigant has a sufficient stake in the outcome of the matter to justify his right to litigate the issue in court.[80]

In response to the 'What's it to you?'[81] query posed by the doctrine of standing, the United States Supreme Court has developed six tests – three constitutional and three prudential – in deciding whether an individual litigant has standing to bring an action in a court.[82] In Association of Data Service Organizations v. Camp,[83] the Court held

---

[74] This Section has benefitted immensely from, and relied heavily on, Comment, Generalized Grievances: 'The 'Law of Rules' Approach to Standing,' *Ohio Northern U.L.Rev.*, 19, 927 (1993).

[75] US Const. Art. III, §'2.

[76] Flast v. Cohen, 392 US 83, 101 (1968).

[77] See Erwin Chemerinsky, *Federal Jurisdiction*, 50 (1989) [hereinafter 'Chemerinsky'].

[78] *Id.*

[79] See Flast, 392 US at 99–100.

[80] *Id.*

[81] See Antonin Scalia, 'The Doctrine of Standing as an Essential Element of Separation of Powers,' *Suffolk U.L. Rev.*, 17, 881, 882 (1983).

[82] The original test for standing was first articulated in very broad, abstract terms in Baker v. Carr, 369 US 186 (1962), where standing was defined in terms of whether the plaintiff has 'alleged such a personal stake in the outcome of the controversy as to assure that concrete adverseness which sharpens the presentation of issues upon which the court so largely depends for illumination of difficult constitutional questions.' *Id.*, at 204.

[83] 397 US 150 (1970).

that standing requires that the plaintiff be 'injured in fact.'[84] By 'injury in fact' the Court meant any cognizable injury including an injury of a purely aesthetic nature.[85] Two more tests were added to the injury in fact test of Sierra Club in 1973: causation and redressability. In Linda R.S. v. Richard D., the Court held that the mother of an illegitimate child did not have standing to compel state officials to prosecute the child's father for failure to make child support payments.[86] According to the Court, plaintiff's success on the merits of her case did not guarantee receipt of child support but 'would only result in the jailing of the child's father.'[87] Implicit in the Court's reasoning was the view that to have standing the plaintiff must be able to show that her injury was caused by the defendant's conduct and that judicial intervention would redress the harm.[88] In Allen v. Wright, the Court made explicit what it had implied in Richard D. that causation and redressability are two separate elements of standing.[89]

The elements of injury in fact, causation and redressability had come to be accepted as the only elements required by the US Constitution to support the standing doctrine.[90] However, the Supreme Court has also introduced three additional 'prudential' elements to the traditional 'constitutional' tests of standing: the bar on third-party suits, generalized grievances, and zone of interests.[91] In McGowan v. Maryland, where department stores were raising a First Amendment objection to Maryland's Sunday closing laws (so-called 'blue laws'), the Court found standing absent on the ground that none of the plaintiffs had alleged that their personal religious beliefs were infringed.[92] The banning of third party suits were consistent with the pragmatic policies of improving judicial decisions[93] and fairness.[94]

In Frothingham v. Mellon,[95] a case which involved a claim by a taxpayer that the way government was using her taxes was in violation of the Tenth Amendment, the Court introduced the ban against 'generalized grievances'[96] as another prudential element to standing. Here the Court held that a mere showing of injury 'in some

---

[84] *Id.*, at 152.

[85] Sierra Club v. Morton, 405 US 727, 734 (1972) (the alleged injury was loss of aesthetic beauty of national parks on which ski resorts would be built).

[86] 410 US 614, 614 (1973).

[87] *Id.*, at 618.

[88] See Warth v. Seldin, 422 US 490 (1975).

[89] 468 US 737, 753 n. 19 (1984).

[90] See Richard D., 410 US at 614; United States v. Students Challenging Regulatory Agency Procedures (SCRAP), 412 US 669 (1973); Wright, 468 US at 737. These constitutionally-mandated elements were seen as serving the important pragmatic policies of judicial efficiency, conservation of judicial resources, and fairness as well as the constitutional principle of separation of powers. See Chemerinsky, *supra* note 77, at 49–51.

[91] See Chemerinsky, *supra* note 77, at 72.

[92] 366 US 420, 429 (1961).

[93] See Singleton v. Wulff, 428 US 106, 114 (1976).

[94] See Duke Power Co. v. Carolina Envtl. Study Group, 438 US 59, 80 (1978).

[95] 262 US 447 (1923).

[96] See Chemerinsky, *supra* note 77, at 77–78.

indefinite way in common with people generally' will not provide a plaintiff with standing.[97] The ban on 'generalized grievances' was compelled by the policy consideration of preserving judicial resources.[98] Finally, in Association of Data Processing,[99] the Court held that a plaintiff whose injury stems from the violation of a statute must show that he is within the 'zone of interests' protected by the statute.[100] This prudential element of standing has as its aim that of establishing whether the plaintiff belongs to the class of persons Congress intended to protect. It also serves the desirable policy of improving judicial decision making by 'providing a detailed fact setting that corresponds to the problems most likely to be encountered in the area of dispute, and … by yielding [to] parties sensitive to the perhaps conflicting interests of those most directly involved.'[101]

The purpose of the standing doctrine is the concern about 'the proper – and properly limited – role of the courts in a democratic society.' It is animated by the belief that '[j]udicial power exists only to redress or otherwise to protect against injury to the complaining party.'[102] Essential to the standing doctrine is that plaintiff must have a 'personal stake in the outcome' sufficient to 'assure that concrete averseness which sharpens the presentation of issues upon which the court so largely depends for illuminating difficult … questions.'[103] In short, '[a]bstract injury is not enough. It must be alleged that the plaintiff has sustained or is immediately in danger of sustaining some direct injury as the result of the challenged statute or official conduct … The injury or threat of injury must be both "real and immediate," not "conjectural," or "hypothetical."'[104]

Lujan v. Defenders of Wildlife[105] alters the traditional formulation of standing to some extent.[106] Lujan involved a challenge to an agency regulation[107] that prohibited the extraterritorial application of the Endangered Species Act of 1973[108] by a group of environmentalists. According to the Court, Article III requires an 'irreducible constitutional minimum of standing,' with three elements: (1) an injury in fact that is both (a) concrete and particularized and (b) actual or imminent rather than conjectural

---

97 *Id.*, at 488.

98 See Flast v. Cohen, 392 US 83 (1968) (held that standing in a taxpayer's challenge to subsidies to parochial schools was in violation of the Establishment Clause of the US Constitution).

99 397 US at 150.

100 *Id.*, at 153.

101 *Id.*

102 Warth v. Seldin, 422 US 490, 498–499 (1975).

103 Baker v. Carr, 369 US 186, 204 (1962).

104 O'Shea v. Littleton, 414 US 488, 494 (1974) (quoting Golden v. Zwicker, 394 US 103, 109–110 (1969)).

105 112 S. Ct. 2130 (1992).

106 See Proctor and C. Sunstein, 'What's Standing After Lujan?' *Mich. L. Rev.*, 91, 163 (1992) [hereinafter 'Proctor & Sunstein'].

107 50 CFR §402.01 (1991).

108 16 USC 1531–44 (1988).

or hypothetical; (2) a demonstration that the injury is fairly traceable to the acts of the defendant, rather than to some third party; and (3) a showing that it is likely that the injury will be redressed by a decision favorable to the plaintiff.[109] The Court went on to say that the three requirements will ordinarily be met when the plaintiff is actually an object of the action at issue.[110] However, when the 'injury arises from the government's allegedly unlawful regulation (or lack of regulation) of someone else, much more is needed,'[111] and that 'causation and redressability ordinarily hinge on the response of the regulated (or regulable) third party to the government action or inaction – and perhaps on the response of others as well.'[112]

The Court dismissed the case because the plaintiffs lacked personalized injury[113] and because they could not show redressability.[114] Justice Scalia, writing for the majority, held there must be 'a factual showing of perceptible harm,'[115] and that plaintiffs did not meet this as a matter of fact. Writing for only a plurality, Mr. Justice Scalia held that redressability was a problem because the Court was incompetent to resolve 'generalized grievances,' even when Congress specifically granted jurisdiction by statute.[116] Further, 'Congress had no authority to convert the public interest in having the laws properly enforced into an individualized injury for all persons' because doing so would in fact violate the separation-of-powers requirement of the Constitution.[117] Professor Sunstein explains this decision as manifesting the Court's fear that allowing standing here would turn judges into overseers and thereby usurpers of the essential power of the Executive, that is, enforcing the laws.[118] If taken up, Lujan essentially says that Congress cannot grant standing to citizens, and instead that the entire standing test must always be applied even given standing established by statute.[119]

Successor Government as a Proper Party[120]

General Status of the Law

The involvement of foreign states and their representatives in federal judicial proceedings and other federal activities[121] is expressly contemplated in the US

109 Proctor & Sunstein, *supra* note 106, at 198–99 citing 112 S. Ct. at 2136.
110 112 S. Ct. at 2137.
111 *Id.*
112 *Id.*
113 *Id.*, at 2138–2139.
114 *Id.*, at 2140–2145.
115 *Id.*, at 2139.
116 *Id.*, at 2143–45.
117 Proctor & Sunstein, *supra* note 106, at 938–939, *citing* 112 S. Ct. at 2144–2146.
118 *Id.*, at 201.
119 *Id.*, at 209.
120 This section relies heavily on Lori Damrosch, 'Foreign States and the Constitution,' *Va. L Rev.*, 73, 483 (1987) [hereinafter 'Damrosch'].
121 *Id.*, at 487.

constitutional scheme. Article III provides that the federal judicial power shall extend to cases 'between a State, or the Citizens thereof, and foreign States, Citizens or Subjects.'[122] Other clauses refer directly to foreign states or implicitly acknowledge their interaction with the United States.[123] Although the Supreme Court has not directly addressed the question of the rights of foreign states under the Constitution; however, several cases support the notion that foreign sovereigns should be treated essentially the same as any other juridical person.[124] The executive branch has at different times reflected two essentially contradictory positions.[125] The Executive lawyers have sometimes unequivocally proclaimed that foreign states have no rights to attack foreign policy decisions on constitutional grounds, but at other times where such a constitutional argument would be helpful they have suggested the relevance of constitutional concerns.[126] Congressional approaches also vary.[127] The Restatement of Foreign Relations Law of the United States adopts the view that foreign states and international organizations are generally treated as 'persons' for most statutory purposes but not for constitutional purposes.[128] And as Professor Damrosch points out, '[t]here are strong considerations favoring judicial application of constitutional values when the political branches have given no contrary indication,' including promoting

---

[122] US Const. art 111, §2, cl. 1.

[123] Damrosch, *supra* note 120, 487 n10. 'The congress shall have Power ... To regulate Commerce with foreign Nations,' US Const. Art. 1, §8, cl. 3; 'No State shall, without the Consent of Congress … enter into any Agreement or Compact … with a foreign power,' *id.* Art. I, §10, cl. 3; and '[The President] shall have Power, by and with the Advice and Consent of the Senate, to make Treaties … and … shall appoint Ambassadors, other public Ministers and Consuls …,' *id.* art II, §2, cl. 2.

[124] Damrosch, *supra* note 120, at 490. See, for example, Pfizer, Inc. v. India, 434 US 308 (1978) interpreting 'person' in §4 of the Clayton Act (current version at 15 USC. §18 (1982)) to include foreign states); cf. Russian Volunteer Fleet v. United States, 282 US 481 (1931) (foreign corporation permitted to sue for just compensation under stature authorizing suits against the United States for wartime requisitioning). In Russian Volunteer Fleet, the Court noted that the issue presented was 'not one of a claim advanced by or on behalf of a foreign government or regime,' 282 US at 492, but lower courts have extended the doctrine of that case to include suits by a foreign state, see Swiss Confederation v. United States, 70 F. Supp. 235 (Ct. Cl.), *cert. denied*, 332 US 815 (1947), and by an agency or branch of a foreign state. See Swiss Fed. Rys. v. United States, 112 F. Supp. 357 (Ct. Cl. 1953). Damrosch, *supra* note 120, at 490 n10.

[125] Damrosch, *supra* note 120, at 491.

[126] *Id.*. at 491–492.

[127] *Id.*, at 493. The Foreign Sovereign Immunities Act suggests that due process constraints should and do apply. 28 USC §1 note, 1330, 1332, 1391, 1441, 1602–1611 (1982). For an approach singling out unfavorable treatment to foreign states, see 15 USC 15(b) (1982) (amending the antitrust laws following Pfizer, Inc. v. India, 434 US 308 (1978)).

[128] *Restatement (Revised) of Foreign Relations Law of the United States* §453 Reporter's Note 3 (Tent. Draft No. 2 (1981)); §721 comment 1 (Tent. Draft No. 6; Vol. 1 (1985)). These sections were done under Louis Henkin who is one of the few to have written on the subject. See generally L. Henkin, *Foreign Affairs and the Constitution* (1972).

these values world wide, fostering good relations with foreign states, and being consistent with the overall trend in executive, legislative and judicial actions to treat foreign sovereigns similarly to private persons.[129]

A solid line of cases establishes that foreign states may sue as plaintiffs in United States courts.[130] In Banco National de Cuba v. Sabbatino[131] Mr. Justice Harlan based his reasoning for allowing foreign states to sue in US courts on policy reasons: promotion of good relations with foreign states, encouragement of equal access elsewhere, and the problems entailed in trying to apply a test of reciprocity under which the United States courts would need to evaluate foreign states' judicial systems.[132] Standing to sue, however, requires recognition by the Executive:[133] '[i]t has long been established that only governments recognized by the United States and at peace with us are entitled to access to our courts, and that it is within the exclusive power of the Executive Branch to determine which nations are entitled to sue.'[134] Numerous cases hold that the Executive power to recognize or not to recognize is both exclusive and nonreviewable.[135] Finally, entitlement to constitutional rights is not based upon a showing that the foreign state affords United States interests reciprocal treatment, that is, comity.[136]

In 1986, the Republic of the Philippines brought a civil suit against former President Ferdinand Marcos and his wife, Imelda, alleging violations of the Racketeer Influenced and Corrupt Organizations Act (RICO).[137] On 25 June 1986, the District Court entered a preliminary injunction forbidding the Marcoses from disposing of any

---

[129] Damrosch, *supra* note 120, at 496.

[130] See, for example, Pfizer, Inc. v. India, 434 US 308 (1978); Banco Nacional de Cuba v. Sabbatino, 376 US 398 (1964) and cases cited therein.

[131] 376 US 398 (1964).

[132] Damrosch, *supra* note 120, at 498. In other words, comity is not required. See *supra* note 32 and accompanying text.

[133] 'An unrecognized government has been called 'a republic of whose existence we know nothing,' Baker v. Carr, 369 US 186, 212 (1962), and has been denied access to US courts.' Damrosch, *supra* note 120, at 499. See Republic of Vietnam v. Pfizer, Inc., 556 F.2d 892 (8th Cir. 1977) (dismissed after the fall of South Vietnam, in the absence of recognition of successor government) and cases cited therein.

[134] 434 US at 319–320.

[135] See, for example, Sabbatino, 376 US at 410; United States v. Pink, 315 US 203 (1942); Guaranty Trust Co. v. United States, 304 US 126 (1938); United States v. Belmont, 301 US 324, 328 (1937).

[136] Damrosch, *supra* note 120, at 505. But cf. Hilton v. Guyot, 159 US 113, 227–228 (1895) (doctrine of reciprocity applied to enforcement of foreign judgments). According to Damrosch, 'Hilton was given a limited reading by Sabbatino, 376 US at 411–412, and most courts in the United States will now enforce foreign judgments without proof of reciprocity.' Damrosch at 505 n83. *See* RESTATEMENT (REVISED) OF THE FOREIGN RELATIONS LAW OF THE UNITED STATES §491 Reporter's Note 1 (Tent. Draft No. 4 (1983)) (§481 in Tent. Final Draft (1985)).

[137] 18 USC §§1961–1968 (1988).

assets except for attorneys' fees and normal living expenses.[138] The Marcoses appealed, and a panel of the Ninth Circuit vacated the injunction.[139] The Ninth Circuit then heard the case en banc and reinstated the district court's injunction.[140] In Marcos 11, the court addresses standing under RICO and finds such standing in a matter of a few sentences because the Republic is a government body within the meaning of 18 USC 1961(3)[141] and because its foreign nature does not deprive it of statutory personhood.[142]

Application to Successor Governments Suing Former Dictators for Domestic Spoliation in US Courts

Given the above state of the law, a successor government must first be recognized by the United States in order to have standing. This is an absolute requirement, but its answer will obviously vary from situation to situation. If this preliminary test is met, the successor government must then meet the requirements of standing, both constitutional and prudential. The plaintiff government must first show injury in fact, causation, and redressability. Under Lujan, the injury must be actual or imminent – a test which under Lujan must be plead specifically.[143] Under this test, the State will have to show specifically that the spoliation of resources had in fact taken specific opportunities and wealth that the State would have had access to had it not been stolen by the previous regime. The State cannot plead merely general injury but must in fact list specific damages and specific opportunities lost. It must also show that the person charged in fact caused the damages averred. Finally, the damages must be redressable. Lujan requires that in order for this requirement to be met, the state must actually charge a party from whom relief can be granted.[144] In Lujan, the members did not charge the agency actually responsible for the projects, but only the Secretary of the Interior who it was unclear whether actually had any control over the desired outcome. The suing State by charging the responsible ruler should meet this requirement, but if the ruler was not in fact directly responsible the State should name all who were involved. Obviously, if none of those involved are within the jurisdiction of the court, this will be a problem. If the State is seeking action from the United States itself, it

[138] See Republic of the Philippines v. Marcos, 818 F.2d 1473, 1477 (9th Cir. 1987) (Marcos II). The question of standing is not even taken up in Marcos 1, Republic of the Philippines v. Marcos, 806 F.2d 344 (2d. Cir. 1986), except for the brief statement that since no restitution to private individuals will take place, no such question arises. *Id.*, at 357.

[139] *Id.*, at 1490.

[140] Republic of the Philippines v. Marcos, 862 F.2d 1355 (9th Cir. 1988) (en banc), *cert. denied*, 490 US 1035 (1989).

[141] 862 F.2d at 1358, citing Illinois Department of Revenue v. Phillips, 771 F.2d 312 (7th Cir. 1985).

[142] *Id.*, citing Pfizer, Inc. v. Government of India, 434 US 308 (1978).

[143] H. Cox, 'Note: Standing to Protect the Global Environment: A Call for Congressional Action,' *J. Energy Nat. Resources & Envtl. L.*, 13, 475, 484 (1993).

[144] *Id.*

must carefully name individuals and agencies who are specifically involved in distributions of funds or who have other direct involvement in the situation. Moreover, the successor government must name specific remedies that these parties are capable of providing.

Besides the constitutional requirements, the state must also meet the prudential requirements of no third-party suits, no generalized grievances, and must fit within the zone of interests provided by the statute. Essentially, Lujan makes these all aspects of the injury in fact requirement.[145] Given this, the State-plaintiff must show that those presently suing were themselves injured by the actions of the spoliator. While it is clear under international law that States can sue States for injuries, Lujan may bring into question whether the State can sue for general injuries or must plead specifically. Given the decision in Lujan, it would make sense for the State to plead very specific and lengthy injuries because otherwise its standing to sue may be challenged as a generalized grievance. Finally, the injury must fall under the zone of interests that Congress intended to protect under the specific statute that the state chooses to sue under. This will be based on judicial interpretation of the statute and will vary from case to case. Given careful pleading, this is probably surmountable at least in antitrust, RICO, and Alien Tort cases. However, the suing State must be careful that it does fall under the zone of any chosen statute.

Overall, given specific and careful pleading a foreign government should have standing to sue a former high-ranking public official in US courts.

THE INDIVIDUAL AS A PROPER PARTY SUING IN THE NAME AND ON BEHALF OF ALL CITIZENS OF THE VICTIM STATE

The Class-Action[146]

Legal Requirements

The class action mechanism under the US Federal Rules of Civil Procedure (FRCP) Rule 23[147] was intended to reduce duplicate claims and provide access to the courts for plaintiffs who would be unable to bring their cases individually.[148] The mechanism has served to conserve judicial resources and increased redress for widely scattered harms by aggregating large numbers of smaller claims.[149]

In order to maintain a class action, the representative party must fulfill all of the

---

145 *Id.*, at 487.

146 This section relies heavily on D. Towns, 'Comment: Merit-Based Class Action Certification: Old Wine in a New Bottle,' *Va. L. Rev.*, 78, 1001 (1992) [hereinafter 'Towns'].

147 Fed. R. Civ. P. 23.

148 Towns, *supra* note 146, at 1001.

149 See P. Schuck, *Agent Orange on Trial: Mass Toxic Disasters in the Courts*, 3–15 (1986); F. Kirkham, Problems of Complex Civil Litigation, 83 FRD 497, 499–504 (1979); S. Williams, Mass Tort Class Actions: Going, Going, Gone?, 98 FRD 232, 324–25 (1986).

requirements of Rule 23(a):[150] numerosity,[151] commonality,[152] typicality,[153] and adequacy of representation.[154] The action must also fit into one of three types of claims

[150] Rule 23(a) provides in pertinent part:

One or more members of a class may sue or be sued as representative parties on behalf of all only if (1) the class is so numerous that joinder of all members is impracticable, (2) there are questions of law or fact common to the class, (3) the claims or defenses of the representative parties are typical of the claims or defenses of the class, and (4) the representative parties will fairly and adequately protect the interests of the class.

Fed. R. Civ. P 23 (a); see Fed. R. Civ. P. 23, Advisory Committee's Note, reprinted in 39 FRD 98, 99–100 (1966); B. Kaplan, 'Continuing Work of the Civil Committee: 1966 Amendments of the Federal Rules of Civil Procedure' (pt. 1), *Harv. L. Rev.*, 81, 356, 380–386 (1967); G. Rutherglen, 'Title VII Class Actions,' *U. Chi. L. Rev.*, 47, 688, 696–697 (1980). See generally Sherman L. Cohn, 'The New Federal Rules of Civil Procedure,' *Geo. L.J.*, 54, 1204, 1213–1228 (1966) (discussing the procedural requirements of Rule 23).

[151] This requirement asks whether joinder of the parties is practical under the circumstances. There is no specific number that will satisfy the numerosity requirement. *Board of Educ. v. Climatemp, Inc.,* 1980–81 Trade Cas. (CCH) para. 63863, at 78578 (N. D. Ill. 1981). A class of 40 has been held sufficient to meet the numerosity requirement. Swanson v. American Consumer Indus., 415 F.2d 1326, 1333 n.9 (7th Cir. 1969). A group of 350 plaintiffs, however, has been denied class status. Utah v. American Pipe and Constr. Co., 49 FRD 17, 21 (CD Cal. 1969).

In determining the relative advantages of joinder and class action, courts will often take the geographic location of the parties into account. See Climatemp, 1980–81 Trade Cas. (CCH) at 78579. Thus, a group of 40 plaintiffs in several states or countries would be a more likely candidate for class status than 40 plaintiffs domiciled in one judicial district. Towns, *supra* note 146, at 1004 n17.

[152] In order to reach the goals of efficiency and conservation of judicial resources, the representative must establish that the questions of law or fact are common to all members of the class. Towns, *supra* note 146, at 1004 n18.

[153] The typicality test focuses on the degree of interrelation between a representative's injuries and claims, as compared to the rest of the class, while the commonality requirement focuses on the degree of similarities and differences among class members, their injuries, and causes of action. Towns, *supra* note 146, at 1005 n19. The two requirements do merge sometimes. See General Tel. Co. v. Falcon, 457 US 147, 157 n13 (1982).

[154] This requirement is based on constitutional guarantees, and even though individuals usually cannot be bound by a judgment to which they were not a party, the Supreme Court has recognized that 'the judgment in a 'class' or 'representative' suit, to which some members of the class are parties, may bind members of the class or those represented who were not made parties.' Hansberry v. Lee, 311 US 32, 41 (1940). Due process requirements therefore require close scrutiny of the class certification to avoid possible operation of res judicata to members not party to the suit. *Id.*, at 41–42. The standard is (1) the representative have no interests that are antagonistic to those of other members of the class, and (2) the representative's attorney be capable of prosecuting the claim with a certain degree of expertise. Wetzel v. Liberty Mut. Ins. Co., 508 F.2d 239, 247 (3d. Cir.), *cert. denied*, 421 US 1011 (1975).

recognized under Rule 23(b).[155] To qualify as a Rule 23(b)(1) class, the prosecution of individual suits must create a risk of inconsistent standards for the party opposing the class or prove dispositive of the interests of proposed class members not party to the adjudication.[156] To qualify as a Rule 23(b)(2) class, class wide declaratory or injunctive relief must be appropriate.[157] To qualify as a Rule 23(b)(3) class, common questions of law and fact must predominate over individual issues[158] and the class action must be a superior method of adjudicating the cause of action.[159]

Besides requiring an analysis of class certification, Rule 23 also imposes

---

[155] 150 Rule 23(b) provides:

> An action may be maintained as a class action if the prerequisites of subdivisions (a) are satisfied, and in addition:

(1) the prosecution of separate actions by or against individual members of the class would create a risk of

(A) inconsistent or varying adjudications with respect to individual members of the class which would establish incompatible standards of conduct for the party opposing the class, or

(B) adjudications with respect to individual members of the class which would as a practical matter be dispositive of the interests of the other members not parties to the adjudications or substantially impair or impede their ability to protect their interests; or

(2) the party opposing the class has acted or refused to act on grounds generally applicable to the class, thereby making appropriate final injunctive relief or corresponding declaratory relief with respect to the class as a whole; or

(3) the court finds that the questions of law or fact common to the members of the class predominate over any questions affecting only individual members, and that a class action is superior to other available methods for fair and efficient adjudication of the controversy. The matters pertinent to the findings include: (A) the interest of members of the class in individually controlling the prosecution or defense of separate actions; (B) the extent and nature of any litigation concerning the controversy already commenced by or against the members of the class; (C) the desirability or undesirability of concentrating the litigation of the claims in the particular forum; (D) the difficulties likely to be encountered in the management of a class action.

Fed. R. Civ. P. 23(b).

[156] This is typically called the 'common fund problem.' See 7A C. Wright, A. Miller & M. Kane, *Federal Practice and Procedure* §1774 (2d ed. 1986).

[157] This is typically called the 'civil rights class action,' and while it is not specifically limited to this context, the advisory notes indicates that private remedies for civil rights cases was a primary motivation. *See* Advisory Committee's Note, at 102.

[158] To distinguish commonality under 23(a)(2) from the 23(b)(3) requirement, one court noted '[a]pparently it is not sufficient that common questions merely exist, rather the common issues must outweigh the individual ones in terms of quantity or quality. In deciding the issue of predominance, this Court must predict the evidence likely to be introduced at trial.' Ryan v. Eli Lilly & Co., 84 FRD 230, 233 (DSC 1979).

[159] The key question is manageability as a class versus manageability through some other method such as joinder. See 7A Wright et al., §1779.

procedural limitations.[160] Rule 23(c)(1) directs the court to determine 'as soon as practicable' whether the suit may be maintained.[161] Rule 23(c) also requires the class representative to notify all members of a proposed Rule 23(b)(3) class and allow them the opportunity to opt out of the suit.[162] The cost of individual notice must be paid by the representative after certification, and this requirement has been consistently upheld by the Supreme Court as necessitated by the Due Process Clause of the United States Constitution.[163]

Due to its nature, Rule 23 provides a significant amount of discretion to courts.[164] Rule 23(d) grants judges broad authority to 'prevent undue repetition or complication in the presentation of evidence' and to ensure 'the fair conduct of the action.'[165] Rule 23(e) requires court approval to dismiss or otherwise compromise a class action that

---

160 Towns, *supra* note 146, at 1006.

161 Rule 23(c)(1) provides:

> As soon as practicable after the commencement of an action brought as a class action, the court shall determine by order whether it is to be so maintained. An order under this subdivision may be conditional, and may be altered or amended before the decision on the merits.

Fed. R. Civ. P. 23(c)(1).

162 Rule 23(c)(2) provides:

> In any class action maintained under subdivision (b)(3), the court shall direct to the members of the class the best notice practicable under the circumstances, including individual notice to all members who can be identified through reasonable effort. The notice shall advise each member that (A) the court will exclude the member from the class if the member so requests by a specified date; (B) the judgment, whether favorable or not, will include all members who do not request exclusion; and (C) any member who does not request exclusion may, if the member desires, enter an appearance through counsel. Fed. R. Civ. P. 23(c)(2).

163 See, for example, Eisen v. Carlisle & Jacquelin, 417 US 156, 177 (1974).

164 Towns, *supra* note 146, at 1008.

165 Rule 23(d) provides:

> In the conduct of actions to which this rule applies, the court may make appropriate orders: (1) determining the course of proceedings or prescribing measures to prevent undue repetition or complication in the presentation of evidence or argument; (2) requiring, for the protection of the members of the class or otherwise for the fair conduct of the action, that notice be given in such manner as the court may direct to some or all of the members of any step in the action, or of the proposed extent of the judgment, or of the opportunity of members to signify whether they consider the representation fair and adequate, to intervene and present claims or defenses, or otherwise to come into the action; (3) imposing conditions on the representative parties or on intervenors; (4) requiring that the pleadings be amended to eliminate therefrom allegations as to representation of absent persons, and that the action proceed accordingly; (5) dealing with similar procedural matters. The orders may be combined with an order under Rule 16, and may be altered or amended as may be desirable from time to time.

Fed. R. Civ. P 23(d).

has been certified.[166] Overall, the open nature of most of the language along with the significant discretion given to judges allows wide use and applicability of the class mechanism as may be needed from situation to situation.[167]

Application to an Individual Citizen of a Spoliated State Suing on Behalf of all Injured Citizens

Obviously, an individual citizen will have to meet the legal requirements for class certification. Most likely, numerosity will not be a problem given the huge numbers of individuals affected and their probable wide geographic spread. Typicality looks to how much in common the individual has with the class they claim to be a member of. If they are claiming a generalized economic injury since all citizens would have the same injury, this may not be a problem; however, they may have to face questions of standing to sue under generalized grievances. If they claim specific injury as is probably required under Lujan, they must be sure that the specific injuries claimed are in fact typical of members of the claimed class. If the injuries of each member are significantly different, then the suit may be adjudicated individually; however, given the policy of judicial economy, class certification is probably more appropriate. They must show commonality which rests on common questions of law. Once again, the claims of each member of the class must be similar enough to involve the same essential questions of law. Finally, the individual must choose a class type to bring suit under. Overall, the choice will probably depend more on the remedy desired, because the general requirements should be manageable for each type in most domestic spoliation issues.

While the pleading requirements of the class action are probably manageable for an individual, the notice requirement depending on the size of the class may be a severe problem – both due to expense and difficulty. Further, unless a statute can be located that provides a remedy for each individual and those individuals were in fact specifically injured, the bar against generalized grievances and falling within the required zone of interest may be a bar to standing. One way around this may be a class action derivative suit, although this mechanism has its own problems.[168]

---

166 Rule 23(e) provides:

> A class action shall not be dismissed or compromised without the approval of the court, and notice of the proposed dismissal or compromise shall be given to all members of the class in such a manner as the court directs.

Fed. R. Civ. P. 23(e).

167 Towns, *supra* note 146, at 1008–1009.

168 See 2A, *infra*.

The Derivative Action[169]

The Legal Mechanism

Derivative suits permit shareholders to sue derivatively on their corporation's behalf.[170] These suits date back at least 150 years.[171] According to Roger Magnuson, these suits permit minority shareholders to champion the cause of an artificial entity.[172] According to the traditional common law distinction between direct and derivative suits, shareholders in derivative actions seek to redress injuries sustained by the corporation.[173] The injury to the corporation then only has a derivative impact on the shareholders, who own the corporation through their shares of stock, and any damages

---

[169] This section relies heavily on C. Swanson, 'Juggling Shareholder Rights and Strike Suits in Derivative Litigation: The ALI Drops the Ball,' *Minn. L. Rev.*, 77, 1339 (1993) [hereinafter 'Swanson'].

[170] Cohen v. Beneficial Indus. Loan Corp., 337 US 541, 548 (1949) (noting that the derivative shareholder suit 'step[s] into the corporation's shoes'); Hawes v. Oakland, 104 US 450, 460 (1881) (noting that derivative suits are 'founded on a right of action existing in the corporation itself, and in which the corporation itself is the appropriate plaintiff'); H. Henn & J. Alexander, LAWS OF CORPORATIONS AND OTHER BUSINESS ENTERPRISES §360, at 1044–1045 (1983) (noting that shareholders sue derivatively '[w]hen the corporate cause of action is for some reason not asserted by the corporation itself').

[171] D. DeMott, *Shareholder Derivative Actions: Law and Practice* §1.01 (1987) [hereinafter 'DeMott']. Historically, courts treated derivative actions as being 'two suits in one' – the first by the shareholder seeking an equitable order compelling the corporation to bring a second action for legal damages. This notion survives in the current practice of making the corporation a nominal defendant and permitting the corporation to raise various objections. R. Clark, *Corporate Law* §15.1 (1986).

[172] 1 R. Magnuson, *Shareholder Litigation XXX* §8.01 (1992) [hereinafter 'Magnuson']. Such actions are rooted both in metaphysics and in common sense. The corporation as a person, albeit a fictitious one, has a life and interests distinct from those of its temporary managers. Those who control it must do so with good faith and exercise good stewardship. If they do not, a minority shareholder may come to the corporation's defense as a representative of its true interests. *Id.*, at 2.

[173] See Principles of Corporate Governance: Analysis and Recommendations (Proposed Final Draft 1992) [hereinafter ALI Final Draft].

> [A] wrongful act that depletes corporate assets and thereby injures shareholders only indirectly, by reason of the prior injury to the corporation, should be seen as derivative in character; conversely, a wrongful act that is separate and distinct from any corporate injury, such as one that denies or interferes with the rightful incidents of share ownership, gives rise to a direct action.

Id. 7.01 cmt. c.

recovered will go to the corporate coffers and not to the individual shareholder plaintiff.[174]

Shareholder derivative plaintiffs can assert legal rights against a variety of possible wrongdoers, including directors, management, other shareholders, and third persons who have damaged the corporate entity.[175] Typically, derivative suits target self-serving officers or directors for breaching their fiduciary duties either through intentional abuse of the corporate form or by negligent 'garden variety mismanagement.'[176] Shareholders of a corporation that is guilty of criminal wrongdoing may seek through the derivative action to make the corporation whole by holding those fiduciaries who caused the corporation to violate the law liable for the resulting injury.[177] As such, corporate directors and officers have a fiduciary duty to promote their corporation's best interests and protect it against loss.[178] These fiduciary duties require corporate officers and directors to refrain from engaging in or causing their corporation to engage in illegal activities in the conduct to the corporation's business,[179] and failure to properly discharge these duties may result in liability to the corporation.[180]

It is fairly agreed that '[t]he duty of loyalty – the obligation of corporate fiduciaries to act with disinterested independence and to exercise judgment unaffected by personal financial interest in making business decisions – has existed since the inception of the corporate vehicle as an entity used to efficiently aggregate "capital from numerous investors" and operate a "large business with numerous owners and employees."'[181]

---

[174] See ALI Final Draft, supra note 173, at §7.01 cmt d, at 606.

[175] See, for example, Ross v. Bernhard, 396 US 531, 538 (1970); see also C. McLaughlin, 'The Mystery of the Representative Suit,' *Geo. L.J.*, 26, 878, 897 (1938).

[176] 1 Magnuson, §8.01, supra note 172, at 2. See *id.* §8.04, at 8–9 (listing 14 'obvious examples' of wrongdoing in shareholder derivative actions).

[177] R. Werder, 'A Critical Assessment of Intracorporate Loss Shifting After Prosecutions Based on Corporate Wrongdoing,' *Del. J. Corp. L.*, 18, 35, 39 (1993).

[178] *Id.* 'Upon accepting the office of director or officer of a corporation, a person assumes a duty of loyalty to the company and its shareholders, and a duty to act with care in fulfilling his responsibilities.' E. Brodsky & M. Adamski, *Law Of Corporate Officers and Directors* §2:1 (1984).

[179] See, for example, Wilshire Oil Co. v. Riffe, 409 F.2d 1277, 1285–1286 (10th Cir. 1969); Clayton v. Farish, 73 N.Y.S.2d 727,744–745 (Sup. Ct. 1947); Simon v. Socony-Vacuum Oil Co., 38 N.Y.S.2d 270, 274 (Sup. Ct. 1942), aff'd mem., 47 N.Y.S.2d 589 (App. Div. 1st Dept. 1944); D. Block et al., *The Business Judgement Rule 34* (3d ed. 1989); W. Knepper & D. Bailey, *Liability of Corporate Officers and Directors* §§1.14, 4.15 (4th ed. 1988); 18B Am. Bus. Jur. 2d, Corporations §1687, 1688 (1985).

[180] Interestingly, according to Werder, liability may also arise under the rule that an 'agent who subjects his principal to liability because of a negligent or other wrongful act is subject to liability to the principal for the loss which results therefrom.' Werder, *supra* note 177, at 40, citing Restatement (Second) of Agency §401, cmt. d (1958).

[181] D. Block, M. Maimone, S. Ross, 'The Duty of Loyalty and the Evolution of the Scope of Judicial Review,' *Brooklyn L. Rev.*, 59, 65 (1993), citing R. Clark, *Corporate Law* 2 (1986) [hereinafter 'Block'].

The duty of loyalty along with the duty of care are the principle fiduciary duties of corporate officers and directors.[182] 'In simplest terms, the duty of care requires that directors exercise the care that an ordinary prudent person would exercise under similar circumstances,[183] and the duty of loyalty prohibits faithlessness and self-dealing.'[184]

Under the business judgment rule, courts will not interfere with a business decision if it is made in good faith by disinterested directors after reasonable investigation and does not constitute an abuse of discretion.[185] The burden is on the party challenging the board's decision to establish facts that rebut this presumption.[186] Once this burden is overcome, the business judgment rule will not be applicable, and the court will look to the transaction at issue.[187]

Arguably, shareholder derivative suits like all tort actions serve two principal goals: compensation and deterrence.[188] Absent derivative suits, individual shareholders would have no access to compensation for injuries directly inflicted on their corporation,[189] and the American Law Institute (ALI) has acknowledged that 'the derivative action may offer the only effective remedy in those circumstances where a control group has the ability to engage in self-dealing transactions with the corporation.'[190] While commentators disagree on derivative suits effectiveness as a means of compensation,[191] most courts and commentators justify derivative suits in the

---

182 *Id.*, at 67. See generally D. Block et al., *The Business Judgement Rule: Fiduciary Duties of Corporate Directors* (3d. ed. 1989 & Supp. 1991).

183 See, for example, Norlin Corp. v. Rooney, Pace, Inc., 744 F.2d 255, 264 (2d. Cir. 1984); Model Business Corp. Act '8.30 (1991) [hereinafter MBCA].

184 Block, *supra* note 181, at 67.

185 *Id.* Delaware courts frequently describe the business judgement rule as a 'presumption' of regularity, that is, it 'is a presumption that in making a business decision the directors of a corporation acted on an informed basis, in good faith and in the honest belief that the action taken was in the best interests of the company.' *Id.*, at 68, citing an extensive list of Delaware cases. *Id.*, at l.

186 See Spiegel v. Buntrock, 571 A.2d 767, 774 (Del. 1990).

187 See, for example, Norlin, 744 F.2d at 264; Gearhartindus., Inc. v. Smith Int'l Inc., 741 F.2d 707, 720 (5th Cir. 1984); see also Grobow v. Perot, 539 A.2d 180, 187 (Del. 1988) ('fairness becomes an issue only if the presumption of the business judgment rule is defeated.').

188 Swanson, *supra* note 169, at 1345.

189 See Home Fire Ins. Co. v. Barber, 93 N.W. 1024, 1034 (Neb. 1903).

190 ALI Final Draft, supra note 173, at 588.

191 See ALI Final Draft, *supra* note 173, Reporter's Note at 596 (summarizing inconclusive statistics); G. Hornstein, 'The Death Knell of Stockholders' Derivative Suits in New York,' *Cal. L. Rev.*, 32, 123 (1944) (discussing findings which concluded that the costs of derivative suits outweighed their benefits); T. Jones, 'An Empirical Examination of the Resolution of Shareholder Derivative and Class Action Lawsuits,' *B.U. L. Rev.*, 60, 542, 545 (1980) (noting that shareholder plaintiffs receive some relief in 75% of cases); R. Romano, 'The Shareholder Suit: Litigation Without Foundation?' *J. Law Econ. & Org.*, 7, 55, 84 (1991) (emphasizing the relative infrequency of derivative suits and the importance of settlement).

absence of provable damages as a way to curb managerial misconduct.[192]

Derivative suits are criticized despite these benefits due to the potential for strike suits[193] and the potentially significant social costs,[194] and courts often suggest that the derivative remedy should only be available under extraordinary circumstances where the plaintiff has no other means of redress.[195] This tension has led to the imposition of significant procedural restrictions on derivative suits – mostly statutory although the derivative suit began as a common law action.[196] The statutes of most jurisdictions include such requirements as contemporaneous stock ownership, verification of pleadings, and security for the corporation's defense expenses.[197] In addition, many jurisdictions require shareholder notice and court approval for any settlement, dismissal, or compromise of derivative actions.[198] The shareholder demand requirement is perhaps the most important of these requirements.[199]

All jurisdictions require that shareholders make a demand on the corporation's board of directors before a derivative suit can be brought.[200] The demand rule is typically embodied in a procedural rule such as FRCP 23.1, which provides that a derivative suit complaint must 'allege with particularity the efforts, if any, made by the plaintiff to obtain the action … or for not making the effort.'[201] This requirement is built on the fundamental policy of corporate law which holds that directors, and not individual shareholders, manage the corporation.[202]

A demand gives management the opportunity to address the shareholder's allegations. If

---

192 The ALI has recently noted that 'properly structured derivative suits may enhance management accountability by: (1) ensuring a measure of judicial oversight, (2) providing for a remedy that does not depend upon the ability of widely dispersed shareholders to take coordinated action, and (3) protecting the market for corporate control from unreasonable interferences.' ALI Final Draft, supra note 173, at 588. See also G. Hornstein, 'Future of Corporate Control,' *Harv. L. Rev*., 63, 476 (1950) (noting that the availability of derivative suits deters managerial wrongdoing).

193 See 1 Magnuson, supra note 172, §8.01; Note, 'Extortionate Corporate Litigation: The Strike Suit,' *Colum. L. Rev*., 34, 1308 (1934).

194 See ALI Final Draft, *supra* note 173, at 588–589.

195 1 Magnuson, *supra* note 172, §8.01 (citing Bell v. Arnold, 487 P.2d 545 (Colo. 1971); Winter v Farmers Educ. and Coop. Union, 107 N.W.2d 226 (Minn. 1961).

196 1 Magnuson, *supra* note 172, §§8.02–.03; Daniel J. Dykstra, 'The Revival of the Derivative Suit,' *U. Pa. L. Rev*., 116, 74, 80 (1967). The statutes can be found in state business corporation acts and civil procedure rules. See, for example, Fed. R. Civ. P. 23.1.

197 See 1 Magnuson, supra note 172, §8.02.

198 DeMott, *supra* note 171, at §1.01.

199 Swanson, *supra* note 169, at 1349.

200 See ALI Final Draft, supra note 173, §7.03 cmt. a.

201 Fed. R. Civ. P. 23.1.

202 See, for example, Aronson v. Lewis, 473 A.2d 805, 809 (Del. 1984) (noting that the demand requirement rule is a rule of substantive right); Del. Code Ann. tit. 8, §141(a) (1991); Cramer v. General Tel. & Elecs. Corp., 582 F.2d 259, 275 (3rd Cir. 1978), *cert. denied*, 439 US 1129 (1979).

> corporate management believes the claims have merit, it may choose to pursue corrective actions or take charge of the litigation. If management disagrees with the shareholder's contentions, the demand requirement gives the corporation the chance to reject the proposed action and if necessary, seek early dismissal of any related derivative suit.[203]

Most jurisdictions will excuse the demand requirement if the shareholder can establish that presenting such a demand to management would be futile.[204] While the standards for excusing demand vary from jurisdiction to jurisdiction, as a general rule some level of directorial involvement in a challenged transaction will excuse demand.[205] Unfortunately, courts disagree on how to apply this principle.[206] As a reaction to these difficult threshold questions, many advocate a standard of universal demand.[207]

Application to an Individual Citizen

Today, most derivative actions are addressed by corporations statutes although the action began as a common law remedy and as such may be open to expansion into new areas. Overall, the derivative suit seeks to protect individual members of a large entity who are not responsible for its management and control. As such, taking the analogy of the trust territory and the fiduciary duties it gave to the administering State, a citizen could argue that public officials are in fact fiduciaries responsible for the overall welfare of the Nation as an entity. While this is a novel application, the example of the trust territories does give some precedent. Unfortunately, strong policy arguments to the effect of 'Would we want our own elected officials held to such a judicial standard?' could be made. The answer would be that so long as these individuals were engaged in public functions, they would be immune from suit, but that if they broke the law they should be held accountable for their actions – especially in something like the spoliation context. In general, the United States has enough legal mechanisms in existence that the derivative suit would rarely be an option, especially since it is generally considered a mechanism of last resort. In the case of spoliated developing countries, such domestic remedies do not in fact exist, and the derivative suit would be more appropriate.

The derivative suit is intuitively appealing in this situation. As we have argued already high-ranking State officials by virtue of their office assume responsibility for

---

203 Swanson, *supra* note 169, at 1349–1350.

204 *Id.*, at 1351.

205 ALI Final Draft, supra note 173, §7.03 cmt. d, at 652.

206 *Id.* Delaware uses a complex test which presents alternative inquiries: '(1) whether threshold assumptions of director disinterest or independence are rebutted by well-pleaded facts; and, if not, (2) whether the complaint pleads particularized facts sufficient to create reasonable doubt that the challenged transaction was the product of a valid exercise of business judgement.' See Levine v. Smith, 591 A.2d 194, 207 (Del. 1991). The latter standard, which has been called the 'reasonable doubt' test, see Aronson v. Lewis, 473 A.2d 805, 815 (Del. 1984), invites judicial subjectivity. Swanson, *supra* note 169, at 1352.

207 Swanson, *supra* note 169, at 1353–1356 (discussing the arguments for and the trend towards universal demand as a threshold requirement in derivative suits).

the general well-being of the nation that they represent. As such, they owe a fiduciary duty to their citizens to protect their interest and should be held accountable for their illegal actions. Further, any remedy would accrue to the successor government and not to the individual citizen, and this to some extent at least mediates problems of self-interested suits. Notice to management either could be made or excused if futile. Further, citizens would not have a problem with contemporaneous share ownership, although this could be potentially analogized to contemporaneous residence in the damaged country. The derivative action is further available under the class action form and therefore could have general applicability.

Overall, despite its immense appeal, it is highly unlikely that a US court would be willing to expose itself to potentially endless litigation over the fiduciary duties of domestic officials, and therefore while this is perhaps the most appropriate form of action in this situation it may simply not be recognized in US courts.

The Citizen as a Private Attorney General

Traditionally, the *Qui Tam*[208] action has offered a means by which Congress may enlist the aid of private citizens in enforcing Federal law.[209] Following the 1986 amendments to the Federal Civil False Claims Act,[210] Congress signaled its intention to pay renewed attention to this traditional form of 'citizen suits.'[211]

---

[208] *Qui tam* is an abbreviation from the Latin '*qui tam pro domino rege quam pro sic ipso in hoc parte sequitur*' meaning 'who as well for the king as for himself sues in this matter.'

Black's Law Dictionary defines a *qui tam* action as 'an action brought by an informer, under a statute which establishes a penalty for the commission or omission of a certain act, and provides that the same shall be recoverable in a civil action, part of the penalty to go to any person who will bring such action and the remainder to the state or some other institution.'

[209] See E. Caminker, Comment: 'The Constitutionality of Qui Tam Actions,' *Yale L.J.*, 99, 341 (1989). *Qui tam* is a provision of the Federal Civil False Claims Act, 31 USC §§3729–3733 (2000), that allows private citizens to file a lawsuit in the name of the US Government charging fraud by government contractors and others who receive or use government funds, and share in any money recovered. This unique law was enacted by Congress in order to effectively identify and prosecute government procurement and program fraud and recover revenue lost as a result of the fraud. The *qui tam* provision has had the effect of privatizing government legal remedies by allowing private citizens to act as 'private attorneys general' in the effort to prosecute government procurement and program fraud. Although most of the early successes in *qui tam* actions have been against defense contractors, more and more actions are being filed that involve other governmental agencies such as Health and Human Services, Environment, Energy, Education, NASA, Agriculture and Transportation. US recoveries for *qui tam* cases, as of the end of 2003, has totaled $7.8 billion. During the same period, relator shares, as a result of the recoveries, has totaled $1.3 billion. In a 2000 decision the US Supreme Court resolved any doubts about the constitutionality of the *qui tam* suit. See Vermont Agency of Natural Resources v. US ex rel. Stevens, 529 US 765 (2000).

[210] Pub. L. No. 99-562, §2(1).

[211] 31 USC §§3729-3733.

Going About Filing a Qui Tam Complaint

A *qui tam* relator (plaintiff)[212] files a complaint, under seal,[213] in a US District Court that has jurisdiction over the case, on behalf of the US Government.[214] Along with the complaint, the relator must also file a 'written disclosure of substantially all material evidence and information the person possesses' concerning the allegations in the complaint.[215] The primary purpose for the written disclosure is to provide the Government with enough information to properly investigate the claim in order to

---

[212] The Civil False Claims statute allows a wide variety of people and entities to file a *qui tam* action. The more common types of relators are as follows: **employees:** an employee who blows the whistle on his or her employer is one of the most common types of relators. Experience has shown that employees normally file *qui tam* actions against their employers as a last resort after repeated attempts to resolve the issues internally (very often through so-called internal 'hotlines') have met with negative results. An important provision of the 1986 amendment protects employees who file an action, or assists in furthering an action, against job retaliation by the employer; **former employees:** who can be viewed as another common type of whistle-blower who files a *qui tam* action based on his or her direct knowledge of fraud on the part of their former employer. In many cases, the former employee was terminated or quit under duress as a result of trying to blow the whistle internally; **competitors and subcontractors:** such as, the competitor of the company being charged or an employee of the competitor who has direct knowledge of the fraud being committed. Also, companies or persons who subcontract with a government contractor have filed *qui tam* actions against the contractor; **state and local governments:** the 1986 Amendments gave state and local governments the power to be relators in *qui tam* actions. Since then, there have been a number of *qui tam* actions filed by local and state governments against contractors and medical providers as a means of recovering state or local revenue lost as a result of the schemes; **federal employees:** as amended in 1986, the false claims statute does not exclude federal employees from being a relator. However, when a federal employee does file a *qui tam* action, it results in considerable controversy and numerous court challenges as to whether the employee, due to his or her responsibilities, are obligated to disclose the fraud. The courts have been mixed on whether a federal employee has standing under the Act and the Justice Department remains hostile toward this type of relator. Concerns have been raised as to whether a federal employee filing an action presents a type of conflict of interest.

Other types of *qui tam* relators have included **public interest groups, corporations** and other **private organizations**. However, organizations as relators have raised questions as to whether they can meet the 'public disclosure' provision of the law. Some courts have dismissed organizations as relators for not being able to meet that provision.

The Act also allows a relator to file a *qui tam* action even if a 'public disclosure' was made prior to the action being filed as long as the relator meets the 'original source' test – the relator had 'direct and independent knowledge' of the information on which the allegations were based and the relator 'voluntarily provided the information to the government' prior to filing the action. See 31 USC §3730(e)(4).

[213] 31 USC §3730(b)(2).

[214] 31 USC §3730(b)(1). Actually the suit is filed in the name of the government and on behalf of both the relator and the government.

[215] *Id.*

determine if it will join in the lawsuit.[216] Once a complaint and written disclosure is filed under seal, the government has 60 days to investigate the information disclosed and determine whether it will join in the lawsuit. The government can, and often does, request the court grant extensions to give it more time to investigate.[217] Once the preliminary investigation is completed, the results are analyzed by the government in order to determine whether it wants to join in the lawsuit, decline to join, move to dismiss the action,[218] or attempt to settle the action prior to a formal investigation.[219] Under the statute, if the government elects to join in the lawsuit, it controls the action and has the primary responsibility for prosecuting the case. The government, under the circumstances, can limit the relator's participation during the case. The government can also dismiss the complaint, but rarely does so. Instead, the government will usually just decline to join if it feels there is no merit to the complaint or there is a lack of resources or for political reasons. At this point, the relator has the option of continuing with the case on his or her own.

If the government declines to join in a *qui tam* action, the relator may continue the action as the sole plaintiff. [220] However, the statute gives the Government the right to intervene in the action at a later date if it feels there is a good reason to do so. A relator who elects to go forward with the case has full discovery rights (court approved access to contractor and government records and sworn testimony of witnesses) as provided under the Federal Rules of Civil Procedure. If the Government does not join and the relator is successful in pursuing the case, the relator, generally, will receive a larger percentage of the award.[221] The size of the relator's share of the award depends on several factors:

---

[216] 31 USC §3730(b)(3).

[217] It is not unusual for a complaint to remain under seal for as long as two to three years before the government makes a decision. However, a relator does have the right to challenge extension requests and to have the seal lifted. The government will then assign the case to an investigative agency that has jurisdiction over the allegations. During the period of time the complaint is under seal, the government investigators will conduct a preliminary investigation based on the information disclosed by the relator. This usually includes a comprehensive interview of the relator and review of relator's records if any exist. It also will include interviews of any corroborative witnesses, reviews of appropriate government records and interviews of government officials. The investigation can also be expanded to include obtaining and reviewing the records of the defendant through the subpoena process.

[218] 31 USC §3730(c)(2).

[219] In most cases, the government will involve civil and criminal resources from the US Attorney's office within the area where the case was filed. In some cases, the US Attorney will decide to open a criminal investigation based on the qui tam allegations. If that occurs, the civil qui tam case will be stayed until the completion of the criminal investigation. 31 USC §3730(c)(4).

[220] 31 USC §3730(c)(3).

[221] The 1986 Amendment to the False Claims Act increased the relator's share of the award in *qui tam* actions to a minimum of 15 percent and a maximum of 30 percent. Prior to 1986, relators were not guaranteed any more than 10 percent of the award.

1 If the Government joins, and successfully prosecutes the case, and the relator was not involved in the wrongdoing, the relator can receive between 15 and 25 percent of any settlement or judgment obtained from the defendant, depending on the extent of the relator's contribution to the case.[222]
2 If the Government does not join and the relator successfully prosecutes the case, the relator will receive between 25 and 30 percent of the settlement or judgment.[223]
3 If the recovery is based primarily on information obtained not from the relator but from public disclosure of the allegations, the relator's award will be ten percent or less of the settlement.[224]
4 If it is determined the relator was involved in the wrongdoing, the court can reduce the relator's share at its discretion depending on the circumstances of the relator's involvement. [225]

The court will dismiss a relator out of an action and deny receipt of any share of an award if the relator is convicted of criminal conduct arising from the wrongdoing alleged in the lawsuit.[226]

In addition to receiving a percentage of the award, the False Claims Act also provides that the relator, if successful, will be reimbursed for expenses incurred, including attorneys' fees and costs.[227]

The appeal of *qui tam* actions is somewhat limited for indigenous spoliation cases under US statutory law. Section 3729(a) of the False Claims statute lists seven specific acts that may provide a basis for a *qui tam* action. Indigenous spoliation is none of these. But as a common law right of action available to private citizens it remains a powerful tool for bringing on behalf of victim-governments against high-ranking state officials for acts of indigenous spoliation. And the prospect of receiving a bounty in the process makes the effort not only worthwhile but provides a powerful incentive to close associates of such officials to blow the whistle on them.

The Status of US Law Following Lujan[228]

Lujan creates specific problems in the environmental context because environmental injury is by nature a public injury rather than a personal injury.[229] Basically, environmental protection stems from a long belief in public stewardship of the

---

222 31 USC §3730(d).
223 Id.
224 31 USC §3730(d)(e).
225 31 USC §3730(d)(3).
226 31 USC §3730(d).
227 *Id.*
228 This section relies heavily on H. Cox, 'Note: Standing to Protect the Global Environment: A Call for Congressional Action,' *J. Energy, Nat. Resources, & Envtl. L.*, 13, 475 (1993) [hereinafter 'Cox'].
229 *Id.*, at 486.

environment.[230] Unfortunately, Sierra Club v. Morton[231] while establishing a nexus between public injury and injury in fact opened itself to wide interpretation, and the court in Lujan has done just that by requiring highly specific pleading of injury in fact. Lujan requires pleading specifically planned future uses of areas that are specifically involved. Evidence of past use is not enough, nor is unspecified future use of unspecified portions, although previous cases have allowed just such formulations.[232] The Court further rejected plaintiff's 'ecosystem nexus,'[233] 'animal nexus,' and 'vocational nexus' theories in its requirement of actual injury.[234]

Application to an Individual Citizen Seeking to Sue for Domestic Spoliation

Following Lujan, an individual must plead very specifically any injury received due to domestic spoliation. Merely alleging lost future opportunities will not be enough, and the plaintiff if possible should plead actual lost opportunities – denial of health care, absence of state-funded educational establishments, lack of employment – due to spoliation of the nation's wealth and resources. If the individual is in the United States, they should plead specifically when they are returning to her country and what activities have been impaired due to spoliation. Under the redressability standard, they must specifically plead relief from those directly responsible – whether private or government. Finally, they would be unwise to rely on general citizen suit provisions in any statute and should in all cases plead specific injuries as specifically as possible. Lujan suggests that Congress may in fact not have the power to grant standing for generalized grievances at all.[235] If this is in fact the case and Congress does not take steps to remedy this aspect of citizen suits, then any plaintiff must very carefully plead all allegations of injury in order to gain standing.

Tax-Payer Standing[236]

Status of the Law

Four cases are generally grouped under the heading of 'federal taxpayer standing.'[237]

[230] See J. Kodwo Bentil, 'General Recourse to the Courts for Environmental Protection Purposes and the Problem of Legal Standing – A Comparative Study and Appraisal,' *Anglo-Am. L. Rev.*, 11, 286 (1982).

[231] 405 US 727 (1972).

[232] Lujan v. Defenders of Wildlife, 112 S. Ct. at 2138. See Cox, *supra* note 228, at 493.

[233] The ecosystem nexus theory gives standing to any person using any part of a threatened ecosystem. Lujan v. National Wildlife Fed'n, 497 US, 871, 887–889 (1990).

[234] The animal nexus theory gives standing to anyone with an interest in studying the threatened animal, and the vocational nexus theory gives standing to anyone with a professional interest in studying the animal. Defenders of Wildlife, 112 S. Ct. at 2138–2140.

[235] *Id.*, at 2145–2146.

[236] This section relies heavily on Fletcher, 'The Structure of Standing,' *Yale L.J.*, 98, 221, 266 (1988).

In Flast v. Cohen, the majority formulated a two-part test designed to separate cases in which federal taxpayer standing should be granted from those cases in which it should not. Under that test a federal taxpayer has standing to challenge a federal expenditure if (1) the challenged expenditure is an exercise of the federal government's taxing and spending power under Article I, Section 8 of the US Constitution and (2) the challenged expenditure exceeds specific constitutional limitations on the taxing and spending power.[238] Valley Forge also involved the establishment clause but involved a grant of federally owned real property rather than federal funds spent.[239] The Court applied the Flast test strictly, holding that the first part of the test was not satisfied because the plaintiffs were challenging an action by the Department of Health Education and Welfare rather than a 'congressional action,'[240] and because the grant was an exercise under the property clause[241] rather than an exercise of the taxing and spending power.[242] More importantly, the Court repeated the statement in Flast that "the requirement of standing 'focuses on the party seeking to get his complaint before a federal court and not on the issues he wishes to have adjudicated.'"[243]

In Richardson, the plaintiff contended that the Central Intelligence Agency Act which allowed the CIA to account for its expenditures 'solely on the certificate of the Director,'[244] violated the statement and account clause of the Constitution which requires 'a regular Statement and Account of the Receipts and Expenditures of all public Money shall be published from time to time.'[245] The Court applied the Flast test and held that the plaintiff lacked standing as a federal taxpayer because there was 'no "logical nexus" between the asserted status of taxpayer' and the claimed constitutional violation.[246]

In Schlesinger, plaintiffs charged violations of the incompatibility clause of the

---

237 Flast v. Cohen, 392 US 83 (1968) (granting standing to a federal taxpayer to seek an injunction against spending federal funds allegedly in violation of the establishment clause of the First Amendment); Valley Forge Christian College v. Americans United for Separation of Church and State, Inc., 454 US 464 (1982) (denying standing to federal taxpayers to challenge a grant of federally owned real property to a religious college allegedly in violation of the establishment clause); United States v. Richardson, 418 US 166 (1974) (denying standing to a federal taxpayer to require the Central Intelligence Agency to provide an account of its expenditures under the 'statement and account clause' of the Constitution); Schelsinger v. Reservists Committee to Stop the War, 418 US 208 (1974) (denying standing to federal taxpayers to enjoin members of congress from simultaneously sitting in Congress and holding positions in the military reserve allegedly in violation of the 'incompatibility clause' of the Constitution).

238 392 US at 102–103.

239 Fletcher, *supra* note 235, at 268.

240 454 US at 479.

241 USC Art. IV, §3, cl. 2.

242 *Id.*, at 480.

243 *Id.*, at 484 (quoting Flast, 392 US at 99).

244 50 USC §403j(b) (1982).

245 USC Art. I, §9, cl. 7.

246 418 US at 175.

Constitution, which provides that 'no person holding any Office under the United States, shall be a Member of either House during his Continuance in Office.'[247] Here, the court denied standing, both as citizens and as taxpayers.

Application to a US Taxpayer Claiming Relief from Spoliation of Tax Money by Foreign Rulers

Overall, Fletcher suggests that these cases equate to 'a presumption that federal taxpayers ordinarily should not have standing to challenge the activities of the federal government on constitutional grounds.'[248] Given this, an American taxpayer claiming that tax money has been illegally appropriated by public officials of a foreign government receiving US financial assistance will have an uphill battle to establish standing. First, the taxpayer must carefully focus on a congressional action, and second that it violates the taxing and spending power. Further, the taxpayer must show a nexus between her status as a taxpayer and the alleged violation. Finally, the challenged violation must be one that is in fact generally enforced. The court will focus on the taxpayer specifically and not her claims. Given this, in all likelihood a taxpayer would be denied standing to sue.

---

[247] USC Art. 1, §6, cl. 2.

[248] Fletcher, *supra* note 236, at 271.

Conclusion

THE INTERNATIONAL LAW CRIME OF INDIGENOUS SPOLIATION

The last decade of the twentieth century has been, in the words of one commentator, 'a decade of remarkable international activity aimed at combating official corruption.'[1] It was during this period that the problem of corruption by high-ranking state officials was finally 'outed.'[2] The veil that was drawn over this subject has now been pushed aside to expose the horrific nature of this crime. The next step in this long journey is the designation of 'indigenous spoliation' as a crime under international law. We have tried to make that case in the preceding chapters of this book: that state practice at both the national and international levels together with the writing of publicists as well as judicial decisions, all seem to point to the emergence of a customary law norm proscribing corruption involving individuals who are entrusted with prominent public functions, such as heads of State and Government, senior government, judicial and military officials, senior executives of publicly-owned corporations, and so forth. Let us briefly review the evidence.

State Practice

Corruption has long been prohibited by the laws[3] and in the Constitutions of most

---

[1] See Cecil Hunt, *Recent Multilateral Measures to Combat Corruption,* Paper Prepared for the American Law Institute-American Bar Association Program *Fundamentals of International Business Transactions*, 1,4 Boston, May 2004.

[2] See Ndiva Kofele-Kale, 'The 'Outing' of 'Grand' Corruption: A Decade of International Law-Making to Combat a Threat to Economic and Social Progress,' *The Quad*, 35, 56 (Summer 2004).

[3] For a representative sample of domestic anti-corruption laws, see The Prevention of Bribery Act, ch. 81; The Tracing and Forfeiture of Proceeds of Drug Trafficking Act, ch. 86; The Dangerous Drugs Act, ch. 223; The Public Disclosure Act, ch. 9; The Penal Code, ch. 77; Money Laundering (Proceeds of Crime) Act (No. 8 of 1996), (Bahamas) Criminal Code, RSC 1970, c. C–34, §§ 118–23, (Can.). Interim Provisions on Administrative Sanctions for Corruption and Bribery by State Administrative Personnel, the Implementing Regulations for the Interim Provisions on Administrative Sanctions for Corruption and Bribery, the Provisions Prohibiting State Administrative Offices and Personnel from Giving and Accepting Gifts, and the Supplementary Provisions Relating to the Punishment of Corruption and Bribery to the Criminal Law of 14 March 1997, (China). Anti-Corruption Statute—Law 190 of 1995, (Colo.) Penal Code §§ 161–162, 165, Prevention of Corruption Act of 1947, (India). Law No. 11 of 1980 Regarding Bribery; the Penal Code, 1915; Law No. 3 of 1971 Regarding Suppression of Criminal Corrupt Deeds, (Indonesia). The Criminal

States;[4] in the old democracies of Western Europe and North America, the new democracies of Central and Eastern Europe and the proto-democracies of Asia and Africa. It is expressly prohibited in the Constitutions of Haiti,[5] Nigeria,[6] Paraguay,[7] Peru,[8] the Philippines[9] and Sierra Leone[10] to mention but a few. Because of the gravity of the problem, special tribunals and commissions of inquiry have been set up in various countries to probe into and try cases of corruption by public officials.[11] These developments evidence expressions of *de lege feranda* for treating corruption as a crime punishable under international law.

Expressions of International Concern

Pronouncements by States in recent years also evidence a universal condemnation of corrupt practices by public officials and a general interest in cooperating to suppress them. This widespread condemnation of acts of corruption is reflected in the preambles of a number of multilateral anti-corruption conventions and resolutions of international organizations.[12] Reading through them leaves one in no doubt as to the seriousness with which the international community as a whole attaches to the problem of corruption is a subject of global concern.

Code of the Kazak Soviet Socialist Republic of 22 July 1959, amended 12 June 1986, Article 147; Decree No. 9 of the Plenum of the Supreme Court of the Republic of Kazakstan on the Practice of the Application by Courts of the Legislation on Responsibility for Corruption 22 December 1995 (Kazakstan). Korean Criminal Code, articles 129, 133; Criminal Code, Economic Crimes Law No. 2; Socialist People's Libyan Arab Jamahiriya, April 1979, Art. 226 (Libya). Criminal Code (Federal Republic of Nigeria, Cap. 77) (1990) § 98; Code of Conduct Bureau and Tribunal Act (Federal Republic of Nigeria, Cap. 56); The Organic Law for the Protection of the Public Patrimony (Venezuela). Criminal Code of the Socialist Republic of Vietnam; Criminal Law No. 12 of the Yemen Arab Republic, 1994.

4 See Ndiva Kofele-Kale, *The International Law of Responsibility For Economic Crimes: Holding Heads of State And Other High Ranking State Officials Individually Liable For Acts of Fraudulent Enrichment*, 183–215 (1995).

5 *Constitution of the Republic of Haiti*, 1987, Art. 21.

6 *1989 Constitution of the Federal Government of Nigeria*, schedule Fifth.

7 *Constitution of Paraguay*, Chapter IV, General Provisions, Art. 41.

8 *Political Constitution of Peru*, Art. 62.

9 *Constitution of the Republic of the Philippines*, Art. XI, §1.

10 *The Constitution of Sierra Leone*, §97(b) (1991).

11 See for example, *Constitution of the Republic of Panama*, Title V, Legislative Organ. Chapter II, Art. 142 (creating a permanent judicial commission to try constitutional officers under Art. 171 for economic crimes (corruption, embezzlement and misappropriation) among other crimes); *Constitution of the Republic of Panama*, Art. XI, §4 (establishing Anti-Graft Courts and the Independent Office of the Ombudsman).

12 In interpreting a treaty, the preamble and annexes are included as part of the text of the treaty. See generally, Vienna Convention on the Law of Treaties (with annexes). Concluded at Vienna, May 23, 1969. Entered into force, 27 January 1988. 1155 UNTS 331; 1969 UNJYB 140; 1980 UKTS 58, Cmnd. 7964; reprinted in *International Law Materials*, 8, 679 (1969), Art. 31, paragraph 1.

The Criminal Law Convention sets outs in its preamble a concise outline of the serious and varied forms of damage caused by corruption and the urgent need to combat it through a multi-disciplinary national and international approach. The Parties to the Criminal Law Convention expressly acknowledge that 'corruption threatens the rule of law, democracy and human rights, undermines good governance, fairness and social justice, distorts competition, hinders economic development and endangers the stability of democratic institutions and the moral foundations of society.'[13] Similarly sentiments permeate the 2003 Civil Law Convention On Corruption. Indeed, the push to draft this instrument was the recognition that corruption is a problem shared by most, if not all, the members of the Council of Europe and the obvious threat corruption poses to the basic principles the Council stands for: the rule of law, the stability of democratic institutions, human rights and social and economic progress; and the responsibility of the Council of Europe as the preeminent European institution defending these fundamental values, to respond to that threat. In the 1994 Summit of the Americas Declaration of Principles and Plan of Action, the Heads of State of thirty-four nations of the southern hemisphere pointedly linked the survival of democracy to the eradication of corruption. 'Effective democracy,' they declared, 'requires a comprehensive attack on corruption as a factor of social disintegration and distortion of the economic system that undermines the legitimacy of political institutions.'[14] In the preamble to the Inter-American Convention that followed the 1994 summit, again the leaders of the OAS came back to the theme of corruption as a phenomenon that undermines the legitimacy of public institutions and strikes at society, moral order and justice, as well as the comprehensive development of peoples. Acknowledging that corruption has international dimensions, the signatories of the Convention agreed on the need for prompt adoption of an international instrument to promote and facilitate international cooperation in fighting corruption and the responsibility of States to hold corrupt persons accountable.

On 16 December 1996, the United Nations General Assembly, acting on an earlier recommendation of the Economic and Social Commission, adopted the United Nations Declaration against Corruption and Bribery in International Commercial Transactions. The Declaration highlights the economic costs of corruption and bribery, and points out that a stable and transparent environment for international commercial transactions in all countries is essential for the mobilization of investment, finance, technology, skills and other resources across national borders. Member States pledge in the Declaration to criminalize bribery of foreign public officials in an effective and coordinated manner and to deny the tax deductibility of bribes paid by any private or public corporation or individual of a Member State to any public official or elected representative of another country.

---

[13] See Council of Europe, *Preamble to the Criminal Law Convention on Corruption* (visited Feb. 26, 2000) <http://www.coe.fr/eng/legaltxt/173e.htm>; reprinted in *International Law Materials*, 8, 505 (1999).

[14] See Summit of the Americas: Declaration of Principles and Plan of Action, 11 December 1994, *International Law Materials*, 34, 808, 811.

Corruption was also the subject of a 1997 United Nations General Assembly Resolution entitled Action Against Corruption. The resolution underscored the General Assembly's concern about the serious problems posed by corrupt practices to the stability and security of societies, the values of democracy and morality, and to social, economic and political development.[15] The resolution also drew a link between corruption and organized crime, including money laundering. Interestingly enough, the preamble of the Inter-American Convention called attention to the 'steadily increasing links between corruption and the proceeds generated by illicit narcotics trafficking … which undermine and threaten legitimate commercial and financial activities, and society, at all levels.'[16] Acknowledging that corruption now has trans-border effects, the General Assembly's anti-corruption resolution recommends a multilateral approach to combat it.

When the United Nations finally got around to drafting its own binding multilateral treaty against corruption, the Preamble boldly acknowledges member States' concern about (i) the seriousness of problems and threats posed by corruption to the stability and security of societies, undermining the institutions and values of democracy, ethical values and justice and jeopardizing sustainable development and the rule of law; (ii) the cases of corruption that involve vast quantities of assets, which may constitute a substantial proportion of the resources of capital-poor States; and (iii) the acceptance that the prevention and eradication of corruption is a responsibility of all States requiring mutual cooperation and assistance.

The African Union anti-corruption convention in its preamble expresses the concern shared by the continent's leadership about the negative effects of corruption and impunity on the political, economic, social and cultural stability of African States and its devastating effects on the economic and social development of the peoples of Africa; the need to formulate and pursue a common strategy to protect African societies against the destructive effects of corruption; and the determination of the continent's leaders to build partnerships between governments and all segments of civil society in the fight against the scourge of corruption.

Not to be left out the nations of Asia also jumped on the anti-corruption bandwagon when they committed themselves to the Anti-Corruption Action Plan

---

15 Available empirical evidence suggests a correlation between corruption and economic growth and investment. Statistically, the relationship is negative: a one standard deviation improvement in the corruption index is associated with a four percentage point increase in investment and over a half percentage point increase in the annual growth rate of per capita GDP. See Global Coalition for Africa, *Corruption and Development in Africa*, GCA/PF/N.2/11/1997, 12 (1997).

16 In the same vein, a 1995 Resolution on Combating Corruption in Europe adopted by the European Parliament also stressed the ties between corruption and organized crime while expressing the view that combating the latter can help to curb the former. European Parliament Report of the Committee on Civil Liberties and Internal Affairs on Combating Corruption in Europe, DOC.EN\RR\287\287701 (1 December 1995).

for Asia and the Pacific and its Implementation Plan.[17] While not a legally binding instrument, the Action Plan contains a number of principles and standards towards policy reform which interested governments of the region politically commit to implement on a voluntary basis. The Action Plan also recognizes that corruption has become a widespread phenomenon that undermines good governance, erodes the rule of law, hampers economic growth and efforts at poverty alleviation and distorts conditions in business transactions. In committing to the Action Plan, the Southeast Asian nations have resolved to eradicate corruption in their region through mutual cooperation.

The Perspective of Publicists

Bribery of foreign public officials is listed as one of twenty-two international crimes by a leading publicist.[18] This crime meets Professor Bassiouni's ten penal characteristics of an international crime: (1) explicit recognition of proscribed conduct as constituting an international crime, a crime under international law, or a crime; (2) implicit recognition of the penal nature of the act by establishing a duty to prohibit, prevent, prosecute and punish; (3) criminalization of the proscribed conduct; (4) duty or right to prosecute; (5) duty or right to punish the proscribed conduct; (6) duty or right to extradite; (7) duty or right to cooperate in prosecution, punishment (including judicial assistance in penal proceedings); (8) establishment of a criminal jurisdictional basis (or theory of criminal jurisdiction or priority in criminal jurisdiction); (9) reference to the establishment of an international criminal court or international tribunal with penal characteristics (or prerogatives); and (10) elimination of the defense of superior orders.[19]

---

17 Agreed to at the 3rd Annual ADB/OECD Anti-Corruption Conference for Asia Pacific, held in Tokyo in December 2000. As of 30 January 2004, the following governments have endorsed the Action Plan: Australia; Bangladesh; Cambodia; Cook Islands; Fiji Islands; Hong Kong, China; India; Indonesia; Japan; Kazakhstan; Kyrgyz Republic; Malaysia; Mongolia; Nepal; Pakistan; Papua New Guinea; Philippines; Republic of Korea; Samoa; Singapore; and Vanuatu.

18 See, for example, the collection of essays in Nouvel Observateur, *La Corruption Internationale: Colloque Du Nouvel Observateur* (1999).

19 It is interesting to note that the noted publicist, Cherif Bassiouni, classified bribery and corruption of public officials as an economic crime under international law at a time when the international legal regime for this conduct consisted only of four instruments of questionable binding force: (1) a resolution from regional organization: Organization of American States Permanent Council, Resolution on the Behavior of Transnational Enterprises, 10 July 1975, OEA/Ser. G., CP/RES.154 (167/75) corr.1 (1975), reprinted in *International Law Materials*, 14, 1326; (2) a declaration from another regional economic organization: Organization for Economic Co-operation and Development, Declaration on International Investment and Multinational Enterprises, June 21, 1976, OECD Press Release, A(76)20, reprinted in *International Law Materials*, 15, 967; (3) an ECOSOC instrument: UN Report of the Economic and Social Committee on an International Agreement on Illicit Payments, UN Doc. E/1979/104 (1979); and (4) a draft code: UN

One can safely conclude that an emerging customary law norm that treats corruption as a crime under international law draws strong support from the following: (a) consistent, widespread and representative State practice proscribing and criminalizing the practice; (b) the widespread condemnation of acts of corruption reflected in the preambles of these multilateral anti-corruption treaties and in declarations and resolutions of international organizations; (c) pronouncements by States in recent years that evidence a universal condemnation of corrupt practices by public officials. In these pronouncements corruption is described in weighty language: a phenomenon that threatens the rule of law, democracy and human rights; hinders economic development and endangers the stability of democratic institutions and the moral foundations of society; (d) a general interest in cooperating to suppress acts of corruption; and (e) the writings of noted publicists recognizing corruption as a component of international economic crimes.[20] From the foregoing, a strong argument can be made for treating corruption as a crime under international law for which individual responsibility and punishment attach.

PROCEDURES FOR NORM IMPLEMENTATION

We conclude this study by proposing some procedures for implementing the normative processes developed in the preceding chapters. The declaration of acts of indigenous spoliation as a crime under international law must be accompanied by an enforcement system with provisions for individual criminal liability.

The Multilateral Treaty Approach

Having failed to include indigenous spoliation as a crime in the recently concluded United Nations Convention Against Corruption, the international community can still address the problem of indigenous spoliation in several other ways. It can do so by expanding the jurisdiction of the International Criminal Court to include the crime of indigenous spoliation or it can propose it as an addition to the crimes already enumerated in the Draft Code of Crimes against the Peace and Security of Mankind, presently before the General Assembly of the United Nations.

The community of nations can also address this problem through a separate convention or treaty. A decade ago, Professor Reisman proposed the drafting of an international declaration that would (1) characterize acts of spoliations by national officials as a breach of national trust and international law; (2) impose on other

---

Comm'n on Transnat'l Corporations, Draft UN Code of Conduct on Transnational Corporations, UN Doc. E/1993/17/Rev.1.\, Annex II (1983). See M. Cherif Bassiouni, 'The Penal Characteristics of Conventional International Criminal Law,' *Case W. Res. J. Int'l L.*, 15, 27 (1983); 'Enforcing Human Rights Through International Criminal Law and Through an International Criminal Court,' in *Human Rights: an Agenda for the Next Century*. at 347 (L. Henkin & J. Hargrove eds, 1994).

20 Bassiouni (1983), *supra* note 19, at 27.

governments an obligation of supplying information and cooperation; and (3) treating the failure of other governments to prevent such funds from being cached in their jurisdiction and to aid in their recapture as complicity, after the fact, and as itself, an international delict.[21] The idea of drafting an international agreement that would provide the legal framework for restraining and recapturing spoliated wealth and punishing its authors remains the ideal remedy. It is worth pursuing.

Proscribing Indigenous Spoliation as a Conditionality for Foreign Aid and Commercial Bank Credits

Major aid donors have increasingly been including democratic reforms and observance of human rights as conditionalities for extending aid and credits to authoritarian and totalitarian governments.[22] A good number of these countries are also victims of indigenous spoliation. So, why not simply make proscription of this activity together with the requirement of leadership incorruptibility along with democratization as conditions which must be fulfilled before donor governments and multilateral lending agencies can extend financial assistance to the countries concerned? This can be accomplished in one of three ways:

1 By requiring that when extradition treaties between victim-States and States where spoliated wealth is banked or invested are negotiated or re-negotiated, as the case may be, indigenous spoliation should be included as an extraditable crime. The willingness of these States to renegotiate extradition treaties for this purpose can be used as a test of their good faith commitment to democratic reforms. Once a State balks at renegotiating, it leaves itself open to charges that it has no serious intention to pursue democratic reforms and as such should not be eligible for foreign aid and credits.
2 Given the importance developing countries attach to private foreign investment, treaties of friendship, commerce and navigation as well as bilateral investment treaties between investment-starved developing countries and capital-rich industrial countries can be drafted to include a provision to assist a government that has been the victim of indigenous spoliation by former high-ranking officials in recovering and repatriating any funds found stashed in the industrial country.
3 Including in bilateral and multilateral Mutual Legal Assistance on Criminal Matters Treaties a provision for the recovery and return of spoliated wealth. Virtually all the instruments that make up the international regime against corruption now include provisions for mutual legal assistance.

---

[21] See W. Michael Reisman, 'Harnessing International Law to Restrain and Recapture Indigenous Spoliations,' *Am.J.Int'l L.*, 83, 56–57 (1989).

[22] See for example Section 11 B of the Foreign Assistance Act of 1961 as amended 22 USC §2151n (1988) (Prohibition of Foreign Assistance to Gross Violators of Human Rights) and Section 502B of the Foreign Assistance Act of 1961, as amended 22 USC §2304 (1988) (Prohibition of Security Assistance to Gross Violators of Human Rights).

Involving Victim States in the Prevention and Punishment of Indigenous Spoliation

Indigenous spoliation will continue unabated unless the countries that are the primary victims are involved in the solution. Towards this end, victim States should be encouraged to pass and enforce national legislation for the prevention and punishment of persons guilty of such acts. Back in 1990 Professor Ann-Marie Burley called for an international convention that among other things would address assisting fragile democratic successor governments to restore 'the legitimacy and effectiveness of their own judicial and political systems.'[23] For such a convention to be effective, it must include an obligation upon victim States to incorporate in their national laws provision for severe penalties for persons guilty of acts of indigenous spoliation. In addition, the convention should also establish national legal guarantees that (a) judgments against high-ranking officials including former heads of state will be enforced, and (b) the courts will not permit a deposed dictator to successfully invoke sovereign immunity or act of state defenses when the new government requests such immunity to be revoked. Many African states have taken the position that economic rights for individuals and peoples take precedence over civil and political (so-called Western liberal) rights. For these countries, there can be no better barometer for measuring their professed commitment to this principle than their willingness to pass and enforce strict laws on leadership conduct.[24] The adoption in 2004 of the United Nations Convention Against Corruption answers some, but not all, of Professor Burley's concerns. Neither this nor any other anti-corruption instrument specifically prohibits the crime of indigenous spoliation. All continue to treat corruption by high-ranking state officials no differently from the rent seeking corrupt activities of the poorly paid customs inspector or traffic cop.

For many of these suggested solutions, Article 2(7) of the United Nations Charter, which prohibits any meddling in the internal affairs of member states may

---

23 See Ann-Marie Burley, Remarks during the panel presentation 'Pursuing the Assets of Former Dictators,' at the *Proceedings of the 81st Annual Meeting of the American Society of International Law*, 394, 402 (Michael P. Malloy ed., 1990).

24 See Limburg Principles on the Implementation of the International Convenant on Economic, Social and Cultural Rights (1986), *Human Rts. Q*., 9, 128, 143 (1987); *World Commission on Environment & Development, Our Common Future* (1987). In 1979, the Assembly of Heads of States and Governments of the Organization of African Unity meeting in Monrovia, Liberia passed a resolution calling for a meeting of experts to draft a human rights charter. The resolution stressed the 'importance that the African peoples have always attached to the respect for human dignity and the fundamental human rights, *bearing in mind that human and people's rights are not confined to civil and political rights, but cover economic, social and cultural problems, and that the distinction between these two categories of rights does not have any hierarchical implications but that it is nevertheless essential to give special attention to economic, social and cultural rights in the future ...*' See On Human and People's Rights in Africa, OAU Document AHG/Dec. 115 (XVI) (emphasis added).

present a problem. The argument has been made that even discussion of a state's human rights violations is prohibited by this Article. This once immovable doctrine that only states not individuals are the proper subjects of international law has been blamed for the position taken by the American Bar Association that the United States could not ratify the Genocide Convention[25] because it dealt with matters within the domestic jurisdiction of the United States.[26] Happily, there has been a steady erosion of this view as external involvement or intervention in areas previously believed to be the internal affairs of a sovereign state has now become a fact of international life. This change in perspective has been forced on the community of nations by several factors.[27] First, the persistent violations of human rights in some countries has forced the victims of these violations to appeal directly to the international community to intervene in their countries in order to put an end to their misery.[28] Such was the case with the Kurdish minority in Iraq or the beleaguered Moslems in Bosnia Herzegovina or the Timorese of East Timor and the list goes on.

Second, the recognition of an emerging right to democracy which the international community is under an obligation to protect by intervening in other countries, if necessary, to prevent the overthrow of democratically elected governments has done much in undermining the notion of the impregnability of sovereignty.[29] The idea of external intervention in support of democracy is found in the Copenhagen Document, one of a series of instruments adopted by the Conference on Security and Cooperation in Europe (CSCE). This document which has been described as 'one of the great documents in the history and development of human rights and international law,'[30] states *inter alia* that (1) the protection of

---

[25] Convention on the Prevention and Punishment of the Crime of Genocide, Dec. 9, 1948, 78 UNTS 277 (entered into force 12 January 1951).

[26] See Malvina Halberstam & Elizabeth F. Defeis, *Women's Legal Rights: International Covenants, An Alternative to Era?* 50–52 (1987).

[27] See generally Claudio Grossman & Daniel D. Bradlow, 'Are We Being Propelled Towards a People-Centered Transnational Legal Order,' *Am. U. J. Int'l L. & Pol'y*, 9, 1 (1993) (arguing that among the forces which are inexorably undermining sovereignty are: technological changes that are facilitating the creation of a global economy and global society; the growing concern about the environment; the expanding role of international organizations in the world; and the changing perceptions of peace and security).

[28] Such interventions have been viewed favorably by some international law scholars; see Anthony D'Amato, 'The Invasion of Panama was a Lawful Response in Tyranny,' *Am.J.Int'l.L.*, 84, 516 (1990).

[29] See Thomas Franck, 'The Emerging Right to Democratic Governance,' *Am.J.Int'l.L.*, 86, 46 (1992); UN General Assembly Resolution demanding the return of Jean-Bertrand Aristide to Haiti following his overthrow by a military coup in September1991, UN Doc. A/46/6/L.8/Rev.l (1991); Organization of American States resolution, Support to the Democratic Government of Haiti, OEA/Ser.F/V.1/MRE/RES.1/91, corr. 1, paras. 5,6 (1991).

[30] See Malvina Halberstam, 'The Copenhagen Document. Intervention in Support of Democracy,' *Harv. Int'l. L. J.*, 34, 163 (1993).

human rights is one of the basic purposes of government; (2) a freely elected representative government is *essential* for the protection of human rights, and (3) states have a responsibility to protect democratically elected governments – their own and other states' – if they are threatened by acts of violence or terrorism.

Finally, the shifting role of the major multilateral agencies – the International Bank for Reconstruction and Development (World Bank) and the International Monetary Fund (IMF) – from a merely lending role to an increasingly law-making institution, able and willing to dictate fundamental institutional change in the borrowing countries through their lending policies, is perhaps the single most important contributory factor to the erosion of the doctrine of sovereignty.[31] The World Bank, it has been observed, has expanded its traditional role as a financial institution to include a new governance role that allows it to dictate legal and institutional change through its lending policies.[32] It has frequently exercised its enormous governance power:

> ... through its financial leverage to legislate entire legal regimes and even alter the constitutional structure of borrowing nations. Bank approved consultants often rewrite a country's trade policy, fiscal policies, civil service requirements, labor laws, health care arrangements, environmental regulations, procurement rules, and budgetary policy.[33]

The World Bank's principal tool in nudging borrowing members towards prescribed social objectives is 'conditionality.'[34] Bank loans impose conditions requiring legislative and policy changes by borrowing governments.[35] As one critic of the World Bank's new and expanded lending policy observed '[t]hese non-financial conditions frequently derive from assumptions about the normative and economic task of development'[36] and are justified on grounds that so long as governance (a euphemism for Western liberal democratic system of government) issues are related to economic development, the Bank may impose conditions on

---

31 See David N. Plank, 'Aid, Debt, and the End of Sovereignty: Mozambique and Its Donors,' *J.Mod.Afr.Stud.*, 31, 407 (1993) (noting that the impact of World Bank and IMF programs of structural adjustment and sectoral policy reform in Mozambique and elsewhere in Africa have thoroughly discredited traditional notions of sovereignty in many parts of Africa); see also discussion in chapter 7.

32 See Jonathan Cahn, 'Challenging the New Imperial Authority: The World Bank and the Democratization of Development,' *Harv.Hum.Rts.J.*, 6, 159, 160 (1993).

33 *Id.*

34 For the origins of the concept of conditionality, see Joseph Gold, *Conditionality* (IMF Pamphlet Series No. 31, 1979); Manuel Guitian, *Fund Conditionality: Evolution of Principles and Practice* (IMF Pamphlet Series No. 39, 1981); John Williamson, 'IMF Conditionality,' in *IMF Conditionality* (John Williamson ed., 1983).

35 The purpose of conditionality has shifted from that of maximizing 'the probability of repayment of a World Bank loan, but rather ... to enable the borrower to remove what the lender sees as fundamental policy induced obstacles to economic growth.' See Paul Mosley, Jane Harrigan & John Toye, *Aid and Power: The World Bank and Policy-Based Lending: Analysis and Policy Proposals*, 1, 66–77 (1979).

36 *Id.*

governance.[37] For its part, the Bank has taken the position that its governance concerns extend from broad macroeconomic policy to the proper structure and role of government institutions that administer the economy, to environmental impacts, and even military spending.[38] Increasingly over the last few years, the World Bank has intensified its anti-corruption activities as it became clear that corruption is a significant impediment to development.[39] To combat corruption in all its manifestations, the Bank has adopted a multi-pronged strategy that is both country- and sector-specific.[40]

Indigenous spoliation is injurious to the economic well-being of a nation by draining it of scarce but vital resources needed for economic development. This activity clearly falls within the World Bank's governance role, therefore, the Bank should include in its loan agreements specific requirements for the repatriation of spoliated wealth in foreign accounts held by high-ranking officials of the borrowing governments.

The IMF has also been active in the global fight against corruption, although it does not have a specific anti-corruption policy.[41] Like the World Bank, the IMF addresses corruption in the broader context of promoting good governance by focusing on (i) transparency of government accounts, (ii) effectiveness of public resource management, and (iii) stability and transparency of the economic and the regulatory environment for private sector activity.[42] Corruption is monitored as part

---

37 *Id.*, at 164; see also Ibrahim Shihata, 'The World Bank and 'Governance' Issues in its Borrowing Members,' in *The World Bank in a Changing World*, 53, 67–72 (Franziska Tschofen & Antonio R. Parra eds, 1991).

38 *World Bank, Governance and Development*, 46 (1992); see also *World Bank, Sub-Saharan Africa: From Crisis to Sustainable Growth*, 60–61 (1989) (the issue of borrowing members' governance raised for the first time whereupon Bank publicly called upon African governments to become accountable to their citizens).

39 See Bernard Funck, Anticorruption Activities of the World Bank in OECD, Combating Corruption in the Asian and Pacific Economies. Papers prepared at the Joint ADB-OECD Workshop on Combating Corruption in Asian and Pacific Economies, Manilla, 29 September – 1 October 1999, 261. Available on www.adb.org/Documents/Conference/Combating_Corruption

40 The first level in the 4-pronged approach is preventing corruption in World Bank projects; the second involves helping countries that request assistance from the Bank in fighting corruption; the third involves integrating anti-corruption concerns in the Bank's country assistance strategies. Finally, the fourth approach is to support international anti-corruption efforts. *Id.*, at 262.

41 The IMF received a formal mandate from its political leaders in 1996 to concern itself with good governance in all its aspects, including (i) ensuring the rule of law, (ii) improving the efficiency and accountability of the public sector, and (iii) tackling corruption.

42 See Anton Op De Beke, 'Anticorruption Initiatives of the International Monetary Fund,' in *OECD, Combating Corruption in the Asian and Pacific Economies*. Papers prepared at the Joint ADB-OECD Workshop on Combating Corruption in Asian and Pacific Economies, Manilla, 29 September – 1 October 1999, at 255 [hereinafter 'De Beke'].

of the promotion of governance through its policy advice (its so-called surveillance activities), technical assistance, and program conditionality. The Guidance Note on Governance[43] developed by the IMF treats corruption as a subset of poor governance which allows the IMF to suspend or delay its support to programs on account of incidents of corruption to the extent that they could have significant macroeconomic implications or they undermine the purpose of the use of IMF resources.[44]

Treating Indigenous Spoliation not as a Property Dispute

The preceding solutions treat indigenous spoliation as essentially a property dispute.[45] But it is much more. Such acts arguably belong to the category of human rights violations. When the wealth and natural resources of a country are diverted by its leadership for its own private use, it is the citizens who are deprived of the full use and enjoyment of the resources which belong to them by right. In these circumstances basic rights are denied. The right of a people not to be dispossessed of their wealth and natural resources through the corrupt activities of their leaders is not just any ordinary human right but *the* fundamental human right.[46] This right transcends all the other rights and gives some semblance of form and shape to, and in a very real sense qualifies, the other rights. In this sense, human rights do not occupy the same plateau and are not all equal. Thus to take the Orwellian view that they are all equal is to ignore the reality that under certain conditions, contexts, and situations, some rights assume far more importance than others. To so state should not be taken as a defense of normative relativism which denies the universality of human rights and holds instead that entitlement to human rights is conditioned by culture and socio-economic conditions, that is, culture determines basic rights.[47]

Rather, the point worth stressing is that acts of indigenous spoliation violate, as it were, the mother of all rights. A people's enjoyment of the other rights within the pantheon of human rights is dependent on their access to the national wealth. One cannot talk realistically of a fundamental right to life when this life can barely be sustained because it is cut off from the most basic necessities of food, shelter and

---

43 See IMF, The Role of the IMF in Governance Issues-Guidance Note (1997). Available on www.imf.org (last visited on 7 March 2005).

44 De Beke, *supra* note 42, at 258.

45 This view was expressed by Peter Weiss, one of the lawyers who represented the Philippines Government in the Marcos cases. He thought that those cases were not property disputes but rather human rights cases. See *Proceedings of the 81st Annual Conference of the American Society of International Law*, *supra* note 23 (remarks by Peter Weiss).

46 See Ndiva Kofele-Kale, 'The Right to a Corruption-Free Society as an Individual and Collective Human Right: Elevating Official Corruption to a Crime under International Law,' *Int'l Law*., 34, 149 (2000) (arguing that the right to a corruption free society is a fundamental human right).

47 See E.F. Teson, *Humanitarian Intervention: An Inquiry into Law and Morality*, 38 ff (1988).

medical care. A hungry woman saddled with a sick child with no money to buy food or medicines can hardly comprehend, let alone enjoy, the right of free expression or of association.[48] For her such rights are simply too abstract and far removed from the reality of her daily existence. And were she faced with the choice between these rights, most certainly she would opt for the one that guarantees her access to food and medicines. Besides, such a choice would make no sense to her since it is a false choice.[49] Her right to enjoy the fruits of her legacy – the wealth of her nation – overrides any other right. This right must be protected because it guarantees the enjoyment of the other rights of life, liberty, and so forth. Those who seek to promote and protect this woman's fundamental human rights can do no better than to ensure that her nation's wealth is not spoliated by public officials. They must ensure that this wealth is not depleted or degraded by those who hold it in trust for her. For the quality of this woman's life, and that of her child, whether it will be a dignified one or not, hangs precariously on the availability of her nation's resources and her right of access to them.

In this vein, it has been suggested that acts of indigenous spoliation should be viewed as an extension of the Filartiga principle[50] which applies international law to violations of human rights in domestic courts.[51] This view informed on the attempts mounted by the Government of Mrs. Corazon Aquino to bring federal court proceedings against the Marcoses under the Alien Tort Statute which authorizes original federal court jurisdiction over 'any civil action by an alien for a

---

[48] These fundamental freedoms are usually the first to go when a country begins to experience economic difficulties. In fact, it can be argued that the basic rights of speech, association and other individual liberties tend to flourish amidst economic plenty.

[49] People begin to develop 'finer aspirations' such as aspiration for political and personal liberties only after the basic necessities for survival have been satisfied. See for example, Peter Berger, *The Capitalist Revolution* (1991). Berger, in explaining the success of the so-called 'development dictatorships' in South Korea and Taiwan, argues that economic progress was achieved at the expense of fundamental human rights. He further goes on to argue that there was relatively little resistance from the population in the 'take off' stages of capitalist development because the latter held out the promise of a better life. And people who are escaping from an economic existence of harsh subsistence and who can see a better life on the immediate horizon are less likely to be interested in political liberation. This comes much later.

[50] *Proceedings of the 81st Annual Conference of the American Society of International Law*, *supra* note 23 (remarks by Peter Weiss).

[51] It is that certain human rights principles have ripened into customary law and therefore part of the law of the United States. Filartiga v. Pena-Irala, 630 F.2d 876, 888-889 (2d Cir. 1980) was a wrongful death action brought under the Alien Tort Claims statute (28 USC §1350) by two nationals of Paraguay (father and daughter) who alleged that their son and brother, a 17-year old Paraguayan was tortured to death in Paraguay by the defendant Pena-Irala while he was Inspector-General of police. The Second Circuit Court of Appeals agreed with plaintiff that the official torture meted out to the deceased violated the law of nations and, therefore, victims are entitled to redress and compensation in accordance with domestic law.

tort committed in violation of the law of nations or a treaty of the United States.'[52] Lawyers for the Philippine Government, however, had a difficult time establishing that the law of nations is violated when a head of state steals virtually all his country's wealth.[53] In the event, elevating this type of conduct to the level of a human rights violation[54] transforms it into an obligation *erga omnes* which entitles any state to bring an action before its courts against high-ranking officials who engage in acts of spoliation under the color of the law.[55]

The willingness of victims of human rights violations to defy the odds by inviting foreign governments to intervene in their countries, by force if necessary, to put a stop to such violations;[56] the fairly widespread recognition by the world

---

52 Alien Tort Claims Act, 28 USC §1350 (1982).

53 However, a group of Philippine and US citizens who sued the Marcoses in the United States District Court for the District of Hawaii alleging that Ferdinand Marcos participated in a campaign of murder, torture, kidnapping, and prolonged arbitrary detention of the plaintiffs and their relatives in the Philippines may have fared slightly better. The plaintiffs asserted federal court jurisdiction under the Alien Tort Claims Act (ATCA). Marcos moved to dismiss the cases on the grounds of 'head of state' immunity, lack of personal jurisdiction, and lack of subject matter jurisdiction under the ATCA. The court held that Marcos did not enjoy immunity and assumed that jurisdiction existed under ATCA but nevertheless held that all claims were nonjusticiable and dismissed under the act of state doctrine. See Trajano v. Marcos, No. 86-0207 (9th Cir. 1986), Sison v. Marcos, No. 86-0225 (9th Cir. 1986), and Hilao v. Marcos, No. 86-390 (9th Cir. 1986); see also R. Haron, 'Alien Tort Claims ActAct of State Doctrine-Act of State Doctrine Requires Dismissal of Human Rights Claims Brought Against Former Philippine President Residing in the United States,' *Va.J.Int'l L.*, 27, 433 (1987).

54 Indigenous spoliation can be included among the list of crimes against the peace and security of mankind enumerated in Part II of the 1991 ILC Draft Code of Crimes, *supra* Chapter 2.

55 In the Barcelona Traction case, the International Court of Justice elaborated on the concept of obligations *erga omnes* when it said:

> [A]n essential distinction should be drawn between the obligations of a State towards the international community as a whole, and those arising vis-a-vis another State in the field of diplomatic protection. By their very nature the former are the concern of all States. In view of the importance of the rights involved, all States can be held to have a legal interest in their protection; they are obligations *erga omnes.* Such obligations derive, for example, in contemporary international law, from [the] rules concerning the basic rights of the human person.

Barcelona Traction, Light and Power Company, Limited (Belg. v. Spain), 1970 ICJ 6, para. 33 (5 February).

56 Although the call for humanitarian intervention has thus far gone unheeded in Bosnia-Herzegovina, such was not the case with the Kurds in Iraq. In the wake of Saddam Hussein's defeat in the Persian Gulf war and as millions of Kurds took desperate refuge on the bleak border mountainsides bordering Iraq and Turkey, the United Nations Security Council responded with Resolution 688 which *inter alia* authorized the creation of an enclave

community of an emerging right to democracy and the duty that it imposes on all states to intervene anywhere to ensure its flourishing; and the increasing interventionist policy of the major multilateral funding agencies, support the view that the concert of nations has an affirmative duty to intervene to prevent acts of indigenous spoliation in countries where these have occurred or are occurring.

Looking back some sixty years when the word 'genocide' was first introduced into our everyday lexicon, it is worth recalling that Lemkin coined the term as 'a kind of speech-act.'[57] As Laura Secor points out in her review of Samantha Power's evocative work on the history of genocide,[58] Lemkin's preoccupation was not simply the naming of a 'crime whose magnitude, combined with its sweeping singularity of motive, distinguished it even in the annals of coldblooded mass murder. He meant for the crime's very name to be a call for universal opprobrium – one that would inspire, if it did not mandate, punishment and prevention.'[59] This is precisely what we hope *patrimonicide* will accomplish in the not-too distant future. The rapacious appetite displayed by constitutionally-responsible leaders for the collective wealth simply has no parallel in human history.

The contrast between the outrageous personal fortunes of leaders and the abject poverty of the people they lead deserves to be called something different so as not to confuse it with conduct associated with such terms as corruption or embezzlement or illicit enrichment. None of these old and venerable crimes can adequately describe the brazen theft of national wealth engaged in by constitutionally-responsible leaders. They cannot begin to convey the paradox of a president who can crisscross the globe in a $30 million presidential jet yet his country can boast of only 100 kilometers of surfaced roads; or a president who dies en route to Europe for a medical emergency because in 38 years in power– during which time he raided the national treasury mercilessly – he could not endow his country with a single decent state-of-the-art hospital; or a head of state who together with family members and close associates control billions of dollars of oil revenues, a sizeable portion of which has been diverted to their private foreign bank accounts, yet prefer to send qualified nationals to study in foreign universities because the country does not boast an institution of higher learning! Only a new term can capture the outrage that the crime of indigenous spoliation represents and the breadth, scope and depth of the destruction it wreaks on peoples and societies.

---

for the Kurds inside Iraq, protected by international forces. See S.C. Res. 688, UN SCOR, 46th Sess., 2982d mtg. at 189, UN Doc. S/Res/688 (1991); see generally Michael Stopford, 'Humanitarian Assistance in the Wake of the Persian Gulf War,' *Va. J. Int'l L.*, 33, 491 (1993) (noting that Security Council Resolution 688 'constituted a watershed, breaking fresh ground in insisting that Iraq allow access by humanitarian organizations to those in need.').

57 See Laura Secor, 'Turning a Blind Eye,' *New York Times Book Review*, Sun., 14 April 2002.

58 See Samantha Power, *The Problem From Hell* (2002).

59 Secor, *supra* note 57.

Index